The Handbook of
Organization Development
in Schools

The Handbook of Organization Development in Schools

THIRD EDITION

Richard A. Schmuck
Philip J. Runkel

University of Oregon

WAVELAND
PRESS, INC.
Prospect Heights, Illinois

For information about this book, write or call:

Waveland Press, Inc.
P.O. Box 400
Prospect Heights, Illinois 60070
(708) 634-0081

Contents

Chapter 3 Clarifying Communication 91

Chapter 4 Improving Meetings 151

Chapter 5 Solving Problems 195

Chapter 6 Making Decisions 231

Chapter 7 Working with Conflicts 295

Chapter 8 Microdesigning 329

Chapter 9 Diagnosis and Readiness

Chapter 10 Evaluation

Chapter 11 Institutionalizing OD in School Districts

Preface

This book emerges from fifteen years of collaboration among more than 150 people working in a program of research, development, and dissemination on OD in schools at the University of Oregon. From 1967 to 1982, that program produced data, theory, practices, and techniques from work with over two thousand educators in more than fifty elementary and secondary schools in the United States. Out of that experience, we speak to school administrators, students of educational administration and curricula, school counselors and school psychologists, classroom teachers and their department heads, state and county departments of education (and their counterparts in other countries), and to organizational researchers in universities, research and development centers, and regional educational laboratories.

We have designed this book both as a text for college classes and as a tool kit for educators. It can be used in classes in curriculum and instruction, educational administration, public policy, school counseling, school psychology, and the social psychology of education. It can also be used as a resource for inservice training of school administrators, staff personnel, and teachers.

Most important, this book has been written for educators who want to bring about constructive organizational change in their work settings. We have in mind administrators and teachers who hope for better organizational climates, educators who strive for more effective schools, and organizational specialists who have been specially trained to operate as helpful facilitators with their colleagues. Indeed, this book addresses anyone who wants to lift morale and raise achievement levels of students through more humane, consistent, and effective teaching. We should no longer think of organization and curriculum as separate fields; good organization offers the soil for good teaching.

We have written each chapter and major section to be understood and used independently from the rest of the book. Curious readers who do not have time to read the whole book over and over can easily use any section. In addition to the table of contents, we have prepared a detailed index to make topics easily accessible. One particular topic is often indexed under two or three key words. Throughout, we have tried to compensate for the inevitable redundancy by providing different perspectives on the same phenomena.

The third edition is more mature and tightly written than the first two editions—offering a more coherent and concisely stated theory, a more completely tested technology, more exercises and procedures, more information about diagnosis and evaluation, and much more conceptualization and techniques for designing. We have tried, too, to make the third edition useful for both small and large consultations. Clusters of chapters offer ideas, exercises, and procedures for moderate-sized chunks of work—for example:

- Chapters 1 (theory), 2 (macrodesigning), 8 (microdesigning), and 9 (diagnosis) introduce readers to the tasks of the organizational specialist.
- Chapters 3 (communication), 4 (meetings), and 5 (problem solving) offer materials for a workshop on effective work in groups.
- Chapters 5 (problem solving), 6 (decision making), and 7 (conflict) offer materials for an advanced workshop for a group dealing with difficult problems.
- Chapters 9 (diagnosis) and 10 (evaluation) constitute a guide for evaluating an educational program.

In this edition we have also revised and expanded Chapter 11 (institutionalizing). We describe several local self-help groups of organizational specialists; we call them *cadres* or *peer cadres*. These specialists are able to bring OD into effective use at surprisingly little cost. They are able to transfer the fruits of research and development on OD in schools from researchers and professors to administrators and teachers. We think they are the key to the institutionalized dissemination of OD. To them, indeed, we dedicate this book.

Since the second edition of the *Handbook*, the use of OD in schools has continued to spread. The appearance of new cadres of organization specialists is one obvious part of the evidence. But perhaps more important, OD has become commonplace in recent work on staff development, effective schools, teamwork in middle schools, and citizens' advisory boards. What is done in such settings might not be labeled OD, but it nonetheless concerns team building, clarifying communication, group problem-solving, and collaborative decision-making—activities central to OD. Many new techniques have appeared, too, and we have included some of these in this book. Further, both practice and research on OD have been paying more attention to the interactions between subsystems in schools and the community environment, and to the task-centered side of what organizational theorists call sociotechnical systems. This third edition takes account of these trends.

Some cadres of OD specialists in schools have formed their own network. Once a year in Eugene, members of those district cadres gather to exchange experiences, information, and friendship. The eighth such conference was held in early February, 1984. For information about the network, or for permission to copy parts of this book for educational purposes, write to either Richard Schmuck or Philip Runkel at the College of Education, University of Oregon, Eugene 97403.

Although the third edition of the *Handbook* is the sole responsibility of Schmuck and Runkel, portions of it naturally remain the contributions of our coauthors of the previous two handbooks. We are grateful to Jane H. Arends, Richard I. Arends, C. Brooklyn Derr, Ronald T. Martell, and Steven L. Saturen for their contributions. In addition, we appreciate the thoughtful reading of a preliminary draft of the manuscript given by William G. Cunningham of Old Dominion University and Fred C. Feitler of Youngstown State University. And to Phyllis Wells and Barbara Platz, our dedicated typists, we extend a very special thanks.

The Handbook of
Organization Development
in Schools

1

Theory and Technology

Schools are social organizations. Without interdependence, collaboration, and commitment among their participants, schools are only wood, concrete, and paper. Typically, educational improvement requires less change in the paper, and more change in the patterns of human interdependence, collaboration, and commitment. Deliberate efforts at school improvement usually affect not only the principal and faculty as individuals, but also relationships between the principal and faculty and their collective relationships with students and parents. For example, improvements in curriculum or instruction are almost always accompanied by changes within the school in such relationships as authority, communication, status, and even friendship. Consciously capitalizing on such social phenomena to bring about and stabilize a desired innovation is a major concern of organization development (OD).

EXAMPLES OF OD

Every two weeks for the past three months, Mike has been driving from a nearby college of education to the central office of a school district, where he consults with the superintendent's cabinet.

I

Before each visit, he talks with the convener of the upcoming meeting, both to coach the convener in ways to run the meeting and to find out what has happened in the cabinet since his last visit.

Once the meeting begins, Mike observes the way the cabinet members work through their agenda. He observes the norms and attitudes they exhibit toward one another—in what they say or don't say, in the way they phrase questions and comments, and in their nonverbal behavior. From time to time, he comments on the distribution of the participation, the clarity of the decisions, the commitment to the decisions, or the ways in which the group is collecting information to solve its problems. Occasionally he offers a summary of his observations to support his comments or to encourage cabinet members to talk with one another about how the group is working. Mike is using the OD technique of *process observation and feedback.*

Paula chairs the English Department and Don is a counselor at a large senior high school. Both received training in organizational consultation from a nonprofit organization while on their respective sabbaticals last year, and both became aware of their shared frustration with the low parental involvement in their school. Working together, they persuaded their principal to allocate money so that other faculty members could join them in planning a new parent-involvement strategy. They then addressed a faculty meeting to explain what they wanted to accomplish and to recruit volunteers for a task force. During the following month, Paula and Don convened a three-day retreat at which task-force members developed a formal proposal to create a representative group composed of one administrator, three teachers, and three parents, all to be elected by their constituencies. The function of this newly formed group would be to coordinate activities in the school that already did or could involve parents. The faculty adopted the proposal, and the principal agreed to try out the new organizational structure if Paula and Don would train the group in collaborative problem solving and joint decision making. After elections to the group were held, Paula and Don carried out a four-hour training session with the new group that included practice in the skills of communication, problem solving, and consensual decision making. Paula and Don were using the OD techniques of *training.*

Pat (an elementary school principal), Lee (a junior high counselor), and Lynn (a senior high biology teacher) are members of a cadre of organizational specialists in their school district. As an ad hoc consulting team, they are collaborating with an elementary school faculty—the principal, teachers, counselor, reading specialist, three aides, and a secretary—that agreed last year to try out team teaching. Pat, Lee, and

Lynn volunteered to help those faculty members move out from their self-contained classrooms and to help them take on new role relationships as team leaders and team members.

These OD specialists attend all team meetings at the school and frequently serve as facilitators when conflicts surface. A lot of conflict has erupted this year as faculty members try to articulate their goals and negotiate the sharing of materials, space, and resources. Plenty of time in staff meetings is left open to permit team leaders and members to discuss how instruction should be supervised in the school. The specialists help organize these role-clarification discussions so that the faculty can uncover differences and arrange to work collaboratively on important instructional problems. Pat, Lee, and Lynn are making use of the OD techniques of *constructive confrontation*.

Vera, an elementary school teacher, and Dick, a senior high counselor, are also members of a cadre of OD specialists in their school district. They have been asked by their cadre coordinator to help a planning team at a middle school with an effort to improve the climate of the entire school. As a first step, the team prepares a climate questionnaire to collect data from everyone in the school. Vera and Dick's role is to offer the planning team examples of climate questionnaires, to help the team prepare its own questionnaire, to facilitate collecting and analyzing the data, and to collaborate with the planning team in feeding back those data to the staff. After the data are discussed by the entire staff, Vera and Dick will help the staff form into problem-solving groups to create action plans for climate improvement. Vera and Dick are using the OD technique of *survey-data-feedback*.

OD DEFINED

Certain features of those four projects are characteristic of organization development in schools. All four projects were *systematically planned* by the prime movers (Mike, Paula, Lee, Vera, etc.) in collaboration with school participants. All showed *sustained effort* over time and encompassed arrangements for continued effort. All focused on altering the dynamics of the *social system* in which the individual were embedded. All showed *self-study*—conscious examination of present social conditions, actions, and procedures in the school. All instituted *planned change*. Two of the projects brought about new *organizational structures*. All four projects dealt with *formal and informal procedures, processes, and norms*. All had the *intent* of improving *organizational functioning*. Finally, all had a *direct or indirect focus on educational issues*.

The italicized words are features of a definition of organization development in school summarized by Fullan, Miles, and Taylor (1980, p. 135) from dozens of definitions in the literature:

> Organizational development (OD) in school districts is a coherent, systematically planned, sustained effort at system self-study and improvement, focusing explicitly on change in formal and informal procedures, processes, norms, or structures, and using concepts of behavioral science. The goals of OD are to improve organizational functioning and performance. OD in schools has a direct focus on educational issues.

Although the four examples are similar in the several ways listed above, they also demonstrate the variety of possible approaches to OD in schools. For example, by sitting with the cabinet during its meetings and offering his perceptions of the cabinet's group dynamics, Mike was using the technique of process observation and feedback. Paula and Don, in contrast, designed and executed a four-hour training session in which they took on the high-profile role of trainers. Pat, Lee, and Lynn dealt primarily with uncovering conflict, constructive confrontation, and role negotiation, while Vera and Dick employed the classical OD approach of collecting survey data from the school staff and feeding it back to all for subsequent problem solving.

The undertakings in our four examples might seem of a kind that arises ordinarily in schools. They might not seem to deserve a special label such as organization development. But one more feature of the definition makes the important difference: *the use of concepts from behavioral science.* Many educators assume that some people are skillful at working in groups like superintendents' cabinets, and some are not, and that's it. Mike, however, believes that skill in group work can be learned. He knows that people can learn to talk about their group processes and that they can be encouraged to practice new skills. Furthermore, he knows that he can help by modeling skilled participation and by stopping the work occasionally to enable cabinet members to talk explicitly about what they see themselves doing. In carrying out the responsibilities of his role as consultant, he uses the concepts of observable group processes and techniques of process observation and feedback.

Paula and Don believe that work is more likely to get done if the people who will do it have a voice in planning it. Some principals, if they agreed with Paula and Don in wanting parents to participate more in the school, would simply appoint a group to recruit parents to work. Paula and Don, knowing that the success of such a venture requires active participation by faculty, asked for volunteers from the faculty to form a working core, and then allowed three days for those teachers to agree about and commit themselves to action. That group, knowing that parents are best recruited by parents, insisted that some members of the task force be parents elected by parents. Finally, Paula and Don, like Mike, know that skill in problem solving and joint decision making is needed if the task force is to be effective. They therefore trained the new group.

Pat, Lee, and Lynn are alert to the conflicts that inevitably arise when teaching teams are formed. When people find themselves in conflict with others, they often begin to fear they will lose something they want. They find that demands are made upon them that they do not want to satisfy, and they begin to worry. Naturally, they wish the fears, demands, and worry would go away. Pat, Lee, and Lynn, however, believe that conflict is inevitable when people participate in innovation, and they know that it can be an occasion for creativity. They know that fears, strong language, demands, and worries are side-effects of resolving an array of differing goals, values, and ways of working, and they know that skills in working with conflict are usually poorly developed. Thus, they choose to conduct confrontation sessions, in which the conflicts can be dealt with in a disciplined way.

Vera and Dick believe that data collected from everyone on a staff permit the sort of self-analysis in a school that can lead to productive change. They also believe that staff members won't come to "own" such data unless they have some say in the sorts of data that are collected. These two have therefore adopted a strategy in which a planning team participates collaboratively with them in developing and executing survey-data-feedback. Vera and Dick believe that problem clarity and ownership are prerequisites to problem solving and school improvement.

Mike, Paula, Don, Pat, Lee, Lynn, Vera, and Dick all believe that the well-meaning professionals, service personnel, parents, and students who make up schools often form into ineffective and poorly coordinated groups. They understand, too, that people in schools typically do not make deliberate efforts to examine their communication patterns, their customary ways of working together in meetings, or the ways in which they are linked together to get their work done. To legitimize the examination of these important phenomena, the OD facilitators bring to their clients both a conceptualization of organizational life and a strategy for change.

An underlying assumption of OD is that schools consist of behavioral and programmatic regularities that do not depend for their existence primarily on particular personalities. Further, organization development theorizes that many efforts at educational reform have collapsed or have been absorbed without effect precisely because of the limited attention given to the organizational context in which the reforms have been attempted. The assumption follows that major innovation in curriculum or instructional techniques requires alterations in the school's behavioral and programmatic regularities—in short, educational innovations require changes in the "culture" of the school.

The tenacity of a school's culture lies in the power of norms, how well they are adhered to, and how resistant they are to change. Norms are shared expectations, usually implicit, that help guide the psychological processes and the behaviors of group members. Note that this definition of norm emphasizes *sharing*; norms occur in groups and are not merely intrapsychic processes. When a norm is present, most people know that their view of things is shared by others, and that the others expect them to have the same viewpoint and to behave accordingly.

The following additional assumptions guide our thinking and action in relation to school improvement and the work of most OD consultants:

1. *Groups differ from a sum of individuals.* A group has a character that is more than the pooling of its members' personalities. The ability of a group to do work stems not merely from the individuals' abilities and attitudes, but also from the ways in which the individuals coordinate, dovetail, and complement the uses of those abilities and attitudes. Working together socially requires skills that cannot be contained within a single individual. Those interpersonal skills come into play when two or more individuals are acting in concert. A school's potentiality is greater than the sum, but its performance can be less than the sum.

2. *Change occurs through subsystems.* Because a work group is more than an assembly of individuals, an organization can change its way of working more surely by directing the effort to "intact work groups"—to its *subsystems*—than to individuals.

3. *Members' goals and motives have relevance.* The actions of individuals are influenced by their goals and social motives. Since coordination depends on knowing what actions people are likely to take, knowledge of others' goals and motives aids coordination. Knowing the goals and motive satisfactions of its members can be as useful to a school staff as knowing members' knowledge, skills, or other capabilities.

4. *Member's feelings have relevance.* Humans become emotionally aroused when they encounter frustration or gratification, and those feelings affect their actions. Since coordination depends on knowing what actions people are likely to take, knowledge of others' feelings can aid coordination. Knowing members' feelings can be as useful to the school staff as knowing members' knowledge, skills, or other resources.

5. *Untapped resources have relevance.* Individuals and groups usually possess abilities, information, and skills beyond those typically expected of them. If tapped, these resources can be used to facilitate improved organizational functioning. The where-

withal for problem solving, for example, frequently already resides within the members of the school staff.

6. *Change comes from within.* Although initial help toward changing the school organization often comes from an outside consultant, people within often possess much of the knowledge and skill needed to create and implement new programs, especially when the change involves reorganizing the structure of the school or altering ways in which staff members work together. The long-range goal of OD is to transmit necessary knowledge and skills to the group members themselves. A school staff that has internalized OD knowledge and skills and that has members who can facilitate the staff's joint work can be regarded as *self-renewing* and as possessing *adaptability.*

THE HISTORY OF OD

Organization development has been used in industrial and governmental organizations since the mid-1950s. Its use continues to spread. As good a marker as any for the beginning of OD is the workshop directed by Kurt Lewin at Teachers' College, New Britain, Connecticut, in June 1946. The workshop was conducted as an experiment in change and as training for workers in intergroup relations. The following summer, the National Training Laboratories were established at Gould Academy in Bethel, Maine.

In the early part of this century, the dominant theory of organizational design was that of "scientific management," which too many people interpreted as meaning that the work of humans, after analysis by time-and-motion studies, should be made as machinelike as possible. That view was weakened, however, after a series of studies was conducted from 1924 to 1932 at the Hawthorne plant of the Western Electric Company. Several social scientists writing between 1933 an 1947 interpreted those experiments as showing that workers would respond favorably, with higher production, to interested and sympathetic attention from supervisors and managers. Though the validity of that interpretation has been challenged, there is no doubt that the Hawthorne experiments drew intense interest from social scientists nor that the experiments prompted further studies and theorizing that became a part of the "human relations movement"—one important strand in the history of OD.

The human relations movement fit nicely with the results of the training and experimentation conducted at Bethel by the National Training Laboratories. It was discovered at Bethel that members of groups could examine explicitly the social processes that made their groups effective. In group after group, it was also discovered that members cared a good deal about the relationships with one another. Especially when the group was given no explicit task to carry out and when it was free from a close time limit, members spontaneously made known their feelings toward one another. That discovery led to "sensitivity training" in "T-groups," a way of purposely training people to become more aware of the emotions that typically develop in groups.

The early development of OD was in part a reaction against "scientific management," and it was therefore natural for some of the early consultants to pay attention almost exclusively to the "human" side of the work, giving short shrift to the technical side. For some years, OD had the reputation of ignoring the work that had to be done, focusing instead on participants' emotions and going round in interminable circles to reach consensual decisions. One heard the derogatory phrase "touchy-feely" and stories of hours spent in seeking consensus on picayune matters.

Organization development is not sensitivity training, and its designs typically do not include T-groups. OD honors people's feelings *when they are relevant to their work.* Feelings *are* aroused when people find strong satisfactions or experience deep frustrations in doing their jobs and working with others. Those feelings become one—only one—of the interpersonal *conditions* affecting the course of action people choose.

Seeking consensual decisions is important when the success of a task depends on coordinated action by all. People are more likely to carry out the actions called for by a decision when they understand the implications of the decision and when they have committed themselves publicly to shouldering their parts of the task. That principle has been shown to hold not only in schools, but in industry, government, human services, and the military. It is one of the reasons that OD facilitators advise that decision making occur low in the hierarchy, at the level of those who will do the work called for by the decision.

But that principle does *not* imply that all decisions should be made consensually or, in schools, only by teachers. Sometimes teachers are willing to carry out a decision no matter which way it goes. In a large school, for example, teachers know that putting together the schedule is a very complex matter, with many criteria to be balanced against one another. They know that the schedule is best made by only a few people—that trying to get the details ironed out in a large group would require more time and energy than the benefits would justify.

Nowadays, OD facilitators still respect the importance of members' feelings and consensual decision making, but only as they relate to solving the school's educational problems. Teachers' feelings are brought into OD meetings when they are relevant to getting the work done effectively, and consensual decision making is used only under special conditions. Contemporary OD gives balanced attention to all sides of work, adopting the view of the school as a *sociotechnical system*.

While organization development in schools has been strongly influenced by the earlier developments in industry, numerous modifications of industrial methods have been made to suit the special characteristics of the educational setting. In particular, three social-psychological conditions set schools off from most industrial organizations: (1) the nature of educational goals, (2) the amount and types of structural differentiation in schools, and (3) the school's unique vulnerability to short- and long-term pressures.

1. *Educational goals.* In contrast to industrial organizations, the goals of schools are special in at least three ways. First, educators exert a great deal of effort toward ends that are seldom concretely defined. For example, while tests measure student achievement, considerable debate goes on continually among educators about how to measure intellectual outcomes. And such outcomes as mental health, creativity, and citizenship are abstract and difficult to measure. Second, the goals of public education are immensely diverse, and their number is steadily increasing. Indeed, each new critic of public education as well as each new alternative program provides evidence that another list of pedagogical and social goals is being articulated. Teachers do not typically have time or energy to understand the new goals as fast as they are promulgated. Third, even the agreed-upon citizenship goals of the public schools take considerable time—usually twelve years or more—to become actualized in the behavior of large numbers of students. Educators must face the frustration of coping with this time span with a huge new cohort of students each year; this perennial frustration is further complicated by the absence of indicators and a sophisticated technology for assessing progress at interim points.

2. *Structural differentiation.* A second organizational characteristic that distinguishes schools from industries is the amount and type of role differentiation that exists in each. Jobs in public schools tend to be much less highly differentiated than jobs in many industrial organizations in which organization development has flourished. Even with increased emphasis on differentiated staffing in schools and the movement to unionize teachers, the number of levels of role differentiation in schools is small. Particularly noticeable in elementary schools is the absence of middle-level managers and of status levels among the

paraprofessional or support staff. While even in secondary schools differentiation among these levels is minimal, specialization—based on real or imagined content differences—by subject matter is extreme. Neither differentiation nor specialization supports norms of active collaboration and cooperation in many schools since teachers and others prefer sharing the functions performed by superordinates and subordinates over sharing responsibility with one another.

3. *Social pressures.* Compared with many industrial organizations, schools are typically less vulnerable to competition but more vulnerable to short-term community pressures. Although public schools are not required to compete against one another to sustain themselves, the effects of many of their day-to-day procedures are readily visible to parents. Still, though their institutions stand largely in a noncompetitive relationship to other public schools, educators often respond either laggingly or defensively to shifts in their cultural, social, and intellectual environments, and tend to respond as public relations experts or emergency brush-fire fighters to short-term crises brought on by students and parents. It is difficult to fit organization development into either of these educator perspectives.

These special features of school organizations—features that in many ways run counter to the theory and technology of organization development—have been at least partly responsible for the slowness with which organization development has caught on in schools. It was not until the 1960s, therefore, that the first systematic effort to carry out and conduct research on organization development in school districts was launched, by Miles (1963). His three-year project on organization development in schools, at Teachers College, Columbia University, involved collaboration with two school districts near New York and Pittsburgh, respectively. Since that historic project, organization development in schools has grown slowly but steadily. It has now established sufficient credibility and legitimacy to make it an important part of the educator's repertoire.

THE GOALS OF OD

The chief goal for organization development is that the school achieve a sustained capacity for solving its own problems. Such a school monitors its environment and takes action to control inputs from the environment. The problem-solving school finds, maintains, and uses its resources, ideas, and energy. It is conscious of the skills it needs and takes steps to improve them when necessary. It periodically reviews its goals and alters them to suit its capacities and circumstances. The subgoals of OD, which take a school along the road to a sustained capacity for solving its own problems, are to clarify communication, establish clear goals, uncover and resolve conflicts and problems in groups, make clear decisions that capture commitment, and self-consciously assess the directions the work is taking.

Above all, OD consultants value the collaborative effort among themselves, educators, students, and parents in striving to create new, more democratic social structures and more humanized interpersonal relationships. Other values include expanding all the participants' consciousnesses about how others think and feel and continually finding more choices for new action. Other important values are authenticity in interpersonal relations; a collaborative, democratic conception of freedom and control; participation and interpersonal respect; and, finally, a commitment to new directions the school might take.

Why do we insist that schools should be able to sustain a heightened capacity for solving their own problems? After all, some might say, schools do solve problems, if only in the sense of muddling through. We do not object to muddling through if staff members have, with some consensus, deliberately chosen that method for dealing with a particular problem. Staff members, however, often let themselves in for much wasted effort, frustration, and conflict when they expect to progress from A to B to C but in fact are only muddling. The methods of OD in a school can save much effort from being wasted, solve some sorts of educational problems more surely than is typical now, and yield to the staff feelings of competence, solidarity, and pride.

Organization development aims at improving the interpersonal and group procedures used by administrators, teachers, students, and parents to reach their educational objectives. It focuses primarily on the *how* of interpersonal and group interactions rather than on the *what* of their content. The success of organization development as a school-improvement strategy is measured by the effectiveness with which the recipients—whether they be educators, students, or parents—work together in reaching their respective objectives. This success is determined by how effective the recipients are in defining their problems and goals (which may, for example, have to do with the content of a program of remedial reading); how resourceful they are in devising ways to reach their goals (which may include conferring with a content consultant in reading methods); and how stable, adaptive, and effective the group's products are over time (as indicated, for example, by measuring the long-term effectiveness of a reading program).

STRATEGIES OTHER THAN OD

Three fundamental strategies employed today for school improvement will clarify OD further: (1) consultative assistance, (2) content consultation, and (3) process consultation.

Consultative Assistance

The strategy of *consultative assistance* employs consultants to fulfill an educational need usually, though not always, considered temporary by the school participants. An expert may be hired to teach a course, or a management firm might be hired to help administrators decide on optimal allocations of money for classrooms or athletic facilities. Sometimes business firms are hired to take over instruction when they guarantee to improve students' mastery of certain subjects. Consultative assistance can help schools fill a temporary gap, but it does not typically improve the skills of other educators in the school. Nor does this strategy give the educators a personal understanding of the nature of the assistance. As a result it is difficult for the educators to pick up any of the consultant's skills and become more self-sufficient. Indeed, most consultants who do short-term work on limited problems have a vested interest in keeping their skills to themselves. OD consultants, in contrast, try to make their consultations long enough and their methods participative enough to enable educators to acquire some OD skills and lessen their dependence on outside consultants.

Content Consultation

The strategy of *content consultation* employs consultants to train educators in the direct content of their jobs to improve their performance as individuals. The consultant sets out to raise participants' cognitive understanding of new procedures and their commitment to the change. The most typical way the content consultant works is through an in-service workshop in a subject such as reading, mathematics, social studies, or the arts. In other examples, a psychologist might teach teachers about child development, a mathematician could help teachers develop new instructional strategies, a mental health consultant could help teachers cope with students having emotional problems, and a management consultant might offer administrators practice in leadership skills. Although the potential for organizational change is present, content consultants do not focus directly on system improvement. Rather, they try to bring about changes in cognitions, attitudes, and skills within individuals, and therefore do not directly facilitate organizational changes. OD consultants spend only a little time with individuals apart from the working group and almost no time with individuals collected for schoollike instruction. OD consultants do take some time to heighten participants' cognitive understanding of the new collaborative processes, but only enough time at one sitting to enable participants to move with more awareness into the next stage of practice.

Process Consultation

The strategy of *process consultation* employs consultants to improve the *procedures* used to reach educational objectives. Process consultants deal with such phenomena as patterns of communication, leadership attempts, underlying tensions, and decision-making procedures. Process consultants do not deal directly with the subject matter—the immediate content—of the interactions. In that respect, they work like OD consultants. Indeed, OD makes use of many of the techniques of process consultation. We list process consultation here as a strategy separate from OD, however, because it can be used—as indeed it often is—with one small group in an organization without touching the organization as a whole. Though OD usually includes process consultation with small parts of the organization, it goes much beyond that. OD consultants do not expect their work to have long-term effects until it reaches throughout an organization—to the entire school or even the entire district.

OD THEORY IN SCHOOLS

Like any organization, a school contains individuals. In one sense, individuals constitute the most fundamental subsystems of the educational enterprise, but we shall spend little time in this book on the individual participant per se. For, while school districts seem by and large to be attuned to the challenges of individual development, they are notoriously weak in their abilities to nurture their own social subsystems for organizational development. School staffs are also weak in their abilities to cooperate, and often even the school's smallest groups, its departments, teams, and committees, experience difficulties. By and large, schools need to give more attention to their own organizational development.

Subsystems

By *subsystems* we mean an intact group—several individuals organized to carry out one or more tasks. Subsystems have tasks to perform, require interdependence among the members, and exhibit a structure through which patterned social interaction occurs. A curriculum committee, the administrative cabinet, the classroom containing students and teacher, and the custodial staff are all subsystems. An individual usually belongs to more than one subsystem. The name of a subsystem is often a good clue to its primary function.

Schools are composed of subsystems that perform various functions, from designing curricula to ordering supplies, and each subsystem includes people, supplies, space, and information. Some subsystems are easy to draw on an organization chart, some are not. People belong to a subsystem if its function depends on them, regardless of where they lie on an organization chart. That is true of equipment, too, no matter what room it is in. The boundaries of subsystems are both formal and informal. To be sure where the boundaries lie, where they are unyielding and where they are permeable, a consultant must often do a good deal of prowling about.

Some subsystems have vague, easily penetrable boundaries. The subsystem in a district that serves the function of socializing new teachers, for example, might not have a designated space in which to carry out its task, a budget, or a stable roster of members. Other subsystems have more definite boundaries, which make them easier to locate. For example, the counseling staff is different from the math department, and that is obvious to everyone. In some cases, legal arrangements involving contracts and credentials prevent outsiders from penetrating the boundaries of an educational subsystem.

Classifications. Miller (1978) divides subsystems into three kinds: those that deal with matter or energy (e.g., bringing coal to the furnace or printing diplomas); those that deal with information (e.g., teaching); and those that deal with both (e.g., maintaining a physical boundary around the organization by erecting walls or by screening the information that goes through the principal's office). Miller (p. 3) goes on to describe nineteen subsystems according to their functions. His list is exhaustive and offers a good guide to the functions an organization must provide, but we will not elaborate his subsystems, because our purpose is to focus attention on those features of schools that now get short shrift and that the methods of organization development can help.

Some OD facilitators find the classification by Katz and Kahn (1978) to be helpful. Their scheme categorizes the organization's functions as *production, support, maintenance, adaptation,* and *management.* The production subsystem carries on the fundamental work of the organization—in schools, that is teaching students the curriculum. The support subsystem provides the material needed by the production subsystem to operate—library, classroom aides, curriculum specialists, texts, and supplies. The maintenance subsystem coordinates and motivates action close to production (instruction)—committees, informal helpfulness among teachers, and norms about "the way we do things around her." The adaptation subsystem anticipates changes in the environment and alters internal processes accordingly—the superintendent's dealings with the school board, curriculum committees anticipating the demands of parents or technological changes in the society, budgeting decisions to anticipate tax revenues, and so on. The management subsystem coordinates the school as a whole—making decisions to convert policy into procedure, specifying job descriptions, and allocating funds.

However one prefers to classify subsystems, the key concept for the OD practitioner is that of the *intact group*. Whenever one wishes to improve some function in a school, the facilitator almost always encounters interdependence among several people whose work carries out that function. The work proceeds partly because the members of that group can predict adequately one another's actions, and because they demand certain actions from one another. Those predictions and demands hold the work in place. If the manner of work is to be changed, there must be changes in the predictions and demands *among* the individuals who work together, and the *intact group thus becomes the best strategic target of change.*

Feedback. Subsystems act to control their inputs. A classroom group, for example, acts to optimize the input of information through the teacher, books, field trips, and other means. It also acts to get maximum favorable information about students' learning by way of test results and comments of students, parents, administrators, and other teachers.

In every subsystem, the members want feedback from those their actions affect so they can anticipate the future input those others will give in return. System theorists call this the *cybernetic* principle. Feedback that encourages the subsystem to continue what it is doing is *positive* (regardless of whether what it is doing is considered by anyone to be good or bad), and feedback that discourages what the subsystem is doing is called *negative*. Feedback is a core concern of OD.

Conflict Among Subsystems. Most OD facilitators assume that conflict is inevitable in organizations, and some say that organizations cannot be creative unless they allow participation that exposes conflicts. Kouzes and Mico (1979) write persuasively that schools have conflicts built into their structure. They say that three kinds of subsystems are inevitably in conflict—those in the domains of *policy*, *management*, and *service*. For school districts, the policy domain is primarily occupied by the school board. In the main, the administrators make up the management domain, and the teachers the service domain.

Typically, people working in the policy domain are elected representatives. They measure their success by whether they make just, impartial, and fair decisions. Their work modes involve negotiating, bargaining, and voting. Those in the management domain view the organization as hierarchy and bureaucracy. They measure their success in terms of cost efficiency and organizational effectiveness. Their work mode is linear and rational. Those in the service domain typically operate by autonomy, collegiality, and self-regulation. They measure their success by the quality of instruction and by whether they act according to professional standards. Their attention goes to process more than product, and their work mode is client-specific and oriented to problem solving.

Management's insistence on conformity to rules conflicts with the service domain's focus on the needs of students. The policy domain's norm of airing disagreements in public conflicts with the management's norm of refraining from doing so. The norm of fair and equitable treatment among the policy makers conflicts with the demand for cost efficiency in the management domain, and that conflicts with the maintenance of professional standards in the service domain.

Representation among the policy makers, bureaucracy in the management, and collegiality for those performing service require different kinds of interpersonal norms, and conflicts arise when a participant in one domain expects to be treated by norms that seem inappropriate to persons in another domain. The linear work modes in the management domain, the individualized treatment of complex human problems in the service domain, and the mode of negotiation and bargaining in the policy domain call for different interpersonal norms and values. It would be fruitless for participants in all three domains to try to adhere to the same work norms and professional standards.

Meyer and Rowan (1977) argue that the school board and the administrators (policy and management domains) have the job of looking outward toward the public, while teachers (service domain) have the job of looking inward toward students. Board and administrators must deal with the public through a large—and simplified—picture of the district. Teachers must deal with students through detailed and technical procedures. That difference, too, is a source of conflict.

One important way to reduce the likelihood of conflict is to arrange work so that people from different domains do not often interact with one another. Division of labor is the typical strategy—among individuals, committees, departments, and so on, with specific resources allocated to each. To the extent that interdependence among persons or groups of diverse domains can be minimized, the occasions for conflict can be minimized. Weick (1976) and others call that reduced interdependence *loose coupling*. Schools are notoriously loosely coupled.

Features of School Organizations

One or more features of schools distinguish them from industrial firms, the military, and churches. These features generate both opportunities and restrictions not found in other organizations. We have already mentioned the "natural" conflicts among the policy, management, and service domains, and the school's loose coupling. Below are some other features that OD facilitators have found noteworthy.

Nonvoluntary. Although faculty members join schools voluntarily, the membership of students is coerced. Hirschman (1970, p. 4) points out that members can express their dissatisfaction with an organization in two ways: they can leave it or they can voice their complaints. Teachers can quit and find employment elsewhere, even though it is sometimes difficult. Up to a specified age, students are constrained from leaving. They often express their complaints by word or action while staying in school. Some of those words and actions (vandalism, for example) become a main source of problems for the school.

Funding. The funding of public schools is loosely coupled to its performance. If a manufacturing firm turns out a poor product, it loses customer revenues. Schools can experience a drop in funding, too, if parents become dissatisfied, but the action is delayed, and it is often difficult to trace the connection between the dissatisfaction and events in a particular school.

Near-monopoly. Competition among schools, even where it is felt, has in the past had little effect on joining or leaving by teachers or students. Recently in many parts of the nation, however, a greater proportion of parents have been sending their children to private schools.

The Membership of Students. Students are members of the organization in some ways, and in other ways they are clients. Students are like clients in that they receive services from the professional faculty. They are also like clients in that they have little voice in the operation of the school, no career line within the school (they cannot be promoted to teacher), an officially limited tenure, and no possibility of being paid for their work.

Permeability. Schools are highly permeable to the environment. Customers of an industrial firm have very limited ways of making known their dissatisfactions. Parents and others with special interests, however, can do many things: vote against levies, vote for different board members, voice complaints at board meetings, initiate meetings of interest groups and demand that administrators attend, visit the school and complain to administrators, complain to teachers, and instruct their children to make various kinds of demands on the teachers.

Multiple and Unclear Goals. Typically, factions in schools have differing visions of educational goals, sometimes radical differences, and it is difficult for one group to describe its goals clearly to another. Whatever other goal a commercial firm may have, the "bottom line" is making a profit. Perhaps the bottom line for schools is maintaining order, though most educators are not satisfied with that. But it is difficult to be specific, when framing educational goals, about the kinds of behavior the education should produce, the preferred domains of behavior, acceptable evidence, and the point in the student's career when a judgment of success should be made.

Information, Not Goods. Almost the whole business of schools is to deal with information and the skills to use it. Schools do not manufacture goods or provide services connected with goods such as washing laundry, repairing typewriters, or transporting groceries. The stuff schools deal with is information, by which we mean more than the formal curriculum. When teachers transmit skill in reading, painting, or basketball, they do the *transmitting* by communicating information and values. Some business firms or churches come close to schools in having information and values as their sole stuff but schools are the purest case.

Formal and Informal Structures

The formal structure of the school, the result of tradition and rational planning, often limits the school's capacity to deal with unpredictable contingencies. Even when administrators try to provide jobs, communication channels, committees, ombudsmen, personnel directors, or some other scheme for adapting to the uniqueness of different individuals, unusual problems still arise that cannot be contained within the formal routines. When unusual demands stir urgent demands, when the formal arrangements become too cumbersome, people find help quickly by opening their own communication channels to informally offered helping roles. No doubt, too, people sometimes feel safer with the informal than with the formal arrangements. In sum, the informal "structure" arises because the school's members have abilities, needs, and feelings that cannot be encompassed by the formal structure.

Although it is true that the informal subsystems sometimes subvert the operations of the formal subsystems, we should not look upon the informal side of the school as clandestine or always subversive. Since rational planning and formal structure is inevitably inadequate, the informal structure is a necessary part of the complete organization. OD facilitators work with both the formal and the informal subsystems with equal openness.

Norms, Roles, Structures, and Procedures

A *norm* exists when, within a collection of people, certain ranges of behavior are approved, others are disapproved, and still others are neither approved nor disapproved. If, in a high school class in writing, most students express acceptance of a student who writes an essay of ten pages but make resentful remarks both to a student who "tries to get away" with five pages and also to one who "tries to show us up" with twenty pages, then a class norm exists regarding essay length. For a norm to have effect, people must express approval or disapproval about certain ranges of behavior. If the norm is to be clear, it must be *shared*—that is, most people must agree on the ranges of behavior to be approved and disapproved. Where people give mixed approval and disapproval, the norm is weak because it is confusing.

Norms hold together the organization's patterns of behavior. Some norms are official rules and regulations. Such formal norms have effect when a large proportion of the members of the school give approval to those who conform and disapproval to those who do not. The rules are ineffective or "on paper only" when they are contravened without disapproval.

Roles are norms about how a person in a particular organizational position should perform—or, more exactly, how two or more persons should interact on the job. Schools have norms, for example, about how teachers should behave toward students and how students should behave toward teachers; there can be no teacher's role without students and no student's role without teachers.

Structures are norms about roles assigned to several interrelated jobs: about performance in those jobs, responsibilities among jobs, and so on.

Procedures are the actions taken through the structure. They are "the way we do things around here." Procedures can be formal or informal, and they are held in place by norms.

When innovations are undertaken in schools, norms must be changed, because they hold the current structures and procedures in place. Since norms exist among role takers, not within individuals, the OD facilitator should expect to work mostly with the intact group to change them. The OD facilitator strives to help school staffs become explicit about the norms they wish to have in their school.

OD STRATEGY IN SCHOOLS

To change norms, roles, structures, and procedures so that a school can become self-renewing, the OD facilitator keeps three goals in mind: (1) organizational adaptability, (2) individual motive satisfaction, and (3) effective subsystems.

Organizational Adaptability

The ultimate goal of developing an organization is to bring it to a sustained capacity to solve its own problems. We call this quality *organizational adaptability*. By *adaptability* we mean that the school constructively manages change, that it does not merely adjust or acquiesce to externally imposed change. By *adaptable*, we mean what Gardner (1963) meant by *self-renewing*, what Buckley (1967) called *morphogenetic*, what Williamson (1974) called *inquiring*, and what Hedberg, Nystrom, and Starbuck (1976) called *self-designing*. We see organizational adaptability in schools as composed of four metaskills: the ability to (1) diagnose the functioning of groups in the school, (2) gather information and other resources from within and outside the schools, (3) mobilize synergistic action in the school, and (4) monitor the other three metaskills. A school with high levels of those skills can deal productively with changing demands and circumstances.

Diagnosis. Diagnosis is the systematic inspection by school participants of their own current functioning. In diagnosis, participants ask whether what the group or school is actually doing matches the way the members talk about what they are doing, and whether what they are doing is what they want to be doing. Diagnosis does not merely mean a yearly review, though that is usually a good idea. Rather, formal and informal diagnosis should be done as often as necessary to prevent stressful responses to crises.

By *systematic diagnosis*, we refer to two things. First, we mean collecting data in a manner that will give answers in which one can have reasonable confidence. If information is sought about what frustrations staff members are feeling, for example, it will not do to ask only the principal, or simply to ask for statements at a faculty meeting. Methods are needed that will survey all important segments of the staff and that will enable the respondents to feel safe in answering.

Second, we mean using a checklist, written or mental, to make sure that important aspects of school functioning are covered. The make-up of the particular list used is less important than the fact that a list exists that does in fact itemize all the important features of school life. (See the list below in "Effective Subsystems" for an example.)

Searching for Information and Other Resources. Searches are initiated whenever currently available information or any other resource is inadequate to plan an effective solution to a problem. A group skillful in dealing with problems will assess the degree to which later action depends on resolving an uncertainty. ("Do we need to know what might happen at that juncture?") If the possible answers to an uncertainty will have little effect on further action, the skillful group ceases discussion of the uncertainty. If clarifying the uncertainty can make a difference, the skillful group decides when the uncertainty must be resolved, how to get information to resolve it, and who will take the necessary steps. Those are the components of searching out information and sources.

Obviously, skill in gathering information and other resources is important in solving problems. A solution to a problem can founder if it turns out that staff members have less than they need of information, status, affection, services, materials, or money.

Mobilizing Synergistic Action. Even if a school were to exhibit well-developed norms, structures, and procedures for systematic diagnosis and for getting information and resources from inside and outside, it would still not show an exemplary capacity for solving problems. Even when all concerned had agreed on an accurate diagnosis of the present situation, when they had consensually chosen a clear and specific target, and when participants had declared their commitment to realistic and well-understood steps of action, a crucial step would still remain. Some staff members would actually have to take the first, risky, irretrievable action in the new mode.

We emphasize the necessity for *synergistic* group action in organizational change, because new norms and role relationships are more than the sum of all individual actions. Administrators, and others too, often try to bring about change by instructing every individual what to do and then saying, in effect, "On next Monday morning, do things the new way, not the old way." As everyone but a few top administrators seems to know, that method often thrusts people into high risks. Participants may lack the confidence that they can do the new thing correctly—in a manner that will please the others involved in the change, or at least not draw their wrath. It is often safer for them to go on doing things in the old way.

If change is to proceed, staff members must be in frequent communication up, down, and laterally to keep up with the latest developments. Collaboration must replace isolation and hierarchical direction so that all concerned can be aware of new action when it occurs, see for themselves who committed it, and give it their own support. Cooperation in processing problems and making decisions will yield new patterns of coordinated action that directives to separate individuals could not possibly have brought into being.

Monitoring the First Three Metaskills.   The monitoring ability is the crowning skill necessary to sustaining a capacity for solving problems in the school. The skill consists of the ability to observe one's own group and to ask, "Are we as skillful as we need to be in diagnosing our functioning, getting appropriate information and resources, and mobilizing our action? Are we able to move ourselves in the direction we want to go?" Answering those questions gives the participants in a school an awareness of their shared capacity to deal productively with problems and change.

Individual Motive Satisfaction

In choosing ways to improve schools, we must not disregard the satisfaction of human motives. Most of us would agree that a strong, resilient school that is able to meet internal and external challenges with competence will be populated by staff and students who are satisfied with their lives in the school.

Though many people work at jobs they find dissatisfying, many others look to their jobs for greater personal satisfaction than they find elsewhere. And it is not generally true that people dissatisfied at work make up for it at home or elsewhere. Indeed, when work is dull and passive, people usually do *not* choose leisure pursuits that answer needs for variety and vigorous activity, but turn instead to activities that are as undernourishing as their work. To ignore the satisfaction of human needs in the school is inevitably to bring about two undesirable results: students and staff will in one way or another increasingly remove themselves from serious work, and they will drag through each additional unrewarding day with growing discouragement.

Individuals act, when they can, to maximize their chances of taking initiative and being successful (the *achievement motive*), of enjoying friendship (the *affiliation motive*), and of exercising influence over their own fate (the *power motive*). They make choices: between behavior producing more achievement and that producing less; between behavior that is helpful and affectionate and that which is obstructive and expresses hostility, and between behavior that yields mastery of the environment and that which requires acquiescence to the will of others. OD facilitators believe that people are more likely to remain motivated, to keep more paths open to further satisfaction, and to become more productive if their motives for achievement, affiliation, and power can be expressed and satisfied in their work.

Effective Subsystems

Because the functions of schools are carried out through coordinated effort within subsystems, understanding what makes subsystems effective is crucial to understanding what makes schools adaptable. Indeed, improving subsystem effectiveness, coupled with efforts to improve interpersonal skill and satisfy human motives, constitutes the core of organization development. The following list describes seven highly interdependent capabilities of an effective subsystem. When one capability is increased, it is easier to increase others.

1. *Clarifying communication.* Because skill in communication opens channels within the subsystem and between it and other subsystems or segments of the environment, clarity of communication is essential to subsystem effectiveness.

2. *Improving group procedures in meetings.* The face-to-face meetings in which most organizational activity occurs need not be frustrating or unproductive. Procedures to facilitate task productivity and group maintenance can make meetings more satisfying.

3. *Establishing goals.* Because educational goals are diffuse and ambiguous, sharpening goal definitions can lead to exploring the differentiation and integration of effort needed to achieve them. Recognizing the pluralism of goals within a subsystem, school, and community can be a vital step toward an acceptance of differences and a greater commitment to common goals.

4. *Uncovering and working with conflict.* Just as clarifying communication and goals will lead to increased awareness of areas of conflict, so confronting conflict can help to clarify the norms that will aid the organization in accomplishing its tasks. Norms for collaboration can replace norms for avoiding conflict.

5. *Solving problems.* Adaptability implies continual active engagement in problem-solving cycles for identifying, analyzing, and

acting on environmental contingencies. Subsystems that harness human resources to extract creative solutions are more successful than are those that merely extrapolate past practice.

6. *Making decisions.* Effective subsystems, like adaptable organizations, must be capable of moving decisions into action; this can be done effectively only when people clearly understand a decision and are committed to it. Although it is not necessary for some to have less influence and others to have more, it is sometimes helpful to reduce authority that is not based on knowledge and competence.

7. *Assessing changes.* Change for its own sake does not necessarily lead to adaptability. Schools must develop criteria for measuring and evaluating progress toward meeting short-range and long-range goals.

OD TECHNOLOGY IN SCHOOLS

OD facilitators try to increase the clarity with which school participants choose what they want to do, the steps through which they will do it, and the signs by which they can decide whether they have succeeded. Facilitators help school participants to visualize those organizational procedures that will help and those that will hinder, to bring into open discussion opinions or feelings that can affect the job at hand, and to find ways the participants themselves can put to use conflicts that are ordinarily suppressed. Above all, OD facilitators *teach* participants how to work with their colleagues in solving organizational problems together.

Types of OD Designs

We distinguish four designs for organization development— (1) training, (2) survey-data-feedback, (3) constructive confrontation, and (4) process observation and feedback. The four call for different behavior from the OD facilitator.

Training. The type of OD design carried out most often with schools is training. As trainer, the OD facilitator determines the learning goals for a particular period of time and organizes and directs the activities. Thus, training involves highly planned teaching and experience-based learning in structured formats that often feature lecturettes and assigned readings. In our examples of OD in action presented at the beginning of this chapter, Paula and Don were engaged in a training design.

Certain *skills*, *exercises*, and *procedures* are regarded as the building blocks of organizational training. A *skill* may be one of communication, such as paraphrasing what a speaker has said to allow the speaker to verify your understanding of the message. Other examples of communicative skills are the ability to guide a group through a quick oral survey of opinion and to write interview queries that successfully elicit diagnostic information about a school.

An *exercise*, or simulation, is a structured, gamelike activity used to enable participants to be consciously aware of their own interpersonal behavior and that of others. Participants usually find it easy to see parallels between their experience in the exercise and their previous workday experience in school. Exercises have two important advantages: they can be designed to produce specifiable learning, and they typically have content very different from that of a school's ordinary day-to-day work. By enabling participants to learn the advantages of one form of behavior over another, an exercise helps them plan to establish more productive behavior.

Unlike exercises, whose content is determined by the trainer, *procedures* are content-free and are used for the purpose of making work more effective toward a specific goal chosen by the group. Under most conditions, experiencing an exercise takes a group away from its primary tasks. Procedures, on the other hand, are introduced to accomplish a task the group is already facing. As steps or routines by which a group can move forward in its actual business, procedures are less gamelike and also less obtrusive to the group's normal functioning. Procedures such as taking surveys and doing systematic problem solving are useful in schools, departments, and cabinets, and sometimes to teachers who have tried them with their students to improve the learning environment.

Survey-Data-Feedback. In *survey-data-feedback*, information is collected systematically and then reported back to appropriate subsystems as a basis for diagnosis, problem solving, and planning. Three aspects of survey-data-feedback are central to its success. First, the facilitator must be adept at collecting data and at putting the data into a feedback form that will be understandable and energizing to the participants. Second, the facilitator must strive to show essential significance in mundane data to capture participants' interests. Third, the facilitator must find ways of incorporating data feedback into the natural ebb and flow of larger consultative designs. Vera and Dick were using a survey-data-feedback design in our earlier examples.

Constructive Confrontation. The social relationships between two or more groups can often be classified by a *constructive confrontation*. This strategy also sharpens and clarifies problems that are causing conflicts between the groups. The facilitators bring together the conflicting groups and help them to make explicit the perceptions that each has of the others; to spell out the ways each views the others as helpful or unhelpful; to increase the openness, or at least the clarity, of communication; to propose procedures for problem solving that can facilitate collaborative inquiry into mutual problems; and to find common concerns, if any, among the parties. Pat, Lee, and Lynn were using elements of a constructive-confrontation design in their consultation with the elementary school that was converting to team teaching.

Process Observation and Feedback. In carrying out *process observation and feedback*, the purpose of which is to help group members become more aware of how they are working together, the facilitator sits with the client group during its work sessions, observes the ongoing processes, and offers occasional comments and questions to turn the clients' attention to their way of working and its effects on getting the job done. The goal of this type of facilitation is to involve participants in talking about their working relationships and in making group agreements to modify their ways of working together in the future. Mike was engaged in this sort of design with the superintendent's cabinet.

The Stages of OD

Although one or another type of OD design can be used to help solve small problems over short periods (to improve meetings, for example), a project in organization development that reaches throughout a school and aspires to bring to maturity its organizational adaptability is inevitably complex. Such a project typically goes through six stages.

Start-up and Contract Building. A school acknowledges a problem when some influential person or group within it conceives a state of affairs significantly more satisfactory than the current one. In our view, productive change is unlikely to occur unless the school personnel acknowledge a discrepancy between an ideal and actual state of affairs before an outsider arrives on the scene. That is, a sizable portion of the school staff, and especially its more powerful members, should accept the problems as their problems and become reasonably committed to solving them instead of merely acquiescing to a project that originates on the initiative of an outside consultant. OD facilitators should make it a rule to enter into contact with educational subsystems that are to some extent reaching out for help.

What happens during the first phase foreshadows those in later phases. If the project is to have support, a facilitator must get at least oral commitment to the enterprise from all the key groups that will participate in it. To that end, it is critical for the facilitator to establish rapport, credibility, and legitimacy at the outset, and to arrive at clear statements about motives, competencies, and shared expectations. Facilitators should be explicit about their role, their goals, the project's budget, and the time they are willing to devote to the project.

Although a facilitator may initially be contacted by an individual at any level of the organization, interactions are best begun between the faciltator and key leaders, because those leaders hold crucial gatekeeping power and can control subsequent contacts with other members of the system, and it is therefore helpful if they become allies rather than enemies. In districts, powerful parties typically include the school board, the superintendent and his or her cabinet, the principals, and teachers' organizations. In individual schools, the powerful parties may be the teachers, department heads, counselors, principal, and, increasingly, students' groups.

Although gaining the approval and collaboration of key authorities is essential, that alone will not necessarily win commitment or acquiescence from others in the client system. Facilitators must keep in mind that they are working not just with individuals but with a system, and they will want to test the willingness of authorities to carry to others introductory discussions of the potential program.

During the first phases of entry, it is vital that the facilitator communicate with an entire client subsystem, and not allow the less powerful participants to believe that they are less important to the facilitator than administrators or others in authority. If the project is districtwide, the facilitator will want to get acceptance from the significant groups within the district. If it is limited to a single school, it will be necessary before proceeding to win support not only from the powerful persons on the faculty but from as many other staff members as possible. Consultants can often win staff acceptance for OD by working in close collaboration with a schoolwide steering committee composed of administrators and teachers representing both formal groups and informal factions of the school.

Although discussions of organizational processes, consultative techniques, OD designs, and schedules are important, a sound relationship between consultant and client is not forged by agreement about tasks alone. The dynamics of entry and contract building can arouse intense feelings ranging from suspicion to trust, dissatisfaction to well-being, caution to a willingness to invest, and reserve to complete openness. Directly acknowledging those feelings is a prime requisite for making valid contracts.

Diagnosing Current Functioning. OD facilitators must have detailed information on which to base their macrodesigns. Furthermore, they must communicate to the client school's staff members the importance of having particular data on the school both for designing a tailored consultation and for enhancing the staff's problem solving. In fact, collecting relevant data on goal setting, conflicts between groups, processes at meetings, methods for solving problems, and procedures used for reaching decisions often demonstrates the foci of OD far better than an introductory lecture.

Resistance to diagnosis, however, is typical, even when participants manifest great interest in becoming involved in OD. Nowadays, for example, school personnel who have experienced diagnosis and consultation frequently in the past may regard them as old hat. It is also true that although the innovative *zeitgeist* has reigned supreme in many districts, promises of change have often failed to materialize. If resistance, consultation, and a subsequent failure of change have been part of a school's history, the consultant must nevertheless insist that diagnosis of the current situation is still critical, since no rational change design can be developed without an accurate picture of the here and now.

Diagnosis should occur with even the most sophisticated faculty. Indeed, pessimistic comments by faculty members are important data in themselves. Consultants need to take special care with cautious or cynical faculty members to assess the amount of resistance to OD in general and to the diagnosis in particular. Facilitators should strive to discover the kinds of workshop events that occurred within the school before, the kinds of organizational problems that were targeted, and the reasons, from the clients' point of view, previous problem-solving efforts were aborted. Attacks on problems that occur later in the consultation, such as ineffective meeting procedures, can take into account the frustration of previous problem-solving efforts.

During the diagnostic period, the OD facilitator should make use of multiple methods, of which self-report questionnaires, interview guides, and planned observations are the most typical. In addition to those formal methods, conversations with organizational members also bring important information, and so do organizational memos and letters.

Collecting formal data can strengthen organizational members' view of the validity and legitimacy of the OD consultation. Ideally, OD facilitators will let their first impressions, however they are obtained, guide the selection of formal questionnaires, interviews, and observations. The results of these data-gathering efforts will be augmented in turn by insights gained from further data informally collected.

Designing the OD Project. OD designs can usually be divided into macroaspects and microaspects. *Macroaspects* include the design's overall structure and outline, sequence of parts, and the general forms through which activities flow. *Microaspects* include the specific activities carried out during a limited period such as a week, a day, or even an hour of consultation. Tailoring macroaspects and microaspects of the design to specific objectives and participants is a major challenge for the OD facilitator, who must be able to distinguish between what is most effective for particular clients and what the facilitator personally is most comfortable doing.

Different diagnoses usually call for different emphases in macrodesigns—that is, different sequences of training, survey-data-feedback, constructve confrontation, and process observation and feedback. For example, although facilitators should deal early with actual organizational problems among sophisticated staffs, with unsophisticated staffs they might choose to offer more simulated skill-training in the beginning phases of consultation. A lack of goal clarity, as another example, might lead the facilitator to begin with an agenda-building activity that would enable participants to deal with very short-term goals as a prelude to dealing with those of longer term.

When designing, the facilitator always does some detailed, rational planning in advance. We have found it useful during initial meetings, for example, to attempt to describe the total OD effort or to post the agenda and plans at the beginning of an event to invite clarification from clients. Still, even the best-laid plans must allow a certain amount of free time to accommodate the unanticipated. This slack allows an unexpected event to turn a highly task-oriented, unexciting consultative session into one in which clients can arrive at their own insights, invent creative solutions to their problems, and find the confidence and zeal to go on.

An effective OD effort must meet the challenges of improving interpersonal and group skills, changing subsystem norms, and improving organizational structure. These goals are often dealt with in the following sequence.

First, the facilitator focuses on interpersonal and group skills, typically trying to increase openness and ease of interpersonal communication by training participants to paraphrase, describe behavior, describe their own feelings, and confirm their impressions of others' feelings. In addition, the facilitator tries to build skills in conceiving problems and in responding, until clients are able to exhibit constructive openness and confidence that communication with colleagues can be worthwhile.

Second, the facilitator focuses on norms. Even while improving interpersonal and group skills, facilitators can raise participants' awareness of the functioning of norms. They can point out the discrepancies between what is being approved and what everyone wants to approve. By giving members a chance to applaud one another for moving plans into action, for example, facilitators can evoke pressures to "put up or shut up" that create new norms in support of responsiveness. In addition, they can show how deviations from norms help to identify problems and resources in the school. Helping people in a school to see that deviation from norms is a resource rather than a threat can move the school a long way toward organizational adaptability.

As a lever for changing work norms, the facilitator can attempt to ameliorate actual problems by asking participants to describe some of the frustrations they encounter in their jobs and then to practice a sequence of cooperative problem solving to reduce them. Cooperative problem solving not only reduces frustrations but also yields the satisfaction of knowing that one's contribution toward reaching a solution is valued by others. When staff members behave in new ways (according to new norms), they enable one another to see the new norm taking hold. They see that others are not only *saying* they are willing, but that they are *acting* willingly.

Third, the OD facilitator turns to the organization as a whole—the school or district. Now, using the same techniques, strategies, and skills as before but in larger scope, participants arrive at the time for building new functions, roles, procedures, policies, or subsystems and making them formal and institutionalized, with budgetary support, so that these new structures become part of the basic fabric of the school.

Assessing Designs and Monitoring Progress. As we see it, OD designs cannot be expected to fit well if they are made in Peoria and shipped to Little Rock, or vice versa. They should be tailored to fit the local diagnostic data. Two parts of tailoring are to assess the feasibility of a design before it is carried out and to assess progress after each event in the design is carried out.

OD facilitators assess a design before putting it into motion by scrutinizing it and trying to anticipate what could go wrong before it does go wrong. They ask how the macrodesign relates to the diagnosis and how it furthers the overall goals of the project. They might also invite two or three colleagues to examine and criticize the plan for possible weaknesses. Moreover, facilitators assess progress by watching alertly both during each microaspect of the design and during the first few hours afterward for signs of unwanted side-effects. If the episode turns out to have fallen short of what was hoped or to have gone well beyond, the OD facilitator redesigns the next episodes accordingly.

Terminating the Consultation. Inevitably, participants in an OD project develop some amount of dependency on their facilitators. The latter must prepare participants for the facilitators' eventual withdrawal by giving repeated advance notice of their date of leaving and then sticking firmly to schedule. The macrodesign should move toward increasingly greater client control over the course of the OD effort, and the facilitators should give participants ample practice in taking over the functions of organization adaptability before they leave.

Institutionalizing OD. If an innovation is to continue in a school for some years, it must be made a more or less routine part of the organization's operation. That is, if a school does not want a new way of doing things to fade quickly away, it must institutionalize it. OD itself can be institutionalized by establishing procedures, roles, and structures to maintain the metaskills necessary for organizational adaptability. For a school district, perhaps the most powerful support for OD, as well as the most economical one, is the cadre of organizational specialists, which we describe in Chapter 11.

2

Macrodesigning

The overall sequence of a comprehensive OD project is this: startup, contract building, diagnosis, macrodesigning, implementing and monitoring microdesigns, evaluating outcomes, and institutionalizing the school's capability for continuous problem solving. Initial contact is with administrators and boards of education to gain approval for the OD effort. Then, a planning committee for the OD project is formed within the target school to guide the OD process. Typically, the planning committee is made up of the principal, a representative group of teachers, and perhaps representatives of classified staff, parents, and students. The planning committee works with the OD consultants to obtain agreements from the staff about involvement in the OD project. Next, diagnostic data on the school's organizational functioning are collected and fed back to the staff by the consultant and the planning committee. At this point, the task of macrodesigning becomes prominent. Whatever macrodesign is chosen, it eventually facilitates active problem solving among staff members. After several cycles of problem solving, the consultants encourage staff members to agree on ways of institutionalizing problem solving so that the whole OD cycle can repeat itself in the school after the consultants are gone.

A *macrodesign* comprises the overall structure and outline, sequence of parts, and general forms through which activities flow. Examples include improving group skills, changing norms through problem solving, and changing the organization's structure for continuous problem solving. Other examples are the steps of a survey-data-feedback procedure, explained later in this chapter, and the constructive confrontation design described in detail in Chapter 7. The present chapter deals with building effective macrodesigns. *Microaspects* refers to the specific activities played out during any limited period of consultation. Some useful microdesigns for training in skills, exercises, and procedures, along with instruments for survey-data-feedback and for process observation and feedback, are offered in Chapters 3 through 7; Chapter 8 presents guidelines for microdesigning.

There is no more important skill for OD consultants than designing. This skill requires knowledge of alternative designs, a sensitivity to the unique characteristics of the clients, and a delicate balance between insight into one's own motives and empathy for the clients. Although matching macroaspects in effective combinations and microaspects with specific objectives and clients is an important skill of the OD consultant, an even rarer skill is the ability to monitor one's own proclivities. The ability to recognize one's own defenses, for example, and to use this recognition as information about the conduct of the consultation greatly enhances a consultant's effectiveness.

SYSTEM DEVELOPMENT

For us, a developing system—whether a group, individual, or organization—is one that is engaged continually in problem solving. This does not necessarily mean that a developing system is also a troubled system. Rather, problem solving here refers to an active striving to meet new challenges, seek improvement, and measure progress. When viewed from such a fundamental perspective, *problem solving* can refer to the thoughtful reflections of individuals as well as to planned evaluations by staff of organizational achievements.

Elements of Problem Solving

We view as a problem any discrepancy between an actual state of affairs (a situation) and some ideal state to be achieved (the target). Since both the situation (S) and target (T) are in flux, problem solving must be continual. In many circumstances, moreover, as progress is made in moving S closer to T, participants switch their perception of T to an even higher level of aspiration, recycling the problem and again making the process continual. One might argue that problem solving is so fundamental to a system's life and health that when problem solving is stopped, the system stops developing and loses its vitality.

Organizations and their subgroups should be detecting and working on problems continually, not just during times of crisis, failure, extreme tension, or pain. Furthermore, they should be aware that their understanding of the situation and the target will change as they work toward solutions. As group members reach new clarity about the problem that brought them together, they will become aware of problems they had not apprehended earlier. This process, however natural in system functioning, has stages, and it is a responsibility of the OD consultant to provide a macrodesign that will enable a group to agree on its present stage and to move ahead in a coordinated manner from stage to stage.

But even as we write about stages, we must point out that those stages are less like steps moving forever upward and more like rolling circles moving forward but also continually recycling. Problem solving is continuous partly because progress is slow and difficult. Problems must be cycled and recycled as the system pursues a better state.

Working toward a target tests how well the original situation has been understood. New information brought to light while a plan for change is being carried out may call for revising either plan or target. As people approach their target and form a clearer picture of what it might be like to live in the more ideal state, they may not find it as desirable as they did originally, or perhaps they will judge reaching it to be too costly. The second thoughts do not necessarily mean that they had planned poorly or chosen the wrong target. Rather, they point to the fact that no plan or target stays good for long, and that even if a group's vision does not change, circumstances will.

For that reason, participants should tackle concrete problems first, pick targets of moderate scope, and avoid the trap of overplanning. The danger of large-scale problem solving is that after people expend an immense amount of effort, they are reluctant either to waste the spent energy or to put still more into reconceiving the goal or changing the plan. If they succumb to the temptation to carry out the plan to the last detail even though the facts show that things are going badly, they face the worse danger of losing the norms and skills of openness. Thus, instead of problem solving on the grand scale, we advocate incremental problem solving informed by regular feedback and replanning. School participants should develop their new world in moderate steps, repeatedly surveying both the wider horizon and the immediate path.

Long-Range and Short-Range Objectives

It is important for the OD consultant to keep in mind the larger, long-term objectives of developing a client system's capacity for continuous problem solving while simultaneously recognizing the shorter-term benchmarks of development. Stated most generally, organization development enables the school to solve its own educational problems more effectively (1) through building more effective communication patterns, group meetings, and joint decision making; (2) by using those more effective group skills to modify at will its own roles, norms, and procedures; and (3) by putting together the improved skills and norms in systematic group problem solving.

To be more specific, some examples of long-range objectives include (1) increasing understanding of how staff members with different jobs interrelate and affect one another; (2) developing clear communication networks up and down and laterally; (3) increasing understanding of the different educational goals in different parts of the school; (4) uncovering organizational conflicts for constructive problem solving; (5) developing new ways of solving problems through creative uses of group dynamics; (6) involving more personnel at all levels in decision making; and (7) establishing procedures for searching out innovative practices, both within and outside the school.

Short-range objectives would be (1) clarifying communication; (2) establishing clear goals; (3) uncovering and working with specific conflicts; (4) improving group meetings; (5) making clear decisions; and (6) assessing progress toward goals.

Both kinds of objectives are subordinate in range and scope to establishing norms, structures, and procedures in the school that support the condition described in Chapter 1 as organization adaptability. The four metaskills of adaptability are (1) diagnosing the functioning of groups in the school, (2) gathering information and other resources from within and from outside the schools, (3) mobilizing synergistic action in the school, and (4) monitoring the other three metaskills. Table 2-1 depicts the several kinds of objectives for OD.

BEFORE THE CONSULTATION STARTS

Readiness to accept the OD process is of course an important variable at all stages of an OD project, but readiness is crucial at the outset, when members of a school or district are asking themselves whether they want to undertake a serious project of change and to accept a consultant's help. It is very unwise to begin even a short OD

Table 2-1. The Goals of OD

Short-range	Long-range	Ultimate Metaskills
Clarifying communication	Understanding different	Institutionalized norms,
Establishing clear goals	roles	structures, and
Working with specific	Developing clear	procedures for:
conflicts	communication	Diagnosing
Improving group meetings	networks	Gathering information
Making clear decisions	Understanding different	Mobilizing synergistic
Assessing progress	goals in the school	action
	Uncovering larger	Monitoring other
	conflicts for	metaskills
	problem solving	
	Developing new ways to	
	use groups for problem	
	solving	
	Involving more personnel	
	in decision making	
	Establishing procedures	
	for searching out	
	innovative practices	

project if it calls for nonexistent resources, skills, commitments, or values that are not there. At the same time, it often falls to the consultants to raise the readiness for OD in an unready school.

Readiness at Various System Levels

As we have pointed out, the school is a social institution composed of many parts. It is a complex organization with diverse individuals and small groups connected to each other by formal and informal relationships, roles, norms, and routine interactions that provide stability. The interrelationships of these organizational features—not primarily the personalities or sheer stubbornness of staff members—create stability and resistance to change in schools.

We identify these interrelationships and interactions by observing the behavior of staff members on three system levels: *individual, group,* and *organization.* In determining a school's readiness for OD, the behavior can be interpreted in different ways depending on your point of view. For example, a staff member who volunteers to work on the planning committee for an OD effort might be seen as satisfying a personal need for affiliation, or adhering to group norms about taking one's share of responsibility, or fulfilling the organization role of a staff member in that particular position. All of these interpretations could be simultaneously true. An important skill is deciding which level of interpretation offers the most useful viewpoint for understanding the behavior and taking effective action. The consultant should be attuned to all three levels of the social system of the school in diagnosing its readiness for OD.

The Individual Level. It is useful to concentrate on two influences shaping individual members' responses to OD—namely, motivation and perception. As we wrote in Chapter 1, under "Individual Motive Satisfaction," people need affiliation—experiencing feelings of friendliness, warmth, and inclusion; achievement—feeling a sense of accomplishment; and influence—exercising some control over their lives and interactions with others. They seek to satisfy these motives in work and play. For teachers, the need for affiliation might be met by joining with other teachers to work on a committee, that of achievement by producing a creative lesson plan or an innovative plan for scheduling students, and that of influence by shaping the learning of students or by influencing parents in positive ways. Of course, an individual always risks the possibility that his or her overtures to satisfy a motive will be frustrated. Thus, one's involvement on a committee might lead to hostilities and the loss of friends, a new lesson plan might fall on its face, and attempts to influence parents might backfire. It becomes clear, then, that any impending change might on the one hand be a welcome opportunity for motive satisfaction and on the other an exasperating ordeal sure to end in motive frustration. The OD consultant must be attuned to the hopes, fears, and concerns of staff members as they look forward to the OD project.

Along with motives, other factors affecting participants' responses to OD will be their perceptions of themselves, their school situation, their understanding of OD, and the OD consultants. In particular, staff members' views of OD will be significantly colored by their experience with previous similar efforts. Staff members will be highly sensitive, in this regard, to how OD might disrupt their own personal routines in the school. Teachers, for example, will be especially concerned with the impact of OD on classroom management, the curriculum, and the time and energy they have to work effectively with the students. Teachers' images of OD will be shaped by their estimates of how it will fit their classroom routines and their relationships with students.

It is important for OD consultants to remember that they will not necessarily be seen as they are (or want to be seen), but will be perceived in terms of staff members' experience with similar sorts of outside consultants. When staff members find the label or image that fits the OD consultant, they act accordingly. They think, "Oh, you're the sort of person who . . .; now I know who and what you are." A significant part of the OD consultant's task is to establish an open and trusting relationship with staff so that the images become more accurate.

The Group Level. Even though staff members spend most of their time alone in their own offices or classrooms, their membership in departments, grade-level groups, and committees influences much of their behavior. In particular, norms, roles, and cohesiveness make groups powerful molders of behavior. Norms, for example, enable us to predict how others will respond to our actions and how they will behave toward us. Norms protect group members from the embarrassing consequences of inappropriate behavior. They provide a measure of safety by defining the range of acceptable behavior. Since norms are created— implicitly or explicitly—to give stability in groups, introducing OD means abandoning some of the old norms and creating new ones.

Just as norms are expectations for how groups members should behave, roles are shared expectations about the behavior of people in particular positions. Staff members behave toward one another according to their images of their roles. School staff members typically develop rather stable role images of one another, so it can be difficult, as in an OD project, for one person to take on new behaviors unless others also alter their role conceptions and behaviors.

Group cohesiveness is another important variable in a staff's readiness for OD. When people identify themselves with others as members of a group, they come to have feelings of solidarity and loyalty to one another. They value their membership in the group and want to protect it. Those feelings of cohesiveness can be a powerful force that keeps individuals from changing their behavior in violation of group norms, but cohesiveness can also be an influential source of support if the group supports the OD effort. The OD consultant will seek to identify the cohesive groups in a school, note the role takers in them as well as their norms, and determine their orientation and images in relation to OD.

The Organization Level. The school as an organization is, of course, made up of the individuals' motives and perceptions as well as the groups' norms, roles, and cohesiveness, but it is instructive for the OD consultant to look beyond such microvariables to see characteristics of the school as a totality. Among the relevant variables are the school's goals, structure, "climate," and environment.

Although schools exist to reach certain goals, agreement on the priority of these goals is frequently low. Schools strive to reach several goals simultaneously—for example, high reading scores, good citizenship, employable students, fiscal accountability, high staff morale, a winning basketball team, and so on. Moreover, OD consultants nearly always find themselves working with staff members whose energy and enthusiasm for a proposed change is severely limited by other goals and demands on their time. Even in the face of such complexity, in most schools during any two- or three-year period certain goals will be advocated over others. It is crucial for the OD consultants to point out how OD processes could help the school move toward at least a few of its highly rated goals.

Structure is the sum of the relationships of various roles to each other in terms of influence, authority, responsibility, function, and so on. Small elementary schools have simple structures; large high schools are more complex. In contrast to organizations like the military which have tightly controlled structures, schools are *loosely coupled*—that is, individuals and groups within them have a good deal of autonomy. Superiors such as central office administrators can rarely mandate a change such as OD. At the same time, the necessity to go through channels can be a major barrier to getting OD going. OD consultants and a school planning team need to identify the important parts of the organizational structure affected by OD and work with them to make the adjustments needed.

A school's *climate* has to do with staff members' feelings about being part of the school, the state of interpersonal relationships, the level of motive satisfaction, shared feelings of success or failure, and so on. The principal plays a key part in setting the climate of a school, but so do the staff, the district norms and policies, the parents, and the like. Climate is the product of a school's norms, and, as the more global phenomenon, is not as easily assessed and altered as its components. The level of readiness for OD is particularly affected by norms about openness in communication (especially in emotional high-pressure situations), collaboration, willingness to spend extra time in meetings, and willingness to experiment with innovations.

The school's *environment* also can play a significant part in the staff's readiness for OD. Two potent factors can be parents' desires for improvements in the school and legislative changes that have implications for school programming—for example, those having to do with desegregation and mainstreaming. On the other hand, change within the school organization often requires some sort of change or accommodation within relevant parts of the environment. For example, involvement in an OD project requires support from the board in some districts, and changes in grade-reporting systems require new understandings and behaviors from parents.

Raising Readiness Levels

It is frequently unwise to pursue an OD project in an unready school. The effort would probably be wasted. Our experience indicates that some degree of readiness is necessary at the outset to ensure future success. Still, raising the readiness of a school for OD is often feasible, and should be tried wherever it does not threaten to become too expensive.

The administrators or OD consultants who attempt to raise readiness levels in local schools should be guided by the three system levels described above. The arguments in favor of trying OD are best approached by considering the organization level first, the group level next, and the individual level third. This strategy involves working initially with site administrators, next with key staff members, and finally with the entire staff.

It is possible to persuade administrators, principals, and assistant principals to consider OD by facing them with issues in their schools related to goals, structure, climate, and environment. Goal achievement is problematic for many administrators. They wonder how they can get their staffs to move together in focused directions and how they might build the synergy and motivation for concerted, goal-directed action. Answers to such challenges are embedded in OD theory and technology. Through participation and self-diagnosis, staff members can be brought to attend to the school's goal achievement. Survey-data-feedback in particular allows staff members to recognize how they view the school's goals, and constructive confrontation can help them resolve differences and conflicts of interest.

Organizational structure is another aspect of school life that can lead administrators to become involved in OD. Administrators usually feel challenged to make the ideal organizational structure function effectively. But how should they go about encouraging staff members to follow through on their assignments and to communicate effectively through the structure? OD can encourage staff members to look with curiosity at their own functioning. In many macrodesigns that use training activities, for example, a simulation or "serious game" is included during which participants can see and discuss difficulties of functioning that characterize their own school, and can do so without yet risking new action in the real workplace. OD can also help schools to build entirely new structures such as team teaching and multiunit or multihouse structures. OD helps staff members to feel that they "own" the new structures—that they want to protect them. Traditional hierarchical decision making too often produces structures on paper that are subverted and undermined in practice.

School climate, a concern of a great many site administrators, offers an obvious invitation to OD. After all, OD asks the staff members themselves to assess their own school culture, to decide on ways in which the culture is lacking, and to take new actions to improve its quality. In this regard, OD is virtually synonymous with a climate-improvement program. Many districts and many site administrators more readily accept a project to improve school climate than something called OD. The wise administrator or consultant will always think of such semantic distinctions when approaching other administrators or staff members about an OD effort.

One can also look to the environment. For example, perhaps the legislature demands desegregation, mainstreaming, or parent advisory boards. The school is pressured to make genuine modifications in structure. How should it go about making such changes? By fiat, by edict, or by participation? Typically, some form of participation is viewed as essential by administrators. OD offers the sort of techniques that can work in building staff commitment.

Another way to raise readiness is to work with site administrators and key staff leaders in the school on the challenges of running effective groups. Perhaps the most universal frustration in schools stems from ineffective meetings, whether staff, departmental, or committee meetings. An OD effort might be started by zeroing in on improving meetings and moving to larger issues after that. Actually, no matter how effective subgroup meetings are in a school, the adept OD consultant can facilitate their improvement through process observation and feedback. But if staff members are not ready for a process observer, the OD consultant might begin by focusing on helping the subgroup's leader to act as a more effective convener of meetings. Here the consultant acts temporarily as a coach to the subgroup leader—in a sort of one-to-one helping relationship—while keeping his or her mind on the potentialities of a larger OD effect.

Large secondary schools often show low readiness for OD. One tactic is for the consultant to work with just a part of the staff, perhaps the principal's cabinet or a particular academic department or committee. The focus of such a consultation would be on improving meeting skills, clarifying roles and norms, and building heightened cohesiveness or team spirit. In the short run, the consultant would be carrying out a team-building effort, but in the long run, this effort could lead to an OD project for more and more parts of the school.

We must also be concerned with individual variables when trying to raise readiness for OD in schools. The consultant needs to keep individual motives and perceptions in mind when trying to persuade site administrators to use OD, but should take care to keep the same variables in mind when approaching entire staffs in introductory meetings and OD demonstrations. The consultant's talk should include concrete illustrations of how the OD project might increase affiliation, achievement, and influence among staff members. One might propose, for instance, a retreat that would give staff members a chance to get to know one another better, some consultative coaching that would help the staff finish a highly valued task, or some new communication channels that would convey more influence to the administration.

Although pointing out expected motive satisfactions is important for raising readiness for OD, the more important task is clarifying staff members' understandings of what OD is, what it is not, and how it works. It is important to explain that OD is not on the one hand direct help on curriculum, or on the other hand, sensitivity training. The OD process aims to help staff members come together and have open and constructive discussions that could lead to beneficial changes for the school.

THE OD CONTRACT

Productive school change is unlikely to occur unless staff members acknowledge a discrepancy between an ideal and actual state of affairs (a gap between S and T) *before* an outsider becomes formally involved as consultant. That is, a sizable portion of the staff (more than 50 percent as a rule of thumb), and especially its more powerful members, should accept the school's problems as their own and become reasonably committed to solving them instead of merely acquiescing to a project that originates on the initiative of the external consultant. OD consultants should make it a rule to enter into contract only with those educational subsystems that are reaching out for help and that exhibit other signs of readiness as described above.

Consultants should be aware that what happens during the first phase of OD can foreshadow much of what is to come, and that, if the OD effort is to be built on a solid base of support, it is necessary to gain at least an oral commitment to the enterprise from all key participating groups. To this end, we cannot overstate the critical importance of establishing at the outset relaxed rapport, credibility, and legitimacy, and of arriving at clear statements about motives, competencies, and shared expectations. Consultants should be explicit about their role, the goals of OD, the project's budget and probable length, and the amount of time per week the consultant will devote to the project. Also early during start-up, the consultant should discuss with staff members their own hopes, concerns, and expectations for the project. Those discussions should be two-way, with the consultant giving informal instruction to staff members about OD and how it works, and with staff members coaching the consultant in the perspectives of people in their school. During such discussions, the consultant should note the extent to which staff members adopt a collaborative attitude and are ready to collaborate with one another in new ways.

Although a consultant might be contacted initially by an individual from any level of the organizational hierarchy, interactions are best begun formally between the consultant and the legitimate leaders, because those personnel hold crucial gatekeeping power over later contacts with other members of the system, and it is therefore helpful, even critical, for them to become allies rather than enemies. The principal is, of course, the most important single leader in the school, and frequently consultants spend several hours with the principal defining OD, discussing the role of the consultants, and sharing hopes, concerns, and expectations about a change project. There are, however, other relevant gatekeepers. In districts, powerful parties typically include the school board, the superintendents and the superintendent's cabinet, and teachers' organizations. In individual schools, the powerful parties other than the principal might be department heads, counselors, teachers in general, and parent groups. Particularly powerful in many schools are personnel whose work is seen as having unalterable routines to which other teachers must defer; athletic coaches are a good example.

Although gaining the approval and collaboration of key authorities is essential, this alone will not win commitment or even acquiescence from others in the client system. OD consultants must keep in mind that they are working not just with individuals but with a system, and they will want to test the willingness of authorities to carry introductory discussions of the potential program to others. How the consultant is introduced to more subordinate personnel will naturally influence subsequent support and program effectiveness, and consultants should not be slow in moving their attention to less powerful groups.

During the first phases of start-up, and at every subsequent stage of the OD sequence, it is vital to work with the whole client subsystem in mind, and less powerful participants should not be led to believe that they are of less importance to the consultant than are administrators or others in authority. If the OD effort is districtwide, the consultant will want to gain the support of every significant subsystem or group within the district. If the OD is limited to a single school, it will be necessary before proceeding very far to get approval not only from the powerful persons on the faculty, but from as many other staff members as possible. Toward this end, the consultant should hold at least one, if not two, meetings with the whole staff in order to publicly poll every staff member about the project.

The OD consultant should almost never agree to hold a meeting with only "those who can come." Potential participants who are deciding whether to commit themselves to the OD effort will need to know how others involved are judging the prospects. People always want to know which way their colleagues are leaning. That is one reason why consultants should poll the intact work groups about OD before going very far. Another reason is that since personnel who work together will be consulted within their intact groups at the later stages of the project, it is advantageous to begin early to deal with the groups, thereby setting a precedent as well as facilitating later conceptualization.

Many projects are greatly facilitated by a "memorandum of agreement" signed by client and consultant. The memo might include a general description of the goals of the OD effort, a paragraph on the role of the consultant, a rough time schedule for the macrodesign, and a statement about decision points—that is, points at which decisions will be made about continuing or stopping the project. A memo of this sort should be no more than a page or two in length. It is important that the signers include a representative committee of teachers, if not the whole staff, and that the document be reproduced and given to every staff member involved in the OD project.

Although a memorandum of agreement is important in formalizing the OD project, sound consultant-client relationships are *not* forged by agreement on tasks alone. The consultant should be mindful that the dynamics of start-up and contract building can arouse intense feelings. Directly acknowledging these feelings at the right time is a prime requisite for valid contract making.

The OD consultant should realize, too, that any improvement of organizational processes will take time. Research by Wyant (1974), for example, indicated that less than twenty-four hours of staff training in communication skills and problem solving can actually have detrimental long-run effects. In contrast, staffs that receive more than thirty hours of such training typically show favorable gains.

PORTRAYING OD DURING START-UP

As we conduct it, OD is largely experiential. Although consultants should take a few minutes to describe what OD consultation will be like, they should not expect their listeners to get an accurate picture from words alone. The best way of conveying this information is actually to demonstrate OD consultation via laboratory training activities that communicate experientially the nature of OD to those relatively inexperienced in it.

Some staff members think of OD as highly emotional sensitivity training; others think of lectures and discussion on administrative sciences and group dynamics; still others think of relaxed fun and games having little relevance to the real life of the school. Most staff members probably hold no very clear idea about OD, and these unclear expectations often plague the start-up and contract-building phases of an intervention. By helping a target group to understand OD theory and to experience OD technology, the following sample design for a demonstration workshop should increase the reliability of the decision as to whether the consultation should continue in earnest.

A complete demonstration calls for two days, but shorter modifications can be designed. The clients are told that the demonstration is being presented to help them determine whether they would like to become involved in an OD project. They are asked to suspend judgment until the two days are over, since the demonstration events must move along a bit before a clear picture of OD will emerge.

Demonstration goals include (1) developing clients' understanding of the possible benefits of OD to their schools; (2) presenting an accurate picture of a self-renewing organization; (3) helping members of the client group see how they can confront current problems through OD methods; (4) helping them understand the unique functions of OD in contrast to those of management consultation or sensitivity training; (5) acquainting them with the skills to be gained through OD consultation; and (6) establishing the beginning of a collaborative relationship between clients and consultants, communicating that the former are expected not only to influence the project but eventually to own and run it themselves. Demonstrations shorter than two days will have fewer stated goals.

Early in the event, following some warm-up and getting-acquainted activities, participants can be given the handout shown in Figure 2-1. A consultant guides them through the material, telling them that aspects of the consultative strategies will come alive for them during the next day and a half and calling attention to supplemental reading materials available on a display table.

After introducing the handout, the facilitator proceeds to episodes that involve more active client participation. Every subsequent activity should commence with experiential activity and be followed by a debriefing with the help of client or consultant observers that focuses on both the here-and-now aspects and interpersonal dynamics of the experience. Clients are then asked to comment on the similarities and differences between the OD activity and their actual school experience. Finally, the consultant shows how the activity is relevant to the real organization, presents some research concepts and results related to the activity for group members to apply to their own organization, and suggests more detailed readings on relevant theory and research. This generic sequence from experience to comparison to theory can be used profitably with every episode or microaspect of the demonstration.

Many alternative macrosequences can be effective, including the

Figure 2-1. Handout #1 for Start-up Demonstration

What Is OD?

Organization development (OD) is a planned and sustained effort at system self-study and improvement, focusing on change in norms, structures, and procedures, using behavioral science concepts and methods. OD involves system members themselves in the active assessment, diagnosis, and transformation of their own organization.

The following outline shows some of the conceptual plan of OD and summarizes the points of today's workshop:

Organizational development enables the school to solve its own educational problems more effectively—by . . .

- Improving its capabilities to modify its own roles, norms, and procedures—through . . .
- Building more effective communication patterns, group meetings, and joint decision making—by experiencing . . .
- Systematic group problem-solving processes—through . . .
- The consultative strategies of

   1. Training in skills, exercises, and procedures
   2. Data collection, feedback, and action planning
   3. Constructive confrontation and problem solving
   4. Process observation and feedback

following example, which makes use of materials supplied later in this book (see index): (1) practice in communication skills; (2) feedback on the results of a survey of norms, using, for example, the Team-Expectation Survey; (3) an exercise on group decision making using the Lost at Sea exercise; (4) an exercise on effectiveness between groups using the Planners and Operators exercise; and (5) practice in uncovering conflicts using an imaging procedure. If aspects of the Imaging exercise are used toward the end of the two days, the consultant must allow time for collaborative problem solving so that conflicts do not remain troublesome at the end of the demonstration. Problem-solving sequences using the *S-T-P* paradigm, also supplied later, can usefully be introduced as the last object for group study.

Midway through this sequence of activities, at the end of the first day or at the beginning of the second, the consultant should hand out Figure 2-2 for discussion. The contents of this handout will help to deepen and extend the participants' understanding of where the consultants hope to go by using the activities. And during the early part of the second afternoon the facilitator should hand out Figure 2-3 for discussion. This handout will help bring alive the steps of OD proposed. As a

Figure 2-2. Handout #2 for Start-up Demonstration

Goals of OD
The goals of OD can be of at least two types: long-range objectives and short-term:

Long-range Objectives

1. To increase understanding of how staff members with different jobs interrelate and affect one another
2. To develop clear communication networks up, down, and laterally
3. To increase understanding of the different educational goals in different parts of the school
4. To uncover organizational conflicts for constructive problem solving
5. To develop new ways of solving problems through creative uses of group dynamics
6. To involve more personnel at all levels in decision making
7. To establish procedures for searching out innovative practices, both within and outside the school

Such long-range objectives are reached gradually through small steps. The following is a list of some short-term objectives:

Short-term Objectives

A. Clarifying communication
B. Establishing clear goals
C. Uncovering and working with conflict

D. Improving group meetings
E. Making clear decisions
F. Evaluating progress toward goals

Figure 2-3. Handout #3 for Start-up Demonstration

Summary of the OD Sequence
1. Consultants make initial contact with administrators and the board of education for approval of the OD consultation.
2. A planning committee is formed within the school to guide the OD effort.
3. Agreement is solicited from the school staff to join the OD effort.
4. Consultants diagnose existing organizational processes and climate of the school.
5. Consultants and planning committee feed data back to the school staff.
6. Consultants, planning committee, and others establish specific goals for the OD effort.
7. Consultants and planning committee build a plan for the OD effort and carry it out. It may include one or more of the strategies of training, survey-data-feedback, constructive confrontation, and process observation and feedback.
8. Staff members engage in active problem solving.
9. Staff members come to agreement about ways to institutionalize problem solving.
10. Staff gathers data to evaluate the progress of the problem solving. At this point, the external consultants withdraw from the consultation. A staff committee takes the next steps for OD in the school.

final event, a twenty-minute audio tape slide show on OD in schools (Arends et al., 1973) can be presented to summarize and provide a springboard for group questions and discussion. In addition, an Arends, Phelps, and Schmuck (1973) booklet on OD in schools might be handed out at the end of the demonstration in preparation for a discussion of whether the staff should enter a full-fledged OD project. Since both the slide show and booklet are somewhat out of date, however, district consultants might wish to use them as prototypes to build their own tailored materials. We will discuss more fully the means of introducing OD in Chapter 11 when we cover cadres of OD consultants in districts.

THE OD DIAGNOSIS

Our research indicates that the most effective organizational diagnoses are carried out collaboratively by the consultants and an OD task force in the school. The task force serves as a steering committee for the OD project and is composed of a representative body including teachers, assistant administrators, counselors, and in some cases parents. The consultant serves as a technical assistant to this team, bringing to it examples of questionnaires, interview formats, and observation strategies, and helping the task force to make wise and practical choices in tailoring its own diagnostic strategy.

The purposes of the OD diagnosis are several. First and foremost, OD theory stipulates that making a meaningful diagnosis of one's own situation increases feelings of ownership of the data and enhances one's motivation to seek change. This is the central idea behind most "needs assessments" in education. Those who participate in defining their needs will work harder to seek new ways of satisfying those needs. But in OD a second purpose of diagnosis is as important and central as the first—to uncover data from all around the social system of the school that will permit colleagues to enlighten one another about their diverse and often contrasting views of the situation. It is easy for people in power to believe that all is going well in a school, particularly if most participants collude to keep quiet about their perceptions and feelings. An OD diagnosis helps make public the views and feelings that typically are not brought out into the open. By focusing on a few of the differences among the staff, the task force can often mobilize energy and involvement for productive change.

A third purpose of diagnosis is to help build a workable agenda for system-wide problem solving. Most organizations, including schools, have a myriad of organizational problems related to communications, goals, meetings, decision making, and the like. A diagnosis can help to rank the problems, according to both importance and feasibility for change. After a diagnostic exercise in a school, the staff should feel motivated to work on very specific targets of change. Moreover, the inspiration of the initiators of the effort should have started to spread to others in the school.

Specific information about the uses and procedures of diagnosis is reviewed in Chapter 9.

THE SELECTION OF AN OD DESIGN

As we discussed in Chapter 1, the OD consultant can follow four themes for macrodesigns in tailoring the right OD design for a particular school—training, survey-data-feedback, constructive confrontation, and process observation and feedback—each of which calls for special sorts of skill on the part of the consultant. Training formats are highly structured, requiring that the consultant adopt a strong leadership role similar to that of an expert scholar or a coach. Training works best when the participants expect to be taught and when the organizational problems of the school are not terribly pressing. Of course, at some point during the OD process, training will be necessary in most schools, but as a point of departure it should be used only with staffs that are very new to OD and that can set aside a few days to retreat from the school for a serious course of study.

Survey-data-feedback has become the most frequently used OD design, in part because of Bowers's (1973) research, which indicated that it was the most effective kind of OD design in industry, but also because it fits very well into the OD philosophy of sharing power with participants at all stages of the change process. In schools where the consultant works with a task force to construct an instrument, collect data, analyze data, feed back the data, and lead faculty committees in problem solving, each of the steps of the data-feedback design involves the participants. Such complete involvement is not typical of training, confrontation, or process observation and feedback.

Furthermore, data-feedback designs can work effectively when the consultant takes a rather low profile, which is not possible in the other three designs. In data feedback, a necessary skill is that of finding or designing a suitable data-collection instrument and advising staff on the construction of the final instrument. (The instrument is usually a questionnaire or an interview guide, but it can also include a guide to direct observation of behavior or to sources of information in existing records.) Persons trained in research and evaluation frequently have the needed expertise.

Once the data-feedback cycle gets going, active participant involvement on the part of a task force is often enough to move toward action planning. We do not mean to imply, however, that it is easy for consultants to play a low-profile role. The effective consultant learns to exert influence and to back off gracefully at appropriate times; doing so requires a level of personal skill typically acquired through consultative experience.

Several pitfalls are frequently encountered in data-feedback designs. First, participants in the school might find the first drafts of diagnostic instruments confusing, irrelevant, or even silly. Careful pilot testing can counteract such reactions. Second, data analysis and feedback can be hindered by respondents who don't fill out the instruments as requested. Again pilot testing will help, but task forces should also try to supplement closed-ended questionnaire items with open-ended items, and even with brief interviews whenever feasible. Third, during discussions of the data, participants can get bogged down in petty arguments about items, formats, and so on. The consultant and task force should take care to keep the discussions focused and to discourage significant deviations from discussions about the school itself. After all, the data are only "windows on the school"; it is the school itself that should be discussed during the staff's OD meetings.

Of the four kinds of designs, constructive confrontation is used least, but this form can be very effective if the circumstances warrant it. It is appropriate when there are obvious disagreements between subsystems in the school and when these disagreements become disruptive. We use the word disagreement because apparent conflicts between groups are often more subjective than objective, and confrontation works best in eliminating hostilities stemming from imagined oppositions and schisms. For confrontation to be effective, however, the consultant must be perceived as a trusted leader by the participants. Moreover, it is important that the participants view the consultant as neutral and disinterested.

Because constructive confrontation calls for dominant behavior by the consultant, it is often difficult for a peer to assume the role of consultant during confrontation. More than in the other three designs, success in constructive confrontation is more sure when it is carried out by an expert outsider, or at least with the help of one. In fact, our research indicates that constructive confrontation is most effective when it is carried out by a team composed of both inside and outside consultants. The outsiders are needed to get the confrontation off the ground, to keep participants on task during the early stages, and to play a significant role in controlling the natural defensiveness that arises during confrontation. Insiders are more important for the latter stages of the confrontation sequence and are crucial for supporting follow-through.

Of course, confrontation designs are risky; they bring into open discussion conflicts that might otherwise have been covered and held down for several years. The catharsis of opening such conflicts can be highly emotional for some participants; it can be so upsetting, in fact, that some people can lose psychological control, however temporarily. Outbursts might be so extreme that the participants reject the whole experience. To control such disruptive outbursts, the consultant must be strong in keeping the confronting parties on task.

The last design category, process observation and feedback, is omnipresent in OD. The astute consultant is always an observer and is always looking for appropriate opportunities to give feedback. However, the most important place for this sort of design is in the second half of most macrodesigns. Process observation and feedback is most useful after problems have been made public and problem solving has proceeded to a point where the group has agreed on new actions. Process observation and feedback can serve to keep participants honest about their action agreements. The consultant observes the group's behavior and gives structured feedback on how closely the observed behavior conforms to the spirit of the previously made group agreements. Thus, this form of OD design serves as a sort of evaluative monitoring.

Process observation and feedback is often used successfully at the very start of an OD design. Generally, the consultant sits in on a series of regular meetings and gradually offers constructive feedback to the group to encourage problem solving. In such circumstances, the group must perceive the consultant as an astute expert and as one who won't hurt the status positions and rewards of the group members. Although on the surface, process observation seems to call for a low-profile role, the consultant's inevitable responsibility to offer feedback means that he or she must have a certain degree of charisma to be effective. The need for charisma, however, diminishes as the group accepts as natural and usual the role of process observer. It is the external consultant's objective, then, to move group participants gradually into being process observers for themselves, giving feedback to one another as an ordinary feature of their meetings.

We should point out that it is frequently impractical to use process observation and feedback with an entire staff, especially when the school is large. OD consultants prefer to do what they call team building only when subsystems are small enough for face-to-face meeting. It is there that process observation and feedback are especially useful.

THE EXECUTION OF AN OD DESIGN

OD consultations consist of a series of organized social events carried out by school people who have continuing, committed interrelationships with one another. Consultants, too, look forward to continuing interaction with their clients and with one another during most of a macrodesign. If the consultation is of sufficient length and scope, all participants become in effect a temporary society that not only serves as a vehicle for the OD work but can itself exemplify many of the interpersonal procedures and structural forms that consultants want to teach.

When designing an OD intervention, consultants should see to it that this temporary society maintains in good condition the four organizational features that affect interpersonal and subsystem effectiveness: (1) differentiation and integration, (2) norms, (3) role relationships, and (4) satisfaction of motives within the organization. They should also see to it that the macrodesign presents clients with conceptual lessons that can be used to support organized action.

Differentiation and Integration

People in schools perform a variety of differentiated functions, from receiving and transmitting information about the working of the school district to shaping students and materials. For differentiated roles to function effectively, they must also be integrated. Consultative events can raise differentiation and integration to the level of conscious awareness in a number of ways. First, selecting as participants people from a variety of jobs and then communicating across this variety invariably reveals to clients the profit inherent in integrating diverse functions. Indeed, that people from heterogeneous but interdependent positions are included in the same intervention events at all helps to make salient the concept of integration.

Second, rotating combinations of people through the various subgroups that form during a consultation so that everyone will eventually have interacted at least once with everyone else can have an important multiple effect. In the course of an intervention, people from every level of the school or district will reveal both competence and incompetence in performing OD tasks, in perceiving organizational functions, and in perceiving how OD tasks relate to everyday life in the organization. By interacting with many people with whom they have either never before communicated or have communicated only superficially, clients have a chance to learn the following: that differentiation of role and function is primarily an organizational reality and not necessarily a matter of personal endowment, that effective interpersonal and group performance is not necessarily more difficult in some positions than in others, and that other people are as worried about interdependence with them as they are about their interdependence with others.

Depending upon the complexity of the macrodesign, rotation can often be achieved by instructing clients to form themselves into groups containing at least one person with whom each individual has not interacted before. When the sequence of consultative events is complicated and the consultant wants the cluster to satisfy goals other than mere spread of interaction, it may be prudent to lay out beforehand a complete schedule describing in detail the groups and their individual members.

Finally, consultants can design exercises and other activities to ensure both division of labor (differentiation) and active collaboration among different roles (integration). For example, the Fishbowl technique (see Chapter 3 under "Communication in the Subsystem") can be used to bring together representatives from different teams to discuss a common problem while they are observed by other members of the team. Or each subgroup can appoint its own convener, recorder, and process observer before a meeting, giving these people time to debrief on how they worked together and with others in their subgroup. In a large event requiring four or five or more consultants, the use of the consultants themselves can be designed to exhibit differentiation and integration.

Norms

A school organization becomes able to change its routines by learning how to replace old norms with new. In outline, this is done by reaching agreement in the relevant groups on what the new norm should be, simulating the new action patterns a few times, and then trying out the new actions a few times on the job. When clients feel rewarded by the new pattern, the new norm has become a reality. In practice, however, establishing new norms causes stress, not only because it means discussing matters that are seldom publicly discussed, but also because older norms may not support the changes being attempted. Clients are less likely to withdraw from an OD design either physically or psychologically if the consultant guides them through a series of steps that arouse an appropriate amount of anxiety. Specifically, a design can move staff members to new norms if it begins with structured, gamelike interpersonal exercises, proceeds to group simulations, and then moves on to real procedures.

At the beginning of one senior high school project, for example, staff members told us through interviews that their school had no problems and ran like clockwork. At a series of discussions with all department heads, however, after it was agreed that further discussions could be profitable, members began to discuss the organization for which the consultant worked and their school as a whole. At a later meeting they mentioned problems they had had in the past and problems they regarded as other people's. In the course of time, the discussion moved closer to people who were present, and from problems present somewhere in the school to participants' current problems. Over the series of meetings, the time perspective moved gradually from the past and a vague future to the present and specified future dates ("Ted and I will see the principal on Friday to tell him what we want to do about this").

As simple as such time focusing is in both concept and action, it could not have occurred at the first meeting because the group's norms did not support it. Uncertain of the extent to which their frustrations were shared and of the degree to which others were willing to invest energy in change, and having as yet no reason to trust the consultant, the group had regarded committed action involving themselves and the principal as inappropriate and too risky at the outset. For these reasons, early discussions had been conceptually vague, general, and interpersonally distant; they were concerned with other people and other times. For the same reasons, early steps in a design encouraging clients to try new norms must allow them, at least initially, to practice at some distance from their ordinary daily involvements.

Working with functioning units or subsystems, in which group norms tend to be very powerful, we do not typically place two different faculties into close interaction with each other, or members of two separate central office departments into the same training group. Instead we bring together interdependent persons who either have the same supervisors or are bound to one another by some shared function, such as supervising the playground or selecting new staff members. In this way clients are already much closer in their interdependence or common fate than are strangers from different subsystems.

Specifically because they are closer, however, it is important that they be given some protective distance from one another—distance that allows them to protect their views of themselves, that requires no commitments affecting other parts of their lives, and that does not require them to take a stand on matters of school policy or to make specific commitments about what they will do on the job. One way of placing protective distance between school members is to begin a consultation during the summer hiatus when the routines and commitments of the new school year are not yet fully established. Another way is to remove clients from the building or rooms in which they usually work, away from telephones or other continual interruptions (although we have found little to be gained by moving them out of town or to a nonschool ambiance). Probably the best technique is to be found in the highly structured game such as those described as exercises in Chapters 3 through 7, which, in relation to their daily work on the job, can be seen as "then and there" rather than as "here and now." If exercises are to be effective in changing norms, however, they must be introduced early in the OD effort.

For example, exercises offered early with an OD design can help to establish a norm that supports *debriefing*—that is, examining the effectiveness of interactive processes in a group soon after every meeting. Even when done during make-believe activities, debriefing encourages adaptability, because it makes explicit the norm that procedures are alterable. That is, if a survey during debriefing shows agreement that a certain procedure is impeding progress toward a goal, the question of whether to change the procedure arises, and the questioning opens the door to productive self-renewal. Thus exercises that facilitate debriefing, if conducted after every meaningful unit during the first few hours of consultation, can cause debriefing to become an accepted norm among the clients. Further, the consultant should provide time for debriefing on all written agendas and encourage its use by listing a number of leading questions for group discussion.

The consultant can also confront norms among clients by modeling behavior that is contrary to their norms—for example, by exhibiting openness, directness, and authenticity about the organization's dynamics to clients who are unwilling to do so themselves. To this end, the macrodesign of data feedback is a useful strategy. The consultant interviews organization members individually about the variables discussed in Chapters 3 through 7, and subsequently feeds group data back to all members of the school using a style that is direct and open, using living examples, and asking for clients' reactions. Clients are often sufficiently relieved that someone is finally telling them the truth about the school to begin concerted problem solving on the newly revealed problems.

Roles

Because role taking always occurs in interactions with other role takers, an OD macrodesign should address itself not only to relationships among organization members but also to the relationship between the consultant and clients (many of whom may expect an "expert" to behave in a more authoritarian manner). At an early stage of execution of the macrodesign, consultants should therefore distinguish between their own goals and those of the clients in order to distinguish between their respective roles as well.

The role of clients is to state the problems and goals of their school or district; to assign priorities, schedules, and deadlines; and to choose whom they will work with and trust. The consultant's primary goal is to maximize the clients' ability to deal consciously and purposefully with their own organizational processes. On the question of appropriate group processes, clients will usually defer to consultants, but on matters of substance, the consultant will defer to the clients. In addition to drawing attention to role structure during consultation, the very process of arriving at an understanding of the proper granting of expertness—group process to the consultants and substance to the clients—will exemplify the introduction of new group-process activities, such as debriefing, that will later prove useful to clients.

Clients can gain wider practice in putting new roles into effect if consultants treat them equally, without regard to previous deference patterns in the school or district. This is not to say that consultants should ignore the jobs that people hold or the realities to which they will return, but only that they can give practice in flexible role taking if they give special privileges to no one. They should not ask administrators, for example, to act as leaders more often than others or excuse their absences more readily. Treating everyone alike demonstrates that a role relationship established for one purpose in one subgroup of the organization need not apply for other tasks or in other parts of the organization.

Motives

Although individuals differ in the extent to which they attempt to satisfy achievement, power, and affiliation needs in their jobs, clients and consultants alike bring their own motives with them to a consultation, and consultants should not allow their own needs to bias them against the needs of others. Indeed, consultants who work with, not against, the needs of all parties will maximize the consultants' influence on a consultation. Let those with strong achievement motives be initiators and planners; let those who enjoy power be coordinators and conveners; let those enjoy the warmth of affiliative satisfactions who wish to do so.

One way in which all three motives can be expressed is through the exercise of charismatic leadership, a quality that is more cultural than psychological in its dynamics and that can characterize a group as well as an individual leader. When David Berlew was a consultant to our research team in 1971, he set forth three principles underlying the attraction of the charismatic leader (or group), all of which related to the motives of achievement, power, and affiliation:

1. The charismatic leader expresses for other people their own mute longings in a way that makes their longings clear to them.
2. The charismatic leader shows people that the object of their longing is attainable—and not by waiting for someone else to bring it, but by taking matters into their own hands.
3. The charismatic leader inspires people with the conviction that significant action can be taken now, today, not next year or in heaven, and that the action should be taken together.

Insofar as the achiever seeks to reach a goal or outcome, and the achievement of specifiable outcomes is a school's *raison d'être*, the achievement motive, especially, can energize the planning of innovative programs. Achievement motives are active when problems are real and important, so that requiring clients to choose realistically attainable goals provides the best possible field of action for people with high achievement needs. Indeed, the high achievement motivation of many educators, parents, and students is one of the forces acting in the consultant's favor. When asked to state their goals, most people can reply with some specificity. When they are asked to do so, many groups of teachers can seek consensus on some near subgoal. When asked to construct plans for reaching a goal, most groups of teachers will put in extra hours in the eager hope of reaching a subgoal.

At the same time, however, program planning and problem solving may not satisfy people whose primary motivations are power or affiliation. These motives are somewhat more difficult to use because many educated Americans believe that it is somehow shameful to exhibit them in public, although inhibiting norms can be considerably weakened by use of appropriate warm-up activities such as those described in this book.

Even action- or achievement-motivated people may not enjoy large-scale problem solving if their motives have been repeatedly frustrated and their patience for finding gratifying outcomes has grown short. People who have had a great deal of frustrating experience are less likely to seek a problem-solving approach to real problems than to indulge any of several common attitudes: the scapegoat attitude (blame or punish someone for the problem, and the problem will go away); the savior attitude ("Don't worry, our leader will take care of us"); the prayer-wheel attitude ("If we continue doing what we've always done when threatened, after a while the problem won't look as bad"); or the rabbit attitude ("Freeze, and maybe the problem will go away without noticing us").

Bridging the gap between consultation and independent action is the most far-reaching way of making use of clients' motives. That is, never design a consultation so that clients go away feeling satisfied and fulfilled, because doing so leaves them no reason to undertake further action. Design each event so that they have committed themselves to action, have formed a clear plan of action and a clear picture of the nature of the action, have expressed mutual expectations, and have perhaps made a first step in the action phase, but have neither completed nor approached completion of the action; doing that leaves them with the motivation to act even in the consultant's absence.

Learning Themes

When designing a macrosequence,, consultants should consider the abstract significance of even the most mundane events in the interests of leaving clients with one or more conceptual lessons that support organized action. While the exercises described in Chapters 3 through 7 teach small lessons, it is in the larger lessons taught by the OD event as a whole that consultants demonstrate their ability at macrodesigning.

The Planners and Operators exercise (p. 283), for example, teaches among other things that, no matter how carefully people may organize their lectures, one-way instructions are less effective than most people believe them to be. The larger session that includes this exercise, however, may carry the additional lesson that principals either do or do not care about the effect of unilateral communication on their relations with teachers and that they are or are not willing to take action on the matter. This further lesson is likely to be clear and strong if the exercise is conducted with principals and their actual teachers, if it is preceded by a few activities centered on communicative efficacy, and if it is followed by activities and exercises that cause clients to probe their present relationships so that participating principals get an opportunity to demonstrate their own perceptions and hopes.

Again, a consultative session that aims at moving into action innovative ideas requiring the collaboration of teachers and administrators might convey the following related lessons. First, while the ordinary routines of the school do not facilitate conferring, gathering information from those with veto power, arranging logistics, or planning committed action to begin on a certain date, it is nevertheless possible to design a setting that does facilitate these steps. Second, the behavior of staff members toward one another is almost always more a function of organizational structures and the given situation than of individual interests and personality styles.

A macrodesign that presents clients with cognitive messages they can carry into the school can leave them feeling that their potentialities are different or that their relationships with others are new. By this we mean that new actions are now possible and that some old actions are now less probable. We mean, for example, that during the next few days the principal and a committee will invent and try out some new modes of bilateral communication, systematically assessing the results of their efforts; that within a few days clusters of teachers will begin doing new things collaboratively; and that the principal or superintendent will support the new ventures. In short, the lesson we seek always to impart is that new and more worthwhile interdependent actions are not only conceivable and feasible but imminent.

By participating in one particular aspect of a group's plan of actions, consultants can also help clients move toward their goals. If, for example, teachers in a group set a goal of learning how to design meetings they themselves can carry out with students, a particular part of their macrodesign might be a planning session in which outside consultants sit in as facilitators, intervening only when asked or when the meeting process appears unproductive. Participating teachers should leave this kind of OD activity feeling closer to their goal than before and more competent to make progress toward it in the future.

The problem-solving sequence described in Chapter 5 provides a useful learning theme, one we used in 1970 during the first week of a design to launch the conversion of several schools from traditional individuated structures to multiunit team-teaching structures. Essentially, the design comprised four stages:

1. During the first five days, skill practice, exercises, and focused training aimed at helping the faculty to articulate its present and ideal conditions, to reach group agreements both for subgroups and for the school as a whole, and to be clearer with one another about their yearnings and frustrations.
2. The staffs were asked next to state formally some problems that were within their power to solve.
3. While working on actual school problems, they were taught the problem-solving sequence. By the time their plans had been detailed and first steps taken in accordance with the plans, the week had ended.
4. During the final day, staff members told one another about the faculty strengths that they believed would help move the school toward its new goals. By adding personal abilities to the list of helping forces, this activity also made some of the staff's diverse resources more accessible.

SUCCESSFUL MACRODESIGNS

This section offers general guides to good designs.

Eight Techniques for Macrodesigning

Include Key Members. Especially with small subsystems such as teams, departments, committees, cabinets, and building staffs, designs for OD consultation work best when all group members begin and participate in all phases together; even a few days' difference can raise barriers between those who participate and those who come late. When all members experience the intervention goals, skills, and activities simultaneously, they are better able to remind one another of what happened at the workshops and to transfer what was learned to the school situation.

When the organization is large, it is not feasible to include all members in one event. It is difficult, for example, to induce all members of a large secondary school to attend an individual OD event, and it is logistically impossible for all members of a school district to attend all training events. The nonparticipant will understand that a great many people cannot be accommodated at one meeting and will not feel threatened when an OD event is held with one fraction of the district before others.

Thus, when beginning an OD project with a large organization, invite key members—those who are regularly interdependent and who hold formal positions of power in the district—and select them in ways that will be viewed as legitimate and appropriate. If you ask teachers or students to attend a district OD event with the superintendent's cabinet, for example, either invite those holding formal positions of leadership, invite a random group, or choose the participants by some other method that will cause them to be viewed as legitimate representatives and not as chosen by some faction. If people do attend an OD event as representatives of a larger body, see to it that they regularly report the content of the consultation to their constituents.

Clarify OD Goals, Theory, and Technology. The ultimate aim of OD is to develop in the school a self-renewing culture in which discrepancies between actual and ideal conditions are viewed as target problems and in which creative solutions are sought both inside and outside the organization as problems arise. To bring these goals to life, the macrodesign should include both explicit descriptions (cognitive) and lively experiences (affective). Clients should see that clarifying communication and developing new group norms for working together more effectively are prerequisites to carrying out innovative educational programs, and they should come to view defining and solving problems as a regular repetitive cycle in the school. Handouts can be used to introduce and clarify these concepts: Figures 2-1, 2-2, 2-3, and 2-4, and some of the exhibits in the other chapters as well. Exercises are sufficiently removed from the reality of the school to allow staff members to participate with little personal risk or anxiety, but they resemble reality enough to spark discussions of the ways the experience in them resembles or differs from what really happens in the school.

Move from Structured Activities to Application. Skill exercises effectively demonstrate in microcosm organizational issues of role relationships, group norms, and human motivation. Indeed, structured exercises enable organization members who attend a training event out of duty rather than by choice to find new interpersonal modes more easily than do freer experiences demanding more personal commitment and initiative. Exercise results often stimulate thought about familiar problems and thus encourage problem solving about real issues as a next step. By means of skillful debriefing, the consultant can bring participants to the realization that more work is needed to improve oral and written communication, to overcome difficulties in listening, and to gain skill in working together in groups.

Move from Shared Information to Action Planning. Reporting systematically collected information back to appropriate organizational units as a basis for diagnosis, problem solving, and planning is one of the most important intervention modes for OD projects in schools. In both survey-data-feedback and constructive confrontation designs, start by sharing important information within and among appropriate subsystems and role takers. Then help group members practice communication skills to assure a flow of clear information across subsystems and persons. Move next to problem solving, and lead clients toward making specific action plans. Continually point out this macrosequence, which can be labeled *action research*, in the hope that clients will adopt it as a regular organizational process.

Rotate Subgroup Memberships. When small subsystems such as a building staff or smaller groups are involved in OD consultation, successful macrodesigns rotate participating members through different groups, especially during the opening days of the intervention. Rotation increases the potential networks of workable relationships on the staff, diminishes the possibility that groups in relative isolation from one another will come to perceive an in-group and out-group (which can occur with surprising speed), and helps to increase members' identification with the whole staff. The latter is necessary to sustain motivation through the project's follow-up phases and to increase group cohesiveness so that members pull together and share resources during problem solving.

When consulting with large groups, such as the staff of a very large building or a complex district made up of people with a number of jobs, rotating subgroup memberships is impractical. In this case it is best to begin with homogeneous job groups, introducing occasions for participants to communicate about their performances during the exercises and skill activities. Next, arrange a period when they can discuss district organizational problems similar to those in the exercises, allowing each group to list its own problems and to tell the others about them. Then, organize problem-solving activities within heterogeneous job groups. Finally, schedule planning of the application of OD techniques to school situations so that homogeneous groups can practice new skills, norms, and actions. Later consultation should bring heterogeneous groups together again to assess how well the problem solving has been going.

Treat All Ranks Equally. People in educational institutions are generally attributed higher or lower status on the basis of impressions of how much or how well they contribute to valued group goals. Some status differences are both relevant and useful, as when parents are accorded high status for knowing their way around the community or when principals are accorded high status for knowing their way around complicated budget procedures. Other status differences are meaningless, however—as when it is believed that only an administrator can convene a meeting or that only the school secretary can take minutes— and an effective macrodesign reduces such unnecessary differences in the context of the OD events. That is, the consultant responds to organization members in terms of their performance in intervention activities and not in terms of their job titles.

Consultants should explain that every participant is potentially important in carrying out a task and that stereotypes based on job titles can impede effective group functioning. Rotating participants through groups can bring teachers, administrators, and nonprofessional personnel into closer communication with one another and thus reduce the distance between them. Equal treatment during an OD event will bring them closer psychologically, a prime prerequisite to achieving openness and improved communication for performing the tasks of the school.

To be sure, consultants sometimes offer special coaching or training to people in certain positions. For example, a principal might welcome recommendations for building bilateral communication into a personal supervisory role. For other examples, we have trained a parent group to give feedback in ways that aroused less defensiveness among teachers and have also helped students to practice effective meeting procedures before joining teachers and parents on a school's advisory body. Consultants should not encourage clients to ignore status or other differences that enrich a school's variety pool or resources. Instead, they should together create norms that support retention of differences that are relevant and useful for accomplishing the school's work.

Exemplify New Organizational Forms. A successful macrodesign deliberately includes activities that, in their own structure and process, exemplify organization forms potentially useful to clients. Practice in summarizing, group exercises in decision making, procedures such as the Fishbowl or problem solving—all should be living representations of techniques that can be used in the everyday life of the school. In other words, the consultant should plan activities that give clients new and improved organizational structures that they can bring to their regular work.

Set Out Continuing Work for the Future. The effective macrodesign should culminate with work specifications that clients will be facing as they leave the OD event. That is, consultants should design in such a way that school people feel both some sense of closure about matters learned and interim tasks completed and some unresolved tension concerning important tasks still incomplete. A shared feeling of incompletion, the conviction that continued problem solving will be useful, and a sense of urgency to get on with it are all powerful motivations for self-renewal.

The Design Team

Intervention teams are typically composed of one consultant to ten or fifteen clients. When the target group offers special challenges or when less-experienced consultants are included in the consulting team, working in pairs can increase the ratio to one consultant to six or seven clients, lend emotional support and additional skill to the consultants, and leave each client unit less susceptible to errors.

Especially during brainstorming, the design team will gain in total strength if its composition is heterogeneous with regard to information, skills, interests, and personal styles. Because such diversity can also create difficulties in building openness and interdependence, the team should spend time developing itself as an effectively functioning adaptive group, and the consultant should strive to create the kind of team culture that is expected of the target group. Both goals require frank discussion of process as the team fashions the OD design.

No matter how large the team becomes, it is important that consultants who will implement the design participate in some of the planning, although it is unnecessary and often inefficient for all team members to be involved in all phases of planning. When the design team exceeds four members, a division of labor is required. Subteams of two, for instance, can work on diagnosing the target group, defining OD goals, and developing alternative sequences.

Before the rest of the macrodesigning takes place, the whole team should react to the diagnosis and goal setting and should brainstorm microdesigns for increasing facilitating forces and reducing restraining forces. Finally, the whole group should react to the proposed sequences, select one, and enlist members for refining and implementing each microaspect of the design. After this is done, individual members or two-person subgroups may finalize the specific steps of each small part of the total design.

Seven Building Steps

The seven steps for building an effective macrodesign are not unlike the steps employed in problem solving (see Chapter 5).

1. The design team starts by discussing its general view of organizational self-renewal, using as guides the concepts introduced in Chapter 1. Talk about conceptions of adaptability in relation to how the target group will look at the end of the OD consultation. Important aspects of this discussion will already have occurred during the entry-and-startup phase, when the contract with the target group was built.
2. Using the instruments and data-collecting procedures described in Chapters 3 through 7, collect data on selected organizational attributes of the target group, and seek information about the clarity of communication and education goals (Chapter 3), hidden intergroup and interrole conflicts (Chapter 7), and meeting effectiveness (Chapter 4). Although these data can be collected by means of questionnaires, interviews and observations are generally more useful for consultants, allowing them to gather sufficient additional data on the spot to commence characterizing the target group during the interviewing or observing process.
3. List for the particular event being designed consultative goals that are more specific than those discussed during entry. Ideally, observable behavioral evidences for the goals are specified in advance (Chapters 3 through 7).

4. List forces present in the target group that will facilitate or restrain the achievement of OD goals. These forces can be categorized as group, interpersonal, or intrapersonal (see Chapter 6 for a discussion of Force-Field Analysis).
5. Use brainstorming to generate microdesigns that might increase facilitating forces or reduce restraining forces (see Chapter 8 for details about microdesigning).
6. Prepare alternative sequences for the microdesigns.
7. Finally, accept one sequence and assign implementation duties for each microaspect to a specific member of the consulting staff. Let the consultant responsible for each microaspect refine the design of his or her part.

Ten Questions

Designing an OD event requires creativity, knowledge, and flexibility; it is in many ways the most challenging and exciting part of the intervention process. Although the history of designing OD events is brief and its empirical basis is limited, there are nevertheless ten questions that should be answered affirmatively before any design is put into action.

1. Will the design allow clients to feel rewarded, challenged, uplifted, and inspired?
2. Does it clearly connect training and consultation to the actual work of the target group?
3. Will it increase communicative clarity, a sense of pulling together, and energy for continuing collaborative work?
4. Does it aid in clarifying problems involving unclear roles, norms, and decision-making procedures?
5. Does it offer activities through which achievement, affiliation, and power motives can be satisfied?
6. Does it offer a description of some goals of the total organization so that members can recognize and identify with superordinate goals?
7. Does it feature a learning theme to leave clients with one or more conceptual lessons?
8. Does it include procedures for monitoring consultative events as they are occurring?
9. Does it build structures and schedules that will continue after consultation?
10. Does it offer a sense of closure while leaving some tension related to work still to be accomplished?

The Centrality of Problem Solving

Problem solving is fundamental in all OD macrodesigns. It is present in all OD virtually from start to finish and, we always hope, even beyond the departure of the consultants. Small cycles of problem solving occur during the making of a contract, the system-wide diagnosis, the selection of a macrodesign, and the execution of an OD design.

During contract making, for example, the consultant offers information about the goals of OD. That gives participants a direction toward targets; it also helps them focus upon the current situation in their school. And the contract presents guidelines for the ensuing problem solving. Thus, even during contract making we find the rudiments of problem solving: the description of the situation (S), specification of target (T), and proposals for the path (P) to the target.

Collecting diagnostic data also requires several cycles of problem solving. First are the task force's discussions on which items and strategies to use in data collection. Often, the best format is one that requires participants to reflect on discrepancies between S and T in the school. Second is the task force's choice of the issues to be given the most attention during the OD. And third are the feedback sessions with all members of the client system that help everyone to see and understand the organizational problems their school faces.

The problem-solving mode of thought comes into play even more significantly during the selection and execution of the macrodesign. Regardless of the macrodesign chosen—training, survey-data-feedback, constructive confrontation, or process observation and feedback—they all help build the structure and motivation for collaborative problem solving among colleagues in the client system.

During training, the organizational problems of the clients are brought into view both indirectly and subtly. During the first few days of training, and particularly toward the end of each minicycle of experiential learning, participants compare and contrast their behavior during the foregoing exercise and their typical behavior in the school. These discussions often give rise to problems that, if worked on, can help the staff strengthen the school's organizational processes. The OD consultant keeps a list of those problems as they arise and later reminds the clients about them before proceeding into problem-solving groups.

Compared with training, survey-data-feedback leads straightforwardly to problem solving. The data themselves typically allow participants to see discrepancies between their S and Ts, so that during survey-data-feedback, problems can be listed both by the consultant and by the participants themselves.

In a different manner, problems also arise from constructive confrontation. Here the consultant helps subsystems in conflict to see the norms, structures, or procedures that are blocking effective collaboration. Through a stepwise progression from social distance through catharsis to reflection, the confrontation design gradually increases participants' realization that system-wide problems are shared and that if they are to be solved, they must be attacked collaboratively.

Finally, process observation and feedback also facilitates problem identification. The consultant watches the client group work, noting process problems and giving feedback to raise participants' awareness of the problem. In structure, that procedure is similar to data feedback, except that in process observation and feedback the consultant replaces the questionnaire as the instrument of problem identification.

Although problem solving goes on continuously from the start, formal problem solving starts, from the participants' point of view, after one of the four macrodesigns has helped the participants to make a list of central organizational problems. Our research indicates that it is necessary for client systems to go through at least two cycles of formal problem solving for lasting outcomes to occur in the school.

The initial cycle of formal problem solving should address pressing school issues that, if worked on, can give rather rapid and visible results. Examples could include communication breakdowns between particular subsystems or role takers, confusion over some of the school's goals, ineffective meetings, and a lack of group agreements about certain role relationships.

A later cycle of formal problem solving should focus on what has to be done to ensure that collaborative problem solving will take place continually in the school. Here, participants explore the norms, structures, and procedures required to maintain an effective capacity for continual problem solving. We discussed examples of such norms, structures, and procedures in Chapter 1.

Figure 2-4 is an abbreviated flow chart summarizing relationships among aspects of a macrodesign.

EXAMPLES OF MACRODESIGNS

Although the number of possible macrodesigns is virtually infinite, we have chosen to present here some that have shown promise in our own work and the work of others with which we have been associated. We distinguish among three sorts of designs: classical, complex, and special interest. *Classical designs* are rather pure examples of survey-data-feedback, training, constructive confrontation, and process observation and feedback. Complex designs are mixtures of those; they are larger in scope and frequently longer in duration than the classical designs. While some differences between classical and complex designs

Figure 2-4. Main Points of OD Macrodesigns

Making the OD contract
↓
The OD diagnosis
    Data collection
    Data feedback
↓
The OD macrodesign
    Data feedback
    Training
    Confrontation
    Process observation and feedback
↓
Pressing organizational problems
are identified
↓
Problem-solving cycle 1
(pressing problems)
↓
Problem-solving cycle 2
(problem-solving capacity)

---

appear obvious, the distinctions are only a matter of degree. *Special-interest designs* commence with a focus on a specific social or educational problem or challenge—for example, desegregation, mainstreaming, or parent involvement. More and more attempts to use OD in schools get their impetus from the presence of a new societal or educational challenges confronting our educational systems.

Classical Macrodesigns

Here are illustrations of the four kinds of strategies.

Survey-Data-Feedback: Developing Renewal Processes in Urban High Schools*

Bassin, Gross, and Jordan (1979) have developed a practical model based on organization development for strengthening urban high schools. This New York-based project differs from other efforts to apply

*Adapted from Richard A. Schmuck, "Organization Development in the Schools" in Cecil R. Reynolds and Terry B. Gutkin (eds.), *The Handbook of School Psychology* (New York: John Wiley, 1982).

OD to schools in several ways. First, it is the largest organization-development effort in inner city schools anywhere in the world; specifically, there are thirty-five participating schools and most of them are very large. Second, it is the largest effort to apply organization development to secondary schools. And third, it is the longest organization development effort in inner city schools, in operation since 1969.

Bassin, Gross, and Jordan describe their "renewal model" as involving participatory, systematic planning, and problem solving. The model calls for members of the school—including students—to identify, analyze and develop solutions to school problems. The process requires start-up, diagnosis, planning, and implementation, and offers an excellent example of how to apply OD for urban school improvement. The plan works as follows.

Following exploratory conferences with the principal and other key staff members, the organization-development consultant decides whether the school is ready. *Start-up* officially takes place when the consultant meets with the principal and other staff to explore the segments of the school that should commence the renewal process.

Next, the principal, a few staff members, and the consultant design procedures for selecting an *internal renewal coordinator*. The coordinator initiates, energizes, and manages the project (see Porterfield and Porterfield, 1979, for details). The first task of the coordinator is to enlist the aid of a voluntary committee drawn from the school and its surrounding community. The start-up is completed when the consultant, coordinator, principal, and the committee design the details of the remaining stages of renewal in terms of who will do what and when.

Diagnosis is the data-collection or needs-assessment stage of renewal. The committee decides on issues of concern about which to collect data, carries out an extensive survey of the issues, and thereby diagnoses the school problem. Several methods of collecting data are used to produce both opinion data and baseline or quantitative data. Most common among the collection methods are survey instruments, group brainstorming, interviews, and observation. The data are used by the renewal committee to establish priorities for planning.

Planning involves developing ideas and programs to solve priority problems. Bassin, Gross, and Jordan indicate that in their schools planning typically consists of five steps. First, potential implementers of innovative programs are invited to collaborate with the committee in the planning process. Second, "research and development" is carried out by examining effective practices relevant to the issues in question that are being tried elsewhere. Third, an action plan is created that includes a carefully phrased set of objectives, an accountability scheme, and a specific time line listing tasks and people. Fourth, a formative evaluation procedure is established. And fifth, administrative approval is sought to assume that the project is consonant with the goals of the school and to enlist support of the administration during implementation.

Implementation involves putting the action plans into effect. It often encounters resistance, particularly in the urban school environments where it is being tried. Resistance is often due to political problems in the school, but just as frequently is due to poor management procedures. The consultant can be helpful in facilitating the prevention or resolution of implementation problems. For example, renewal committees often find fault with the principal for what is perceived as a lack of support. Principals, on the other hand, often tend to view the committee as another pressure group that must be balanced along side of many others. These perceptions may lead to hostilities that obligate the consultant to act as a third-party facilitator.

Training: Organizational Training for a School Faculty

The following design, carried out in a junior high school, is fully reported in Schmuck and Runkel (1970); its purposes were to stimulate improved group problem solving among faculty members and generally to help the school, as a human organization, to become more responsive to students and parents. The training began with a six-day laboratory in late August 1967 with almost the entire building staff present. The fifty-four trainees included all the administrators, all but two of the faculty, plus the head secretary, the head cook, and the head custodian.

The first two days were devoted to group and intergroup exercises and communication skills—e.g., Lost on the Moon, the Five-Square puzzle, and the Planners and Operators exercise (use the index to locate specific exercises) along with paraphrasing and other communication skills described in Chapter 3—all of which aimed at increasing awareness of interpersonal and organizational process and at demonstrating the importance of effective communication in accomplishing tasks collaboratively. After each exercise, small groups discussed how the experiences were like or unlike their normal relations in school. All staff members then pooled their experiences and analyzed their relationships as a faculty. Each small group chose its own way of reporting what it had experienced, and the consultants supported openness in giving and receiving feedback about perceptions of real organizational processes in the school.

During the next four days the faculty pursued a problem-solving sequence, working on real issues that were thwarting the school's organizational functions. On the third day, after a morning of discussion and decision (which also served as practice in decision-making skills), three significant problems emerged and three groups formed, each to work through a problem-solving sequence directed toward one of the problems.

Working substantially on its own, each group followed a five-step procedure: (1) identifying the problem through behavioral description, (2) further defining the problem by diagnostic Force-Field Analysis (see index), (3) brainstorming to find actions likely to reduce restraining forces, (4) designing a concrete plan of action, and (5) trying out the plan behaviorally by means of a simulation activity involving the entire staff. The consultants served as facilitators, seldom made substantive suggestions, and never pressed for results. The first six days of training culminated with a discussion in which members described their own strengths and those of their colleagues and reflected on what their school could be like if all faculty resources were used.

Early in the fall, during the active school year, the consultants interviewed all faculty members and also observed several committees and subject-area groups to determine what uses were being made of the earlier six-day training. Data gathered at this point indicated that problems still unresolved were closely related to communicative misunderstanding, an overload of duties in some jobs, and a limited capability for group problem solving.

At the next follow-up consultation with the entire staff, held for one-and-a-half days in December 1967, the consultants sought to increase the effectiveness of area coordinators as communication links between teachers and administrators, to increase problem-solving skills of the area groups and the principal's advisory committee, to help the faculty explore ways of reducing its duty overload, and to increase effective communication between service personnel and the rest of the staff. OD activities included communication exercises, problem-solving techniques, decision-making procedures, and development of skill in observing and giving feedback to work groups.

On the first day, departmental groups applied problem-solving techniques to their own communication difficulties and received feedback from other observing groups. The problems raised were brought the next day to a meeting of the principal's advisory committee held before the staff. The staff observed the committee in a Fishbowl Arrangement (see index), participated with its members in specially designed ways, and later reflected on how effectively the committee had worked and how accurately its members had reflected them.

The main objectives of the third follow-up event in February 1968, which also lasted one-and-a-half days, were to evaluate staff progress in solving the problems of resource utilization, role clarity, and staff participation and to reanimate any lagging skills. A group discussion was held for each problem, and all teachers were invited to work in the group considering the problem that interested them most. Each group discussed the favorable and unfavorable outcomes associated with its problem and wrote examples of improvement, instances of no change, and cases of regression. The groups tried to devise ways to halt backsliding by modifying the school's organizational procedures. Faculty members continued with this activity in small groups during the spring without help from the consultants.

Survey-Data-Feedback: The Charismatic Day

The personal qualities of a charismatic leader, who excites the imaginations of others, encourages them to share in feelings of relevance and power, and imparts a sense of urgency to them, can also become part of the culture of a group. The Charismatic Day, a one-day macrodesign built on this concept, can be carried out with a school faculty (or groups of parents or students) late in a year-long OD effort, following a series of training and consultative events such as those described in this chapter.* The intent of the design is to excite the hopes and imaginations of staff members, to help them feel powerful and confident, and to instill in them a pervasive sense of urgency. It encourages organization members to put new ways of working together into immediate action and is also useful in stimulating a staff to upgrade classroom group processes in new ways.

First, the outside consultants, with the help of insiders who have participated in planning the event, quickly list in the form of goals some changes currently under serious consideration in the school, each of which must have the vocal support of at least one small group. Staff members are asked to express their understandings and feelings about these goals in buzz groups and soon afterward to report the discussions to the total staff.

Again in a small group, each person is asked to tell others specifically and realistically what he or she personally wants to do to achieve these broader goals. Then each individual prepares a list headed "what I can contribute toward achieving my preferred action plan." These lists are posted, and staff members try to find others with whom they can profitably work to achieve their personal plans. Clusters of four staff members are encouraged but not required, and time is allowed for the clusters to form.

To induce a sense of urgency, each cluster is asked to produce a plan of action that can be initiated in the next week. After an hour or two of planning, participants are asked to talk about the new things they

---

*For our use of this macrodesign, see Schmuck et al. (1975).

believe they can do with others in school as a result of this procedure. If nothing they have done in planning has been important, or if they feel discouraged about their action plans, they are asked to talk about their disappointments. The design can end here, or, if group members seem ready, ten to fifteen minutes can be spent at some trust-building procedure.

Constructive Confrontation: Bringing a School Staff and Parents into Effective Interaction*

During the 1971–1972 school year, Schmuck teamed with a cadre of organizational specialists within a school district to facilitate conflict resolution at a beleaguered elementary school. The context of this intervention was a national reaction to the presumed dehumanization in school classrooms and the need for parent involvement at the local level to turn things around. About ninety parents at an elementary school attended informal neighborhood meetings in the fall of 1971 to discuss concerns they had with their own school. The outgrowth of these meetings was the formation of a group that called itself the Parents' Advisory Committee.

The committee sent a letter to the school's principal in November that described "wide-spread concerns with school-to-parent communication, curriculum—especially in the arts—and the quality of the staff and its training." The principal passed on the letter to the school's twelve teachers who greeted it with disbelief, resentment, and disappointment. The principal then called on the coordinator of the district's cadre of organizational specialists, asking for "assistance in dealing with the parents' complaints."

Members of the cadre, along with Schmuck, developed a design that had as its overall theme a confrontation between parents and teachers. Within the theme of confrontation were elements of training, data feedback, and process observation and feedback. The macrodesign included six stages:

1. Forming and meeting with a steering committee composed of some teachers and a few parents to explain the macrodesign and get approval to proceed.
2. Providing demonstrations of organization development to the

*Adapted from Richard A. Schmuck, "Organization Development in the Schools," in Cecil R. Reynolds and Terry B. Gutkin (eds.), *The Handbook of School Psychology* (New York: John Wiley, 1982).

staff and to all interested parents so they understand the goals and procedures of the intervention.

3. Training parents and staff separately in the skills of interpersonal communication and group problem solving and helping each group identify top-priority concerns. Collecting data on impressions of intergroup climate and influence.

4. Bringing the two groups together and feeding back data on climate, concerns, and influence. Helping the groups clarify intergroup communication and agree upon top-priority mutual concerns.

5. Forming problem-solving groups of parents and teachers to design proposals to solve important mutual problems. Serving as process facilitators to these groups.

6. Bringing all problem-solving groups together to share their proposals and to make decisions and plans for implementation.

The six stages were carried out as scheduled, beginning with Stage 1 in November and ending with Stage 6 in June. Details about microdesign elements and the intervention's outcomes can be found in Schmuck et al. (1977). In general the outcomes were very favorable.

Three kinds of outcomes were documented. The first set had to do with implementation of proposals designed by the parent-staff problem-solving groups. Within a year, there were (1) a new parent organization that included parents in the process of making decisions about curriculum and staffing, (2) new forms of written communication from school to home, (3) improvements to the building and grounds, (4) parties for welcoming new and foreign families to the community and school, (5) many parent volunteers in classrooms and the library, and (6) an artist-in-residence program.

A second set of outcomes had to do with improvements in the climate of interaction between staff and parents and in the climate of interactions among staff members. After the intervention, parents reported that they had better impressions of the school, could now get the information they wanted, and thought their input was welcomed by the staff. When asked about changes they saw in the school, more than two-thirds of the parents singled out the atmosphere as being very different.

The third set of outcomes concerned changes in perceived and attributed influence. Parents perceived an increase in their own influence after the intervention and did so without attributing less influence to the staff. Staff members, by contrast, did not think they had gained or lost influence but attributed more influence to parents. To both parents and the staff, the PTA in its new structure was the vehicle through which the total amount of influence available to be shared had been increased.

Process Observation and Feedback: Improving
the Meetings of a Teaching Team

Schmuck helped a team of teachers in a middle school to improve its meeting procedures by using techniques of process observation and feedback.

After meeting with the team leaders and subsequently with the team itself, a joint decision was made to use an in-service day to get the consultation going. Schmuck suggested that the team meet the evening before the in-service day to give him an opportunity to observe the team in action. He recommended that the team run a regular meeting that evening with its own agenda and typical procedures. He would observe the procedures used, offer some immediate feedback, and work up other feedback after that meeting for discussion on the next day. From then on, the team was to do problem solving and to make some new group agreements about its meetings on the in-service day.

The work proceeded well as planned. Schmuck observed the team work for ninety minutes. After a break he offered behavioral descriptions of what he saw, along with some of his feelings about the group behaviors. His feedback sought a balance between favorable and unfavorable reflections about the team. While he saw concerted attention to task and participation by all, he also noted that when a few people spoke no one responded to them, that the agenda for the meeting wasn't written down, that no paraphrasing or gatekeeping occurred during the meeting, and that no one checked with others to reinforce decisions that seemed to be made by the team. After a short discussion about the meeting, the session ended.

The next morning, at the start of the in-service day, Schmuck led off by asking team members for their reflections and feelings about the meeting on the previous evening. This question gave rise to quite a few critical comments about the team's functioning. Schmuck then asked how typical the meeting had been—how it resembled or differed from other meetings. Some participants saw similarities with other meetings in the team's lack of a clear agenda and its failure to clarify who was to do what after decisions were made. Others saw contrasts with other meetings, chiefly insofar as the team was trying to perform well in front of Dr. Schmuck. Typically, they remarked, the team drifted away from its task more than it had the night before.

Next, Schmuck engaged the participants in a discussion to identify key process problems during the team's meetings. The list that developed included (1) a lack of clarity in the agenda; (2) too much dependence on the leader for running the meetings; (3) some sloppy communication; (4) hidden feelings that came out only after the meetings; and (5) unclear decision-making procedures, throwing most of the responsibility for follow-through on the shoulders of the team leader.

Then, each person was paired with another and each pair selected one of the above-listed problems to work on. Schmuck introduced the *S-T-P* problem-solving process (described in Chapter 5). Each pair proceeded through the steps of problem solving while Schmuck moved around the room again acting as a process observer. Finally, the initial cycle of problem solving ended with each pair reporting back its ideas to the whole group.

Schmuck next asked that each individual spend thirty minutes alone listing the actions he or she would like to see the team take to improve its meetings. At the end of the half-hour period, each participant presented his or her list on a large piece of newsprint paper so the others could see it. Schmuck suggested circling any ideas that were on three or more lists. The circled ideas were then discussed by the team and either consensually accepted or tabled for later consideration. No idea was immediately rejected. Schmuck ended the day by asking each team member to state his or her willingness to try out the new ideas, and by scheduling his next visit to the school when he would again act as process observer at a meeting.

Schmuck visited the school once a week for three weeks to do process observation and feedback at team meetings. He used as a guide to his observations the lists of ideas that the team had agreed upon during the in-service day. During the third week, he suggested that team members themselves start to serve as process observers at future meetings, and suggested choosing a member to pair off with him and observe at the next meeting. Schmuck asked the team members to count off, and then arbitrarily chose a number; the person whose number matched his would collaborate with him as an observer of the next meeting. This kind of pairing with Schmuck took place twice, and then all participants felt capable of observing and feeding back information on their own. Schmuck departed from the school six weeks after the in-service day.

The following macrodesigns contain one or another mixture of training, survey-data-feedback, constructive confrontation, and process observation and feedback.

Complex Macrodesigns

Establishing OD Specialists in a School District

As part of a two-year intervention from 1968 to 1970, consultants from the Center of Educational Policy and Management (CEPM)—then known as the Center for the Advanced Study of Educational Administration (CASEA)—established an internal cadre of organizational specialists within a school district. Before the specialists were in place, however, CEPM consultants carried out organizational training events for several key parts of the district for one year. The goal of the OD events was to increase the communication and problem-solving skills of teams of personnel in a variety of influential positions; an early auxiliary goal was to clarify and define the complex relationships between line and staff personnel. The results of this districtwide effort are described by Runkel, Wyant, Bell, and Runkel (1980).

Training Personnel with Line Functions

In April 1968 the CEPM consultants invited all the key personnel performing line functions in the district to the first training event. These included the superintendent and his cabinet, the elementary and secondary school principals, and selected teachers who were leaders within the local education association. At least one teacher from every building attended the meeting along with the higher officers in the association. The event lasted for four days, but only the superintendent's cabinet was present all the time.

On the first day, before others had arrived, the superintendent and his cabinet first discussed ways in which their communication was breaking down, the lack of clarity in their role definitions, ambiguous norms within the cabinet, and also their strengths as a group.

On the second day, the principals joined the cabinet in a specially designed Imaging procedure that brought into the open the organizational problems that each group felt involved the other (see Chapter 7 for details). The issues uncovered were earmarked for future problem solving. Now the cabinet and principals divided into three units: cabinet, elementary principals, and secondary principals. Each group met separately to list the other two groups' helpful and unhelpful work-related behaviors toward their own group. At the end of two hours, all agreed-upon behaviors of the other groups were written in large letters on sheets of newsprint. This session ended with a brief period of training to sharpen the communication skills of paraphrasing and behavior description.

Next, one of the three groups sat in a circle surrounded by members of the other two groups. Those in the outer ring read aloud the descriptions they had written of the inner group. A member of the inner circle then paraphrased the descriptions to make sure everyone in the ring had understood. After all items describing the inner group were read, each of the remaining two groups took its turn in the inner circle. Throughout this procedure, inner-circle members were *not* allowed to defend their group against the allegations made by the others.

Next, the three groups met separately to find evidence supporting the descriptions—that is, to recall examples of their behavior that could have given the other group its impressions. Returning to the Fishbowl Arrangement, each inner group reported evidence it had recalled to verify the others' perceptions. Again, inner-group members were asked simply to describe the evidence without attempting to defend themselves.

On the evening of the second day, teachers joined the principals and cabinet for four hours, and thus, for that period all the line personnel in the district with formal authority were together. A modified Imaging procedure was carried out, culminating in a meeting at which the three groups specified the organizational problems that they believed existed in the district. Discussion was lively, penetrating, and constructive; most had never so openly confronted persons in other positions with their perceptions of district problems. The principals returned to their buildings the next day, leaving time for teachers and cabinet to interact. On the fourth day the cabinet met alone to schedule dates for problem solving.

Training Personnel with Staff Functions

Personnel in staff roles in the divisions of Student Personnel Services and Curriculum Development attended a three-day conference in September 1968 during which they were joined for a half-day by the principals. This event began with the staffs of Student Personnel and Curriculum meeting separately to discuss the helps and hindrances occurring within each of their groups, with special attention to obvious interpersonal helps and hindrances. Afterward, the two groups plus the principals participated in a period of confrontation. As in April, the confrontation unearthed a number of problems needing work. Finally, each group undertook a systematic process of problem solving, planning to continue these efforts back home.

Demonstrating OD Consultation to Selected School Staffs

From September 1968 to April 1969, CEPM consultants worked with five of the school staffs in the district. More than the trainings with line and staff personnel, these brief OD events demonstrated to many of the teachers the benefits of consultation in reaching district subsystems. Although as demonstrations they were probably not as successful as that portraying OD during entry, they had the effect of increasing awareness of the meaning and procedures of organization development. Perhaps the most significant result of these events was that many of the volunteers to be trained as future specialists came from the buildings in which the consultation took place.

Preparing the Specialists

In the spring of 1969, district personnel were informed that a workshop would be held in June 1969 for those who wished to become OD specialists. A mimeographed circular stated that the trainees would become skilled and knowledgeable in group processes and would serve on committees to give feedback or as trainers for special groups within the district. The CEPM consultants solicited applications from all hierarchical levels of the district, and the twenty-three persons selected represented a wide cross-section of the district, including teachers, counselors, elementary and secondary principals, specialists in curriculum and student personnel, and assistant superintendents who were members of the superintendent's cabinet.

The first (and major) training event was a two-week workshop in June 1969. The goals of the first half of this workshop were to introduce the trainees to many of the skills, exercises, and procedures that later appeared in the first edition of this book; to provide them an opportunity to explore the effect of their behavior on a group; to establish the cadre as a cohesive, supportive unit; and to give practice in leading training activities.

Trainees spent the first three days experiencing many exercises in small groups, rotating the role of cotrainer for training experience. Each exercise focused on a certain type of group process, such as interpersonal control, sharing of resources, or coordinating efforts to make certain "lessons" easy to comprehend. During the last two days of this week, group members designed exercises that would help strengthen their group as a cadre of specialists. They carried out the exercises with their peers, engaged in critical discussion afterward, and reviewed and practiced the skills of paraphrasing, behavior description, describing one's own feelings, and checking one's impressions of the feelings of others.

For the second week, they divided into six subgroups, each convened by a CEPM consultant. The entire group determined potential target groups within the district, and each subgroup chose one for its work. Among the targeted groups were several schools that were changing their programs in the coming academic year, the principal and department heads at a senior high school, the principals and counselors serving elementary youngsters, and a community advisory group made up of parents. The remainder of this week was spent establishing goals for the training to be conducted with the target groups, gathering diagnostic data about them, analyzing the data to determine the forces operating within the target groups, and designing training events. The CEPM consultants worked closely with these subgroups, anticipating the follow-up they would give during the academic year.

During the first two-thirds of the 1969/70 academic year, the CEPM consultants continued to work with the new specialists, withdrawing in March 1970. Thus, many training events engineered by the specialists were observed and criticized by the outside consultants to support the development of training skills within the cadre. Approximately ten different training events occurred with their assistance, most of them successful in raising district interest in improving communication, group processes, and organizational problem solving. Other features of this project are described in Chapter 11.

Launching Multiunit Elementary Schools

Future elementary schools are likely to be increasingly characterized by a multiunit structure in which teams of teachers work in flexible ways with large groups of students. Ideally, this format will make fuller use of individualized instruction, differentiated staffing, and group decision making. The transition, however, from the self-contained to the multiunit style will not be easy, nor will the abilities and customs developed in the traditional school be sufficient in themselves to make the new organization work. Relying on differentiated staffing and dispersed decision making will require that roles and norms be well understood and that greater attention be paid to coordination among teachers. This in turn will require that all staff members exhibit improved skills in communication and group problem solving.

The following design aims at helping a largely self-contained school move effectively toward the multiunit structure. This intervention calls for a series of consultative events over about nine months. The first, week-long event of approximately forty hours occurs in August and is followed by several events during the academic year that total another forty hours.

The first five days in August commence with group exercises, such as Grievances of Black Citizens (Chapter 6) and a diagnosis of the school's organizational structure through the use of Tinkertoys in groups. During the same period, consultants teach clients communication skills to use during debriefing. To generate organizational concerns, consultants attempt to make group agreements in teaching teams by means of intergroup exercises. On the third day, problems are identified and problem solving occurs in heterogeneous groups. Finally, staff strengths are identified and shared. Staff members discuss their group agreements within teams and continue problem solving in the heterogeneous groups after they return to school. Consultation during the school year should emphasize four major themes in this sequence, with approximately ten hours of process facilitation devoted to each theme.

1. *Supporting successful performance of the heterogeneous problem-solving groups.* As a skill, problem solving will not be successful unless it leads to reduced frustrations and new satisfactions among the staff. The plans made during the last few days of the first week of consultation should now be reexamined to meet the schedules of the school day. In general, plans should either be carried through, modified as necessary, or dropped by explicit agreement.

2. *Helping the teaching teams work effectively.* Continued organizational problem solving depends upon norms of interpersonal openness and helpfulness in the teaching teams. During this phase, the teams should be strengthened by continued consulting and coaching in communication skills, group agreements, meeting skills, and decision making.

3. *Building the leadership team.* The aim of any OD consultation should be to build new functions, roles, procedures, or policies so that the new structures become part of the basic fabric of the school. Because the principal, team leaders, counselor, and resource teacher are crucial to success or failure in the new organization, special process consulting should be extended to them in such functions as the role of the effective group convener, the role of process analysis during a work session, and differences between being the leader and merely performing leadership functions.

4. *Involving the leadership team in designing an OD learning experience for the rest of the staff.* Consultants should attempt to establish expectations and skills within the two staffs that support continued consultative efforts initiated and carried out by fellow staff members. During this phase, the outside consultants might co-plan and co-consult with the leadership team to help the staff solve problems, to help the staff improve group processes in its subgroups (e.g., teaching teams), and to help the entire staff improve organizational processes across subgroups.

Collegial Consultation

Cameron (1982) described the details of an experiment in collegial consultation in Australian schools. Eight experienced teachers, three of whom were principals, volunteered to receive training in OD consultation from experts on the staff of the New South Wales State Department of Education. Those eight, who were to act as OD facilitators in schools other than their own, received seven days of intensive workshop training before forming into four pairs, with one consulting pair to serve each of four schools. The decision to participate in the experiment rested with the staffs of the four schools, with the understanding that once in the project, the school would remain in for two years. For their part, the neophyte consultants were released from their own schools for one half-day per week to carry out the consultancy functions and to receive continued training over the two years.

In general, the new consultants followed a survey-data-feedback design. After they discussed with the staffs the purposes of the consultation, they asked staff members to complete a questionnaire about their schools. At several subsequent meetings in each school, results from the questionnaires were given back to the staffs for understanding and discussion. Then, each school retreated for a three-day weekend workshop that was intended to teach a structured approach to problem solving, to gain a commitment to collaborative problem solving for planned change, and to gain further acceptance of the consultants as credible process helpers. The consultants deliberately played low-key roles. While they tried to keep the participants to the task of problem solving, they avoided confrontations and refrained from becoming involved in the content of the discussions.

After the retreat, temporary task groups of staff members were formed, each to work in earnest on one of the problems identified at the retreat. Examples of problems were role confusions, communicative difficulties, ineffective meetings, need for curriculum revision, inadequate counseling services, poor relationships among departments, and the like. The task groups brought suggestions for change back to the whole faculty after doing their own problem solving. In many instances, staffs tried some modifications in work patterns.

The assessment of the change effects revealed some interesting outcomes. While there were some reservations, the majority of responses indicated that, compared with non-OD schools, staffs of the four OD schools felt that there had been an improvement in the problem areas in which change was attempted. The improvements had to do with knowledge, skills, and attitudes for staff members in various aspects of their teaching roles and professional relationships. Also evident were improvements in both the organization of schools and their use of resources. At the same time, the data indicated that the staffs of the OD schools in general tended to be more critical of their work procedures as staffs than those of non-OD schools. Cameron interpreted that result as an indication that the staffs of the OD schools developed higher standards by which to evaluate their work than those current in the non-OD schools. Other features of this project are described in Chapter 11.

A Design for Renewing Urban Elementary Schools

Scheinfeld (1979) offered a complex macrodesign that shows promise for dealing with the difficult problems of school improvement in inner-city settings. His strategy assumes that the quality of classroom life is multiply determined and that it is advisable to explore improvement strategies that take into account as many factors as possible.

Scheinfeld's design uses interventions into three key aspects of school life: the classroom, the organizational climate of the school, and school-community relations. The design employs the roles of classroom advisor, OD consultant, and school-community organizer working together as a coordinated consulting team. Specific features of the design were developed during a three-year action-research project in which Scheinfeld's team worked with two public elementary schools in Chicago.

The most effective approach, largely developed during the team's engagement with the second school, used an OD framework for the overall coordination of consulting efforts. An OD facilitator first helped a staff reflect on its problems, needs, and desires. During that activity, diagnostic data were unearthed that the consultants and the participants could share. Some of the problems raised were high rates of vandalism, poor student discipline, low student achievement, a lack of staff coordination in relation to the students, and poor relationships with parents. The OD facilitator was assisted by the consulting team's community organizer, who helped members of existing parents' groups to formulate their own concerns and wishes.

The OD facilitator and the community organizer worked closely with the principal to bring the staff and parents into formal meetings to discuss the problems and to formulate a list of challenges. Tightening discipline and raising achievement were included in the list. Once the challenges were chosen, the OD facilitator provided process observation and feedback to the staff to improve communication and group meetings within the school. In addition, the OD facilitator coordinated the use by the parents of the community organizer and the consultative assistance of the classroom adviser.

As the OD process with the staff moved along, teachers made more and more requests for help from the classroom adviser. The classroom adviser typically consulted with individual teachers, helping them set specific goals for their teaching, observing them, and giving them feedback. Later, after several teachers had worked with the classroom adviser, the OD facilitator convened them to talk about what they were doing and to what extent the school's challenges were being met by their new classroom practices.

Later, the school-community organizer invited parents and teachers together to parcel out ideas about how best to dovetail procedures at the school with family support of the student at home. This effort led some parents to volunteer as aides at the school and to more dialogue between parents and teachers about the students. There was a noticeable increase in attendance at parent-teacher conferences.

Special-interest Macrodesigns

Here are four designs built to alleviate particular problems: desegregation; faulty group processes in the classroom; interpersonal conflicts; and dissension among parents, students, and teachers.

Desegregation

Milstein (1979) described a project in the Buffalo public schools that used a cadre of internal OD specialists to facilitate court-ordered desegregation in that district. The cadre, called the School Improvement Resource Team (SIRT), was patterned after the project designed by Schmuck and Runkel and described above under the heading "Establishing OD Specialists in a School District." The Buffalo district was obliged to desegregate the elementary schools before desegregating the secondary schools. District administrators believed, however, that it was primarily in the secondary schools that careful preparation of the staff and community was essential, and that is where the SIRT began work.

The rationale was that if desegregation was to succeed in Buffalo, staffs would have to come together to support the change process. Teachers and administrators would have to share their hopes, concerns, and expectations; to anticipate obstacles to good human relations in the school; and to develop a plan together for working with students and the community. The consensus was that it would be disastrous if staff members were in conflict about the desegregation process. The SIRT was created to facilitate staff problem solving.

We can classify the activities of the first year into three relatively sequential phases: team selection and school identification, SIRT development and maintenance, and a first round of OD projects in several schools. In his 1979 paper, Milstein indicated that after two years of operation, the SIRT was working very well. The SIRT became very cohesive, schools were actively using its consultative services, and the district's administration had become supportive and understanding. During the second year, the services of the SIRT became more diversified; the team worked with a variety of school subsystems including teaching teams, administrative cabinets, grade-level teacher groups, and student groups. SIRT continued to employ a variety of designs, including a considerable amount of training and process observation and feedback and smaller amounts of survey-data-feedback and constructive confrontation.

Improving Group Processes in the Classroom

Although so far we have barely touched on the classroom, successful OD consultation for a school can have favorable direct effects there (for evidence, see Schmuck, 1971 and Bigelow, 1971). As Schmuck and Schmuck (1974) point out, macrodesigns that deliberately plan for the transfer of OD training and that also include consultation on classroom group processes will have the greatest impact. This section offers two illustrative designs.

The first design, which lasts eighteen months, commences with an OD event in late August, just before the beginning of the school year. The design for the August laboratory could resemble that described in the subsection above headed "Organizational Training for a School Faculty." Teachers are then asked to volunteer for a program of consultation and training in classroom group processes, and a consultant skilled in interpersonal relations theory and classroom processes works with them for two hours each week throughout the academic year. During the following summer, a teacher development laboratory is held; it might cover communication skills, group techniques, problem solving, and role playing as applied directly to the classroom. Follow-up discussions could occur during the fall semester to help the teachers try out new procedures and to reinforce any insights or new skills developed during the previous year.

The second design, which lasts about six months, is launched with a one-week OD laboratory two weeks before school begins; this is followed by a week of consultation in classroom group processes. Since many districts now grant some days before the opening of school for in-service training, it may be possible to use these days as part of the second week, which is devoted to facilitating the translation of group processes found useful during the OD phase into classroom innovation. During the fall semester, consultants can lead supportive discussions, emphasizing the problem-solving process and encouraging teachers to implement their plans in the classroom. For action plans for the classroom, see Schmuck and Schmuck (1983).

Interpersonal Conflict

Schmuck helped a high school staff work through some very tense conflicts that had existed for several years. Four years prior to the consultation, the faculty had been divided into two subparts. One subgroup stayed in an older building that was a few hundred yards from a new structure in which the other half of the staff worked. Although the newer structure was more desirable because of larger classrooms, better office space, and a brand new library, the older building carried the nostalgia and school spirit of a generation of educational activities. Gradually the two subgroups grew apart psychologically; they also began to develop intergroup stereotypes and feelings of antagonism toward each other. Members of both groups made fun of colleagues in the other group but shared a cohesiveness with the colleagues in their own subgroup. Several times, interpersonal antagonisms between members of the two subgroups came out into the open, and, to the embarrassment of the principal and a number of teachers, students and parents were becoming aware of the intergroup hostility among the teachers. Indeed, the public face of faculty conflict had become so serious that the superintendent and principal, not to mention more than half the staff, thought that some sort of action was necessary.

Because time and money were limited, Schmuck's macrodesign could span only a few months. Schmuck asked first that a representative steering committee be formed of the principal and a counselor from the school at large and three influential teachers from each of the two subgroups. This group of eight met with Schmuck several times for a total of four hours to share perceptions of the school's conflicts and to react to Schmuck's ideas for design. The major event of the design was a three-hour clearing-the-air meeting of the entire staff on a Friday morning when the students were released from school.

This clearing-the-air event was made up of six parts:

1. Schmuck's introduction, during which his ground rules for the session were explained
2. Small-group discussions on "perceptions of staff cultures in the two parts of the school"
3. Other small-group discussion on "old behavior that accentuates misunderstanding and conflict between the two parts of the school"
4. Small-group brainstorming on "new behaviors to try to increase understanding between the two parts of the school"
5. Suggestions from the entire staff about possible future behavior
6. Feedback about this session and expectations about next steps

As staff members entered the meeting room, they picked up a name tag which indicated, along with their names, the small group to which they were assigned for the entire session. The small groups were made up of four staff members each, two members coming from each of the two parts of the school. The chairs were arranged in clusters of four for the small groups, and the clusters were arranged in a large horseshoe with the opening of the horseshoe reserved for Schmuck, his chalkboard, and his easels of newsprint paper. The chairs were arranged so that at first everyone would be facing Schmuck but later could easily be turned for small-group discussions. There were forty-four staff members at the meeting.

Schmuck's introduction covered the following points: "First, a public relations problem exists in this school. No longer are your conflicts simply internal to the staff. Increasingly, students and parents are being affected by your difficulties. There is a need for more understanding on this staff, a need to alter what has become a frustrating climate, and a need for more accurate and more supportive communication. The time to act is now, today. Second, the ground rules for this session are very important. I will expect you to abide by them. Since this is serious business, we must not beat around the bush; we must be open, straightforward, direct, and succinct. There should be absolutely no kidding or joking. I won't be able to understand the in-jokes around here, and they will get in the way of our communication. Today, we should have direct statements about your perceptions and feelings, not how you think others feel. When we don't understand one another, we should ask for clarification or try to paraphrase. I will try to do a lot of paraphrasing. Time is very precious; we must move along."

Next, Schmuck directed small groups to talk about the two staff cultures in the school. What are they like? What are the most favorable and the most unfavorable characteristics of each? The groups were given twenty minutes each. Then each of the eleven groups proceeded with their discussions, and Schmuck circulated personally, asking one member in each group to act as the recorder. Next, he asked the recorders to report to the whole group about their discussions. With the help of several assistants, Schmuck recorded the main points on newsprint in front of everyone.

Similar procedures were employed for the next parts of the design, described as "old behavior that accentuates misunderstanding and conflict between the two parts of the school" and "new behaviors to try to increase understanding between the two parts of the school." Before beginning the second part of the design, Schmuck exhorted the participants to leave the past behind and to think creatively about possibilities for the future.

The fifth part of the design was carried out with all forty-four participants acting together in a brainstorming session. Since ideas about "new behaviors to try" were fresh in people's minds, Schmuck asked everyone to reflect on that list and to suggest the most important actions to take first. As the brainstorming proceeded, index cards were passed around to everyone. One side of the card was reserved for ideas for new behavior that didn't get onto the lists, while the other side was for giving feedback about the session.

One week after the clearing-the-air meeting, the steering committee met to debrief and to cluster the action ideas for further work. The decision was made to cluster the action ideas into seven categories and to form seven parallel task forces on the faculty. The seven clusters were (1) developing a more effective total faculty council, (2) establishing an attractive, common faculty room, (3) dispersing staff collaboration in extracurricular student activities, (4) developing an attractive social calendar for the whole faculty, (5) rearranging classroom and office locations to bring different faculty members physically closer, (6) scheduling classroom visits and designing team teaching, and (7) developing a more effective program of community relations.

At a two-hour faculty meeting the following week, the list of task forces was approved unanimously, and virtually all participants agreed to sign up for one of the committees. Steering committee members were designated as the conveners of the task forces, with the principal serving as convener of the conveners. To ensure that all faculty members would have an opportunity to select a committee that interested them, each participant was asked to rank the three committees they most preferred and to jot that information down on their name tags as they left the meeting.

Bringing Parents and Students into School Management

The gap between the sporadic, generally ineffective ways in which parents and students currently participate in educational decisions and the well-organized procedures available to this end constitutes a major problem in contemporary public schooling. As the following sketchy macrodesign indicates, however, the methods of OD consultation can be adapted to narrow the gap.

First, train each separate body—educators, parents, and students—in communication skills, establishing objectives, uncovering and working on conflicts, conducting meetings, solving problems in groups, and collecting data. Second, bring all three together to explore goals, uncover differences, and agree on problems that impede joint decision making and other uses of human resources. Third, allow small heterogeneous problem-solving groups (with students, parents, and educators all represented as members) to work collaboratively on problems previously identified. Fourth, build new structural arrangements out of the multiple realities shared during the second and third stages and as part of the solutions to problems worked out during the third stage. The four stages are to be recycled several times and the whole design can last for more than a year.

3

Clarifying Communication

For members of school staffs to be clear about educational
goals, solve important problems, make effective decisions, and put plans
into action, many acts of communication are required. Understanding is
particularly important when complex plans are to be developed—plans
requiring many people to coordinate their actions. If the school is to
remain responsive to demands of all sorts, an open flow of information
from and to the various groups must be maintained.

A school with organizational adaptability has open and direct
channels of communication within the staff as well as between the staff
and other groups. Members have interpersonal skills that facilitate clear,
open, and candid communication. They have norms that support directness, tact, and authenticity. They have procedures for helping those
outside the staff understand "what the school stands for" and for encouraging members to listen well to what those outside are saying.

Although many different activities, from ringing a school bell to
reading a printed page, may be categorized as communication, this
chapter will focus mainly on the kinds of face-to-face verbal and nonverbal interactions between people in subsystems by means of which educational functions are carried out. The first section explains what is meant
by unilateral, directive, and transactional communication; the second

section describes interpersonal communication; the third describes communication processes in subsystems; and the fourth considers communication in the organization as a whole. Instruments that the OD consultant can use to assess communication are enumerated in the fifth section. The sixth describes exercises and procedures that we have used to enhance clear communication in schools, and the seventh section summarizes designs the consultant can use in raising the level of communicative effectiveness in schools.

TYPES OF COMMUNICATION

In its simplest form, *unilateral communication* is initiated by a speaker and terminated at a listener; examples in schools include reading the morning bulletins over the loudspeaker or making announcements at faculty meetings. But much unilateral communication involves a second step as well. In studying the mass media, for example, Katz (1957) found that information from the media reaches certain opinion leaders who in turn relay it, as they understand it, to others in face-to-face interactions. Although this second step involves two-way communication, the event remains unilateral because the person who is the original source of information is unable to clarify any misunderstandings that may have occurred during the transmission of the information. Indeed, any error in transmission is likely to be amplified during this second step.

In their study of the transmission of rumors, Allport and Postman (1945) describe three psychological processes that occur in the course of two-, three-, and four-step communications. In the first process, called *leveling*, the receiver tends to reduce contrasts between parts of a message—by omitting qualifying phrases, for example. In the second, the receiver *sharpens* certain parts of the information so that a few high points are remembered while most of the rest is forgotten. In the third, the receiver *assimilates* much of the message into his or her personal frame of reference, coloring memories and interpretations of the message by his or her own thoughts and feelings. For all these reasons, unilateral communication is not an efficient way of transmitting information even when it is supplemented by a second step.

In *directive communication*, which occurs face-to-face, the exchange is complete when the receiver indicates to the sender that the message has been received and understood, as when a teacher gives an assignment and students indicate that they understand the assignment. The distinguishing feature of a directive communication is that the sender influences while the receiver merely complies, as when one student tells another to get out of his way and the second obliges. McGregor (1967)

Figure 3-1. Transactional Communication

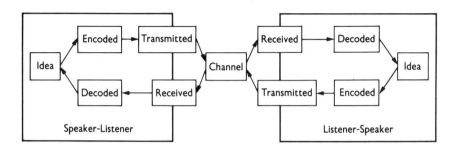

calls this kind of communication coercive because there is no provision for mutual influence and exchange. It is assumed that the source's position is correct. The listener is required only to understand the message; acceptance is implied.

As Figure 3-1 demonstrates, *transactional communication* is a reciprocal process in which each participant initiates messages and attempts to understand the other. Information travels in both directions rather than in one direction only; each message has some impact on the next message, and the roles of source and receiver shift rapidly back and forth as communication takes place. Participants in transactional communication engage in active listening as well. The listener attempts to grasp both the facts and feelings of a message, attempts to increase his or her understanding by discerning the speaker's point of view, and tests this understanding by advising the speaker of personal reactions to the message, thereby helping the speaker know whether the meaning was or was not communicated. Elsewhere in this book we usually refer to this kind of communication as *two-way communication*.

While many misunderstandings can be resolved through transactional communication, carrying out effective transactions takes a high degree of communicative skill. Participants must be able to state their thoughts and feelings clearly, ask each other for specific information, read the relevance of gestures, and make sure that the message was apprehended correctly. This mutual feedback and spirit of helpfulness between participants is of crucial importance.

INTERPERSONAL COMMUNICATION

People in schools communicate many different kinds of information to one another. They talk about the tasks they perform, the methods they use to get tasks accomplished, and sometimes, though rarely, their relations with one another. The content of face-to-face conversations can also be viewed as belonging to one or another aspect of a problem statement—that is, people talk about how things are (situations), how things ought to be (targets), or how to move from the situation to the target (proposals). As mentioned earlier, this is known as the *S-T-P* model of problem analysis and will be explained in detail in Chapter 5.

Features of Effective Interpersonal Communication

Openness, communication during emotion, eliciting personal resources, and trust are features that cut across the three levels of interpersonal skill, subsystem effectiveness, and organizational adaptability described in Chapter 1, and are extremely important signs of a readiness to begin organization development. Their presence not only sets a context for interpersonal communication but also oils the way for improving the interpersonal skills and other subsystem processes on which improvements in organizational adaptability depend.

Openness. Luft (1984) depicts openness by means of the following useful illustration known formally as the Johari Awareness Model and informally as the Johari Window (see Figure 3-2). In this model, a behavior, feeling, or motivation is assigned to one of four quadrants on the basis of who knows about it. Quadrant 1 refers to behavior, feelings, and motivation known both to oneself and to others (open); Quadrant 2 refers to that which is known to others but not to oneself (blind); Quadrant 3, to that which is known to oneself but not to others (hidden); and Quadrant 4, to that which is known neither to oneself nor to others (unknown). Openness is the skill that increases the area of Quadrant 1 in relation to other quadrants.

Openness does not mean telling all, confiding indiscriminately, or giving information that is irrelevant to the work situation. It means giving information that both parties need in order to get work done or the feelings that are generated by people working together. By disclosing information that has heretofore been hidden, and by attempting to understand their blind spots, people can increase the total amount of information in the open quadrant.

As Figure 3-3 indicates, people communicate more or less openly depending upon the emotional closeness or distance they feel toward one another. In emotionally distant interactions, people know little about one another and view one another as objects that can either fulfill or frustrate their wishes and expectations. In emotionally close interac-

Figure 3-2. Johari Awareness Model

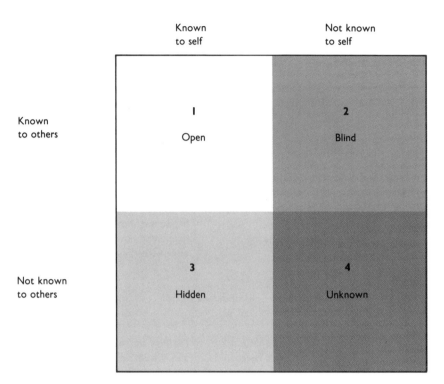

Source: Luft (1984).

tions, people recognize their interdependence with others, realizing that other people's behavior simultaneously influences and is influenced by their own behavior.

Communication During Emotion. It is extremely important to know how to communicate during emotion, whether it is you or another person who is hurt, angry, or embarrassed. Alberti and Emmons (1975) call this ability *assertiveness* and contrast it with nonassertive (acquiescent) and aggressive behavior. In their view, aggressive behavior enhances the sender's position at the receiver's expense; nonassertive behavior expresses the sender's self-denial and forces the receiver to make choices without any help from the sender; assertive behavior allows the sender to be direct and open while encouraging the receiver to respond in a similar fashion.

Thus, if parents want teachers to behave in new ways, they must

Figure 3-3. Emotional Closeness and Distance

Degree of closeness depends upon ↓

	Close				**Distant**
The *topic* we are talking about	Concerns our relation, you and me.	Concerns you or me.	Concerns people or things we both know directly.	Concerns people or things known to one of us directly.	Concerns people or things known directly to neither of us.
The *time* perspective	*Now:* Topic is happening now or something that helps us understand what is happening now.			*Then:* Topic is past or future happening, not related to what is happening now. *Or:* No time perspective, as in generalizations, jokes, etc.	
The *importance* of topic	Important to *both* of us.		Important to *one* of us.		Important to *neither* of us.
How we use our *feelings*	Feelings are seen as natural; openly stating one's own feelings is viewed as helpful to both persons; each accepts the other's feelings.			Feelings are seen as unfortunate and disruptive; openly stating one's own feelings is avoided, so feelings are indirectly reflected in intellectualizations and judgments about the external world, including the other.	
How close the conversation is to *direct experience*	Conversation is composed of specific, tangible reports of observations and examples from direct experience.			Conversation is composed of abstract, vague generalizations without illustrative examples; no evidence is presented. The language is remote from any direct experience.	
How much *coercion* enters the interaction	Personal autonomy is respected; because each knows that the other must lead his own life, make his own decisions, face his own consequences, he offers information but does not try to persuade him to follow a certain course of action.			One or both attempts to convince, persuade, coerce, or manipulate the other to be like him or to do what he thinks should be done.	

work with teachers and not against them to make the necessary changes. If teachers want administrators to make fewer unilateral decisions, they must work together to change this condition. The systemlike nature of schools requires one part to change along with other parts if changes are to be sustained. Wresting power from an administrative subsystem and giving it to parent-controlled subsystems, for example, will not in itself produce important or lasting changes in education, although skillful collaboration between parents and administrators might.

Eliciting Personal Resources. Effective interpersonal communication also requires an awareness of one's need for the resources of others, and an awareness, too, of the virtue of offering one's own strengths, preferences, ideas, and feelings in finding solutions to problems of mutual concern. But people are far more reticent about some of their personal resources than others, and they frequently require strong encouragement to state their feelings.

Wallen (1972) suggests several reasons that it is difficult to discuss one's feelings. First, many people have an unfavorable attitude toward emotion, often responding to someone else's expression of strong feelings with a variation of "please don't feel that way." Second, while actions and thoughts seem controllable, feelings seem to have a life of their own. Third, we too often think that others have more control over our feelings than we have ourselves. To believe that others can make one angry, for example, is to acknowledge a surrendering of some control over oneself. Feelings, in short, seem to threaten voluntary, planned control over one's own affairs.

Some people think that typically the teaching of communication skills overemphasizes trust and truth and underemphasizes power and conflict, but we like to stress both areas in our consulting. Helping participants to voice their wants and at the same time helping problem-solving groups collaborate to reach a group consensus are both OD services, and it is true that people in schools should not shy away from the conflicts that often accompany differences in values. At the same time, in schools where interdependence is increasing, we value skillful collaboration over confrontation and believe that collaborative goals can best be achieved through methods that emphasize trust building and open communication.

Consultants must convince clients that feelings—whether of attraction, anxiety, interest, or resentment—provide important information that a group needs if work is to proceed efficiently and effectively and that to feel emotion toward another person is a sign of relatedness and interdependence. Acknowledging one's own feelings and the feelings of others eliminates unnecessary guesswork and releases energy that is otherwise spent in concealing emotions.

Of course, there is much more to eliciting personal resources than hearing another's feelings. It also is important to help others tell about their experience and ideas and make suggestions about courses of action. Consultants must convince clients that ideas, however incomplete they might be, must be articulated and discussed if grass-roots participation is to work. The consultant's skill involves both showing understanding and appreciation for the ideas and linking clients' ideas one to another during group deliberations.

Trust.   Being open, communicating during emotion, and offering one's personal resources involve taking risks, and risk taking depends in turn on the presence of interpersonal trust, which is in many ways the key to enhanced communication even where true differences exist. A fragile quality on which a single action can have profoundly destructive consequences, trust is built very slowly and in small increments, is established more by deeds than by words, and is sustained by openness in interpersonal relations. But it is very difficult to achieve this quality in interpersonal relations, because being genuinely honest when an existing level of trust is low involves taking a very great risk. Perhaps this helps to explain why trust develops slowly and incrementally; if only small risks are taken, only small amounts of trust are built.

McGregor (1967) defines trust as the knowledge that the other person will not take unfair advantage of one, either deliberately or accidentally, consciously or unconsciously. Trust is built between two people when each person is convinced that the other is both motivated and competent enough to sustain the relationship. Binding responses that diminish the other person's autonomy are likely to destroy trust; freeing responses that increase a sense of equality are likely to promote it. At the same time, however, the amount of gain or loss in trust depends on the amount that was present at the beginning; that is, a binding response is less binding and a freeing response less freeing when trust is low. Following is a list of interpersonal effects of various responses:

FREEING RESPONSES

- Listening attentively rather than merely remaining silent
- Paraphrasing and checking your impressions of the other's inner state
- Seeking information to understand the other
- Offering information that is relevant to the other's concern
- Describing observable behaviors that influence you
- Directly reporting your own feelings
- Offering your opinions or stating your value position

BINDING RESPONSES

- Changing the subject without explanation
- Interpreting the other's behavior by describing unchangeable experiences or qualities

- Advising and persuading
- Vigorously agreeing or obligating the other with "how could you?"
- Approving the other for conforming to your standards
- Claiming to know what motivates the other's behavior
- Commanding the other or demanding to be commanded

INTERPERSONAL COMMUNICATION SKILLS

The six skills described in the following subsections are neither new nor unique; indeed, they are tried and true methods of helping openness, communication during emotion, and an exchange of communication during emotion, to permit an exchange of personal resources to occur. Those who regard the skills as gimmicks and use them perfunctorily should not be surprised when results are disappointing. Merely becoming aware of communication skills will not in itself improve the ability to communicate. The skills must be applied consciously and strategically if they are to help overcome some of the difficulties in communication, and they must arise out of a genuine desire to understand the other person as an individual.

Of the six skills, *paraphrasing* (checking your understanding of the other person's meaning) and *impression checking* (checking your impression of the other person's feelings) are ways of helping you understand the other person. *Describing the other's behavior, describing your own behavior, making clear statements of your ideas*, and *describing your own feelings* aim at helping others to understand you. The six skills shown in Figure 3-4 are highly interdependent, so much so that it is virtually impossible to imagine a relationship of trust in which all six are not used at one time or another. The term *public information* refers to that which should already be known to oneself and to others. *Private information* is similar; it refers to what Luft has called blind or hidden in the Johari Awareness Model.

Every message and behavior has both a public and a private component, and senders, receivers, or observers always have seven choices: to say nothing, to describe their own behavior, to state their own ideas, to describe others' behavior, to describe their own feelings, to paraphrase, or to check an impression of what the other is feeling. Consider, for example, the question of whether it is normal to feel sad at the end of the school year. If a student asks that of a teacher on the last day of school, the teacher might wish to check an impression that the student is feeling sad, describe his or her own feelings at the time, or even describe his or her own behavior in the past in relation to closing school. If a student teacher asks the same question in an introductory methods class, the professor might paraphrase to determine whether the student teacher is considering a research problem, and later perhaps give his or

Figure 3-4. Relationships Among Six Communication Skills

	When the Information Is Public or Visible	When the Information Is Private and Concerns Inner States
To Be Open	Tell what you did that might have affected others by *describing your own behavior.*	Tell what you think by clearly *stating your own ideas.*
To Be Candid	Tell what others did that affects you as a group participant by *describing another's behavior.*	Let others know as clearly and unambiguously as possible about your own inner state by *describing your feelings.*
To Be Receptive	Check to make sure you understand the ideas of the other person by *paraphrasing.*	Check to make sure how the other person feels by *impression checking.*

her own ideas about the issue. If a colleague sticks his head in your office for the fifth time one morning to ask the same question, and if you are annoyed by the repeated interruptions, you might describe his behavior and your own feelings about it.

To acquire the six skills, the key to success is practice. OD consultants should introduce the skills early and reinforce their use at every opportunity. With continuing practice, clients will become more skillful, and increased clarity of understanding will result. There is no given point at which one finally becomes skilled at communication, however. Each new person, relationship, and situation calls for practicing the skills anew, and no one should be excused on the grounds that he or she has "had that" elsewhere.

Paraphrasing

Many people mistakenly assume that they understand what another person has meant to convey without troubling to check whether the remark means the same thing to both of them or without giving the sender any evidence that the remark has in fact been understood. As used here, paraphrasing denotes any method of showing other people how you have apprehended their meaning. By testing your understanding against their intentions you show them that you want to understand and you invite them to clarify their meaning if you have not understood them correctly.

As the following example demonstrates, simply repeating another person's ideas in different words can result in a mere illusion of mutual understanding.

> SARAH: Jim should never have become a teacher.
> FRED: You mean teaching isn't the right job for him?
> SARAH: Exactly! Teaching is not the right job for Jim.

Instead of trying to reword Sara's statement, Fred should have asked himself, "What does this statement mean to me?" In that case the exchange might have gone this way:

> SARAH: Jim should never have become a teacher.
> FRED: You mean he is too harsh on the children? Maybe even cruel?
> SARAH: No, I meant that he has such expensive tastes that he can't earn enough as a teacher.
> FRED: Oh, I see. You think he should have gone into a field that would have ensured him a higher standard of living.
> SARAH: Exactly! Teaching is not the right job for Jim.

A general statement may convey something specific to you.

> LARRY: I'd like to own this book.
> YOU: Does it contain useful information?
> LARRY: I don't know about that. I meant that the binding is beautiful.

A very specific statement may convey a more general idea to you.

> RALPH: Do you have twenty-five pencils I can borrow for my class?
> YOU: Do you just want something for them to write with? I have about fifteen ball-point pens and ten or eleven pencils.
> RALPH: Great. Anything that will write will do.

The comments of another person may possibly suggest an example to you.

> LAURA: This text has too many omissions; we shouldn't adopt it.
> YOU: Do you mean, for example, that it contains nothing about the role of ethnic minorities in the development of America?
> LAURA: Yes, that's one example. It also lacks any discussion of the development of the arts in America.

Skillful paraphrasing thus requires an ability to make generalizations, identify examples, and think of opposites. Developing these abilities requires trying out different ways of discovering the kinds of responses most helpful to you.

Impression Checking

Inferences drawn from the words, tone, gestures, or facial expressions of another person are often inaccurate, not least because we may unconsciously attribute to that person our own feelings, attitudes, or desires. Impression checking involves describing what you perceive to be the other person's emotional state in order to determine whether you have accurately decoded his or her expressions of feeling. That is, you transform expressions of feeling into tentative descriptions, such as, "I get the impression that you're angry with me. Are you?" "Am I right that you're feeling disappointed because no one commented on your suggestion?" "I'm uncertain as to whether your expression means that my comment hurt your feelings, irritated you, or confused you. Can you help me?"

Skillful impression checking requires reading nonverbal clues, drawing tentative inferences from them, clearly describing the inferred feeling, and indicating that you recognize the inferential character of the impression. An impression check aims to convey the fact that you wish to understand the other person's feelings in order to avoid actions based on false assumptions about them; it does not express approval or disapproval of the feelings.

Describing Another's Behavior

For most of us it is not easy to describe another person's behavior clearly enough for that person to understand which actions are affecting us. Indeed, instead of describing behavior, we usually discuss attitudes, motivations, and personality traits, often unaware that our conclusions are based less on observable evidence than on our own feelings of affection, insecurity, irritation, jealousy, or fear. Accusations that impute undesirable motives to another, for example, are usually not descriptions at all but are rather expressions of the speaker's unpleasant feelings toward the other. Yet if we are to discuss the way we work together or what is occurring in our relationships, we must be able to talk about what each of us does that affects the other.

Behavior description means reporting specific observable actions of others without judging those actions as good or bad or right or wrong, and without making generalizations or accusations about the other person's motives, attitudes, or personality traits. As the following examples illustrate, it also means describing the actions clearly and specifically enough for others to know what you have observed. To remind yourself to describe specific actions, it is helpful to begin with "I see that . . ." or "I noticed that . . ." or "I heard you say . . ."

- *Example:* "Jim, you've talked more than others on this topic. Several times you've cut off others before they had finished." (Not "Jim, you're too rude," which identifies a trait and gives no evidence, or "Jim, you always want to hog the center of attention," which imputes an undesirable motive or intention.)
- *Example:* "Bob, you've taken the opposite position on nearly everything that Harry has suggested today." (Not "Bob, you're just trying to show Harry up," which is an accusation of an undesirable motivation, or "Bob, you're being stubborn," which is name calling.)
- *Example:* "Sam, you cut in before I had finished." (Not "Sam, you deliberately didn't let me finish," which implies that Sam knowingly and intentionally cut you off. All that anyone can observe is that he cut in before you had finished.)

To develop skill in describing behavior you must sharpen your observation of what actually occurred, pay attention to that which is observable, recognize when you are making inferences, and be able to couch them in language that reflects both their tentative nature and your desire to check them out.

Describing One's Own Feelings

Reporting one's own inner state provides more information that is necessary if two people are to understand and improve their relationship; certainly, others need to know how you feel if they are to take your feelings into account. Negative feelings should not be ignored because they signal that something may be going wrong in a relationship and that the two parties need to check for misunderstandings or faulty communication. The aim of describing your feelings is to open a dialogue that will improve a relationship; it should not be an effort to coerce the other into changing so you won't feel as you do. Although the other person may behave differently on learning what distracts, bothers, or pleases you, you may also discover that your feelings are based on false perceptions and should themselves be changed.

To communicate your feelings accurately is very difficult because emotions can express themselves in bodily changes, actions, and words; because a specific expression of feeling can indicate a myriad of different feelings (as a blush may indicate pleasure, annoyance, embarrassment, or uneasiness); and because a particular feeling is not always expressed in the same way. The communication of feelings is often misleading as well. What may appear to be an expression of anger, for example, might turn out to result from hurt feelings or fear.

One way to describe a feeling is by naming it and by referring to *I, me,* or *my* to indicate that you own the feeling—for example, "I feel angry," "I feel embarrassed," or "I feel comfortable with you." Another way is to report the kind of action that the feeling urges you to take: "I feel like hugging you," "I'd like to slap you," or "I wish I could walk off and leave you." A feeling can also be specified by means of simile ("I feel like a tiny frog in a huge pond") or of metaphor ("I just swallowed a bushel of spring sunshine"). Finally, as the following examples demonstrate, any one expression of feeling can actually represent a number of quite different descriptions of feeling.

EXPRESSIONS OF FEELING	DESCRIPTIONS OF FEELING
Person blushes and says nothing.	"I feel embarrassed." "I feel pleased." "I feel annoyed."
Person suddenly becomes silent in the midst of a conversation.	"I feel angry." "I'm worried about this." "I feel as if I've been slapped."
"She's a wonderful person."	"I enjoy her sense of humor." "I respect her abilities." "I love her but feel I shouldn't say so."
"Shut up!"	"I hurt too much to hear any more." "I feel angry at myself." "I'm angry at you."
"You shouldn't have bought me such an expensive gift!"	"I really like your gift." "I feel obligated to you and I resent it." "I feel inferior to you when I think of the cheap present I gave you."

Describing One's Own Behavior

This skill is similar to that of describing another's behavior. The actions described might have occurred previously in the same group or they might have occurred in another setting. The intent of the skill is to reveal weaknesses or inadequacies in one's own behavior that will help to establish empathy and understanding with the others.

We think of this skill under the more general label of openness. The speaker shows that he or she is aware of personal mistakes or errors of judgment and is willing to announce them publicly in the group. At times such revelations can be accompanied by humor as long as the receivers understand that the sender is also being serious. To use the skill is to say, "Look, I did some things myself in this group that weren't so helpful. Remember when I did _____." This indicates that to make an error is human and to be expected and that we should all be open to feedback and willing to change.

Sometimes, too, the skill of describing one's own behavior is used to clarify what the sender is trying to convey. It stands as an example of the main message. By way of illustration, one might wish to check impressions of how another is feeling. In the course of such checking, it could be useful to present an example of one's own behavior and the feelings that accompanied it.

Stating One's Own Ideas

This skill might appear to be the easiest of all, but for many people it is difficult. The skill involves using words that are understandable to the receivers, putting the words together in a logical flow, and limiting the length of one's string of words. This calls for putting a check on one's jargon and use of special language, defining terms that might be misunderstood, thinking through the major points in the fashion of an outline, pausing to check impressions of others' understanding, and being succinct.

Giving and Receiving Feedback

Giving or receiving feedback is not a single skill in the way the six are we have described above. All six of the basic skills come into play when one is giving or receiving feedback. At the same time, many communicative acts using one of the six basic skills becomes feedback. Feedback is so intertwined with the six basic skills that we include it here as a kind of wrapping around them.

The concept of feedback originated in the field of cybernetics, the study of automatic control mechanisms in machines and living organisms. It refers to an error-correcting process in which information about a system's output is returned as input so that the system can control its own performance. Because of its circularity, the term *loop* is often used to describe the feedback process.

In human communication, feedback consists of information sent by the receiver back to the source of a message so that the original sender can gauge the effect of the message. By comparing this effect with the intention behind the communication, the original sender can adjust his or her subsequent message, which can serve as the stimulus for further feedback, which in turn can be used to modify the succeeding message, and so on. Ideally, sender and receiver will continue to use this circular mode of interaction until the desired level of accuracy is achieved.

The feedback process is a two-way endeavor and should not be regarded primarily as a way for the listener to aid the speaker. Mutual feedback, a cardinal feature of transactional communication, is achieved when the person giving feedback is also given information that will help gauge the effect of the feedback. Thus each communicator can help the other to become skillful in using feedback to the benefit of their mutual communication. To communicate transactionally with another person requires a great expenditure of time and energy, although limited evidence suggests that the need for great amounts of feedback diminishes with continued use (see, for example, Leavitt and Mueller, 1951).

Without mutual feedback, miscommunications—discrepancies between intended and received messages—occur frequently, partly because certain behaviors are more difficult than others for some persons to perform, partly because of the confusion that arises from an effort to express oneself authentically while attempting to perform in ways meant to be attractive to others. To try to impress others is not necessarily to be phony; it is a natural phenomenon that enables people to cope more easily with superficial social events. But superficiality and self-concealment are often detrimental to effective transaction communication.

Whether it is given or received, feedback can best be carried out if the following guidelines are observed:

1. *Noncoercive.* Feedback should be given so that it does not require the recipient to change his or her behavior.
2. *Consideration.* Feedback should be given after a careful assessment has been made of the recipient's feelings. This does not mean, for example, that you should avoid showing anger to the other person; it means that the other should be ready to deal with it productively.
3. *Descriptive.* Feedback should involve a clear report of the facts rather than an explanation of why things happened as they did.
4. *Recency.* Feedback should be given close to the time of the

events causing reaction. Gunny sacks of grievances are hard to carry and can burst at inopportune times.

5. *Changeability*. Feedback should be given about behavior that can be changed. It is not helpful, for example, to tell people that you are bothered by the color of their eyes.

Finally, mutual feedback must arise out of a true concern about and interest in the other person. Each participant should want to find ways of moving psychologically closer to the other and of helping that person to grow, for without such concern transactional communication will be hollow. Even when concern is keenly felt by all parties, however, the decision of whether to give feedback is not easy to make, perhaps because feedback seems to imply a desire to change the receiver. To say, for example, "You've been quiet all through the meeting, and I feel anxious" is to imply that the receiver should speak up more often. To this, the receiver might reply, "I'm comfortable speaking no more than I do. Why don't you learn to accept my quietness?" If the same feedback with its implied demand for change had been given many times before, an irritated receiver might snap, "Get off my back! I like being quiet!"

In such a case, senders must decide whether to pursue a request for change or to accept the other person's behavior. If senders consider their own values, explore the possibility of accepting the other, and still experience the other's behavior as a violation of certain basic values, the receiver deserves to know that. If senders can widen the band of behaviors that they find acceptable, feedback can be withheld until something more important happens. Senders might also reexamine their own values to find reasons why the behavior initially appeared unacceptable and thereby change themselves instead of trying to change the receiver. In other words, feedback is not just a process of requesting another person to change but can often begin the process of changing oneself.

COMMUNICATION IN THE SUBSYSTEM

Although much of the work in schools is accomplished through communication exchanges between two persons, the work of people in groups—cabinets, departments, committees, and teams—is very important as well. As groups increase in size, especially as they exceed three or four members, new issues and communication problems arise. Since only one person can speak at a time and since speakers must follow one another serially, it is inevitable that some members will have more air time than others. Indeed, group norms develop that influence the amount of talking time considered appropriate for each member of the group. When a norm supports speaking by the leader but by few others, for example, communication will be confined to a very small subgroup, with the rest of the group participating as a passive audience.

Group members who remain silent at formal meetings may nevertheless do a great deal of informal communicating with colleagues based on such factors as shared responsibility, personal attraction, and the physical location of the work space. Although informal communication often serves a social function rather than the function of promoting work, at most schools communication at formal meetings is so poor that informal communication is necessary for tasks to be completed adequately.

Problems arise when informal communications run counter to formal communications. Most formal communication is followed by interactions in small informal groups that strive to achieve an adequate understanding of the original message. When the original message is distorted by these informal discussions, problems of coordination arise for the organization. When the most influential members of the informal networks disagree with the views and decisions of the formal leaders, the messages from the informal leaders often take precedence over the formal communications. A breakdown in authority then occurs and norms about decision making become ambiguous, leading to the development of distrust in a work situation, the more so when differences of opinion and belief are kept private.

OD consultants should gather data on both formal and informal communication networks to help group members become more aware of the effects of these patterns. Examining how communication structures affect small-group performance, Leavitt (1951) found that differences in degree of satisfaction, accuracy, time spent at problem solving, and the emergence of a leader were all related to the type of network involved. The quality of performance in Leavitt's groups improved when one person or a subgroup in the group had communicative contact with all other members of the group, and the satisfaction of members increased as each gained some power through communication to influence the way the group performed.

The OD consultant also gives attention to the type of information that passes through communication channels and networks: the amount of time that the group devotes to sharing information about a task, the methods to be used, the interpersonal feelings that emerge, as well as the situations, targets, and plans. Figure 3-5 shows these six kinds of information in a matrix of nine combinations. Examples of the kinds of statements that fall in each cell accompany the figure. The ultimate payoffs for groups result from high-quality work in Cell 3, although

Figure 3-5. Content of Subsystem Communication

Aspects of problem analysis

		Situation	Target	Proposal
Level of analysis {	Task	1	2	3
	Methods	4	5	6
	Interpersonal	7	8	9

Cell 1: There are more children in Class A than in Class B.
Mary doesn't like to teach large classes.

Cell 2: We ought to interest more children in taking Class B.
Mary should have a smaller class at least one period a day.

Cell 3: We can get more students to elect Class B by adding two field trips.
Mary can have the first chance at encouraging her students to transfer into that class.

Cell 4: Our staff meetings usually last two hours.
The principal observes in most classrooms only once or twice a year.

Cell 5: We should come to meetings prepared to discuss agenda items.
The principal should spend more time in classrooms before evaluating teachers.

Cell 6: We will start our meetings a half-hour later to give people time for preparation.
Teachers will rotate playground duty so that the principal is freed for observations.

Cell 7: I'm pleased that everyone participated at this meeting.
Only half of us feel influential regarding decisions about X.

Cell 8: We should always make sure that everyone who has something to say gets a chance to speak.
We should reconsider who is to be involved in decision making about X in the future.

Cell 9: The convener of the meeting will periodically ask if all who wish to speak have had a chance.
We'll give two days' notice before making another X decision so that interested persons can be contacted.

high-quality task proposals do not come out of thin air; groups must share information in all cells on a fairly regular basis.

The amount of energy a subsystem expends on each topic of communication is governed in part by communication norms. In some groups, for example, no one expects anyone to exchange information about the interpersonal feelings that emerge from members working together. Other groups might exhibit a norm supporting regular interpersonal-process debriefings. Norms also specify rewards for openness, communicating during emotion, and eliciting statements of personal resources. Subsystem norms specifying what people should or should not talk about greatly influence the degree to which interpersonal communication skill will be displayed.

It should be noted, however, that information is always distorted to some degree as it passes from one person to others. When most group members distort a message in the same way, as when a majority of group members believes an untrue thing to be true, a condition of pluralistic ignorance is said to exist. In many groups, an effective strategy for dealing with pluralistic ignorance in relation to interpersonal matters is to use the Team-Expectation Survey described later.

The OD consultant could collect interview or questionnaire data that illustrate pluralistic ignorance. By feeding these data back to the group and encouraging discussion of obvious discrepancies, the consultant can help the client group to improve the accuracy of information at its disposal. To facilitate clearer communication, the consultant can also teach groups to use the following procedures or activities during their regular meetings. (For further discussion of some of these procedures, see Chapter 4 under "Exercises and Procedures for Improving Meetings.")

1. *The Right to Listen.* Typically, meetings are run so that members have their say without much regard to whether they are understood by others. A procedure that can help to ameliorate this situation is to require a member before speaking to paraphrase what the last person has said, both to indicate understanding of the previous speaker and to ensure some continuity in the discussion. If the speaker cannot paraphrase the previous speaker's remark, the remark was probably either too vague or too rambling. The remark should be repeated, but with amplification if it was too short and fewer words if too long. The convener or chair can assume the duty of ensuring each participant both the chance to be heard and the chance to listen or to paraphrase.

2. *Time Tokens.* To assure that members initiate no more than their share of comments, poker chips can be equally divided among

group members with the stipulation that one chip be tossed into the "pot" when a member begins to speak. In addition to sensitizing the group to frequency of participation, this procedure often leads members to make long speeches, so that the group also becomes aware of the negative effects of a series of prolonged monologues.

3. *High-Talker Tap-Out.* In this procedure, a group monitor notifies a speaker when he or she has exceeded a given time limit, either by giving a tap on the shoulder or by handing over a card on which an explanation has previously been typed. At the monitor's signal, the person notified drops out of the discussion by moving back a few feet. When only two people are left and have had their chances to contribute, the entire group discusses feelings and responses to the process. Such an activity often makes it easier to confront established patterns of discussion and decision making, offering an opportunity to discuss reasons for infrequent participation and perhaps to increase the number of persons involved in decision making.

4. *Thumbs Up.* It is often difficult for groups to carry on meaningful discussion while simultaneously monitoring their group functioning. If group members have trouble recognizing when they are ready to make a decision, for example, members might give a thumbs-up signal when they are ready to state their opinions and test whether others agree with them. If a group decides to monitor the use of a newly acquired communication skill, each member would display thumbs up when another member uses a skill effectively and thumbs down when an unhelpful comment is expressed. The use of this procedure can create stress, particularly when a unanimous thumbs-down signal is presented, but some of this stress can be productively harnessed if the group periodically discusses the procedure and its implications.

5. *Taking a Survey.* In a survey, one member of the group asks for the opinions of all others on a specific issue ("I'd like to know what everyone thinks of this proposal right now"); then some other member paraphrases the request until all members understand what they are being asked. All members in turn state their positions on the topic in two or three sentences. The members might also express uncertainty, confusion, a desire to hear more, or they might admit they have nothing to say. Each person must say something, however, and as soon as everyone has stated a position, someone summarizes the group's position—for example, "Only two people seem to have reservations about the proposal," or "Only the third, fourth, and ninth ideas

seem to have captured our interest." Group members should not confuse a survey with a vote, although a survey may be used in this way. Sometimes a survey is used to test the water instead of as a way of ascertaining commitment. In any case, the person requesting the survey should make clear what it is intended to accomplish.

Generally, a survey should be taken at the time it is requested, superseding any other activity. If group members using this procedure for the first time find it too cumbersome or too mechanical, they might take a minute to plan their response before the survey starts, or flash thumbs up if they think a survey is a good idea at that time and thumbs down if they would prefer to wait. This procedure, like all others, should periodically be talked about by group members.

6. *Sitting in a Circle.* Because arranging group seating in a circle soon becomes automatic behavior for the consultant, group members sometimes forget the importance of this procedure and begin to place barriers, such as tables, between themselves. Close circular seating has two advantages: nonverbal behaviors are more easily sent and received when each person has an unobstructed view of everyone else, and equal participation is encouraged when there is no podium or head of the table to suggest that any particular member should assume leadership. When it is desirable to record information on a chalkboard or on newsprint, the circle can be opened into a horseshoe arrangement so that all have an unobstructed view of the recorder.

7. *Fishbowls.* In large groups too much air time may be used if everyone speaks on an issue. In this case the consultant may institute a procedure whereby those in an inner circle talk while those in a concentric outer circle listen. Those on the outside may still contribute if there is an empty chair in the inner circle to which they can move when they have something to say, or if those in the inner circle occasionally turn around to confer with or receive coaching from them.

8. *Video Taping or Audio Recording.* Video-taped and (the less dramatic) audio-recorded segments of a meeting can provide excellent feedback and stimulate a group to review its own functioning. But both techniques require a skilled technician who can judge what to record and can quickly find important bits of interaction to play back. Replaying a two-hour meeting is usually time-consuming and frustrating, while delaying the feedback until someone can edit the tapes could destroy part of the drama. Relying on transcription of tapes as the sole record

of a meeting can cause frustrating delays when important decisions are being made. Nonetheless, well-made tapes are extremely useful for teaching group members to observe communication and other group processes.

ORGANIZATION-WIDE COMMUNICATION

Communication in the organization as a whole can best be observed by attending to the regularized procedures through which it occurs. The OD consultant looks at regular and legitimate channels of communication among subsystems, the regularity with which information from the organization's environment is discussed, the time that elapses between problem identification and responsive action, the regularity with which extra resources in one task group are used by another, and the like.

By formal channels of communication we mean interactions that are sanctioned by the organization and that carry information of the officially relevant acts; examples are announcements in bulletins or over the intercom, faculty or departmental meetings, and teacher-parent conferences. Informal channels—such as coffee-break conversations among teachers or parking-lot debriefings of faculty meetings—are not officially required; nor do they typically carry much of the kind of information that flows through the formal channels. Indeed, informal channels are kept alive precisely for the reason that they carry kinds of communication the formal channels reject.

When the official channels fail to transmit information important to the organization's functioning, or when useful information is crowded out by irrelevancies, the OD consultant can sometimes help by examining the formal channels that are supplementing the official channels. Sometimes a new formal channel can be built on the model of an informal channel.

Likert (1961) has distinguished a form of organizing that he terms "link-pin structure." A link-pin function is performed by a person or subgroup that participates in two or more separate communication networks, carrying information up and down and across groups that would normally not otherwise communicate. To be sure, it is not unusual for a principal to attend teachers' meetings or student council sessions to report decisions of an administrative team; but it is very unusual for a teacher or student to sit with an administrative team or for a group of people (instead of an individual) from one level to engage in face-to-face communication with a group from another level. The consultant should be alert to the possibility of building unique link-pin structures to promote an accurate flow of information within a school organization.

As Chapter 11 will explain, a district cadre of part-time organizational specialists is an important link-pin structure, because its members work in and among different subsystems, thereby gaining access to much important information. Further, representatives of cadre intervention teams serve as link-pins to the cadre coordinator through a steering committee. Finally, another report of our work (see Schmuck et al., 1975) has shown how OD consultation can create team-leader roles and how team leaders can serve as link-pins in multiunit elementary schools.

However laudable increased information flow may be, it is more helpful to identify specific organizational problems first and only then to introduce changes aimed at helping the organization solve the problems. An organized system implies a restricted number of channels that can be used to perform a specific function; to move from one organized state to another may require new norms supporting the use of only certain channels while omitting others or reserving them for organizationally irrelevant purposes.

A way of combining the link-pin idea with the need for dealing with specific organizational problems is to structure the school in the form of a *matrix*. For example, the columns of the matrix could be the grade-level units, or the teaching teams, or the departments. The rows of the matrix could represent some of the overriding tasks or problems faced by the whole school, such as consistency in discipline, continuity from one grade to another or among subjects, parent involvement, racial and ethnic integration, and the like. The key to the matrix structure is for members from each of the basic teaching units to form the membership of a task force, thereby increasing the effectiveness of communication in the whole school.

The larger the organization, the more important it is to provide clarity about channels that carry task-related information. In a group of six persons, for example, each must communicate with five others, so that there are only fifteen channels to contend with altogether; an organization of sixty persons, by contrast, contains 1,770 possible channels. Unless people in larger organizations know clearly to whom they should go for what kinds of information, the results are likely to include overloaded channels, pluralistic ignorance, and insufficient information to do the job. A matrix structure in which every staff member takes part in at least two formal subsystems (an instructional unit and a schoolwide task force) can be an effective form for facilitating communication in schools.

Though we advocate clear designation of the channels to be used for formal organizational purposes, we also value freedom to use any channel for informal purposes. In our view, organizational life is better when hierarchical lines and differentiated subsystems do not prevent people from reaching out to one another for support, comfort, or good times. Although teachers may have to go to administrators for information about budget procedures, for example, they should not be prohibited by either time or architectural constraints from interacting with one another.

GATHERING DATA ABOUT COMMUNICATION

The first source of data about communication in schools is the consultant's own informal observations. The consultant should be alert to note how staff members relate with one another in meetings, in the hallways, and in the teachers' lounge. Are people trying to make their positions known and to persuade others while actually talking past one another and showing an unwillingness to hear what others are saying? Are unpleasant feelings remaining hidden, are feelings of others being ignored, is little checking done to ascertain what others are thinking, are voices quickly becoming loud and emphatic regardless of the issue, and is there a lot of talk about trivial issues while little attention is paid to important needs and issues? If so, the staff's communication skills are probably weak, and a fair amount of conflict will probably come out before any real collaborative problem solving is possible.

On the other hand, the consultant must keep in mind what would be the ideal staff communication and seek out illustrations of it. For example, are there people checking to make sure they understand what others are saying? Do people seem to feel free to report directly to others the sorts of things that are bothering them? The consultant could find such behavior in the very first meeting with a staff committee. If so, he or she should make a special effort to comment on how helpful and difficult it is to be open during meetings in most schools. The consultant should also stay alert to the kinds of topics that come up for discussion. Do they involve instruction, the curriculum, the students' quality of life, parental responses to the school, and the like? If so, the consultant should tell the staff how unusual and special it is for groups of teachers to collaborate on such critical issues.

All this observation and reaction to staff members comes prior to a formal diagnosis. The questionnaires and observation forms that follow can be used to diagnose problems of communication in a much more formal and systematic manner. They can also be used, of course, by principals and staff members for gathering data from their own groups. In some cases, the data can be presented to the group immediately after they have been collected, or a questionnaire can be administered and scored during a single meeting. In other cases, the consultant or participants can summarize lengthy questionnaires or the data from several observation periods and present the summary to the group later. Guidelines for feeding data back to the group are detailed in Chapter 8.

The Knowledge and Use of Communication Skills

The questionnaire below was developed by Crosby and Wallen to assess a participant's recognition of communication skills. Members of the group may wish to compare their answers and discuss their differences.

Concepts About Communication _____

Communication is much more than words. It includes tone of voice, facial expressions, posture, gestures, and eye contact or lack of it. But words are also important. If they match the tone of voice, etc., one's communication message is clear and congruent. This test is about communication by words. Please do not infer tone, etc., but rather focus on the words.

Section I: Description of the speaker's feelings. Before each sentence which represents a description of feelings below put an X. (Make no mark otherwise.)

1. _____   What a lovely day!
2. _____   I'm bored and confused!
3. _____   Cut it out!
4. _____   I feel like I'm on a pedestal.
5. _____   Why can't you ever be anyplace on time?
6. _____   You're a very interesting conversationalist.
7. _____   You shouldn't have bought me such an expensive gift.
8. _____   I feel that he didn't care if he hurt my feelings.
9. _____   Go jump in the lake!
10. _____   I feel this is an easy text.

Section II: Behavior description. Put an X before each sentence which represents a description of behavior.

11. _____   Joe interrupted Harry.
12. _____   Harry was sincere.
13. _____   Harry misinterpreted Joe.
14. _____   Joe was discouraged.
15. _____   Harry's voice got louder when he said, "Cut it out, Joe."

16. _____ Joe was trying to make Harry mad.
17. _____ Harry talked more than Joe did.
18. _____ Joe was dismayed by Harry's statements.
19. _____ Joe said nothing when Harry said, "Cut it out."
20. _____ Harry knew that Joe was feeling discouraged.

Section III: Impression check of speaker's perception of another's feeling. Put an X before each sentence representing an impression check.

21. _____ Are you angry with me?
22. _____ I can tell that you're embarrassed.
23. _____ Why are you mad at me?
24. _____ Did my statement cause you to feel put down?
25. _____ What Jim said obviously upset you.
26. _____ You seem unhappy.
27. _____ Your feelings get hurt pretty easily, don't they?
28. _____ Oh, heck, are your feelings hurt again?
29. _____ What is it about Bill that makes you resent him so much?
30. _____ You're not getting mad again, are you?

Section IV: Personalness in which the speaker reveals something about his private life versus openness in which the speaker shares his reaction to the other person. Put an X before each sentence expressing openness.

31. _____ I've enjoyed our time together tonight.
32. _____ I'm annoyed at your making fun of me.
33. _____ I've never been able to cope with authority figures.
34. _____ I'm seeing a counselor regularly.
35. _____ Sometimes I feel so discouraged and frightened that I'm afraid I'll commit suicide.
36. _____ I envy you.
37. _____ I'm beginning to tune out because you are telling me so much detail.
38. _____ I'm afraid people would disapprove of me if they knew my background.
39. _____ I'm very fond of you.
40. _____ I felt hurt and disappointed when you said you didn't want to hear about my difficult childhood.

Cognitive awareness is insufficient in itself to ensure the use of communication skills. The observation form shown in Figure 3-6 can be used to provide information regarding the use of these skills by specific individuals and to obtain frequency counts for the use of each type of

Figure 3-6. Instances of Use of Communication Skills

Name of group: _____

Time at start of tally: _____   Time at end: _____

Tally each instance of initiation of each skill by each person.

Names or symbols of participants	Para-phrase	Behavior description (other)	Behavior description (own)	Feeling description
_____	_____	_____	_____	_____
_____	_____	_____	_____	_____
_____	_____	_____	_____	_____
_____	_____	_____	_____	_____

Names or symbols of participants	Impression check	State idea (own)	Give feedback	Ask for survey
_____	_____	_____	_____	_____
_____	_____	_____	_____	_____
_____	_____	_____	_____	_____
_____	_____	_____	_____	_____

skill per unit of time. The latter measure can be used to compare use of the various skills by two different groups or by the same group on two separate occasions.

Actual and Perceived Participation

Participation in a group discussion may vary over the course of time because of differences in task involvement, in feelings about the group, or in such factors as fatigue or preoccupation with matters outside the life of the group. The consultant must sample participation

Figure 3-7. Members' Participation: Observer's Form

(1) Take three ten-minute samples at early, middle, and late stages of each meeting observed. (2) Tally at ten-second intervals to indicate who is talking at that instant. (3) Write the times that observation begins and ends in the spaces provided.

Sample Observation Form

Observer: _____   Date: _____

Page no.: _____

Time begun: _____

Time ended: _____

Persons in group
(Name or code number)   Tallies of participation

_____   _____

_____   _____

_____   _____

_____   _____

several times during a meeting, and perhaps at several different meetings, before arriving at an adequate measure of actual and typical participation. The form in Figure 3-7 can be used to sample actual participation in a task-centered group. The consultant may also wish to have group members provide subjective estimates of member participation by means of the form in Figure 3-8, even though the objective and subjective measures will often be highly correlated. In any case, the subjective data may be compared with an observer's more objective tallies, or it may be fed back to group members as a stimulus for group self-analysis. The estimates should represent participation during a specific time period, usually the time just before the ratings are made. (See Figure 4-2, Chapter 4, for another tallying method.)

Norms About Communicating

If they are to perform effectively, all group members must know what behaviors other members expect. This section offers three questionnaires that can be used to identify norms about communication in the group and to determine the amount of agreement that exists about a specific norm.

Figure 3-8. Members' Participation: Estimate by Group Members

Each member should be given enough copies of the rating form to rate everyone in the group. After the ratings are completed, all members are given all the estimates of their participation so they can study and total their individual ratings.

Sample Rating Form

Name of member being rated: _____

Please rate other members in the group on the following scales. Circle the appropriate number from 0 (low) to 6 (high).

1. How much did he or she participate?

0	1	2	3	4	5	6
None						A great deal

2. How well did he or she listen to other members?

0	1	2	3	4	5	6
Little or none						Very well

Do's and Don'ts _____

In any school district (or school or group), there are informal "do's and don'ts." They are rarely written down anywhere, but they serve as a kind of code, making it clear what people in the system should and should not do if they are to be accepted by others.

Below is a list of specific things that a person—an administrator, a teacher, a staff member—might do or say. We would like you to estimate what most people in your system would feel about each item. That is, we want you to tell us whether the predominant feeling of most of the people is that one should or should not do or say the thing in question. You can indicate your answer by placing a check mark in the appropriate column beside each item.

	Should publicly	Should privately	Should not publicly	Should not privately
1. Ask others who seem upset to express their feelings directly.	____	____	____	____
2. Tell colleagues what you really think of their work.	____	____	____	____
3. Look for ulterior motives in other people's behavior.	____	____	____	____

4. Always ask, "Why?" when you don't know.

5. Avoid disagreement and conflict whenever possible.

6. Question well-established ways of doing things.

7. Disagree with your superior if you happen to know more about the issue than he or she does.

8. Withhold personal feelings and stick to the logical merits of the case in any discussion.

9. Push for new ideas, even if they are vague or unusual.

10. Ask others to tell you what they really think of your work.

11. Keep your real thoughts and reactions to yourself, by and large.

12. Trust others not to take advantage of you.

13. Be skeptical about things.

14. Point out other people's mistakes, to improve working effectiveness.

15. Try out new ways of doing things, even if it is uncertain how they will work out.

The next questionnaire is excellent for checking the pervasiveness of pluralistic ignorance in a group. People not only answer for themselves but estimate how others will answer. The content of the expectations can be changed to fit the situation. If, for example, teachers were asked how many parents they would be willing to work with and how many parents would like to work with them, parents in turn would be asked how many teachers they wanted to work with and how many teachers wanted to work with them.

Team-Expectation Survey

Directions: In the blanks before each of the items below enter a number from the following rating scale that best expresses your opinion at this time.

Rating Scale
  5 = All members of this group
  4 = All members except one or two

3 = A slight majority of the members of this group

- -

2 = Slightly less than half the members of this group

1 = One or two members of this group

0 = None of this group

A. Others' Candidness

How many members of this group do you expect will candidly report the following information during future group sessions?

_____ 1. When they do not understand something you said?

_____ 2. When they like something you said or did?

_____ 3. When they disagree with something you said?

_____ 4. When they think you have changed the subject or become irrelevant?

_____ 5. When they feel impatient or irritated with something you said they did?

_____ 6. When they feel hurt—rejected, embarrassed, or put down—by something you said or did?

B. Your Candidness

With respect to how many members will you candidly report the following information during future group sessions?

_____ 7. When you do not understand something a member said?

_____ 8. When you like something a member said or did?

_____ 9. When you disagree with something a member said?

_____ 10. When you think a member has changed the subject or become irrelevant?

_____ 11. When you feel impatient or irritated with something a member said or did?

_____ 12. When you feel hurt—rejected, embarrassed, or put down—by something a member said or did?

C. Others' Interest in Directness

In your opinion, how many in this group are interested in knowing . . .

_____ 13. When you do not understand something a member said?

_____ 14. When you like something a member said or did?

_____ 15. When you disagree with something a member said?

_____ 16. When you think a member has changed the subject or become irrelevant?

_____ 17. When you feel impatient or irritated with something a member said or did?

_____ 18. When you feel hurt—rejected, embarrassed, or put down—by something a member said or did?

D. Your Interest in Directness

With respect to how many members are you interested in knowing . . .

_____ 19. When they do not understand something you said?
_____ 20. When they like something you said or did?
_____ 21. When they disagree with something you said?
_____ 22. When they think you have changed the subject or become irrelevant?
_____ 23. When they feel impatient or irritated with something you said or did?
_____ 24. When they feel hurt—rejected, embarrassed, or put down—by something you said or did?

Answers to the twenty-four questions from two teaching teams from each of two elementary schools are shown in Figures 3-9 through 3-12. The dotted lines show the average response to items 19–24: "With respect to how many members are you interested in knowing . . . ?" The lines made with short dashes show the average response to items 13–18: "How many in this group are interested in knowing (from you) . . . ?" The lines made with long dashes show the average response to items 7–12: "To how many members will you candidly report . . . ?" And the solid lines show the average response to items 1–6: "How many members of this group do you expect will candidly report (to you) . . . ?" The results in group after group in schools and elsewhere are like those shown here. The number of others to whom respondents say they are willing to tell their reactions (the long dashes) is larger than the number of others respondents think are ready to return the favor (the solid lines). The number of others from whom respondents say they are interested in getting reactions (the dotted lines) is larger than the number whom respondents think want reactions from them (the short dashes). The number of others from whom respondents want reactions (the dotted lines) is almost always dramatically larger, for items at the right side of the graph, than the number of respondents whom respondents think will actually tell their reactions (the solid lines). And so on—you can compare any two lines. Also notice that the discrepancies generally get larger with the items toward the right side of the graph—the items that deal with the more emotional reactions. Those are the reactions most respondents want from almost everyone else but expect to get from very few. This graphic illustration of pluralistic ignorance can be useful feedback to teams during an OD project.

**Figure 3-9. Team-Expectation Survey
Elementary School I, Third- and Fourth-Grade Team**

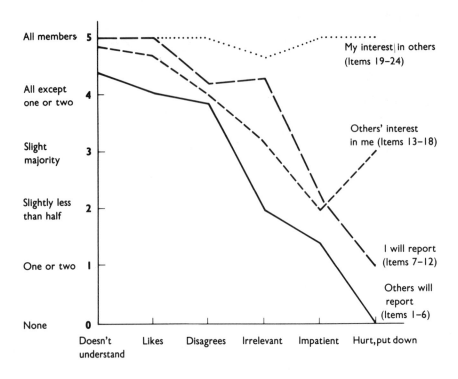

In the questionnaire below, Questions 1 and 2 ask the respondent to predict the actions of others; Questions 3 and 4 ask the respondent to predict his or her own response. The consultant may wish to write additional questions so that respondents provide both types of prediction for a single situation. The two predictions can then be compared to see how much the individual agrees with what he or she perceives to be a group norm and how much pluralistic ignorance exists in the group.

Communication in Problem Situations _____

1. Suppose Teacher X feels hurt and put-down by something another teacher has said to him. In Teacher X's place, would most of the teachers you know in your school be likely to . . .

    1a. Tell the other teacher that they felt hurt and put down?
    ( ) Yes, I think most would.
    ( ) Maybe about half would.

Figure 3-10. Team-Expectation Survey
Elementary School 1, Fifth- and Sixth-Grade Team

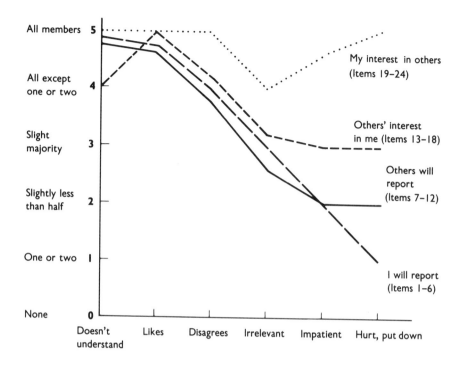

( ) No, most would not.
( ) I don't know.

1b. Tell their friends that the other teacher is hard to get along with?
( ) Yes, I think most would.
( ) Maybe about half would.
( ) No, most would not.
( ) I don't know.

2. Suppose Teacher X strongly disagrees with something B says at a staff meeting. In Teacher X's place, would most of the teachers you know in your school . . .

2a. Seek out B to discuss the disagreement?
( ) Yes, I think most would do this.
( ) Maybe about half would do this.
( ) No, most would not.
( ) I don't know.

**Figure 3-11. Team-Expectation Survey
Elementary School 2, First- and Second-Grade Team**

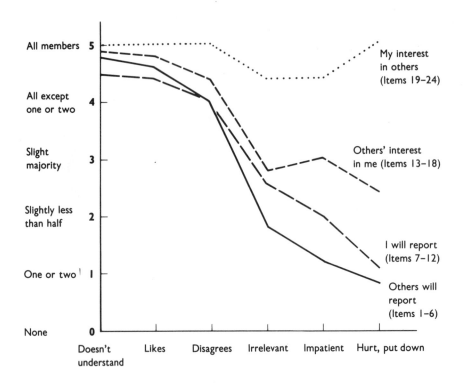

2b. Keep it to themselves and say nothing about it?
   ( )   Yes, I think most would do this.
   ( )   Maybe about half would do this.
   ( )   No, most would not.
   ( )   I don't know.

3. Suppose you are in a committee meeting with Teacher X. The other members begin to describe their personal feelings about what goes on in the school, but Teacher X quickly suggests that the committee get back to the topic and keep the discussion objective and impersonal. How would you feel toward X?

   ( )   I would approve strongly.
   ( )   I would approve mildly or some.
   ( )   I wouldn't care one way or the other.
   ( )   I would disapprove mildly or some.
   ( )   I would disapprove strongly.

Figure 3-12. Team-Expectation Survey
Elementary School 2, Third- and Fourth-Grade Team

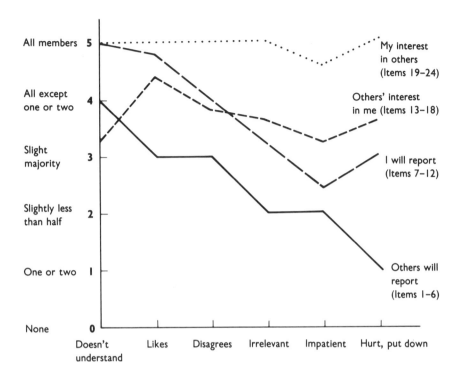

4. Suppose you are in a committee meeting with Teacher X. The other members begin to describe their personal feelings about what goes on in the school. Teacher X listens to them and tells them his own feelings. How would you feel toward X?

( )   I would approve strongly.
( )   I would approve mildly or some.
( )   I wouldn't care one way or the other.
( )   I would disapprove mildly or some.
( )   I would disapprove strongly.

Communication Networks

Questions like the following can be used to determine the number, size, and complexity of communication networks within an organization.

A. Perhaps there are some people in your organization with whom you talk rather frequently about matters important to you. Please think of people with whom you talk seriously about things important to you, inside or outside formal meetings, once a week or more on the average. Write their names below. (If there are fewer than six people, write down only as many as there are; if none, write "none." If there are more than six, list just the six with whom you feel your conversations are most satisfying.)

1. _____   4. _____

2. _____   5. _____

3. _____   6. _____

B. Now look back at question A. Each name is numbered. Listed below are all the pairs that can be made among six numbers. Perhaps you know whether some of the six people talk to each other about matters important to them. Please look at each pair of numbers below, look back to see what names they represent, and circle the pair of numbers if you have good reason to believe that the two people talk to each other once a week or more about matters important to them.

1-2				
1-3	2-3			
1-4	2-4	3-4		
1-5	2-5	3-5	4-5	
1-6	2-6	3-6	4-6	5-6

Feedback in the School

The following questions provide information about the availability of feedback. Question B is less direct than Question A, but if many teachers indicate that they do not know whether others agree with them on important issues, the consultant can be relatively certain that the level of interpersonal feedback is low.

A. Do you get any information from other professionals that helps you to tell whether you are doing an effective job of teaching?

( ) No, none.
( ) Yes, about once or twice a year.
( ) Yes, about once a month, maybe.
( ) Yes, about once a week.
( ) Yes, more than once a week.

B. Would you say there is some particular aspect of the school's functioning where new ideas are especially needed?

( )   No, things are working about as well as they can.

( )   No, no particular aspect more than another. We just need things polished up a bit all over.

( )   Yes. If yes, please describe a feature of the school's functioning that needs attention:

_____

_____

C. If you wrote in an answer above, how many people would you say agree with you?

( )   Many.

( )   Some.

( )   Only one or two.

( )   None.

( )   I don't know.

Communicative Roles

Communicative acts in work-oriented groups fall into two general categories. The task-centered category includes acts that promote getting a job done; the social-emotional category includes acts that lower tension and increase group cohesiveness. Figures 3-13 and 3-14 are observation forms for task-centered and interpersonal processes. Using these forms, an observer can tally all group interactions during a specified time period or focus on each member successively.

An observer sometimes wishes to code unproductive communication processes as well. The following list, while not exhaustive, includes some of the unproductive processes commonly seen in groups.

- Recognition seeking, claiming expertise because of seniority, etc.
- Self-confessing, apologizing repeatedly
- Pleading a self-interest that is irrelevant to the task
- Side talking
- Seeking help, asking for special favors

Another useful observation and feedback tool can be created from the matrix of Figure 3-5. Observers can tally the incidence of communi-

Figure 3-13. Categories for Task-centered Process

Tallies

I. Helps group collect data related to task

    A. Contributes data, defines terms, gives
facts, states objectives and goals,
gives opinions and generalizations   _____

    B. Asks questions, asks for survey   _____

    C. Suggests actions and alternatives   _____

II. Helps group use data

    D. Organizes, combines, compares, points
out relations in data   _____

    E. Summarizes: identifies points of agreement
and disagreement   _____

III. Tests for consensus

    F. Checks to see if group agrees   _____

Figure 3-14. Categories for Interpersonal Process

Tallies

I. Acts to increase shared understanding

    A. Paraphrases   _____

    B. Impression check   _____

    C. Helps others paraphrase or make perception
checks   _____

II. Acts to provide data about interpersonal process

    D. Describes interpersonal behavior   _____

    E. Reports own feelings directly

        1. Positive feelings   _____

        2. Negative feelings   _____

    F. Helps others to describe interpersonal behavior
or to report their own feelings directly   _____

cation about the situation dimension of the convening tasks, target statements about methods, proposals for improving interpersonal relations, and so on. They can also record the kinds of contributions made by each group member to give feedback on the roles that are or are not being filled in the group.

The role-perception questionnaire below, which can be completed by group members near the end of a work session, provides subjective data to complement the data collected by an outside observer.

Directions: For each of the ratings below, imagine that the value of the contributions from all members equals 100 percent. Then, beside each member's name, show what percentage of the total effort you would attribute to that person. You may give any member a score from 0 to 100 on each question. Remember that the scores for all members must add up to 100. Be sure to list your own name and to score yourself.

Question A: Show how much each member has contributed to making this a smoothly working, friendly, comfortable group by such acts as encouraging others to participate, showing interest in the feelings of others, helping to resolve tensions and misunderstandings, providing support when members were feeling uneasy or upset, and, in general, showing concern for how well the members of this group got along together.

	Members	*Score*
1.	_____	( )
2.	_____	( )
3.	_____	( )
4.	_____	( )
5.	_____	( )
6.	_____	( )

Total must equal 100

Question B: Show how much each member contributed to the group's achievement by such acts as providing good ideas, suggestions, and information, by keeping the group on the ball, by summarizing what had been accomplished and what still needs to be done, and, in general, by showing concern for productivity, or getting a lot of work done.

	Members	*Score*
1.	_____	( )
2.	_____	( )
3.	_____	( )
4.	_____	( )
5.	_____	( )
6.	_____	( )

Total must equal 100

Again, the questions can be changed to reflect the observation scheme being used, as, for example:

A. Show how much each member contributed to clarifying the *situation* in which the group found itself by such acts as describing the purpose of the meeting, reporting an observation of how the meeting was going, or describing his or her own feelings toward another at the time.

B. Show how much each member contributed to making the *methods* used in this meeting effective by such acts as describing methods that were being used, suggesting better methods, or proposing that the group take a survey or meet in buzz groups.

EXERCISES AND DESIGNS FOR INTERVENTIONS

Basic Communication Skills

In practicing the following exercises, the consultant should not only encourage correct use of the skills but should help group members learn ways of correcting one another. It is useful if participants identify their attempts to use the skills by stating, for example, "I'd like to paraphrase what I heard you say," and so on. Of course, all the exercises and designs presented at the end of this chapter will reinforce points discussed earlier, just as exercises and designs presented elsewhere in this book should highlight or otherwise encourage discussion of communication.

Paraphrasing. For the purpose of paraphrasing, members cluster into circles of no more than eight persons. The consultant or someone in the group suggests a topic that is relevant and important to the group, such as "What is the most important problem facing our team?" One member answers the question briefly; the next person in the circle accurately paraphrases this before giving his own answer, and so on around the circle. This exercise is also effective in two-person units, especially if the two join still another pair and each speaks from an understanding of his partner's answer.

A variation on this exercise can be particularly useful with a new group or with groups that have new members. Here, each person writes five to ten answers to the question "Who am I?" on either a five-by-eight-inch card pinned to the person's chest or on a piece of newsprint taped to the wall. All members mill around for a few minutes silently reading one another's answers. Then, in dyads or triads, individuals paraphrase items from the other persons' lists, perhaps limiting themselves to items that are most like or unlike items on their own list.

Impression Checking. Two exercises are useful for practicing impression checking. In the first, the consultant might ask group members to take turns conveying their feelings to others by means of gestures, expressions, and nonsense language and then ask others to check to make sure that they read the emotion correctly. In the second, called the Alter Ego Procedure, half the group members sit in a circle while the other half take their places behind specific members of the circle. While those in the center discuss an agreed-upon topic, those in the outer ring whisper their impressions to their partners ("Are you upset because you can't get a word in edgewise?" or "Am I correct in inferring that you're slumping because you're uninterested?"). Partners in the inner circle respond only by nodding their heads yes or no to these questions.

Describing Behavior (Own or Other's). The nonverbal exercises in this book can provide data for practicing this interpersonal communication skill. After a five-member group completes the Five-Square puzzle, for example, members might begin their debriefing process by describing orally a behavior that was conspicuous to them. Members should be encouraged to start with descriptions of their own behavior and go on to descriptions of others' behaviors. If group members appear to be withholding significant oral reactions from one another, the consultant might ask each person to write a behavior description instead. The consultant then collects these statements and reads them aloud anonymously.

Stating One's Own Ideas. A simple exercise for practicing this skill is to arrange participants in pairs and to ask each pair to practice simultaneously the skills of stating their own ideas and paraphrasing. The topic for discussion can be far from or relate closely to the school; for example, "Discuss what you consider the most important challenges facing education today," or "Discuss what you consider the most important problems in your school today." The consultant should stress clarity of communication, not agreement between the participants. If the receiver can't paraphrase quickly and accurately, the sender must restate the idea again, using different words.

Describing One's Own Feelings. Many of the nonverbal exercises in this book arouse strong feelings that can later be expressed by means of an oral debriefing, a technique that works especially well when group members describe the nonverbal behavior that triggered their feelings. Written self-tests can also help clients in this skill. In the following example, group members individually mark a *D* (for *describe*) by sentences that describe feelings and an *N* (for *not describe*) by sentences that convey but do not describe a feeling. When all participants have marked Item 1, they share their responses in trios, and then check against explanations of what is correct. The explanations appear out of order so that the eye is not drawn to the list of answers. After everyone in the trio understands the explanation, the trio marks Item 2, and so on. This self-test takes about forty-five minutes to complete.

Self-Test

_____ 1(a). Shut up! Not another word out of you!

_____ 1(b). I'm really annoyed by what you just said.

_____ 2(a). Can't you see I'm busy? Get out!

_____ 2(b). I'm beginning to resent your constant interruptions.

_____ 2(c). You have no consideration for anybody else's feelings. You're completely selfish.

_____ 3(a). I feel discouraged because of some things that happened today.

_____ 3(b). This has been an upsetting day.

_____ 4(a). You're a wonderful person.

_____ 4(b). I really like you.

_____ 5(a). I feel comfortable and free to be myself when I'm around you.

_____ 5(b). We all feel you're a wonderful person.

_____ 5(c). Everybody likes you.

_____ 6(a). If things don't improve around here, I'll look for a new job.

_____ 6(b). Did you ever hear of such a lousy outfit as this is?

_____ 6(c). I'm afraid to admit that I need help with my work.

_____ 7(a). This is a very poor exercise.

_____ 7(b). I feel this is a very poor exercise.

_____ 7(c). I'm confused, frustrated, and annoyed by this exercise.

_____ 8(a). I feel inadequate when teaching that particular subject.

_____ 8(b). I am inadequate in teaching that particular subject.

_____ 9(a). I am a failure; I'll never amount to anything.

_____ 9(b). That teacher is awful. He didn't teach me anything.

_____ 9(c). I'm depressed and discouraged because I did so poorly on that test.

_____ 10(a). I feel lonely and isolated in my group.

_____ 10(b). For all the attention anybody pays to me I might as well not be in my group.

_____ 10(c). I feel that nobody in my group cares whether I am there or not.

Answers and Explanations _____

1(a): *N.* Commands such as these convey strong emotion without describing what kinds of feeling evoked the commands.

1(b): *D.* The speaker conveys feeling by describing himself or herself as annoyed. Thus, the statement not only expresses feeling; it also names the feeling.

7(a): *N.* This statement expresses a negative value judgment. It conveys some kind of negative feelings without describing them.

7(b): *N.* Although the speaker begins by saying, "I feel . . . ," he or she does not then tell the feeling. Instead the speaker passes a negative value judgment on the exercise. Note that merely tacking the words "I feel" onto the front of a sentence does not turn it into a description of feeling. People often say "I feel" when they mean "I think" or "I believe." For example, "I feel the Red Sox will win" or "I feel it will rain tomorrow."

7(c): *D.* The speaker specifies the feelings of confusion, frustration, and annoyance. The speaker describes feelings but does not evaluate the exercise itself.

Although we can disagree with value judgments expressed by another person, we should not deny that the person feels whatever he or she feels. If Joe says the exercise is poor and Jill says it is good, an argument may ensue about which it "really" is. However, if Joe says he was frustrated by the exercise and Jill says she was pleased and stimulated by it, no argument should follow. Each person's reaction is what it is. Of course, discussion about what causes each to feel as he or she does may provide important information about each person and about the exercise itself.

Many persons who say they are unaware of what they feel habitually express value judgments about others without recognizing that they are thereby expressing positive or negative feelings.

10(a): *D.* This statement conveys feelings by describing the speaker as feeling lonely and isolated.

10(b): *N.* This statement conveys negative feelings without telling whether the speaker feels angry, lonely, disappointed, hurt, or any other specific way.

10(c): *N.* Because it begins with "I feel," this kind of expression is often thought to describe the speaker's feelings. Notice, however, that the last part of the sentence really tells what the speaker assumes the others in the group feel about him or her and not what the speaker feels.

Expressions 10c and 10a relate to each other as follows: "Because I believe or assume that nobody in my group cares whether I am there or not, I feel lonely and isolated."

4(a): *N.* This sentence states a value judgment. It conveys positive feelings toward the other without describing what they are. Does the speaker like the other, respect the other, or what? The expression does not tell us.

4(b): *D.* The speaker conveys positive feelings by describing it as liking for the other.

2(a): *N.* Strong feeling is conveyed by the question and accompanying command, "Get out!" but the feeling itself is not described.

2(b): *D.* The speaker's feeling is described as resentment.

2(c): *N.* The speaker makes charges and accusations about the other. The accusations certainly convey strong negative feelings. However, because the feelings are not identified we do not know whether the accusations stem from anger, disappointment, or hurt feelings.

6(a): *N.* This statement conveys negative feelings about the organization without specifying them. It alludes to the condition of things in this organization but does not clarify the speaker's inner state.

6(b): *N.* This is a rhetorical question that expresses a negative value judgment about the organization. It certainly conveys some kind of negative feeling but does not describe what it is.

6(c): *D.* This is a clear description of how the speaker feels in relation to his job:

Expressions *6a* and *6b* are attacks or criticisms of the organization that could result from the kind of fear described in *6c*. Notice that expressions conveying anger result from fear. Many expressions of anger result from fear, hurt feelings, disappointments, or loneliness, but because the speaker's basic feelings are not described, the other person does not understand them.

9(a): *N.* This is another example of the subtle distinction introduced in Item 8. The speaker is conveying a strong negative feeling about himself or herself ("I am a failure"). The statement does not, however, describe the feeling. Is it dejection, fear, resignation, or what?

9(b): *N.* Instead of taking it out on himself, the speaker blames the teacher. His value judgment conveys negative feelings, but it does not describe what the speaker feels.

9(c): *D.* This conveys feelings by describing the speaker's emotional state as depressed and discouraged.

Expressions *9a* and *9c* illustrate the important difference between labeling oneself and describing one's feelings. Feelings can and do change. To say that I am now depressed and discouraged does not imply that I will or must always feel the same. However, if I label myself as a failure, if I truly think of myself as a failure, I increase the probability that I will act like a failure.

One person stated this important insight for herself this way, "I always thought I was a shy person. Now I have discovered that I am not shy although at times I *feel* shy." No longer did she keep herself from trying new things she wanted to by reminding herself that she was too shy.

5(a): *D.* This is a clear and specific description of how the speaker feels when around the other.

5(b): *N.* First, although this conveys positive feelings toward the other, it does not say that the speaker feels this way. To be a description of feeling, the statement should use "I," "me," "my," or "mine" to make clear the feelings are in the speaker. Second, "you're a wonderful person" is a value judgment which does not specify what feeling is behind it (see Item 4a).

5(c): *N.* The statement is not about the speaker's own feelings but refers to everybody. It is true that a feeling is named in the statement but the speaker does not make clear that the feeling is his or her own. A description of feeling must contain "I," "me," "my," or "mine."

Note how much more personal and warm you feel when another says to you that *he* likes you rather than *everybody* likes you. Do you find it more difficult to tell another "I like you" or "everybody likes you"?

8(a): *D.* This conveys feeling by describing the feeling as one of inadequacy.

8(b): *N.* Careful! This sounds much the same as *a*. However, it really says the person *is* inadequate. The person labels himself or herself as inadequate. It is true that a negative feeling about self is conveyed but the person does not describe the feeling.

This subtle difference was introduced because many people confuse *feeling* inadequate with *being* inadequate. A person may feel inadequate when teaching a certain subject and yet do an excellent job of it. Likewise, a person may feel adequate and competent in a subject and perform poorly. One sign of emotional maturity may be when a person functions adequately while feeling inadequate.

3(a): *D.* This describes the speaker as feeling discouraged.

3(b): *N.* Conveys negative feelings without describing what they are. The statement appears to be about the kind of day it was when, in fact, it is an expression of the way the speaker is feeling. We cannot tell from this expression whether the speaker is feeling depressed, annoyed, lonely, humiliated, or rejected.

Giving and Receiving Feedback. In this section we offer two exercises that enable people to practice giving and receiving feedback. In the first exercise, group members form trios in which one member is assigned to give feedback, the second to receive the feedback, and the third to observe both the giving and receiving. The giver describes two helpful and two unhelpful kinds of behavior he or she has seen in the receiver; the receiver paraphrases, and the observer sees to it that the two continue to use communication skills correctly.

The second exercise demonstrates the importance of giving and receiving feedback by showing that close-mouthed behavior is more often interpreted as disapproving than as approving. Participants select partners and decide which of them will be A and which will be B. The consultant tells A privately, "Your partner was supposed to contact you for lunch yesterday but failed to do so, and you are disappointed. On a scale of feeling ranging from 1 (extremely distant) to 9 (extremely close), portray a feeling of 3 in the one-minute conversation that you'll be having soon." To B the consultant says privately, "In the one-minute conversation that you'll soon be having with your partner, whom you like, respect, and value, pretend that you think it would be nice to share a ride to an evening meeting. You think the probability that your partner likes you is about 8."

The partners then come together to talk for one minute about whatever they choose. At the end of that time the consultant tells all Bs to assign their partners a number from 1 to 9 based on the scale of feeling from extremely distant to extremely close. Before it is divulged that all the A partners had been asked to portray a 3, all the B estimates are recorded on newsprint. Almost invariably, the average B estimate will be less than 2. The consultant can then initiate a discussion of why this is so, pointing out that silence or lack of candor about feelings can strain trust in even a one-minute interaction.

Unilateral and Transactional Communication

This section describes two exercises in unilateral and transactional communication (defined at the beginning of the chapter, under "Types of Communication"). The first exercise, commonly known as the One-Way, Two-Way Communication Exercise and adapted from Bass (1966), is designed to provide a group with a springboard for discussions of communication in the school within a brief period of time (see Figure 3-15). In this procedure, one member is designated as the coordinator; another is asked to be the sender; the remaining members are receivers. The coordinator signals when to begin, keeps track of how much time is spent during each phase of the activity, and observes the nonverbal reactions of the receivers.

To commence the activity, the coordinator gives the sender two patterns of rectangles, being careful not to show them to the receivers. The first pattern is presented to the receivers as a unilateral communication during which they must remain silent and refrain from asking questions as they draw the pattern as accurately as possible. The second is given through transactional communication, during which the receivers are encouraged to break in at any time, to raise questions, and to interact orally with the sender.

Figure 3-15. Handout for Unilateral and Transactional Exercise

Phase I: Unilateral Communication

Handout for Sender:

Directions for sender:
1. Be sure that none of the receivers sees the overall design below.
2. Sit with your back to the receivers.
3. When you are ready to start, describe the diagram below so that the receivers can duplicate it on their own papers.
4. None of the receivers may communicate with you in any way at any time.
5. When you are through, take several minutes to record below your degree of satisfaction with the activity just completed.
6. Hand this sheet to the coordinator.

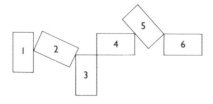

Figure continued on next two pages

Satisfaction scale (circle one):

Very	Rather	Rather	Very	Don't
dissatisfied	dissatisfied	satisfied	satisfied	know

What factors caused the reaction you circled above?

Handout for Receivers:

Directions for receivers:

1. Sit with your backs to the sender.
2. Your task is to reproduce on this paper whatever the sender instructs you to.
3. Only the sender can talk. You may initiate no communications and make no audible signals of any type.
4. It is best to use only your own ideas about what the sender is saying. A neighbor's understanding of the task may be wrong.
5. When the sender has finished, answer the two items below and give the paper to the coordinator.

A. How many pieces of the diagram do you think you completed accurately? Circle the appropriate response: 1 2 3 4 5 6
B. If you felt any frustration during the exercise, circle the number below that best describes your feelings:

1	2	3	4	5
Not at all	A little	Some real	Very	Don't
frustrated	frustrated	frustration	frustrated	know

Handout for Coordinator:

Directions for coordinator:

1. Prior to the exercise
   A. Check back-to-back seating so that receivers cannot see the sender's paper.
   B. You may answer questions before exercise begins.
   C. Tell sender to begin when all are ready.
2. During the exercise
   A. Record starting time _____
      Completion time _____
      Elapsed time _____

B. Record below apparent evidences (including nonverbal) of feelings such as satisfaction, frustration, interest level, high or low morale, and so on, of:

Sender	Receiver

3. After the exercise
    A. Note elapsed time for exercise completion in 2A.
    B. Complete your own notes in 2B.
    C. Collect completed papers in your group.
    D. Record on the back of this sheet any on-the-job implications of the exercise you have just observed.

Phase II: Transactional Communication

The handout for the *sender* differs from the one for unilateral communication in only two ways:

1. Rule 4 now reads, "The receivers may interrupt your directions with questions or comments at any time."
2. The diagram to be transmitted is this one:

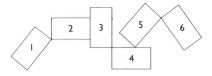

The handout for the *receiver* differs from the one for unilateral comunication only in Rule 4, which now reads, "You may question the sender about instructions at any time and as often as you wish."

The handout for the *coordinator* is identical to the one for unilateral communication.

After the two episodes are completed, the coordinator assists the receivers in determining the number of correct placements in their drawings. A correct rectangle touches one or two other rectangles at the matching location on the sides of the other rectangles and should also be oriented vertically, horizontally, or diagonally as on the sender's page. One point is granted for each rectangle drawn correctly. Scores can range from 0 to 6 for each communication episode. Or if you wish, you may count one point for each correctly oriented rectangle (maximum of 6) and one point for each correct point of contact between rectangles (maximum of 5) for a maximum of 11 points.

After the receivers score their own drawings, receivers and senders are asked to answer the following questions for discussion: With which communication were you most frustrated or tense? Which type would you prefer to use as a sender? Which type would you prefer to receive? (To each question, three alternative answers are possible: unilateral, transactional, or no difference.) When is unilateral communication efficient in our work, and how might we improve it? When is transactional communication necessary in our work, and what can we do to improve it? What are other implications of this activity for our work? What keeps us from using transactional communication more often in our work?

When using the exercise with multiple groups, coordinators are asked to report the primary outcomes of their teams to the entire staff so that all group members can discuss what they learned from the activity and recommendations can be made for continued work on improving communication clarity. Finally, before meeting with the total group, the consultant may meet with the coordinators during a scheduled break and prepare summary charts of the time required, accuracy, and attitudes associated with each communication mode in each of the groups. These summaries can be used to supplement individual reports by the coordinators during the meeting with the entire group.

The Blind Walk is another exercise that highlights the differences between unilateral and transactional communication. In this procedure, each member of the group is asked to pair with a person whom he or she does not know well or would like to know better. One member of the team is blindfolded and is silently guided by the other through, over, or around things. After several minutes the roles are reversed, but during this second phase talking is allowed. When the walk is completed, participants share their mutual reactions about the two ways of communicating and about their relationship. In a variation of this exercise, half the members of the entire group are blindfolded, and the sighted members choose a partner. Each leads one blindfolded member around without identifying himself or herself, which seems to augment the impact of the nonverbal phase of the walk. In still another variation, no touching

Figure 3-16. The Five-Square Puzzle

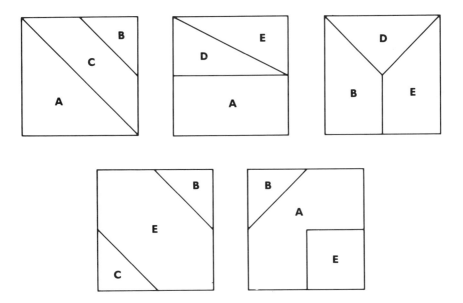

is allowed during the verbal phase, which makes clear verbal instruction imperative.

The Five-Square Puzzle

The Five-Square puzzle exercise (adapted from Bavelas, 1950) demonstrates cooperation in a group task characterized by nonverbal communication. It is administered to participants in groups of five. Observers are instructed to look for ways in which participants communicate nonverbally and for ways in which cooperation is helped or hindered.

Participants occupy five chairs around a table on which, before each person, are laid some flat, mostly irregularly shaped pieces of plastic or cardboard. In an unordered pile before one person are three pieces marked A; before another are four pieces marked B; before another, two pieces marked C; before another, two marked D; and before the fifth person are four pieces marked E. The participants are told that there are exactly enough parts distributed among them to make five complete squares (see Figure 3-16). The task is completed when a square has been composed in front of each member of the group.

The procedural rules are as follows: (1) each member must construct one square at his own work place; (2) no member may talk, signal, or gesture in any way that would provide guidance, direction, or suggestions to any other member—for example, no member may signal for a piece from another member; (3) any member may give any piece to another member; (4) except for any piece given to another member, members' pieces must be in front of them at work places. Only giving is allowed, no taking.

This exercise is frustrating for individuals who are accustomed to managing others as well as for people who are accustomed to guiding themselves by watching for signals of the expectations of others. To the extent that rules are observed (and it is very difficult for most participants to apply this discipline to themselves), the exercise focuses participants' attention on discovering ways in which they can be helpful to one another. The most direct contribution members can make is to give appropriate pieces from their places to the appropriate people, but they must allow the others to find for themselves the way in which the desired pieces fit with those before them.

This exercise points up the great difficulty of allowing other people to do things in their own way and the great extent to which we rely on language to influence the behavior of others. At the same time, it provides very useful information about how group members act toward one another under the frustration the exercise produces. When the performance is completed, the ensuing discussion should focus on problems of coordinated effort and on the implications of the exercise for relations among group members in their daily work. To guide the discussion, the consultant might ask the following questions: What were some of your feelings during the exercise? Do you have similar feelings when you are working in groups in the school district? Under what circumstances do these feelings arise? What implications does this exercise have for our work in the school?

The Five-Square puzzle also can be employed for giving practice in the communication skills. For that purpose, an observing group of five persons sits in a Fishbowl Arrangement around the group doing the puzzle. The inside group members are told to keep track of their feelings during the exercise and to note the behavior of others in their groups as accurately as possible. The observers watch behavior and make notes about their impressions of the insiders' feelings, and after the insiders have finished their work, the insiders paraphrase and verify or contradict the observers' impression checks. The consultant might then ask if the behavior observed during this exercise is similar to or different from what typically goes on in the school.

Figure 3-17. Handout for Group Agreements

Group functioning is improved when members have clear expectations of what kinds of behavior are expected of them as group members. Here are two examples of agreements that a group might accept.

1. *Directness:* If I am dissatisfied with the way the group is going, I will report my reactions directly to the group when it is in session. If, outside of a regular session, another member expresses to me dissatisfactions with the group, I will suggest that that member bring the matter before the total group at a regular session.
2. *Sharing:* Any member may request a survey at any time. The requesting member states what he or she wants to know from the total group; another member paraphrases or otherwise clarifies the topic until all concerned are clear about what is being asked of them; then each person in turn states his or her current position on the topic in two or three sentences. A survey is not a vote that will bind the group or its members. A survey must be taken at the time it is requested, with all other activity suspended.

You should now discuss and decide whether you wish to conclude any group agreements and, if so, what they are to be.

Group Agreements

An exercise in making group agreements about communication not only encourages discussion about the behavior expected from group members but also serves to introduce survey procedure. (We described taking a survey in the section headed "Communication in the Subsystem.") If it is feasible, members who will continue to work as a team should be grouped together for this exercise (adapted from one by Hale and Spanjer, 1970). The exercise requires little preparation beyond providing each participant with a copy of the handout instructions (see Figure 3-17), although the consultant may wish to point out that the outlined agreements are only examples.

Emotional Distance and Closeness

The purpose of this exercise is to heighten awareness of how degrees of distance and closeness in communication affect human relationships. The exercise is most effective if group members are skilled at describing their own feelings, objectively describing the behavior of others, and checking their own inferences about the feelings of others.

Groups form two-person units to engage in a series of three-minute conversations on one of the following topics:

1. A topic that is of interest to only one of you and is unrelated to this day or event.
2. A topic that is of interest to both of you and is unrelated to this day or event.
3. A topic that is of interest to only one of you and is closely related to your life today or to this event.
4. A topic that is of interest to both of you and is closely related to your life today or this event.
5. What is happening between the two of you right now—the way you are relating, your feelings, and your inferences about your partner's feelings. Emphasize your experience of this moment.

When the five conversations are completed, the consultant can guide the debriefing using the following questions: How did your experiences change over the series of conversations? Did you find some conversations easier or more difficult than others? Why? What is happening between you right now? After the debriefing, the consultant might give a lecturette highlighting the dimensions of closeness and distance or might distribute a handout similar to Figure 3-3. The exercise can be concluded with a discussion in quartets of the ways in which emotionally distant and emotionally close communication affects the everyday lives and relationships of people, groups, and organizations. It should be emphasized that close communication does not require intimate friendship between persons and that emotionally close communication cannot be achieved immediately but is based on a step-by-step increase of mutual trust.

Improving Communication Skills

With the consultant's help, communication skills can be improved directly and indirectly. As an example of the former, the following sequence of events emphasizing the use of these skills helps a group to identify issues and problems for additional work. The design takes about seven hours to complete and can be divided into morning and afternoon sessions.

The day begins with a general meeting introducing an overview of training goals and activities followed by an introduction to paraphrasing. The group is divided into small subgroups to discuss what should be changed to help their school operate more effectively. Following this discussion, members concentrate on paraphrasing and attempt to identify its difficulties and potentialities. After the unilateral and transactional communication exercise is introduced, participants discuss it within their subgroups, giving special attention to impression checking and describing one's own feelings. The total group is then reassembled, and the consultant reviews all the skills introduced so far before the group adjourns for lunch.

The afternoon session begins with an introduction to the Five-Square puzzle, following which the group is again divided into small subgroups but of different participants. After completing the exercise, the subgroups discuss it using the skills of behavior description, impression checking, and describing one's own feelings. The total group reconvenes for an introduction to the Group Agreements Exercise, and participants are reassigned to new subgroups. Emphasis is placed on using communication skills correctly during the task and during discussion as well. The small groups then report their various discussions to the total assembly.

The final activity of the day is introduced by a lecturette on the Johari Awareness Model, and the subgroups form helping trios to practice giving feedback on helpful and unhelpful behaviors. If time permits, group members may redistribute themselves into new helping trios and continue practicing. The consultant ends the meeting by reviewing the day's activities, distributing handouts on communication skills, and suggesting possible directions for future OD activities.

Occasionally a consultant will discover that processes other than those of communication are so seriously impaired that the school's functioning is impeded. In this case initial training efforts must be directed to these processes if the training is to benefit the organization. For the consultant who is designing a training sequence, however, this poses a problem, because clear communication is essential to the success of other organizational training events. The solution to this dilemma is to plan the training activities in such a way that communication skills can be introduced even when the focus of the activities is elsewhere.

For example, the authors once worked with an elementary school in which conflict between parents and staff was so intense and goals so ambiguous that collaborative problem solving and decision making were impossible to initiate. To use the terms of Gibb (1961), the climate was defensive rather than supportive. Parents and staff were only interested in the amount and kind of communication skill training that would move them out of this situation rapidly. We decided to work separately with the two groups in a series of meetings distributed over two months.

At the first meeting individuals were asked to write behavior descriptions and statements of their own feelings about the situation in the school. Participants took turns sharing what they had written while others in their group practiced paraphrasing and impression checking.

At other meetings we asked staff and parents separately to describe their behaviors and feelings when the school situation was as they wished it to be. Again they took turns sharing what they had written while everyone had a turn to practice paraphrasing and impression checking. At all these meetings we collected cards, eventually categorizing their content into seven major areas including the reporting system, building and grounds, extracurricular activities in the arts, and so on.

All staff and parents were given handouts describing interpersonal communication behaviors characteristic of defensive and supportive communication. According to Gibb, defensive climates are characterized by evaluation, control, strategy, neutrality, superiority, and certainty; supportive climates are characterized by description, problem orientation, spontaneity, empathy, equality, and provisionalism. Both groups were encouraged to consider how their own behaviors contributed to defensive reaction by members of the other group.

After all participants had attended at least two meetings—in extra training events, the staff worked on organizational issues not directly related to relationships with parents—we brought the two groups together for a seven-hour meeting at which they performed the Imaging exercise described in Chapter 7. This exercise required them to use the communication skills to give and receive feedback. The content of the feedback was then compared with seven kinds of problems participants had discussed earlier, and that comparison helped them choose problems for further work. Small problem-solving groups of parents and staff subsequently met for several months to generate proposals that were ultimately reported back to the total group. Throughout these meetings we continually urged people to use the communication skills and taught them how to coach one another when they used the skills improperly.

In contrast, we have also consulted with several staffs that were unaware that communication in the school needed improvement. They had simply not given much thought to their procedures for communicating. With such groups we have found that the exercise on unilateral and transactional communication is a good place to start. This exercise demonstrates the respective advantages and disadvantages of two organizational forms of communication. In discussing the implications of the exercise, most staffs seek ways of improving one-way communication in the school and of increasing the amount of two-way communication. Their interest in the latter offers a good opportunity to introduce the practice of basic communication skills. Once the six communication skills have been rehearsed, the consultants can ask participants to talk about strengths and weaknesses in the school's current communication patterns. While selecting strengths and weaknesses, staff members are urged to practice the communication skills again. Finally, such a design leads to the identification of organizational problems in communication for future problem solving.

Improved communication is a fundamental objective of consultation in organization development. Because a school's adaptability depends in part upon effective communication among individuals, within subsystems, and in the organization at large, most OD efforts in schools begin with practice in new forms of interpersonal communication and proceed to the use of new communication skills, norms, and structures within the school's subsystems.

4

Improving Meetings

In schools, as in most other organizations, we spend a considerable portion of our time in meetings. Rarely, however, do we or our colleagues speak favorably of them. Most people speak of meetings as a burden to be endured.

That negative attitude is unfortunate. Although all channels of communication can be useful, formal meetings are singularly important for staff communication. Meetings give staff members the opportunity to coordinate information about problems and decisions while satisfying motivational needs for achievement, affiliation, and power.

Meetings provide an opportunity for participation not found in memos, newsletters, loudspeaker announcements, and the like. They permit us to check reactions immediately to a speaker's contribution and to our own utterances as well. If managed effectively, meetings can be the principal channel for bringing staff members into collaboration to reach common understandings and for that reason can be highly productive and satisfying events in the life of the organization.

Yet most school staffs and subgroups use meetings infrequently and ineffectively, often inhibiting clear communication and wide participation. Indeed, since many educators regard meetings as a dull waste of time or as a burden to be endured while more interesting work awaits elsewhere, it is not surprising that mismanaged meetings can arouse distaste and even hatred. There are many traps that prevent meetings from being effective: holding meetings merely because they are scheduled, clinging strictly to Robert's Rules of Order, failing to deal with feelings, blocking members' help in planning the meeting or compiling the agenda, failing to keep a record of things done, attempting to cover too many items on an agenda, allowing a few members to do all the talking, allowing only those with high status to conduct the meetings, and neglecting to carry the group's decisions into action. All these pitfalls inhibit meetings from realizing their potential.

OD consultants, who conduct most of their training in meetings and who are called on in the course of the school year to give help and consultation at ordinary school meetings, should make their training sessions models of effective meetings. This chapter introduces methods that consultants can use to help school people organize meetings for the most effective mobilization of human resources.

PURPOSES OF MEETINGS

Most educators recognize the potential benefits of forming committees, departments, and teams for organizing curricula and developing policy. They see, too, that present trends in school organization, such as team teaching, curriculum committees, and direct citizen involvement with teachers, will bring about a greater need for effective problem solving and decision making in groups. Although individuals can usually reach more efficient decisions on issues that are relatively simple, have objective and easily separable elements, and require a strict sequence of acts that can readily be performed by one person, on more complex issues groups have some advantages over individuals working alone.

Where issues with many alternative subtasks are involved, where elements are not easily conceptualized, where one person cannot perform a subtask without relating to others, and particularly where efficiency depends on the continued coordination and interaction of a number of persons, a group decision will almost always be superior to one produced by even the most capable individual. Groups can usually produce more ideas, stimulate more creative thought among members, pool ideas to develop more realistic forecasts of the consequences of decisions, and generally produce bolder plans than can individuals working alone. Perhaps most important, group members can commit themselves to action in one another's presence.

In a school organization that requires intelligent coordination among staff, one-way communication is not enough; the percentage of people responding constructively to messages must be high. It is important for an organization member to know how many people have "bought" a message, who these people are, and why they have found the message to be either inspiring or distasteful. Beyond getting a message accepted, it is often important for many people to know firsthand that the transmission occurred and that others know it occurred. The face-to-face meeting is the only setting in which all these functions can take place quickly.

Perhaps the greatest value of meetings is that they draw out and coordinate staff resources for a systematic exchange of creative ideas. They can also be useful for planning action that will require the consistent coordinated effort of several staff members. Even the simplest matters, such as using audio-visual equipment or art supplies, are often difficult for staff members to coordinate and might be facilitated by staff discussions. If the transmission of simple information at meetings wastes valuable time, another mode of communication, such as a clearly written memorandum, would be more appropriate, require less time, and be available for later reference.

Chapters 5 and 6 provide further discussion of the assets and debits of participative involvement in problem solving and decision making.

Finally, meetings provide one of the few means by which people in schools can come together to satisfy emotional needs. Observers such as Jackson (1968) and Lortie (1975) have noted the social isolation, the vagueness of outcomes, and the relatively low degree of power associated with teaching and working in schools. The traditional self-contained classroom requires teachers to work apart from other adults most of the time. Vague but demanding educational goals are often set by the larger society of which the school is a part but on which teachers have little influence. Joining with other adults in meetings to solve mutual problems and share common frustrations can greatly improve the chance for school members to take initiative, feel successful, experience affiliation with others, and feel that they are exercising some influence over their own and shared fates.

Because meetings are confined in time, space, and have limited membership, they bring many group processes that are elusive in the larger organization into full view for the consultant to observe. Thinking of meetings as microcosms of the organization will enable the consultant to anticipate many of the norms manifested outside meetings. Moreover, in initial contacts with clients, consultants should make observations at regularly scheduled meetings in which real work is taking place. It is better to see clients in action than to hear them talk about how they work together, and meetings are among the most easily observable group actions in schools.

By observing interpersonal interaction at meetings, consultants can discern roles and norms that reflect the organization's goals, approved procedures, and affective climate. The kinds of communication encouraged at meetings, for example, can reveal the expectations and skills that members use to coordinate their efforts. The amount of time devoted to goal setting can indicate the importance that members attach to this in relation to other activities. Shared assumptions about the functions of conflict can be noted in the ways in which opposing views are uncovered and handled. To understand how staff members have organized to accomplish their tasks, comparisons of problem-solving and decision-making activities can be made at staff meetings, smaller group meetings, and informal sessions. Finally, consultants can watch the degree to which participants comment on how they conduct their meetings and how they assess changes in their group processes.

Meetings that are handled ineffectively often have unfortunate repercussions elsewhere in the school. Principals who receive a policy decision at a district meeting without a clarifying discussion may misinterpret the policy and transmit wrong directions to teachers. When educational goals are seldom discussed at building meetings, teachers may find themselves working at cross-purposes. When small conflicts over disciplining students are not discussed at staff meetings, they may grow into hostilities. When problem solving and decision making during meetings are confined to only a few staff members, nonparticipants are likely to experience frustration and to tune out; those who stay out of the discussion may be unwilling or unable to carry out the action steps that others have developed. Finally, if staff members fail to discuss changes occurring in the community and student body, their instructional programs will lose effectiveness.

EFFECTIVE MEETINGS

Effectiveness at meetings is uncommon, especially when issues are not easily resolvable. But ineffectiveness should not be punished when it occurs. Instead, consultants should go beyond helping groups to develop effective meetings and on occasion help them to lower their expectations so that mutual recrimination does not consume an inordinate amount of time.

Four Features

Effective meetings are characterized by at least four features: (1) a balanced mixture of task and maintenance functions, with an edge given to sticking to the task; (2) many more group-oriented actions than self-oriented actions; (3) wide dispersal of leadership roles; and (4) adequate follow-through to permit decisions made at the meeting to result in the expected actions.

A Balance of Task and Maintenance. To have effective meetings, groups must learn to fulfill both task functions, which carry forward the meeting's work requirements, and maintenance functions, which help group members develop satisfying interpersonal relationships. Task functions include initiating ideas on work procedures, seeking information or opinions from others, giving information or opinions, and summarizing what has occurred in the meeting. Maintenance functions include ensuring that others have a chance to speak, ensuring that listeners have a chance to check on what they have heard, reconciling disagreements, sensing group mood, and being warm and responsive toward others. Since most groups have difficulty staying on task, the consultant will wish to emphasize task functions. At the same time, without maintenance functions the group will not continue to act as a group. The consultant will have to perform maintenance functions in some groups and trust that group members will model some of their behavior after those of the consultant.

Meetings are most effective when some members attend to how well the group is accomplishing each part of its work and others stop working on their tasks periodically to discuss the group's process. Symptoms of difficulty include excessive nitpicking, repetition of obvious points, ignoring suggestions for improvement, private conversations in pairs or subgroups, domination of discussion by two or three people, polarization of members, general inability to paraphrase others' points of view, attack against ideas before they are completely expressed, and apathetic participation. When such symptoms are present, the group should set aside the original task and place emerging maintenance issues on the agenda. It must also learn to deal effectively with its processes and to shift easily back to its main work. Most if not all staff members should be capable of performing both task and maintenance functions.

Group Orientation. The second feature of effective meetings is the degree to which members engage in self-oriented rather than group-oriented behavior. Unproductive behaviors such as fighting, withdrawing, blocking, avoiding, depending on the formal leader, expressing indifference, sandbagging, and keeping agendas hidden are directed toward individual needs rather than toward the task at hand. Schein (1969) theorizes that self-oriented behavior occurs when groups fail to recognize or to deal with any of four underlying emotional issues of members: identity, control, needs and goals, and acceptance of intimacy. Such behavior also probably reflects low trust in the group.

Self-oriented behavior may be a problem when it delays accomplishment of the main task and leaves members dissatisfied, but groups often allow individuals to take up everyone else's time for individual purposes. If this can be done aboveboard, the group should not avoid it and an individual should not be afraid to ask. Everyone should be clear that it is happening and be willing to delay the original group task so that a discussion of the individual's concern, like attention to group process, will pay off later.

Shared Leadership. The third feature of effective meetings is shared leadership—that is, any behavior that helps the group carry forward its work or satisfy members' needs in constructive ways. Leadership is needed for (1) planning and preparing for the meeting, (2) setting goals by building an agenda, (3) coordinating task business, (4) keeping records of what happens, (5) helping attend to group and interpersonal processes, (6) evaluating how well activities meet goals and how satisfying and helpful interpersonal processes are, and (7) planning ways of following through on plans.

In our view, these functions should be shared by all members of a group at the same time that individual members are assigned primary responsibility to see that certain special roles are performed effectively. These special roles—meeting organizer, convener, recorder, process observer, and follow-up monitor—are described later in this chapter.

Follow-through. The fourth readily observable feature of effective meetings, follow-through, occurs after the meeting. If requests pour into the secretary's or principal's office for information about items discussed at the meeting, the meeting was probably ineffective in relaying that information. If staff members grumble in the faculty room about a decision made at a meeting, they probably did not feel free to contribute their own views. Tasks that are implemented with commitment and dispatch, however, give evidence of adequate preparation at the meeting.

The Consultant's Roles and Functions

Two factors encourage consultants to improve meeting skills at a very early phase of an OD effort. First, although most school staffs cannot easily call off work, even for brief periods, to practice new group and organizational processes, consultants can often gain admission to regularly scheduled meetings to help with the ongoing work of the school. Second, any initial successes achieved at moving group members from chaotic to productive meetings can increase their trust in the consultant's competence and encourage them to work toward resolving the larger issues confronting their organization. Four methods are available to the consultant to improve meetings: (1) modeling an effective group member, (2) providing information about effective meetings, (3) providing training, and (4) providing consultation and feedback.

Modeling. By attending the meetings of a school staff or other group within the client system, consultants to some extent become temporary members of these meetings and, as such, may act as models of effective group members. If members seldom clarify one another's statements, for example, consultants may repeatedly clarify what others are saying. If agendas are loosely described and consultants are themselves on the agenda, they may insist that the purpose of their agenda topic be clarified and that definite time requirements be imposed for them. If a group leaves decisions dangling with no clear indication of who is to be responsible for follow-up actions, consultants can ask leading questions that focus on this lack of specification.

For purposes of modeling, consultants can sometimes assume important leadership roles as well. As convener, the consultant can demonstrate assertive behavior, help the group warm up, organize its agenda, and encourage wide participation; in other roles, consultants can exhibit the careful recording of events or demonstrate careful observations of group processes. Unless considerable trust exists between members and the consultant, however, this type of modeling should be avoided. The role of consultants is not to furnish leadership functions for the group but rather to help the group establish effective meetings by passing on their own skills to group members.

Providing Information. If group members already perceive the nature of their problems, consultants can often help by providing information about the characteristics and procedures of effective meetings, especially the guides for conveners, recorders, and process consultants described later in this chapter. After giving this information, they can lead discussions about the advantages and disadvantages of the recommended procedures or techniques and then coach members as they conduct their meetings in new ways. In this way, too, consultants can help a group find resources that none of its members individually can provide by assisting in a search beyond the group for other people and materials.

Training. When group members are unhappy with their meetings and have committed themselves to improving them, the consultant is in a good position to offer training in alternative modes and roles. Training events can be set up at which members practice the exercises and procedures connected with various leadership roles and functions described in this chapter.

Providing Consultation. Finally, group members are often unaware of how they are influenced by group norms and processes. Members of a faculty, for example, may know that their meetings are going poorly but may not understand why. Some members may be upset because the group cannot work effectively on its agenda in a brief period of time; others may criticize meetings because they are all work and no fun. In such instances, process consultants can collect and feed back data about meeting processes so that members can perceive, understand, and act in ways that will improve their meetings.

GATHERING DATA ABOUT MEETINGS

The first source of data about meetings is the consultant's own informal observations. The consultant might keep the following questions in mind: Do meetings start late, with members straggling in? Or do the meetings start promptly, with most members ready to work? Is there an atmosphere of confusion and muddling through? Or is there a clear direction to the meeting guided by a publicly shared agenda? Do members compete and act coldly toward one another? Or do the members cooperate and act warmly toward one another? Do only a few members talk? Or do most members seem to be involved and getting a chance to talk? Do members interrupt one another, talk at the same time, and use sarcasm, ridicule, or put-downs to express disapproval? Or is the communication open and direct, with favorable and unfavorable feelings being described explicitly?

Answers to such questions will help the consultant to get an initial sense for what this staff is like. Subsequently, however, the consultant will need to collect more formal data for purposes of diagnosis and feedback. In this section we present several questionnaires, interviews, and observation schedules that we have found useful for gathering data about meetings in schools. We have tried to describe the context in which each instrument works best and the settings in which many have been used successfully. Many of the instruments can be adapted to meet special situations. Items from the Meetings Questionnaire, for example, might become part of an interview schedule or might suggest behavior the consultant can observe and report in a process-feedback session.

Instruments for Diagnosing Problems

Meetings Questionnaire. We have used the Meetings Questionnaire, developed by Matthew Miles for the Cooperative Project on Educational Development, in numerous settings to diagnose the quality of clients' meetings. In the normal procedure, each member of a group that meets regularly responds to the thirty-seven items on the questionnaire. The consultant can then tabulate and display these data on newsprint to present means and frequency distributions for each item. Members can be encouraged to diagnose their own meetings by discussing items on which high agreement exists or items with mixed responses. In the questionnaire below, the introductory paragraph can be modified to suit the type of meeting to be described.

Meetings Questionnaire ──────────────────────

Schools hold a lot of meetings, and much depends on their quality. Please think specifically of the meetings you have in your school.

How often are these meetings usually held? _____

How long is the typical meeting? _____

Now, please consider what usually or typically happens in these meetings. Some possible happenings in meetings are listed below. Before each item below, please write one of the following numerals to indicate how usual or typical it is in your group.

5 This is very typical of the meetings; it happens repeatedly.
4 This is fairly typical of the meetings; it happens often.
3 This is more typical than not; it happens sometimes.
2 This is more untypical than typical, though it happens now and then.
1 This is untypical; it rarely happens.
0 This is not typical at all; it never happens.

1. _____ When problems come up in the meeting, they are thoroughly explored until everyone understands what the problem is.
2. _____ The first solution proposed is often accepted by the group.
3. _____ People come to the meeting not knowing what is to be presented or discussed.
4. _____ People ask why the problem exists and what the causes are.
5. _____ Many problems that people are concerned about never get on the agenda.
6. _____ Participants have a tendency to propose answers without really having thought through carefully the problem and its causes.

7. _____ The group discusses the pros and cons of several different alternate solutions to a problem.

8. _____ People bring up extraneous or irrelevant matters.

9. _____ The average person in the meeting feels that his or her ideas have gotten into the discussion.

10. _____ Someone summarizes progress from time to time.

11. _____ Decisions are often left vague as to what they are and who will carry them out.

12. _____ Either before the meeting or at its beginning, any group member can easily get items onto the agenda.

13. _____ People are afraid to be openly critical or make good objections.

14. _____ The group discusses and evaluates how decisions from previous meetings worked out.

15. _____ People do not take the time to really study or define the problem they are working on.

16. _____ The same few people seem to do most of the talking during the meeting.

17. _____ People hesitate to give their true feelings about the problems discussed.

18. _____ When a decision is made, it is clear who should carry it out and when.

19. _____ There is a good deal of jumping from topic to topic—it's often unclear where the group is on the agenda.

20. _____ From time to time in the meeting, people openly discuss the feelings and working relationships in the group.

21. _____ The same problems seem to keep coming up over and over again from meeting to meeting.

22. _____ People don't seem to care about the meeting or want to get involved in it.

23. _____ When the group is thinking about a problem, at least two or three different solutions are suggested.

24. _____ When there is disagreement, it tends to be smoothed over or avoided.

25. _____ Some very creative solutions come out of this group.

26. _____ Many people remain silent.

27. _____ When conflicts over decisions come up, the group does not avoid them but really stays with the conflict and works it through.

28. _____ The results of the group's work are not worth the time it takes.

29. _____ People give their real feelings about what is happening during the meeting itself.

30. _____ People feel very committed to carry out the solutions arrived at by the group.

31. _____ When the group is supposedly working on a problem, it is really working on some other "under the table" problem.

32. _____ People feel antagonistic or negative during the meeting.

33. _____ There is no follow-up on how decisions reached at earlier meetings worked out in practice.
34. _____ Solutions and decisions are in accord with the chairman's or leader's point of view but not necessarily with that of the members.
35. _____ There are splits or deadlocks between factions or subgroups.
36. _____ The discussion goes on and on without any decision being reached.
37. _____ People feel satisfied or positive during the meeting.

Expectations about Meeting Behavior. The Team-Expectation Survey in Chapter 3 (under "Gathering Data About Communication") enables participants in meetings to discover what kinds of information they want from others and what kinds of information they are willing to give to others. Fosmire and Keutzer (1968) discuss protocols collected from a wide range of groups showing that (1) meeting participants usually say they are receptive to interpersonal feedback but perceive others as unwilling to give it, and (2) meeting participants usually say they would report their feelings candidly but doubt that others would do so. Our experience confirms Fosmire and Keutzer's findings. This survey is useful not only for measuring and reporting data for discussion but also for showing meeting participants that attempts at openness might be safer than they had formerly believed. We have used this questionnaire with a variety of staffs and faculty subgroups that meet regularly. When each member has completed the questionnaire, we calculate the mean scores for each item and feed the results back to the group for analysis and discussion during a regular meeting. Figure 4-1 illustrates how the data might be displayed for feedback.

Instruments for Process Observation and Consultation

The instruments in this section consist mainly of observation schedules that the consultant can use to facilitate process consultation during meetings. With these instruments, an observer can record both descriptive and quantitative data during a meeting, and these can later be fed back to group members for their own analysis and discussion.

Observing Participation. Effective groups make use of their members' resources during meetings. All members participate although in different and complementary ways. By means of the observation schedule illustrated in Figure 4-2, the consultant can record the frequency with which individuals speak to other individuals, to the total group, or not at all.

Figure 4-1. Displaying Results of the Team-Expectation Survey

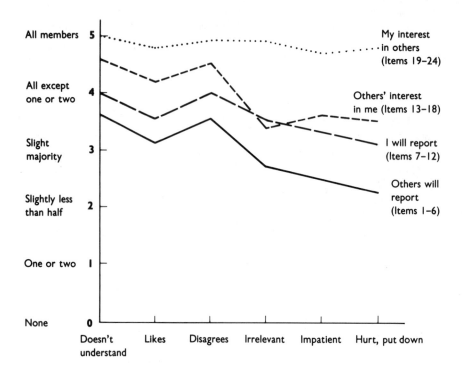

Observing Leadership Functions. The following observation schedule can be used to observe particular leadership functions in groups. In this instance, the observer makes a tally every time a member performs a leadership function in the specified categories listed in the schedule. At the end of the meeting, tallies can be counted and fed back to members. The numbers in Figure 4-3 illustrate how the tallies might turn out.

Interaction Process Analysis. Another way of observing and analyzing leadership functions in meetings is to collect information on the task and socioemotional behavior of group members. Bales (1950) developed an instrument with categories similar to the task-maintenance functions described earlier in this chapter. His categories were as follows:

SOCIAL-EMOTIONAL: POSITIVE
1. Shows solidarity, raises others' status, gives help, rewards
2. Shows tension release, jokes, laughs, shows satisfaction

Figure 4-2. Observer's Frequency Chart: Patterns of Communication

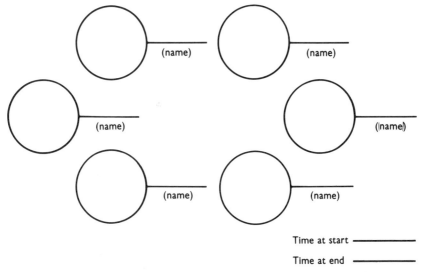

Record at the bottom of the chart the time interval during which the observations are made. Label the circles with the names of group members. The first time a person speaks to another person, draw an arrow from the speaker to the receiver of the message. The first time a person speaks to the total group, draw an arrow to the center of the cluster of circles. Indicate additional messages from the speaker to that individual or to the total group with tally marks on the arrow. Place an *X* in a person's circle if he or she interrupts another to speak. Place a check mark in the circle to indicate that the person's remark encouraged another to participate.

3. Agrees, shows passive acceptance, understands, confers, complies

TASK: NEUTRAL

4. Gives suggestions, direction, implying autonomy for others
5. Gives opinions, evaluation, analysis, expresses feeling, wishes
6. Gives orientation, information, repeats, clarifies, confirms
7. Asks for orientation, information, repetition, confirmation
8. Asks for opinions, evaluation, analysis, expressions of feeling
9. Asks for suggestions, direction, possible ways of action

SOCIAL-EMOTIONAL: NEGATIVE

10. Disagrees, shows passive rejection, formality, withholds help
11. Shows tension, asks for help, withdraws, leaves the field
12. Shows antagonism, deflates others' status, defends or asserts self

Figure 4-3. Leadership Functions in Meetings

While observing the group, make a tally mark every time you hear or see behavior (verbal or nonverbal) that approximates one of the following.

			Member			
Categories	S	W	E	R	J	O
1. Setting goals		3				
2. Proposing problems	8	2		20	3	12
3. Asking for information	3	8				2
4. Giving information		2	1	2		2
5. Proposing solutions	4			2		2
6. Asking for clarification	2	1				
7. Giving clarification	3	1		15	3	6
8. Testing for consensus		1				
9. Supporting				1		
10. Asking about group progress			1			
11. Summarizing		1		2		
12. Evaluating	5	1		20	2	9

The consultant can collect information on these categories using the observation schedule in Figure 4-4. The data can be reported to group members, who can discuss the task and socioemotional activities they usually perform or identify those they would like to practice to gain greater proficiency.

Instruments for Evaluating Meeting Effectiveness

The following questionnaires measure participants' reactions to meetings. The first three were developed to help a group analyze a

Figure 4-4. Cumulative Interaction Form

Date _____ Group _____

Time _____ to _____ Observer _____

	Behavior	Members									Totals
Positive Emotions	Shows solidarity										
	Shows tension release										
	Agrees										
Task	Gives suggestions										
	Gives opinions										
	Gives orientation										
	Asks for orientation										
	Asks for opinions										
	Asks for suggestions										
Negative Emotions	Disagrees										
	Shows tension										
	Shows antagonism										
	Totals										

single meeting; the fourth has been used to measure perceptions and expectations about a series of meetings.

Example 1. Several consultants have used this questionnaire for feedback to school groups.

Directions: Mark an X in the space that best shows your reaction to this meeting.

Agreement		Disagreement		
Strong	Mild	Mild	Strong	
( ) YES!	( ) yes	( ) no	( ) NO!	1. The results of this meeting were worth the time.
( ) YES!	( ) yes	( ) no	( ) NO!	2. I was given adequate opportunity to state my beliefs about subjects discussed by the group.
( ) YES!	( ) yes	( ) no	( ) NO!	3. Our meeting was efficient.
( ) YES!	( ) yes	( ) no	( ) NO!	4. I am satisfied with the attention and consideration that others gave to my ideas and opinions.
( ) YES!	( ) yes	( ) no	( ) NO!	5. We wasted too much time in this meeting.
( ) YES!	( ) yes	( ) no	( ) NO!	6. The group effectively used my knowledge of the subjects discussed.
( ) YES!	( ) yes	( ) no	( ) NO!	7. The most important topics were never discussed.
( ) YES!	( ) yes	( ) no	( ) NO!	8. I had adequate opportunity to influence our conclusions and decisions.

Example 2. The following items were developed by Runkel.

1. Do you feel that anything of value happened during this meeting?

( ) Yes, quite a lot.
( ) Yes, something.
( ) Not much.
( ) Nothing.

2. If you found something of value in this meeting, does any particular happening or idea stand out in your mind?

( )   Nothing of value happened.
( )   It was a valuable meeting, but no particular thing stands out.
( )   Yes, something does stand out for me—namely,

_____

3. If you found something in this meeting to be of *no* value, was there a particular happening or idea that stands out in your mind as being valueless?

( )   Most everything was of some value.
( )   Some parts of the meeting had no value, but no particular thing stands out.
( )   Yes, something stands out for me as having no value—namely,

_____

4. Was there any feature about the way this group operated that you thought particularly effective?

( )   No   ( )   Yes—namely,

_____

_____

5. Was there any feature about the way this group operated that you thought particularly *in*effective?

( )   No   ( )   Yes—namely,

_____

_____

Example 3. This form is based on an instrument developed by Schein (1969).

Answer the items according to *your own opinions* about the meeting. There are no right answers. Circle the number on the scale that corresponds to your opinion.

1. Goals of the meeting

Poor____1_____2_____3_____4_____5____Good

(Conflicting; unclear;   (Clear; shared by all, en-
diverse, unacceptable.)   dorsed with enthusiasm.)

2. Participation in the meeting

Poor_____1_____2_____3_____4_____5_____Good

(Few dominate; some passive; some not listened to; several talk at once or interrupt.)

(All get in; all are really listened to; open and lively discussion.)

3. Leadership of the meeting

Poor_____1_____2_____3_____4_____5_____Good

(Group needs for leadership not met; group depends too much on one or a few persons; no direction or no leadership.)

(A sense of direction is in evidence; leaders are allowed to emerge as needs for leadership arise; everyone feels free to volunteer to lead.)

4. Decisions made during the meeting

Poor_____1_____2_____3_____4_____5_____Good

(No decisions were made; decisions were made to which I feel uncommitted; bad decisions were made.)

(Good decisions were made; everyone felt a part of the decision-making process; people feel committed to the decisions.)

5. Your feelings during the meeting

Poor_____1_____2_____3_____4_____5_____Good

(I was unable to express my feelings; my feelings were ignored; my feelings were criticized.)

(I freely expressed my feelings; I felt understood; I felt support from the participants.)

6. Organization of the meeting

Poor_____1_____2_____3_____4_____5_____Good

(It was chaotic; it was too tightly controlled; very poorly done; I felt manipulated.)

(It was very well organized; it was flexible enough to enable us to influence it; all went smoothly.)

7. Relationship among meeting participants

Poor _____ 1 _____ 2 _____ 3 _____ 4 _____ 5 _____ Good

(My relationship with them is the same as before; I feel antagonistic toward many of them; I don't trust them; there is little potential for a future relationship.)

(Our relationship is much improved; I trust them more than I did prior to the session; I feel I got to know and understand many of them better; there is good potential for the future.)

8. Attitude about the meeting

Poor _____ 1 _____ 2 _____ 3 _____ 4 _____ 5 _____ Good

(Boring; it was a waste of time; I don't like the way it was presented; I disliked it.)

(Interesting; was helpful; I liked it.)

9. Content of the meeting

Poor _____ 1 _____ 2 _____ 3 _____ 4 _____ 5 _____ Good

(Uninstructional; I did not learn much; not informative; too much process; not enough content.)

(I learned a lot; was informative; I'll be able to use the content; content was appropriate to our needs.)

10. Productivity of the meeting

Poor _____ 1 _____ 2 _____ 3 _____ 4 _____ 5 _____ Good

(Did not accomplish much; no useful ideas emerged; it got us nowhere.)

(Got a lot done; very fruitful; something will come of this session.)

Example 4. The following questionnaire can assist group members in analyzing members' contributions to meeting effectiveness. The information might be sensitive for groups with low degrees of openness and trust, so the consultant should strive to accentuate the helpful and favorable aspects of the meeting.

Role-Perception Survey ——————————————

Which members, in your judgment, contributed most to meeting effectiveness by:

Helping to get started on time? ——————————————

—————————————————————————————— (names).

Sticking to the agenda? ——————————————

—————————————————————————————— (names).

Performing acts of encouragement, warmth, friendly interest, and support?

—————————————————————————————— (names).

Bringing in ideas, information, and suggestions? ——————————

—————————————————————————————— (names).

Helping us to stay on the track, summarizing, checking to make sure we

understood one another? ——————————————

—————————————————————————————— (names).

EXERCISES AND PROCEDURES
FOR IMPROVING MEETINGS

This section offers exercises and procedures that consultants can use either in formal training sessions or during regular meetings. Although some might prefer another scheme, we have categorized these exercises and activities according to their effectiveness in helping group members (1) warm up for meetings; (2) plan, conduct, and evaluate meetings; (3) broaden participation; (4) stimulate creativity; and (5) deal with hidden agendas and game playing. Consultants will want to adapt them to their own particular applications, although each has been successfully tried as described here.

Helping Members Warm Up

Fatigue, illness, or other preoccupations can prevent participants from becoming involved in the tasks at hand. Procedures that help them to become attentive to the here and now will increase the efficiency of meetings. To this end, we have found the following five warm-up activities to be effective.

Naming. This activity enables strangers to learn the names of others in the group while their own names are being learned. One person states his or her own name; the next person to the left or right repeats this name and adds his own, the next person repeats the first two names and adds his own, and so on until all names are given. Because connecting names and faces (or whatever other aspect of appearance is mnemonic) requires alertness, the exercise has the effect of focusing eyes on people instead of on note paper or out the window.

Announcing Preferences for the Agenda. This activity, which is also designed to focus attention on persons and their directions of thought, can be used rapidly to yield a quick acquaintance with persons and their ideas, or it can be used thoughtfully, with deliberation, to get more depth. Each person addresses a particular other person, expressing what he or she believes to be a preferred agenda item that the two of them share. The person addressed is obliged to agree or disagree with the first speaker, and then turn to another person and announce another agenda item to be agreed on by both. The procedure continues in the same manner.

Milling. In this procedure, each person walks about the room looking at other members without speaking to them. After a few minutes, participants are asked to choose someone they would like to know better and to talk about their hopes for the meeting. After another few minutes the milling begins again and each person chooses someone else with whom to repeat the activity. After a while, all group members are asked to summarize their hopes for the meeting.

Billy Goat. This activity is helpful for loosening people up in preparation for some creative task. The group stands in a close circle; the consultant steps into the center of the circle and says, "When I point to someone and say 'billy goat,' that person must place her hand beneath her chin to resemble a goat's beard and bleat *baa*. The persons to her immediate left and right must at the same time form a goat's horns by each holding an index finger to the head. The last person of the three to do this must then step to the center of the circle and choose the next billy goat." After a few rounds the facilitator may introduce variations such as Elephant (middle person makes a trunk by holding two fists to his nose while neighbors form floppy ears) or Kangaroo (middle person makes a pouch by cupping hands while neighbors hop up and down). There are endless variations, and the group should be encouraged to create a few.

Walk Across the Circle. In this exercise, eight to twelve persons are seated in a circle and, at a signal from the consultant, all walk across the circle and sit in the chairs of the persons opposite them. But only one step may be taken at the first signal, only one step at the second signal, and so on. After each single step, participants must hold their positions until the next step is called. As soon as everyone has taken one step, call the next step promptly, although not while someone is still off balance. Keep calling until the last person has reached a chair and is seated. You may join the exercise yourself while calling the steps. After the first step, participants will get in one another's way and will have to choose whether to circumnavigate or to plow through the scrimmage. Those who prefer bodily contact will get it; those who do not will easily avoid it. This exercise requires only an average feeling of friendliness and good will among group members. During the debriefing, some of the participants will quickly offer descriptions of behavior and feelings.

Helping Members Plan, Conduct, and Evaluate Meetings

We have already noted the leadership functions needed for effective meetings and the several leadership roles that should be assigned to individual members in rotation. Here we discuss how consultants can help members plan, conduct, and evaluate their meetings and how they can strengthen the ways in which leadership functions are managed and leadership roles assumed.

Planning and Preparing. Before a meeting is called, the convener should give thought to clarifying goals, to issues of appropriate membership, and to matters of time scheduling and physical facilities. If the purpose of a meeting is not clear to everyone involved, prepare relevant contributions beforehand to accomplish that purpose. If goals are unstated or unclear, some people whose presence is necessary may not be invited; some will discover that their presence is unnecessary; others may feel little desire to attend the meeting at all; and many who attend will present concerns irrelevant to the major purpose.

Goals are also important to consider with respect to scheduling. A group that wants to generate fresh ideas for teaching should probably not plan to meet at 3:00 P.M. after a hard day's work. And time allotments must be considered as well. Too often groups spend hours discussing a five-minute report only to find themselves forced to make a major decision in a few minutes. Finally, most meetings for problem solving and decision making require physical arrangements that encourage participation. Chairs should be placed in circles or around tables so that face-to-face communication can occur, and materials such as newsprint and felt pens should be available for illustrating and recording members' contributions.

As simple as these items appear, in many schools they are ignored by those responsible for meetings. Consultants can help to improve meetings by going over the planning prerequisites and by encouraging an individual member, not necessarily the formal leader, to assume responsibility in guiding the meeting. Meeting organizers can use the three planning sheets displayed in Figures 4-5, 4-6, and 4-7 (developed by Schindler-Rainman, Lippitt, and Cole, 1975, pp. 23–25) to increase the effectiveness of their efforts.

Organizing an Agenda. Most meetings involve several topics or activities that vary in their respective time requirements. Some items will be presented for information only; others will require longer discussion and planning for action. A group can greatly improve efficiency by spending a brief time at the beginning of the meeting to set priorities, designate time allotments, and decide what kind of action each item requires. Unfortunately, many people are inexperienced at running meetings in a disciplined way. Those accustomed only to the free-for-all style will need repeated explanations of the disciplined step-by-step method and will learn faster if others in the group help to model and explain this style.

The following procedure allows everyone to contribute to building an effective agenda. (1) Ask group members to name the items they want to deal with at this meeting. (2) When you are reasonably sure that all members understand each item, order the items according to their similarities and place them in homogeneous clusters. (3) Select the order by asking group members for their priorities, trying at the same time to establish rough time estimates for each agenda item. You can accomplish some of this before the meeting begins by posting an agenda sheet in a central location and encouraging group members to write on it items for the next meeting's agenda. In this way participants can both contribute their own items for the group's consideration and think about other people's items in order to offer informed questions and decisions.

The best strategy we have found for helping groups improve their ability to organize an agenda is to assign that responsibility to the convener, gain the group's agreement to follow that procedure, and then coach the convener over several meetings. Consultants can recommend that the convener use the meeting format exhibited in Table 4-1 or some modification of it.

Figure 4-5. Diagnostic Planning for Designing Participatory Meetings

Thinking about the participants or members (e.g., how many, subgroups and individual differences, needs, readinesses, interests, expectations)	Some desirable outcomes of the meeting (e.g., skills, information, values, concepts, actions, plans, recommendations, decisions)	Ideas for activities, experiences, resources, to facilitate the outcomes (e.g., exercises, projects, resources, facilities, work groups)
*Star most important characteristics and differences among participants to keep in mind when designing	*Star highest priority outcomes	*Star what seem to be most appropriate, effective, feasible ingredients of design

Summary statement of desired outcomes:

Source: Reprinted from Eva Schindler-Rainman, Ronald Lippitt, and Jack Cole, *Taking Your Meetings Out of the Doldrums*, San Diego, CA: University Associates, Inc., 1975. Used by permission.

Figure 4-6. The Meeting Design

Time estimate	Activities, methods, groupings	Who is responsible	Arrangements of space, equipment, materials

1. Premeeting and start-up of the meeting

2. Flow of session after start-up activities

(continue on additional sheet as needed)

Source: Reprinted from Eva Schindler-Rainman, Ronald Lippitt, and Jack Cole, *Taking Your Meetings Out of the Doldrums,* San Diego, CA: University Associates, Inc., 1975. Used by permission.

Figure 4-7. Commitments, Follow-ups, Supports

1. *Plans for ending the meeting* (e.g., closing activities, evaluation, reports of back-home plans, deadline commitments, etc.)

2. *Follow-up:* Who will do what? When? Where?
   (e.g., often a directory of names, addresses, telephone numbers of participants is very important at this point; make sure any follow-up dates are recorded in everyone's calendar)

3. *Clean-up and other immediate commitments*
   (e.g., what has to be returned, thank-you calls made, bills paid, etc.)

Source: Reprinted from Eva Schindler-Rainman, Ronald Lippitt, and Jack Cole, *Taking Your Meetings Out of the Doldrums,* San Diego, CA: University Associates, Inc., 1975. Used by permission.

Table 4-1. Sample Agenda Format

Agenda Item	Order	Time	Person	Required Action
United Way	4	5	Sue	Information only
Hall passes	2	10	Lee	Discuss, appoint study committee
Selection committee for new vice principal	1	15	Lynn	Advise principal on membership criteria
New science textbook	3	35	Task force	Decision
Debriefing	5	10	All	Discuss

Convening. Using a chairperson or convener to lead the discussion and rotating the role throughout the membership are common procedures for providing some of the leadership functions previously discussed. Conveners have the legitimate authority to conduct the meeting. They should facilitate discussion by gatekeeping, asking brief questions, and summarizing concisely. They should move groups efficiently through their tasks, steering discussions of group processes when that appears helpful and bringing hangers-back into the discussion, though remaining conscious of the necessity of moving the group along. They should see to it that someone is recording minutes, writing on the chalkboard, and assigning tasks to individuals and subgroups. Although they should be forceful and definite, not hesitant and apologetic, conveners should be aware that their role is to facilitate, not to dominate, and they should avoid arguing down others or writing on the board only that which meets their approval.

The convener's primary duty is to remind the group of its pact to discuss certain items during the meeting and to stop at a stated time (although this pact can be altered by common consent). If the group is taking too much time on one item, the convener should point this out, asking something like, "Do you wish to subtract time from other items, cancel one or more items, extend the meeting, or what?" Conveners should not choose or even suggest a solution but should demand procedural decisions from the group. When the group is not capable of making such decisions, it is useful to discover this fact.

Over a series of meetings each group member can practice guiding the group. This procedure is most helpful if group members give the convener feedback after the meeting about how well this individual met their needs. The following guide for the convener has proved very easy to use for those with a fair amount of previous experience at conducting deliberative meetings. Conveners should think about all these tasks but should not try to use them all if the meeting is brief or attended by very few.

GUIDE FOR THE CONVENER

Before the meeting:
- Review the agenda.
- Make sure a recorder is assigned to document proceedings at the meeting.

During the meeting:
- Get it started promptly.
- Lead the group to establish priorities among items on the agenda and to specify the time to be spent on each item.
- Keep the group at the task (i.e., monitor discussion and inform the group when it strays from the agenda at hand).
- Keep the group to its time commitments for each agenda item.
- Be attuned to feelings of confusion and try to clarify them.
- At the end of each agenda item:
  Check to be sure that everyone who wanted to has had a chance to contribute to the discussion.
  Check to see whether everyone understands where the matter now stands.
  Summarize or ask someone else to summarize. Be sure the recorder records the summary.
- Take process checks whenever they seem appropriate: if a process observer is present, employ that person's services (see the guide for the process observer below).
  Check to see whether group members are satisfied with their participation.
  Check the decision making being done.
- Conduct or ask someone else to conduct a debriefing session during the last ten minutes of the meeting.

Recording Activities and Decisions. Activities initiated at a meeting are seldom completed at the same meeting, because most such issues require some sort of procedure for storage and retrieval of information at a future time. Since groups cannot rely on individual memories, recording and distributing minutes are crucial for continuity. Effective groups assign recording tasks to one individual but rotate the role throughout the membership just as the convener role is rotated. The following guide is appropriate for most school meetings but can be adapted for brief informal meetings attended by few people.

GUIDE FOR THE RECORDER

Before the meeting:
- Review the agenda and the record of previous meetings for unfinished agenda items.

- Gather materials necessary to record what happens at the meeting (e.g., pencil and paper, large newsprint and felt pens, and perhaps a video or audio recorder).

During the meeting:
- Describe the setting for the meeting (place, date, time) and list the participants.
- Copy down the agenda in the order finally agreed upon.
- During each agenda item, record the major views expressed and points of information shared.
- At the end of each agenda item, record a short summary containing decisions made, understandings achieved, and action to be taken.

After the meeting:
- Collect any newsprint used by group members during the meeting (e.g., for brainstorming ideas) and prepare to attach a typed copy to the record.
- Meet with the convener to check the clarity and completeness of the record.
- Have the records typed, duplicated, and transmitted to group members.
- Make sure a debriefing item gets on the agenda.

Facilitating Process. A group can usually improve its meetings by appointing one of its own members as process observer with functions that complement those of the convener, and if the consultant has been successful in transferring to group members the skill and responsibility for observing and analyzing their own process. The consultant can coach the process observer over several meetings by using the guide below and by helping this person become proficient in using the instruments for process observation and feedback described earlier in this chapter. Groups new to process observation and discussion might take a look at how they are doing every twenty to thirty minutes, with the observer leading a brief discussion at each process break about how satisfying and productive the meeting has been so far. The following guide suggests important tasks for the process observer. That individual should not attempt to squeeze all these tasks in at once, however, but should choose among them in accordance with the size and type of meeting.

GUIDE FOR THE PROCESS OBSERVER

Before the meeting:
- Collect and practice using appropriate observation schedules for gathering data on meetings.

- Ask the group the kind of information it would like you to look for and when you could make a process check or report back observations.

During the meeting:
- Attend to the group process rather than to the content of the work.
- Record your observations and impressions about why the meeting is going as it is. Look at communication patterns, breadth of participation, atmosphere of the group, apparent satisfaction of group members, decisions being made.
- Organize your observations so that you can convey them to the group. Coding similar observations may help to make sense out of a clutter of notes.
- Report your observations to the group when appropriate, and make sure you describe observed behavior to support your interpretations of what was happening in the group.
- If the group gets bogged down at any point, ask members to stop and discuss what is preventing them from accomplishing their purposes.

At the close of the meeting:
- Conduct a debriefing session during the last few minutes of the meeting, asking members to consider the following:
  Did we accomplish our goals for this meeting?
  Did we use our resources effectively?
  Did we avoid pitfalls such as wasting time?
- Ask members for feedback about how well you served as their process observer.

Group Agreements. Rewards and punishments come into play when groups have definite but inexplicit norms about behavior. If people believe that they will suffer rejection or punishment by failing to conform to these norms, it will be difficult for them to practice new behavior or to take creative risks unless doing so is explicitly encouraged. Hence, norms controlling collaboration, use of power, and especially openness about feelings should be made explicit if they are to have a beneficial influence on meeting effectiveness. If, for example, group members deal with feelings of boredom or frustration when they arise, the conditions that produce these feelings can be changed to create a better climate for accomplishing the tasks at hand. The following procedures are helpful for clarifying norms.

1. *Forming group agreements.* Each member states a norm or custom that he or she would like others to practice. The group dis-

cusses each proposal until it reaches consensus on several of them. Because it is important to describe the behavioral content of a proposed norm, the consultant may wish to provide samples like the two that follow.

a. For directness, I will report dissatisfactions with the way the group is going during the meeting. I will not discuss these dissatisfactions with nonmembers. If outside a regular session another member tells me of his dissatisfaction with the group, I will suggest bringing the matter before the total group at the next meeting.

b. Any member may ask for a survey at any time. The member will state what he or she wants to know from the total group, and someone else will paraphrase the request. Each person will state a position in two or three sentences. A survey is not a vote and will not bind us. A survey must be taken when it is requested and all other activities will be suspended for it.

New norms are made by establishing group agreements. Members discuss the explicit ways in which they have been rewarding and punishing one another for certain behavior in the past. They say that they want to give up some of the behavior that was maintained in that way, that they want certain other behaviors to be rewarded, and that they will join in new common patterns of encouraging and discouraging one another's behavior. It's as simple and as difficult as that.

2. *Continuing group agreements.* Periodically a group should review its agreements and discuss whether they are being kept. Agreements should not be regarded as sacrosanct. An effective group will change its agreements often and will plan actions to build commitments for new agreements. Above all, the group should be clear and explicit about what kinds of behaviors are expected.

3. *Listing inhibited and induced behaviors.* Each group member answers the following questions in writing:
a. What have I wanted to do in this group but have not done because it seemed inappropriate?
b. What have I done in this group that I didn't want to do but to which I couldn't say no?

After sharing the answers aloud, the group looks for common patterns that suggest norms. The members then make consensual agreements about which existing norms are dysfunctional and which new norms would be better. In the final step, members plan for instituting the new agreements by stating steps and dates for actions that will reflect them.

Broadening Participation

Most meetings could be more effective if all group members were encouraged to participate actively. Accurate communication demands active listening, and effective decision making requires at least minimal participation by those who will carry out decisions. Members should not have to guess what others think of their ideas; if they are to improve the way they participate in the group, they must know the effects of their remarks on others. The following procedures are useful for broadening participation.

The Chance to Listen. By time-honored democratic tradition, the right to speak is everyone's basic right at a meeting. But parliamentary rules and procedures do not ensure our right to understand what has been said. To ask a question for clarification, you are first required to "get the floor," and getting the floor is hedged about with numerous rules, restrictions, protocols, customs, and protections. By the time you have fought through the channels to be allowed to ask your question, you have had a ten-minute debate with the meeting's chairman or parliamentarian, three other speakers who were awaiting their turn at the floor have made long speeches, and the earlier speaker of whom you wished to ask your question has gone out to lunch.

One way to alter this situation is to insist during crucial periods that before someone speaks, he or she must paraphrase the person who just finished speaking. Before a proposal is decided upon, several people should paraphrase so that everyone is clear about what is being decided. The chance to listen means that you are allowed at any moment to interrupt a speaker for clarification. This procedure works, however, only when the group as a whole genuinely values mutual understanding.

In the other situations, particularly those in which the consultant is taking a strong role, the consultant can require that before one contributes to the discussion the contributor must paraphrase what the last person said. Also, it can be beneficial to ask subgroups reporting on their discussions to paraphrase or summarize the last subgroup report before making their own.

High-Talker Tap-Out. It is not uncommon to find during small-group discussions that only a small percentage of the group is involved in a large percentage of the interaction. The High-Talker Tap-Out, described in Chapter 3 under "Communication in the Subsystem," deals with this problem by evening out participation. Appoint someone to watch for anyone seizing more than a reasonable share of the discussion. When that happens, give the person a note requesting that he or she refrain from further comments on content (comments on group process may still be permitted).

Time Tokens. The Time Token, also covered in Chapter 3, is another device for dealing with people who contribute too little or too much. Distribute tokens to participants, each token to be redeemed for a specific amount of discussion time—say fifteen seconds. Participants who use up their tokens may say nothing more unless other members are willing to give some of their own. This less obtrusive procedure has certain advantages over the tap-out. It allows an exceptional contributor to overcontribute with the consent of the other group members; it makes each member's degree of participation obvious and salient, and it encourages participants to make their contributions more concise. Participants monitor their own talking and need not wonder at the meaning of certain other members' silence.

Beach Ball. Still another procedure for dealing with those who contribute too little or too much is the Beach Ball. Only the person holding the ball is permitted to speak. Others who wish to contribute must nonverbally attract the attention of the person with the ball and induce the speaker to toss it to them. Instead of a beach ball, a wad of newspaper or another harmless object can be used.

Fishbowl. Another procedure discussed earlier that employs some of the advantages of the small-group discussion within the setting of a larger meeting is the Fishbowl. As noted in Chapter 3, in this procedure a small group forms a circle within a larger group to discuss whatever is on the agenda as the other participants observe. To allow wider participation, the arrangers can provide empty chairs in the central group so that any observing members can join the discussion, with the understanding that their visits will be only temporary. The onlookers are themselves arranged in a circle so that they can all see and hear the inner group clearly and also get to a visitor's chair quickly.

This procedure is useful when those in the encircling group can see an obvious reason why those in the interior circle were selected—if, for example, they are a regularized group within the organization, if they are temporary or regular representatives of segments of the onlookers, or the like. If members of the inner group are not obviously different from the rest, assigning them special seating will usually seem unjustified.

Fishbowl seating can also be used during training on leadership or group process. Each member of the outer circle pairs with a member of the inner circle. The outsider observes the group behavior of the insider. At planned intervals, the pair gets together to discuss what is happening in the group. The outsider gives feedback while the insider makes plans about new behavior to be tried in the group.

Buzz Groups. Buzz groups are effective in diffusing participation in a large group, especially when important decisions must be made and some members hesitate to express opposing views before the entire assembly. Suppose, for example, that a faculty is at the point of setting priorities among several goals. Some teachers have stated their preferences, but most have remained silent. The chairperson may interrupt the meeting temporarily while groups of four to seven persons form to discuss the issue briefly, seeking to discover whose opinions are opposed and whether they are ready to reach agreement. When opinions are difficult to bring out, have reporters from each buzz group summarize the ideas and feelings of their groups without indicating who expressed them. Such summaries also discourage any one group of members from dominating the flow of interaction.

An Exercise to Encourage Participation. The following eight-step exercise* shows the importance of maintenance functions in a decision-making group, emphasizes the necessity of involving all members in group decision making, and gives practice in observing leadership behavior in a group. It concentrates on encouraging group members to become involved in group activities.

I. Introduce the exercise by reviewing the task and maintenance functions in a group and by telling participants that the exercise focuses on leadership behavior in a decision-making group. Inform them that there is a "best" solution to the problem, based on research, which they will learn after they have completed the first six steps.

II. Form groups of ten to fourteen members—large groups are essential in this exercise—with two additional observers for each group. Distribute copies of the following case study.

Overcoming Resistance to Change ─────────────────

In American industry, competition makes change necessary—like changing products and the way in which jobs are done. One of the most serious production problems at the Sleep-Eze pajama factory has been that production workers have resisted necessary changes. The upshot has been grievances about the piece rates that went with the new methods, high job turnover, low efficiency, restriction of output, and marked aggression against management. Despite these undesirable effects, methods and jobs must continue to change at the Sleep-Eze company if it is to remain a competitor in its field.

The main plant of the Sleep-Eze Manufacturing Corporation is in a small town in a

---

*Originally created by Hall (1969); here adapted from Johnson and Johnson (1975, pp. 39–40 and 351–54). A similar exercise appears in Johnson and Johnson's second edition (1982, pp. 68–71, 473).

southern state. The plant produces pajamas and, like most sewing plants, hires mostly women; there are about 500 women and 100 men employees. The workers are recruited from the rural areas around the town, and they usually have no industrial experience. Their average age is twenty-three, and their average education is ten years of formal schooling. Company policies in regard to labor relations are liberal and progressive. A high value has been placed on fair and open dealing with the employees, and they are encouraged to take up any problems or grievances with the management at any time. Sleep-Eze has invested both time and money in employee services, such as industrial music, health services, lunchroom facilities, and recreation programs.

The employees of Sleep-Eze work on an individual-incentive system. Piece rates are set by time study and are expressed in terms of units. One unit is equal to one minute of standard work: 60 units per hour equal the standard efficiency rating. The amount of pay received is directly proportional to the weekly average efficiency rating achieved. Thus, an operator with an average efficiency rating of 75 units an hour (25 percent more than standard) would receive 25 percent more than the base pay. The rating of every piece worker is computed every day, and the results are published in a daily record of production that is shown to every operator.

The average relearning time for workers who are transferred to a new job is eight weeks. The relearning period for experienced operators is longer than the learning for a new operator.

The company now recognizes that the time has come to make changes again. Although they are to be minor ones, changes heretofore have been met with extreme resistance by the employees involved. Such an expression as "when you make your units [standard production], they change your job" is heard all too frequently. As in the past, many operators will refuse to change, preferring to quit.

Some examples of the changes to be made are:

1. Eighteen hand pressers have formerly stacked their work in half-dozen lots on a flat piece of cardboard the size of the finished product. The new job calls for them to stack their work in half-dozen lots in a box the size of the finished product. An additional two minutes per dozen will be allowed (by the time study) for this new part of the job.
2. Thirteen pajama folders have heretofore folded coats with prefolded pants. The change calls for the pants to be folded too. An additional two minutes per dozen will be allowed.
3. Fifteen pajama examiners have been clipping threads and examining every seam. The new job calls for pulling only certain threads off and examining every seam. An average of 1.2 minutes per dozen will be subtracted from the total time.

What is the best procedure for management to take to make sure the least amount of resistance results from these needed changes? Listed below are several different ways of handling this problem. Rank these alternatives in terms of their effectiveness for bringing about the least resistance to change. Place a 1 by the most effective alternative, 2 by the second most effective, and so on through 5, the least effective. Remember that after the exercise you will be told what researchers have found to be the "best" ranking.

_____ By written memo, explain the need for a change to the employees involved, and allow extra pay for transfers to make up for the usual drop in piece rate after a change.

_____ Before any changes are made, hold meetings with large groups of the employees involved, and give a lecture explaining that the change is necessary because of competitive conditions. Have the time-study man thoroughly explain the basis of the new piece rate. Then put in the change as planned.

_____ Before any changes take place, hold meetings with large groups of the employees involved. Using demonstrations, dramatically show the need for change. Present a tentative plan for setting the new job and piece rates, and have the groups elect representatives to work with management in making the plan final.

_____ By written memo, explain the need for the change, put the change into operation, and make layoffs as necessary on the basis of efficiency.

_____ Before any changes occur, hold meetings with small groups of the employees involved. Employing demonstrations, dramatically present a tentative plan for setting the new job and piece rates, and ask everybody present to help in designing the new jobs.

III. Meet with the observers and give them copies of task- and maintenance-functions observation sheets. Explain that their role is to give their attention to the leadership and decision-making behavior of the group.

IV. Give the groups thirty minutes to arrive at a decision on the case study, indicating that their decision should be based upon accurate information and facts.

V. At the end of the thirty minutes, have every group member fill out the form below, circling the number in front of the answer chosen.

1. How much did you participate in making the decisions reached by your group? I participated:

7 Completely or thoroughly
6 A lot more than others
5 More than others
4 About as much as most others
3 Less than others
2 A lot less than others
1 Not at all

2. How satisfied did you feel with the amount and quality of your participation in reaching a joint decision? I felt:

7 Completely satisfied
6 Generally or mostly satisfied
5 A little more satisfied than dissatisfied
4 Neutral, as satisfied as dissatisfied

3 A little more dissatisfied than satisfied
2 Generally or mostly dissatisfied
1 Completely dissatisfied

3. How much responsibility would you feel for making the decision work? I would feel:

7 Completely responsible
6 Generally or mostly responsible
5 A little more responsible than irresponsible
4 Neutral, as responsible as irresponsible
3 A little more irresponsible than responsible
2 Generally or mostly irresponsible
1 Completely irresponsible

4. How committed do you feel to the decision your group made? I feel:

7 Completely committed
6 Generally or mostly committed
5 A little more committed than uncommitted
4 Neutral, as committed as uncommitted
3 A little more uncommitted than committed
2 Generally or mostly uncommitted
1 Completely uncommitted

5. How much frustration or fulfillment did you feel during the work on the decision? I felt:

7 Completely frustrated
6 Generally or mostly frustrated
5 A little more frustrated than fulfilled
4 Neutral, as frustrated as fulfilled
3 A little more fulfilled than frustrated
2 Generally or mostly fulfilled
1 Completely fulfilled

6. How good was the decision your group made? It was:

7 Completely accurate
6 Generally or mostly accurate
5 A little more accurate than inaccurate
4 Neutral, as accurate as inaccurate
3 A little more inaccurate than accurate
2 Generally or mostly inaccurate
1 Completely inaccurate

7. How much influence did you have on the group's decision? I influenced:

7   Completely or thoroughly
6   A lot more than others
5   More than others
4   About as much as others
3   Less than others
2   A lot less than others
1   Not at all

8. When members had differences of opinion, to what extent were all sides carefully listened to and the conflict directly faced and resolved?

7   Completely listened to
6   Generally or mostly listened to
5   A little more listened to than not listened to
4   Neutral, as listened to as not listened to
3   A little more not listened to than listened to
2   Generally not listened to
1   Completely not listened to

9. To what extent are you willing to work effectively with this group in the future?

7   Completely willing
6   Generally or mostly willing
5   A little more willing than unwilling
4   Neutral, as willing as unwilling
3   A little more unwilling than willing
2   Generally or mostly unwilling
1   Completely unwilling

Questions 1 through 9 above are phrased to make lessons in the exercise explicit. Examining those dimensions of group functioning, however, is also useful in diagnosing decision making in actual working groups. A Personal Reaction Index suitable for use with intact groups is available from Teleometrics International, 1755 Woodstead Court, The Woodlands, Texas 77380.

VI. On the basis of the response to question 1, divide the reaction forms from all groups into two categories as follows: place in the high-participator category any person who responded 5 or higher on the first question and in the low-participator category anyone who responded 4 or below. For each category, determine the mean response to the rest of the questions by totaling the responses for each question and dividing by the number of persons in the category. Enter the mean response in the table below.

	High participators	Low participators
Amount of satisfaction obtained from participation	_____	_____
Feelings of responsibility for making the decision work	_____	_____
Feelings of commitment to the group's decision	_____	_____
Amount of frustration felt during group meeting	_____	_____
Appraisal of decision quality	_____	_____
Influence felt on the group's decision	_____	_____
Direct dealing with conflict	_____	_____
Willingness to work with the group in the future	_____	_____

Present the results to the participants, ask each group to discuss them, and propose a theory concerning both the effects of participation in group decision making on the implementation of a decision and the effects of maintenance functions (especially encouraging participation) on group decision making. Give each group up to thirty minutes to formulate its theory.

VII. Gather all into one meeting and ask that someone from each group describe orally the group's theory. Encourage a general discussion about the importance of maintenance functions in groups. Only after this discussion, present participants with the correct ranking of alternatives presented in the case study, as below:

This case study was an actual situation studied by Coch and French in the late 1940s. From the results of their study, they considered the correct ranking to be 4, 3, 2, 5, 1. The two principles involved are (1) group discussion is more effective than lectures and memos in influencing change, and (2) belief that one is participating in making the decision leads to commitment to putting the decision into practice.

VIII. Have each group analyze the leadership behavior in its group using the information gathered by the observers. Review the leadership behavior of group members in terms of the theories just formulated in step VI. Of special interest should be information on who encouraged the participation of other members.

Stimulating Creativity

Brainstorming. Members of groups have a wealth of ideas about most problems, but their ideas too often remain untapped. The purpose of this technique is to get as many ideas as quickly as possible and to elicit ideas that would remain hidden in free-for-all criticism. The consultant can help group members identify the problem to be brainstormed and then discuss the following principles with them. (1) Groups will be more productive if they refrain from evaluating ideas at the time they are proposed; critical judgment should be suspended until all ideas are out. (2) Group production of ideas can be creative. Wild ideas should be expected, and people should build on one another's contributions. (3) The more ideas the better. Quantity is more important than quality during brainstorming.

The Self-Inquiry Method. Schindler-Rainman, Lippitt, and Cole (1975) have used the self-inquiry method to help members think through those problems that might inhibit open communication and inquiry during meetings. The steps include explaining the purpose of the activity and having members spend a few minutes alone answering these questions:

- What are some of the factors in this meeting that will inhibit free and open exchange?
- What might a member like yourself propose to reduce the barriers to openness and creativity?

The final step is having members share the results of their self-inquiry with others at the meeting. If certain factors are repeatedly identified, or if group members want to find ways of carrying out their individual proposals, group problem solving might follow.

Dealing with Hidden Agendas

Consultants will sometimes observe behavior that has nothing to do with the immediate goals of the group or with the agenda posted before the meeting. Perhaps two teachers have had a running feud for years and delight in putting each other down at every opportunity. The principal may have information members need but may be withholding it, afraid of some or other consequence. Two members may be carrying on a flirtation with each other. When these relationships are played out in meetings, we say that people are dealing with *hidden agendas,* and the energy that goes into these agendas saps energy from the public agenda of the group.

The following exercise is designed to create an awareness of hidden agendas and how they affect the accomplishment of group goals.* The exercise requires a minimum of five role players and two observers and can be done within an hour.

1. Introduce the exercise as a way to think about differences between individual and group goals. Select five role players and two observers (or multiple sets of seven with large groups).

2. Present the following instructions to all role players. Read your instructions alone, and do not reveal them to other role players. When thinking about how you will play your role, think of ways to emphasize the role while remaining natural and not overacting. You are all playing actors at a meeting of a special fact-finding committee of the Community Action Program (CAP) Governing Board in Middleburg. Your committee was established to study the suggestion that CAP revise its procedures for electing board members. At present, representatives are elected for three-year terms and must run in a general-area election. Your committee is to consider two questions: (1) What would be the best electoral basis? the general-area election? smaller district elections? even smaller neighborhood elections? (2) How long should representatives serve? The chairwoman of your committee is LaVerne Turner; she will make your recommendations to the city council.

3. Present the following instructions to individual role players:
   (a) Instructions for Carol Stone: You are a social worker with the Middleburg Department of Welfare and would like some of your welfare clients to become active in CAP. You want some of your clients elected to the CAP governing board so that your department head will be impressed with your efforts and you will have more power in CAP. Because your assignment and those of other social workers are determined by districts, you want board members to represent districts and the terms of board representatives to remain at three years.
   (b) Instructions for LaVerne Turner: You own and operate a store and are an ambitious community leader. You think poor people are lazy and want their representatives on the CAP governing board to be divided about goals so that business and professional members can run things their own way. You support citywide elections for board members so there will be more representatives without support from small-interest groups, and you support one-year terms to minimize continuity among members from poverty areas.

*Adapted from Johnson and Johnson (1975, pp. 91–92 and 365).

    (c) Instructions for Roberta Stevens: You are a mother of five on a federal benefit called Aid to Dependent Children and want a greater role for poverty representatives on the CAP governing board. You support the concept of neighborhood elections and one-year terms for board members so that more people from poverty areas get a chance to serve. You want more poverty representatives on the board to minimize the influence of business and professional members.

    (d) Instructions for Lou Haber: You are a dentist who is also on the city council. You feel that government officials and professional people know what they are doing and should have a greater voice on the CAP governing board. Your objective is a weaker group of poverty representatives on the board, so you would support general-area elections and one-year tenure for board members.

    (e) Instructions for Ed Simon: You are vice president of the chamber of commerce and are not really interested in this committee. You joined only to meet Carol Stone so you could ask her for a date. During the meeting you plan to agree with and support every point she makes. Your behavior is guided by your desire to impress her.

4. While individual role players are studying their individual instructions, tell the observers that they are to answer the following questions:
   - What is the basic goal of the group? How did each member contribute to or hinder goal accomplishment?
   - Toward what goals were the individual members working?
   - What task and maintenance behaviors were present and absent?
   - What was the group atmosphere like? Did it change from time to time?
   - Was participation and influence distributed throughout the group? If not, who dominated?
   - How far did the group get in attaining its goal?

5. Set the stage for role players by reviewing the situation and setting up the space for the meeting of the fact-finding committee. Instruct them to begin.

6. End the role playing after fifteen minutes whether or not the group has come to a decision about what to recommend to the city council. Ask observers to report, and encourage role players to join in a discussion of the observers' questions.

7. Have role players read their individual instructions with Ed reading his last. Then ask role players and observers to discuss answers to these questions:
   - How do hidden agendas affect the group; how do they affect each group member?

- What are some of the indications that hidden agendas are operating?
- Is the recognition of hidden agendas necessary to understand what is going on in the group?
- How can hidden agendas be productively handled to help in accomplishing the group's goals?

Good skill in conducting meetings is the foundation for skill in the special tasks groups undertake such as making decisions, solving problems, and resolving conflicts—matters to be discussed in later chapters.

5

Solving Problems

Problem solving is the heart of OD. All else is preparation, follow-up, or recycling.

When we speak of problems, we mean problems that concern the group or organization—for example, when members of a high school come to believe their departmental organization is not working well. Individuals have problems, too—for instance, when a teacher puzzles over the best way of describing the economy of colonial America or the best way to bring a student's attention back to academic matters. But in this book we deal with problems that require cooperation in a group or in the school as a whole.

This chapter lays out the steps of the systematic problem solving we call the *S-T-P*. The basic idea is that a problem is the gap between an unsatisfactory present situation (*S*) and a more desirable goal or target (*T*). The problem is solved (or at least reduced) when we find a path (*P*) from *S* to *T*.

AN ILLUSTRATION

The following is an instance of problem solving carried out by a very skillful group—a team of first-grade and second-grade teachers in

195

a school we will call Spartan School. The episode began when two members of the team visited another school, Palmer, and saw there a reading program they liked. We quote a memorandum* written by a member of the team:

> Two members of the 1–2 unit visited Palmer School on November 30, 1970, and returned very excited about their reading program. Others in the school became interested in learning about it, too. This type of reading program was discussed at a unit meeting. It was thought that this type of program would improve the reading in the low grades and would also bring the unit closer together. A survey was taken to see if everyone in the unit was willing to participate in planning and operating this program. Everyone was eager to begin.
>
> The entire unit worked out a schedule of classes which half the children would attend for forty minutes while half the class had reading with their classroom teacher. After a schedule had been worked out the unit broke into four subgroups to plan a scope and sequence for each class (art, PE, questioning strategy, guidance, reading games). Each teacher joined the subgroup in which she was most interested or felt she could contribute the most. We also listed some of the problems we would have to face. They were (1) extra personnel would be needed; (2) would the children be able to move? (3) we would have to switch gym periods with the 3–4 unit; (4) music schedule would have to be changed because it conflicted with the new gym schedule; and (5) auxiliary personnel would have to be willing to participate in the program.
>
> At the next meeting, we attempted to solve some of these problems. The 3–4 unit was contacted and they agreed to change gym times if we could change the music schedule. The principal—through the leadership team—scheduled ways in which needed art and ditto work would be completed for the 1–2 unit.
>
> To find the extra rooms we needed, we listed all possible choices and decided to have a first-and-second grade teacher move to the rooms next door, sharing the room with the teachers there. Because of the lower class numbers this was possible. This left two classrooms free to hold Art, reading games and two other groups. This also answered the question of whether children can move to other parts of the school. The classes they would move to will be right next door, and it was felt that the children could handle this.
>
> To find the extra personnel, parents were contacted and enough volunteered to cover the classes. The classes would be on questioning strategies, group counseling, reading games, art, and PE. The principal agreed to take part in the PE program.
>
> A meeting for everyone involved in the program was held on Friday (workday) at 10:00 A.M. The entire program was explained and the group

*Quoted from Schmuck, Murray, Smith, Schwartz, and M. Runkel (1975, pp. 89–90).

was then divided into subgroups to discuss different subjects each would cover.

In essence, this new 1–2 program, which came to be known as the *back-to-back reading program*, allowed each teacher to focus on reading with one half of the class, while the other half was engaged in another, interesting activity with a large group. The program made use of the previously untapped resources of teachers, parents, auxiliary staff, and the principal. An article describing this program, complete with a picture of the principal teaching PE to six and seven-year-olds, appeared in the local newspaper.

That episode illustrates several features of good problem solving. It illustrates collaborative goal setting and commitment: "A survey was taken to see if everyone in the unit was willing to participate in planning and operating the program." That is, the group determined whether every individual accepted the goal of putting the new reading program into effect. The writer of the memorandum noted the result: "Everyone was eager to begin." The next sentence indicates commitment: "The entire unit worked out a schedule of classes. . . ."

The episode illustrates how the team gathered information and other resources, one of the metaskills described in Chapter 1. The 1–2 unit gathered information from outside when two of its members visited Palmer School to see what was going on there. The unit used resources from outside again when "the program made use of previously untapped resources of . . . parents. . . . " And the unit called upon resources outside itself but within the school: "The 3–4 unit . . . agreed to change gym times." In general, the unit made use of the "untapped resources of teachers, . . . auxiliary staff, and the principal." The unit also made discriminating use of its own internal resources: "Each teacher joined the subgroup in which she was most interested or felt she could contribute the most."

The episode illustrates how an effective group explicitly anticipates obstacles: "We also listed some of the problems we would have to face." And it shows how the unit acted to deal with those obstacles: "we attempted to solve some of these problems. The 3–4 unit was contacted. . . . "

The episode illustrates collaborative coordination: The "program was discussed at a unit meeting." The tasks necessary to reduce obstacles were planned in the group. Then, though the memorandum does not say so, the various tasks were assigned to individuals. The unit used its meeting on the Friday workday to be sure everything was ready to go. The writer of the memorandum shows the group's explicit attention to maintaining its collaborative norm when she writes, "It was thought that this type of program would . . . bring the unit closer together."

The episode illustrates skill in conducting meetings (see Chapter 4): "After a schedule had been worked out, the unit broke into subgroups to plan a scope and sequence . . ." and "a survey was taken. . . . "

The episode illustrates another metaskill: mobilizing synergistic action. The memorandum says the unit "attempted" to reduce obstacles, and it is clear that its actions succeeded in doing so. "The 3–4 unit . . . agreed . . . ," "the principal agreed . . . ," "the principal . . . scheduled ways . . . ," "parents were contacted and enough volunteered . . . ," and rooms were rescheduled.

The episode illustrates the group's attention to motive satisfaction; it celebrates its achievement: "An article . . . appeared in the local newspaper."

The episode shows that a problem is not solved at one sitting. The unit's solution took shape as it planned its adaptation of Palmer's reading program to Spartan School, as it took sequential actions to reduce the obstacles it foresaw, and as it moved the new program into actual operation.

Finally, the episode shows that problem solving does not always begin with a formal review of "what problems do we have?" In this case, when it sent two of its members to Palmer School, the group was simply exhibiting its routine (but lively) metaskill of gathering information that might be useful. These two members liked the reading program they saw at Palmer better than the one they had been using at Spartan. Upon discussing the discrepancy between the existing program's results and those they expected from the Palmer program, the members of the 1–2 unit decided that the improvement would be great enough to justify considerable effort. They then chose the discrepancy as a problem and Palmer's program as their target.

THEORY

Let's begin our theoretical discussion with a very brief description of the *S-T-P* procedure for solving problems in groups. We will go into detail later in the chapter.

1. *Agree on the problem.* Effective problem-processing demands attention to two kinds of questions at the outset: Where are we now (the situation, *S*)? and Where do we want to be (target, *T*)? An effective group must reach a working agreement early about what constitutes its *S* and *T*. At the same time, the effective group realizes that agreements about both the *S* and *T* are inevitably temporary. Situations do not stand still; targets move into new definitions as they are approached. Further, as a group

reaches new clarity about the problem that brought it together, its members become aware of problems they had not thought about earlier. The process is a natural one in human awareness and thinking.

2. *Generate alternative paths.* The group chooses a target and tries to think of steps or paths or plans (*P*) to get from the existing situation (*S*) to the target (*T*). Brainstorming is often used in this phase. This is the phase (though it may also occur earlier or later) in which a group typically envisions a benefit from reaching deeper into its members' personal knowledge and resources or from reaching outside itself for information and resources. A skillful group can begin at any point and then oscillate among *S*, *T*, and *P* in its discussions.

3. *List helping and hindering forces.* Once the group has agreed firmly on the desirability and feasibility of a target (and by considering *P*s helps to clarify the desirability and feasibility), it can move into considering the forces that will work for and against its efforts. Among the kinds of helping forces groups sometimes name are publicly announced support from certain authorities, support from interfacing groups, some available money, some time already set aside for problem solving, some people already committed to the target, and some necessary skills already existing in the group. Among the kinds of hindering forces sometimes named are a debilitating history, political blocks, anticipated lack of support, anticipation of too much cost of change, and lack of knowledge or skill.

4. *Choose action steps.* The group next chooses the hindering forces that seem feasible to reduce and generates ideas for reducing them. The group agrees on the forces to be attacked first and on the best steps to use from among those proposed. Again, brainstorming is useful to generate ideas.

5. *Act.* This is the phase of mobilizing for committed action. The group assigns people to the various agreed-upon actions and assigns schedules.

6. *Monitor and recycle.* Meetings are scheduled at which progress will be reviewed. Working toward a target tests how well the situation has been understood.

That is the scheme in brief.

All schools deal with problems in one way or another, but our observations convince us that most schools use up a great deal of energy unproductively. Schools often flounder through problems instead of using systematic procedures that save time. Schools sometimes put the wrong people to work: they give a problem to a group when almost everyone is willing to accept a solution chosen by the principal or the school's secretary, or, conversely, the principal imposes a solution that actually requires the initiative and commitment of groups. Schools sometimes undertake to solve a problem within the school that cannot be solved there. They sometimes expect to solve a problem once and for all when in fact work on the problem must be recycled year after year. Schools sometimes use methods that alleviate one problem only to make others worse. Finally, schools often engage in "fire-fighting"—they try to cope with a great many very difficult problems at the same time by trying to stop-gap one after another. All those ways of coping are understandable, but the waste of effort is prodigious. A sustained problem-solving capacity requires ways of working that avoid those wastes and that enable participants to devote most of their energy to the rewarding parts of their jobs.

Converting Frustrations into Problems

A problem is more than a frustration. Some frustrations go away by themselves, and some remain but only as minor irritations. Part of the problem-solving skill is the judicious selection of frustrations to be made into problems. In our view, people are likely to flounder in frustration interminably until they explicitly conceive a problem as a gap between a specified undesirable present situation (What do I want to get away from?) and a more desirable specified future state of affairs (Where do I want to go?).

When we listen to educators discuss their frustrations, we hear them say or imply that they would prefer something to be different. They sound as if they find something unpleasant about the current state of affairs and as if they believe some alternative state of affairs would be more pleasant. Often, however, they are not able to specify the features of that improved state of affairs. From our point of view, educators who primarily complain about the present without conceiving a better alternative have not yet conceived a problem and are therefore not ready to solve a problem.

Life is full of frustrations. You may not enjoy driving ten miles to work every morning, but if you accept the commuting as a reasonable price for living in a neighborhood you want to live in, it is not a "problem" in our sense, not something you are motivated to *solve*. Since our topic is solving problems, we want a concept that opens the door to doing something that is new.

We use the word *problem* to mean a discrepancy between a present state of affairs and a more preferred state of affairs—sufficiently more preferred that one is ready to spend some energy to get there. Without the two parts—the current situation and the more desirable one—no problem has been specified. Frustration, irritation, anger, or confusion is often a feature of a problem—part of the present state of affairs—but it is not in itself a problem.

Usually, people feel frustration, irritation, or anger before they can put a discrepancy into words, because those feelings are typical symptoms of underlying problems. But not all disgruntlements are worth converting into problems. Most of us, almost without thinking, make a judgment about whether a frustration is worth the energy required to remove it or whether the frustration will remove itself in the natural course of events.

Often, a frustration does indeed signal a problem worth working on. It is a profitable habit to give at least a little thought to any feeling of frustration that does not go away in a few minutes or an hour to see whether an important problem might be lurking under it. It may be that the source of the frustration is not the condition most evident to the eye when the frustration arises. It may be that a problem more worth working on lies elsewhere. For instance, if a teacher feels frustrated by the application of a school policy and is unwilling to discuss it with the principal, the problem worth working on may be not the teacher's unwillingness to confront the principal, but rather the absence of a school norm enabling the teachers to feel free to describe their frustrations to the principal. That is, while the feeling of frustration itself, being a psychological condition, lies within the teacher, the proper place to conceive and solve the problem may lie in the interpersonal skills and norms of the school staff.

Finally, it should be clear that in our view the problem lies inside people's heads, not in the real world. When someone says that a school has problems, to us that means some people in the school react to the state of affairs there by wishing they were different. But different individuals in the school may have very different images in their heads of the present state of affairs, the more desirable state, and the steps necessary to move from the one state to the other. The implication is obvious; one of the first steps in problem solving is to ascertain with some precision the images the people concerned have of the present state of affairs and the alternatives.

School participants perceive a problem—in our use of the term—when they perceive a discrepancy between what they diagnose to be actually happening in the here and now and what they would prefer to be happening in the future. Whatever the degree of discrepancy, optimal problem solving occurs as those who perceive troubles are motivated to do something productive about them by designing proposals and then taking action. Along with awareness of a discrepancy, "having a problem" also means contemplating change and taking action. The person or group with a problem is energized to move from the present state of affairs to a happier, more satisfying state.

From this point of view, a problem has three aspects: the present situation, the valued state or target, and the proposals or paths that might be taken to reduce the discrepancy between the present and the desired states. Any of the three aspects may be unclear when school participants first feel a frustration. A problem begins to take shape when participants begin to conceptualize situations and targets and explain their images of them to one another. Participants become energized when they can conceive alternative proposals to bring the situation closer to the target. Achieving clarity about the three aspects of problem solving is necessary for effective group action.

Rationality and Creativity

Many observers of human problem solving are impressed with individuals' insights—the sudden leaps to valid solutions that seem to short-cut all rationality. Indeed, the brain seems to work in two fairly distinct ways. One is logical, analytic, systematic, rational, and usually verbal. The other is the intuitive, insightful, quick apperception of relationships, patterns, and recombinations, usually in a nonverbal mode— the kind of cerebration we usually associate with art and invention. It is not much of an overstatement to say that we would waste the creativity and speed of half the brain if we required *individuals* to work at problems only systematically, rationally, and verbally. For that reason, a systematic procedure for solving problems in a group should allow some time for individual intuition—for example, a period for brainstorming.

In schools, problem solving that affects the school can benefit immensely from the intuitions and insights of individuals. If those capacities are to be brought out, individuals must be given time to be creative without being held down to rationality, ritual, or "reality." If those capabilities are to be salvaged for use by the group, interpersonal skills and group skills must be used delicately to prevent the creative ideas from being submerged in conformity to whatever thinking is most evident in the group at the moment.

But solutions that depend for their success on the group or the school as a whole cannot be reached merely by bringing out individual creativity, no matter how brilliant it may be. Chaos results when one person wonders aloud whether there is a problem worth working on, another says the problem is how to oil the present mechanism, another urges throwing away that mechanism, another advocates an action step she thinks is likely to have pay-off regardless of what the problem is, another asks whether there is consensus on a goal, another asks whether the right people are represented at the meeting, and so on. Chaos grows when all those cross-currents occur while participants are unaware that they are occurring. Often, many members of a meeting assume that all the others are talking about the same part of the problem-working process without checking whether that is true. The result is that many of the remarks sound like nonsense.

At some point, individuals must be able to direct their actions toward a common goal, taking steps in unison toward it. At some point, therefore, there must be time for every group member to come to understand the images others see and to feel familiar with them. There must be time for members of the group to compare images and explore their potentialities. There must be time to agree on the advantages and disadvantages of proposed solutions and on the best bets. There must be time, too, to ascertain the willingness of every member to commit the energy and take the risks necessary to make the adopted solution work.

A Vicious Circle

Many schools encounter frustrations and impediments to their work: low achievement scores, uninspired teaching, decreasing tax bases, poverty in the community, desegregation, demographic shifts, ethnicity mixes, mobility and attrition among students and staff, over-large districts and schools, decay of facilities, politicization of the community, crime among youth, dropouts, truancy, drug abuse, and so on. But some schools are burdened with more of those difficulties at any one time and in more severe degrees than others. Most urban schools, for example, contain larger stockpiles of troubles from which their members can extract problems than do most nonurban schools.

When troubles pile up and the stew of difficulties becomes so constant, intrusive, and demanding that it tears out the vitals of the school's work, teachers and administrators become distraught, anxious, and bone weary. Even the constant perplexity about the difficulties that should be chosen as problems is anxiety-provoking and wearing. Teachers' energies are drawn away from their teaching into worrying and fire-fighting. They have little energy left for the demanding task of reconceiving their stresses as problems about which something might be done.

Under stress and enervation, members of schools often turn in one of two directions. One reaction is to stop taking action and to become deeply pessimistic and cynical about the possibility of fruitful change. It is not surprising that teachers, in particular, should react that way. Often, they have suffered from too much fruitless upheaval. Superintendents declare new policies, programs, and procedures and appoint new functionaries. Consultants come in and demand teachers' time for a myriad of projects. Teachers' associations and unions make demands for new rules they think will reduce stress on teachers, but the new rules often add other stresses. Parental groups add their demands, and so it goes. And too often the efforts make no difference. Teachers come to look upon any new proposal as almost certain only to add to their burdens and to drain their energies without any benefit. They want desperately to be left alone. Posing a problem to be worked on becomes a threat, not an opportunity.

The other frequent response to stress and enervation is to demand miracles from outside helpers. Some educators still believe that a half-million-dollar project will cure their woes with little effort on their own part. Or they may hire in consultants, but, mindful of consultants in the past who have drained their energies to no profit, say to the new consultants, in effect, "Show results quickly or leave." The attitude is understandable, but unrealistic nevertheless.

Both reactions to stress and enervation lead to further abortive efforts. Neither sluggish participation in a new project nor unrealistic demands upon it improves the likelihood of its success. And the projects that fail simply add to the burden of difficulties urban educators suffer. The vicious circle feeds upon itself; the difficulties mount and become harder and harder to alleviate.

This is not the place to paint all the details in their terrible colors. Still, we take space for one brief example of the vicious circle. In the more stressful school districts, superintendents often have rather brief tenure. They burn out and look for easier jobs, or they make enemies during their heroic efforts to improve matters, and those enemies engineer their expulsion. (In Oakland, one superintendent's tenure was cut short by assassination.) When a superintendent goes, the school board looks for a new superintendent who can clean the Augean stables that the previous one could not. The new superintendent declares a new policy, reorganizes the district's personnel, and imposes new programs of work—typically curricular improvement programs. Many of the teachers, however, have seen all this happen before. They remember putting in a lot of hard work in the past only to find their jobs as difficult as ever. Or perhaps they remember a program that was improving matters and their dejection when a new superintendent came in, threw out the program under way, and started a new one. The teachers protect themselves against a repetition of that experience. They obey the new superintendent superficially, but spend the least energy possible. The new program is not their idea anyway, and they have little stake in its success. Many teachers, intentionally or unintentionally, sabotage the program by doing too little too late. Some teachers persuade others to join the resistance. The program fails. Some teachers who were in favor of the program decide, "You can't do anything worth while around here. There are too many old fuddy-duddies." They look for jobs elsewhere. Some who must stay in the city retreat to their classrooms and join the resistance when the next new program comes along. The superintendent leaves, and a new debilitating cycle begins.

Breaking the Vicious Circle

Luckily, schools are loosely coupled systems. That is, action in one part of the school does not immediately or necessarily produce a specified action in another part. Connections are only probabilistic. Some probabilities are rather high, such as the probability that absence lists will reach the office by 9 A.M. if the principal orders them to be there by then. Other probabilities are rather low, such as the probability that teachers will observe one another's teaching and give advice for improvement if the principal suggests that it would be a good idea. Some probabilities are rather high if a time lag is allowed. For example, some time usually elapses between the decision to adopt a new curriculum and its first actual use in a class. The result of the loose coupling is that not all members of a school get caught in the vicious circle to the same degree or at the same time. At any one time, some members of the school may be enjoying a respite off at the edge of the main vortex of turmoil.

Adding to the dispersing effect of the loose coupling is the natural variability in the amount of threat that different individuals perceive from the vicious circle. Persons who perceive less threat will be less immobilized than persons who perceive more. Some members may even perceive more opportunity than threat, finding stimulation where others find incapacitating confusion. In sum, though aspects of the vicious circle may immobilize some or even most, others may remain able to act with deliberation, and still others may be aroused to new energy.

Even though the school as a whole may be unready to begin energetic problem solving, smaller efforts can begin with subsystems containing individuals who are more ready. Here is a list of some signs to look for:

1. Look for school participants with some time and energy who are willing to discuss their troubles and whether fruitful problems might be built from them.
2. Look for administrators, in particular, who realize that short projects will only continue to waste their energy and who are ready to plan at least a year ahead and to bear their troubles as best they can in the meantime.
3. Look for teachers who have not yet succumbed to pessimism

and cynicism and who still have energy. Often they are the newer teachers.

4. Look for those who can be motivated by a vision of joint achievement, greater control over their work, and camaraderie.

5. Look for those who understand that schools are complex systems with complex dynamics and that the norms in work groups are the key to productivity and change.

6. Look for those who have faith that there must be a better method of dealing with difficulties than blundering through.

7. Look for those who know that school improvement will require extra and sustained energy, that some kinds of change will require skills they do not now have, and that some ways of doing things now disapproved must become approved if they are to shake loose from an old way and lay the basis of a new one.

Those seven signs reveal opportunities within the school. They indicate places where problem solving can usually start with a fairly good chance of gaining a beachhead, even though the school as a whole may be unready to muster all its members for a sustained and concerted attack upon a major problem. If a small project by one subsystem succeeds, it can do a good deal to counter pessimism in other parts of the school or district.

GATHERING DATA ABOUT PROBLEM SOLVING

Because picking the right problems and finding solutions to them is the heart of OD, every skill we describe in this book helps in problem solving. Gathering data about any of the skills is a way of gathering data about an aspect of problem solving. For that reason, the methods of gathering data offered in other chapters are good diagnostics for problem solving. Chapter 3 gives ways of ascertaining whether the communicative norms in the group or school are appropriate to support good problem solving, Chapter 4 describes ways of gathering data about a group's effectiveness in problem-solving meetings, Chapter 6 describes ways of assessing the decision-making skills necessary to choose paths toward targets, and Chapter 7 presents ways of assessing a school's readiness to deal with the conflicts that arise as coordination is sought. Chapter 9 on diagnosis offers ways of assessing a school's readiness to tackle problems.

It will suffice here to present two more problem-solving aids. The following is another set of interview questions. You might use them for a quick reconnaissance among members of a school or group.

Interview Questions for Finding Problems _____

1. What are some things you would like to see this school working toward that it isn't doing now?

_____

_____

2. [If named something:] Which staff members do you think could help accomplish these things?

_____   _____

_____   _____

3. Have you received any information recently about your work or about the school that you found surprising? [Yes, no] [If yes] Please describe one or two such kinds of information:

_____

_____

4. To make things operate more effectively, which people do you think ought to work together more closely? [Write names. Show each cluster of names the respondent says should work more closely together by encircling that cluster.]

_____   _____

_____   _____

_____   _____

5. What are some aspects of the current situation in the school that need changing?

_____

_____

_____

6. What are some target conditions that you would like to see your staff attempt to achieve?

_____

_____

_____

_____

7. Do you have any proposals for action in mind right now for moving toward those targets?

_____

_____

_____

In the heat of solving problems, groups often become strongly task oriented. The following is a brief questionnaire that might be useful to help a group stand back and examine its group dynamics.

Questions to Check on Group Effectiveness _____

You have been working on a task. Like an automobile, a group needs maintenance. While working on a task, a group needs to stop occasionally to be explicit about its _interpersonal processes_. Please circle one number in each of the following scales.

What I say is prized and valued here.	6	5	4	3	2	1	What I say is being ignored here.
Our group is falling into traps.	6	5	4	3	2	1	Our group is avoiding traps.
I have participated often.	6	5	4	3	2	1	I have participated very little.

Discuss your responses on the three scales with the group. Try to be helpful. You will tend to be *helpful* when you are specific (e.g., "I felt valued by you, John, because you often asked me to say more when I spoke," or "An example of when I thought we fell into a trap was . . . ," or "I felt put down when you . . . "). You will tend to be *unhelpful* if you are general and evaluative (e.g., "You're the kind of person who puts people down," or "This group isn't working well," or "This group is the greatest I've ever been in").

TWO EXAMPLES OF SYSTEMATIC PROBLEM SOLVING

This section presents two examples of how groups in schools use systematic problem solving. We reproduce here actual records of group work made by teachers who had received five days of training, mostly in communication skills, group and intergroup exercises, and problem solving. About half of the five-day period was devoted to the problem-solving procedure. We reproduce the participants' own words so that you can see how ideas come out in actual instances.

Clarifying the Principal's Role

This example is taken from the newsprint records kept by a team of teachers and their principal in an elementary school. Although the statements below are just some of those the group wrote on the newsprint, they do include the agreements that enabled the group to move from stage to stage.

Stage 1. Specifying the Problem

Where we are: Lack of clarity in the role of the principal.
Where we want to be: We (the staff) know where the principal stands, and he knows where we stand.
Our task: To clarify the role of the principal.

Stage 2. Listing Helping and Hindering Forces

Forces that are helping us move toward our target:
1. Many of the staff are open and want to know about the principal's philosophy.
2. The staff's willingness to be open is enhanced by our new communication skills.
3. The principal is willing to clarify his philosophy and his role.

Forces that are blocking our movement toward where we want to be:
1. Lack of time.
2. Some staff members' willingness to be the principal's "mouthpiece" and the feeling that he does nothing to discourage this.
3. Lack of complete openness of the staff, including the principal.
4. Confusion about our own roles.

Stage 3. Specifying Multiple Solutions

The most important ideas that we brainstormed were as follows:
1. We need more time for process and problem-solving meetings
2. We need to practice openness.
3. We should let the principal know if we like something he is doing.
4. We should let the principal know if we do not like what he is doing.
5. We want the principal to give us feedback.
6. We need to clarify roles and expectations of each other and with the kids.

You must do some hunting to find the correspondences between the items in one stage and those in earlier stages. For example, Item 1 in Stage 4 (below) says, "The principal will make a statement to the staff. . . ." That plan for action takes advantage of Helping Force 1 under Stage 2 above: "Many of the staff . . . want to know about the principal's philosophy." By getting the word directly from the principal, the plan reduces Hindering Force 2 in Stage 2: "Some staff members' willingness to be the principal's 'mouthpiece'. . . ." Because it says the staff will "interact with" the principal, it offers a chance for Solution 2 in Stage 3 to operate: "We need to practice openness." And it carries forward the task the group set for itself in Stage 1: "To clarify the role of the principal."

In Stage 4, you will note that the group permitted discussions of the principal's role to arise several times. Members were realistic about recycling.

Stage 4. Planning for Action

Our intended actions, developed from elaborations on our brainstormed ideas, are as follows:

1. The principal will make a statement to the staff about his educational philosophy and role expectations, and the staff will have a chance to interact with him. Observers [names specified] will record the interaction and check on the communication processes between the principal and staff. All will evaluate the process and progress at the meeting. These actions will occur during our forthcoming workshop.
2. During the last week of summer vacation, we will go to Mabel's place on the Klakitaw River for a debriefing and planning session after the leaders' workshop. The whole staff is invited.
3. A school handbook will be written with everyone participating. It will contain:

   a. Role descriptions.
   b. A statement of how we hope to operate (openness).
   c. The principal's philosophy and expectations.
   d. Each group's summary of what it did and felt during this workshop.
   e. Operational procedures.
   It should be flexible and changeable and written in behavioral terms.
4. A teacher's workday in the fall (statewide In-service Day) will be used to do follow-up consultation with the whole staff in communication with the help of a few outside consultants—preferably in some location away from the school.
5. During the first week of school we will conduct a day of orientation for children and:
   a. Take students on a tour of the total building (nothing, including faculty areas, will be out of bounds).
   b. Introduce all the staff to students.
   c. Provide some heterogeneous group activity (mixed-grade groups) for students.
6. On the first day of school, the students, interested parents, and staff will report to the gym for an hour of welcome.
7. Following all staff meetings, communication and procedural matters will be checked by:
   a. Having a couple of people observe the meeting and report back on how we did.
   b. Including total staff in staff meetings.
   c. Training students to answer the phone and to greet visitors.
8. All students will be sent home at lunchtime on the last Friday of each month. Staff will bring sack lunches, eat together, and practice sharing communication skills and ideas. On those days all students will leave school at the same time.
9. One meeting a month will be set aside for sharing ideas, innovations, and failures. Seating will be arranged to prevent staff teams from isolating themselves.

Stage 5. Anticipating Obstacles

[The group presented the information produced above to the rest of the staff and asked for reactions and criticisms.]

Stage 6. Taking Action

[The staff implemented Action-Plan 7 (evaluating staff meetings) immediately. They also formed several ad hoc groups to develop the other plans and to try them out.]

Stage 7. Evaluating

[Most of the ideas for action had built-in evaluation plans. The staff was careful to allow time for evaluation as each sequence of actions unfolded during the school year.]

Sharing Strengths and Encouraging Variety

This example is taken from the problem-solving activities of a group of teachers attempting to move from teaching in self-contained classrooms to teaching in teams. The experience of this group reinforces our admonition not to give up when things don't seem to be going according to plan. For a time, the group seemed to have stalled after Stage 5, but the returning consultants helped the group proceed to action and evaluation.

Stage 1. Specifying the Problem

Situation: Lack of established procedures for sharing innovative ideas and supporting one another in experimentation. *Target:* We shall have adequate procedures for developing, sharing, supporting, and protecting innovations.

Stage 2. Listing Helping and Hindering Forces

Facilitating forces: (1) physical plant conducive to sharing within units, (2) staff is willing to try new things, (3) principal encourages innovation, (4) new staff is willing and enthusiastic, (5) young staff has good ideas, (6) interns and others have experiences that will bring in outside ideas, (7) experienced staff is supporting changes and participating in them, (8) there is ready access to equipment that can be used for innovations, (9) there is willingness to know and communicate because of our new staffing arrangements (esprit de corps), (10) shared experiences brought us together during planning weeks, (11) kids serve as communication channels for ideas, (12) kids are very open to new experiences and sharing them, (13) some parents are very supportive, and (14) consultants work directly with students.

Restraining forces: (1) noise carries, (2) units are physically cut off from one another, (3) three of four units (or unit rooms) are separated, (4) some kids resist sharing, (5) facilities are overcrowded, (6) procedures for flexible use of space have not been worked out, (7) there is limited access to consultants for planning and execution, (8) failure to pass budget threatens many contracts (e.g., consultants and interns), (9) funds are lacking for supplies and field trips, and (10) the fear of a lack of supplies sometimes leads to hoarding. [In addition to the above, the group listed the most important restraining forces in this order:]

1. Lack of procedures for sharing knowledge between and within units about what each teacher has done, can do, and wants to do regarding innovations.
2. Competition and a lack of procedures for seeking support result in feelings of inadequacy, mistrust, and failure among staff members.
3. Teachers feel inadequate to innovate and are forced to fall back on traditional methods when confronted with large groups of students.
4. Some parents lack a view of the total picture at the school, and they feel

apart from what we are doing; consequently, teachers fear parental nonacceptance.

Stage 3. Specifying Multiple Solutions

[The group brainstormed ideas for overcoming each of the most important restraining forces.]

Stage 4. Planning for Action

[The group reviewed its list of solutions, discarding many ideas and categorizing the rest as follows.]

1. Procedures for sharing knowledge:
   a. Ideas for immediate action: (1) take a survey at a staff meeting of each person's desires and strengths, (2) set up a card file of past and future ideas for innovations, and (3) set up tours. Ensure that staff members get to walk through the building to all rooms regularly.
   b. Ideas for future committee action: (1) make a list of strengths and have staff members put a check by the ones they feel they possess, (2) release each teacher once each week to go around and visit other classes (i.e., observe and interact), (3) have everyone tack a big sheet of newsprint up with his own strengths and hopes, (4) allow each person to add to other lists by writing perceptions of others' strengths, (5) put the lists into a file of "resources" in our building, (6) share lists stating "what I feel like doing today," (7) keep a record of what is being done (include critiques), (8) update the outside resource file, and (9) use outside resource people more often.
   c. Ideas for future individual or team action: (1) inform your team leader about what you have done, can do, want to do, (2) establish time at each team meeting for sharing such information, (3) set up memory refreshers throughout the year, (4) send your students to find out what is going on elsewhere in building, (5) use intercom to invite others to visit your lesson, (6) create central displays about what is going on in your team, (7) tape record events and let others listen, (8) make posters advertising all events, (9) encourage classes to visit other classrooms, and (10) set up and exchange student programs within and between teams.
2. Procedures for seeking support, decreasing competition, and reducing feelings of inadequacy, mistrust, or failure:
   a. Ideas for immediate action: (1) use direct expression of feelings, (2) acknowledge own or others' feelings, (3) hold brainstorming sessions on these problems, (4) wear signs saying how you are feeling, (5) keep signs saying "I need support," and wear them when you do, (6) wear button with smile on one side and frown on the other, and (7) help staff to share crazy ideas.
   b. Ideas for future committee action: (1) arrange staff parties, (2) arrange demonstrations by faculty (e.g., of lessons), (3) plan a trust-building day, and (4) use student questionnaire on feelings and evaluation.

    c. Ideas for future individual or team action: (1) establish positive reinforcement outside building, (2) eat right, get sleep, (3) survey periodically for feelings, (4) know own strengths and limitations, (5) give positive reinforcement to your colleagues, (6) accept others' limitations, (7) work together in unit groups, (8) let others accept you—be open-minded, (9) openly express feelings, (10) try to get success from apparent failure, (11) talk about your failures and weaknesses, (12) avoid secrecy, (13) share feelings with your team leader, (14) paraphrase, describe behavior, and check impressions, (15) share long-range plans across units, (16) establish as a goal the expression of a certain number of statements about your feelings, and (17) share your feelings with principal and auxiliary staff.

3. Ways to facilitate innovations with large groups and overcome teachers' feelings of inadequacy:
    a. Ideas for future committee action: (1) set up a committee to implement the use of student helpers, (2) set up procedures for using parent volunteer groups, and pass them around the building for additional information, (3) talk to people at other schools doing similar things, (4) enlist help of student teachers, university students, and high school students for large meetings, and (5) observe other large groups.
    b. Ideas for future individual or team action: (1) use the skills of a partner, (2) plan with auxiliary staff to cooperate during large meetings, (3) use rooms as research centers, (4) strive to use new materials, (5) forget that you are a teacher, (6) use district coordinators, (7) try one new method each week, (8) visit the Curriculum Materials Center more often, (9) look for successes, point them out to your colleagues, and praise one another, (10) appreciate individual differences among teachers (e.g., let some work with large groups and some with small), (11) value student concerns and student feedback, (12) use large groups to free staff, (13) remove or rearrange furniture, (14) have principal help teachers, (15) use machines, (16) read, (17) lengthen school day, (18) innovate in area where you are comfortable, (19) teach outdoors, and (20) have a problem-sharing session each week.

4. Ways to increase the support of parents:
    a. Ideas for immediate action: (1) evidence a lack of phoniness, (2) complete parent questionnaires, and (3) consider the parent knows something about his child.
    b. Ideas for future committee action: (1) set up newsletters, (2) set up conferences (have parents come to school for feedback about students), (3) use room helpers, (4) hold an open house, (5) establish a teacher-parent social time (parents bring nonparents), (6) present precise information about student progress to parents, (7) hold parent workshops, (8) work cooperatively with Education Center in framing news items for the press, (9) plan carefully for meeting with parents (e.g., work in role-playing situations with others and critique, meet with public during staff meeting, and establish sessions in which teachers role-play parents and parents role-play teachers),

(10) keep school facilities open for community use during nonschool hours, (11) do not combine too many activities in one parent-teacher meeting, (12) plan for greater informality at PTA meetings, and (13) plan Dad's Night and Mom's Night.

c. Ideas for future individual or team action: (1) invite parents to observe special projects, (2) encourage school visits any time and at special times, (3) make phone calls to children's homes when all is going well, (4) ask parents for suggestions and use them, (5) plan teacher-parent-team potlucks, (6) send room newsletters home, (7) send notices about new team planning, (8) be open with children, (9) have kids write letters to parents, (10) establish school newspaper, (11) take an interest in parents' interests, (12) have a parent "share day," (13) learn to live with parental nonacceptance, and (14) encourage team mothers to meet.

Stage 5. Anticipating Obstacles

[Unfortunately, members of this group neglected to anticipate the barriers to carrying out their plans. Excited and committed to following up their ideas, they did not recognize the many constraints that would hold them back when school began, with the result that most of the ideas they developed were either lost or placed in suspended animation. As it happened, they had written their ideas in a form they could retain, so later in the school year they were able to recapture many of these plans and use them effectively.]

Stage 6. Taking Action

[The group wrote out its plans on ditto masters, assembled booklets for each staff member, and described its work to the rest of the staff at a special meeting.]

Stage 7. Evaluating

[This stage received scant attention. During the follow-up OD consultation in the fall, the group reconvened to assess the current state of its problems. Several members were too busy to attend; the remaining members attempted to act on some of the simpler plans, but they, too, soon abandoned the task. Seven months later, however, the school staff was ready to recoup many of the resources they had discovered during the summer. Staff members spent a good part of one Saturday in April reaffirming the goals they felt to be most urgent and finding others with whom to collaborate in planning for action. For a description of the microdesign used on that Saturday, see the section headed "The Charismatic Day" in Chapter 2.]

SOLVING PROBLEMS WITH THE *S-T-P*

Good problem solving requires readiness. Before starting actual problem solving, you may wish to use survey-data-feedback to provoke discussion and focus attention, thereby heightening readiness. The technique is explained in Chapters 2 and 8.

The group should have reasonable skill in communicating, some skill at watching its own processes in meetings, and some hope of agreeing on goals. Before asking the group to undertake systematically to solve a serious problem, you may find it advantageous to improve some of those conditions or skills (already discussed in Chapters 3 and 4). Systematic problem solving will certainly go badly if the group is split into distrustful or hostile factions. If it is, you will probably want to use one of the methods described in Chapter 7 for reducing conflict. With reasonable readiness, however, and a little luck, systematic problem solving can be successful, invigorating, and fun.

In our previous problem-solving examples we labeled the stages, and for convenience we will use the same labels here. But be warned that problem solving is not neatly sequential. As we go along, we will call attention to the recycling—the oscillating between one subtask and another—that is likely to occur. Working on problems is a juggling act that has been nicely described by Cohen, March, and Olsen (1972, p. 2): "An organization is a collection of choices looking for problems, issues and feelings looking for decision situations in which they might be aired, solutions looking for issues to which they might be the answer, and decision makers looking for work."

Nevertheless, the stage labels help participants to stick to one part of the task at a time. Participants can use the labels to help one another answer such questions as "Are we clear about what the problem is?" "Are we talking about helping forces, or are we planning action steps?" "Do you want to shift now from planning for action to anticipating obstacles?"

Stage I. Specifying the Problem

To reiterate, by a problem we mean a gap between a present situation and a desired target. We specify a problem by describing the existing situation (S) and the desired target state (T). In our first example in the preceding section, the participants specified the S as a "lack of clarity in the role of the principal" and the T as a state in which norms and procedures in the school would enable staff to say at almost any time, "We know where the principal stands, and he knows where we stand." As we noted, a solution is a procedure, plan, or path (P) that will enable participants to get from S to T.

When people state something they do not like about the present situation (S), they are also likely to think of how things might be better (T) and of actions (P) that might move in that direction. When people state something they think the school ought to do (*P*), they are also likely to think of something about the present situation (*S*) that they think might be improved by the action, and they are likely to think of how things might get better (*T*) after the action is taken. When people describe a state of affairs they wish existed (*T*), they are also likely to think of how the present state (*S*) fails and of something they might do (*P*) to move toward the better state. That is the way our minds work, and it is how we ordinarily discuss problems with others—cycling among *S*, *T*, and *P*. That is what Cohen, March, and Olsen meant when they said that an organization is full of choices (*T*s) looking for problems (gaps), issues and feelings (about *S*) looking for an airing, and solutions (*P*s) looking for issues (problems) to which they might be the answer.

In this first stage, we deal with *S*, *T*, and *P* all at once—that is, cyclically.

A group may come together to discuss a problem that is already pretty well delimited in their minds—for example, the gap between an existing method of assigning students to classes that generates a lot of reassigning during the first two weeks of classes (*S*) and a more desirable method that would settle all students in their classes during the first couple of days (*T*). Group members may also come together to survey all significant problems they feel and pick the most pressing for immediate work. We treat here the case in which the precise problem has not been picked. For the more limited problems, the procedure can be compressed.

Step 1. Put up three sheets of newsprint and label the one at the left *S*, the one at the right *T*, and the one in the middle *P*. You can write on the newsprints yourself or appoint a recorder. Have more sheets ready.

If you think the important thing is to get the participants working as fast as possible, don't start with a lecture about *S*, *T*, and *P*. Simply get the discussion going and write down on the appropriate sheet what people say. They will understand the *S*, *T*, and *P* better after they see all the examples you have written down.

If part of your purpose is to teach the participants how to use the problem-solving procedure themselves, then you might spend three minutes explaining the *S*, *T*, and *P* before starting the discussion.

You can start the discussion at any of the three places. Use simple language and perhaps a question, such as one of these:

- (*S*) What's wrong with the way things are now?
- (*T*) What would you like to be doing in your work that you are not doing now—or doing too little of?
- (*P*) What would you like to do to improve things?

When you get a statement that seems to be a clear instance of S, T, or P, write it on the proper sheet. If someone wants to argue about wording, remind the group that the sheets are not for publication, that they are only a beginning stage. The words are there only to remind the group of what has been talked about. There will be plenty of time for careful wording in later stages.

In this first step, get everybody's ideas onto the newsprints. Try to get statements that fit clearly into one of the three classifications, but don't work so hard for clarity that you slow down the generation of ideas. If two or three short questions don't clarify what a participant is saying, write whatever you have on the sheet that seems best at the moment. Alternatively, you could put up a fourth sheet for unclassifiable statements and return to them later.

Don't let a discussion start about whether an idea is good or bad. Write down everything.

When the contributions are slow, ask whether anyone wants to change an item from one sheet to another. If you have not yet done so, you can explain now the labels S, T, and P. The important thing here is not to get the group to agree on where the statements best belong, but to generate additional items. If someone thinks that having a group discussion with the principal about her role is a T, and someone else insists it is a P, write it down on both sheets. The group can agree in a later stage on how to classify the item. Being flexible here is a good introduction to the cycling in Step 2.

Step 2.   Tell the group you now want to use the ideas on each sheet to generate ideas for other sheets. It is not yet time for participants to agree on what they want to take as Ts and build toward with action steps. You want everyone to hear all the group's ideas about how the statements on the newsprints are connected. Talking about the connections will clarify for everyone how the group is coming to think about the present situation, about what would be a happier state, and about how to get there.

The ideas here for cycling among S, T, and P are taken from a handout written in 1971 by Fred Fosmire and John Wallen. The questions we use below are adapted from theirs. Much of the handout has been put into print by Pilon and Berquist (1979).

You might begin by generating more ideas for the shortest list, or you might want to add more specific ideas to the list containing the vaguest items.

To get more Ts, you can point to an item on the S list and ask questions like these:

- If you could change this feature of the present situation, what would you want to accomplish?

- What would be your goal in improving this feature of the situation?
- What does this fact make you think is missing? What is it you want?

To get more *T*s, you can also point to an item on the *P* list and ask,

- What will that accomplish?
- What goal does that aim at?
- What will this bring that you really care about?

To get more *P*s, you can point to an item on the *S* list and ask,

- What might be done to improve that?
- What kind of action would you say that requires?
- What kind of plan would use that resource?

To get more *P*s, you can also point to an item on the *T* list and ask,

- What might be a possible way to get started toward that?
- What steps might move toward that goal?

To get more *S*s, you can point to an item on the *P* list and ask,

- What would that improve about the present situation?
- What would that deal with, or take account of, that is part of the present situation?
- What resources do we have that will help do that?

To get more *S*s, you can also point to an item on the *T* list and ask,

- In what ways does the present situation fall short of that goal?
- What in the present situation is holding us back from that goal?
- What in the present situation can help us move toward that goal?

If your participants are at all lively, they will begin to volunteer translations among *S*, *T*, and *P*. If they are not so lively, you can ask them to join the game: What do you see in one list that gives you an idea for another list?

When contributions slow, begin cleaning up the lists. In each list, cross out the duplicate items or items that are clearly included in others. Add a few words to clarify items you wrote too fast. If the group seems in the right mood, appoint a committee to do this work. If there is time, ask them to copy everything neatly to make the list more legible. Because of the rush to get everyone's ideas written down, newsprints often get very messy, and it becomes hard to read words that are squeezed hurriedly into small spaces.

Step 3. Now the group focuses on the target statements. Ask participants to delete target statements that are simply not feasible in the reasonable future or that are the least urgent. Use consensus to reach the choices if at all possible. (By consensus, we mean getting everyone's view with sufficient clarity to show that it is plain no one will work against the decision. For a full explanation of consensus, see Chapter 6 under "Group Decision Making.") If full consensus does not seem feasible, use voting, but set the necessary vote closer to 80 percent than to 51. Give time—five seconds instead of one—for persons in the minority to voice serious objection. If they do so, point out that the objections should be remembered for Stage 2. Make a note.

The group now examines the remaining target statements. The members discuss the statements to clarify them. "Joe, did you mean by Number 6 that _____?" "Amy, does your statement overlap with Joe's?" Members give their opinions on the desirability and feasibility of the targets. Sometimes it helps to have the group write numerical ratings beside the targets, calculate the totals or averages, and then resume the discussion. Urge the group to envision (and talk about) what their working lives will be like after the target is reached. Rewrite any targets the group wants rewritten.

The goal of Step 3 is to come out with at least one target, but not more than, say, four that everyone agrees are both urgent and feasible. Copy the agreed-upon targets onto a fresh sheet.

Helping the Group Through the First Steps

Start with participants' own problems, not the problems you think they have. Action can spring only from the reality the participants perceive.

Help participants to loosen their thinking about causes. When they think of things that are wrong with the present situation (S), their Ps will spring from their ideas about what *causes* the bad things. When they think about how to get to a target (T), their Ps will also spring from their ideas about what causes human action. Most people's ideas about why things go wrong fall into three types: (1) it's the way things are (it's fate, that's the way people are built); (2) it's somebody's fault (make Joe behave properly); and (3) it's the system (we're all in this together).

You won't have to do much about "it's fate." Somebody else will think of something that can be done.

You may have to help now and then with "it's somebody's fault."

Some difficulties certainly do center upon one or a few persons—or on a group. Some people *are* bottlenecks, at least sometimes, and changing the behavior of a particular person or group may be key to solving the problem. The key person may be at a point where work flows converge, or the key person may be an administrator. The person may be one of the participants present. But if difficulties seem to center upon a particular person or group, it is important to get a lot of information about what is going on in the neighborhood of that person or group.

The danger in blaming a person or group is that it is easy to take it for granted that the problem, and its solution too, lies solely with that person or group. It is too easy to say, "We've just got to put the pressure on Joe," or "Somebody's got to go in there and straighten that bunch out."

You can remind the group about systems and norms. If a problem hasn't faded away of its own accord, it is likely that some regular routines somewhere in the organization are holding it in place. When you take this view, you are thinking about the whole *system*—all the ties and expectations and norms and communication links that keep things going—both the things you want kept going and the things you don't.

If your cuckoo clock squeaks, it squeaks *because* the pendulum is swinging, the gears are going around, and the clock is keeping time. Both what you want it to do (keep time) and what you don't want it to do (squeak) come from the whole system. The clock repairer's task is to find a way to stop the squeak *without stopping the time keeping* and without introducing a squeak in another part of the clock. Think how much more complicated your organization is than a cuckoo clock.

In the short run, maybe the cheapest thing you can do is nothing—just accept your fate. But that could be the most expensive thing in the long run. It's not very expensive in the short run to scold somebody or even to fire somebody, and if you are lucky the work may even go better for a while after you've taken those actions. In the long run, however, you may find yourself chasing the squeak all over the district.

Dealing with the system is usually more expensive, at least in the short run, than dealing with a few individuals. But if you can avoid merely pushing a squeak from one person to another and instead rearrange roles or work flows so that squeaks become rare everywhere, you won't have to go on paying for that same squeak the rest of your life.

Most problems can be categorized according to whether they reside predominately within one person (intrapersonal), among a few people (interpersonal), within a group, between two or more groups, throughout a subsystem, or among several subsystems. But most organizational problems in schools actually exist at several levels at once. When a faculty is concerned about a discrepancy between its current and an ideal set of disciplinary procedures, for instance, the discrepancy exists not only at the level of the entire school but also among various grade levels, among several sets of individuals, and within many individuals. In addition, this problem can involve district policy and discrepant expectations among parents, students, and staff.

Although a problem can be categorized chiefly within a particular issue such as goal setting or conflict management, each content area is interrelated with all others. Goal setting, for example, overlaps with issues of communication, managing conflict, running meetings, and making decisions. Since schools are multifaceted and their organizational problems are multidetermined, solutions will necessarily be multiple.

Stage 2. Listing Helping and Hindering Forces

Now the group chooses one of its highest priority targets (listed in Step 3 of Stage 1) and lists both the existing forces that will help it reach the target and those that can hinder its efforts. It lists forces within individuals (attitudes, feelings, values, typical behavior); within the group (norms, roles, interpersonal skills); within the school or district (norms, roles, rules, procedures, organizational "climate"); and within the community or society (economic trends, political "climate," pressure groups)—anything that can help or hinder.

The group can choose to work toward a single target until reaching it before beginning work toward another. Or the group can choose to work toward several targets simultaneously. If the group makes the first choice, it carries the first target through the remaining stages of problem solving, including action and evaluation, and then returns to its list of highest priority targets. If it makes the second choice, it carries the first target at least through Stage 5 (anticipating obstacles) before recycling to the next target.

Put up a newsprint bearing the diagram shown in Figure 5-1. Have extra newsprint ready.

The vertical line in the diagram represents the current state of affairs (S). There are forces at the left pressing toward the target (T) and forces at the right resisting that movement. Listing the helping forces at the left will remind the group of valuable resources and allies. Listing the hindering forces at the right will remind the group of obstacles to be surmounted. It is usually easier to move into action by weakening the hindering forces than by increasing the helping forces.

Step 1. List all the forces anyone can think of. Avoid argument and evaluation. Suspend critical judgment, but encourage paraphrasing for clarity. Strive for an accepting, inventive mood.

Figure 5-1. The Force Field

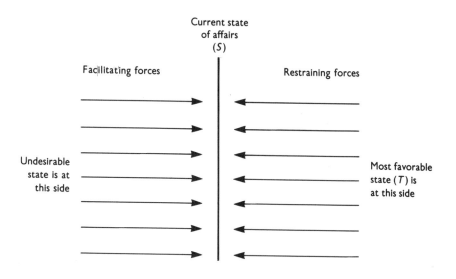

Work back and forth. A force of one sort named by one person will remind someone else of a force of the other sort. Some forces have both helping and hindering aspects. List such a force on both sides of the diagram.

This is the time to recall any objections voiced by outvoted persons during Step 3 of Stage 1.

Step 2. Ask the group to agree on the forces they think can hinder their efforts the most. Try to keep the number to six or fewer. If the hindering forces are insightfully chosen, reducing only a few of them will almost always suffice to get the group moving toward its target. Choosing too many hindering forces to overcome will make the task seem too formidable, and trying to keep too many forces in mind will be confusing.

Rate the forces according to how feasible it will be to reduce them. You will end with a few hindering forces that the group believes are both important and possible to reduce.

It is not necessary to choose and rate the helping forces. The group will recall them easily as the need arises.

Sometimes there will be disagreements about the fact. Is there or is there not some loose money in the budget? Does the law prohibit a certain action or does it not? Will a certain community organization or pressure group see our change project as something they'd like to help with, or won't they?

Avoid arguing about fact. Delegate someone to get on the telephone immediately and find out. If finding the answer is likely to take more than half an hour, write down the uncertainty as a hindering force: "We don't know whether. . . . " Finding the answer can become an action step later.

Sometimes pluralistic ignorance gets confused with fact. A member of the group may say it is not feasible to reduce a particular hindering force because of something "everybody knows." Maybe "everybody knows" that the counselors will have a certain opinion, or that the principal won't permit a certain action. Often, "everybody" goes on believing something for months or years because each takes the others' word for it without testing the matter. It is usually a good idea to ask for evidence or go get some.

Stage 3. Specifying Multiple Solutions

The purpose of this stage is to generate as many ideas as possible for reducing the hindrances selected in Stage 2. It is easy, in this stage, for people to get bogged down in arguing about the feasibility of actions or their likely efficacy. It is important to tell participants at the outset, therefore, that they will get their chance to be critical later on. The important thing now is to be inventive. Some very good ideas seem crazy at first glance.

This stage is a time for creativity and fun. Now is the time for brainstorming. Withhold critical judgment and evaluation; rather, encourage one another to be creative, playful, even wild.

Consider each hindering force in turn, and think of ways to reduce its strength. Use the following ideas to increase your creativity:

1. *Get ready.* Loosen up. Stretch your body; reach for the ceiling. Try some warm-up activity such as Billy Goat described in Chapter 4.
2. *Get set.* Have lots of newsprint tacked to the wall. Appoint a recorder who can hear well and write rapidly. If it will speed the recording, appoint two recorders.
3. *Go.* Brainstorm ideas for eliminating the first hindrance. Be silly and wild, and pool your wildness. Don't say no to any idea. Don't even take time to express approval beyond exclamations like "Hurray!" "Hear! Hear!" "Wow!" or "Go! Go!" Proceed to the next force in the same way.

Limits

Either in this stage or the next, some people will have worries about particular points of feasibility. They will worry that some of the ideas for action might push them into untenable positions. Likert and Likert (1978) remind us that people do face limits to their actions. It is a good idea to find out the limits on individuals before getting very far into serious planning for action.

A principal might need to make it clear that he or she cannot violate certain laws or is constrained by district poicy not to delegate certain responsibilities. A department head might point to the state's requirements for certain curricula. A counselor might insist that no plan is acceptable that reduces the hours available for personal counseling with students. Others might demand that their ethical, moral, or religious values not be violated. They might require that any plan show promise of increasing their freedom to make choices about their own work. In short, one or more participants might have nonnegotiable requirements—Likert and Likert call them "essential conditions"—that any solution must satisfy. It is better for the group to learn those requirements sooner instead of later.

Usually, no one will name a condition that brings the problem solving to a halt. Should that occur, however, it is usually possible to plan a solution that gives the objector limited participation that does not violate his or her essential condition. If that is impossible, only two courses of action remain: (1) ask the member to withdraw from the problem-solving group or (2) cease trying to solve the problem as a group and turn it over to an administrator to solve by fiat.

As essential conditions are listed, it will sometimes happen that people forget to restrict themselves to essential, nonnegotiable conditions and will name a few that they actually hold only as desirable. After the list is made, therefore, it is a good idea to ask a questions such as, "Are these now the conditions which, if violated, would cause you to withdraw from the project?" Once the essential conditions are settled, the group should take them as given and not to be questioned.

Use you own judgment about the best time to list the essential conditions. If you list them just before brainstorming possible solutions in Stage 3, you will forestall possible anxieties on the part of the people who might see violations of their essential conditions appearing on the newsprints, but you might also put a damper on the group's freedom to be creative. If you wait until after the brainstorming in Stage 3, it will be easier to generate playfulness in the brainstorming, but a few people could be anxious and therefore reticent, and it might be more difficult to draw them out later.

Stage 4. Planning for Action

Now is the time to be critical and hard-nosed.

Step 1. Pick out the solutions from Stage 3 that seem most feasible—likely to bring good results for a reasonable amount of effort. Make a new list of those ideas that seem within the capacity of the group and its allies to carry out. Use consensus if possible. (For the characteristics of consensus, see Chapter 6 under "Group Decision Making.")

In Step 3 of Stage 1, we chose targets—states in which a problem would no longer exist. In Stage 2, we listed hindering forces whose removal would allow us to move toward the targets. In Stage 3, we listed actions (solutions) that would put us in motion toward the targets. Those solutions were large chunks of action—large actions, so to speak. The large actions we choose in this step of Stage 4 can be thought of as subtargets. We must now think of smaller actions that will move us into the larger actions (solutions). Just as the solutions called for more specific and immediate actions than the targets, so now the smaller actions we will list in Step 2 will be more specific and immediate than the solutions. These smaller actions will be so specific, immediate, and clear that everyone will be able to take action tomorrow morning.

You can see that in effect we are recycling the first three stages, but now with the subtargets. Indeed, Stage 5 will be part of the recycling.

Step 2. Specify dates and persons:

1. For each solution selected, put its necessary steps of action into a time sequence.
2. Designate the groups or persons who will take each step.
3. List the materials and other resources needed.
4. Plan to begin the sequence as soon as possible.
5. Estimate specific dates on which each step will be taken.
6. Make plans for periodically evaluating the effectiveness of the actions as they are taken. Agree on criteria where they are not obvious: "We will know this action is successfully completed when we see (or hear) that. . . . "
7. Be prepared to revise the plans as the action sequences unfold. Specify dates for review.

Stage 5. Anticipating Obstacles

Now we recycle to hindering forces, but new ones. We anticipate what might go wrong with our plans. The step-by-step planning in

Stage 4 will have revealed some possible difficulties not apparent when we were generating hindering forces in Stage 2.

Step 1. Once more, weigh the probabilities of success against the probable effort required. Do that for each proposed action.

Step 2. Try to imagine all possible things that might go wrong. Remember to anticipate barriers in the environment (district regulations, economic trends, political "climate," pressure groups) as well as in individuals, the group, and the school.

Simulate the actions by asking friends to role-play persons who will be affected by the planned actions and to tell you their reactions.

Step 3. Go directly to the actual persons who will be affected and ask them how well they think your plans will work.

The steps in this stage are arduous, and you will be impatient to get on with the planned actions. It is easier to deal with obstacles that are realistically anticipated, however, than to deal with obstacles that come as surprises.

Stage 6. Taking Action

Do not delay taking the first step. The best time is tomorrow morning, even today. Many of the forces affecting the problem are changing from day to day. Your solutions may not remain appropriate for long.

Under Stage 5, we urged you to ferret out every possible obstacle. Now we temper that advice. Do not overplan. A group sometimes gets so fascinated with the planning or so anxious about the obstacles that it seems to want to leave not the slightest detail to chance. It seems willing to go on planning forever (see "Mobilizing Synergistic Action" in Chapter 1). But the current of events flows on while you are planning. You cannot anticipate everything. You must leave a good deal to the skill and judgment of the people who will carry out the action steps. Indeed, too much planning sometimes indicates too little trust in the group.

No plan can be perfect. Have the courage to go forward with an imperfect plan.

Stage 7. Evaluating

Things can go wrong. Something usually does go wrong. Without tracking, monitoring, and evaluating, the finest plan can founder when no one is looking. Planners should establish criteria for evaluating the effectiveness of their actions (see Item 6 under Step 2 of Stage 4). They should review their progress (or appoint someone to do so) as each action step occurs.

Working toward a target tests not only how well a plan has been conceived but also how well the original situation has been understood. New information brought to light while a plan is being carried out may call for a change in the plan itself, a modification of target, or revised ideas about the desirability of the target as first conceived. As people approach their target and form a clearer picture of what living in the ideal state might actually be like, they may not find it as desirable as they had originally thought. Or perhaps reaching it will have come to seem too costly. This does not necessarily mean that they planned poorly or chose the wrong target. It means that no plan or target stays good for very long, and that if the group's vision does not change, circumstances will.

For that reason, participants should tackle concrete problems first, pick targets of moderate scope, and avoid the trap of overplanning. The danger of large-scale planning is that after devoting an immense amount of effort to it, people feel reluctant either to "waste" any of it or to put still more effort into reconceiving the goal or changing the plan. If they succumb to the temptation to carry out the plan to the last detail even though the facts show that things are going badly, they face the worse danger of losing the norms and skills of openness. Thus, instead of planning on the grand scale, we advocate incremental planning informed by regular feedback and replanning. School participants should build their new world in moderate steps, repeatedly surveying both the wider horizon and the immediate path.

PROMOTING EFFECTIVE PROBLEM SOLVING

Here are some admonitions and ideas that can be useful at various stages of solving a problem.

1. At intervals, as the group goes through the stages, it should take time out to discuss how well the problem solving itself is going. Doing this will ensure that the systematic process is serving the group well instead of becoming a burdensome ritual. As a group becomes skillful, it looks at its own process, briefly or at length, whenever someone comes to feel that a step should be short-cut, lengthened, or conducted in a more fruitful way.

2. The group should attend to the feelings of its members as they work at the task.

3. Because disagreement can be a valuable tool for creative problem solving, encourage respect for its use as a stimulant for new ideas. The convener should help group members distinguish among disagreements over beliefs about facts (S), disagreements that involve different value positions (T), and disagreements concerning different proposals for action (P).

4. Because conveners have great power even when they lack formal authority, be aware of your domination as a convener and try to limit it.

5. Because leadership is a set of functions, the convener should encourage the group to share responsibility for the functions.

6. In describing a systematic problem-solving procedure for groups, we do not mean that the procedure will be serviceable only where individuals all conceive the problem in exactly the same way, agree wholly on the strengths of the facilitating and restraining forces, and so on. Nor do we mean that every individual must be enthusiastically committed to the steps agreed upon. The procedure is serviceable whenever no one is so opposed to the conception or so fearful of the action steps that he or she will take action to sabotage the sequence of action. Part of the skill of solving problems in groups is the ability to ascertain whether anyone feels that sort of opposition. Success in ascertaining that requires trust.

7. When we say that getting work done requires coordination and agreement on how to do things, we do not mean that people must swear undeviating commitment to long-term goals, short-term goals, and all the myriad small steps for reaching them. We mean only that there is inevitably some minimal orderliness in what people expect from one another today, next week, and next month. Planning in a group, for example, probably yields its greatest benefit when it enables people to test the trustworthiness of those expectations. Dowling (1978) interviewed Fletcher Byrom, chairman of the board and chief executive officer of the Koppers Company. Byrom said:

> We do quite a bit of [long-range planning] ourselves . . . but to us, it's a discipline more than it is a guide to future decision making . . . If you have taken the trouble of anticipating something, you should at least be able to recognize that it hasn't happened that way. If you hadn't done the planning, you wouldn't have realized that what happened was unexpected. As a regimen, as a discipline for a group of people, planning is very valuable. My position is, go ahead and plan, but once you've done your planning, put it on the shelf. Don't be bound by it. Don't use it as a major input to the decision-making process. Use it mainly to recognize change as it takes place (p. 40).

6

Making Decisions

Solving problems requires that proposals for action be generated. Because humans hold different goals, see the same circumstances in different ways, and think differently about different plans, choices between alternatives become necessary. Indeed, decision making can be defined simply as choosing among alternatives.

The preceding chapter described problem solving as the bringing together of information about situation and target and the generating of proposals to move school participants from their present state to an ideal state. Problem solvers become decision makers when they determine the validity of situational information, select their preferred targets, or choose among alternative plans of action. In other words, decision making follows problem solving whenever a choice arises. Problem solving requires gathering, filtering, and processing information; decision making requires assigning priorities and acting on them.

Although problem solving and decision making are often viewed as a single process, we have chosen to distinguish them for four reasons. First, we believe that increased awareness of decision-making methods can alleviate the tensions and frustrations that arise when the methods are imperfectly understood, when decisions are made by default, or when decisions are made but not implemented. Second, we believe that people who are aware of how decisions are made can participate more effectively in making those that require their aid and that such decisions will be more likely to be carried out. Third, we think that a school group that has been trained to employ multiple decision-making modes effectively can better select the mode most appropriate to the kind of decision to be made. Fourth, we believe that school resources will not be adequately shared unless school participants in all important roles can at least sometimes take part in collaborative decision making.

Although a school's ability to maintain access to resources, to act responsively, and to assess its movement toward goals is critically linked to the clarity and explicitness of its decision making, few schools regularly examine their norms, structures, or procedures for exerting influence or making decisions. This chapter describes concepts and skills that can clarify these processes for achieving shared influence and collaborative decision making in schools.

MAKING DECISIONS IN SCHOOLS

Traditional theories of organization located the major sources of power at the top of the organizational hierarchy and consequently limited the power and influence of those at lower levels. Early organizational and management theorists believed that workers were motivated primarily by economic incentives and job security, that efficient organizations developed rational rules and procedures to keep subordinates under control and protect the organization from human caprice, and that participation in decision making and shared influence were incompatible with organizational effectiveness.

For many organizations now, however, those traditional views are mistaken. In particular, there are school districts in which power is not located exclusively at the top but is shared among principals, teachers, students, and even parents. And there are schools with very active neighborhood boards that include educators and parents in equal numbers. Indeed, there is a good deal of evidence that a wider distribution of influence yields measurable benefits. In addition, problem solving and decision making are not always sequential, deliberate, orderly, rational processes carried out by people tightly connected with one another. We support the view of Weick (1976), who describes schools as systems that are loosely coupled rather than "coupled through dense, tight linkages." Using Weick's imagery, consider the implications of this view.

> Imagine that you're either the referee, coach, player, or spectator at an unconventional soccer match: the field for the game is round; there are several goals scattered haphazardly around the circular field; people can

enter and leave the game whenever they want to; they can throw balls in whenever they want; they can say "that's my goal" whenever they want to, as many times as they want to, and for as many goals as they want to; the entire game takes place on a sloped field; and the game is played as if it makes sense. . . .

If you now substitute in that example principals for referees, teachers for coaches, students for players, parents for spectators, and schooling for soccer, you have an equally unconventional depiction of school organizations. The beauty of this depiction is that it captures a different set of realities within educational organizations than are caught when these same organizations are viewed through the tenets of bureaucratic theory.

Consider the contrast in images. For some time people who manage organizations and people who study this managing have asked, "How does an organization go about doing what it does and with what consequences for its people, processes, products, and persistence?" And for some time they've heard the same answers. In paraphrase, the answers say essentially that an organization does what it does because of plans, intentional selection of means that get the organization to agree upon goals, and all of this is accomplished by such rationalized procedures as cost-benefit analyses, division of labor, specified areas of discretion, authority invested in the office, job descriptions, and a consistent evaluation and reward system. The only problem with that portrait is that it is rare in nature. People in organizations, including educational organizations, find themselves hard-pressed either to find actual instances of those rational practices or to find rationalized practices whose outcomes have been as beneficent as predicted, or to feel that those rational occasions explain much of what goes on within the organization. Parts of some organizations are heavily rationalized, but many parts also prove intractable to analysis through rational assumptions. (p. 1)

If entire states, districts, or even large schools are unlikely to be moving in the same direction at the same time, it is important for groups solving problems and making decisions to be substantially independent of other subsystems while they marshal their commitment and take their first steps. It is unrealistic to believe that people in loosely coupled systems are able to commit themselves to one another over long periods of time. For this reason, problem solving and decision making must occur in brief cycles in which people take small first steps, assess progress, and only then move on to further action.

INFLUENCE AND DECISION MAKING

In an organization, a decision is a directive, a promise, or an agreement asserting that particular people will carry out particular acts.

A decision, therefore, is a channel of influence. When an administrator makes a decision that certain other people will do something, the administrator is seeking to influence those people. When a group decides that it will do something, the group members are seeking to influence themselves as a collectivity.

Many writers have speculated about the sources of social power or influence. In an article for the *Encyclopedia of Educational Research* (Runkel and Schmuck, 1982), we argued that thought about influence, aided by a good deal of empirical research, has begun to converge.

French and Raven (1959), from whom we have borrowed some of our ideas about power sources, postulate five potential sources of power that people can use to influence others in social settings:

1. *Reward power:* The control and distribution of rewards valued by others
2. *Coercive power:* The control and withholding of rewards valued by others
3. *Legitimate power:* Authority legally vested in or assigned to a position
4. *Expert power:* The expertise of special knowledge, skill, or experience
5. *Referent power:* Personal attractiveness or membership in someone's primary reference group

In general, the more such sources people can marshal, the more powerful they will be, although expert and referent power tend to be especially important. Bachman, Smith, and Slesinger (1966) have shown, for example, that the satisfaction and performance of subordinates improve as organizational leaders rely increasingly on expert and referent power bases. According to Hornstein and his colleagues (1968), teachers find more satisfaction working under principals who employ expert or referent power than those who impose legitimate or coercive power. These findings support Weick's position that reward, coercion, and legitimacy are less tightly coupled to action than are expert and referent power.

Foa and Foa (1974) say there are six kinds of resources we exchange with one another: goods, money, information, status, love, and services. We gain influence over another person by giving (or offering to give) or withholding (or threatening to take away) one or more of those six resources. Harrison (1978) identifies four styles of influence: reward and punishment, assertive persuasion, participation and trust, and common vision or charisma. Here are some ways in which those ideas and some others come together.

Reward and Punishment

In one circumstance or another, people find many kinds of things rewarding or punishing. The Foas make that clear when they point out that you can reward or punish by giving or taking away any of the six interpersonal resources. French and Raven (1959) also list reward and punishment (coercion) as sources of power. In the same vein, Longabaugh (1963) has written about dominance versus submission, and Boulding (1978) has written about the polity and the "threat system."

McClelland's (1958) concept of power emphasizes the negation of punishment—not being subject to punishment or threats from others, being in control of one's own destiny. When you are not at the mercy of others, you can bargain from a position of strength. Similarly, Harrison and Kouzes (1980) list disengaging as a form of power, saying that it enables us to avoid emotionally draining involvements and to conserve energy. DeCharms (1968, 1976) points to the same positive and negative faces of power when he writes of being an origin (making one's own initiatives) or being a pawn at the mercy of others.

Information

"Knowledge is power," we often hear. Harrison's (1978) influence style of assertive persuasion includes using information when proposing courses of action and arguing about them. Having special information is an important part of French and Raven's category of expert power. The Foas make information one of their six interpersonal resources. The power of having information comes not only from knowing facts that others do not have, but also from how we are able to connect the facts to matters at hand and from our persuasiveness in doing so.

Affiliation

McClelland refers to the immemorial need we have to find bonds of affection with others. Harrison and Kouzes call this joining. The Foas include it in their category of love. Maslow (1954) includes it when he writes about social relations, Longabaugh when he writes about love versus hostility, Alderfer (1972) when he writes about relatedness, and Boulding when he writes about the integration of society. When we affiliate ourselves with others, when we join them to do work, we must to some extent put ourselves at their mercy. We take a risk that others will not have our welfare in mind. Influencing others to work both for our benefit and their own, therefore, requires cooperation and trust. Developing a group in which work is shared, participation is widespread, trust is high, and personal ties are strong is a way of magnifying our own powers through the powers of the group. Working with a cohesive group of that sort is the style of influence that Harrison calls participation-and-trust. French and Raven call this referent power—power through being an attractive figure, one with whom people can identify. It is the kind of influence or power that is implicit, and sometimes explicit, when we write in this book about the following topics: effective subsystems, group maintenance, participation, interdependence, trust, openness, sharing resources, using conflict constructively, emotional closeness, two-way communication, third-party helping, consensus, and similar matters.

Status

Status includes, among other things, the common notion of authority (but not authoritativeness, which belongs better with informational or expert power). French and Raven call this concept legitimate power. The influence that accrues to status comes from the culture, customs, or laws of society; from the norms or regulations of an organization; or from the agreements within a group. The influence that goes with status is bestowed by others. To persons in certain positions, we delegate, so to speak, the use of one or another of the kinds of influence we described above.

When we put a person into a position of authority, we grant that person the use of certain kinds of influence with us. School administrators can reward teachers with money, goods (materials), services, information, and status (recognitions of merit) or punish them by withholding these. Teachers can reward (or punish) students with information, services, status, and affection.

But status can come from positions other than those of formal authority. A person of high achievement (a captain of industry, say) can attract the allegiance of others who hope for a share in the achievement. An expert can command deference because of the information or know-how he or she has to give or withhold. Status can come through respect prescribed by culture or custom, as when we give respect to age. Status can even accrue to sheer munificence of love, as in the case of Eleanor Roosevelt.

A special case of status comes not as much from position, expertness, or control of resources as from personal qualities and leadership skill. It is the status of the charismatic leader. The charismatic leader articulates our yearnings and inspires us to action. Harrison calls this the influence style of common vision. French and Raven include personal attractiveness under referent power. Although charisma brings the emotional ties that also arise in what we called affiliation, the ties are not a network in the group, but are usually focused on one person. Still, charisma need not reside solely in a leader. Berlew (1974) has argued that charisma ("organizational excitement") can characterize an entire organization.

Many people grow up thinking of power and influence as attached to authority and position. As we have seen, however, influence arises from many sources, and all of us can reach out to some of them. Furthermore, as Harrison and Kouzes say, "Many people now recognize that the authority of an office is not sufficient to get things done in organizations and in society. We see people at all organizational levels having to use their skills of persuasion, negotiation, personal charisma, and trust building in order to influence others" (1980, p. 44). The industrial literature is full of reports substantiating Harrison and Kouzes's claim. The educational literature on the point is meager, but Hornstein and his colleagues (1968), as noted above, reported that teachers find more satisfaction working under principals who employ expert or affiliative power than under those who impose positional or coercive power.

Participative Decision Making

The OD consultant can help clients to identify the sources of power at their disposal, to develop sources they do not have, and to rely more often on those that have strong intended effects and few undesirable side-effects. For example, the consultant can help a parent group gain legitimacy by getting them school-board approval to give feedback to the faculty of a school. Or staff members can describe one another's resources and rewarding behavior to become aware of those sources of influence. The consultant can also help those in positions of legitimate power—principals, for example—to begin distributing part of their power to others. Forming new organizational structures such as special decision-making bodies or ad hoc steering committees can encourage teachers and others to assume leadership and responsibility for what goes on in the school. Particular problems in moving toward more shared influence are discussed later in this chapter.

It is not necessarily true that if some people become more influential, others must become less so. Powerful people who subscribe to this view often fear organizational development as a threat to their power. In the effectively functioning organization, however, members of all hierarchical levels can gain in power and influence as the power and influence of their subordinates increase. In other words, influence is reciprocal in effective organizations.

March and Simon (1958) theorize that expanding the influence of lower echelons not only increases the power of those members but also allows management to participate more fully. According to Likert (1961, 1967) who describes much the same phenomenon in connection with his link-pin model for organizations, more influence is given to subordinates by communicatively linking all organizational levels. Researching the relationship between organizational power and effectiveness, Tannenbaum (1968) found it feasible for more influence to be exercised at every hierarchical level in what he called *polyarchic organizations*, and has shown that when more people exert influence, the extent to which they are influenced by others increases as well.

The creation of management or leadership teams and multiunit structures are attempts by people in schools to organize themselves according to these principles. The multiunit school developed by the Wisconsin Research and Development Center for Cognitive Learning provides procedures for teachers to work in teams rather than in isolation, and it creates the position of team or unit leader. Regular meetings between the principal and unit leaders provide a forum for broader involvement in decision making and a communicative link between unit teachers and the principal. The total organization becomes mores integrated as information goes directly from its source to where it is needed, and all levels gain more actual operating power from the increased interaction.

Indeed, there is a definite trend for elementary schools and middle schools, in particular, to exhibit increasing formal collaboration and cooperation among staff members. Such changes in the social structure of the school are driven by an assumption that innovative curricula and instruction will flourish in group arrangements that facilitate greater interdependence among the professionals. Increasingly, teachers are expected to work together and to share their resources to provide a broadened range of learning opportunities for children. We have shown how OD consultation might facilitate the development of such relationships among teachers (see Schmuck, Murray, Smith, Schwartz, and Runkel, 1975). In that project we also learned a great deal about striking the right balance between high interdependence and loose coupling. Close collaboration can be overdone in schools; increased influence should not be unremittingly exercised from everyone to everyone every hour of every day.

It is better, for example, to place a leadership team between the teachers and the principal than to have the total body of teachers making demands on the principal every week. In the latter case, the principal, learning too much about every week's details, would be tempted to get into the teachers' roles, which would destroy necessary differentiation. For the same reason, it is better for principals to meet the superintendent with serious demands every month or two instead of every week. The OD consultant can help clients explore how influence is distributed in their organization and compare this to their images of ideal distributions. By helping them learn to exert and receive influence, give and receive feedback, and recognize the existence of interdependencies, the consultant can help clients create more effective and satisfying decision-making structures.

A number of empirically oriented organizational theorists have challenged the traditional notion that participation deters rather than enhances organizational effectiveness. Lewin (1951) and Coch and French (1948) indicate how participation satisfies social needs; Maslow (1954), Schein (1965), and McGregor (1967) suggest that participation satisfies growth needs as well. Research carried out in industry, voluntary organizations, and schools alike has demonstrated that the satisfaction of organization members increases when they can influence decision making.

Our consultative experiences lead us to believe that people in schools not only want but need to offer critical input and to participate in decision making. Like members of other organizations, teachers who have access to powerful people in the district feel better about their jobs and their schools and are more willing to display their capabilities to others. Teachers report greatest satisfaction with principals when they perceive some degree of mutual influence. There is even a positive correlation between student satisfaction with school and their perceptions of mutual influence with teachers.

But organizational effectiveness means more than satisfied people; it means improvement in the quality of decisions and increased likelihood of implementation as well. Maier (1970) provides some of the best evidence that shared decision making produces more acceptable decisions of higher quality than those made by individuals alone. Participative decision making enhances organizational effectiveness, because people who feel the support of a group are more willing to take risks in pursuit of creative solutions. Another reason is that the possibility of finding the best solution is greater in a group than with an individual. In short, decision-making procedures that allow more people to risk sharing their good ideas can yield decisions that are worth implementing. To this end, OD consultants can help clients explore the kinds of decisions made in school, pinpointing those that must be of high quality and that require high acceptance for implementation, and calling attention to situations in which participative decision making is especially important.

One of the most significant obstacles to participative decision making is the size of a large organization. Katz and Kahn (1966) suggest solutions to the problem of size. We can apply their ideas to big schools. Most large schools—those with more than forty teachers—can profitably experiment with decentralizing decision making in substructures such as departments or "houses." Feedback about decisions in the substructures can be communicated through unit heads, who function as link-pins between the substructures. Job enlargement is often possible within existing structures so that, for example, teachers can take on some of the functions of administrators and vice versa. Committee or team responsibility for a set of tasks can ensure greater psychological involvement of individual staff members in the school. The key idea in managing a big school is to conceive of it as composed of groups working on specific tasks and linked together by members of more than one group.

GROUP DECISION MAKING

Three Modes

How influence is distributed in an organization depends upon how decisions are made in face-to-face groups. Although groups vary considerably in their composition and procedures, three decision-making modes occur most often: (1) decisions made by a single person or by a minority, (2) decisions based on the ability of a majority to overrule a minority, and (3) decisions based on acquiescence and support of the total group after discussion and debate (here called consensus). Although it is difficult to obtain these patterns in their purest forms even under controlled laboratory conditions, behavioral studies indicate that each affects a group's performance differently.

Although many kinds of school decisions are best made by one person or by a small committee, these are either about matters that do not require committed action by all or most of the members of the school, are not so complex as to require subtle coordination and understanding among those implementing the decisions, or are those whose outcome is a matter of indifference to most people. Examples include the form on which to report absences, the date on which a particular school assembly will be held, the time to call a committee meeting, or the advice to give architects of the new home economics wing. The efficiency of such decisions is widely understood and does not require discussion here.

Relegating discussions to a minority subgroup is the method most frequently practiced in everyday school life. This method is the least effective in using members' resources, obtaining their commitment, or in achieving high quality. Decisions made by one or a minority of persons may be welcome when contestants find strife so unpleasant that merely resolving the matter is more attractive than the quality of the solution. It is nevertheless true that when only a few members contribute to making a decision, the final decision will depend upon the limited resources of only those few.

When problems are too complex to be solved by simple sequential decisions, a minority does less well than the total group, partly because it lacks the total group's resourcefulness and partly because the mutual probing and stimulation of the total group are missing. The inferiority of minority decision making is especially evident in complex organizations like large schools, whose central organizational tasks cannot be carried out in face-to-face groups containing most of the members.

Because it allows more resources to be introduced into discussion, decision by majority vote is superior to minority decision making in producing decisions that require wide commitment for implementation. Where commitment by everyone is not required, a majority vote can also serve very well. If, for example, a school faculty decides to hold a picnic on a certain day with the understanding that not everyone will attend and that there will be no penalty for nonattendance, a majority vote will enable the picnic to be held with no damage to the undertaking by those in the minority.

It should be remembered, however, that a majority vote ascertains only those alternatives that people find more or less preferable; unless there is extended discussion, it does not uncover the alternatives that certain people find insupportable. To the extent that the outvoted minority is unable to use its resources to influence the decision, some resources are still not being brought to bear on the decision. Indeed, when nonsupport or sabotage by one or more members could seriously damage an undertaking that requires total group support, a decision by majority vote could be dangerous.

Group consensus is, for us, a process in which (1) all members can paraphrase the issue under consideration to show that they understand it; (2) all members have a chance to voice their opinions on the issue; and (3) those who continue to doubt the decision or disagree with it are nevertheless willing to try it for a prescribed period without sabotaging it. Consensus is therefore different from a unanimous vote. It does not mean that everyone agress or even that the decision represents everyone's first choice. It means that enough people are in favor for it to be carried out and that those who remain doubtful nonetheless understand the decision and will not obstruct its implementation.

Because consensus requires fairly advanced skill in two-way communication, in coping with conflict, and in the use of paraphrasing and surveying, it is more difficult to achieve than majority vote, although its emotional benefits in many ways outweigh the cost. Majority vote hides pain. Members who may be hurting silently vote one way or another without having to reveal their dismay, with the result that the group is unaware of their pain and is surprised by subsequent foot-dragging and sabotage. But pain is far more likely to find expression and to be dealt with during the consensual process. Thus, majority rule sacrifices pain to efficiency, while consensus takes pain into account but at the expense of considerable time and discomfort.

Where there are pronounced status differences among staff members, a minority decision is often employed in the hope of short-circuiting conflict and saving time. For avoiding conflicts that arise from differences of opinion, the majority vote holds great attraction for many. Consensus, however, is designed neither to avoid conflict nor to overcome group resistance in the short run. Perhaps for that reason consensus is often discounted as impractical or unfeasible. Although consensus usually results in more resourceful decisions for complex tasks, it is a form of decision making seldom attempted in schools.

For our part, we are convinced that decisions about instructional matters, for example, can be made more effectively when staff members are able to stimulate and encourage use of one another's resources during decision making. To this end, a number of procedures described in this book are extremely useful for uncovering minority views that might otherwise not surface easily. Surveying, for example, can be carried out by tactfully inviting silent members to express their views. Paraphrasing, summarizing, and checking the feelings of others can also be used to elicit responses. Those who hold the majority position can assume the role of the minority and express this view to the rest of the group, asking minority members to say whether the expression of the role player was accurate.

Alternative Structures

Members of teaching teams and small faculties with common values can readily learn to use the consensual mode of decision making. But techniques and procedures that facilitate consensus in small groups are difficult to apply successfully when value orientations are pluralistic or when the group is too large for easy interaction in face-to-face discussion. In such organizations, the OD consultant and organization members may wish to create alternative structures that allow for different modes of decision making. Three alternative arrangements that have been used in large organizations include the management team, the decision-making body, and ad hoc groups.

The Management Team.   We know of a senior high staff of seventy teachers that was involved for several years in an OD effort. The administration team, composed of the principal and three vice principals, found that some staff did not wish to be involved in shared decision making. The latter viewed the process as too complicated, time-consuming, and frustrating. After considerable experimentation, the administrative team agreed to continue providing overall leadership to the staff.

Each member of the team now holds certain fixed responsibilities related to student services, physical plant, curriculum, and so on, but avoids making unilateral decisions about matters that have ramifications for someone else's responsibility. For example, the vice principal in charge of student services does not decide whether students can hold an assembly in the gym without first conferring with the vice principal in charge of physical plant to see that the gym is available. The group still meets regularly, any member can suggest items for the agenda, and all decisions are made by consensus.

The Decision-making Body. In this same school, most decisions are made by a group called the DMB (decision-making body). Composed of all department chairpersons, head teachers, the principal, and the three assistant principals, this body meets regularly to make schoolwide policy, make curriculum decisions that affect more than one department, and allocate the school's total budget. Any staff member or student may initiate agenda items and speak on any issue during open meetings. The positions of convener and recorder are rotated every nine weeks or less so that almost everyone shares in leadership roles. The principal counts only as one member of the group unless he clearly states in advance that he will take responsibility for making a unilateral decision; otherwise decisions are made by consensus.

Ad hoc Groups. In the same senior high, staff or students who think that the administrative team and DMB are inadequate forums for particular issues have the right to form ad hoc groups, whose proposals are placed before the total staff for a majority vote. This arrangement, while seldom used, is nevertheless always present as a backup when consensus for decision making appears to be too costly to someone involved. We also know of a large research and development organization that used an ad hoc group when it was faced with a major policy decision about its mission and organizational staffing pattern. The creation and use of this group involved a four-stage activity spread over two days.

First, the program's director described the issues and problems facing the organization. All professional staff, assisted by two OD consultants, discussed this presentation and the extent to which any means of resolving the issues would affect organization members, continuing until all were able to report clear understanding. In a method approximating consensus, they used a survey to agree that no solution would be acceptable until everyone in the group could vote 3 or 2 on a scale in which 3 meant wholehearted support, 2 meant support with some reservations, and 0 meant no support for any part of the solution.

Second, an ad hoc group was formed of individuals who stated either that they had special resources or expertise to contribute to decision making or that they cared greatly about the decision's ultimate outcome; a survey identified these persons among the total group. Third, the ad hoc group met in a Fishbowl until its members agreed consensually to recommend a single proposal to the total group. An open chair in the Fishbowl allowed persons in the outside circle to make process observations or comments about the proposal being developed. The consultants monitored reactions of other group members, occasionally providing feedback to members of the ad hoc group.

Fourth, the ad hoc group presented its proposal to the total group. When a survey of the total group indicated that several people were still reluctant to support the proposal, the ad hoc group reconvened to refine it and to plan a way of taking the reservations into account. Again, all other group members could occupy the empty chair in the Fishbowl or otherwise observe the meeting. A second presentation was followed by a survey indicating that the proposal now had sufficient support to become the basis of a new policy statement.

Readiness for Joint Decision Making

Changing the norms and procedures associated with decision making is not easy for consultants or clients. Discussions of how influence is exercised and received are often the most prolonged, painful, and conflict-producing parts of an intervention. Indeed, as influence becomes more widely dispersed through collaborative decision making, more rather than less conflict can occur. This does not mean that consultants should avoid dealing with the decision-making process, but only that they should be aware of several potential difficulties.

Leadership. The amount of participation in joint decision making by people in schools is determined in part by the leadership style of the formal leader—for example, the principal, team leader, or department chairperson. Schmidt and Tannenbaum (1958) list six leadership styles:

Telling: The leader makes the decision autonomously, announcing only its substance.

Selling: The leader makes the decision autonomously but provides rationale to encourage others to go along with it.

Testing: The leader makes a tentative decision and elicits reactions before deciding finally and autonomously.

Consulting: The leader elicits input before making the decision and explains how input was used or why it was ignored.

Joining: The leader asks others to take an equal part in decision making and agrees to go along with what the group decides.

Abdicating: The leader lets others make the decisions either by delegating the responsibility or by default.

Evidence from several of our projects indicates that unless the formal leader is willing and able to join with others, efforts toward joint decision making are likely to fail. In one school that was moving toward a multiunit organizational structure, for example, decision-making authority was to rest within grade-level teaching teams. The teams were to be coordinated by a special leadership team composed of the principal and three team leaders. But satisfaction with the principal and the school declined over the course of the OD project, primarily because of the principal's unwillingness to allow others to exert influence on decisions affecting the school (see Chapters 4, 6, and 13 of Schmuck et al., 1975). In another school pursuing the same goal, the principal valued joint decision making. Initially lacking the skills to join effectively with others, he went through a period of indecision that led to staff frustration and dissatisfaction, but by the second year he had gained enough skill and confidence for himself and the staff to work out a way in which decisions could be made to their mutual satisfaction.

OD consultants should carefully assess the readiness and capability of formal leaders to join others in decision making, and they might arrange a variety of special experiences to help them become more comfortable and skillful in doing so. These experiences might include special skill-practice sessions, opportunities to discuss leadership behaviors, or coaching. The consultant can also serve as a counselor merely by being supportive or by actually helping a leader link with other leaders in a peer-support system.

In one project in which parents were forcing a principal to share influence, we not only helped the principal plan meetings and develop interpersonal communication skills, but we also arranged for her to talk with the principal of a neighboring school about the problems of sharing influence and of joining with others in decision making. In another project, we brought principals from several elementary schools together in monthly meetings to share their concerns and to role-play difficult situations that they were facing. We gave special coaching to some of these principals, sitting with them as they convened decision-making meetings, explaining our observations of the group's dynamics, and making suggestions about what they might do to improve participation and performance.

Motivation and Skill. Since few teachers are trained to make decisions outside their classrooms, it is not surprising that many members of a school staff or team may themselves lack the motivation or competence needed to make shared decision making work. Some teachers may lack commitment to school goals, be uninterested in certain decision issues, distrust the formal leader's motives, or otherwise have little investment in finding solutions or taking action. Since the spread of influence is likely to increase conflict, some group members may be unwilling to pay the cost of involvement in time and energy. Finally, some teachers simply prefer being at home with their families to participating in long decision-making meetings.

Many of the instruments presented in the next section of this chapter can be used to assess the readiness of group members to participate in joint decision making. Several of the exercises presented in the final section can be used to build this readiness when it is low. Group members can see the advantages of using the consensual process by participating in one or more of the consensus exercises described later in this chapter. They can specify the areas of decision making that are the most important to them by helping to develop a decision-making matrix. Procedures such as surveying can alleviate many of their fears about inability to handle conflict.

Environment. Several factors within the larger organization or larger environment may impede movement toward joint decision making. Members of school districts or communities that exhibit highly diverse goals, unsupportive polarized subgroups, and a history of continued conflict or management by crisis may hesitate to change their decision-making norms and structures. In such cases, the consultant might provide evidence that groups in the environment are not invariably obstructive, or might collect data from these groups to help in designing a new decision-making structure. The Imaging exercise described in the next chapter can help to clarify real environmental constraints and reveal those that are only imagined.

GATHERING DATA ABOUT DECISION MAKING

An important source of data about decision making is the consultant's observation of school processes. The consultant watches, for example, for signs that the decision-making responsibilities are unclear and for instances of decisions made without appropriate amounts of staff involvement. The consultant also looks to see how much consensus is used and evaluates the staff members' clarity about who is to do what and when. The consultant is particularly concerned when staff members express frustration over not being heard, or even being ignored, by the leader or by a minority. Such instances are hints of alienation and powerlessness in the school.

The consultant keeps in mind a few ideal targets when making initial observations. Such targets might be decision making by those with the necessary information, the formal specifying of decision-making responsibilities so that staff members understand them, and wide recognition by staff members that several decision-making methods exist and that different procedures are useful for different issues or circumstances.

Certain questionnaires and observation schedules can help in assessing an organization's ability to make group decisions. By using the instruments provided here, the consultant can design intervention strategies or gather information to feed back to clients.

Actual and Preferred Decision Making

The following questionnaire reveals how respondents think decision making *is* handled and how they think it *should* be handled by three levels of the organization—the team or department level, the school level, and the overall district level. Discrepancies between what is and what ought to be provide a focus for group problem solving about decision-making processes and procedures.

Instructions: Circle one number at the left and one number at the right.

The way things are							The way things should be					
Always					Never		Always					Never
1	2	3	4	5	6	1. Decisions are made through teamwork.	1	2	3	4	5	6
1	2	3	4	5	6	2. Facts from those who know are used to make decisions.	1	2	3	4	5	6
1	2	3	4	5	6	3. You take a part in making decisions that affect you.	1	2	3	4	5	6

The way things are							The way things should be					
Always					Never		Always					Never
1	2	3	4	5	6	4. You or your peers help make decisions.	1	2	3	4	5	6
1	2	3	4	5	6	5. When decisions are made, they are based on information that you think is right and fair.	1	2	3	4	5	6
1	2	3	4	5	6	6. Decisions are made by those who know most about the problem.	1	2	3	4	5	6
1	2	3	4	5	6	7. The people who make decisions that affect you are aware of the things you face.	1	2	3	4	5	6
1	2	3	4	5	6	8. Decisions are made in such a way that you do not mind carrying them out.	1	2	3	4	5	6
1	2	3	4	5	6	9. Leaders work with their peers and people below them to make the decisions.	1	2	3	4	5	6
1	2	3	4	5	6	10. Things are organized so that you or your peers can help make decisions.	1	2	3	4	5	6

Actual and Preferred Influence

The first question below measures the amount of influence a staff member believes occupants of different positions in the school district now exert. The second question measures how much influence the respondent thinks each occupant ought to have. Results from the two parts can be compared and used for feedback to members of the school organization. Discrepancies between the two parts can stimulate discussion and problem solving to reduce the differences. Other phrases can be substituted for "in determining what innovations get attempted in your school." For example, the consultant might ask about influence in determining curriculum policy, influence in determining codes of conduct, or influence in determining what books, supplies, and equipment will be purchased.

1. In general, how much actual influence do you think each of the following groups or persons has now in determining what innovations get attempted in your school? Please indicate how much influence each person or group has by circling the appropriate number.

	None	A little	Some	Con-sider-able	A great deal
Local school board	1	2	3	4	5
The superintendent	1	2	3	4	5
Principal of your school	1	2	3	4	5
You yourself	1	2	3	4	5
A small group of teachers	1	2	3	4	5
Teachers in general	1	2	3	4	5
Curriculum personnel (supervisor, director, or coordinator)	1	2	3	4	5
Students	1	2	3	4	5
Parents	1	2	3	4	5
Teacher unions	1	2	3	4	5
PTA	1	2	3	4	5
Other (specify)	1	2	3	4	5

_____

_____

_____

_____

2. How much influence do you think these groups or persons *ought to have* in determining innovations attempted in your school?

	None	A little	Some	Con-sider-able	A great deal
Local school board	1	2	3	4	5
The superintendent	1	2	3	4	5
[and so on, as in 1 above]					

Participation in Decisions

Answers to the first three items below help to draw a picture of influence structures and networks of interdependence. Item 4 elicits perceptions of the power of various people in the school and helps assess how autocratic, democratic, or polyarchic the influence structure is perceived to be by the staff. Item 5 elicits the staff's perceptions of the principal's sources of power. Is the principal influential because of his or her expertise, or what?

1. Please mark an X before the *one* statement below that best describes *your* part in deciding upon the teaching methods you use.

    _____ I choose my own teaching methods without assistance or direction.
    _____ The final choice of teaching methods is left to me, but there are others whose job includes making recommendations or suggestions.
    _____ Within certain limits I can choose my own teaching methods.
    _____ As a member of a group or committee, I share with others the job of deciding the teaching methods to be used.
    _____ I do not choose my own teaching methods. They are laid down for me by others.

2. If you choose answer 2, 3, 4, or 5 in the question just above, you were indicating that some other person or persons were somehow involved in deciding upon the teaching methods to be used in your classroom. If you choose answer 2, 3, 4, or 5, please write below the names and positions of the other persons involved.

    _____   _____

    _____   _____

    _____   _____

3. When you want to receive approval in your school for an idea you are proposing, it is sometimes helpful to enlist the support of certain individuals in your school. Please list below, by name and position, the individuals whose support would help most in obtaining approval for your ideas.

    _____   _____

    _____   _____

    _____   _____

4. Please check the column that indicates your best estimate of the influence of teachers and principals on the areas of school life listed at the left.

	None	A little	Some	Con-sider-able	A great deal
In general, how much influence . . .					
Does the principal have on how the school is run?	—	—	—	—	—
Do teachers as a group have on how the school is run?	—	—	—	—	—
Does the principal have with teachers when it comes to activities and decisions that affect the performance of their classroom duties?	—	—	—	—	—
Do teachers have on the principal's activities and decisions?	—	—	—	—	—

5. Listed below are five reasons commonly given when people are asked why they do what their superiors suggest or want them to do. Read all five, then number them according to their importance to you as reasons for doing what your principal suggests or wants you to do. Write 1 by the most important factor, 2 by the next, etc., using each of the numerals 1 through 5 only once.

I do what the principal suggests or wants me to do because:

_____ I admire the principal's personal qualities and want to merit his or her respect and admiration.

_____ I admire the principal's competence, good judgment, and experience.

_____ The principal can give special help and benefits to those who cooperate.

_____ The principal can apply pressure or penalize those who do not cooperate.

_____ The principal has a legitimate right, considering his or her position, to expect that suggestions will be carried out.

EXERCISES AND PROCEDURES IN DECISION MAKING

The exercises presented here can be used to highlight influence patterns, decision-making procedures, the behavior of decision makers, or some combination of these. Ideas for sequencing or combining these exercises with those in other chapters appear in the final section of this chapter.

Nonverbal Procedures and Exercises

The following procedures and exercises work only with people in pairs. Repeating them with a sequence of partners can generate data for considering how individual influence in decision making varies in different situations.

Hand Mirroring. Spread out so that their outstretched arms do not collide, participants face their partners and present their hands palms out and fingers up about two inches from the other's hands. When they have agreed who will lead the first round, the leader moves his or her hands and arms while the partner follows as in a mirror image. After three minutes the partners reverse roles. For the final round, roles are left unspecified, and partners discover nonverbally who will lead and who will follow. At the end of each round, partners describe their feelings and check their impressions of the other's thoughts and feelings. At the end of the exercise, all describe thoughts and feelings.

Influence Line. Participants nonverbally arrange themselves in rank-order according to the amount of influence each one has. The rank-order can be recorded on newsprint before the group debriefs its experience. Questions to guide the debriefing might include the following: In what ways does the rank-order surprise or not surprise anyone? What are the consequences of this particular influence structure on the way the group makes decisions? How did it feel to be where you were in the line?

Exercises on Influence Styles

The following two exercises can be used in training designs to expose participants to alternative styles of influence and to help them explore both their own preferred styles and the styles of others.

Role-Playing Three Leadership Styles (Democratic, Authoritarian, and Laissez-faire). The goal of this exercise is to help participants recognize different styles of leadership and their effects. It should lead participants to become more aware of influence processes and help them talk about leadership in staff discussions. This exercise attempts to replicate the spirit of the classic experiment of 1939 by Lewin, Lippitt, and White.

The consultant arranges the seats so that participants are sitting face to face in pairs. Three pairs are closely clustered. Half the participants are called leaders and half are called followers. The followers must

Figure 6-1. Interaction I

Rank the following eight traits in the order of their importance for being a competent parent. Place a 1 by the most important trait, 2 by the second most important trait, and so on down to 8, which will be the least important trait.

	Tact		Compassion
_____	Tact	_____	Compassion
_____	Honesty	_____	Energy
_____	Ambition	_____	Intelligence
_____	Courage	_____	Sense of humor

have available to them another room where they can go while the consultant coaches the leaders about their roles. Another consultant can help with the logistics by taking the followers to the other room.

Before the followers leave, give each a copy of the sheet headed "Interaction I" (see Figure 6-1). Ask them to rank the traits while they are waiting to be called back. Tell them they will be interacting with three different leaders in three different decision-making tasks, and that the first task will deal with this sheet. Tell them also that after each task, they will fill out a questionnaire about what happened during the task.

After the followers have left the main room, give each leader three copies of the sheet headed "Reaction to Leadership Exercise" (Figure 6-2), one copy of the sheet headed "Interaction I," and one copy of the sheet headed "Instructions for Leader I" (Figure 6-3). Tell the leaders briefly about the experiment by Lewin, Lippitt, and White. Tell the leaders that this exercise will replicate the leadership styles used in that experiment, beginning with the democratic style.

Success in the exercise does not depend on your knowledge of the experiment by Lewin, Lippitt, and White. It should suffice that you have a clear understanding of the three leader styles as described on the three sheets of instructions.

Ask the leaders to read "Interaction I," "Instructions for Leader I," and "Reaction to Leadership Exercise," in that order. Give them any further explanation you think they need, and answer their questions.

Call the followers back. Each follower sits with one leader. Ask the pairs to begin deciding upon the best ranking of the traits.

After the pairs have made their decisions, distribute sheets headed "Reaction to Leadership Exercise" to the followers. Ask both followers and leaders to fill out those sheets. Collect them.

Then give sheets headed "Interaction II" (Figure 6-4) to the followers. Ask them to go to the other room, rank the items on the sheet, and wait to be called.

Figure 6-2. Reaction to Leadership Exercise

Check one: Discussion 1 ___ 2 ___ 3 ___ Check one: Leader ___ Follower ___ For each question, please circle the number that best summarizes your opinion.

1. Who led in the interaction?
   9 Superior led completely.
   8
   7 Superior led somewhat more than the subordinate.
   6
   5 Leadership was shared; each led about equally.
   4
   3 Subordinate led somewhat more than the superior.
   2
   1 Subordinate led completely.

2. How much satisfaction did you derive from the discussion?
   9 Completely satisfied
   8
   7 Moderately satisfied
   6
   5 Neutral: neither satisfied nor dissatisfied
   4
   3 Moderately dissatisfied
   2
   1 Completely dissatisfied

3. How much responsibility do you feel for the ranking you made as a pair?
   9 Feel complete responsibility
   8
   7 Feel some responsibility
   6
   5 Neutral
   4
   3 Feel very little responsibility
   2
   1 Feel no responsibility

4. How much hostility did you feel toward your partner?
   9 Felt completely hostile
   8
   7 Felt somewhat hostile
   6
   5 Neutral
   4
   3 Felt somewhat friendly
   2
   1 Felt completely friendly

5. Rate the quality of the ranking you made as a pair.
   9 Best possible ranking
   8
   7 Moderately good
   6
   5 Average
   4
   3 Moderately poor
   2
   1 Worst possible ranking

After the followers have left, give each leader copies of "Interaction II" and "Instructions for Leader II" (Figure 6-5). Let them read the sheets, give them any further explanation you think they need, and answer their questions.

Call the followers back. Ask the followers to sit with leaders they did not sit with before. After the pairs have made their decisions, distribute reaction sheets to the followers. Ask followers and leaders to fill out the sheets.

Then give sheets headed "Interaction III" (Figure 6-6) to the followers, and send them to the other room. Give each leader copies of "Interaction III" and "Instructions for Leader III" (Figure 6-7). Proceed as before.

At the end of the third interaction, display to the total group the responses on the reaction sheets. You can shorten the task of compiling

Figure 6-3. Instructions for Leader I

This interaction is a joint undertaking. Develop an acceptable basis for working together before you start into the rankings. For example, you and your subordinate might set the goal of agreeing first on the items that lie at the extremes of the scale and then resolving any differences in the intermediate categories. Be sure every item gets a reasonable amount of consideration. Give your subordinate a full chance to participate. Even though you are the leader, you have high respect for the quality of your subordinate's thinking and ability; your goal, therefore, is to weigh his or her opinions and your opinions equally. Discourage the use of chance, like coin tossing, in any doubtful cases.

Keep in mind that after you finish you will be asked to evaluate the efficiency of your subordinate in helping your pair develop the most adequate list. At the same time, your subordinate will be asked to evaluate *your* efficiency in acting according to these instructions. You are both responsible for getting a good list by working together in the manner described.

Remember, it is your responsibility to use the authority of your leadership to ensure that you and your subordinate come up with a ranking of the list that represents your collaborative thinking and that matches in quality the best ranking of the list. In the final analysis it is a joint effort.

Figure 6-4. Interaction II

Rank the following eight items in order of importance for being a competent principal. Place a 1 by the most important, a 2 by the second most important item, and so on down to 8, which will be the least important item.

_____ Has a good understanding of the structure of the organization
_____ Is able to give clear-cut understandable instructions
_____ Keeps all parties who are concerned with a decision fully informed on progress and actions taken
_____ Is willing to change own viewpoint when it proves to be wrong
_____ Is able to make decisions based on facts rather than personal feelings, intuition, hunches, etc.
_____ Is able to make good decisions under time and other pressures
_____ Is able to delegate effectively
_____ Is able to resist making a decision before all the facts are in

the responses at the end if you compile what you have after each interaction.

Finally, ask questions for discussion: (1) What are the helpful and unhelpful aspects of each style of leadership? (2) Under what circumstances in the school is it good for the principal to be democratic, autocratic, or laissez-faire? (3) What about the staff members in the school—when should they use one leadership style or another?

Figure 6-5. Instructions for Leader II

In this interaction _you_ are responsible for the activities and procedures followed by your pair. Assume that you have more knowledge, background, and skills than your subordinate. Take into your own hands whatever responsibility you consider necessary to get the job done. Your goal is to give greater weight to your own opinions than your partner's. You tell your subordinate the procedure you wish him or her to follow in working for you. As the supervisor in this situation, you have a better grasp of things, and it is perfectly proper for you to bring the subordinate around to your point of view. In the final analysis _you_ are responsible for the list. You will receive the criticism if your list is not good. Discourage the use of chance, like coin tossing, in any doubtful cases.

Keep in mind that after you finish you will be asked to evaluate the efficiency of your subordinate in helping you develop the most adequate list. At the same time, your subordinate will be asked to evaluate _your_ efficiency in acting in accordance with these instructions.

Remember, you are responsible for using the authority of your leadership to ensure that you come up with the best ranking of the list. In the final analysis this is a situation of authority-obedience.

Figure 6-6. Interaction III

Rank the following eight items in order of importance for being a competent teacher. Place a 1 by the most important, a 2 by the second most important item, and so on down to 8, which will be the least important item.

_____ Communicates effectively
_____ Treats each student as an individual with unique abilities, interests, etc.
_____ Improves himself/herself by continuing formal education, reading current journals, attending workshops, training programs, etc.
_____ Relates well with colleagues, superiors, and subordinates
_____ Does research in his or her specialized field
_____ Takes an active part in community affairs concerned with education
_____ Is able to effectively handle the "administrative" aspect of teaching
_____ Is willing to try new teaching techniques and methods

Figure 6-7. Instructions for Leader III

In this interaction your goal is to avoid active participation in the content of the discussion as much as possible. You are, however, to see that the work is done efficiently. If discussion gets off target, bring your subordinate back to the task. As much as you can, avoid giving your opinions beyond expressing agreement when you feel it. You don't really care what order is produced, as long as your pair can establish an order or priority for the items. Your goal is to weigh your follower's opinions much more heavily than your own. Discourage the use of chance, like coin tossing, in any doubtful cases.

Keep in mind that after you finish you will be asked to evaluate the efficiency of your subordinate in helping your pair develop the most adequate list. At the same time, your subordinate will be asked to evaluate *your* efficiency in acting in accordance with these instructions.

Four Styles of Influence.* People influence one another in many ways, and various authors categorize the ways variously. David E. Berlew and Roger Harrison have put styles of influence into four categories that we find especially useful. The descriptions of the styles require only common language, and participants can quickly connect the styles and substyles to their own experience. After only about half an hour of

---

*This section was composed from ideas in Harrison (1978) and Harrison and Kouzes (1980), from conversations with Harrison, and after using the influence categories in our own consulting. You can engage consultants to conduct exercises that will increase your personal skill in the four styles of influence by contacting Situation Management Systems, P.O. Box 476, Center Station, Plymouth, MA 02361, or Harrison and Kouzes, 1214 Walnut Street, Berkeley, CA 94709.

explanation and discussion, most participants can begin using the categories.

The purposes of this exercise are to help participants to (1) become more aware of the extent to which they and others use the four styles of influence, (2) practice watching for influence styles that people use in groups, and (3) make conscious choices of influence styles that are suitable in various circumstances.

The exercise can be conducted with any number of people, though the minimum is probably six.

Begin by passing out copies of the sheet headed "Influence Styles" (Figure 6-8).

Point out to the participants that they all know what assertive persuasion is. Teachers, managers, and others who work through words spend most of their time using assertive persuasion. Beyond reminding the participants of how dull meetings full of proposing and reasoning can get, you won't need to say much about *AP*.

You won't have to tell them much about reward-and-punishment, either. We all get it and give it. You might give some examples. You might also remind the participants that one style can wear the clothes of another. When an administrator interrupts someone and says in a loud voice, "I think the money is the first thing to think about," the words seem to have the form of making a proposal—*AP*. But in the ensuing silence the listeners may hear a threat: "—and you'd better do it my way or else!" The kind of influence a communicative act conveys depends less on the speaker's phrases or even on the speaker's intentions than on the way the listeners interpret the message.

Charisma will take a little explaining, because many people believe it to be a mysterious quality beyond analysis. If charisma is to be effective, there must actually be some common yearning in the group. (You often discover a common yearning during diagnosis.) The job of the person who wants to use charisma is to find that common yearning and then express it simply and clearly so that participants exclaim, "That's it! That's the way it is! You hit the nail on the head! Right on!" The capacity to use language simply and directly can be developed; you don't have to be born with it. The next job is to show the group members (or remind them of) their capacities—to show them that their present abilities can move them in the direction they want to go. The final part is to inspire action. With the common goal and the capability, the time is *now*. You don't have to wait until you die to find a better life. It is here for you to grasp.

You use participation and trust when you use the power of the group—when you use the influence of all upon all to carry the work forward to a goal cherished. Two prime features characterize a group that works through participation and trust: (1) the group draws out from

Figure 6-8. Influence Styles

Assertive Persuasion (AP)

Proposing: Giving your ideas; proposing what should be done; asking questions that show where you stand.

Reasoning: Telling why your ideas are good or others' are not as good; agreeing or disagreeing with others' arguments.

Charisma (CH)

Articulating the vision: Finding the common goal and describing the common yearning simply and clearly.

Inspiring confidence: Convincing people they can themselves do what is necessary. *You* can do it.

The time is now: We don't have to wait. You can do it *now*.

Reward and Punishment (R&P)

Approving and disapproving: Showing your values; making moral judgments.

Setting standards: Telling what you expect from others; setting goals; setting forth requirements; making demands.

Offers and threats: Offering rewards; threatening punishments; offering to bargain or negotiate; invoking power, authority, or status.

Participation and Trust (P&T)

Openness: Describing own emotions; admitting mistakes, lack of knowledge, uncertainty.

Trying to understand: Paraphrasing; describing others' behavior; checking your perceptions of others' emotions.

Appreciating others: Inviting others to contribute; using what they offer; showing you value others as whole people.

---

its members all the resources of individuals that can be used to do the work better and (2) the group does not allow the task to become a juggernaut that grinds individuals under its wheels. The group values individuals for *all* their capacities and qualities—not only those that are useful now, but also those that may be useful in the future. If a group is to work that way, its members must openly make known their strengths and weaknesses, constantly check their understanding of one another's intentions and commitments, and repeatedly invite and use everyone's skills.

Because very strong interdependence arises in such a group, every member's fate is to a great degree in everyone else's hands. That means that members feel more willing to take risks than in a more formal and hierarchical group. Members know they will get help from others during periods of difficulty, because their troubles are the troubles of all. The willingness to take risks enables the group to carry out tasks that a more hierarchical and bureaucratic group would not attempt, but the strong interdependence also requires more time for group maintenance. It takes time to develop a strongly interdependent group, and it takes time to maintain it in that condition. This book contains many exercises and procedures for helping participation and trust to develop in a group.

The next step is to give participants practice in observing influence styles. Pass out the "Influence Tally Sheet" (Figure 6-9).

Participants should get practice very soon after hearing about the

Figure 6-9. Influence Tally Sheet

Write one person's name over each of the columns. Make a tally when someone exhibits one of the influence categories. Sometimes you will make more than one kind of tally for one utterance or act. But do not make extra tallies just because someone takes a long time to say something.

Influence category

Reward and punishment (R&P)								
Approving and disapproving								
Setting standards								
Offers and threats								
Participation and trust (P&T)								
Openness								
Trying to understand								
Appreciating others								
Charisma (CH)								
Articulating the vision								
Inspiring confidence								
The time is now								
Assertive persuasion (AP)								
Proposing								
Reasoning								

four influence styles. You can ask them to observe actual workaday groups or you can set up a simulation.

If there is going to be a break of a few days in your consultation with the participants, you can ask them to observe an actual group and make tallies. For good practice, participants need to observe a group discussion in which a variety of influence styles will be shown. Some actual working meetings exhibit a variety and some do not. Some faculty meetings, for example, exhibit almost unrelieved assertive persuasion, with the principal doing most of it. Other kinds of meetings show more variety. In a meeting of department heads, for example, the members might show approval and disapproval, tell what they expect of one another, make promises and threats, reveal their uncertainties, check their understanding of one another, show excitement about common purposes, and so on. Other meetings might serve—a curriculum committee, a building-and-grounds committee, the school board. If a group of that sort will allow observers, you could send participants to its meetings.

You can also ask participants simply to make tallies in gatherings they attend as part of their regular work. Many participants will belong to committees, for example. Further, participants who are teachers may have classes in which they encourage some talk among the students. If so, they can observe some variety there. Young students are often very free, for example, with approval and disapproval, telling their expectations, their sense of urgency, and the like.

But you might want to give practice immediately. Here are a couple of simulations you can use. One will draw out influence of the reward-and-punishment (*R&P*) sort, the other participation and trust (*P&T*). Let some of the participants take roles in the simulation, and let the remainder sit around them and make tallies. While those on the outside are getting practice in observing the influence attempts, those playing roles will be noticing their own choices of influence styles.

The handouts needed are shown below, first for the *R&P* Simulation and then for the *P&T* Simulation. They require no more instruction than "Read your instructions and then begin."

R&P SIMULATION: Instructions for the Principal

You are about to attend a regular meeting of the school's leadership group made up of the principal, a representative of the counselors, and the department heads. No agenda has been preplanned for this meeting. The principal typically develops an agenda during the first five minutes of the meeting.

You are the *principal* of this school.

It never rains but it pours, and as it happens, two of your department heads are sick today, and one has jury duty. But you are going to hold the meeting anyway. The people present will be the department heads of English, Science, Physical Education, and Arts and Music, and one of the school's counselors.

You have a couple of guesses about what might come up. It is getting on toward time to think about next year's budget, and somebody might be wanting more money for next year—someone usually does. Also, some teachers have complained to you that the counselor too often pulls students out of their classes for counseling sessions. That matter might arise.

As to the budget, there isn't money to throw around, but there is a little slack. You might be able to shift a little money here and there if they don't want too much.

R&P SIMULATION: Instructions for the Counselor

You are about to attend a regular meeting of the school's leadership group made up of the principal, a representative of the counselors, and the department heads. No agenda has been preplanned for this meeting. The principal typically develops an agenda during the first five minutes of the meeting.

You are one of the school's *counselors.*

As well as conducting some classes or group sessions in career counseling, you also have a heavy case load of students who need help with personal problems or with difficulties they have with teachers. You and your counseling colleagues cannot see all the students you need to see in their free periods or after school. You frequently make appointments for them during their class time. Some teachers complain to the counselors that doing that interrupts their classes and makes it difficult for the students to keep up with their lessons. An art teacher says students can't leave an art project half done. A math teacher says that if a student misses one lesson, he or she can't do the next. The principal has told you of receiving similar complaints from teachers.

You want to clarify your role during this meeting. You want the principal to make it clear that your work is just as important as the teachers', and you have to call students out of class.

R&P SIMULATION: Instructions for the Head of Arts and Music

You are about to attend a regular meeting of the school's leadership group made up of the principal, a representative of the counselors, and the department heads. No agenda has been preplanned for this meeting. The principal typically develops an agenda during the first five minutes of the meeting.

You are the *head of Arts and Music.*

Your teachers have been telling you that their budgets for materials are always too low. They have to spend a lot of time, they say, scrounging for free art materials or having two students look on at the same sheet of music.

At this meeting, you want to convince the principal to increase the budget for materials in your department for the coming year.

R&P SIMULATION: Instructions for the Head of Physical Education

You are about to attend a regular meeting of the school's leadership group made up of the principal, a representative of the counselors, and the department heads. No agenda has been preplanned for this meeting. The principal typically develops an agenda during the first five minutes of the meeting.

You are the *head of Physical Education.*

You believe strongly in the educational value of sport and outdoor recreation. Young people can enjoy nature more if they are physically fit. They can learn cooperation and group effort in team sports. They can learn perseverance in the discipline of body building. You want to have more hiking, jogging, canoeing, weight lifting, and gymnastics.

But sometimes winning gets in the way. Sometimes students doing weight lifting give up because, they say, players in basketball get all the glory, and nobody cares about weight lifting. Hikes are hard to do during school hours. When you take a group out for hiking during a weekend, they too often don't seem to see anything around them. They just trudge. When you point out the beauty of a vista, they don't pay any attention.

You suspect you are doing something wrong, but you don't know what. You respect the psychological acumen of the counselor, with whom you have had a couple of talks about your perplexity and who seemed to have a good idea or two. You would like the counselor to come into your classes and on a couple of hikes, observe what you do, and make some suggestions for better ways to bring about your larger educational objectives.

At this meeting, you want to persuade the counselor, with the principal's help, to take some time with your classes.

R&P SIMULATION: Instructions for the Head of Science

You are about to attend a regular meeting of the school's leadership group made up of the principal, a representative of the counselors, and the department heads. No agenda has been preplanned for this meeting. The principal typically develops an agenda during the first five minutes of the meeting.

You are the *head of Science.*

Two of the teachers in your department have many students who have developed very fine projects that they want to exhibit proudly to parents. You would like to mount a "science fair" about two or three weeks from now and invite parents to come and see the fine work your department has been doing with its students. The only room in your school large enough to set up all the exhibits and leave space enough for visitors to walk about is the combination lunchroom and gymnasium. So you expect some opposition from the head of Phys Ed, because the Phys Ed teachers use the room every day after school for extracurricular weight lifting, ballet, tumbling, and the like. But you are eager to get your fair scheduled before the semester is too far gone.

R&P SIMULATION: Instructions for the Head of English

You are about to attend a regular meeting of the school's leadership group made up of the principal, a representative of the counselors, and the department heads. No agenda has been preplanned for this meeting. The principal typically develops an agenda during the first five minutes of the meeting.

You are the *head of English.*

You and your departmental colleagues in English have been working very hard to get the students to write competently. Still, their papers and scores on verbal tests show considerable weakness. You believe that good writing must be taught in other classes beside English. You want the science teacher, for example, to grade science reports on their quality of writing. You would like history teachers to do the same.

At this meeting, you are going to propose your idea and try hard to get it adopted.

P&T SIMULATION: Instructions for the Principal

You are at a task-force meeting of six appointed by the principal to prepare for an important evaluation of your school's program. The evaluation will be carried out by a state accreditation committee that plans to visit your school for some days in a few months. If your school does not receive a favorable evaluation, the staff will be under the gun from the district to make changes. It is in the interest of the entire staff to pull together to pass this evaluation with flying colors.

You are the *principal.*

You have been the principal here for five years. You are deeply committed to your job and to the school. You want very much to look good on this evaluation. But you are worried that the staff might not pull together during the next few months. You've been hearing some bothersome complaints. For example, some staff members have been complaining that the counselors are working at cross-purposes with the classroom teachers and that the coaches have too much power over class scheduling. You worry that the evaluation committee will see the school's program as being fragmented and that some of the interpersonal tensions on the staff will show up during the evaluation process.

P&T SIMULATION: Instructions for the Librarian

You are at a task-force meeting of six appointed by the principal to prepare for an important evaluation of your school's program. The evaluation will be carried out by a state accreditation committee that plans to visit your school for some days in a few months. If your school does not receive a favorable evaluation, the staff will be under the gun from the district to make changes. It is in the interest of the entire staff to pull together to pass evaluation with flying colors.

You are the *librarian*.

You are one of the youngest people on the staff. You came to the school three years ago, fresh out of a master's program in library science. You view the library as an integral part of the school, but worry that your colleagues will forget about highlighting it to the evaluation committee. You can see how the library functions in helping the departments reach their educational goals, but you're not sure that others do. Maybe they just take you for granted. You hope that everyone pulls together in showing the evaluation committee that the school is more than the sum of its parts.

P&T SIMULATION: Instructions for the Science Teacher

You are at a task-force meeting of six appointed by the principal to prepare for an important evaluation of your school's program. The evaluation will be carried out by a state accreditation committee that plans to visit your school for some days in a few months. If your school does not receive a favorable evaluation, the staff will be under the gun from the district to make changes. It is in the interest of the entire staff to pull together to pass this evaluation with flying colors.

You are a *science teacher*.

You have been at the school since it started seventeen years ago, and you are the oldest staff member in the school. You believe that while your own department is not great, the school is very effective. You worry that the skills of the older teachers will be criticized by some of your colleagues during the evaluation and that the oldsters' skills won't be given proper credit by the evaluation committee. You want everyone to pull together and to support one another during the evalution.

P&T SIMULATION: Instructions for the Mathematics Teacher

You are at a task-force meeting of six appointed by the principal to prepare for an important evaluation of your school's program. The evaluation will be carried out by a state accreditation committee that plans to visit your school for some days in a few months. If your school does not receive a favorable evaluation, the staff will be under the gun from the district to make changes. It is in the interest of the entire staff to pull together to pass this evaluation with flying colors.

You are a *mathematics teacher*.

This is your first year of teaching, and you like your job and this school very much. You believe that this math department is one of the strongest in the state. It has a very good reputation, and you judge your departmental colleagues to be very effective teachers. You worry, however, that the science teachers do not give proper credit to the worth of the math department, and that the science teachers might ignore the obvious tie between math and science during the evaluation. You want the evaluation committee to see a constructive synergy between math and science. In fact, you want all departments to support one another. You are going to show your appreciation of other departments at this meeting.

P&T SIMULATION: Instructions for the Athletic Coach

You are at a task-force meeting of six appointed by the principal to prepare for an important evaluation of your school's program. The evaluation will be carried out by a state accreditation committee that plans to visit your school for some days in a few months. If your school does not receive a favorable evaluation, the staff will be under the gun from the district to make changes. It is in the interest of the entire staff to pull together to pass this evaluation with flying colors.

You are an *athletic coach.*

You believe that your school has a sound athletic program for boys and girls that emphasizes physical development and cooperative effort, but you aren't sure that your colleagues in the academic departments recognize its value. You worry that some staff members hold derogatory stereotypes about the coaches and that they might let their attitude show during the evaluators' visit. But even if they don't bad-mouth the coaches during the evaluation, you worry that the evaluation committee won't take proper note of the educational value of the athletic program.

At the same time, you have strong confidence that your school's faculty can pull together during the evaluation. You think others feel that way, too. In this meeting, you are going to express your solidarity with the faculty and test the solidarity of the group.

P&T SIMULATION: Instructions for the Counselor

You are at a task-force meeting of six appointed by the principal to prepare for an important evaluation of your school's program. The evaluation will be carried out by a state accreditation committee that plans to visit your school for some days in a few months. If your school does not receive a favorable evaluation, the staff will be under the gun from the district to make changes. It is in the interest of the entire staff to pull together to pass this evaluation with flying colors.

You are a *counselor.*

You see yourself and your counseling colleagues as doing a top-notch job with the students. You know you couldn't do that were it not for the excellent cooperation you get from teachers. The principal has told you of a few complaints, but they seem minor, and you are sure you can straighten them out in a few visits tomorrow. But you wonder whether there might be some conflict elsewhere in the staff that needs to be aired and alleviated before the evaluators get here. You are going to do your best in this meeting to help people speak frankly and understand one another.

Once the participants have had some practice in observing the influence styles, you can help them become more aware of their own predilections. To do this last part of the exercise, participants need to have had some experience in working together. Merely working at the same school will not necessarily be enough, because teachers often communicate little. But perhaps the participants will have been on the same committees, the same teaching team, or the same administrative team. If they have not worked together intimately, delay this part of the exercise until they have participated in several group exercises, such as Planners and Operators or the consensus exercises in this chapter, the Imaging exercise in Chapter 7, or actual planning sessions for real work in the school.

Ask participants to gather in groups in which all members have worked together before. Groups of four are best, but three or five are acceptable. Ask everyone to draw a diamond like that in Figure 6-10 (a). Then explain that the corners of the diamond represent the greatest frequency possible of using the four influence styles. A person who uses reward and punishment all the time would be located at the corner marked "R&P," and so on.

But situations differ in the amount of opportunity they offer for using the various influence styles. Any of us may use more *R&P* in one setting and more *P&T* in another. Ask every group, therefore, to agree on an imaginary setting to keep in mind as they mark their diagrams— the curriculum committee, this workshop, or whatever.

Now each person should estimate the amount of each style he or she has been using in the agreed-upon setting. A person who has been using none of the styles would mark the very middle of the diagram. Someone who has been using nothing but a particular style would mark a corner. Figure 6-10(b) shows how a person might mark the diagram.

Now ask the participants to connect the marks and shade in the inside area, as shown in Figure 6-10(c). The shaded area shows the portion of the influence domain the person has been using. The unshaded area is the portion that person might want to explore in further work with the group.

And now ask the participants to make a similar diagram for all the others in their groups. Each person makes a diagram to show the kinds of influence he or she has felt from each group member. Then each person hands out the diagrams about the others to the members the diagrams describe. All will then have in hand the diagrams they made about themselves and those the others made about them. They can then compare their perceptions of themselves with the perceptions others have of them.

If the perceptions from others agree with the self-perceptions, participants will feel that their own perceptions have been verified. If

Figure 6-10. The Influence Diamond

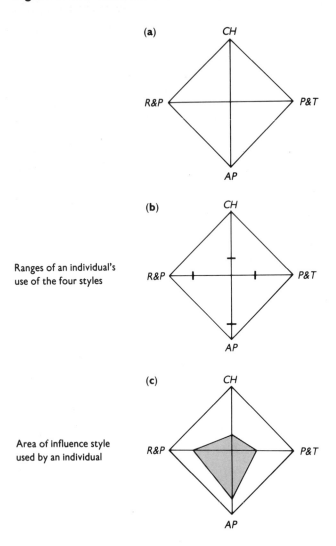

Ranges of an individual's
use of the four styles

Area of influence style
used by an individual

perceptions from others agree among themselves but differ from the self-perceptions, participants can conclude (1) that they have been using more or less of a particular style than they thought or (2) that their skill is low, and they have been "coming across" in a way they did not intend. If perceptions from others do not agree among themselves, then (3) participants can conclude that their ways of using the influence styles affect some people some way and other people another. For the last two outcomes, participants could ask others for more paraphrasing to help them grow more sure of the effects they are having.

Finally, participants will inevitably get into a discussion of the uses of the four styles. They will say that a particular style works better in one setting or for one purpose than another. And they will be right. You might want to pass out copies of "When to Use the Four Influence Styles":

WHEN TO USE THE FOUR INFLUENCE STYLES

Assertive Persuasion

Use it when

1. Getting the task done depends on having the facts and on getting the technical detail properly ordered.
2. In a group, when the task is so complex that more than one person's information or judgment is necessary.
3. Others *want* to have influence on the decision or solution. (Don't ask a group to argue about what brand of pencils to buy.)
4. The norms of group process permit all to put forth their ideas and all to be honestly heard.
5. The group is ready to judge proposals on their technical merit.
6. When you are not simply giving a persuasive speech, but want full participation from the group, and when the group is reasonably small—say, three to twelve members.

Do *not* use it when

1. Almost everyone agrees that the task or decision is simple enough for one person to do it or to make the decision.
2. Most people prefer that you do it yourself. (If they want you to do it yourself but you think it would be better done by having more ideas than your own, then you need a meeting in *P&T* style to get more ideas.)
3. The norms within the group are competitive or strongly *R&P*.
4. The group will judge proposals chiefly by *who* makes them. (In this case, use *R&P* or *P&T*.)

Benefits

1. Puts attention on technical detail.
2. Brings to bear a range of facts, proposals, and chains of reasoning beyond what any single member is likely to bring: expands resources.

By itself, it *won't* usually bring you much.

1. Energizing or inspiration.
2. Quick action.
3. Trust or commitment.
4. Long-term control.

Reward and Punishment

Use it when

1. Time is short.
2. You have set standards for others, and you will not change them.
3. You actually have rewards or punishments that are in your power to give or withhold, and you are ready to do so. (Promises or threats not carried through have very temporary effect.)
4. You actually cannot get what you want unless others get less than they want—that is, when the situation is objectively win–lose.

Do *not* use it when

1. You are searching for the best standards to apply. (Then use *AP* or *P&T*.)
2. The rewards or punishments you might apply are weak or will be considerably delayed.
3. You need creativity, initiative, and risk taking from others. (Then use *P&T*.)

Benefits

1. Puts attention on the immediate task.
2. Usually makes decisions and effects quick—though not in complex negotiations and bargaining.
3. Locates control simply. Bureaucratic controls can be built in for the long term.
4. Maximizes getting what you yourself want, at least in the short term.
5. Useful with one person or ten thousand.

By itself, it *won't* usually bring you much.

1. Benefit of others' ideas, creativity, or risk taking. (Use *AP* or *P&T*.)
2. Solidarity, espirt de corps, or trust. (Use *P&T*.)
3. Long-term organizational resourcefulness. People will wait to find out what will bring them rewards and punishments. (Use *P&T*.)

Participation and Trust

Use it when

1. You need the continuing commitment of the group to follow through and get the task done.

2. You want initiative, creativity, a range of resources, or risk taking.
3. There is enough mutual trust and acceptance in the group so that members will make some personal disclosures, will want to involve one another, and will want to understand one another at some depth.
4. The group is no larger than, say, twenty, or the task is such that the people needed can be organized into separate but linked small groups.
5. There is ample time.

Do *not* use it when

1. Immediate action is necessary; when time is very short.
2. You do not need initiative, creativity, risk taking, trust, solidarity, or a range of resources.
3. Trust in the group is low.
4. The group is too large to be brought together face to face, or too large for everyone to participate even if the group is in one room (say, larger than twenty, or if the task cannot be done by separate but linked small groups.
5. You yourself are not ready to self-disclose, etc.

Benefits

1. Solidarity, trust, long-term commitment to group and task.
2. Generates creativity, initiative, risk taking, drawing-out of members' resources (synergy).
3. Flexible use of members' abilities. Members can move from one role to another as needed.
4. When combined with *AP*, groups can solve their own problems.

By itself, it *won't* usually bring you much.

1. Clarity of control from the top (because members will make decisions and take action on their own or in small groups; you will hear about it *after* it is done).
2. If skill in *P&T* is low in your school, it may take you a year or more to develop it to the point where it is an effective way to get things done.

Charisma

Use it when

1. There is a clear possibility of a common vision (also called "superordinate goal").
2. You can articulate the vision clearly and simply.
3. It is within your power and that of others to take significant steps toward realizing the vision.
4. When you want to energize people (though if you are doing it by yourself, you have to do it repeatedly).

Do *not* use it when

1. Visions within your staff are in conflict—when people are not merely in disagreement about *how* to get there, but when one faction can move toward its vision only if another is prevented from doing so.
2. You are not skillful at articulating the vision. (Get someone else to do it, or brush up your *CH* skill before you depend on it.)

Benefits

1. Energizes. Gets things moving.

By itself, it *won't* usually bring you much.

1. Detailed problem solving.
2. Clarity of control.
3. Solidarity within subgroups. (*CH* brings allegiance to the leader who articulates the vision. The only kind of solidarity it brings is that common allegiance. But through the use of *P&T, CH* can become a method of influence used *within* groups *by* groups as well as a method used by you.)
4. Carry-over to the next leader when you leave.

A Resource-sharing Exercise

Many of the exercises in this book enable participants to observe the extent to which they use the resources in the group, including their own. The card-discovery problem, however, is especially effective in showing the use of resources. Unless the group succeeds in drawing out accurate information from every member in the exercise, fatal errors are almost inevitable. The card-discovery problem will go well with five to seven persons in the group. The consultant prepares a deck of thirty cards for each group of participants. Each card has printed upon it a 12 × 12 matrix of points, and each point is designated either *X* or *O*. If each of the 144 points is randomly assigned either an *X* or an *O*, the problem is very difficult and time-consuming. The problem is simplified if you assign the same symbol to all the points in a small area. For example, the 12 × 12 matrix can be divided into 36 smaller 2 × 2 squares, with all 4 points in a given square containing the same symbol. Or the 12 × 12 display can be divided into 3 × 3, 4 × 4, and 6 × 6 squares. The examples in Figure 6-11 show that the complexity of the display diminishes as the size of the squares increases. You can further reduce the difficulty of the problem by labeling one edge of the card as its top. We strongly recommend doing so, because not knowing which way is up, so to speak, can slow the solution. You need not use the word

Figure 6-11. Several Levels of Display Complexity

```
O O O O O O X X X X X X        O O O O O O O O O O O O
O O O O O O X X X X X X        O O O O O O O O O O O O
O O O O O O X X X X X X        O O O O O O O O O O O O
O O O O O O X X X X X X        X X X X X X X X X X X X
O O O O O O X X X X X X        X X X X X X X X X X X X
O O O O O O X X X X X X        X X X X X X X X X X X X
O O O O O O O O O O O O        O O O O O O X X X X X X
O O O O O O O O O O O O        O O O O O O X X X X X X
O O O O O O O O O O O O        O O O O O O X X X X X X
O O O O O O O O O O O O        X X X X X X O O O O O O
O O O O O O O O O O O O        X X X X X X O O O O O O
O O O O O O O O O O O O        X X X X X X O O O O O O

            6 × 6                            3 × 3

X X X X X X O O O O O O        X O X O O X X X X X X O
X X X X X X O O O O O O        O X X O O X O O O X X X
O O O O O O X X O O X X        X X O O O O O X O O O X
O O O O O O X X O O X X        X O X X X X X O O O X O
X X X X X X X X X X X X        X O X X X X X O O O X O
X X X X X X X X X X X X        X O X O O X X O O O X X
O O X X O O O O X X X X        O O O O O O O O X X X O
O O X X O O O O X X X X        X X X O X O O X O X O O
O O X X O O X X X X O O        X X O X X X X O X O O O
O O X X O O X X X X O O        O X O X O O O X X O X X
O O X X X X O O O O X X        X X X X O O O X X O X O
O O X X X X O O O O X X        O O X O X X O O O O X X

            2 × 2                          Random
```

top; any symbol in the same place on every card will serve. Finally, for quick verification that the group has solved the problem correctly, you may wish to print a number on the back of the card identifying the pattern, assigning identical cards the same identification number.

The deck contains varying numbers of duplicate cards at the several levels of complexity. Below is the list of pattern types to use in making up the deck. Notice that the deck contains more than one card of every pattern except one; one card with a 2 × 2 pattern is unique.

LIST OF TYPES

Two cards of a 6 × 6 pattern
Two of another 6 × 6 pattern
Two of a 4 × 4 pattern

Three of another 4 × 4 pattern
Two of a 3 × 3 pattern
Two of another 3 × 3 pattern
Four of still another 3 × 3 pattern
Two of another 2 × 2 pattern
Two of another 2 × 2 pattern
Three of still another 2 × 2 pattern
One card of yet another 2 × 2 pattern (the unique card)
Two of a random pattern
Three of another random pattern

Total: Thirty cards

The consultant introduces the exercise by reviewing the instructions below with the group and, if desired, passing out copies. The consultant then mixes the cards and distributes them as equally as possible. Forty minutes is an average time for solving the problem.

The Card Discovery Problem

Instructions: A set of cards will be distributed among you. One card in the set is a *singleton;* it is unique. In other words, each card in the entire set has one or more duplicates except the singleton card. Your task as a group is to discover the singleton card in the set. When your group indicates that the unique card has been identified, the task is ended whether or not you are correct, so be sure that everyone is confident of your choice before you declare.

You may organize yourselves any way you wish to complete this task, except for the following restrictions:

1. You may not show your cards to another member.
2. You may not pass cards to another member.
3. You must not look at another member's cards.
4. You may not draw pictures or diagrams of the designs.
5. Pay no attention to the numbers on the back of the cards.
6. Do not pool your discards. Keep your own discards in your own separate pile.

While it is very important that you do not make an error in selecting the unique card, you will be scored also for the amount of time it takes you to complete the task.

After participants reach a decision, they should discuss the influence and decision making that occurred during the exercise, compare their way of working on this problem with the way they usually work as a group, and give their ideas about the barriers that reduced the effective use of group resources. Fosmire (1970) has noted four common errors among groups that try to solve this problem: (1) failure to agree on a common language for describing the displays, (2) attempting to work in pairs or trios instead of remaining in a single group, (3) passive listening, and (4) silent acceptance of nonunderstanding. The two latter errors he describes as follows:

> If one member describes a card and another replies, "I've got one; let's throw it out!" the group may be making two mistakes. First, the member may not be hearing the description correctly, but he does not paraphrase, so no one catches the error. Second, there may be a third card in the set. If a more passive member has the third card, he may fail to speak up to double-check his suspicion that he holds the card, silently accepting his nonunderstanding, only to run the risk of erroneously identifying that card as the singleton later in the task (pp. 21–22).

Consultants should watch for those errors, but should not prevent them from happening and should present their observations to the group for discussion during the debriefing phase of the exercise.

Consensus Exercises

The exercises in this section allow participants to practice consensual decision making. The first exercise is described in complete detail, but we have condensed others by eliminating some information about procedures. Using the first exercise as a pattern, the consultant can create handouts and scoring sheets for the others.

Grievances of Black Citizens. In the long form of this exercise, participants predict the order in which a large group of mostly black citizens identified the most significant grievances of American blacks in 1968. Distribute to participants the instruction sheet headed "Grievances of Black Citizens." Participants first rank-order the items individually and then discuss them to achieve a consensual order. Use the instructions for consensus and guided debriefing given below; see also the section "Group Decision Making" earlier in this chapter. The ordering of the grievances given by the National Advisory Commission on Civil Disorders (1968), from most to least grievous, is as follows. The letters are those used on the handout.

1. (D) Discriminatory police practices
2. (H) Unemployment and underemployment
3. (E) Inadequate housing

4. (A) Inadequate education
5. (G) Poor recreational facilities
6. (L) Unresponsive political structure
7. (B) Disrespectful white attitudes
8. (I) Discriminatory administration of justice
9. (J) Inadequate federal programs
10. (C) Inadequate municipal services
11. (K) Discriminatory consumer and credit practices
12. (F) Inadequate welfare programs

Grievances of Black Citizens

During the fall of 1967 the research staff of the National Advisory Commission on Civil Disorders (the Kerner Commission) studied conditions in twenty cities that had experienced riots during 1967. The group consisted of nine cities that had experienced major destruction, six New Jersey cities surrounding Newark, and five cities that had experienced lesser degrees of violence.

A majority of the interviewees in each city was composed of black residents living in or near the disorder areas. Also interviewed were people from the official sector (mayors, city officials, policemen and police officials, judges, and others) and the private sector (businessmen, labor leaders, and community leaders). Altogether, more than 1,200 persons were interviewed, the large majority being black citizens living in or near the riot-torn areas.

Using the answers to the interviews, the investigators identified and assigned weights to the four types of grievances that appeared to have the greatest significance to the black community in each city. For each city they made judgments about the severity of particular grievances and assigned ranks to the four most serious. Their judgments were based on the frequency with which a particular grievance was mentioned, the relative intensity with which it was discussed, references to incidents exemplifying the grievance, and estimates of severity obtained from those interviewed.

Four points were assigned to the most serious type of grievance in each city, three to the second most serious, and so on. When the point values were added for all cities, a list of twelve rank-ordered grievance types emerged. The type of grievance considered the most serious in the most cities was number 1. The one that seemed generally least serious was number 12. Following are the twelve grievance types reported by the Kerner Commission. Your task is to guess how they were ordered by the commission staff.

Put a 1 beside the type of grievance you believe the staff judged that black citizens felt to be the most serious to them across all twenty cities. Put a 2 beside the second most serious and pervasive, and so on down to a 12 beside the least widespread and least serious.

_____ A. Inadequate education: de facto segregation, poor-quality instruction and facilities, inadequate curriculum, etc.

_____ B. Disrespectful white attitudes: racism and a lack of respect for the dignity of blacks.

_____ C. Inadequate municipal services: inadequate sanitation and garbage removal, inadequate health care facilities, etc.

_____ D. Discriminatory police practices: physical or verbal abuse, no grievance channels, discrimination in hiring and promoting blacks, etc.

_____ E. Inadequate housing: poor housing-code enforcement, discrimination in sales and rentals, overcrowding.

_____ F. Inadequate welfare programs: unfair qualification regulations, negative attitude of welfare workers toward recipients.

_____ G. Poor recreational facilities: inadequate parks and playgrounds, lack of organized programs, etc.

_____ H. Unemployment and underemployment: discrimination in hiring and placement by organizations or by unions, general lack of full-time jobs, etc.

_____ I. Discriminatory administration of justice: discriminatory treatment in the courts, presumption of guilt, etc.

_____ J. Inadequate federal programs: insufficient participation by the poor, lack of continuity, inadequate funding.

_____ K. Discriminatory consumer and credit practices: blacks sold inferior-quality goods at higher prices, excessive interest rates, fraudulent commercial practices.

_____ L. Unresponsive political structure: inadequate representation of blacks, lack of response to complaints, obscurity of official grievance channels.

The short form of this exercise, which takes less time, offers participants only eight grievances to rank instead of twelve. The same instructions can be used, but all designations of twelve should be changed to eight. The eight items we have used and their correct ranking are as follows:

1. (C) Discriminatory police practices
2. (F) Unemployment and underemployment
3. (D) Inadequate housing
4. (A) Inadequate education
5. (H) Unresponsive political structure
6. (B) Disrespectful white attitudes
7. (G) Inadequate federal programs
8. (E) Inadequate welfare programs

To begin, instruct participants to work individually, without conferring, and to rank-order the items according to the instructions they read on their sheets headed "Grievances of Black Citizens." Next, give the participants "Instructions for Consensus." After they read this sheet, instruct them to come to a consensual decision of the best way to rank-order the twelve items (or eight in the short form).

INSTRUCTIONS FOR CONSENSUS

Consensus means general agreement and concord. For consensus to exist, it is not necessary for every participant to agree in full, but it is necessary for every person to be heard and, in the end, for none to believe that the decision violates his or her convictions. It is not necessary that every person consider the decision the best one.

Consensus is a decision process for making full use of resources and for resolving conflicts creatively. Consensus is difficult to reach, so not every ranking will meet with everyone's complete approval. Complete unanimity is not the goal—it is rarely achieved. But each individual should be able to accept the group rankings on the basis of logic and feasibility. When all group members feel this way, the group has reached consensus as defined here, and the judgment may be entered as a group decision. This means, in effect, that individuals can block the group if they think it necessary; at the same time, they should use this option in the best sense of reciprocity. Here are some guidelines for achieving consensus:

1. Avoid arguing for your own rankings. Present your position as lucidly and logically as possible, but listen to the other members' reactions and consider them carefully before you press your point.
2. Do not assume that someone must win and someone lose when discussion reaches a stalemate. Instead look for the next most acceptable alternative for all parties.
3. Avoid simply voting; don't try to resolve differences arithmetically. Through discussion, try to find a decision that has an objective and logical foundation.
4. Differences of opinion are natural and expected. Seek them out and try to involve everyone in the decision. Disagreements can help the group's decision because, with a wide range of information and opinions, there is a greater chance that the group will find a better solution.

Allow groups approximately forty-five minutes to reach consensus about their rank-orderings, and then ask them to tabulate the results. In each group let one person act as secretary. As members of the group call out their private rank-orderings of the twelve (or eight) items, the secretary records them on the scoring sheet shown in Figure 6-12. When each person's rank-ordering has been recorded, the secretary sums the ranking for each of the items and rank-orders the sums, thus arriving at an

Figure 6-12. Scoring Sheet for "Grievances of Black Citizens"

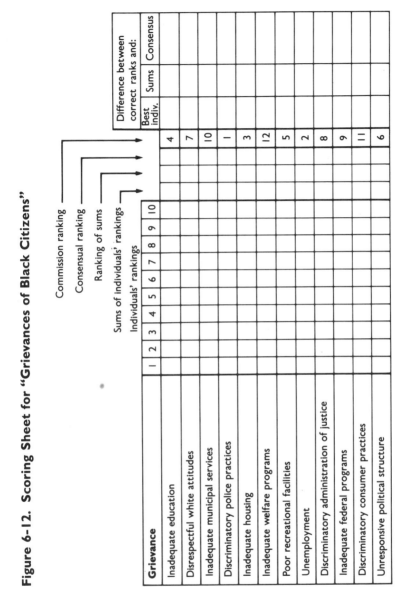

average rank-order for the group. (This is the rank-order that might have been obtained had the group merely voted and not held a discussion.) The secretary also records the rank-order that the group has reached by consensus.

It is best if all groups work in one large room in circles that are separated to minimize mutual distraction. When the secretaries in each group have completed their work, the correct answer to this exercise according to the Kerner Commission is announced. The secretaries also record this rank-ordering on their sheets. Each group then computes three scores by summing the differences (ignoring whether the differences are plus or minus) between the correct rank-order and (1) the rank-order obtained through consensus, (2) the average rank-order of the group before discussion, and (3) the individual rank-order that came closest to the rank-order. Each group then sees whether its "best" individual, its average produced before discussion, or its consensual product is superior. The smaller sums of differences are the superior scores.

After the participants have inspected and informally discussed the charts for a few minutes, each group should discuss three questions. The highlights of these discussions should be made known to the total assembly of participants.

1. What were my reactions to the exercise? How did I feel? What was I thinking?
2. How similar was our behavior here to our usual behavior in school? How different? What are the implications of this exercise for our staff?
3. How well did we use our group resources? What prevented us from using them better? How could the obstacles to better use of resources have been avoided?

Occupational Prestige in the United States. The following instructions can be used in the same way as the foregoing as an exercise in consensus. The numbers in parentheses are the correct rankings and should not appear on the sheet given to the participants at the outset.

Occupational Prestige in the United States _____

Instructions: In 1963 the National Opinion Research Center at the University of Chicago conducted a study of the prestige accorded ninety occupations. A national sample of the American adult population was interviewed, and all interviewed were asked their personal opinions of the general standing of each job. Below is a list of fifteen occupations included in this study. Your task is to rank them in the same order of prestige as did the sample of the American public. Place a 1 by the occupation that you think was ranked as most prestigious by the national sample; place a 2 by the second most prestigious occupation, and so on, through the number 15, which will be your estimate of the least prestigious of the fifteen occupations.

_____ Priest (8)
_____ Nuclear physicist (2)
_____ Author of novels (11)
_____ Banker (9)
_____ Member of the board of directors of a large corporation (7)
_____ Carpenter (15)
_____ Owner of a factory that employs about 100 people (10)
_____ Physician (1)
_____ Electrician (13)
_____ Lawyer (5)
_____ Architect (6)
_____ College professor (4)
_____ Official of an international labor union (12)
_____ State governor (3)
_____ Undertaker (14)

Below is an alternate list of occupations taken from the same source as the one above.

_____ Banker (6)
_____ U.S. representative in Congress (2)
_____ Public school teacher (8)
_____ Railroad engineer (11)
_____ Sociologist (7)
_____ Musician in a symphony orchestra (10)
_____ Dentist (3)
_____ Radio announcer (14)
_____ Insurance agent (15)
_____ Minister (4)
_____ U.S. Supreme Court Justice (1)
_____ Farm owner and operator (12)
_____ Policeman (13)
_____ Airline pilot (5)
_____ Building contractor (9)

The Desert-survival Problem. Another consensus exercise has been developed by J. C. Lafferty, P. M. Eady, and A. W. Pond of Human Synergistics. The exercise involves a situation in which a plane has crashed in the Sonoran Desert, seventy miles from an inhabited mining camp. The crew is left with twelve items. Again, participants are asked to rank the items first alone and later as a group using the norms of consensus. Unfortunately, we have not been given permission to print the specifics of the exercise. If you wish to use the exercise for educational (nonprofit) purposes, write to us for details.

Lost at Sea. Pfeiffer and Jones have collected a great many exercises, including consensus exercises, into two very useful series of books: the *Handbook of Structured Experiences for Human Relations Training* (1969 to present) and the *Annual Handbooks for Group Facilitators* (1972 to present). Volume 4 (1973) of the *Handbook of Structured Experiences* collects eight consensus exercises into one section. A consensus exercise we particularly like is "Lost at Sea"; it appears in the 1975 *Annual Handbook*. Because "Lost at Sea" is easily available in the Pfeiffer and Jones volume at no cost for educational purposes, we do not reproduce it here.

Characteristics of a Successful Teacher. The following can also be used as an exercise in consensus. Although there are no correct rankings, the topic is of real relevance to people in schools, and reaching consensus on the most important characteristics of a successful teacher often brings out major value differences useful as foci for discussion.

Characteristics of a Successful Teacher _____

Following is a list of eleven characteristics of a successful teacher plus one space for adding any characteristic you think has been overlooked. Rank-order the characteristics according to your opinion of their importance in contributing to successful teaching.

Your rank-order		Group's rank-order
_____	Encouraging creativity among students.	_____
_____	Maintaining an orderly and quiet classroom.	_____
_____	Enriching the course of study or curriculum of the class-room.	_____
_____	Giving individual attention to students.	_____
_____	Experimenting with new teaching techniques.	_____
_____	Diagnosing learning problems of students.	_____
_____	Coordinating classroom activities with other parts of the school program.	_____
_____	Ensuring that students learn basic skills.	_____
_____	Solving personal problems of individual students.	_____
_____	Developing student ability in analytical reasoning and problem solving.	_____
_____	Developing the aesthetic potential of students.	_____
_____	Other (specify): _____	_____

Intergroup Exercises

The exercises that follow show the effects of hierarchical decision making. Both require that more than one group work together in the same organization. Suggestions for forming the groups are included in each description.

Planners and Operators. By simulating problems that arise when one team makes decisions about another team's work, this exercise demonstrates the difficulties of using a formal hierarchy in group problem solving. Participants learn about the processes of team planning, about communication problems between a planning and an implementing group, and about the problems an implementing group confronts when carrying out a plan that is not its own.

The exercise is performed by clusters of nine to twelve persons divided into three subgroups of four planners, four operators, and one to four observers. The planners decide how they will carry the task through as best they can; and the observers watch the process, making notes of efficiencies and difficulties. The task consists of joining sixteen puzzle pieces designed to form a 12-inch square, leaving an empty 1-inch square in the center. The diagonal lines on the diagram given to the planners (see Figure 6-13) are made thicker than the others to hint to the planners how they might organize their instructions for the operators.

Each member of the planning team is given four pieces of the puzzle; the planning team has the diagram shown in Figure 6-13. In placing the pieces in four piles, the exact distribution is not of great importance; the following combinations are possible—(1) A, B, I, G; (2) A, C, D, H; (3) A, D, F, J; (4) A, E, J, G—although the actual pieces should not be labeled. The key restriction on the planning group is that its members may not move the pieces, put the puzzle together, or give a drawing of the design to the operating team; they may only tell the operators orally or in written words how to fit the pieces together.

The consultant explains that this is a simulation in which planners instruct operators to carry out a task, and divides the group into four-person planning teams, four-person operating teams, and observers. Observers leave the room to be briefed by a consultant later. Operators go to another room. Planners gather around their tables to get acquainted.

Out of hearing of both the planning and operating teams, the consultant briefs observers on what to look for in the planning, communicating, and implementing stages of the exercises, giving each a copy of the "Briefing Sheet for Observing Team" (see Figure 6-14).

To planning teams the consultant hands out briefing sheets (Figure 6-15) and puzzle materials, reads the briefing sheets aloud, and empha-

Figure 6-13. Planner's and Operator's Puzzle

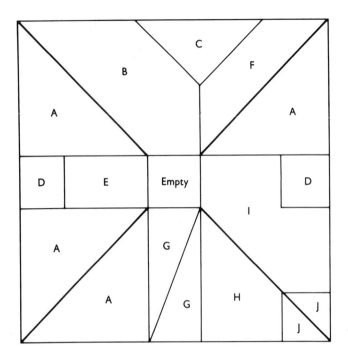

sizes that the planning must end in forty minutes. The planning now gets under way.

The consultant then goes to the operating teams to distribute briefing sheets (Figure 6-16) that explain their task during the waiting period. Essentially this task is to discuss how they feel while waiting to be instructed and how they can prepare themselves for an unknown task. They are told that their planning team may summon them at any time but that if they are not called by five minutes before the task is to begin, they are to report for work anyway. If the participants ask about visiting the other groups or passing notes, some consultants will carry notes between groups and allow planners to visit operators (but not vice versa).

When the planning is completed, whether in forty minutes or sooner, the planning team calls in the operating team and gives instructions.

The consultant now calls time to begin, instructing planners to step back from the table and to remain silent as the operating team begins its work.

Figure 6-14. Briefing Sheet for the Observing Team

You will be observing a planning team decide how to solve a problem and give instruction to an operating team so that they can carry out the solution. The problem consists of assembling sixteen flat pieces into the form of a square containing an empty square in its middle. The planning team is supplied with a diagram of the assembled pieces. This team is not to assemble the pieces itself, but is to instruct the operating team how to assemble the parts in minimum time. You will be silent observers throughout the process.

Suggestions

1. Each member of the observing team should watch the general pattern of communication but give special attention to one member of the planning team (during the planning phase) and one member of the operating team (during the assembling period).

2. During the planning period watch for the following behavior:
   a. Is there a balanced participation among planning team members?
   b. What kinds of behavior block or facilitate the process?
   c. How does the planning team divide its time between planning and instructing? (How early does it invite the operating team to come in?)
   d. Does the team decide that certain members should do one thing during the instructing and other members other things? If so, how do they decide?

3. During the instructing period, watch for the following behavior:
   a. At the beginning of the instruction, how do the planners orient the operators to their task?
   b. What assumptions made by the planning team are not communicated to the orienting team?
   c. How effective are the instructions?
   d. Does the operating team appear to feel free to ask questions of the planners?

4. During the assembly period, watch for the following behavior:
   a. What evidence do the operating team members exhibit that instructions were clearly understood or misunderstood?
   b. What nonverbal reactions do planning team members exhibit as they watched their plans being implemented or distorted?

Operators complete the task according to their instructions, taking as much time as necessary.

Discussion includes reports from the observers, planners, and operators and observations of similarities between the exercise and other organizational and group experiences.

Planners and operators both experience several kinds of learning in the course of this exercise. Planners learn that it is frustrating to plan a task that someone else has to carry out and that they are themselves

Figure 6-15. Briefing Sheet for the Planning Team

Each member of the team sits by a packet containing some pieces of a puzzle. When all the pieces from all four packets are properly assembled, they will form a large square containing an empty place in the middle. A sheet bearing a diagram of the completed puzzle is provided for your team.

Your task is to do the following

1. Plan how the sixteen pieces distributed among you can be assembled to make the puzzle.

2. Decide on a plan for instructing your operating team how to assemble the puzzle.

3. You may call the operating team and begin instructing them at any time during the next forty minutes.

4. The operating team must begin assembling the puzzle forty-five minutes from now, and you are required to give them at least five minutes of instruction.

Before you start, read these rules

During planning:

1. Keep the pieces in your packet and in front of you at all times.

2. Do not touch the pieces nor trade any with other persons, either now or during the instruction phase.

3. Do not assemble the square; that is the operators' job.

4. Do not mark on any of the pieces.

During instruction:

1. Give all instructions in words. Do not show the diagram to the operators; hide it. Do not draw any diagrams yourselves, either on paper or in the air with gestures. You may convey your verbal instructions either orally or on paper.

2. The operating team must not move the pieces until the signal is given to start.

3. Do not show any diagram to the operators.

4. After the signal is given for the assembly to begin, you may *not* give any further instructions; stand back and observe.

---

prohibited from performing. They frequently spend so much time planning the activity that they do not allow enough time to communicate their plans adequately to the operators, with the result that a good deal of the planning effort is wasted. In addition, planners often place limitations on themselves that are not in their instructions and fail to use all the resources at their disposal. Indeed, their very preoccupation with giving information under pressure often reduces the efficacy of the communication. They sometimes use geometric or other terms that the operators do not understand, and they frequently give cumbersome

Figure 6-16. Briefing Sheet for the Operating Team

1. Your team of four people will have the responsibility of carrying out a task according to instructions given you by your planning team.

2. Your task will begin forty-five minutes from now.

3. Your planning team may call you in for instruction at any time during the next forty minutes.

4. If they do not summon you during the next forty minutes, you must report to them at your own initiative at the end of the forty minutes.

5. While you wait for a call from your planning team, do the following:

   a. Individually, write on a piece of paper the concerns you feel while waiting for instructions.

   b. As a group, think of anything you can that might help you follow instructions or hinder you in doing so. Write the things that are working for you on one sheet of paper and the things that are working against you on another.

   c. How can the four of you organize as a team to receive and follow the instructions? Make notes on a sheet of paper.

   d. Keep handy the sheets on which you have written your ideas. You may find them useful during the discussion that takes place after you have completed the task.

6. You may send notes to the planners, and they may send notes in reply. Give notes to the game leader or to an observer to be carried to the planners.

7. Once you have begun the task your planners give you—forty-five minutes from now—your planning team will not be allowed to give you any further instructions.

8. Finish the assigned task as rapidly as possible.

---

instructions in writing instead of taking the time to give them aloud. At the same time, planning is a very seductive task, which so absorbs the interest and attention of planners that they often forget what the operators are experiencing, and fail to take into account their anxieties, their need to feel physically comfortable in the environment, and so forth.

For their part, operators often feel anxiety about performing an unknown task and usually develop some antagonistic feelings toward the planning team. This is particularly true when several groups are engaging in the exercise in one large room and one operating team is called by its planners after seeing other teams called in earlier. Sometimes an operating team sets up its own organizational structure, selecting a leader to receive their instructions and give them guidance; but this structure is typically ignored by the planners, who usually never suspect that such an organization exists.

When the exercise is completed, the ensuing discussion may be guided by questions such as the following: Did you feel that your behavior during this task was typical, or were you surprised by some of your behaviors or feelings? Which actions of the planners and operators surprised you? What was most frustrating about the task, and what do you think is the key to its successful completion? What could planners or operators have done to improve their own or the other group's performance? What occurred during the exercise that was like or unlike what occurs at our school? Did any ideas arise that might be used to improve our school's organizational functioning? If no one else does, the consultant may summarize the important points raised during the discussion.

The Prisoners' Dilemma. This exercise simulates a risk-taking situation like that experienced by two guilty prisoners being questioned separately by the police. Each is told what the other has confessed and that a similar confession will get them both off easier. Each prisoner's dilemma is whether to confess. The exercise allows groups to explore win-lose, zero-sum-influence situations and dramatizes the merits of collaboration and competition in intergroup relations. This exercise is adapted from Pfeiffer and Jones (1974, pp. 52–56).

Two teams of three to eight persons are seated far enough apart so that they cannot overhear or communicate with each other unless told to do so. One team is designated Red and the other Blue. The exercise consists of ten rounds, in each of which the Reds vote either an *A* or *B* and the Blues vote either an *X* or *Y*. Teams have three minutes to make the decision for each round before reporting their choices and discovering their scores.

Points are awarded for each round as follows: (1) if Reds choose *A* and Blues choose *X*, both teams win 3 points; (2) if Reds choose *A* and Blues choose *Y*, Reds lose 6 points and Blues win 6; (3) if Reds choose *B* and Blues choose *X*, Reds win 6 and Blues lose 6; (4) if Reds choose *B* and Blues choose *Y*, both teams lose 3 points. (See Figure 6-17.) Points won or lost are doubled in the fourth round and quadrupled in the ninth and tenth rounds. Points for each round and a running total for each team are recorded on newsprint. If desired, teams may appoint representatives to "negotiate" before the fourth and eighth rounds. Negotiators meet for one minute where they cannot be overheard by either team. Other than imposing a time limit and designating the meeting place, the consultant does not limit what happens in those sessions.

Final debriefing can begin with questions like these: How were decisions made in our team? Who was most influential in our team? What were the advantages and disadvantages of collaborating with, competing with, being suspicious of, trusting, defeating, or losing to the other team? How was our work method in this exercise like or unlike everyday life in this organization?

Figure 6-17. Scoring Chart for the Prisoner's Dilemma

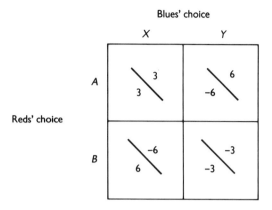

Examining Influence and Participation

The next three procedures can be used in sequence to examine influence and group-participation patterns. Like High-Talker Tap-Out, Beach Ball, and such instruments as Communication Roles (see Chapter 3), these procedures provide good transitions from communication skill to decision-making process.

Influence Group. Participants form three groups of equal size composed respectively and exclusively of high influencers, moderate influencers, and low influencers. The members decide among themselves by consensus who is to be in which group. Consensus on the final grouping is very important and ends the active part of the procedure. Debriefing can begin in a Fishbowl arrangement, with each group taking a turn in the center to discuss how it feels to be in this group and how its members feel toward the other two groups. The total group then explores the likely effects of the grouping on the functioning of the subgroups and total group.

Self-assessment of Participation. Group members form three groups of equal size composed of high talkers, moderate talkers, and low talkers, each group to discuss a regular item on the agenda in the presence of the two other groups. The Fishbowl arrangement allows all members to see how persons of high, middle, and low talkativeness deal with issues and also to see what the problems of communication are in these three groups.

Knutson (1960) has demonstrated that highly loquacious persons get the greatest attention from others, including their own kind; that worthwhile contributions from low talkers are often inhibited or buried by the garrulousness of high talkers; and that high and low talkers alike come to believe that low talkers have little to offer. Asking high talkers to be quiet while low talkers speak can expand possibilities for both listening and interaction.

After every subgroup has had its turn in the center, the entire group discusses what has happened (Knutson's points will usually emerge in the discussion). Finally, the entire staff proceeds with the rest of the agenda. At the end of the meeting, members are asked whether the exercise had any effect on the later portion of the meeting.

Influence Roles. Two kinds of influence on group functions must be present for meetings to be effective: task functions, which answer the work requirements of the meeting; and the maintenance functions, which help the group with its interpersonal feelings and internal cohesion. Ideally, all staff members should be capable of performing both of these functions. Usually, however, only a few perform task functions and even fewer perform maintenance functions. In this exercise, group members individually nominate one person as the one who most often performs one or the other function in their group. Below, we have itemized each of the two functions into six subfunctions. Twelve names are written down, one for each influence role below, and all nominations are listed on newsprint.

INFLUENCING TASK

1. Initiating: proposing tasks or goals; defining a group problem, suggesting a procedure for solving a problem, suggesting other ideas for consideration.
2. Information or opinion seeking: requesting facts on the problem, seeking relevant information, asking for suggestions and ideas.
3. Information or opinion giving: offering, facts, providing relevant information; stating a belief, giving suggestions or ideas.
4. Clarifying or elaborating: interpreting or reflecting ideas or suggestions, clearing up confusion, indicating alternatives and issues before the group, giving examples.
5. Summarizing: pulling related ideas together, restating suggestions after the group has discussed them.
6. Consensus testing: sending up trial balloons to see whether the

group is nearing a conclusion or whether agreement has been reached.

INFLUENCING MAINTENANCE

1. *Encouraging:* being friendly, warm, and responsive to others; accepting others and their contributions; listening; showing regard for others by giving them opportunity or recognition.
2. *Expressing group feelings:* sensing feeling, mood, relationships within the group; sharing one's own feelings with other members.
3. *Harmonizing:* attempting to reconcile disagreements; reducing tension by oiling troubled waters; getting people to explore their differences.
4. *Compromising:* offering to compromise one's own position, ideas, or status; admitting error; disciplining oneself to help maintain the group.
5. *Gatekeeping:* seeing that others have a chance to speak; maintaining group discussion rather than one-, two-, or three-way conversations.
6. *Setting standards:* expressing standards that will help the group to achieve; applying standards in evaluating group functioning and production.

Debriefing can focus on individual feelings and behavior either causing or resulting from the nominations, or on consequences for the group of the centralized or dispersed structure described by the nomination pattern.

This exercise can also be combined with the self-assessment of participation described earlier. After the group has divided into equal subgroups of high, moderate, and low talkers, there will be twice as many observers as participants in the Fishbowl. Each inside participant can have one outside colleague watching for task functions and another outside colleague watching for maintenance functions. The pairs of outside colleagues can give the inside participants feedback on the functions they did or did not carry out during group discussion.

If this procedure is repeated several times, persons being observed can tell the observers about several functions they would like to try to perform more, and the observers can give feedback in later meetings on the frequency with which they see their colleagues performing those functions. One of the most important conclusions to be drawn from such an activity is that many contributions are influential and helpful to the group even when not focused directly on the task. In addition, the dispersion of influence is likely to increase as more members learn how to keep the discussion circulating widely through the group.

Decision-making Roles

This exercise provides a vehicle for achieving group agreements about the roles each member should assume in decision making. In the matrix that follows, the columns represent different jobs or status levels within the organization; the rows represent functions about which decision making occurs. Participants use their own jobs and functions to head the columns and rows.

	Principal	Assistant principal	Coun-selors	Teachers	Service personnel	Students
Determin-ing goals	_____	_____	_____	_____	_____	_____
Ordering materials	_____	_____	_____	_____	_____	_____
Sequencing procedures	_____	_____	_____	_____	_____	_____

Next, the consultant describes six kinds of influence that persons can have on a decision and tells the group to complete the matrix by discussing the kind of influence appropriately exerted on each function by each position. The kinds of influence are as follows:

KINDS OF INFLUENCE

Blank: May recommend or suggest. Because it is understood in a healthy organization that any person in any position may make recommendations to the person who can authorize action, we enter no special symbol for recommending and suggesting.

I: Must be informed. *I* means that position holders must know the results of a decision to take appropriate coordinating action. *I* usually shows that a position will be affected by a decision or that the position holder will have to implement the decision.

C: Must be consulted. The position must be given an opportunity to influence the decision making by presenting information, demonstration, or proof. Those with *C* power should be consulted early enough so that their information can make a genuine difference in the final decision.

P: Must participate. *P* means that position holders must take part in making the decision and that at least a majority vote of all those with a *P* is necessary before the decision can be final.

V: Veto power. *V* means that position holders have veto power over the function and that their agreement must be obtained before the decision can be made.

A: Authority to make decision. *A* represents the greatest power of all. Those with *A* can make the decision, and others must go along with it.

MACROSEQUENCES FOR DECISION MAKING

In designing macrosequences from the exercises in this chapter, four guidelines will be helpful: (1) begin with feedback, (2) sequence according to the social-psychological level of emphasis, (3) move from exercises to closer approximations of the group's real world, and (4) repeat or provide similar experiences to assess progress.

To help a school group move toward discussion of decision-making processes, first collect systematic data on meetings using the meetings questionnaire or observation categories presented earlier in this chapter. Next, report a summary of the data to the staff. Finally, the staff might do the self-assessment of participation exercise to highlight their own contributions or lack of contributions to decision making at meetings.

Two sequences are useful for acquainting participants firsthand about how the dilemmas of power and decision making look at the interpersonal, group, and organizational levels. One starts with an interpersonal exercise such as Grievances of Black Citizens or Lost at Sea and ends at the intergroup or organization level with the Planners and Operators exercise. Another sequence moves in the opposite direction, beginning with the organizational emphasis, proceeding to the face-to-face group, and ending at the interpersonal level.

The sequence chosen depends upon the level of interaction that participants are most eager to explore at the beginning of a training event and upon the goal toward which the consultant wishes to lead them. Generally, we believe that moving from the interpersonal to the organizational level is the more effective procedure. Participants can easily think about interpersonal influence at the beginning of training and, by proceeding from small group to organization, can be encouraged to analyze the issues of power and decision making in their organization more carefully.

Moving from exercises to procedures helps a group make use of the lessons learned from the exercises. After a consensus exercise such as Grievances of Black Citizens, for example, the consultant can give the group a comparable period of time in which to reach consensus on some actual group issue that requires clarification and decision. In the course of the real decision making, the consultant can ask them to take a self-assessment of participation. After the group has had ample time to reach a decision, participants can discuss how well they used members' resources, diffused participation, and made decisions. Occasional comments on processes by the consultant help participants become more aware of their actual methods of making decisions.

Presenting two or more of the five exercises on consensual decision making one after the other can be particularly useful when participants can meet for only two or three hours at a time and the times are spread over several months or more. Desert Survival, Grievances of Black Citizens, and Characteristics of a Successful Teacher, for example, can be presented sequentially, each followed by a discussion of how well the group used its resources in making the decisions. The repetitive pattern encourages group members to remind one another of the new norms about discussion and decision making that these exercises expose. In addition, a series of exercises makes improvement visible. By seeing how well they perform in subsequent exercises, group members are less likely to deceive themselves about the difficulty of making effective decisions consensually.

7

Working with Conflicts

Conflicts are ubiquitous within school organizations; they occur continually, arise for many reasons, appear in a variety of forms, and affect the educational process both favorably and unfavorably. The presence of conflict is in itself neither good nor bad; it simply exists and should be expected. Administrators, teachers, parents, and students not only react differently to conflict but react differently from case to case and from time to time. Thus, the most effective strategies for dealing with conflicts must also vary according to the conflict, the school, and the parties involved. That is, an appropriate conflict-management strategy will depend on the type of conflict, the intensity of the disagreement, the persons participating in the conflict, the seriousness of the issue for them, and the authority, resources, and knowledge they possess.

Conflicts range from disagreements over important matters to intensely emotional struggles over cherished resources. Conflicts of all varieties do create tension, anxiety, and unpleasantness. But unpleasant experiences in themselves are not always bad for the school. They can supply the punch and push needed for growth and development. Indeed, bringing conflicts into the open can provide a creative tension that inspires problem solving. Moreover, open discussions of conflicts can enhance individual or group performance.

OD consultants must know how to seek out conflicts, how to conceptualize them and make them known, and how to help school participants generate creative solutions to them. The nature of the conflict-management strategy will depend in part on a careful analysis of the conflict itself and in part on the consultant's own skill in working with school people in conflict. This chapter is intended to serve as a guide for diagnosing and analyzing organizational conflicts in schools, for determining when it is appropriate for consultants to intervene, and for selecting designs and specific consultative techniques for managing school conflicts.

One of the primary demands on any school organization is that its various parts should be linked together to achieve overall objectives. To accomplish common tasks and achieve goals generally requires collaboration, and for most educational tasks the need for participant interdependence is great. Teachers in teams must work together; curriculum specialists at the district level must work with teachers; indeed, to facilitate a more open school, groups of teachers and administrators must work interdependently on committees and teaching teams that span grade levels.

Conflict is likely to arise when particular educational goals are perceived as being mutually exclusive (as when teachers believe that counseling is not benefiting students' cognitive learning); when activities undertaken to reach goals are regarded as interdependent (as when teachers and counselors alike believe that student self-concept is the key to cognitive learning); or when two or more parties draw upon the same limited resources to accomplish their goals (as when teachers and counselors compete for time with students).

More specifically, conflict occurs between two people when the goals of each are frustrated by the other, when each is competing for some reward at the other's expense, when they misunderstand or disagree with one another's expectations of conduct, or when they approach a problem from different points of view. Conflict occurs between groups for many of the same reasons, and it occurs between organizations when they compete for scarce resources or when, as in the case of revolutionary movements, the legitimacy of an organization is challenged.

For the OD consultant, conflict should not denote individual distaste, disappointment, frustration, anger, or any of the common forms of miscommunication discussed in Chapter 3. In these pages, conflict refers to a social condition in which two or more persons or groups cannot have the same thing at the same time. Further, OD consultants should regard school conflicts as natural unavoidable occurrences that cannot be expected to vanish of their own accord. Instead, they should be brought out into the open and managed by means of channels or occasions through which adversaries can introduce their conflicting claims into the business of the school.

If conflicts are legitimated, then compromises, trade-offs, and other negotiations can be conducted openly at problem-solving meetings; more realistic educational policies can be achieved, and anxieties diminished as outcomes are more clearly foreseen. If conflicts are not uncovered and managed, informal groups and underground networks (which often greatly distort the truth) will arise to cope with them, often increasing destructive tension and personal hostility between conflicting parties. Thus in many schools teachers cluster to criticize the work of counselors; counselors stay away from teachers, preferring to keep to their own offices and to enjoy informal breaks with one another; and only rarely do criticisms become public enough for problem solving to occur.

Before school conflict can be brought into the open for public discussion, some degree of interpersonal trust and constructive openness must exist. Most school participants, however, are unaccustomed to expressing open disagreement directly to those with whom they disagree. In many schools, direct discussion of conflict is experienced as unpleasant and undesirable both by those involved in the conflict and by those only observing it. This is especially true when staff members find it difficult to distinguish between disagreeing with a colleague's opinion and "putting down" or rejecting the colleague. Indeed, in addition to personal predilections, the norms of many school organizations militate against the open expression of differences. The OD consultant should work toward making constructive openness and the open confrontation of differences new norms within the school. School participants will be more willing to discuss conflict openly when a consultant, whose own skill in dealing with conflicts can serve as an important model, is present to support and legitimate the process.

The consultant should first look for signs of hidden conflict among individuals and subgroups. In some cases, different parts of the school may be unaware that they are competing for scarce resources; in other cases, competitors may be aware of conflict but unwilling to communicate about it publicly or officially. Second, the consultant should ascertain tentatively to what extent the conflict may be obstructing educational goals, making procedures inefficient, and frustrating the personal needs of staff members. Conversely, the consultant should also ascertain to what extent the conflict satisfies the power and achievement needs of some members and demonstrates qualities of inventive resourcefulness in the school. Third, if the consultant decides that the macrodesign should include steps for bringing the conflict into the open, procedures precisely suited to the nature of the conflict, the school, and the school's participants should be devised to make it accessible to direct and constructive dealing.

TYPES AND SOURCES OF CONFLICT

To reiterate briefly, in the *S-T-P* procedure for problem solving, the *S* (situation) refers to the essential features of a current condition, the *T* (target) to a desired condition toward which an individual or group is striving, and the *P* (path) to specific action-plans aimed at bringing about the desired condition. The *S* is commonly associated with facts, opinions, explanations, perceptions, and feelings; the *T*, with goals, aims, ends, values, purposes, and objectives; and the *P*, with paths, plans, strategies, and implementation. The *S-T-P* points us to three kinds of conflict.

Factual conflict (type *S*) involves argument about the realities of a current situation—either debate over easily discoverable facts, such as the number of square feet in a classroom, or over facts more difficult to gather, such as the opinions of math and science teachers about current curricula. *Value conflict* (type *T*) encompasses argument over values, goals, or objectives ranging from highly specific phenomena, such as students' behavior or achievements, to more general events, such as debates between essentialist and progressive educational philosophies. *Strategy conflict* (type *P*) involves argument over the best way of moving from a present condition to a valued future condition with respect to either the major stages of a macrodesign or the microaspects of a specific action-plan.

Conflicts can also be sorted by using the concepts of closeness versus distance, which we discussed in Chapter 3. Disagreement over facts, values, or strategies usually stem from topics or issues that are personally distant from both parties. Stronger conflicts—those conditions we typically call conflict—get down to things personally close to both parties. The question arises, "Can you and I both get what we want?" Those two types of conflict call for different consultative strategies. Talking things through, voting, and agreeing to disagree can be applied successfully to disagreements, while negotiation, bargaining, and finally taking action are often necessary to resolve intense conflict.

The sources of school conflict, whether mild or intense or of fact, value, or strategy, can also be categorized as (1) differentiation of function among parts of the school, (2) power struggles between persons and subsystems, (3) role conflicts, (4) differences in interpersonal style among school participants, and (5) stress imposed on the school by external forces.

Differentiation of Function

Effective adaptation to the community requires school organizations to communicate with their environments through a number of specialized units, and this differentiation of function is often a major source of conflict. Members of different departments or subgroups who have access to different kinds of information from that of their counterparts in other departments are likely to take a different view of the facts of a situation and to entertain different strategies for accomplishing their primary tasks. When the same problem is tackled from widely diverging points of view, the presence of various cognitive, emotional, and attitudinal differences will produce interpersonal and intergroup conflict. All too often, however, conflicts arising from functional differentiation are misunderstood as arising from someone's personal incompetence. This happens because school participants who interact every day are too close to their own parts of the organization to understand easily the parts others work in, and it is only natural for them to associate the source of the conflict with the person toward whom the frustration or irritation is directly felt.

An example of this type of misunderstanding once occurred in our work with a school staff. Over a period of months the staff had repeatedly complained that the counselor was doing such an inadequate job that they had begun to question his competence, although the principal and a school psychologist thought that he was doing a fine job and could not understand the staff's dissatisfaction with him. At a staff workshop designed by a couple of OD consultants, the issue was raised and dealt with as it had been many times before. Defensive, bewildered, and frustrated, the counselor knew that he worked hard but could somehow not get this across to the other staff members.

After listening to the discussion and asking several questions, the consultants realized that the problem had less to do with the counselor as a person than with the fact that his position and functions caused his primary energies to be directed toward community, parents, and other outside agencies. Because of the way their own tasks were organized, the teachers had had little contact with either the counselor himself or with those in the community with whom he worked, and for this reason they were largely unaware of the effects of his actions. The principal and psychologist, on the other hand, had considerable contact with the counselor and his work and were well aware of the effects of his actions. On the basis of this understanding, the consultants were able to educate the staff about the effects of differentiation of function and clear the way for improved communication and understanding between the teachers and the counselor.

In their work on industrial organizations, Lawrence and Lorsch

(1967) concluded that success in achieving both high differentiation and a high quality of collaboration is determined by the organization's processes for resolving conflict. When organizational mechanisms for resolving conflicts are ineffective, the conflicts caused by differentiation can be destructive. When conflict is openly confronted and resolved, both differentiation and collaboration are effectively promoted.

Power Struggles

A common cause of conflict in school faculties and districts, power struggles typically arise when some participants attempt to gain advantage over others. This can occur when adversaries compete for a commonly desired reward, such as a promotion or merit pay for good teaching; when self-interests conflict; when resources are scarce; and when opinions differ on the relative autonomy or interdependence of individuals or subgroups.

In one of our projects, for example, conflicting self-interests and the scarcity of a resource brought about a power struggle over a scheduling problem in an elementary school. One team comprising teachers of the first and second grades, another comprising the third and fourth grades, and still another comprising the fifth and sixth grades all wanted a late-afternoon PE schedule. All had good reasons, but, as only one gymnasium was available for the afternoon periods, the conflicting self-interests developed into a full-scale power struggle.

The lower grade units accused the upper grade team of having dominated the afternoon schedule in the past, claimed that this domination had been typical of numerous other faculty interactions, and coalesced to demand a schedule change, in part because they wanted to exercise their right to a share of schoolwide power. Feelings were heated, the upper grade team resisted, and the ensuing conflict took six hours to resolve. We describe this episode in more detail under "Tactics for Conflict Management" below.

Power struggles also develop over conflicting views of the appropriate power relationships between members of a school organization; that is, who should be accountable to whom, or who should tell whom what to do and when and how to do it? In another school we worked in, a conflict arose between the principal and the teaching staff over a new coordinator role: the principal intended for the coordinator to begin supervising the teachers, while the teachers thought that they had been teaching effectively without external supervision and believed that the principal was treating them unprofessionally.

Finally, power struggles can result from certain people's desire to gain more personal influence over educational goals (value conflict) or over the instructional program (strategy conflict). Some faculty members may wish to put their own stamp on the school's philosophy and curriculum; others may wish to gain influence in order to be seen as more effective professionally. Whatever the particular social-psychological dynamics may be, such desires are typical in many schools.

Role Conflict

Some social scientists argue that insofar as an organization comprises persons interacting in roles, much organizational behavior can be understood by understanding role relationships. Thus, on joining a school faculty, new teachers usually attempt to learn what others expect of them by meeting with the principal, the team leader, other teachers in the same unit, district specialists, the counselor, the custodian, cooks, and students. These others constitute a *role set*, and the behavior of new teachers will be strongly influenced by what those people expect of them. It should be noted, however, that as some jobs allow more leeway than others for individual differences, neophytes have the power to conform to these expectations, to resist them, or to comply with them only partially.

Individuals may fail to conform to role-set expectations for a variety of reasons. First, they may receive from role senders conflicting or contradictory expectations about how they are to perform—following the principal's expectations, for example, might mean violating important norms of a teaching team. Persons within the role set might hold diverse expectations among which the individual will have to choose, as new teachers have sometimes to choose between the faculty's various goals and those they were themselves taught at school. These examples of *intrarole conflict* illustrate conflicting demands that an individual acting in a single role cannot satisfy simultaneously.

Second, *interrole conflict*—conflict between roles—sometimes prevents individuals from conforming to expectations. Because most persons perform multiple roles within a school organization, the individual will often have to choose among the expectations from *different* roles sets. For example, an individual may simultaneously be a teacher, the head of a curriculum committee, a member of a planning committee, a representative of the teachers' association, and the faculty member to whom most students express their dissatisfaction about how the school is run. If this individual is firm about leaving an important curriculum meeting as early as 4:30, members of the committee may express disapproval, while to stay past 4:30 without special arrangement for overtime pay might elicit disapproval or even disciplinary action by the teachers' association.

A third obstacle arises when the role expectations held by others conflict with an individual's own values, perception of the facts, or professional orientation; when they seem merely uninteresting; or when they accumulate to a greater amount of work than the individual alone can discharge. This condition can come about when recruiters overemphasize the favorable aspects of a job and underplay its unfavorable aspects, when recruits interpret the recruiters' messages to suit their own needs, or when there is a strategy on the part of new teachers to change the expectations of others by redefining the role once they are in the school.

During one of our projects, a role conflict emerged when an elementary school staff sought to redefine the role of the school counselor. The three teaching teams in the school presented three sets of targets and action proposals for the counseling role, none of which appealed to the counselor, who maintained that the role, goals, and strategies she had adopted were based on her training as a counselor and offered a more responsible and useful version than those presented by the teaching teams. Hurt and angry, she finally mustered supporters to defend the ways in which she was currently carrying out her functions.

The problem in this case was threefold. First, the goals that the various subgroups held for counseling were themselves in conflict. Second, at the district level the counselor was considered to be performing well and meeting the expectations of that part of her role set. Third, the counselor disapproved of the action proposals made by the teaching teams, believing that her graduate training had prepared her well for what she was doing, that the values articulated by the teaching teams were unimportant, and that the suggested new roles would not be personally fulfilling to her.

Role conflict is a common cause of schoolwide conflict, bringing together organizational, interpersonal, and personal factors as the individual and role set try to find expectations that will be acceptable to all. If the expectations of new teachers conflict with those of others in the school, their own expectations are likely to go unfulfilled. As time elapses, neophyte teachers will conform to the expectations of members of their role set, try to change the expectations, or create tension within themselves and within the school. If the conflict remains strong, they will usually move to another kind of job within the field or leave the field altogether.

Differences in Interpersonal Style

Every participant brings to a school a unique set of needs and experiences, styles of coping with stress, and a rhythm for getting things done. At times these interpersonal styles can work against one another, creating friction and conflict that may destroy productive collaboration. Several strategies can be effective in reducing or resolving these differences. As the following example demonstrates, encouraging open feedback between the parties involved may suffice to alter work patterns or interpersonal behavior for the better.

During consultation with the staff of a school in which we were working, it became evident that, with one exception, all the teachers had developed highly collaborative and flexible team-teaching relationships, while one teacher remained closed off from collaboration with the rest. Uncomfortably aware of the others' anger, he nevertheless did not know how to change the situation. An exercise encouraging open feedback revealed that this man habitually responded to serious matters with a joke. No one ever got a straight answer from him, and many had become so frustrated that they had stopped trying to communicate with him altogether. Bringing this feedback to light enabled him to begin to change his behavior and opened an opportunity for future exchanges of feedback between him and the rest of the staff.

Another common strategy is to arrange the duties of contending individuals in such a way that they need communicate only seldom and then only in very precise and objective terms. When it is feasible, this method often works well enough in the short run, although in the long run the reduction of communication may only increase hostility and cause it to spill over into comunication with others. Still another strategy is to capitalize on the different styles, extracting complementary and mutually supportive styles that will strengthen the capacity of the group as a whole.

External Stress

What school district in America has not been in conflict with groups of citizens over new bond issues, controversial curricula, or issues of school control? Although some external stress may be induced intentionally, as when militant gruops strive to produce revolutionary change in a school district, some stress inevitably accompanies social change, and the demands made by external forces and groups often create conflict for the school.

Disagreements will arise within the school district over the methods to be used in coping with external demands and assuaging external pressure groups, while diverse inputs from the community that lead to increased differentiation within the district will not only increase tension in the school but exacerbate conflicts already in existence. Perhaps the most typical external stress comes from parents who wish for improved conditions in their children's school. Consultants can help schools cope with such stress by working to develop parent-teacher communication channels and by involving parents as aides and facilitators within the school. The most ardent critics in the community can become energetic contributors to the school's program.

ORGANIZING FOR CONFLICT MANAGEMENT

Some conflicts are natural and inevitable, and may even provide a creative tension that has the effect of improving school performance; others, although not helpful to the school, are not so destructive as to require the services of an OD consultant. Still others, however, can significantly weaken a school's instructional program and for that reason should receive a consultant's attention.

As they uncover conflicts between role takers or units in the school, consultants should answer two questions. First, are the conflicting parties required to work together to accomplish an important mission for the district? A teacher in a school with self-contained classrooms, for example, is not required to work much with other teachers on matters of instruction; similarly, the faculty of a school may have little to do with some of the personnel of the central office. Second, how interdependent are the parties who must work together? If a great deal of collaboration is required among them, the consultant should work toward making any conflicts accessible to problem-solving processes.

Whether conflicts should be uncovered at all depends upon the nature of the tension that is present. Some tensions enhance productivity, motivate change, and improve organizational functioning. If extremely high tensions can be reduced through clear communication or effective problem solving, uncovering conflict is likely to have constructive consequences. On the other hand, where tensions can be reduced only over a long period of time, uncovering conflict may have debilitating or even destructive effects.

The likelihood of a destructive outcome is greater when participants exhibit low readiness for dealing with conflict. A low level of communication skill can cause the issues in conflict to become increasingly confused. A low level of skill in problem solving can leave people who feel inadequate in dealing with conflict even more distant and alienated than before the conflict was uncovered. A low level of mutual trust among participants can have similar consequences, especially if the consultant fails to realize that lack of trust and openness is not always the result of ignorance or lack of skill but is sometimes a realistic attitude on the part of individuals. In this case, a participant who is invited by the consultant to state the conflict orally may be punished in some way by the others for doing so. In such a case, the level of trust would decline even more, defensiveness would increase, and the consultant would be in a poor position to help resolve other conflicts.

Uncovering conflict, then, involves a certain risk for the consultant and school participants alike. The staff's attitudes towards conflict, the existing degree of openness and trust, the staff's skill in communication and problem solving, and its experience with conflict in the past are all indicators of whether the risk is worth taking.

In addition to exhibiting staff readiness, schools and districts should themselves be structured to manage conflicts productively. Lawrence and Lorsch (1967) suggest that relatively simple organizations such as elementary schools need only a well articulated, overlapping hierarchy for managing conflicts, but that more complex organizations such as school districts should have special formal structures alongside the regular managerial hierarchy for this purpose. In our view, two very productive structures for managing conflict are the multiunit structure for elementary schools and the cadre of OD specialists for school districts.

How the multiunit school is organized to manage conflict has been described in Schmuck et al. (1975). The key to this structure is that it offers a communicative link among hierarchical levels and formal subsystems. Thus, for example, on the leadership team is the principal, who connects with the school's central office, and team leaders, who connect the leadership team with teachers and students. Everyone in the school knows someone who can communicate directly with the leadership team, and this arrangement permits direct managerial contact with those who may be in conflict. To be most effective, multiunit structures must have administrators who are not only competent at conflict management but who communicate accurately about mundane matters by means of memos and bulletins to forestall or resolve minor day-to-day disagreements.

As Chapter 11 will document, our research and development activities have shown that a cadre of OD specialists can make a major contribution toward managing district-wide conflict. We describe the work of several cadres in that chapter.

Derr (1971) found in one big-city school district, which relied on a highly differentiated hierarchy for managing conflicts, ineffective coordination between subsystems. Little direct contact occurred among administrators to deal with differences, and those in positions of authority were perceived by many personnel as incompetent to handle conflict. Clearly, such a district could benefit from an internal cadre of organizational specialists.

Effective school districts should have within them persons who are skilled at working with conflict and should provide for direct contact between these persons and the contending parties. They should have in addition a well-coordinated hierarchy, an effective formal procedure for settling small disputes, and the ability to build appropriate conflict-management components—such as roles, teams, and departments, depending upon the degree of differentiation—into their own fabric.

TACTICS FOR CONFLICT MANAGEMENT

Many times, when people get into disagreements and arguments about what to do, they find themselves worrying not about what *is* happening to them, but about what *might* happen to them. Dragons that might spring upon us in the future are always more frightful than those we are holding at bay today. To reduce the threat from frightful future dragons, we advocated in Chapter 5 choosing clear, near, reachable goals and clear, orderly steps of problem solving, with clear specification of who is to do what. Clear communication (Chapter 3), productive meetings (Chapter 4), and crisp decisions (Chapter 6) also help.

Often people with opposing views about a proposed action are imagining different future dragons. And frequently when more information is brought to bear, when the goals of individuals and of the organization are brought closer and clarified, when several paths to the goals are accepted as alternatives, and when clear arrangements are made for monitoring the steps of progress, the dragons shrivel and vanish. We gave an example earlier when we described the counselor who, unknown to most of the staff, had been spending most of his time working with community, parents, and other outside agencies. The consultants explained the counselor's work to the staff and conveyed some ideas about differentiation of function that helped them understand the usefulness of the counselor's work, and their worries about the counselor's future behavior dwindled. Many of the techniques we give in this chapter for uncovering conflicts will reveal situations of that sort—oppositions that have grown out of incomplete or wrong information.

Another example occurred in a high school in which the principal had been accusing the staff of five counselors that they were disorganized, were not using their time to the best benefit of the students, and so on (see Francisco, 1979, for an account). We spent three days making an actual minute-by-minute count of how the counselors used their time. We interviewed all the counselors, the principal, and several teachers who worked frequently with the counselors. It turned out that the counselors were very conscientious, and that the things bothering the principal about the way they worked were the very things bothering the counselors. Neither the principal nor the counselors, however, had been able to see their agreement, because both parties had taken an embattled stance. The accusations and defenses had created an opposition—a dragon—that really wasn't there. When we fed back our information and then helped the counselors forge a new way of working together—a way they found more satisfying and productive—the dragon vanished.

We think that most seeming conflicts in schools, and in most places, are of that sort—worries about what is going on that isn't, or worries about what might go on that doesn't have to. But some conflicts are more refractory than that sort.

Some conflicts stem from limited resources—limited materials, space, money, or time. If two secretaries fight over time at the copying machine, no amount of added information or of explaining each to the other will reduce the demand on the machine. You could conceive the conflict as a shortage of materials, and you could resolve it by buying a second copying machine. You could conceive the conflict as a shortage of time, and hire an aide to do the copying. You could conceive the conflict as a shortage of money, and ask for money to buy a second machine or to hire an aide. When a conflict comes down to the matter of limited resources, the solution must deal with the resources in a new way. There are several ways of dealing with limited resources. The parties to the conflict can use one of the following methods or some combination of them.

Reorganize Duties

If two secretaries fight over the copying machine, let one of them do all the copying or hire an aide. Or, if there is no shortage of time, require one secretary to copy in the morning, the other in the afternoon. Rearranging the flow of work is called the *sociotechnical solution*.

The cadre of organizational specialists (or *peer cadre*—see Chapter 11 for its description) is a way of reorganizing duties. If a school district's funds are too limited to hire a succession of outside consultants or to hire some permanent inside consultants to help with organizational problems (including conflict resolution), the district can reorganize the duties of a couple of dozen of its present employees so that they can devote, say, 10 percent of their time to helping with organizational problems throughout the district. That arrangement, as we explain in Chapter 11, can be made at very small cost.

Increase the Resources

You can ask for more money. You can apply to the federal government for funds for special purposes. You can campaign for a special tax levy. And so on.

In one school where we once worked, teachers were in conflict because of demands on their time. They resolved a great many of their conflicts by recruiting parents to take over some of their duties. In their letter to parents, they gave as examples "observing . . . working one-to-one with a student . . . teaching a specialty . . . using handicraft skills . . . typing . . . and leading small group discussions." During one year, that school of a couple of dozen teachers had more than fifty parents working as volunteers.

Where budgets for materials and equipment are tight, many schools have reduced conflicts over money by canvassing local businesses for donations of equipment or materials that can be used in science, business, and industrial arts courses.

Trade Kinds of Resources

If the English teacher needs new books and the science teacher needs new equipment but there is not enough money for both, the science teacher might relinquish enough money for the English teacher to get the new books, and the English teacher might help canvass local businesses for gifts of equipment the science teacher can use.

Compromise

Sometimes both parties can agree to give up a little. The English teacher could agree to get new books for only one course, and the science teacher could agree to get new equipment for only one course. Usually, principals avoid conflicts of this sort between teachers by making the allocations themselves.

Change the Schedule

Often a conflict arises because two or more parties want to use the same equipment or the same space at the same *time*. Sometimes a discussion of respective needs and a negotiation can lead to a trade-off—with each party using the scarce resource at different times.

In 1970–1971, Gaynor elementary school was converting to team teaching and making itself into a multiunit structure. The three teaching teams got into a conflict over scheduling the gymnasium (see pp. 218–225 of Schmuck et al., 1975). The team comprising the teachers of the fifth and sixth grades, a forceful and highly vocal group, had been dominant for some time. To resolve the conflict over the use of the gymnasium, the consultants decided not to use a problem-solving mode, because it "might only help the highly vocal 5–6 unit to achieve its own objectives at the expense of the others. The consultants also wanted the Gaynor staff members to realize that trying to gain power and acting on one's own behalf are realistic dimensions of any complex organization" (p. 219).

The consultants arranged a negotiation procedure that emphasized "selfish bargaining." After the first part of the procedure, "The 1–2 unit got the message that they would have to take a stronger stand to get their desired schedules. Also, the 5–6 unit was somewhat shocked to discover that their hegemony was being questioned and that they would really have to bargain to get their way" (p. 221).

In the next part, the groups tried compromising and trading one kind of resource for another:

> *Initial Intransigence.* At first the parties reiterated their positions and tried to convince the other groups that their cause was the most just. When they saw that nobody would win at this game, the various units began searching for alternatives. Many of the unit members passed notes to their leaders making suggestions and proposing alternatives.
>
> *Giving a Little.* The proposals and counterproposals advanced during this stage were not very significant but represented some give-and-take. For example, one unit which had originally requested an hour for PE was willing to take 35 minutes. Another group said it would also take a shorter period if it could simultaneously use one of the vacant classrooms.
>
> The 5–6 grade unit, as represented by its leader, continued to ask for prime time and was unwilling to bend.
>
> Feelings were running high. The 5–6 unit members thought they owned this prime time; they had always had it. The other two groups thought that the 5–6 unit had usurped the schedule so long that now it was their turn (p. 222).

Finally, the three teams managed to agree on a schedule. It wasn't pleasant. When resources are scarce, it often happens that some people get less than they want:

> After lunch, the three units regrouped to discuss their alternative positions and to make counterproposals. The 1–2 and 3–4 grade units met together and decided to form an alliance that would force the 5–6 grade unit to adopt a morning PE schedule. The negotiators returned to the table after about 45 minutes of deliberation.
>
> The discussion became very heated as the two lower-grade units pushed their position and the upper-grade unit resisted. Two events finally

enabled us to arrive at a settlement. One chair at the negotiation table had been left free for the use of any unit member. One member of the 3–4 grade unit used it to effectively confront the logic of the 5–6 grade leader's position. Second, the consultant suggested that the team leaders change roles and negotiate for the other side in an attempt to use both perspectives in reaching a solution.

It was finally agreed that the 5–6 grade unit would have a morning PE schedule and the other grades would take the gym for PE in the afternoon. The unit leaders checked with their units and all agreed that they could abide by this agreement. The 5–6 grade unit added, "We can live with it but we surely don't like it" (p. 223).

Appeal to Authority

When contending parties believe they cannot find a solution on their own, they can turn over the solution to an arbitrator or an authority. Teachers can say to the principal, or principals can say to the superintendent, "All right, *you* decide."

The decision is not always turned over to a single person. Sometimes it is given to a committee, one that might have been formed especially for that purpose. One elementary school where we worked had a wing that had been built in 1890. The district had almost promised to remodel the wing, but a tax levy failed at the polls, and the expected money was unavailable. The school staff was very disappointed, and conflicts arose over who would be assigned to teach in the old wing. At a meeting, the staff considered various ways of allocating rooms to teachers:

1. Committee composed of representatives from each unit, principal and vice principal. Staff agrees to abide by decision of this committee.
2. Total group decision by consensus.
3. Planning within units—plans submitted, evaluated, and differences resolved by compromising into final form.
4. Decision on allocation made by principal and next year's vice principal.
5. Decision made by principal.

In the end, the staff agreed that each unit would meet and discuss its needs, then the leadership group would meet and make several proposals. Next, the entire staff would react to the proposals and try to reach consensus, but if that failed, the leadership group would finally make the decision.

Get What You Can

If all the above methods fail, you are left with having to fight for what you want as best you can. Or, if you are in a position of power, you are left with having to use coercion. Schmuck et al. (1975, pp. 98–99) describe a conflict among teachers of the fifth and sixth grades over the performance of a paraprofessional:

> But effective meetings did not serve to ward off all organizational difficulties for the 5–6 unit. In October, unit members argued about the role of their paraprofessional. One-half of the team supported what the paraprofessional was doing; the other half was opposed. The conflict centered on the amount of responsibility that the paraprofessional should have for actual teaching. Some team members believed the paraprofessional should teach; others did not. The ones that did not were angry when the paraprofessional refused to carry out routine tasks. The team leader was also concerned because often she ended up doing the menial tasks of the paraprofessional.
>
> Throughout the fall, the 5–6 unit tried a variety of schemes to change the situation. They published a time schedule of expected duties, confronted her when she was not carrying out her tasks, and had a special debriefing session once per week in the unit on the role of the paraprofessional. When these attempts did not work, the team leader took the problem to the leadership group. The leadership team spent several hours discussing possible actions. After gathering information and having the principal interview the paraprofessional, the leadership team decided to ask her for her resignation.

Resolving conflicts over scarce resources is often stressful. But most people do not resent going through a stressful negotiation if they succeed in getting what they want, or at least not losing as much as they feared. Sometimes a negotiation leaves rancor behind it, but it need not do so if each party believes the other is tempering its demands to reduce the loss to the first party. Participants can have confidence in one another's good intentions if they have developed openness and trust before entering the negotiation. The only method of resolving conflict that guarantees resentment is the last—that of fighting to get what you can with all claws bared.

GATHERING DATA ABOUT CONFLICT

Uncovering Conflicts

Collecting data through questionnaires, interviews, observations, or preferably some combination of all three and checking their validity by feeding them back to participants are highly effective methods for uncovering organizational, group, and interpersonal conflicts in schools. While data should be collected in a formal systematic manner, it is not always important that they give a complete or balanced picture of the school. In some instances the only data necessary are those that allow the consultant to produce a picture of significant disagreements.

In giving data feedback the consultant should include interesting quotations from interviews together with tables of quantitative data derived from questionnaires, interviews, or observations. Participants will tell whether the data are correct and whether they agree with the weight the consultant is attaching to them. Data feedback may in itself engender meaningful conflicts that will help to move the consultation along, and the interaction that occurs within the representative group may mirror organizational conflicts that can be discussed at once.

Evaluating Collaborative Relationships

Conflicts can also be uncovered by asking school members to describe the quality of collaborative relationships among them. Here is a question adapted from Lawrence and Lorsch (1967):

We would like to know about relationships that exist between various units in your organization.

Listed below are eight descriptive statements. Each of them might be thought of as describing the *general state of the relationship* between the various units. We would like you to select the statement you believe best describes each of the relationships shown on the grid and to enter the corresponding number in the appropriate square.

We realize you may not be directly involved in all of the possible relationships about which you are being asked. Probably, however, you have impressions about them. We hope, therefore, that you will put in every box a number corresponding to one of the eight statements. Here are the eight kinds of relationships:

1. Sound—a fully sound relationship is achieved
2. Almost full relationship
3. Somewhat better than average relations
4. Average—sound enough to get by even though there are many problems of achieving joint effort
5. Somewhat of a breakdown in relations
6. Almost complete breakdown in relations
7. Couldn't be worse—bad relations—serious problems exist which are not being used
8. Relations are not required

3–4th grade team	1–2nd grade team	Leadership team	Principal	
				5–6th grade team
				3–4th grade team
				1–2nd grade team
				Leadership team

The same sort of grid might be compared in other ways. For example, the names of individuals might be used if one is concerned about interpersonal relationships within a unit with high interdependence, or the titles of groups both within and outside the school might be used to study possible conflicts between the school and the district office.

Ascertaining Interdependence

To determine the importance of conflicts to the school, consultants need information on the degree to which conflicting parties must work together to accomplish educational tasks. (Even serious conflicts may not need attention if they arise between relatively autonomous parties.) The following questionnaire adapted from Lawrence and Lorsch (1967) gives examples of items that help to determine the amount of interdependence required by various units in an elementary school.

Questionnaire for Opinions About Others' Interdependence _____

We are interested in the degree of coordination required between the various units in your school.

1. Make an X by the statement that most nearly describes the extent to which the principal is able to carry out his or her job and make changes in it without having to bring others into the decision.

The principal is able to choose his or her own job activities:

( )   to an extreme extent
( )   to a very great extent
( )   to a considerable extent
( )   to some extent
( )   to a small extent
( )   to a very little extent
( )   not at all

How about the first-grade team? They are able to choose their own job activities:

( )   to an extreme extent
( )   to a very great extent, etc.

The second-grade team? Its members are able to choose their own job activities:

( )   to an extreme extent
( )   to a very great extent, etc.

One might continue to ask this question until all grade levels have been covered. Afterwards the questioner might move to other major working groups:

The leadership team (principal and team leaders):

( )   to an extreme extent
( )   to a very great extent, etc.

The counselor:

( )   to an extreme extent
( )   to a very great extent, etc.

2. Make an X by the statement which most nearly describes the extent to which the principal is influenced by:

The work of the first-grade team (or second or third, etc.):

( )   to an extreme extent
( )   to a very great extent, etc.

The work of the leadership team:

( )   to an extreme extent
( )   to a very great extent, etc.

The work of those in the central office:

( )   to an extreme extent
( )   to a very great extent, etc.

Actions of community groups:

( )   to an extreme extent
( )   to a very great extent, etc.

Actions of parents:

( )   to an extreme extent
( )   to a very great extent, etc.

Actions of consultants and university persons:

( )   to an extreme extent
( )   to a very great extent, etc.

Actions of professional associations and groups:

( )   to an extreme extent
( )   to a very great extent, etc.

We'll give an abbreviated version of the rest of the questionnaire to present general ideas about the kinds of questions that are asked. It is possible in every case to ask similar questions for any particular group.

3. Make an X by the statement which most nearly describes the extent to which the various teams are influenced by:

The work of the principal:

( )   to an extreme extent
( )   to a very great extent, etc.

The work of the leadership team:

( )   to an extreme extent
( )   to a very great extent, etc.

4. Make an X by the statement which most nearly describes the extent to which the leadership team is influenced by:

The work of the principal:

( )   to an extreme extent
( )   to a very great extent, etc.

The work of those in the central office:

( )　to an extreme extent
( )　to a very great extent, etc.

One can also use an interview schedule to find interdependencies, as follows:

Interview About Own Interdependence with Others ____

[To interviewer: Read words in parentheses only if necessary for clarity. Do not read words in brackets; they are instructions to you.]

1. To achieve the school's goals, is it necessary for you to work closely with others? [yes, no] [If yes,] which people? [Try to get names.]

---

2. Are there any important things that you do in the classroom (things important to you) that you think run counter to the school's goals? [yes, no] [If yes,] what things are those?

---

3. [If yes, on item 2:] In achieving these important things in your classroom, is it necessary for you to work closely with any others? [yes, no] [If yes,] what people work closely with you?

---

4. Upon whom, inside or outside your school (not students), do you depend most to perform your job effectively? [Write names.]

---

5. [Taking each name separately:] Does [name] work closely with you? [Circle each name above working closely.]

6. Now I want to ask you about the sorts of help you get from these people [taking each name separately:] What is the chief kind of help

that _____ gives you? _____
that _____ gives you? _____
that _____ gives you? _____
that _____ gives you? _____

Finally, the questionnaire below can be used to measure interdependence in the organization.

Questionnaire About Own Interdependence with Others _____

      Please circle the response that best describes your job:

5 = *Very* characteristic of the job
4 = *Quite* characteristic of the job
3 = *Moderately* or *fairly* characteristic of the job
2 = *Not very* characteristic of the job
1 = *Not at all* characteristic of the job
NA = Does not apply or don't know

1. Other people have to come to me for decisions.	5	4	3	2	1 NA
2. On my job I meet pretty often with my boss.	5	4	3	2	1 NA
3. On my job I meet pretty often with my subordinates.	5	4	3	2	1 NA
4. On my job I am expected to help other people.	5	4	3	2	1 NA
5. If I have to get help from someone, it's an indication I can't do the work well.	5	4	3	2	1 NA
6. My job requires a good deal of cooperation from others.	5	4	3	2	1 NA
7. On my job I have to interact with a lot of other people.	5	4	3	2	1 NA
8. My job depends on how well others do their work.	5	4	3	2	1 NA
9. On this job (assignment) you get to know other people really well.	5	4	3	2	1 NA
10. I work almost exclusively with other people.	5	4	3	2	1 NA
11. I am frequently in contact with other people.	5	4	3	2	1 NA
12. My ability to influence others has to be used on this job.	5	4	3	2	1 NA
13. I spend most of my time managing people.	5	4	3	2	1 NA

Assessing the Organizational Climate

In determining a school's readiness to deal with conflict, it is important to know whether the organizational climate supports open confrontation of differences, supports receiving and giving feedback, and generally fosters an atmosphere of two-way interaction and discussion. Several questionnaires are useful for assessing these characteristics. One, entitled "Do's and Don'ts," was presented in Chapter 3 and is described in greater detail in Fox et al. (1973). The following questionnaire also helps to evaluate the informal norms or the organizational climate with respect to how they help or hinder staff members in uncovering and working with conflict:

Organizational Norms _____

1. Suppose Teacher X feels hurt and "put down" by something another teacher has said to him. In Teacher X's place, would most of the teachers you know in your school be likely to . . .

   . . . tell the other teacher that they felt hurt and put down?

   ( )   Yes, I think most would.
   ( )   Maybe about half would.
   ( )   No, most would *not*.
   ( )   I don't know.

2. . . . tell their friends that the other teacher is hard to get along with?

   ( )   Yes, I think most would do this.
   ( )   Maybe about half would do this.
   ( )   No, most would *not*.
   ( )   I don't know.

3. Suppose Teacher X strongly disagrees with something B says at a staff meeting. In Teacher X's place, would most of the teachers you know in your school . . .

   . . . seek out B to discuss the disagreement?

   ( )   Yes, I think most would do this.
   ( )   Maybe about half would do this.
   ( )   No, most would *not*.
   ( )   I don't know.

4. . . . keep it to themselves and say nothing about it?

( ) Yes, I think most would do this.
( ) Maybe about half would do this.
( ) No, most would *not*.
( ) I don't know.

5. Suppose Teacher X were present when two others got into a hot argument about how the school is run. Suppose Teacher X tried to help each one understand the view of the other. How would you feel about the behavior of Teacher X?

( ) I would approve strongly.
( ) I would approve mildly or some.
( ) I wouldn't care one way or the other.
( ) I would disapprove mildly or some.
( ) I would disapprove strongly.

6. Suppose Teacher X were present when two others got into a hot argument about how the school is run. And suppose Teacher X tried to get them to quiet down and stop arguing. How would you feel about the behavior of Teacher X?

( ) I would approve strongly.
( ) I would approve mildly or some.
( ) I wouldn't care one way or the other.
( ) I would disapprove mildly or some.
( ) I would disapprove strongly.

7. Suppose you are in a committee meeting with Teacher X and the other members begin to describe their personal feelings about what goes on in the school. Teacher X quickly suggests that the committee get back to the topic and keep the discussion objective and impersonal. How would you feel toward Teacher X?

( ) I would approve strongly.
( ) I would approve mildly or some.
( ) I wouldn't care one way or the other.
( ) I would disapprove mildly or some.
( ) I would disapprove strongly.

8. Suppose you are in a committee meeting with Teacher X and the other members begin to describe their personal feelings about what goes on in the school. Teacher X listens to them but does not describe his own feelings. How would you feel toward Teacher X?

( ) I would approve strongly.
( ) I would approve mildly or some.

( )   I wouldn't care one way or the other.
( )   I would disapprove mildly or some.
( )   I would disapprove strongly.

Determining the Seriousness of Conflict

The consultant should attempt objectively to measure the seriousness of a dispute by asking participants, for example, to choose the position on the following scale that represents their perceptions of its seriousness:

1. Not at all serious
2. Not serious
3. Average
4. Serious
5. Very serious

A similar scale could be used to ascertain whether the conflict breeds creative or destructive tensions:

1. Makes me work much better
2. Offers encouraging competition
3. Doesn't affect me
4. Prevents me from being as effective as I could be
5. Is destroying our working relationships

Using an interview method, the consultant can gain a sense of the degree of conflict by asking participants to describe the worst thing that could happen if the conflict were worked on openly. Later, when resolution proposals are being presented, those opposed to particular proposals can be asked to describe their worst fantasies of what would happen if the proposals were undertaken.

PROCEDURES FOR MANAGING CONFLICT

The procedures introduced in this section are designed to serve a variety of purposes related to conflict management. The purposes include uncovering conflicting expectations between individuals and their role sets, managing role conflicts, reducing individual conflicts and other disagreements, bringing subsystem differences into the open, testing the intensity of conflicts and obtaining a quick resolution of those that are easily resolvable, causing perceptions to be verbalized in order to dispel misperceptions and manage real differences, and suggesting structural changes for the effective management of schoolwide conflicts.

Checking Expectations

This procedure is designed to reveal discrepancies between the expectations of individuals and their role set. Focal individuals are asked to write what they expect to be doing in their jobs in one year, five years, and ten years. Members of their role set are asked to write their expectations of what the focal persons should do to make the organization more effective. Consultants may then organize the data and feed them back to the participants to reveal any discrepancies between the two; or they can group the parties together to read their expectations aloud—the focal individuals first and the others second—and then react together to the discrepancies revealed. This procedure is also useful when two parties have differing expectations regarding a third party's role.

Imaging

Because it sets the stage for future problem-solving sessions and provides a good setting for the introduction of communication skills, Imaging can be the introductory activity in a sequence of training events. Depending upon the number of groups involved, Imaging typically requires a day and a half to two days. If more than two groups are involved, it is best to work with them sequentially in pairs of groups until all the combinations have had a chance to meet.

In introducing this procedure, the consultant should emphasize that its purpose is to clarify both the character of the relationship between the two groups and the problems that are contributing to their conflict. Participants are grouped into circles of six to eight persons, with both groups represented in each circle; the skills of paraphrasing and behavior description are introduced, and all participants practice them with the others in their circle.

When intergroup conflict is particularly strong, the groups should meet separately during this first stage. Each group is instructed in the skills of paraphrasing and behavior description. Also, the consultant strongly emphasizes the importance of resolutely continuing to use the skills during the confrontation between groups yet to come.

The groups are then given a four-part assignment. Each group, meeting separately, is to develop descriptive images, both favorable and unfavorable, of itself and of the other group. On the basis of observed behaviors, the descriptions are to be recorded on newsprint sheets that will later be displayed for the other group to see when the two groups reconvene. In sum, each group prepares four newsprints. The newsprints can be headed as follows:

- Helpful Things We (the _____ Group) Do
- Unhelpful Things We (the _____ Group) Do
- Helpful Things They (the _____ Group) Do
- Unhelpful Things They (the _____ Group) Do

As participants develop the images, one or two consultants work with each group, encouraging it to focus on its relationship with the other group and to find behavioral examples that verify their images, reminding members that the newsprint sheets will be shown to the other group later.

When the images are completed, the two groups convene, post their sheets of newsprint, and share their images with the total group.

Members of the two groups sit in rows facing one another. The consultant who is convening this part of the meeting stands at the end and between the two rows. The first member in one row reads a statement from a newsprint that row wrote about itself, and the first member in the row opposite paraphrases. Then the member in the first row (or the next member in that row, if you wish) reads a statement that row wrote about the *other* row, and the member directly opposite in the other row paraphrases. As paraphrases are given, the people in the first row accept or reject the paraphrases in the usual fashion.

The reading moves down the row. When the end of the first row is reached, the reading moves to the members of the second row, and the first row paraphrases. If there are many items written on the newsprints and if they arouse emotion, this session can be long and wearing. Participants will often feel the urge to defend themselves against what they take to be accusations, and the convener will have to act strongly to discipline the communication.

Next the two groups are again divided into several circles of six to eight people to review and practice the skills of checking one's perceptions of another's feelings and describing one's own feelings. Then the two groups are again asked to meet separately to accept the feedback they have been given and to recall examples of their behavior that support the favorable and unfavorable impressions of the other group. Group A takes the sheets Group B has written about it. For each point Group B has written, Group A tries to think of evidence—things its members have done or features of their behavior that would lead Group

B to hold the opinions it does. Group A writes the evidence it thinks of on newsprint.

When this task is completed, the groups reconvene to share behavioral evidence with the total group. This time, inner and outer circles are used in the Fishbowl technique and again participants are urged to use communication skills. The group giving evidence sits in the inner circle. Each member in turn reads off one piece of evidence, and any member of the outer group immediately paraphrases it. The reading and paraphrasing continue until all evidence has been read. Then the other group takes the inner circle, and the process is repeated.

The inner circle contains an empty chair for outer-circle participants who want more information from the inner circle. As their admission ticket, they must describe their perception of the present feeling of someone in the inner circle and ask for a check of this perception. Only after their perception has been verified or corrected may they ask their question or make a contribution.

After each group has given the evidence supporting the opposing group's impressions, the two groups can work jointly with the consultants to specify the issues that require further examination, discussion, or resolution. This work can be followed by a commitment to meet again to work on specific problems. Or representatives may wish to consult with their constituents before making any agreements. Although it is unlikely that Imaging will bring about a complete resolution of existing differences, it does set the stage for future problem-solving sessions, which, if carried out in good faith, can lead to increased trust and the development of a more collaborative relationship.

A Short Version of Imaging

1. Have each group meet separately to consider helpful and unhelpful on-the-job behavior in the other group. At the end of an hour or so, all agreed-upon descriptions of behavior in the other group are to be written on sheets of newsprint. Remind participants to use paraphrasing and behavior description skillfully.
2. Next, bring the two groups together. One group surrounds the other, more or less, in the form of a Fishbowl. Participants sitting in the outer ring read aloud the descriptions they wrote of the inside group. A member of the inner circle paraphrases the description to make sure the others understand it. Participants in the center group are not allowed to defend—their work is to make sure they understand.
3. Reverse the Fishbowl.
4. Next, the groups meet separately again to find evidence that

will support the descriptions received. Members should recall examples of their own behavior that could have given the other group its impressions.

5. The two groups come together again and are asked to tell the insiders what they came up with that proves the insiders to be correct. As these descriptions are presented, an outside consultant attempts to record on newsprint the genotypic issues that seem to be involved (e.g., poor communication, hierarchical decision making, unclear or restrictive norms, ineffective group process at meetings, covered-over conflict, etc.).

6. Problem-solving groups are formed of members from both role groups.

Role Negotiation

Assuming that most school participants prefer a fairly negotiated settlement to a state of unresolved conflict, and assuming that bargaining and negotiation are effective methods for helping adversaries change their behaviors, it is possible to help resolve some role conflicts through role negotiation.

In this procedure each person writes three lists addressed to every other person. In the lists, the writers tell what they would like the others to do more often or better, less often, and about as often as they do now:

To: _____

Here is what I would like you to do more often or better:

_____

_____

_____

Here is what I'd like you to do less often:

_____

_____

_____

Here is what I'd like you to continue doing as you now are:

_____

_____

_____

The "letters" are then given to the addressees. Recipients are allowed to question those who have sent messages but not to argue about the information received. "Communication is controlled in order to prevent escalation of actual or potential conflicts" (Harrison, 1972). It is important at this stage to prevent the occurrence of any hostile, hurtful, or defensive emotional expressions.

When the messages are clearly understood, both sides choose issues to negotiate, with each prepared to offer the other something of equal value in return for a desired behavior change. The consultant can urge that a list of negotiable issues be compiled, asking each side to state its issue priorities and to rank-order the items from most to least important (ordering the agenda is itself a negotiable issue). The items can then be discussed in the order of preference. The negotiation takes the form of an exchange: If A does _____, B will do _____ in return. When all parties are satisfied that they will receive a reasonable return for what they are to give, the negotiation on one issue comes to an end, the agreement is recorded in writing, and another issue is negotiated.

Interpersonal Feedback

Interpersonal feedback is an important process for resolving conflicts that arise from differences in interpersonal style. _Feedback_ is information on how close the recipient's behavior is to achieving its desired effect. Feedback must contain information about progress toward a goal chosen by the recipient, and it will not be effective unless the recipient specifically requests it. The following technique is designed to give recipients maximum control over requesting feedback.

As the procedure begins, all participants list on newsprint features of their own behavior that they regard as strengths or weaknesses, or as helpful or unhelpful, in relation to their work situations. The lists are posted on the walls, and participants mill around, first reading and then adding as feedback helpful or unhelpful behavior they have perceived. In this fashion all participants end with a list of their own helpful or unhelpful behavior as others see them. They then take time to read and think about this feedback.

Next the consultant explains that individuals may choose one of three options in deciding how best to use the feedback. First, individuals can choose to consider their feedback personally, to see whether any of the information will be useful to them for future behavioral change. (If everyone chooses this option, there will be no need to discuss others in the group context.) Second, an individual can request clarification from others if the feedback is unclear, insufficiently specific, or inadequately informative about others' perceptions. In this case, participants may ask what actions of theirs led to a given perception or may request a specific example of behavior. In addition, a person may want feedback from one or two others.

When participants choose to ask for clarification, it is their responsibility to initiate the request and to be clear about precisely what information they want and from whom. Third, the participant can contract for future feedback about a particular behavior if that behavior occurs. This is a useful technique for helping people change behavior they are unaware of and for clearing up interpersonal misunderstandings on the spot.

Throughout this process, the consultant's role is to clarify and facilitate communication. When one person asks another for clarification, for example, the consultant might help the former to state the request clearly and ask the latter to paraphrase it. When the clarification is provided, the recipient might be asked to paraphrase it in turn, to describe specific instances when such behavior occurred, or to check with others to confirm that the behavior in question occurred in these instances.

Consultants should also be concerned with the group's emotional climate during this procedure. Realizing that people might be sensitive to feedback about unhelpful behaviors, they should intervene to ensure that it is given clearly and constructively, and in a way that ascribes neither good nor bad intentions to the recipient. Consultants should be aware, too, of each person's level of receptivity to the feedback and should intervene to regulate the process if too much feedback is given at one time.

Third-party Consultants

The district can make available to its members a list of organizational specialists who are qualified to serve as consultants to individuals or groups in conflict. When a conflict develops that district members believe will be difficult to resolve, or when they deal with a conflict but are unable to resolve their differences, they can call on one of these specialists for help.

Such specialists act as objective, neutral facilitators. They use communication skills, probe for concrete clarification, suggest role negotiation or problem solving, lead the parties toward agreements about new actions, and urge the parties to select a follow-up date to check on how things are going.

Structural Changes

Conflicts arising from differentiation require an appropriate organizational structure to be resolved. In particular, those in the upper echelons of the hierarchy should have direct contact with subordinates to work out their disagreements together. In highly differentiated organizations that require a complex articulated structure, cadres of OD specialists specially trained to manage conflicts and facilitate group processes can help in achieving integration. See Chapter 11 for a description of cadres of organizational specialists.

We have found that too much structural integration within a school can create tensions and conflicts, especially when the philosophies and instructional styles of faculty members are highly varied. In such schools, conflict can be managed successfully by allowing for planned pluralism or school structures in which there are several teams, houses within schools, even schools within schools. During the past decade we have observed a number of schools containing several different structures for carrying out effective instructional programs. For schools seeking the qualities of self-renewal, deliberately decreasing interdependence and increasing differentiation is sometimes the best path to follow.

MICRODESIGNS FOR MANAGING CONFLICT

This section offers possible intervention strategies for resolving problems common to school organizations. When a conflict arises between two interdependent co-workers, determine whether the difference can be quickly resolved by using the communication skills described in Chapter 3, since much of what appears to be interpersonal conflict can be due to miscommunication. If value or strategy differences are uncovered, test the intensity by using questions of the sort we gave earlier in this chapter under "Determining the Seriousness of Conflict." If the conflict cannot be resolved by one person acceding to the stronger feelings of another, try methods of negotiation, bargaining, and compromise. A third-party consultant can be used to sharpen the conflicting issues and help the co-workers proceed through the role-negotiation procedure. Finally, the consultant should get the parties to formally agree to reducing their interdependence, and should see that the new circumstances are tested for a defined period of time. The third-party consultant should later check to see how the relationship is going. See also the section above on "Tactics for Conflict Management."

The Imaging procedure is most useful for uncovering and working with conflicts between interacting groups such as one teaching team and another or between the district office and teachers' associations. In one very effective consultation, we used this procedure to help bring parents and the educators at an elementary school into collaborative problem solving and decision making. Before a seven-hour meeting at which the parents and educators moved through most of the steps of the Imaging procedure, each group received training in communication skills. After that, each group offered its images of the helpful or unhelpful things that members of the other group were doing in relation to the school program.

At the meeting itself, the group followed six steps: (1) verifying the images, (2) presenting the images, (3) thinking of behavior that gave evidence of the images, (4) presenting the evidence, (5) determining issues for problem solving, and (6) choosing key problems for future work as well as forming groups to solve them. In Step 1, both groups examined lists of cross-group images created by the consultants, and modified these images until they found the lists acceptable. In Step 2, the two groups were brought together within a highly structured format to show each other their lists. In Step 3, the two groups spent an hour apart; participants described examples of their own behavior that might have contributed to the other group's image of them. In Step 4, the two groups met again to show each other the behaviors they had each listed during Step 3. This step completed a round of generating and validating factual data, and the participants were ready to move on to identifying targets.

In Step 5, the consultant presented a tentative summary of the kinds of targets parents and staff had been advocating. Then the participants divided into groups to list issues for problem solving, making use of the consultant's summary and their own ideas as well. Finally, in Step 6, a list of seven major issues for collaborative problem solving was developed at a general meeting. For the next several months, seven problem-solving groups, composed of five to eight parents and one or two staff members, met for five three-hour sessions each. Each group spent time carefully clarifying its problem, considering the forces that prevented its solutions, and locating resources that might be brought to bear. The problem-solving steps they followed were described in Chapter 5.

8

Microdesigning

Macrodesigning refers to the overall structure, sequence of parts, and large events of OD consultation. *Microdesigning* refers to particular elements within the structure, specific events in the sequence, and the minute-to-minute steps and activities within any event. Although all those activities are interrelated, microdesigning is more concerned with the *logistical, substantive,* and *methodological* details of the consultation.

By logistical details, we mean the organization of materials and physical facilities before a consultative event begins. For some events this might involve merely providing enough newsprint, masking tape, and felt pens. For others it might require preparing materials for an exercise or simulation, writing and practicing lecturettes, arranging tables and chairs, assigning participants to groups, providing a timepiece, bringing refreshments for activity breaks, or preparing to take telephone messages so participants will not be interrupted in their work. Choosing a location in advance is also part of microdesigning. If furnished with tables and adult-sized chairs, a classroom or the school library is suitable. For very large groups, a school's cafeteria or gymnasium can be used if its acoustics permit both small-group and individual work.

The substantive and methodological details of a microdesign include the particular content of a training event, the interview data to be collected for data feedback, the context of an intergroup confrontation, and certain special conditions to which the consultant must attend during process observation and feedback. The nature of the details will depend upon the goals of the consultation and the requirements for producing significant and lasting change. As consultants turn from macro- to microdesigning, attention to the intervention's ultimate goals and a perspective on what is needed to achieve them are the only matters that should not be allowed to become "micro."

Distinctions between macrodesigning and microdesigning appear in the consultant's use of the *S-T-P* paradigm. In the large, diagnosis assesses *S* and *T*, and the macrodesign embodies the *P*. In the small, the *S-T-P* guides the specific, concrete, detailed steps of the problem solving within a microdesign.

This chapter focuses on microdesigns—that is, on the details and guidelines—within the four classical macrodesigns: survey-data-feedback, training, confrontation, and process observation and feedback. We assume here that the reader is acquainted with macrodesigning (see Chapter 2) and with some of the skills, exercises, and procedures presented in Chapters 3 through 7. The descriptions that follow highlight (1) the distinguishing micro features of the classical macrodesigns, (2) some important considerations for microdesigning, (3) guidelines for carrying out OD consultation, and (4) examples of effective microdesigns within each macrodesign. The chapter also describes a complex macrodesign with elements drawn from all four classical designs. Finally, we list the most important characteristics of successful macrodesigns.

SURVEY-DATA-FEEDBACK DESIGNS

Designs for survey-data-feedback assume that collaborative functioning can be enhanced if organizational members share a common understanding of what is happening in a group, of what they think ought to be happening, and of which proposals will move the group to its goals. A survey-data-feedback design elaborates the first stage of the *S-T-P* (see Chapter 5). Rather than assuming that participants already have sufficient information or that they can quickly get it (as we did in Chapter 5), consultants using a data-feedback design begin by collecting data themselves. Consultants elicit and organize information from individual group members, emphasizing discrepancies between what is actually occurring in the group, what group members think is occurring, and what members would like to see occurring.

The survey-data-feedback does not bear full fruit, however, until the participants go through the steps of problem solving. In the full sequence, the consultants (1) collect the data, (2) organize the data for feedback, (3) create the behavioral setting in which feedback will occur, (4) present the feedback and help members choose the discrepancies upon which problem solving will subsequently focus, and (5) facilitate the actual problem-solving effort.

Just as experiential learning is important in the work of the trainer, inquiry learning is crucial for the consultant using data feedback. Inquiry learning seems complicated, because it requires that participants learn particular concepts while simultaneously developing their skills for inquiring into other, discrepant data. Basically however, data-feedback strategies are rooted in a simple principle: don't tell or interpret for clients what you can get clients to tell or interpret for themselves. You can encourage clients to examine and interpret data by using questions that ask Why? What theory do you have to explain this? or What evidence can you present to back up that assertion?

Guidelines for Survey-Data-Feedback

There is no question about the importance of collecting and feeding back data to client organizations. Because of the extraordinary skills required, however, it is not surprising that this method poses a major challenge to most OD consultants. First, consultants must be clever enough to collect relevant, valid data and to put the information into a form that is at once understandable, engaging, stimulating, and tension producing. Second, they must raise the mundane facts to a level of quintessential significance so that participants regard them as worthy of notice. Third, and perhaps most important, they must introduce the data into the ongoing ebb and flow of organizational life at opportune times. The more naturally and spontaneously they can do all that, the more helpful they will be.

Collecting Data. Scientifically trained consultants may well envy the skill with which the world's great novelists make perceptive observations about human behavior, transform them into word pictures of brilliant clarity and detail, and at the same time create a sense of universality that is larger than the lives of their characters. Amassing relevant data and overcoming the scientific penchant for distant, abstract, and general phenomena are major challenges for OD consultants, who, like anthropologists, must perceive the relationships between highly particularized organizational events and infer from them larger principles about organizations.

To assist clients in solving their unique problems while helping them recognize that their problems have, nevertheless, some points of similarity with problems in other organizations, the consultant should continually collect data, by both formal and informal means, that will yield insights into the operation of the organization. Self-report questionnaires, interview schedules, and observational categories are the primary formal methods for survey feedback. At the same time, however, organizational letters and memos, informal conversations with organization members, and observations made during even the most casual visits yield important information as well. Ideally, consultants allow their first impressions, however they are obtained, to guide their selection of formal questionnaires, interviews, and observations, the results of which will be embellished by insights gained from more informally collected data.

The following principles help formal data collection and feedback.

1. Interviewing clients before collecting data via questionnaires helps to establish rapport and trust between clients and consultant, which in turn supports more authentic responses by clients on self-report questionnaires.

2. Within an interview or questionnaire, ask general questions before specific ones. For example, ask "To achieve the school's goals, is it necessary for you to work closely with others?" before asking "With whom is it necessary for you to work closely?" and ask that before you ask "What is the chief kind of help you get from Mr. Abernathy?" Going from general to specific gets you the respondent's salient, unprepared answer to the general question and helps you form context for the later specific questions. Going in the reverse order can bring back to you mostly the ideas *you* put into the respondent's head through your specific questions.

3. Modeling the communication skills of paraphrasing, describing behaviors objectively, checking impressions of the client's feelings, and describing your own feelings when appropriate during the interview will facilitate the introduction of these skills later.

4. When using questionnaires, collect some data that can easily be quantified and other data that render quotable phrases. Though many clients prefer numbers, an equal number are captivated by the catchy phrases of their colleagues. Ideally, numbers and phrases will support similar themes.

5. Employ the same open-ended questionnaire item several times throughout a sustained consultation in order to engage participants in discussions about how things are changing within the

organization. Force-field analyses of the same phenomena, for example, might be drawn several months in succession.

6. Use only a few categories for feedback. Ten are plenty, but it is better to use even fewer and to keep the tallying process simple. Clients' arguments over a complicated instrument typically siphon off energy and motivation better used for self-analysis.

7. Carefully sift data before presenting them, give only small amounts at a time, and try to elicit discussion about their meaning for the organization.

8. After formally observing a meeting, interview a few of the participants about which events were usual or unusual to give yourself a more balanced understanding of typical interaction in the group's meetings.

9. Finally, observe the client group as it discusses the meaning of the data, voice your observations to encourage the group to discuss its interactions during the data feedback, and ask how typical these interactions are.

Making Feedback Significant. In addition to these principles for increasing the validity and usefulness of survey-data-feedback, there are several ways of giving concrete items in the feedback more significance for participants.

First, the feedback activity should be guided by a simple theory that applies to other social settings as well. "Gunny sacking," for example, is likely to apply wherever two or more persons become reasonably intimate, whether in the home or on the job. This term refers to an accumulation of pent-up and hidden frustrations, irritations, and resentments that participants rehearse only to themselves, afraid that exposing them would be emotionally overwhelming. Built-up interpersonal tensions lead to ineffective collaboration, but they can be reduced in open and direct discussions about them, especially if the consultant points out that interpersonal irritations are inevitable and characteristic of all organizations, including the family. Such a clear, reasonable, simple theory can be used during data feedback to emphasize the importance of exposing even the most trivial on-the-job frustrations and irritations.

Second, the consultant can sometimes increase the significance of variables being measured by clustering them under a label that is interesting to the clients—for example, "Five Features of Organizational Health" or "Three Facets of Organizational Climate." The organization's productivity, its morale, and its use of human resources are other useful summary designations.

Third, particular data sometimes take on higher significance if they are compared with data from similar organizations. Pressures for understanding and action seem to be strongest when members of the client organization view themselves as lying somewhere between the worst and best of the comparison organizations.

Incorporating Feedback into Macrodesigns. To incorporate data feedback into the natural flow of a consultation, consultants should have two basic capabilities. First, they should have (both in mind and in their files) a large and diverse collection of formal questionnaires, interview items, and observation categories. The instruments presented in Chapters 3 through 7 and in Chapter 9 are an excellent basic set; also very useful are instruments contained in Fox et al. (1973). As the following five examples will show, the second capability consists of remembering that methods and instruments for formal data collection and feedback can and should be woven into each of the primary stages of a macrodesign.

1. *During entry, when data can be used to develop understanding and agreement about the intervention's objectives.* Consulting with the staff and a large parent group in an elementary school, we first attended a meeting with a representative group composed of the principal, a few staff members, and representatives of the parent group. Before agreeing that we would help, we met separately with the total staff and total parent group to learn what they hoped to gain by working together and by having us work with them. At a second set of separate meetings, we reported a summary of the data collected during the first meetings, and each group discussed differences in how they perceived the purposes of the consultation. We then met again with the small group of representatives and proposed what the consultation could accomplish in light of those differences. The small group concurred with our proposal and agreed to serve as a steering committee to make decisions about the direction of the macrodesign over the next several months.

2. *During the first major consultative event, when data previously collected might be fed back as part of the planned design, or might be collected on the spot and fed back immediately.* In an intervention with a junior high school faculty, we were invited to conduct a two-day event on the topics of improving meetings and clarifying decision making. Before the event, we interviewed all staff members to find out how they defined meeting and decision-making problems. At the beginning of the event, we fed back a summary of those data and asked the staff to decide which specific problems were most important to deal with now. At the end of their meeting, when they had selected four problems for work,

we gave them feedback about how the meeting had gone and how they had decided which problems to attack first. That on-the-spot feedback confirmed their view that the major problems with their meetings and decision making included infrequent use of listening skills, a lack of group agreements about roles in meetings, sloppy procedures for meetings, and a lack of understanding about who was to decide what.

3. *After the first consultative event but before the follow up.* With another junior high school faculty we followed a two-day consultative event in August with small-group interviews in September. The interview questions enabled us to find the faculty subsystems with the highest degree of mutual interdependence. Determining from the data that the pupil personnel subsystem (composed of counselors and the school psychologist) and the administrative subsystem (composed of the principal, vice principal, and two grade-level coordinators) were more recognizable than various departmental teams and more in need of coordinating their efforts than either was of coordinating its efforts with any other group, we proposed to continue consultation on their interaction and to abandon immediate efforts to consult with the total faculty. To enable other interested individuals to continue working with us, we proposed establishing a new subsystem that would be trained to serve as process consultants to any other faculty group requesting help. Those proposals were accepted at a brief meeting of the total faculty in October.

4. *In doing process coaching with an organizational subsystem during one of its regular work sessions.* This is by far the most common setting in which we have used data-feedback designs—so common, in fact, that we have provided many examples of such designs later in this chapter. At this point suffice it to say that we have frequently distributed abbreviated questionnaires during meetings, quickly tabulated the results, and reported the findings to the total group as a means of focusing debriefing. Our questions have included the following: To what degree have members' ideas been listened to at this meeting? How satisfied are you with your participation so far? Describe one thing that someone has done during the meeting that has been helpful to you. On a scale of one to ten, ranging from very unproductive to very productive, how would you describe the group's work during this meeting? See Chapter 4 for more ideas.

5. *After the consultant has completed work with the organization.* Most of our longer macrodesigns have concluded with a report that

typically recounts the major events of the macrodesign, summarizes major findings from data collection during and after the consultation, and makes recommendations either to the clients or to other consultants who would undertake similar work. When such a report is prepared for an audience other than the client group, we not only shield the identity of the individual participants but sometimes prepare two versions of the report—one for the client group and another for outsiders. Returning to the school to answer questions about either or both versions, we have often had to explain how data are displayed and the meaning of any research or statistical jargon used.

TRAINING DESIGNS

Chapter 1 introduced the view that to become self-renewing, an organization needs to improve interpersonal skill and subsystem effectiveness. Chapter 2 described a macrosequence to do that: improving communication skills, changing group norms through problem solving, and modifying organizational structure to support the new skills and norms. Chapters 3 through 7 described many skills, exercises, and procedures that could be incorporated into a training design. For example, training designs might make use of paraphrasing, the Five-Square Puzzle, the Planners and Operators, to name a few. Training designs consist of step-by-step plans to produce cognitive, behavioral, and normative change. They are used primarily when the consultant aims to refurbish interpersonal, group, or organizational functioning, and they assume that individuals and groups alike can learn to use new behavior, norms, and structures.

Another assumption in training designs is that individuals can alter their habitual behavior when encouraged to act in new ways by colleagues (role senders) and when they internalize concepts to symbolize the new behavior. Yet another assumption is that the organization, too, can make long-lasting change when new norms and structures match and support the new behavior on the part of individuals. Cognitive change can be stimulated by means of information presented in the form of lecturettes or written handouts. Behavioral and structural change arises from experiential learning.

When presenting information and experiences about what ought to occur in an effective group, the consultant should maintain a directive stance, helping group members infer discrepancies between the ideal way of working together and their present way of working together. The consultant should also design training events in a way that permits the organization as a whole to try out new norms and practice new ways of functioning successfully in real organizational life.

Experiential Learning

Since Kurt Lewin's research during the 1930s and early 1940s showed the importance of active group participation in helping people to learn new skills and attitudes, much social-psychological research has strongly supported behavioral tryouts or experiential learning, which is basic to OD training. Experiential learning places the responsibility for learning directly on the client. Only by actually trying out new role behavior and by reflecting on the generalizations and conclusions that it produces can individuals make cognitive or behavioral changes in their interpersonal competencies. Only by means of active practice and conscientious self-reflection or debriefing do groups develop norms in support of, for example, surveying or creating the roles of convener and recorder. Likewise, new organizational structures, such as steering committees, link-pin arrangements for communicating information, or the regular use of buzz groups and Fishbowls in goal-setting conferences, do not emerge unless the organization can experience their utility.

The consultant's job is to organize the training so that learners can experiment with their behavior, try out new skills and ideas, and make their own generalizations. By providing appropriate input, the consultant helps clients summarize and build frameworks that organize what they have learned. In other words, learning occurs as a result of both the experiences themselves and the participants' own conceptualization of the meaning of their experiences. But OD consultation assumes further that cognitive and behavioral change on the part of individuals is insufficient without normative and system change as well. That is, subsystem and organizational change will not occur unless experiential learning opportunities teach new procedures, give practice in operating with new norms and roles, and allow reflection on organizational structures.

Experiential learning requires above all a deep commitment to the client's self-determination. Because democratic values and procedures pervade the experiential learning strategy, consultants must clearly communicate their own intentions so that clients are forewarned about the direction of the consultation. Consultants can do so by means of the demonstration techniques described in Chapter 2. Because the commitment to the client's self-determination further requires that the consultant respect the client's choice of whether to become involved at all, we also encourage clarity and specificity during contract building. We urge, too, that all participants be surveyed to determine whether enough of them will be engaged to justify a consultation at all.

In addition, consultants should not label the client's interpretation of what has been learned as either inaccurate or wrong. Rather, they should show clients who perform an exercise for one purpose but who offer debriefing comments on other matters, for example, how these apparently disparate matters relate. Denying clients' interpretations not only violates the consultant's commitment to the client's self-determination, but also makes it unlikely that important or lasting learning will result.

Finally, it takes more than just skill to facilitate experiential learning successfully. Knowing how to give directions for an activity or exercise, knowing how to ask questions that stimulate thorough debriefing, knowing how to structure a session so that participants get practice in new organizational forms—all these are important, but other qualities and conditions are required as well.

1. Trainers should have internalized a repertoire of conceptual maps and theory, an understanding of research, and so forth. An understanding of how organizations work serves as a context for consultation. Further, it yields sophistication about the methods and substance of consultative inputs and a familiarity with the processes and probable outcomes of various kinds of interventions.

2. Of the several kinds of support that trainers need, one is the client's readiness to benefit from the training. For clients to take responsibility for their own learning, they must want to do so, know how, and understand why, at least to some degree. The ready client organization exhibits norms in support of collaboration and the acceptance of individual differences. If it does not exhibit those norms, preliminary work to raise readiness may be vital to enable even the most brilliant and skillful trainer to attract the environmental support necessary to pursue an effective consultation. See the section on "Raising Readiness for OD" in Chapter 9.

3. Membership in a consultative team can bring forth a third quality that trainers need: one that might be called will, courage, guts, chutzpah, self-initiating action, or "hanging in." Unfortunately, trainer burnout occurs all too often in OD work. Without clearly differentiated and integrated roles, without norms that support lending a hand and giving feedback, consultants will sometimes find it impossible to accomplish their tasks or to maintain a cohesive team with their colleagues. We return to this point when we describe cadres of organizational specialists in Chapter 11.

Guidelines for Training

Chapters 3 through 7 offer numerous exercises and games that can be part of a microdesign for OD training. Each exercise is in some way different from the others. For example, the exercise in Chapter 4 for increasing participation is intended for use in groups, while Imaging, described in Chapter 7, is used when two or more groups are brought together. At the same time, however, all exercises have some basic similarities. All provide some lesson to be learned by practicing with an artificial or trainer-determined content, and all require particular behaviors on the part of the trainer. We set forth below some concepts that trainers should keep in mind and some behavior they should exhibit.

Beginning the Activity. Carefully introducing an exercise or activity helps clients to know what is expected of them and how they might interpret the experience. Imaging, for example, might be introduced by explaining that its purpose is to show the character of relationships between two groups and the problems that are contributing to conflict. Because paraphrasing and behavior description are important in this exercise, consultants might review them briefly or encourage a ten-minute practice session in each group. Next the consultants might present a brief overview of all phases of the exercise, giving greatest attention to the first phase and explaining that detailed instructions for each subsequent phase will be given as they begin. Approximate times for beginning each phase might be posted in some visible place, such as on newsprint or on a blackboard.

If the exercise requires participants to assume different roles, the behaviors expected of each role player and the differences between them should be clarified at the outset. When performing the One-Way, Two-Way Communication Exercise described in Chapter 3, for instance, it is important to clarify what senders and receivers can expect of each other and what both can expect of observers. It is often helpful to encourage group members to paraphrase instructions. All questions about the consultant's expectations should be answered, but those whose answers would reveal the solution to the simulated problem or puzzle should be fielded with the explanation that the purpose of the activity is for clients to discover that for themselves. Inaccurate paraphrasing or repeated questioning need not be annoying if the trainer regards it as evidence that the directions were ambiguous in the first place for those who need most to understand them.

Modeling the expected product of the exercise often helps participants understand what they are supposed to do. In explaining Hand Mirroring, for example, we have sometimes selected partners from among participants to demonstrate what we mean. To introduce the Blind Walk, we have used pairs of consultants to demonstrate their individual styles for the purpose of stressing that many variations are possible in this exercise. If we expect participants to make lists on newsprint during the activity, we exhibit a possible format or a sample created by another group in a previous workshop.

During the Activity. Many relatively uncomplicated exercises allow participants to complete their work without interruption. For more complicated exercises, such as Imaging or the Planners and Operators Exercise, consultants may have to remind clients of the rules or explain next steps throughout the event. In such cases, you should do only what you said you would do at the beginning, as interruptions to give an overlooked instruction or unsolicited comment can be annoying and disrupting to the participants' experience. This is not to say that attention to every detail before and during an exercise will prevent a flop, but only to reiterate that careful planning is very important. At the same time, however, overplanned designs that leave no wiggle room for surprises, freak accidents, or unanticipated side trips can produce a highly "tasky" atmosphere that leaves no room for ownership of learning, inventiveness, or "soul."

On one occasion, for example, we planned for the staff of an elementary school a half-day of training in giving and receiving interpersonal feedback, using the first half of the morning for a third-party helping exercise. We planned to ask participants after a break to brainstorm the organizational forces that prevented them from using interpersonal feedback on their own. As we watched the exercise unfold, however, it became clear to us that many people resisted either hearing themselves described as "tough battlers" (a term used in the exercise) or telling others that they were regarded as tough battlers. In addition, many people seemed to want much greater influence than they currently had over decisions about staffing and assigning students to classes. During the break, several participants told us that there was a "vague something" about our design that did not quite meet their needs. After a brief huddle, we initiated the second half of the event by occupying the center of a Fishbowl and replanning the design. We ended by proposing, with the clients' agreement, that the discussion change to the issue of interpersonal influence in the group.

The rest of the half-day included an activity in which staff members rank-ordered themselves (i.e., lined up) according to the amount of influence they believed they had, following which the total group discussed where it believed various individuals should have placed themselves. As in the earlier exercise, we encouraged giving and receiving feedback. It developed that our willingness to redesign the second exercise on the basis of data collected informally during the first part of the morning spared us the necessity of conducting a training event from which group members would have learned little of importance to them.

Following the Activity. At the end of an activity in experiential learning, consultants should provide concepts that enable clients to connect their generalizations and conclusions with OD theory. This phase begins with debriefing, in which participants share their observations, state their interpretations, or raise issues that the experience brought forth. The consultant may sit in on debriefing merely to observe or to paraphrase what is being said or, more important, may provide reluctant or unskilled debriefers with leading questions, behavior descriptions, or impression checks to help them get started. Debriefing should not, of course, focus indefinitely on descriptions of feelings or behaviors. Questions like, What patterns did you notice? or What generalizations can be drawn? raise the discussion to a higher level of analysis. Final debriefing questions can encourage a group to focus on how its performance in the exercise, or its satisfaction with it, is like or unlike what typically occurs at group meetings in the school.

Once participants have discussed their experiences, trainers may wish to call attention once again to the main purposes of the exercise, relating it to organizational theory. A lecturette to this end may require no more than restating or summarizing what has already been said during debriefing, or this phase may take the form of a prepared presentation with only occasional reference to participants' comments. Examples of lecturettes we have used include the Johari Awareness Model from Chapter 3, task and maintenance leadership functions from Chapter 4, and types of decision making (minority rule, voting, consensus, etc.) from Chapter 6.

The nature of the consultant's comments during the wrap-up will naturally depend upon the group's success in performing the exercise or activity. To a group that completed the Five-Square Puzzle rapidly, and in which members greatly appreciated one another's helpfulness, the trainer may wish to note only helpful behavior. Providing a wrap-up for a less effective group, however, may require very different tactics.

For example, we once asked an elementary school staff to divide into small groups for the purpose of building Tinkertoy models of "who talks to whom on this staff." Only one of three groups was able to build a model; another group's model collapsed as members attempted to describe what it meant to them; after five minutes the third group abandoned the effort altogether and returned their Tinkertoys to the container. The debriefing of the total staff revealed great discouragement and frustration with a task they had thought would be fun. Blaming one another was commonplace during the debriefing.

The lecturette we delivered after those events highlighted the need for sufficient, adequate channels of communication and reassured participants that many groups had far too few such links. We asked them to discuss who talked to whom in the school and who ought to be talking more. The thrust of the lecturette and the shift away from the frustrating Tinkertoy experience freed staff members to discuss issues especially relevant to their group.

Designing for the Transfer of Learning

Because training aims to equip persons and groups with skills that will enable them to function successfully in real life, it is important to design microevents that include simulations or games for transfer of learning. Doing so, however, is complicated by the "cultural island" character of many exercises. It is true that a simulation helps to "unfreeze" daily mindsets, patterns, and expectations, and enables participants to stand off and take a fresh look at themselves. That can happen when a teaching group is asked to make decisions about surviving though lost at sea or when an administrative team is asked to assemble the Five-Square puzzle. But the very distance from ordinary work that such exercises bring about requires the consultant to take special pains to ensure the transfer of learning.

When designing for transfer of learning, several guidelines are helpful. First, do not assume that transfer is automatic, but plan for it and discuss it with participants. Second, immediately after debriefing an exercise, allow participants plenty of time to consider its implications for their home setting. Third, include several of what classical learning theorists call "identical elements." For example, a large staff at a retreat might be grouped into its natural teams for an exercise.

For another example, in teaching some faculty members to design questionnaires for assessing the organizational climate in their school, we divided the group into two teams, each of which was to play both "consultant' and "client" to the other. Each team was given diagnostic information about the "client" team, including a description of the group's own history and problems. By designing questionnaires about and for themselves, the participants learned how to select and combine items to assess dimensions of climate. After trying out their first efforts and getting feedback from their "clients," the total group worked together to design an instrument actually to be used with others in the school.

Fourth, make sure the participants can learn the cognitive, affective, and motoric aspects of what they are expected to transfer. In helping members of a student council become better representatives of their homeroom constituencies, for example, we attended to the cognitive aspects of representation by giving a lecturette on what a good representative would and would not do. We encouraged thought about the affective aspects of being a representative in small-group discussions of hopes, fears, and concerns. Motoric aspects were taken into account as each member made to the rest of the group a practice presentation about the meeting that had just occurred; other council members were told to simulate a homeroom, with one student portraying the teacher.

Fifth, after the behavioral tryout, provide opportunities for debriefing in the real situation. The next workday meeting of the group could begin with a discussion of "how we have worked as a group since our last meeting" and could go on to establish a next set of learning goals.

Themes and Designs for Training

If it is to succeed in teaching something of importance without eliciting cries of "input overload," a training intervention, regardless of its length, should be organized around some major theme. In the interests of clarification, we have often found it helpful during training events to post an agenda listing times, the name of the exercise, and the kinds of concepts the exercise is intended to teach. Note that we do not tell clients *what* they will learn (e.g., "You will learn that transactional communication is superior to one-way communication"); instead, we reveal the topic and purpose of the exercise (for example, "To explore the relative advantages of one-way and transactional communication and to relate the exercises to communication in the school").

One theme could be simply activity or practice. Role-playing certain behavior before it is to be tried in the real setting is one way of using participants' natural urge to be active. A staff that is talking about someday holding parent conferences, for example, may be helped to take initiative in doing so by pairing up and demonstrating such a conference to other pairs. Another design might call for enthusiastically praising the first group member who volunteers to try out the role of convener or those who take initiative in giving feedback to the consultant on how the training session is going.

Achievement themes might include an activity like "strength bombardment," in which each person describes the special strengths that he or she perceives in every other person. Praising or otherwise acknowledging individual achievements that do not directly concern group work—for example, praising faculty members who complete home-improvement projects or who stay on their diets—can satisfy achievement motives by establishing the expectation that work well done will be rewarded. We have also encouraged groups to display activity charts on which to check off each task as it is completed, or to take time during the training event to exhibit their visible products—if only newsprint lists—to demonstrate to even the most product-oriented people that something is in fact being accomplished.

The best way of satisfying the achievement motive, of course, is to help group members find real solutions to real problems. In one of our projects, for example (see Schmuck et al., 1975), first and second-grade teachers in a multiunit school had agreed to find a way for each teacher to teach reading to only half a class at a time while the other students engaged in interesting activities as part of a large group. But a lack of space and of additional personnel to run the large groups impeded achievement of this goal; in addition, schedules would have to be changed for the music teacher's visits to first and second graders and for use of the gym by third and fourth graders.

One problem was solved by brainstorming all possible space arrangements and by choosing those requiring the fewest people to move each day (an important criterion for the group). Sufficient personnel were found through soliciting parent-volunteers. Finally, other staff members were contacted so that the necessary schedule rearrangements and trade-offs could be negotiated. As a result of finding these solutions, the teachers in the first- and second-grade unit were very proud, not only of their new reading program, but of their success in overcoming real problems that had stood in their way.

Opportunities to laugh together while working collaboratively on low-risk tasks can help groups build cohesion that satisfies members' needs for experiencing friendships. Affiliation themes are particularly important in brand-new groups or at the start of temporary systems such as workshops; thus we often include warm-up activities that encourage people to become better acquainted or to get ready to try out new behavior.

The Billy Goat Exercise described in Chapter 4 allows people to try out unusual or unreal role behavior before the serious work begins of experimenting with real day-to-day role behavior. We have divided faculties into temporary teams to plan games that all could play together. One team devised a relay for building the tallest sandpile on a nearby beach in four minutes; another made materials so that everyone could play a popular TV game show; still another wanted each group to write a song parody about group life. We have also asked groups to make chalk murals on large sheets of butcher paper and have suggested to others physical exercises, such as jumping jack or leapfrog. In short, affiliation themes can and should be fun to design and carry out.

Power motives can sometimes be satisfied by pointing out a group's range of goals and encouraging members to think about how influential they are or wish to be, either within or beyond that range. On one occasion, for example, we worked with a parent-staff problem-solving group that was distressed about the unattractiveness of their school building and grounds. Complaining specifically about the drabness of the walls and the blacktop on the playground, their first ideas included placing flowers on the secretary's desk and posting colorful exhibits in the display case.

When the consultants pointed out that they were not talking about painting walls or tearing up blacktop to plant a few trees, group members replied with *yeahbuts*: "*Yeahbut* the district has a policy about who should do the painting," or "*Yeahbut* the steering committee coffers are too empty to pay for landscaping labor or materials." By continually prodding the group to check whether their suggestions matched their complaints, the consultants encouraged the members to get district policy changed so that they could do the painting if they used regulation-quality paint, to sponsor a workday on which parents and teachers were invited to bring tools and seedlings for playground refurbishment, and in general to expand their area of influence.

Many of the goal-setting activities described in Chapter 5 can help groups think about the areas of their environments that they wish to influence. Hand Mirroring and the Influence Line Exercises described in Chapter 6 can be used when issues of interpersonal influence are salient. Imaging (Chapter 7) and the Planners and Operators Exercise (Chapter 6) are particularly useful in uncovering issues related to inter-group influence.

CONFRONTATION DESIGNS

Confrontation becomes necessary when a conflict between individuals or groups has become public, at least to the extent that the conflicting parties can both agree with the consultant that conflict is present and that both parties know it is present. Note that both data-feedback and training designs often bring out conflict. Indeed, those designs are more appropriate than confrontation when conflict is hidden in an organization. Confrontation should occur after the conflict has become public.

Because confrontation designs are most often used in cases of difference or conflict, they usually focus on building a description of the conflict's dimensions, an analysis of the source of the differences, and a consideration of the consequences of the conflict for both parties. Confrontation designs enable consultants to help either or both parties express their perceptions of the other's actions, focus on their differences, and engage in problem solving to resolve their differences. The elements of such designs usually include creating a setting for confrontation, uncovering and clarifying differences, and encouraging problem solving that leads to agreements for managing conflict.*

Arranging the Setting

The elements of a confrontation design that can be influenced by consultants include the place in which the confrontation occurs, the amount of time allotted, and the amount of privacy provided. The place, for example, can be selected to give an advantage to one or to neither party. Neither party would feel more comfortable if Imaging were performed by elementary and secondary school principals in the district's central office. On the other hand, staging an Imaging exercise in the school cafeteria might make outnumbered teachers more receptive to a large and angry parent group, and a teacher-principal confrontation might be appropriately set in the teacher's classroom to offset the principal's power advantage.

A highly formal setting is particularly useful when two groups greatly different in size are brought together in a confrontation. On one occasion in consulting with one group of twelve and one of sixty, we arranged two sets of chairs facing each other—one set in two rows of six chairs each, the other in ten rows of six chairs each. By requiring persons in each front row to move to the back and all others to move forward a row every ten minutes, we equalized participation with each group and minimized the effects of differences in total group size. Participants in the smaller group said that it was less threatening to be "six against six than twelve against sixty."

The amount of time allotted for a confrontation should be sufficient, specified in advance, and as free of interruption as possible, especially if the consultant is to help the parties understand their differences, consider how much can realistically be accomplished in the time available, or determine the amount of time they wish to set aside to accomplish their goals. In other words, it is possible to begin with a clear time limit or a clear goal, but one or the other should be known in advance.

The consultant should consider in advance whether adding extra people will help or hinder a confrontation and should be ready to change if the initial choice is not effective. Although extra persons can add relevant insights and be a source of support for either or both of the confronting parties, a private event avoids the risk that another person

*Confrontation designs are explained in great detail by Walton (1969).

or third major group might inhibit the confrontation or complicate the process with other needs and goals.

Three-way confrontations effect a compromise between maintaining privacy and including others. We once divided the eighty participants in a district demonstration event into three groups—central office personnel, building administrators, and teachers—to do a modified Imaging exercise in which each described its images of the other groups and examined their images of itself in return. We then asked each to describe problems between the other two, finally combining the three lists to find common problems. In addition to accomplishing the purposes of Imaging, this strategy gave a considerable number of people some initial experience in acting as third-party consultants to groups in conflict.

Functions of the Third Party

As third parties to a confrontation, consultants can perform a number of vital funcitons. First, they can equalize the energy that the parties bring to the confrontation by, for example, giving the more impatient party something constructive to do while working with the more passive or frightened party. In one case we planned a practice session in paraphrasing for the group with the clear agenda while helping the less prepared group make up its list of demands.

Second, consultants can equalize the situational power of the two parties. If one party is more verbal than the other, consultants can suggest a nonverbal activity or require both parties to put their ideas on paper first. Many of the suggestions for arranging the setting are intended to equalize situational power. When we conducted a role-clarification and negotiation session between the counselors and administrators of a secondary school, for example, we were aware that the administrators wrote annual performance reviews for the counselors. Therefore, we held the session in a room in which counselors sometimes worked with students and at a time immediately after school when the administrators, but not the counselors, were still on duty.

As it turned out, however, our attempt to make the counselors feel more secure about confronting the administrative team had the effect of shifting the power advantage too much the other way. Although the familiar setting gave the counselors confidence, repeated interruptions by teachers and students looking for an administrator caused the meeting to adjourn after two hours with very little accomplished. An evening meeting, or even a daytime meeting during which students and teachers were otherwise occupied, might have enabled both groups to focus more intently on their work.

Third, the consultant as third party can help participants achieve similar definitions of issues before suggestions are made for resolving the conflict. The *S-T-P* procedure is useful; posting three sheets of newsprint labeled "Situation," "Targets," and "Proposals" and asking each group to complete the first two before working on the third can frequently prevent premature decision making about solutions. By encouraging paraphrasing and impression checking, the consultant can also reduce possible misunderstandings between parties, so that the expression of an unpleasant feeling by one party can be correctly interpreted either as an attempt to perpetuate the conflict or as a gesture of trust.

Fourth, the consultant can maintain an optimal level of tension so that a sense of urgency produces an exchange without either rigidity or distortion. Encouraging the parties to persevere while the information is fresh or suggesting a break may both be appropriate in the same consultative event. During a two-day event in which three groups used the Imaging exercise to uncover and find solutions to common organizational problems, we ended the first day by brainstorming a list of specific problems. Leaving the newsprint on the wall overnight, we encouraged participants to think about major categories that would guide the brainstorming of cross-role groups as they created proposals and action plans to recommend to the larger group.

Fifth, the third party can employ procedures and language that ensure clear communication. Use of the interpersonal communication skills described in Chapter 3 is essential. The third party may have to be particularly active with paraphrasing and impression checking to encourage the clients to use those skills; it may also be necessary to ask questions that require each party to describe feelings or to describe the other's behavior.

The sixth function of the third party is often implicitly to convey a positive message. Simply by being present during the course of a confrontation, the OD consultant can provide emotional support. This implicit way of saying that it is all right to express disagreements and that it is very productive to try to do something about them can be extremely important in organizations whose norms do not support such behavior.

Encouraging Follow-through

One way of stimulating follow-through on agreements or on further dialogue after the initial confrontation meeting is to make explicit the techniques and principles that are being used as the meeting proceeds. By attempting to teach the means of effective confrontation, the consultant should help enable the clients to continue or to repeat the confrontation on their own. Such empowerment must be well planned and well carried out, since parties to a conflict will not themselves normally think about how to avoid unproductive interchanges in the future.

Another means of encouraging follow-through is to change the larger organizational context in which the conflicting parties must survive. In order for them to continue their dialogue or carry out their conciliatory plans, it may be necessary to plan ways of informing others in the organization about the outcomes of the dialogue or to confront others about their lack of support. If participants have strong feelings about keeping their confrontation confidential, however, the consultant should respect their wishes. In any case, the follow-up behavior of consultant and clients alike should be clear before a confrontation meeting is regarded as complete.

A third means of ensuring that a dialogue will continue or action-plan be implemented is simply to "stick around." Just being available may give the parties confidence or remind them of agreements they have made. If the consultant cannot be present continually, it may be wise to build another third party into the process at the beginning. If participants and the extra third party are willing, all may attend the initial encounter to become more familiar with the procedures of third-party consultation. Of course, the most obvious way of facilitating follow-through is to ensure that the parties make an appointment to get together again, clarifying both the time and the purpose of the future meeting.

PROCESS OBSERVATION AND FEEDBACK DESIGNS

Much has been written about process observation and feedback (or more simply, process consultation), because many consultants consider them the heart of any macrodesign. Designs for process consultation focus strongly on the immediate functioning of the group and reflect the view that effective functioning is inseparable from the group's ability to see its problems while actually working on them. Otherwise uninvolved in the group's task, OD consultants monitor group processes and individual behaviors and offer behavior descriptions, questions, hypotheses, and speculations about why the group works as it does. Consultants encourage participants to report their own observations and attempt at the same time to shift attention from tasks to the more deductive processes.

In contrast to training designs, process observation and feedback designs emphasize the inductive approach to learning. By reflecting on many actions in one meeting or on many phenomena over several meetings, group members increasingly understand how to improve their methods of working together. In contrast to the trainer, the process observer maintains a low profile, is generally nondirective, reacts to what is happening rather than to what should be happening, and intervenes to help solve a particular process problem rather than to help beef up group functioning in general.

Foci

The titles of Chapters 3 through 7 offer a basic set of foci for process observation and feedback. As the theme of a particular event, the consultant may also choose the group's interpersonal relationships. Calling a group's attention to its cliques and coalitions, for example, leads to a different kind of discussion than do comments about dispersion of influence, struggle between group goals and individual satisfactions, clarity of communication, or phases of problem solving. Interpersonal or group process may also be enriched by focusing on the structure of the organization, including its integration and differentiation of roles, allocation and limitations of material resources, time-task relationships, intergroup linkages, and the like.

Opportunities

The strategy of process observation and feedback makes the group aware of its own dynamics, usually getting a discussion of process on its agenda. During the initial consultative events it may be suggested that fifteen minutes be allocated for a process debriefing at the end of a meeting; during the later stages, consultants can offer their own comments when any group member makes an observation about the group processes. It may take repeated efforts before a group will agree to an agenda item for discussing how they worked together on other agenda items, but getting them to do so is the process observer's basic function and responsibility.

Because of the immediacy of observational feedback, the process observer seldom has the luxury of building a design with as much care as the trainer, of analyzing data with as much leisure as the feeder back of data, or of structuring a meeting to the extent that a third-party consultant must. At the same time, however, any occurrence in a group provides the process observer an opportunity for feedback, and this quality of "winging it" often gives process consultation an advantage in flexibility. By this means clients come to use their own learnings, to invent creative solutions to their problems, and to find the zeal and confidence to continue. In addition, process consultation can easily include time for clients to analyze and criticize both the behaviors of the consultants and the overall nature of the consultation itself.

Timing

Knowing when to comment on a group event and when to let it pass is a crucial skill for a process observer, and its effective exercise depends upon several factors. Consider, for example, the observer who, having the group's permission to interrupt whenever something "significant" occurs, notices that one member has interrupted another member for the third time in a half-hour.

First, the observer must judge how ready the group is to consider its interpersonal processes at this point. If a slow meeting has only just begun to accelerate, the time may be wrong for process examination. If the interrupted member has complained about interruptions in the past, however, the time may be right. In any event, a group will ignore a consultant's comments until its members are ready for them, and nothing is gained by premature feedback that is ignored or resisted. If the observed event is genuinely significant, it is likely to recur repeatedly.

If the consultant offers an observation and is ignored, it is usually not a good idea to repeat and insist. When a group ignores what the consultant says, it almost always means that the group is busy with other matters and not ready to consider the consultant's statement. The consultant can repeat the observation at a more opportune time and go with the group's flow.

Second, consultants must take their own feelings into account, recognizing that body language may reveal their feelings to clients and thereby make them the property of the group. Whether to be transparent or opaque about one's feelings is a matter of personal preference. Some consultants prefer to initiate a process discussion by saying, "I feel uncomfortable because Joe has interrupted Maria three times so far"; others will prefer to ask Maria how she feels about being interrupted or may ask the total group to discuss who has spoken, who has been interrupted, and who has remained quiet. Although the choice between relative opacity or transparency is largely one of style, consultants should be aware that the choice is theirs, and they should pay attention to the consequences for the group of speaking out or remaining silent about their own internal states.

Third, process observers may decide either to offer or to withhold feedback in the interests of dependency. The ultimate aim of OD consultants is to work themselves out of a job by building into the organization a capability for monitoring its own processes and eliciting its own feedback. Thus, on one occasion, observers may withhold feedback to allow a group member with skill and understanding to do so instead; on other occasions they may encourage a group to examine a particular phenomenon in order to sensitize members to that kind of issue, to reinforce something previously taught, or to model appropriate ways of giving feedback. In both cases the rationale centers ultimately on reducing dependency.

In addition to group readiness, the consultant's preference for personal transparency or opacity, and the need to reduce clients' dependency, a fourth factor depends on the culture of the group. Groups that regard the singling out of individuals as taboo, for example, are not likely to appreciate attempts at behavior description or impression checking. Some groups are more apt to discuss their processes when regularly interrupted to do so, while others seem to profit more from widely spaced interventions. Faculty groups that maintain a slow steady pace and whose norms militate against contributions that lack citations of literary, historical, sociological, or biological data will prefer feedback that is rich in abstract concepts and observable behaviors, while a quickly paced group may profit more from feedback given in small bits.

Although we have implied throughout this chapter that OD consultants alone make decisions about microdesigning, we recognize that they value a collaborative stance with clients in the real world. For that reason, we end this chapter with a brief section on ways of working with clients as an intervention is designed, implemented, and evaluated.

AN ILLUSTRATIVE CASE: BRINGING A SCHOOL STAFF AND PARENTS INTO EFFECTIVE INTERACTION

The following case, written by Jane and Richard Arends for the previous edition of this book, shows how the four classical designs (data feedback, training, confrontation, and process observation and feedback) can be combined. In most actual designs, the consultant will indeed combine features of several of the classical designs. In this instance, the consulting team included members of the Program on Strategies of Organizational Change at the University of Oregon and representatives of a school-district cadre of OD specialists like the one described in Chapter 11. The case nicely illustrates some of the detailed planning that is required for microdesigns of OD consultations. It also illustrates how microdesigns are fitted into macrodesigns.

The Context of the Microdesign

Thomas Elementary School, one of 32 elementary and 12 secondary schools in the district, had a student population of 250 drawn from a middle- and upper-middle-class neighborhood. Students had traditionally scored well above national norms for achievement, and both the parents and staff had expressed pleasure with the school's academic rigor for a number of years.

In the early seventies, some parents began to echo the concerns of popular educational critics who argued for parent involvement and humanized education. About 90 of these parents at Thomas School attended informal neighborhood meetings in the fall to discuss concerns they had with the school. The outgrowth of these meetings was the formation of a group that called itself the Parents' Advisory Committee.

The committee sent a letter to the school's principal in November that described "widespread concerns with school-to-parent communication, curriculum—especially in the arts—and the quality of the staff and its training." The principal passed on the letter to the twelve teachers in the school, who greeted it with disbelief, resentment, and disappointment. The principal then called upon the coordinator of the district's cadre, asking for "assistance in dealing with the parents' complaints."

The coordinator of the cadre called together a team of consultants from inside and outside the district to outline a macrodesign that would guide the intervention. The team came up with a design that had as its overall theme a confrontation between parents and teachers. Within the basic theme were elements of training, data feedback, and process observation and feedback. The macrodesign included the following six stages:

Stage 1: Form and meet with a steering committee comprised of some teachers and a few parents to explain the macrodesign and get approval to proceed.

Stage 2: Provide demonstrations of OD to the staff and to all interested parents so they understand the goals and procedures of the intervention.

Stage 3: Train parents and staff separately in the skills of interpersonal communication and group problem solving and help each group identify top-priority concerns. Collect data on impressions of intergroup climate and influence.

Stage 4: Bring the two groups together and feed back data on climate, concerns, and influence. Help the groups clarify intergroup communication and agree upon top-priority mutual concerns.

Stage 5: Form problem-solving groups of parents and teachers to design proposals to solve important mutual problems. Serve as process consultants to these groups.

Stage 6: Bring all problem-solving groups together to share their proposals and to make decisions and plans for implementation.

According to the macrodesign, Stage 1 was to begin in November and Stage 6 was to be completed by June of the same school year.

Features of the Microdesign

The six stages of the macrodesign did get carried out as scheduled. The following sections describe the microdesign elements that made that possible. This section concludes with a description of the intervention's outcomes and some ideas of things to consider when tailoring the design for other situations.

Meeting with the Steering Committee

On December 14, the consultants met with the newly formed Steering Committee, a group composed of three teachers, the principal, and seven parents. The principal had identified these people as representative of the school and community and as both influential and energetic in their respective groups. Giving special attention to the parents' impressions of the needs of the school and the consultants' definition of their role, the two-hour meeting began with a presentation and discussion of the macrodesign. Steering Committee members were surveyed and agreed that the consultants should proceed with the demonstration events. Parents on the committee agreed to extend invitations to other parents, and the principal agreed to have the consultants attend the next faculty meeting. All Steering Committee members agreed to meet about once a month throughout the school year to discuss progress with the intervention and to give feedback to the consultants.

Demonstration Events for the Staff and Interested Parents

Two members of the consultant team met with the total staff the following week. After informing the staff of decisions made by the Steering Committee, the principal introduced the consultants. The demonstration meeting had two main purposes: to explain OD and the consultants' roles and to elicit the staff's commitment to proceed. A slide-tape presentation on OD, a lecturette on consultants as multipartisan helping agents,* and a question-and-answer session served the first purpose. A total group discussion that concluded with a survey of individuals served the second.

The survey revealed that staff members were generally hesitant and unwilling to become involved because they were concerned about the time it would take for training, whether the parents already involved were "truly representative of all parents," and whether they "as professionals" should listen and respond to parents. In addition, the consultants became aware of the fact that teachers did not trust each other to take a united stand should parents' demands be difficult to implement. The consultants paraphrased these concerns and did not attempt to influence the staff, but the principal did *not* take the same stance;

*Multipartisan helping agents was a term coined by the consultants for this intervention to emphasize that (1) they would not side with parents to attack the staff any more than they would side with the staff to ignore parents' demands, and (2) they were group process and organizational consultants who would not tell teachers how they ought to teach or parents what to do in the school.

he pressed the staff to approve of the project, saying, "We really have no other choice." A second survey showed that all teachers were willing to proceed but were skeptical about possible outcomes.

The first demonstration event for parents occurred at an evening meeting attended by 51 parents. The PTA president and the principal opened the meeting with a short business session and introduced the consultants. After the consultants gave a brief history of the intervention to date, described the interests and roles of the consultants, presented a slide-tape show explaining OD, and outlined the macrodesign, parents formed small groups with members of the consultant team for question-and-answer sessions. A summary of each group's discussion was reported to the total group after about half an hour.

The summaries revealed skepticism on the part of parents as to the staff's commitment and ways to involve other parents. Recognizing a need to keep other parents informed and at the same time to avoid spending a lot of time continually bringing newcomers on board, the parents agreed that all parents should be informed of a second demonstration and that attendance at this or the next meeting be considered a prerequisite for being on the mailing list for future involvement. Parents on the Steering Committee ended the meeting by agreeing to send out invitations to all parents for the next meeting.

The second demonstration for about fifty parents began with a review of what had happened at the first meeting to bring the fifteen newcomers up to date. A lecturette on S-T-P problem solving was followed by work in pairs to describe frustrating situations and valued targets. After twenty minutes with two different partners, parents formed eight groups to list common situations and targets on newsprint. The consultants urged paraphrasing and describing situations and targets in behavioral terms. The evening concluded as some parents volunteered to host training seminars for parents in their homes and all were given a questionnaire intended to elicit their impressions of who had influence in the school as well as handouts on S-T-P problem solving, communication skills, and an article on defensive communication (Gibb, 1961).

Training for Staff and Parents

Training for the staff occurred at a two-day workshop in January when teachers had released time to prepare semester reports. The session began as communication skills were introduced through an exercise that required three groups of teachers to build Tinkertoy models depicting how staff members typically communicated with each other. After the staff assembled the models without speaking, they used communication skills to describe what the models represented. During the second half of the first day, staff members completed the Group Expectation Survey and were interviewed individually by the consultants. The second day began with feedback of data collected and a lecturette on S-T-P problem solving. The staff formed small groups to define more precisely problems related to staff and parent relationships. The consultants urged the staff to postpone brainstorming solutions until the gap between situation and targets was clear. The day concluded with practice in small-group problem solving using the Five-Square puzzle exercise and with staff members listing their individual resources on large sheets of newsprint.

In early February, eleven seminars for groups of four to six parents each were hosted in the homes of volunteer parents. Warm-up exercises and introductions were followed by reviews of communication skills. Parents then described experience they had had at the school so all could practice the skills. After the S-T-P problem-solving model was reviewed, parents summarized their experiences as a definition of the situation and listed their individual goals. By paraphrasing and surveying, the interest others had in their individual goals was ascertained.

There was more training for staff members as they met later in the month for two hours after school in three small groups. These meetings included time for additional practice in communication skills and S-T-P problem solving as well as time to administer the questionnaire on impressions of influence that had been given to parents.

Identifying Mutual Problems

In March a seven-hour meeting was held at the school in the afternoon and evening for parents and the staff.* The session began with feedback of data collected through the questionnaire on influence. The consultants emphasized that both groups saw the other as more influential than either saw itself and explained that this protocol is usually indicative of a history of poor communication. One trainer was assigned to meet latecomers at the door to catch them up; approximately forty-five parents and thirteen staff members were present when the session began and only five or six parents came late.

The Imaging exercise proceeded through the following six steps:

Step 1: Parents and staff went to separate rooms to verify lists of helpful and unhelpful behaviors they thought the other group exhibited. These lists had been prepared in advance by the consultants as their summaries of the comments repeatedly voiced by parents and teachers in earlier sessions. Each group modified its list until they found it acceptable.

Step 2: The two groups came back to the large multipurpose room and sat in chairs that had been arranged so that five parents at the front of the parent group would face five staff members at the front of their group. The groups took turns presenting items from their lists and a member of the receiving group was asked to paraphrase as each item was read. The consultants did not allow debate, explanation or justification of any item. Twice during the session, participants played "musical chairs" so new people got the front-row seats where they were allowed to talk. This structure was designed to equalize participation between two groups that were very unequal in size.

*Students were sent home at noon so teachers and parents could be ready at 3:00. Parents had arranged for their own babysitters at home and the Steering Committee had called everyone to bring something for a potluck supper.

Step 3: The two groups again went to separate rooms for an hour to discuss examples of their own behavior that might have contributed to the other group's image of them. The consultants urged them to avoid defensiveness and to concentrate on why they had been viewed as unhelpful rather than to insist that they hadn't wanted to be.

Step 4: The parent group and the staff each picked six people to represent them in reporting the discussions that had occurred in step 3. The twelve representatives sat in a Fishbowl for this discussion. Parents and staff members took turns reporting items from their lists and a paraphrase was allowed and encouraged after each item.

Step 5: The consultants reported five target areas they had summarized from all earlier staff and parent comments. Participants then divided into four groups in the four corners of the room: parents and teachers of first and second graders, parents and teachers of third and fourth graders, parents and teachers of fifth and sixth graders, and the principal and auxiliary staff with the parents from the Steering Committee. Each group listed five to ten major issues they wished to see become topics for collaborative problem solving. Each problem was stated in the form, "There is a lack of," and was written on newsprint.

Step 6: Members of the consultant team, in a Fishbowl, summarized the issues raised in the four groups. One consultant acted as convener until the forty specific problem statements were combined into a list of seven. The seven were listed on separate sheets of newsprint and parents and staff members signed up to work on the one that interested them most. The Steering Committee members spread themselves among the seven groups and agreed to serve as links across the groups over the next two months.

Joint Problem-solving Groups

During March and April, the seven problem-solving groups, composed of five to eight parents and one or two staff members, met five times in homes of parents. Each group chose its own convener and recorder and had the same consultant each time. During the course of the two months, each group made and worked with its own procedural agreements, carefully defined its problem, considered facilitating and restraining forces operating on the problem and its ability to find solutions, and located resources that might be brought to bear to solve the problem. One group prepared a questionnaire that its members administered to other parents and students, while other groups contacted people in other schools and the district's central office whom they had identified as appropriate technical consultants. Each group brainstormed possible solutions to its problem and planned what would be required in terms of financial, physical, and human resources if its proposal gained acceptance from others.

Total Community Sharing

At the last regularly scheduled PTA meeting of the year—in May—
each group presented its proposal. The meeting was planned and convened by
members of the Steering Committee so that proposals could be considered in
some logical sequence. The proposal to restructure the PTA and to write a new
constitution was quickly adopted and followed by election of PTA officers.
Proposals to establish a parent volunteer program, make improvements to the
building and grounds, and to start an after-school program for students, an
artist-in-residence program, a handbook for students and parents, a regular
newsletter, and a party for welcoming new and foreign families were then presented and adopted. Parents and staff members then signed up for committees
that would oversee implementation of the proposals. The evening ended as the
new PTA president convened a Fishbowl meeting of PTA officers to review
summer activities.

Outcomes of the Intervention

Three kinds of outcomes of the intervention were documented by
the consultant team with methods that included follow-up interviews with forty
participants. The first set of outcomes had to do with implementation of proposals designed by the parent-staff problem-solving groups. Within a year, there
existed in the school (1) a new parent organization that included parents in the
process of making decisions about curriculum and staffing, (2) new forms of
written communication from school to home, (3) improvements to the building
and grounds, (4) parties for welcoming new and foreign families to the community and school, (5) many parent volunteers in classrooms and the library, and
(6) an artist-in-residence program. Parents and teachers favorably evaluated
these innovations.

A second set of outcomes had to do with improvements in the climate of
interaction between staff and parents and in the climate of interactions among
staff members. After the intervention, parents reported that they had better
impressions of the school, could now get the information they wanted, and
thought their input was welcomed by the staff. When asked about changes they
saw in the school, more than two-thirds of the parents noted that the atmosphere
was very different.

Staff members reported being much more comfortable about having parents in the school, inquiring about the school's activities, and being effective in
the PTA. Teachers did not totally endorse parental participation in other than
subordinate roles as volunteer aides, but they did appreciate the efforts of some
parents to make the library more accessible to students. In addition, two-thirds
of the staff reported a year later that working conditions and relationships
within the school had improved. They were proud of their first steps at team
planning and thought that their individual resources had been put to better use
since they had started communicating openly with each other.

The third set of outcomes concerned changes in perceived and attributed
influences. Parents perceived an increase in their own influence after the intervention and did so without attributing less influence to the staff. Staff members,
by contrast, didn't think they had gained or lost influence, but attributed more

influence to parents. To both parents and the staff, the PTA in its new structure was the vehicle through which the total amount of influence available to be shared had been increased.

Considerations for Tailoring

What happened at Thomas School cannot be expected to occur without alteration in other settings. In this case, the involved parents were motivated and competent to confront and collaborate with the staff even though they had been frustrated in their prior efforts to do so. In addition, the staff came to realize—quite early in the intervention—that confrontation and collaboration were inevitable and not as painful as they had expected them to be. Important questions remain, however.

1. What happens with a staff that, compared with that at Thomas School, has even stronger norms in support of autonomy, lower competence in interpersonal and problem-solving skills, a greater inability to recognize the implications of its posture, and more unwillingness to regard the parents' efforts as legitimate?
2. What happens when parents are not motivated or competent to make their wishes known, to suggest proposals to remedy important problems, or to pitch in and help implement new programs?
3. What happens when it is impossible to form a consultant team of district personnel who have credibility and legitimacy with the staff, and outsiders who have credibility and legitimacy with parents?
4. What happens logistically when a higher percentage of parents than at Thomas are employed in nine-to-five jobs, are spread over a much larger community, don't have phones, or don't volunteer their homes as meeting places?
5. What happens if the school, instead of being one of the "best" in the district, is known to be one of the "worst," so that parents and staff members feel discouraged at the outset and have to deal with basic needs before being creative about new, add-on programs?
6. What happens when there is more diversity within the community, so that finding a representative group of parents is a chore rather than a fairly easy task?

Some of the consultants who carried out this intervention began almost immediately to seek answers to these questions. And some of the team members found answers after conducting an intervention during the succeeding school year. In this later consultation—another pilot effort in the sense that it was the team's first in an inner-city school serving seventh- and eighth-grade students—the outcomes sought were not achieved. Efforts to establish a Steering Committee to oversee the project were abandoned midway through the year, and efforts to train a group of teachers as group facilitators were to no avail in the sense that the group disbanded as soon as the consultant team left. Nonetheless, the team learned several lessons in this project which answered questions left over from the Thomas School intervention. These lessons were derived from comparisons of the project with the "ideal" described in theory and research on OD in schools. Seven major lessons were these:

1. Involve the total staff in decisions to conduct a demonstration event about the OD process. Don't take the word of a few—even if they are administrators—that the staff is ready to be helped.
2. Retain initiative for contacting parents until the staff or other parents volunteer to take over this function. Don't leave to chance notification of parents about meetings.
3. Provide training to volunteer subsystems or to ad hoc groups of individual volunteers. To be helpful to some people about some things, you need not wait until the whole staff is ready.
4. Establish new subsystems only when a "critical mass" of the staff agrees and funding to continue training is assured. Don't start to build a new group until others are ready to adjust to its presence and you are ready to stick around and help it become a more permanent structure.
5. Be extremely clear about project goals by portraying the ideally functioning school in a variety of ways. Find out which portrayal best matches the priorities and sequences of priorities that staff members have in mind.
6. Include a variety of people on the intervention team, e.g., local people as well as outsiders, curriculum consultants as well as process consultants. Keep the differentiation among roles clear and present enough variety to make differentiation visible to clients.
7. Provide training that allows staff members to "distance" themselves from traumas of the on-the-job world before encouraging application of learning. Teachers, in particular, invest so much energy in "keeping school" that they find it hard to think of change when they are in the midst of things, as they seemingly always have been.

To be sure, not all of the questions left over after the Thomas School intervention were answered by this second intervention. The consultants from Thomas School still look forward to the day when they and other OD consultants will have a swifter and surer technology to bring about parent involvement in schools. In the meantime, they keep the questions in mind, keep reading new research, and are careful never to assume that what worked at Thomas School or any place else will work in the same way or with the same outcomes in yet another school.

AN INSTRUCTIONAL CASE: MANAGING CONFLICT AT MIDURBAN HIGH SCHOOL

The following case aims to give a neophyte OD consultant practice in macrodesigning. While particular aspects of the case are fictitious, the school's organizational problems are based on fact.

The goals of this activity are to (1) create a macrodesign of a year's duration, and (2) create examples of the microaspects of the macrodesign.

The sequence of this activity enables the participant to (1) become acquainted with the school through the description that follows; (2) draw up an OD contract for the project; (3) think up questions or observations for additional data collection; (4) simulate answers to the questions and observations; and (5) create the macrodesign (which could include alternative streams of activities at different points during the year).

Background Information

Midurban High School is a large urban high school of approximately 2,500 students located in a city of 300,000. The school has a professional staff of fifty-six full-time teachers, eighteen teacher's aides, five counselors, a half-time school psychologist, a school nurse, and, during most semesters, at least ten student teachers.

The student population of the school is well integrated and comes from a variety of ethnic and socioeconomic groups. Though it has no problems of desegregation or other racial sorts of tension, the school does have problems and tension. It is not highly regarded in the community. The absentee rate is the highest in the city, the achievement scores (reading and math) are the lowest, and occasionally there are acts of vandalism.

Staff morale was so low at the start of the year that the teachers from Midurban organized the other high school teachers in the district for a strike. Most neutral observers of the strike seemed to think that the strike had no real issues and was only a statement of frustration. The aftermath of the strike left Midurban High polarized, because some staff supported the strike, while others didn't.

There are now only three more months left in a long and frustrating year. The principal of Midurban does not want to go through another year like this one, and decides that something must be done to improve the school's internal environment and its image in the community.

The principal decides that since teachers cannot be required to do anything differently (the fear is that they may strike again), perhaps a reorganization of the counseling services will help. After all, if better counseling were available, students would not skip school, and if they would stay in the classroom their achievement scores would increase.

The principal sends word to the counselors that he wants them to "shape up" and do something about the student problems. According to the principal, they have failed to address the needs of the Midurban student population. Also, the principal says teachers become very frustrated because they interact with about two hundred kids a day and counselors sit in their nice offices and see about fifteen to twenty a day on an individual basis. If counselors dealt more with the problems of the school, then maybe the teachers would be happier.

The counselors feel irritation at the principal's focus on them. In an effort to respond to the principal's demands, the five counselors decide to request feedback about their work from the teachers at a faculty meeting. At the meeting, not much is said when the counselors ask for feedback. Only two faculty members speak, and both of them say they think the counselors are doing all right. The principal is chagrined; he wonders why the teachers don't complain when they have the chance. Later that week, the principal creates a committee of two counselors and four teachers to discuss ways of improving the working relationships between the counselors and the teachers. The committee decides to collect data from the faculty. The committee collects data from the five counselors and from about three-fourths of the staff. The collected data are as follows.

The Data

Question 1. Imagine that you were working in your ideal school—the school you might sometimes dream about. What would the working relationships between counselors and teachers be like? (Please be specific.) The answers were as follows:

COUNSELORS' REPORT

1. Everyone would work together, not apart.
2. Counselors would consult with teachers about their needs.
3. Teachers would come to counselors when they have problems.
4. Counselors would help in the classroom sometimes.
5. Counselors and teachers work together with problem students.

TEACHERS' REPORT

1. Counselors would know what teachers are teaching.
2. Counselors would work on emotional problems of the students.
3. Counselors would not make many mistakes in placing the students in the class.
4. Counselors would not let problem students off easy.
5. Everyone would work together instead of apart.

Question 2. What do counselors do now at Midurban High that is helpful for teachers?

COUNSELORS' REPORT

1. Try to relieve the stresses between students and teachers.
2. Tell students that they must do what teachers expect of them, not because teachers are always right, but because they have to do it to survive. That's how the system operates.
3. Encourage teachers to send students to the counselors right away if they have any problems.
4. Contact parents for them, though I'd much rather the teacher did it.

TEACHERS' REPORT

1. Work closely with me in programming kids.
2. Sometimes help me program a student.
3. Place kids in the right class.
4. Change class assignments to suit student's needs.
5. Send students for placement tests.
6. Refer gifted kids to me.
7. Come to confer with me when in doubt.
8. Reduce troubles students bring with them from home.

5. Prepare students for the SAT.
6. Stay out of their way. Most teachers I've had dealings with seem okay, but I don't deal with that many. I don't want to be where I'm not wanted.

9. Talk with parents.
10. Reinforce standards—being uniform in their expectations.
11. I get information from some counselors sometimes, and that's helpful. On the whole, though, we don't work that closely.
12. Just knowing that I have their support is help enough.
13. Basically, I've had good vibes with the counselors; I get back good reports from the students.
14. Counselors are flexible; deal with teachers quite well. I have no negative feelings about counselors. They have never gotten in my way; they almost always do as I wish.
15. They are not usually obstructive; they help when they possibly can.
16. I don't think any of them get in my way; they are very helpful.
17. I don't think we ever get in each other's way.

Question 3. What do counselors do that gets in the way of the teachers?

COUNSELORS' REPORT

1. Insist on assigning students to their classes.
2. Pay little attention when I disagree about handling a student.
3. They feel sometimes we are responsible for overcrowding their classes.
4. They don't feel we work as hard as they do and sometimes that gets in the way when asking a favor of them.

TEACHERS' REPORT

1. Not knowing the required sequences of courses.
2. They do not know about prerequisites.
3. They don't make sure students have satisfied the prerequisites for a course.
4. Students get programmed into the wrong class. Sometimes counselors stereotype kids.
5. Misprogram students.
6. They overload my classes.
7. Change students' class assignments too late in the grading period.
8. Don't confer enough with me when programming.
9. They don't have enough career information.
10. They don't know how my classes are run.

11. They don't take care of the really bad kids.
12. They don't have uniform standards among themselves or with the faculty.
13. They have different procedures among themselves; they need a program that all teachers and students understand. Students should know when their counselors will be available.

Question 4. What do teachers do that is helpful for counselors?

COUNSELORS' REPORT

1. Generally, I've found teachers very cooperative; they don't seem to be on any power trip.
2. Some teachers are helpful.
3. Most teachers are cooperative.

TEACHERS' REPORT

1. Counseling students myself about course sequences.
2. Help with programming in my spare time.
3. Keep our own file on students' progress.
4. Work with students.
5. Take care of different needs of students.
6. Help students define their goals.
7. Help counselors with the testing program.
8. Give placement tests on short notice.
9. Join conferences with parents.
10. Visit families.
11. Handle an overcrowded classroom without complaining.
12. Not hassling them because they did not participate in the strike.
13. Stay alert to problems and let counselors know about them.
14. Invite them to sit in on my classes.
15. Are amenable to changes.

Question 5. What do teachers do that gets in the way of the counselors?

COUNSELORS' REPORT

1. Play games with me and with students. I send a student to join a class, and he comes back and tells me the class is full. Now what am I supposed to do?

TEACHERS' REPORT

1. Insist that a class of mine is closed.
2. Changing students' classes late in the year and forgetting to tell the counselor.

2. Teachers are not helpful at all. Teachers will tell me it's too late for a student to get into a class. Sometimes I think they say so only to keep their roll books clean.
3. Shift rooms of classes too soon in the semester.
4. I wouldn't mind visiting a few classrooms; the problem would be with the teachers. They say they want us to help, but they really don't.
5. All any of these teachers seem to "know" about my job is that I'm sitting here with this fat job doing nothing. We get a lot of lip from people about all the stuff we should be doing.
6. When some teachers are not as competent as they ought to be, I hear that from students.
7. Some students tell me that they are not learning anything in a class. If teachers would teach well, there would probably be no problem about attendance.
8. Some teachers, especially the ones behind the strike, don't seem to care about teaching. I hate to put kids in their classes.
9. When we try to add a student to a class.
10. Turn away students I send to join their classes.

3. Not getting grades in on time, leaving blanks in the forms, etc. But I think we have a pretty good record.
4. Not conferring with counselors often enough.
5. Usually what upsets them is not so much talking about one counselor, but talking about something that's wrong with the whole department; that gets in their way.
6. The school gets in their way because they are not directly in charge of registration, so they don't have the chance to meet all the students or even place them.l They need to be more a part of the school.

Where the Consultant Comes In

The committee is pleased with the openness and honesty of the counselors and teachers but is confused about what to do with the data. The committee wants help. The principal discovers that money for consultants is available at the district office and is able to procure enough to hire an OD consultant for twelve days during the next calendar year. The consultant confers with the principal and the committee in April. Now the consultant has the above data, the possibility of collecting additional data, and the requirement that he or she come up with a macrodesign by the middle of May. The consultation can last from this May to the next, and the staff can be available as a total group for OD (if desired) for three days in August, one day in October, and one day in March.

The OD consultant should take it from here, and create a strategy and design for proceeding.

FEATURES OF SUCCESSFUL MICRODESIGNS

OD consultants should keep at least four principles in mind as they create their microdesigns: they should (1) get some clients to participate in the microdesigning, (2) seek ways to increase all participants' motivation, (3) remain aware of the location of all clients and of how the ebbs and flows of change fit in their world, and (4) shift back and forth between the macrodesign and the microaspects to raise clients' consciousness about the nature of the planned OD.

Involving Some Clients in Microdesigning

To the extent that diagnostic data are collected and used, clients can be said to influence the designing process before a consultative event actually begins. But there are several more direct ways in which the consultant can allow clients to influence the event in its early stages. Prior interviews that assess the group's organizational, group-process, and interpersonal problems can also provide information about what the consultant should or should not do during the consultation. During interviews, for example, we have asked clients whether they prefer to work all together or in small groups most of the time. In questionnaires we have asked for advice about when and where workshops and retreats should be held. We have also begun a few training sessions by proposing several different designs and asking clients which would best suit their needs.

Clients can also greatly influence microdesigning in the course of a consultative event. For example, they might refuse to record all their ideas on newsprint but choose instead to record only each person's best idea. They may choose to interrupt the consultant during a feedback presentation instead of waiting until the end or, as in one of our more devastating experiences, reject the consultants' proposals in favor of using the time in their own way. Consultants who pay attention to the clients' behavior during a consultative event can collect a great deal of diagnostic data for later use; indeed, all the factors related to the timing of process observation and feedback have application in this regard.

The importance of involving clients in the designing process in the interests of increasing a staff's capacity for self-renewal has been abundantly demonstrated by our own experience and by much research as well. In a study supported by the Rand Corporation, Berman and McLaughlin (1975) coined the phrase *mutual adaptation* to describe a condition in which a project is modified to fit a local school situation while the local school is changing in the direction of project goals. They found, in addition, that this condition is associated with a number of other conditions.

First, projects that clients view from the beginning as responsive to their needs and as a means of solving their problems have much more staying power than those that begin merely because money or other resources are available. Second, it is important that the project be supported from the beginning by group members whom others regard as having a thorough knowledge of particular local conditions; in other words, most clients believe that the suitability of a project depends primarily upon local conditions, and they are right. Third, and most important regarding designing, mutual adaptation is accompanied by planning that establishes channels of communication between project staff and clients, sets forth initial goals and objectives with the assistance of representatives of the client group, and is maintained continually throughout the project.

Fourth, it is important that practical, how-to-do-it, here-and-now topics have precedence over theoretical or inspirational content during the project. Both design and consultant are likely to be judged unfavorably if they do not meet the clients' immediate needs. Fifth, projects are most often successful when they include what Berman and McLaughlin call "local development of materials." That is, the quality of the finished product, whether it is to be an understanding of what is going on in the organization or a document outlining group agreements, is much less important that is the chance to participate in developing the product. Sixth, mutually adaptive planning and mutually adaptive interventions are likely to occur only when a critical mass of individual staff members is involved.

Finally, we believe that by asking clients to collaborate in the designing process and to criticize the design before it is executed, while it is in progress, and after it is completed, consultants can get important information that will enable them to do a better job next time. We believe that clients will take the risks involved in criticizing and evaluating if time is allowed for the purpose and if consultants are receptive to their feedback. One can begin collaborative planning by asking clients what they think can be done to meet a list of intervention goals and by referring to those goals during postintervention debriefing. The consultant can also ask to what degree each goal has, in fact, been met. Another method of ensuring that clients give feedback is for consultants to involve clients in designing a postmeeting reaction questionnaire before the event begins and to use the questionnaire when the session is ended.

Motivating All Clients

OD designs cannot be sustained without the active involvement of the clients. The consultant must keep in mind the motives discussed in Chapter 1: achievement, affiliation, and power. Microdesigns should be created to raise the clients' feelings of competence and mastery, friendship and social support, and influence and power. Consultants can arrange to enhance those motives by selecting the appropriate exercise or procedure and then, after performing the activity, by leading the debriefing in the direction of the three motives.

In selecting a consultative activity or in leading a debriefing after the activity, the OD consultant should strive to increase clients' engagement and involvement while reducing their reticence and defensiveness. When executing data feedback, for example, the consultant can ask clients for examples of particular issues that the data pointed up. By asking for examples, the consultant acknowledges the clients' closeness to their own system and the fact that they are involved in it and understand it better than the consultant. At the same time, the consultant strives to communicate that issues like those under discussion arise in many organizations and that clients need not feel embarrassed, since the problems are common. The consultant tries to walk a fine line between the poignancy of a concrete problem and the wisdom of viewing organizational problems as universal.

Going with the Flow

To communicate effectively, to obtain a basis for building sound strategy, and to express empathy, the consultant must understand how clients view themselves and how they view the culture of their school. This means "starting where the system is"; it requires that the consultant be adept in fitting into the flow of the change.

An important skill for the consultant is the ability to show understanding for the here and now while communicating respect for the past and excitement for the future. Timing is of the essence. At one moment a summary of current events is appropriate, at another a reminder of past events. And at still another time, painting pictures of the future is necessary to inspire the clients. There are patterns and rhythms to consultations; the competent consultant learns to discern them.

Shifting Between the Macrodesign and Microaspects

The consultant should keep in mind the place of each microaspect within the larger macrodesign, and should articulate such information to the clients as the design unfolds. In this way, the particular OD design takes on a past, present, and future for the clients and serves as a metaphor for more general self-renewal in the organization. At each stage of the OD sequence, the consultant can raise activity to a higher level of significance by relating it to the macrodesign as a whole. The consultant can show the contract, for example, in relation to the past and possible future of the organization. He or she can relate the past to the future through diagnosis by asking what in the present might be changed in the future. Skills, exercises, and procedures serve as transition steps from an older style of problem solving to a new, more systematic type of problem solving. Though each part of an OD sequence is performed for its own sake, no part can be isolated from the whole. The consultant's expertise and credibility are rooted in large measure in an ability to reveal to the clients the interdependencies between macro- and microdesigns.

9

Diagnosis and Readiness

In Chapters 3–7, we described interview items, questionnaire items, and other means of gathering data about openness of communication in the school, role taking in meetings, systematic processes in the problem solving, and so on. All those means of gathering data were varieties of diagnosis. Using those techniques of gathering data, planners can design interventions that take existing levels of skill into account. Most of the means of gathering data presented in the preceding chapters, however, are especially well-suited to microdesigning. In this chapter, we will discuss diagnosis for macrodesigning—for assessing the readiness of the organization as a whole for longer-term change.

DIAGNOSIS, EVALUATION, AND RESEARCH

By *diagnosis*, we mean simply an assessment of an existing state of affairs—of the S in S-T-P. If you want to go swimming, you dip your toe in the water to test its temperature. From what your toe reports, you can not only decide whether to swim in this pool, but also choose a particular strategy for your swimming. If the water is cold, you will choose to swim more vigorously or more continuously. If the water is warm, you will do more lolling about.

Likewise, your diagnosis of a district, school, or department might persuade you, for example, that the organization is not ready for an intervention employing an outside consultant, you or anyone else. Or your diagnosis might tell you that the organization can make profitable use of your consultative skills, but that the waters are likely to be cool. Finally, your diagnosis might tell you that the organization is in optimum condition to receive your help; far from having to drag the participants along, you may have to swim fast to keep up with them.

A diagnosis can be carried out by consultants or by the participants in change themselves. Regardless of who does it, the participants themselves are always the primary audience for a diagnosis, as we use the term.

Diagnosis is a subclass of *evaluation*. When we evaluate, say, a radio, an automobile, a book, a school, a curriculum, or a policy, we gather information about it that will enable us to judge whether using it will be profitable or unprofitable for us, and in what ways. When we diagnose a school, we discover its present state (*S*), and we judge in what ways the school is doing well at present and in what ways we would like it changed. If we want it changed, the diagnosis helps us to anticipate the school's likely response to various kinds of proposed changes.

When we undertake a program of change in a school—what we can call a *change project*—we want to know where our efforts are taking us. Are we bringing about some of the new conditions we hoped for? Are we bringing about some good things we did not foresee? Or are we perhaps bringing about some bad things? Are we discovering goals to yearn for that we could not earlier have conceived? Those are good questions to ask periodically as a change project goes along. When we gather data in the midst of a change project to help ourselves answer those questions, we call the gathering and interpretation of the data *formative evaluation*.

Often, a change project employs a special temporary intervention that has a clear beginning and ending. When a change project or a phase of it has a recognizable ending, we often want to answer the question, "Was the effort worth it?" We can gather data to tell ourselves where we are now compared with when we started, or perhaps to show ourselves how our conceptions of where we were and are have metamorphosed. When we gather data to sum up what we have accomplished at the end of a project or a major phase, we call the gathering and interpretation of the data *summative evaluation*.

Evaluation is a subclass of *research*. When we undertake research, we try to learn something we didn't know before. We might want to assess the magnitude of an event (for example, the percentage of a school's faculty that wants to adopt team teaching), or we might want to discover the extent of a connection between one kind of event and another (for example, how many of the teachers who want to adopt team teaching intend to remain with the school at least three more years?). But questions of those kinds could motivate both an evaluator and a researcher. The difference between the ways most professionals use the words *evaluation* and *research* lies mostly in the connection between the local and wider world.

The evaluator wants to know primarily the practical usefulness of a program (in a school or district) for the people using it, the people paying for it, the patrons of the school or district (students and parents), persons with a professional interest in the outcomes in that locality (legislators or police, for example), and the program's designers. The evaluator wants to know whether the benefits were worth the effort for at least one of those clients, audiences, or publics. And note that those clients, audiences, and publics are all local. The evaluator cares little, or only secondarily, about whether the program would be useful to someone connected with schools or districts in other regions. Furthermore, the evaluator wants to know primarily *whether* and possibly *how much* benefit results, and cares only secondarily about *why* the benefit occurred—that is, about the particular characteristics of the actors, features of the program, and conditions in the environment that caused or permitted the various benefits to happen.

The researcher, on the other hand, wants to know primarily whether the program produces particular outcomes that he or she had in mind at the outset. The researcher cares little, or only secondarily, about whether local audiences also care about those outcomes. And note that the audiences the reseacher has in mind are not primarily local audiences. The researcher wants others everywhere to be able to read the report and reproduce the outcomes. Furthermore, the researcher wants to know primarily the *reasons* for the outcomes and cares only secondarily about whether they are of practical value. Indeed, the researcher is often happy to have correctly predicted the direction of an outcome, even though that outcome is so small that only by statistical calculation can the researcher tell whether it has occurred by sheer chance.

It is easy to write of "the evaluator" and "the researcher" as if the two were easily distinguishable, wearing clearly labeled hats. And, indeed, it is true that the pure cases can be found; they are not rare. But it is also true that participants or consultants in change projects often collect data with purposes in mind that are a mixture of those of the evaluator and the researcher. And it is certainly true that you cannot usually tell by watching a data collection (people filling out a questionnaire, for example) whether the data will be used to serve diagnosis, evaluation, or research.

This chapter deals with collecting data for diagnosis. Chapter 10 deals with collecting data for evaluation.*

A SHORT DIAGNOSIS OF THE ORGANIZATION

A change project in a school can be short or long and involve a few persons or many. The diagnosis should be proportional. It should give sufficient information about the existing situation so that consultant and participants alike can lay plans for the near future with some confidence. For a project fairly small in scope, you might gather diagnostic data in a concentrated and formal way only once. In a larger project, the first formal data collection might yield more data than in the small project, and special time might be set aside repeatedly for more checkups (*formative evaluation*) as the months go by.

In either case, the key is to get information useful in answering the question, "Where are we now and where can we go from here?" In this section, we use a short list of questions to illustrate how an interview can bring out useful information. In a project of small scope, you might use no more than the thirteen questions below when systematically interviewing the participants at the start of the project. We will go into more detail about questions for diagnosis in later sections.

The questions below are adapted from a handout by Dale Lake, Paul Buchanan, and Matthew Miles. The questions are phrased as for an interview guide; that is, the interviewer is to ask the questions orally and write down the answers. In paragraphs following the questions, we comment on the kinds of information the questions might yield.

1. *"Please describe what you do—your area of responsibility."*

Answers to this question would begin to tell us about functions and give us hints about membership in subsystems (see Chapter 1). When a respondent said, "Actually, I'm not very clear about some of my responsibilities," we would learn about role clarity. When a respondent went beyond the letter of the question, we might learn about still other matters. We might learn about the press for change: "I don't think I should be the one to do X; I've been talking to the principal about it." We might learn about the support for change: "I'm willing to change my responsibilities, but I don't know whether other people are willing to

---

*The first manuscript of this book contained a chapter reviewing the research on OD in schools, but in the end there was no room in the book for that chapter. We have, however, retained the references to research reports in the list of references at the end of the book.

ight learn about the stability of the staff:
h leaving next year, and I suppose I'll be
‑‑‑‑ they've been doing." We might learn about
i ‑‑pporting collaboration: "I tried for six months to get the other
people to do their part and then gave up. When you're put in charge of
something, people here seem to think you should do it all yourself." We
might learn about skill in collaboration: "I'm chairperson of the X
committee, but I wish I weren't. We just seem to argue in circles." We
might learn about readiness for taking risks: "The principal says he
wants us to make more decisions ourselves, but at the same time, he says
he can't promise to go along with what we decide, because the responsibility is really his." We write down everything respondents tell us.

2. *"With whom does your work bring you into contact most often? Whom do
you need in doing your work? Are there people in your school (district, department, or other) whom you need to see more often?"*

This, too, helps to chart subsystems—the groups with which you
must work as consultant. The last part of the question can suggest
possible inadequacies in communication that might be parts of other
problems. Again, volunteered comments might give us further information: "We've been having to meet at 6:30 in the morning." "She says
she's willing to give us whatever time it may take if we can come up with
a plan we all like." "Six of us are working out a new committee structure.
I think it's shaping up really well." And so on.

3. *"How would you characterize the amount and type of confidence that
the principal (superintendent, department head, or other) has in you? that she
has in (Person X)?"*

This one, when the answers are tallied, gives us clues about the
distribution of trust and therefore the willingness of people to risk new
collaborations. If there are clear differences among the answers to the
part about confidence in "you," then the principal may favor one faction
in the staff to the exclusion of others, or the communication of confidence may be so sketchy that the answers arise more from desire and
self-deception than from evidence. If there are clear differences among
the answers to the part about confidence in "Person X," then the communication net might be distributing reliable evidence only to a part of
the staff, or again the communication about confidence may be too
sparse to produce agreement. And, again, respondents may volunteer
remarks about additional matters.

4. *"How much influence do you think you have over goals and activities in
your school (district, department, or other)? How are the goals set?"*

This question may draw rich information from some people and
almost nothing from others. Some people simply do not think in terms

of goals; they become either somnolent or impatient during discussions of goals. Those people may answer something like "Oh, I don't know," and mean "—and I don't care." Other people like to feel they can count on companions as they move into the future. They use discussions about goals as opportunities to find out who will join them in the direction they want to go. When those people answer that they have little influence over goals and activities, they mean that they feel isolated and lonely. They may be ready for change. They may want greater affiliative satisfaction and yearn for more companionship in their daily work. They may want greater satisfaction of achievement and yearn for collaboration that would enable them to use more of their skills. And regardless of whether respondents think much about goals, the question may draw out their need for power—their yearning for more influence so that they can control more of what they do.

5. *"How would you characterize the principal's (superintendent's, department head's, or other) leadership?"*

This question can draw out information about many aspects of the school. Some respondents will merely utter an adjective, but most will go on to say more about the principal's style and its effects on what they themselves feel they can do. We will learn about aspects of the press for change, the support for change, the stability of the staff, the norms supporting collaborative group work and the readiness to take risks.

6. *"How are budgets created?"*

This one will tell us where the financial resources lie. It will give us some hint about how money is used for influence (for reward, status, and so on) and about the people who influence the use of money. The question may also uncover some important facts or feelings about centralized and decentralized decision making.

7. *"How do you know when you are being productive? What are the criteria? Who notices? What gives you satisfaction?"*

Be prepared to spend time on this question. Because there are four clearly distinguishable parts to it, almost every respondent will have more than a sentence to offer. The answers are likely to yield a lot of useful information about the norms supporting collaborative work and the skill in it and about the interviewee's readiness to take risks.

8. *"What is currently going very well in the school (district, department, or other)?"*

When respondents name something, we will get clues about what they believe the school does well. If most respondents fail to name something, we will get information about morale. Many respondents, too, in that case, will give us hypotheses about the reasons the school is not doing well. Those hypotheses will be useful in designing the OD consultation.

9. *"In my (our) brief meeting with your group at _____, certain issues came up that were called _____. Could you tell me more about them?"*

This question assumes the consultants will have had one or more meetings with some key people during preliminary negotiations, before undertaking this systematic interviewing. The reference is to one of those meetings. The question will draw out a fuller picture and more viewpoints on the participants' conceptions of their current problems. Our design for OD should have some obvious connection with the local problems as the participants see them—not necessarily as we seem them. On the latter point, see Chapter 2.

10. *"If you were given the principal's (superintendent's, department head's or other) job for a month or a year, what would you change? How would you do that?"*

If many of the answers to this question were no more than "I don't know," we would think ourselves to be in a school unready for serious change. In most cases, we would expect to learn important things about the press for change, the support for change, the stability of the staff, the norms supporting collaborative group work and the readiness to take risks.

11. *"Is there anything you want to add that I haven't covered?"*

This is always a good question, because respondents often hold back, not because they are reluctant to answer, but because they are waiting for a question that will seem more relevant to the point they are holding in mind.

12. *"What specific things do we need to give attention to at the next meeting?"*

Don't ask this question unless you do in fact intend to bring up most of the matters proposed by respondents. Of course, you can reduce the pressure somewhat by altering the question to "as we move into the project?" Either way, this question, like Number 9, will keep us alert to how respondents conceive their problems and to the urgencies they feel.

13. *"Now let's go back over the interview to give you a chance to strike out anything you don't want me to mention in the meeting that's coming up."*

Always be sure to find out what the respondent wants to keep confidential. Often, a respondent will be willing for you to bring up a topic publicly if you don't mention his or her name in connection with it. In addition, this question will often serve the purpose of Number 11, because reviewing what the respondent said will give him or her time to think of what could be added and subtracted.

Those thirteen questions illustrate five good rules about diagnosis:

1. Get clues to interpersonal dynamics early.
2. Get clues to the satisfaction of social motives early (see Chapter 1 for a description of those motives).
3. Take notes of all volunteered information, especially at the beginning of a project, when you don't know yet what you don't know.
4. Elicit the help of the participants in discovering what it is important to know.
5. Maintain confidentiality.

In a large organization, a project expected to last a year or more, or any project expected to make strong changes in norms, the diagnosis should go further than the scope of those thirteen questions. In the section below,* we set forth several conditions of readiness and several indicators of each.

SIX CONDITIONS OF READINESS FOR OD

A widely accepted principle of consultation is that you must start where the people are now. If you act as if the participants know something critical that they actually do not know, or as if they have a necessary skill that they do not have, at least some of them will soon feel confused, deceived, or even betrayed, and your work with them will fall apart. (It will also fall apart if you act as if *you* know everything critical about the local situation when you don't.) Conversely, if you act as if the participants don't know what they need to know when they do, or as if they've not had experience they believe they have had, many of them will be bored or even insulted.

The principle of readiness is an ancient one. It says that people are likely to take a step that is a reasonable distance beyond where they are now, but that they will give up in hopelessness if the step stretches them too far, and they will give up in boredom if they are asked to retrace steps already familiar to them. The principle applies not only to individuals, but also to groups, schools, and districts. Indeed, in spirit if not detail, it even applies to iron ready to be struck and potatoes ready to be mashed.

We describe below six conditions that it is important to assess before undertaking an OD project. Under each condition, we describe

---

*The rest of this chapter draws heavily upon our students, Bell and Wyant (1981).

several variables or indicators that can yield a diagnosis of the condition. We omit conditions arising in the environment or in the society—such as federal legislation—that local people can usually do little about. The theory behind most of the conditions and variables was set forth in Chapter 1.

We do not propose the six conditions as an outline for diagnosis to be followed mechanically. In a particular school or project, some kinds of information will be more critical than others. In some cases, you will have acquired reliable information about one or more of the conditions before you get ready for systematic diagnosis. Instead of proposing them as requirements for all occasions, then, we offer these six conditions as a checklist of the kinds of information you might want to get from your diagnosis.

Condition 1: The Press for OD

If an OD project is to get off the ground, a "critical mass" of people should be dissatisfied with the way the organization is going. This group should also have some confidence that OD is feasible and desirable. But do not forget the principle of the subsystem. The critical mass must exist within the subsystem for which OD is proposed. Those in favor of trying OD must be influential with others in that same subsystem.

We know of no formula by which one can calculate the size of the critical mass. When you find persons in favor of trying OD, ask them to name their allies and opponents. Ask them to estimate their influence with uncommitted and opposed persons. Ask them to help you estimate a time schedule. If you and they are not unduly worried by the answers, you will be reasonably safe in taking next steps.

Indicators

1-1. *How many people are dissatisfied with the present organization?*
It helps if a large portion of the school (or of the subsystem you are working with) wants the present organization or situation (earlier we called it S) to change. It helps even more if most agree about the target (T) toward which they would like the organization to move.

If the portion of the subsystem wanting organizational change is too small, then change will be small or require a long time. If the portion is large, you may be in good shape for a strong OD project. If, however, the portion wanting organizational change is large but the members want the changes to go in different directions, and all are impatient to move *right now*, then the prognosis could be poor.

Consultants can gather information on this point, as on the others below, in various ways. Our first example is Number 14 below,* a questionnaire item that asks directly about desire for change in the school. To ascertain the proportion of people wanting change, the consultant can tally the number of people answering "yes" to this question. The consultant can get clues about their targets from the write-ins.

14. Would you say there is some particular aspect of the school's functioning where new ideas are especially needed?

( ) No, things are working about as well as they can.

( ) No, no particular aspect more than another. We just need things polished up a bit all over.

( ) Yes. If yes, please describe briefly the features of the school's functioning that need attention:

a. _____

_____

_____

_____

_____

b. _____

_____

_____

_____

_____

Our next interview-item examples follow several other questions about goals. Tallying the answers to Items 19 and 20 below will give useful information about the portion of people who are dissatisfied with the present situation, directions they'd like to move in, and their expectations about help from others.

---

*For convenience, we continue numbering our examples from Question 13 above.

[To the interviewer: Read words in parentheses if necessary for clarity. Do not read words in brackets; they are instructions to you.]

15. What are the three most important things you do as a teacher? (The things that really count for something.)

    a. _____

    b. _____

    c. _____

16. Do any of these enhance the (main) goals of the school? [Circle: yes, no.] [If yes,] which ones? [a, b, c]

17. Do you think the school is making progress toward its main goals? [yes, no] Can you elaborate on that? [Include sureness or confidence of answer if ascertainable.]

    _____

    _____

    _____

18. Are there any important things that you do in the classroom (things important to you) that you think wouldn't be thought as important by others? [yes, no] [If yes,] what things are those?

    _____

    _____

    _____

19. What are some things you'd like to see this school working toward that it isn't now?

    _____

    _____

20. [If names something:] What staff members do you think could help in accomplishing those things?

_____

_____

_____

Consultants can also get information from informal observations—for example, from conversations in the teacher's lounge or from topics that arise in committee meetings, PTA meetings, student council meetings, and so on. While remaining alert to the possibility that comments might be unrepresentative or in error, one can profitably combine information from informal sources with more formal information from questionnaires, interviews, and school records. Such a combination is usually more reliable than any single source.

1-2. How many people find organizational change attractive?

If people are to work together in mutual helpfulness, they must agree fairly well on their target. And if you, the principal, or some other key person has proposed OD, a critical mass of participants must find that direction a desirable one.

In our consulting, we have tried to find the answer to this question chiefly by attending meetings at which the potential participants discuss whether they want to undertake OD. That is, we have typically asked the intact groups that would be participating in the change to meet, one after the other, and decide whether they wished to participate. We listen, note how many people speak, and estimate their commitment to the OD project. Agreement on the target can also be assessed using, either in interview or questionnaire form, such questions as Numbers 8, 9, 10, 14, 15, 16, and 19 here.

1-3. How many people believe OD is worth the effort?

To decide whether OD is worth the effort, people usually work through a kind of equation that balances the benefits against the costs. It is important to determine these two aspects, then: the benefits people expect and the costs they expect.

Where you get a commitment to begin the OD project by consensus or from a critical mass of participants, the judgment about benefits and costs is embedded in the commitment. But it is possible to get information about the two aspects, expected costs and benefits, separately. Under indicators 1-1 and 1-2, we discussed the matter of getting information about the benefits participants anticipate. You might get information about the costs they anticipate by asking direct questions such as

21. How many hours per week beyond your normal duties are you willing to give to the OD project?

22. What kinds of conflicts do you think will arise during the course of the OD project?

23. Who do you think is likely to become angry at you before the OD project is over?

We think it best, however, at the beginning of OD, to leave most questions of commitment global and intuitive rather than detailed and analytical. You do not need to know the particular answers to Questions 21, 22, and 23. At the start, what you want to know (and what participants want to know) is whether the project can get started. It is reasonable for consultants to ask the potential participants to discuss among themselves their commitment to the OD project while the consultants are absent or at least sitting quietly on the sidelines. And it is reasonable for the propsective participants to raise questions such as Numbers 21, 22, and 23 during such a discussion. For the consultants to ask them directly, however, might blow things out of proper proportion. The mere fact of the consultants asking for such specific detail might cause the participants to anticipate more trouble than is likely. Later in the project, particularly during systematic problem solving, consultants could raise Questions 21, 22, and 23 without having to worry about exaggerating participants' fears.

1-4. *Does the environment press for OD?*

Outside forces are often very powerful in stimulating change. We mean, for example, parental displeasure over students' low scores on standardized tests, a change in legislation affecting schools, or the acquisition of outside funding for an innovative project. When you are about to start an OD project, it is very helpful if outside forces support the direction of your work. At the least, you will want the outside forces not to be against you—you need a "benign neglect" from the environment.

Often, you have an adequate indication of outside support for OD from such informal sources as board meetings, media reports, visits parents initiate to the principal, notification from the central office of pending federal grants, and so on. Usually, you will not need a complete and accurate profile of all the environmental forces. You will need only know whether, if you begin OD, certain events are likely to interfere with your work. You can usually make such estimates well enough with informal, workaday information.

When, however, you need a precise survey—of opinion in the community, for example—it becomes important to know the technical procedures so as not to waste effort and money. You can hire a survey firm, or you can study technical books such as those by Cronbach (1982), Guba and Lincoln (1981), House (1980), Kidder (1981), Patton (1978), Scriven (1973), and Stake (1975).

Condition 2: Support for OD

OD can succeed when it is supported by the critical resources of money, know-how, and administrative endorsement.

Indicators

2-1. Are resources available within the school?
Most schools have within them resources they do not fully use. One sort is technical competence that can be conveyed from one person to another—competence in teaching reading, counseling, facilitating accurate communication, and so on. Another sort is emotional support—helpfulness, encouragement, and sheer friendliness. Another is more tangible—materials (often lying dusty in closets), space (corridors can be used for more than walking through), and money (priorities can be changed). Once you have sufficient commitment to OD, a simple way to discover the resources within the school is to list what you need on a questionnaire and ask respondents to check those areas in which they are willing to contribute. School staff will be aware of many resources they and their colleagues can offer, but many useful resources almost always remain hidden until someone makes a systematic survey. Even then, some individuals remain bashful. Sometimes resources of Person A becomes known only when Friend B tells the group about them.

2-2. Are resources available from the school's environment?
Will technical knowledge, support, money, and other resources be easy to find? Resources may lie nearby. The question is whether they can be located and used—whether they are readily accessible. An Educational Service District or Intermediate Education District is often a useful channel. So sometimes are professors in colleges of education. A cadre of organizational specialists in the district (see Chapter 11 for a description of the cadre) is of course the most effective channel to resources for OD.

2-3. *Do key decision makers support OD?*

OD is easiest when the superintendent and other important officials publicly announce their enthusiasm for it and back up their words with support in the form of money, services, materials, space, released time for participants, and so on. A kind of support that is often vital is official permission to relax some usual ways of doing things so that new ways can be tried. At minimum, as we said earlier, you need benign neglect from top administrators.

2-4. *Will key administrators provide leadership?*

It is not necessary that the principal or the administrator be versed in the technicalities of OD. The technical competence can lie elsewhere. It is always helpful, however, if the principal or other administrator can provide the quality of leadership sometimes called common vision and sometimes charisma. We mean the ability to express for the members of the organization a vision they have in common, and one that parallels the proposed project. Also covered by the term charisma is the ability to inspire the people with the self-confidence that they can take large steps toward their vision and the ability to kindle a sense of urgency. See Chapter 6 under styles of influence for more on charisma.

It isn't necessary to be analytical to discover whether your administrator has the charismatic style. The test is emotional. If you and several others agree that the administrator inspires you to action, that's enough of a test.

Condition 3: Stability of the Staff

Readiness for OD is probably greatest when the staff is stable. That is, turnover in the staff must be low enough to keep the critical mass necessary for OD intact during the time it takes to complete the OD macrodesign and make the new way of doing things customary and routine. That time could be a year for a small project and five years for a very large project.

A critical mass can stay intact in three ways: (1) by retaining all its active members; (2) by replacing members who drop out with others who are so well trusted by the remaining members and so influential that they require almost no training or socialization; or (3) by being over-staffed at the outset so that new members can be trained or socialized while old members' influence remains effective.

Beyond maintaining a critical mass, it is also desirable that the school (or subsystem) retain the same principal or other administrator during the project and throughout the routinization of the new norms, structures, and procedures.

Indicators

3-1. What is the rate of turnover in the staff?

As we said above, OD goes better when a critical mass of people is eager to use OD from the start. There should also be reasonably low turnover in the rest of the staff, so that the people in the critical mass do not constantly have to begin anew their work of influence.

Turnover, however, can be *too* low. Teachers sometimes settle into repeating themselves year after year. Very low turnover enables teachers and others to help one another repeat comfortable routines. Under those circumstances, OD becomes threatening because it threatens a stable world.

3-2. Do key administrators plan to stay in their positions for the duration of the project?

People know that a new principal may not continue what the previous principal started. Hard work, in that case, can go for naught. When a school undertakes serious OD, it is important that key administrators see it through to the point where it becomes routine in the school. And it is just as important, at the outset, that people *believe* that key administrators will see it through.

We know of no way to predict whether administrators will remain on the job through an OD project. It is not difficult, however, to ask staff to exchange their opinions with one another as to whether the administrators will stick it out.

3-3. Is the school already committed to other change efforts or special programs?

OD requires extra effort. One change program added to the teachers' already full day is enough for most schools.

3-4. Do people feel stress due to the complexity of life in the school?

Life at school may be complex and fraught with conflicts because of a diversity of groups and activities—committees, task forces, programs, student activities, clubs, accountability requirements, and so on. Life may also be complex in a large school because of the sheer logistics of keeping everything going. The more anxiety people feel over the normal day-to-day threats of something going wrong, the less they will be ready for the additional disruptions and demands of an OD project.

You can usually get a good idea of whether people feel overburdened by day-to-day stresses by listening in at meetings where they discuss whether they want to try OD. People who feel overburdened will usually say things like, "I have enough to worry about now," "I can't keep track now of everything I have to do," and "Have you cleared this with the association's committee on extra duty?" Sometimes, however, people who feel overburdened will refrain from speaking because they fear retribution from the principal. In that case, the signals will be clear: almost no one will say anything adverse, but neither will anyone say anything favorable. In that case, you must ask the question under conditions of anonymity.

Condition 4: Norms Supporting Collaborative Group Work

We told what we meant by a *norm* in Chapter 1. To reiterate briefly, a norm is an expected way of doing things that is held in place by expressed approval and disapproval, by rewards and punishments. Serious OD usually requires the weakening or giving up of certain norms and the adoption of certain others. At the same time, however, norms of still a third sort are required to give people approval and to reward them for giving up certain norms and adopting others. Maintaining a norm requires group support, and replacing it with something else requires group collaboration.

Indicators

4-1. *Do the norms support collaboration?*
Do people in the school believe it is all right to share tasks in the sense of depending on one another? Do they approve when others share responsibility, work together, exchange ideas and resources, and seek the best solutions to problems through group discussion?
You can find out about norms for collaboration by asking this question directly. You can also ask what joint work is now going on in the school. And you can ask contrary questions such as, "Do people in this school encourage you to do your own work without bothering others about it?"

4-2. *Do the norms support perseverance in group tasks?*
We refer here to the expectation that group members will stick to a task until it is completed even though the work may be frustrating and difficult. OD requires time and hard work. Overtime is usually necessary.
We do not, however, recommend asking directly about overtime work at the beginning of a project. Participants are rarely able to predict whether they will be willing to work overtime when the need arises. Furthermore, questions about overtime can give the impression that the project requires more time than it actually will. But as the days go by, it is important to be alert to indications of readiness for overtime. You can keep notes of indications: mentions of past projects in which people

worked overtime, frequency with which meetings are cut short regardless of what is going on merely by someone saying, "Well, it's four-thirty," suggestions that the next meeting start before the usual time or run beyond it, and so on.

4-3. *Do the norms support disclosures by individuals of their feelings, worries, and frustrations over their tasks?*

An OD project is more likely to be successful when participants openly communicate their doubts and worries and when they encourage one another to do so. Doubts and worries are often signals of trouble ahead. Trouble can be kept to a minimum if it is anticipated and warded off.

It is usually fairly easy to get a rough indication of readiness for self-disclosure by listening in on a few meetings. You may, however, come into the school just at a time when the staff has very little to worry about or when few meetings are occurring. Then you may wish to fall back on a questionnaire or interview. In the "Do's and Don'ts" Questionnaire* below, Items 24, 28, 31 and 34 elicit answers indicating norms for disclosing feelings, worries, and frustrations.

Do's and Don'ts

In any school district (or school or group), there are informal "do's and don'ts." They are rarely written down anywhere, but they serve as a kind of code, making it clear what people in the system should and should not do if they are to be accepted by others.

Below is a list of specific things that a person—an administrator, a teacher, a staff member—might do or say. We would like you to estimate what most people in your system would feel about each item. That is, we want you to tell us whether the predominant feeling of most of the people is that one should or should not do or say the thing in question. You can indicate your answer by placing a check mark in the appropriate column—should or should not—beside each item.

	Should	Should not
24. Ask others who seem upset to express their feelings directly.	___	___
25. Tell colleagues what you really think of their work.	___	___
26. Look for ulterior motives in other people's behavior.	___	___
27. Always ask "Why?" when you don't know.	___	___
28. Avoid disagreement and conflict whenever possible.	___	___
29. Question well-established ways of doing things.	___	___

*From Matthew B. Miles.

30. Disagree with your superior if you happen to know more about the issue than he or she does.   _____ _____
31. Withhold personal feelings and stick to the logical merits of the case in any discussion.   _____ _____
32. Push for new ideas, even if they are vague or unusual.   _____ _____
33. Ask others to tell you what they really think of your work.   _____ _____
34. Keep your real thoughts and reactions to yourself, by and large.   _____ _____
35. Trust others not to take advantage of you.   _____ _____
36. Be skeptical about things.   _____ _____
37. Point out other people's mistakes, to improve working effectiveness.   _____ _____
38. Try out new ways of doing things, even if it is uncertain how they will work out.   _____ _____

Another kind of questionnaire item for getting indications of readiness for self-disclosure is exemplified by Items 39, 40, and 44 below.*

39. Suppose you are in a committee meeting with Teacher X and the other members begin to describe their personal feelings about what goes on in the school. Teacher X listens to them and tells his own feelings. How would you feel toward X?

    (   ) I would approve strongly.
    (   ) I would approve mildly or some.
    (   ) I wouldn't care one way or another.
    (   ) I would disapprove mildly or some.
    (   ) I would disapprove strongly.

40. Suppose you are in a committee meeting with Teacher X and the other members begin to describe their personal feelings about what goes on in the school. Teacher X quickly suggests that the committee get back to the topic and keep the discussion objective and impersonal. How would you feel toward X?

    (   ) I would approve strongly.
    (   ) I would approve mildly or some.
    (   ) I wouldn't care one way or another.
    (   ) I would disapprove mildly or some.
    (   ) I would disapprove strongly.

*All six items are adapted from items kindly supplied by Ray Jongeward and Michael Giammetteo, then of the Northwest Regional Educational Laboratory in Portland, Oregon.

41. Suppose Teacher X strongly disagrees with something B says at a staff meeting. In Teacher X's place, would most of the teachers you know in your school seek out B to discuss the disagreement?

    (   ) Yes, I think most would do this.
    (   ) Maybe about half would do this.
    (   ) No, most would *not*.
    (   ) I don't know.

42. Suppose Teacher X strongly disagrees with something B says at a staff meeting. In Teacher X's place, would most of the teachers you know in your school keep it to themselves and say nothing about it?

    (   ) Yes, I think most would do this.
    (   ) Maybe about half would do this.
    (   ) No, most would *not*.
    (   ) I don't know.

43. Suppose Teacher X is present when *two others* get into a hot argument about how the school is run. If teachers you know in your school were in Teacher X's place, what would most of them be likely to do? Would they try to help each one in the argument understand the viewpoint of the other?

    (   ) Yes, I think most would.
    (   ) Maybe about half would.
    (   ) No, most would *not* do this.
    (   ) I don't know.

44. Suppose Teacher X feels hurt and "put down" by something another teacher has said to him. In Teachers X's place, would most of the teachers you know in your school be likely to tell the other teacher that they felt hurt and put down?

    (   ) Yes, I think most would.
    (   ) Maybe about half would.
    (   ) No, most would *not*.
    (   ) I don't know.

  4-4. Do the norms support continued communication even in emotional situations?
    Some OD procedures are bound to raise anixety in at least some people, and they are also bound to produce conflict of some sort. Emotions are bound to heat up. Not only should the norms support the

revelation of emotion, but they should also support the continuation of work despite the arousal and exhibition of distress.

In some groups, when members show emotion, the norm is to act as if they have embarrassed the group, and the usual action is to ask them to try not to do it again. But that kind of treatment discourages people from talking about the very matters they care most about. It condemns them to sitting and seething, and that experience makes them want to stay home. At the extreme, meetings become occasions when a few people discuss matters they care nothing about. If work is to get done concerning matters people care deeply about, participants must be allowed to show that they care, and work must continue while they care. We discussed communicating during emotion in Chapter 3.

Again, you can often get a good idea about whether norms support communicating during emotion by listening in at meetings of the participants. If that does not yield enough information, questionnaire or interview items can be used, such as Numbers 28, 30, 31, 33, 34, 35, 37, 40, 42, and 43 above.

4-5. *Do the norms support people in helping colleagues to communicate accurately and work together productively?*

Suppose two members of a curriculum committee, Fred and Sharon, are in the middle of a misunderstanding about the committee's goals. If it is all right in the group for Martha or Bill to step in to help them understand each other (instead of sitting on the sidelines or jumping in to take sides), the answer to this question is yes. Martha and Bill might offer help in clarifying communication, summarizing discussion, resolving differences, proposing procedures, and so on.

Once again, you can observe meetings. Or you can question people in the manner of Questions 14, 41, 42, and 43 above.

Condition 5: Skill in Collaborative Group Work

Working collaboratively in groups requires skill. An OD project can go more rapidly when participants begin it with good skills in collaboration.

Indicators

5-1. *Can people work effectively with others who have diverse views, opinions, and values?*

Tension and conflicts inevitably result when people holding different beliefs, values, and ideas try to work together. Those differences can often be reduced through clarification, but they cannot be eliminated.

In fact, they can be a great source of strength and inventiveness if they are used well. Effective groups turn their differences into motivations for change and into creative solutions to problems. Success hinges on participants' ability to clarify the differences and accept the virtues in the differences. See the more extended discussion in Chapter 7.

Again, you can get clues to the way people deal with differences by observing meetings. But to learn how students see your school in its dealings with diversity, here are some items you can use*:

Circle your answer

45. People listen to each other even if they are not friends. Yes No I don't know

46. No one else will help me if a teacher is unfair to me. Yes No I don't know

47. Most people here believe there is more than one way to take care of problems. Yes No I don't know

48. The principal will not listen to "our side" of an argument. Yes No I don't know

49. When we disagree here, we learn from each other. Yes No I don't know

For adult members of the school, you can use questions like the following in interviews or questionnaires:

50. In any school, there are differences of opinion about the goals of education or how to reach them. Sometimes there are "camps" or "cliques" having members who agree with one another but disagree with people in other camps or cliques. Is that the way it is in your school? Yes No I don't know

51. In committees or other groups containing people with differing opinions about education, does useful work usually get done anyway? Yes No I don't know

52. Do people with differing ideas about education sometimes pick up good ideas from one another despite their differences? Yes No I don't know

5-2. *Can people communicate clearly and effectively?*
Here we refer to the skills we set forth in Chapter 3 on communication and Chapter 4 on meetings. Many of the data-collecting methods

*All the questionnaire items shown on the next few pages, except Numbers 50, 51, and 53, were written by Bell and Burr (1976).

offered in those chapters can be adapted to diagnosis. In addition, here are some questions that can be asked of students about openness of communication:

53. Teachers find it easy to talk to the principal.	Yes	No	I don't know
54. I do not find it easy to talk to the teachers.	Yes	No	I don't know
55. The principal talks with us frankly and openly.	Yes	No	I don't know
56. I can easily get help from teachers if I want it.	Yes	No	I don't know
57. People do not talk to each other here if they are from different parts of the school.	Yes	No	I don't know
58. Teachers say mean things about each other.	Yes	No	I don't know

5-3. Can the group make high-quality decisions that are understood and accepted?

Can the group members usually come to decisions appropriate to the task? Do the decisions capture the commitment of the group's members? The Meetings Questionnaire in the section on "Instruments for Diagnosing Problems" in Chapter 4 contains some good items on decision making—namely, Numbers 11, 14, 18, 27, 33, 34, 35, and 36. And below are some questions to be asked of students that can help you find out their beliefs about who is involved in making decisions:

59. Teachers help decide which adults will work at this school.	Yes	No	I don't know
60. Parents do not help decide about new school programs.	Yes	No	I don't know
61. People from this school give advice to the superintendent and his staff before things are decided about the school.	Yes	No	I don't know
62. I do not get to help decide what to do here in school.	Yes	No	I don't know
63. None of the students gets to help decide what to do.	Yes	No	I don't know

5-4. Can the group be systematic about solving problems?

Systematic problem solving in groups requires several individual and group skills; see Chapter 5. If few people in a school have a conception of group problem solving as a systematic process demanding learnable skills, then an OD project must incorporate training in systematic problem solving.

As with other indicators described here, you can observe meetings. If you want to use a questionnaire in your diagnosis, some items of the Meetings Questionnaire in the section on "Instruments for Diagnosing Problems" in Chapter 4 are relevant—namely, Numbers 1, 2, 4, 6, 7, 13,

15, 23, 24, 25, 30, 31, 34, and 36. Those items can also be rephrased to be used in interviews. And below are some items with which you can find out what students believe about problem solving in the school:

64. People notice when something goes wrong;
   they try to make it right.   Yes   No   I don't know
65. There is no one here who will help me when I
   have a problem.   Yes   No   I don't know
66. Teachers plan a lot together when a change
   needs to be made.   Yes   No   I don't know
67. People here are interested in ideas from everyone.   Yes   No   I don't know
68. Teachers don't solve problems; they just talk
   about them.   Yes   No   I don't know

5-5. *Can the group conduct productive meetings?*
Most of the work of groups and schools is done in face-to-face meetings. We described the skills needed for effective meetings in Chapter 4; we also offered there some ways of collecting data about the skills.

Condition 6: The Spirit of Risk Taking

Nothing ventured, nothing gained. Every OD project is risky, at least to some extent. If people are to commit themselves to participate in OD, they should have an experimental attitude: "Let's see if it will work." They should feel not only that the effort will be worthwhile if the project is successful (see Indicator 1-3 above), but also that the effort will not be wasted if the project fails.

Indicators

6-1. *How many people are willing to risk new action on behalf of the school?*
Serious changes in ways of working together in the school require that at least some people make changes in roles, interrelationships, and routines. Further, some personnel will have to assume new responsibilities not merely for personal advancement, but for the improvement of the school. The risks are aggravated when, as is often the case, the required changes cannot be confidently specified in advance.

It is no good asking people vague questions like, "Are you willing to take a risk for this school?" or even specific questions such as "Are you willing to invest ten hours of hard work to make a plan for converting to team teaching?" People are almost always strongly affected by knowing who else is committed to working on a project. Even then, most people don't know how much they are willing to risk until they have put in some effort and have seen some of the first results. You can get some tentative indications from what people say at the opening of an OD project, but you should not trust those indications beyond a next few hours, and even then you should not trust them much. Better indicators are the small commitments that people make or do not make when they are offered the opportunity.

During a meeting at which a faculty is discussing whether to participate in OD, if no one puts into words any likely benefit from the OD project, you can put one weight in the pan of the balance representing low readiness to take risks. You can also put weights there when people mention losses they might incur. You can put a weight in the favorable pan when someone mentions a possible benefit, when someone says, "I'd like to give it a try, at least for a while," and when someone volunteers to do work not specifically requested. But such indicators become more reliable when they occur after the OD project has been launched.

6-2. *Are key administrators willing to make changes in their own behavior?*

We have repeatedly emphasized the importance of the principal in supporting OD, and we say it again here. Actions speak louder than words. The willingness of administrators to make changes in their own behavior is critical. If administrators say, "You go ahead and change, but don't expect me to do so," then the likelihood that others will risk change is greatly reduced. OD cannot work without the principal's support.

6-3. *How many people are willing to undergo training in a new skill?*

Since OD calls for changed roles and norms, it is almost inevitable that skills will be called upon that were not called upon before, or in greater degree. Our society does not teach many of us the skills of organizational change (as J. S. Coleman, 1971, argues). Almost always, therefore, an OD project will require a certain amount of direct training of participants in the necessary new (or underdeveloped) skills.

As with Indicator 6-1, you can get some utterances from people about whether they are willing to undergo training, but those utterances are not usually very helpful to diagnosis. More reliable indications are simply the counts of those who show up for the scheduled training sessions and who continue to attend.

6-4. *How many people are already feeling anxious or under stress or threat?*

OD brings with it uncertainties, possible threats, and anxieties. If a school faculty or student body is already feeling a pronounced level of uncertainty, anxiety, and threat, adding more with an OD project is not a good idea.

It is very difficult to get a direct indicator of feelings of threat when an OD project is being considered, because that is precisely the time when respondents will be reluctant to trust you with the information. You can yourself make inferences about the probable level of threat in the school by gathering information about the conditions there. If there is a high rate of vandalism, if some students are extorting money from others through threats of bodily harm, if three new programs are under way that will probably affect teachers' eligibility for raises in salary, and if voters have just failed to approve a budget levy, you can reasonably suppose that school staff members are feeling threatened and anxious.

You can also extrapolate from the soundings you took for Indicators 1-3, 1-4, 3-3, 3-4, 4-3, 4-4, and 6-1.

A MAPPING SENTENCE FOR ORGANIZATION DIAGNOSIS

Diagnostic data can be collected by people in different jobs and in different ways. The *information gatherer* can be a consultant, an evaluator, a researcher, or the clients themselves, to mention only those who most commonly play the role. Upon occasion, the information gatherer may also be a funder, a teachers' association, a taxpayers' association, a court, or some other. As to styles of gathering data, the information gatherer can be *visible or invisible* to the participants. People who hand out questionnaires, conduct interviews, or sit at the side of the room taking notes are highly visible. A person who counts the number of windows in the school having glass missing is not very visible. People who get information about the school from the school's records kept in the central office are almost invisible. You can also be invisible by listening through a hidden microphone or by watching through a one-way mirror, but we do not recommend those or any other deceptions.

The information itself can come from any of several *sources*: a client's self-report, the report of an informant, behavior of the client observable now, nonverbal traces of past behavior, public documents, or archives. And the information can be collected by any of several *methods*: questionnaire, interview, information volunteered by clients, existing documents, direct observation during consulting, and direct observation of ordinary day-to-day work. Finally, the *situation* in which the information is gathered can be a natural or spontaneously occurring one—that is, a situation quite beyond the control of the information gatherer. Or it can be partly or wholly under the control of the information gatherer. An example of the latter might be when the information gatherer is alone in the library searching through archives.

All five facets of information gathering can affect the sort of information that is finally gathered, and therefore the usefulness of the information to one or another audience. The sixth feature of diagnostic information, then, is its suitability, or *usefulness*, and the seventh is the *audience* to which the information goes. Most often, the audiences for diagnostic information in OD are the consultants and the clients alone. The audiences for evaluative information, however, often include many more kinds of people, as we will discuss in Chapter 10.

One way to put all this together is to say that a particular kind of information gatherer, visible or invisible to the client, collects information about the client from one or more sources, by one or more methods, in a particular situation (or series of them), and thereby produces information of some degree of usefulness to one or more audiences. Figure 9-1 says the same thing, but restores the detail. When you write a sentence by picking one of the choices listed under each of the facets, you describe a particular way of getting information for a particular audience. The mapping sentence serves as a convenient catalog of all the ways you might choose to get diagnostic information in OD. Here are a few examples of specific sentences you can extract from Figure 9-1, each describing a specific episode of data collection.

- To form an opinion on whether the client is ready to begin actual training with a three-day workshop, for example, the consultant might think of getting information this way:

  A consultant who is visible to the client collects self-report information via interview in a meeting convened by the consultant, and thereby gets diagnostic information useful to the consultant.

- A consultant might get information about how the faculty works together at meetings in this way:

  A consultant who is visible to the client collects information about the client by observing (method) a natural regular meeting (source and situation) of the faculty. The consultant reports what he or she observed to the faculty (audience), and the faculty can use that information to change its methods of conducting meetings.

- Sometimes a consultant asks trainees to participate in an exercise or simulation, the chief purpose of which is to enable the participants objectively to observe their own group dynamics. The

Figure 9-1. Mapping Sentence for Getting Information About a Client

Information Gatherer		_Visibility_	
A consultant evaluator researcher client	**who is**	visible invisible	**to the client**

collects information about the client from

Source		_Method_
client's self-report	**by**	questionnaire
a person or agency within the client's organization or in its environment who is observing or has observed the client and who is not a member of the staff of the information gatherer: an "informant"		interview of individual or group spontaneous communication from client existing documents direct observation during consultation
behavior of the client directly observable now, such as manner of participating in meetings or manner of responding to demands from the environment		direct observation of ordinary day-to-day work
nonverbal traces of past behavior, such as glassless windows or murals by students		
public document, such as a copy of a speech to the PTA		
archives, such as attendance records		

in a situation that is

Situation

natural or spontaneously
  occurring
convened or given structure by the
  data gatherer
one of culling documents

and thereby produces information of

Usefulness		Audience
high	**usefulness to an audience of**	consultant
moderate		evaluator
low		researcher
		client (such as members of
		a school)
		teachers' association
		taxpayers' association
		parents' association
		students' association
		school board
		funder
		court
		legislature
		newspaper readers

mapping sentence for this kind of information gathering would be:

A client group that is visible to itself collects information about itself from its members (source) who are present and observing themselves (method) as a group in a situation that has been organized by the client's having agreed to participate in the exercise. The client group (audience) uses the new awareness to change its own dynamics.

- The debriefing after the exercise, when participants reveal to one another what they saw themselves and others doing, also gives the consultant information about the client's ability at self-diagnosis:

A consultant who is visible to the client collects information about the client from behavior of the client directly observable now (the game and debriefing session) in a situation that the consultant has organized as an exercise. The consultant (audience) uses the information to judge the client's skill at self-diagnosis.

And so on. The mapping sentence is a handy way of reminding ourselves of the many ways in which we can obtain information about clients and in which clients can obtain information about themselves.

TIPS FOR CARRYING OUT DIAGNOSIS

Gathering information about human behavior can be very simple or very complicated. For example, getting information about the likelihood of a certain proportion of the people in the United States acting in a particular way (such as buying a refrigerator) in the near future can be very complicated. It would take a fairly long book to tell you how to do it well. Getting information that can enable you to decide whether to start an OD project isn't always simple, but it often is. We give here some tips we believe to be essential for carrying out even simple sorts of diagnosis.

Choices

Before committing yourself to a particular way of getting diagnostic information, look again through the mapping sentence (Figure 9-1) to see whether you have overlooked a good idea.

You will often choose to use interviewing, not only to make it easier for respondents to volunteer information, but also as a way for you and the participants to begin to get personally acquainted. When you prepare for a series of interviews, be sure to write out a guide for yourself. The guide will make it easier for you—and your associates—to conduct all interviews in the same way. Write out not only the questions you are going to ask, but also the introductions you are going to make, the words you will use to encourage respondents to elaborate on their answers, and the "thank you" at the end. Remember, too, to use the communication skills presented in Chapter 3 during the interview.

Types of Items

There are two general types of items, both of which can be used either in questionnaire or in interviews. The first type is called the open-ended or free-response item. This type allows respondents to answer in their own words. Of the items we have presented in this chapter, the open-ended ones are Numbers 1–13, 15, 16, and 18–23. The disadvantages of open-ended items are (1) it is time-consuming to collect the answers—for such questions you have to record them on tape or write them down— and (2) the answers can be compared only through "coding"; that is, you must invent ways of classifying the answers so you can say that so many respondents gave a "Type A" response, so many a "Type B," and so on. The advantage to this type is that you get the respondent's own way of thinking about the question. You often pick up viewpoints you would not have discovered if you had restricted the respondent to answers you listed in advance.

When you are using an open-ended question in an interview, you will sometimes get an answer that is too brief or that is phrased so unusually that you know you will not be able to get useful information from it. It is then customary to *probe*—that is, to ask a question that encourages the respondent to talk more but does not constrain the direction of the talk. Examples of probes are, "Could you say a little more about that?" and "What did you mean just now by . . . ?" and "Could you give me an example?"

The second type of item is called *closed* or precoded. Respondents are asked to choose an answer from a list you have made up. Closed questions are familiar to everyone. In an interview, consultants use them by reading off the answers (if they are few, short, and simple) to the respondent or by printing them on a card and handing the card to the respondent. Of the items presented earlier, the closed ones are Numbers 24–68. Three of our items, by the way, are mixed. Item 14 is closed, in that it offers three prewritten answers, but if the respondent picks "yes," we then ask for elaboration in a free response. Items 17 and 18 ask first for a "yes" or "no" and then for a free response.

The disadvantage of closed questions is that they force your way of categorizing the answers onto the respondent. You don't find out the respondent's way of thinking about the question. You don't know what category of response the respondent would have generated spontaneously had you not shown him or her your list. The advantage is that closed questions are comparatively easy and quick to answer—if they are written well. That fact also makes them cheaper in two ways: you can ask less time of the respondent than an interview would take, and you need not spend your time coding the answers.

Funnels

If you want to find out how participants think about things privately, and not merely whether they assent to your ideas, and if you want to get simultaneously some precise, countable, and comparable answers from the participants, you can do so by using the Funnel Technique. The image refers to the process of beginning the questions that catch a wide range of answers and ending with questions that permit only a very narrow range of answers.

Questions 15–20 on pp. 381–382 are an example of a funnel. That series was designed to discover whether respondents could name colleagues likely to join efforts for school improvement that the respondents cared about. That idea was too complicated to be conveyed clearly in a single item. Furthermore, we wanted to be sure that respondents gave us answers connected with their own reality—that is, that they named topics they cared about, and not merely ones they thought someone else cared about. So we had to ask questions first that would bring out what the respondents cared about. The first question of the series, Number 15, asks an open-ended question about what the respondent cares about professionally—about as broad a question as one can get. It gives us a frame of "importance"—a first cut—that will eventually put more meaning on the answer to Question 19. The questions following Number 16 narrow the attention of the respondent by asking about the directions other people in the school are going or want to go. Question 18 admits the possibility that there might be disagreements in the school. Question 19 narrows respondents' attention to something they would like to see happen that is not happening now. And, finally, Question 20 asks very specifically and narrowly for a list of names. Of course, respondents can always reply "None" to Number 19 or "I don't know" to Number 20.

K.I.S.S. and Pilot

Whenever you are interviewing or giving questionnaires, remember that participants are giving you the precious gift of a little chunk of their lives. Therefore: *Keep It Short and Simple.* Don't ask questions just because you think the answers might be interesting. Ask a question only if you know exactly how you are going to make use of the information.

Use nickel instead of dollar words: write *use* instead of *utilize*, *simple* instead of *simplistic*. Make *visits*, not *visitations*. Look back through the items to see whether you can simply drop out some words: write *temporarily* instead of *on a temporary basis*, *in case of emergency* instead of *in case of an emergency situation*, *in social studies* instead of *in the social studies area*, *they believe* instead of *they are the kind of people who believe*, *in itself* instead of *in and of itself*, *we hope* instead of *we would hope*, and so on. K.I.S.S.

Before you distribute a questionnaire or set out to interview a faculty, try out your instrument on some friends or colleagues; give it a "pilot test." Ask two or three people to answer the questionnaire or to sit for an interview to find out how long the instrument takes to complete and whether all the questions are clear. Ask another few people to check it for spelling, grammar, and clarity.

Try to make KISSing and pilot testing the two rules of diagnosis you never break.

Reactivity and the Hawthorne Effect

Some of the methods of collecting information are more likely than others to arouse a reaction in clients. Ask yourself how the method you are planning to use may affect the clients' willingness or ability to give information and how giving the information will affect their willingness to participate in the OD project.

If the data gathering is highly reactive—that is, if it causes some sort of relevant change within the clients—you will find yourself with data that tell you what the clients *were* like but what they are like no longer. Although this inconvenience should be avoided whenever possible, it is often worth using a reactive method if it gets a kind of information you need for effective consultation, even at the cost of having to recheck the client's condition before taking the action you based on your earlier diagnosis. You must make that timely check, no matter how informally, to be sure that your design for intervention matches the client's present condition and not a condition that no longer exists. If you do not check, you may pay the still higher price of having to redo that part of the intervention and suffer loss of confidence on the part of the clients. The recheck need not be as formal or extensive as the first assessment, of course; often a simple oral query will suffice.

Information is especially reactive when it is fed back to the client by the consultant; in fact, data feedback is very often a useful strategy for bringing about organizational change—see Chapters 1 and 2.

At the outset of an OD project, things will often seem pleasant enough, but as the clients learn to speak more openly about their feelings and tell more about their disgruntlements with their working conditions, their colleagues may conclude that the consultants have upset them by stirring things up. The onlookers are here noting only an increase in expressed disgruntlement and are forgetting that the trainees may have been as dissatisfied earlier but unwilling to talk about it. In our view, if a school staff does not increase its complaints soon after consultation starts, the consultants should conclude either that the training in openness of communication has been remarkably ineffective or that conditions in the school have remarkably improved very recently.

The famous "Hawthorne effect" is also susceptible to opposite interpretations. When an intervention in a school is followed by an increase in productivity or morale, some onlookers will remark that people almost always do better when they know they are being watched. This observation is only half true. People usually act differently when they know they are being watched, but whether they will do better or worse depends on many other things. Indeed, workers who are subjected to an innovation by management sometimes show the "reverse Hawthorne effect"—they will slow down rather than speed up.

How people will react to attention is not a simple matter. When a classroom is visited by a principal, superintendent, or group of parents, for example, will the students want to be more or less obedient to the teacher than usual? Will they want to show more or less knowledge of the lessons? Will they want to recite with more or less clarity and enthusiasm? Whichever they choose to do, do they choose so as to gain self-approbation without regard to the opinions of others? Do they choose their acts in the hope of pleasing the teacher, other students, or someone not even present? Or do they choose their acts in the hope of displeasing teacher, fellow student, or someone else? If they choose a particular kind of act, are they capable of performing it or will their performance fall short in some way?

Similarly, if teachers are interviewed by central-office persons after three or four months of OD, how are they likely to perform during the interviews? Will they want to please or displease the interviewers, and are they correct about what will please or displease? Suppose the teachers are interviewed by their OD consultants, who want to monitor progress. Do the teachers want the consultants to feel good or bad, and do they know what will make them feel one way or the other?

Arguments about the Hawthorne effect are further complicated by the view that this effect is somehow disreputable—that effects on a faculty, for example, are not due to the consultation, but merely to the attention that faculty are getting from the consultants and from one another. This argument is difficult to refute rationally because it makes a false dichotomy. Communication, training, love, and reward and punishment cannot be carried on without special attentiveness. In fact, one of the goals of OD is to heighten the ability of participants to be more attentive to one another, to give routinely what now seems like special attention. From this point of view, the Hawthorne effect, however double-edged, becomes a tool, not necessarily a debility.

MONITORING PROGRESS

As we said at the beginning of this chapter, when you are part way along in an OD project and you want to know where you are now with respect to where you'd like to be, you can collect some systematic information to get an answer. This is called *formative evaluation*. When you do that periodically, even if informally, it is also called *monitoring progress*. The difference between diagnosis and monitoring progress is that diagnosis is done early in the project, and monitoring progress is done later and repeatedly.

Consultation and training activities can double as opportunities for diagnosis or monitoring progress. Sometimes diagnostic information from an early training event can provide a good baseline against which to compare later assessment of design or later monitoring of progress.

In 1973, for example, we designed for key people in a school district a demonstration intended to yield prognostic information both to us and to them, and their reactions enabled us to go at least part of the way toward answering several questions of importance to us both: To what extent did the organization's members agree on the expectations that they placed on their various roles? Were there conflicting expectations? Did participants typically see their troubles as arising from other people, or did they include themselves as sources of trouble? Were they more concerned with finding out who was right or wrong or with getting problems solved? Were they aware of the productive aspects of conflict? Were the administrators hoping that an OD intervention would answer their own needs and alleviate their own problems, or were they hoping that seeming to approve the project would appease someone who might otherwise be a nuisance to them? How much were various members ready to invest in the project in terms of money, time, prerogatives, status, and other resources? What kinds of risks did people seem ready to take?

Sometimes, to be sure, the direction of an activity's usefulness changes in midstream. In the early 1970s, we designed for a junior high school an initial training event that included the Planners and Operators exercise as a component. Our purpose was to give the participants here-and-now evidence about their manner of working in groups but to elicit this evidence from an exercise that would arouse less anxiety than evidence taken from their performance in actual day-to-day work in the school. As it turned out, four of five groups failed to solve the Planners and Operators exercise even in forty minutes. The debriefing evidenced very little discussion of interdependence, helpfulness or lack of helpfulness to others, explicit attention to influence processes, emotional reaction to personal experiences of release or frustration, or other organizational dynamics.

Instead, participants justified their own behavior and castigated the trainers for having picked the wrong exercise, having given unclear instructions, and so on. The exercise was the wrong medium for the participants to learn about their own interaction during problem solving, but it provided excellent diagnostic information to the trainers concerning the participants' lack of readiness to examine their own interpersonal relations—a diagnosis that was amply verified by our experience with them during the subsequent year.

In sum, consultation and training are never entirely separate from diagnosis and monitoring progress. The skillful consultant uses occasions of assessing progress to provide clients with information they can use for their own diagnosis, to serve as examples of ways they can collect diagnostic or monitoring information for themselves, to enable them to become aware of how they react to having their performance evaluated, or to serve other purposes as the occasion permits. Conversely, the consultant often uses conferences, demonstrations, or training episodes as additional sources of diagnostic or monitoring information for his or her own purposes.

RAISING READINESS FOR OD

Following diagnosis, you and the client can come to one of three conclusions:

1. Readiness is high enough and of the right sort for an OD project; you will proceed with it.
2. Readiness and the likelihood of success are low; you will drop OD.
3. The indicators are mixed; if some features of readiness could be heightened, the chances of success could be good, so you decide to improve readiness for OD.

Suitable Readiness

Since OD will most likely require significant changes in norms among a large proportion of the people in the school (as when schoolwide problem solving is undertaken, for example), you will want high readiness of all six sorts described above.

The following guides will improve the likelihood of success.*

1. *Plan collaboratively.* Bring at least a representative group of the participants into the planning as soon as possible.

---

*These guides are explained in slightly more detail in the appendix to Runkel, Schmuck, Arends, and Francisco (1979). The more important research backing up the guides is also listed there.

2. *Establish a joint steering committee early.* Or you might call it a planning group, a liaison team, or a task force. Try to get people with complementary skills.
3. *Encourage participants to adapt* the OD procedures and materials you bring to them to make them suit the local situation better, or even to create their own. They will use them better.
4. *Model the desired behavior.* Practice what you preach.
5. *Offer training* as you think it appropriate. Establishing norms requires skill in self-observation; training to heighten that skill is often necessary. Mix interpersonal and content skill when you can.
6. *Build support systems.* Get communication and understanding going not only inside the target system, but also between the target system and adjoining systems. If a school is a target for OD, build links to those who will support you in the central office, in the community, among other principals, and so on.
7. *Keep at it.* As long as you see some signs of readiness for OD within some critical mass, keep at it. Even when you are confused, discouraged, and can't come up with a useful next step, do something. Go to the site and talk to somebody. If you don't go away, the participants will have to deal with you somehow.

Lack of Readiness

The indicators may be so bad that you and the client decide not to start the OD project. But don't let the plan fade away in a vague, indecisive manner. After conferring with all the stakeholders, make a clear public announcement of termination. Make the announcement clean, crisp, and conclusive.

Mixed Readiness

If some indicators for OD are good and others bad, offer consultation to the school on *creating a climate for OD* without a commitment to a full OD macrodesign. Below, we offer a few brief remarks about heightening each condition of readiness.

Condition 1: The Press for OD. If a press for OD is indeed latent, waiting to be brought into awareness, the following actions are appropriate.

First, create a shared sense that there are organizational problems, that the problems are serious enough to merit action, and that enough people are sufficiently dissatisfied to guarantee the energy to work on them. By *shared* we mean not only that a lot of people have the same opinion, but also that they know that others have the same opinion.

It is not difficult to know when dissatisfaction exists in a school unless punishment for expressing it is unusually strong. The difficulty lies in discovering the extent and shape of the dissatisfaction and in assessing the possibilities of alleviating the underlying problems. At bottom, it is important to create opportunities for people to talk about their discontents, both with and without administrators present. Often, a participant will be able to serve as facilitator. Sometimes an outsider will be useful. Ideas for Ss, Ts, and Ps (see Chapter 5) should be written down and circulated.

Second, try to find two or three people in the environment—in the central office, among the business community, in a university—who can speak with understanding about the organizational problems that are voiced in the school. They can provide a "social reality," allowing participants to say to themselves, "If that outsider takes our problems seriously, maybe it's reasonable for us to take them seriously, too."

Condition 2: Support for OD. The key thought here is that of resources: money and things are important, but so are information, respect or approval, the support of affection, and services.* It is usually a straightforward task to find out whether money and equipment are in good supply. Officially, money and property are always put in the keeping of particular people; you need simply ask them. The answer will not always be a fully open one, but you can usually find out the approximate range of practicability.

Information, approval, affection, and services can be discovered everywhere. Certain kinds of information, it is true, are entrusted to particular people and are given to others only sparingly, but great ranges of information useful in OD are free for the asking, and some can be found in the head and heart of almost every member of the school. The remaining three kinds of resources cannot be assigned to the safekeeping of any official; anyone, if he or she desires, can give you respect or approval, affection, and favors or services.

Look for the resources within the school that might be available to you in the future. Look especially for information or knowledge that people have that could be useful in an OD project. Look for people who respect the urge toward organizational change in others, for ties of affection, and for people willing to give some of their energy to improv-

*We adapt this list from Foa and Foa (1974, pp. 36 ff.).

ing the way the school is organized. We described a few ways of discovering personal resources in Chapters 4 and 5.

A key source is *energy*—the willingness and ability of people to do work beyond what is routinely required of them. Indeed, every one of the six conditions of readiness touches in one way or another on the availability of energy. And the seven guides we gave under "Suitable Readiness" all require extra energy. Sometimes a charismatic leader will inspire others with energy. At other times you must hunt through the potential participants for those who already have it.

It is always important that key administrators and other leaders give clear signs of approval and support. When you are improving the climate for OD, talk with central-office administrators, members of the school board, leaders of the community groups, and so on. Find out the sorts of OD in which they would invest their energy. Find out how organizational change could alleviate *their* problems.

Condition 3: Stability of the Staff. There is not much you can do quickly about this condition. If staff turnover is high, or if most people are heavily overburdened, or if the school's schedule is so tight that there is not a minute for nonroutine matters, then no project will have much chance of success unless it deals directly with one of those conditions as a problem. Give up other kinds of innovative projects. Mount an effort to reduce the daily burden of work or to loosen up the schedule so that teachers and others have a few unprogrammed hours. If turnover is high and if changing the causes seems beyond your ability, wait until turnover drops to a reasonable level.

Condition 4: Norms Supporting Collaborative Work. Most people yearn for collaborative work, because it enables them to satisfy their needs for affiliation, achievement, and power. That fact gives us several ways of strengthening norms for collaboration:

1. Often, people want to do more collaborative work while simultaneously believing that others do not want to collaborate. Using an anonymous questionnaire or interview can expose such "pluralistic ignorance." For example, see the Team-Expectation Survey in Chapter 3.

2. You can ask groups to make explicit agreements, or contracts, about how work will be conducted within the group. The agreements should be written down. They should be adopted only by consensus (see Chapter 6). For example, they might agree to set aside certain hours of the week for the business of the group, and not schedule anything else for those hours. Or they might agree that for the next three months, no tasks that have to be

done outside the meetings would be given to the chairperson except preparing the agenda for the next meeting. Or whatever seems appropriate to encourage collaboration in the particular group.

3. You can give praise and recognition when collaboration occurs.
4. You can organize tasks so that interdependence is the key to success—that is, so that one member succeeds only when the group succeeds.
5. You can institute training programs for intact work groups.
6. You can institute team building on a small scale, beginning with the key teams.
7. Finally, when it comes time to hire a new person, you can hire the person with a preference for collaboration and skill in it.

Condition 5: Skill in Collaborative Group Work. Generally, doing the things to strengthen norms for collaboration listed above will also give people the opportunity to improve their collaborative skills. Aside from that, every how-to chapter in this book contains some ideas about improving these skills. You can also offer collaborative-skills workshops to individuals in the district.

Condition 6: The Spirit of Risk Taking. Four conditions will encourage people to take risks on behalf of the school. The first is psychological safety—that is, a clear norm that it is all right, even admirable, to experiment, try things, and therefore sometimes fail. The second condition is being buffered from the consequences of failure. Retreats, workshops, and training sessions can give participants opportunities to practice a new norm or a new skill without submitting their work in school to the fumbles or failures of learning.

The third condition fostering risk taking is approval and support; we described that under Condition 2. Here we add that the best kind of support from an administrator is a demonstration in action that he or she is willing to make the behavior changes that the OD project is asking others to make. The fourth condition is calculating costs and benefits; we mentioned that under Condition 1-3. You can teach people how to look at the costs they are already paying as well as the potential benefits of alternative ways of doing things. We add here that calculating costs and benefits gets complicated when the school is already overburdened with projects of various kinds: heavy schedules; interruptions from supervisors, parents, and newspaper reporters; and so on. Potential participants must then calculate the cost of lightening the burden now against the possible benefits of whatever may be done later with the time freed up. That seems like crystal-ball gazing to many. We can only say again: look for the critical mass of those willing to participate in OD and go with those people.

SUMMARY

Consultants should extract information from every relevant source and by every appropriate method. They must diagnose the organizational conditions that exist at entry, monitor the progress of the OD project, and evaluate the outcomes after the OD has ceased.

In initial diagnosis, consultants should ascertain the manner in which the client organization is functioning in its interpersonal communication, in its subsystems, as a whole organization, and in its interaction with its environment. Of great importance to the effectiveness of the project is the presence of certain conditions of client readiness. We described six conditions.

Diagnosis (and evaluation later as well) can strongly influence participants' reactions to the entire OD project. When collecting information for organizational diagnosis, consultants will maintain more effective relations with clients if they allow them to see that they can be trusted with potentially harmful information, if they avoid any role in which they could be perceived as influencing the fate of participants against their will, and if they teach participants how to gather and interpret information about themselves. They should also collect information under circumstances that permit participants' anxiety to be low, and they should encourage participants to collaborate in problem solving.

10

Evaluation

Why should one evaluate an OD project at all? As OD consultants work, they get lots of evidence about what they are doing right and wrong. Isn't that enough? Patton (1978, p. 13) quotes an administrator of a community service agency:

> This scientific evaluation stuff is all very interesting, and I suppose it's something we're going to have to do for funders. But when it comes right down to it, my program is evaluated every night when I get down on my knees and ask God to look into my heart and judge what I do by His criteria. And, by God, as long as His evaluation is positive we'll keep on serving and helping people.

The inner voice of belief is convincing, of course, to the one who hears it. So are the voices of participants throbbing with gratitude for the personal benefits they have reaped from OD. Almost every OD consultant has felt the rightness, even the righteousness, of those voices.

But systematic evaluation is valuable for two purposes. First, those who have endured the rigors of an OD project may want more than their own impressions. They may want some countable data by which to judge the worth of their efforts. The OD consultants themselves and the key leaders in the project will almost always welcome countable data, but other participants will usually be eager to see the data as well.

Second, besides the participants there are always other audiences that have some stake in an OD project. They will not usually feel well informed by a few anecdotes. They will want to know who benefited from the work, how much and how often, and what the benefits were. They will want to know, too, the costs in time, energy, and money. In short, they will want "the facts." And since some of those audiences can give or withhold valuable support to further OD work, it is important for OD consultants and the leaders of OD projects to give those audiences the facts.

Important audiences contain the parent who wants to know how teachers are spending their time, the administrator who is convinced that something good has happened but thinks it may have been accidental and undesigned, and the president of the education association who wonders about the project's effect on the association's bargaining position. Other obviously important audiences are the members of the school district: administrators, counselors, teachers, classified staff, and students. Still other audiences can be important: parent groups, taxpayers' associations, the school board, the local newspaper, and perhaps even state and federal education agencies. A clearly written evaluation can be useful in dealing with all those audiences.

OUTCOMES

When you consider the possible audiences for an evaluation of an OD project, it becomes obvious that they will differ in the outcomes they care about. The consultants will probably want to know whether the project brought about the outcomes they hoped for at the outset. Teachers might want to know whether their working lives have improved in some way—any way at all. The taxpayers' association may want to know whether OD will save more money than it cost. The newspaper reporter may be looking for a human-interest story about OD.

Some writers on evaluation write as if the only outcomes of a change project worth attention are those the project designers originally conceived—were "the goals" of the project achieved? But the designers are not the only people who have a stake in an OD project. The participants, obviously, have a stake as well. So do other people in the district and at least a few of the other audiences mentioned above. A useful evaluation will contain data on effects that the stakeholders care about.

Here are a few questions that various audiences might want an evaluation to answer:

- Did the OD project achieve the goals officially adopted at the outset?
- How much consultation was rendered, and to whom?
- Was the OD work a reasonable load or an overload?
- Could the benefits of OD have been gotten more cheaply through other methods?
- What was the essential specification of the OD project? What parts were necessary? What conditions helped the essential parts to operate?
- Did the OD project deal effectively with those who had a political interest in it?
- Did the OD project uncover new ways of working not originally designed into it?
- Do we have a better appreciation now of how we do or can work together?
- Did the project increase or decrease equitable treatment of one organizational member by another?
- What human satisfactions such as achievement, affiliation, or power did the project increase or decrease?
- What was the effect of OD on the quality of working life?
- Were the original goals worth achieving? Do we have new goals more worth achieving.?

Because the interests of various audiences in an evaluation can be so diverse, we offer next a way of thinking about the variety.

VARIETIES OF EVALUATION

To evaluate OD is to put *value* on it. We try to find out the worth of OD—the benefit or harm it has brought, or is likely to bring, to us or to somebody else. We think that "developing" a school organization is a good thing, at least for many schools under many circumstances. But what is good (or bad) for one person is not good (or bad) for another. When we start to evaluate any policy, program, or cluster of activities in a school, the question should always arise, *For whom* is it good or bad? Who are the benefitted and who are the bereft? Who gains? Who pays?

Ted Aoki (1984) says the evaluation can take three directions. Shortening Aoki's phrases, we will call the three directions the ends-means, the situational, and the critical.

The *ends-means* direction is the one most familiar to most of us. The typical question it takes seriously is, "Did the OD project achieve the goals adopted at the outset?" That question is typical in not specifying *who* adopted the goals. The goals to which ends-means evaluators give first attention, however, and sometimes their only attention, are typically those chosen by the people with the most power—administrators, funders, and the like. Ends-means evaluators also ask such questions as, "Did we spend more money than we had to?" Ends-means evaluation looks for goal-achievement, comparisons against objective criteria, and favorable cost-benefit ratios. It seeks control in the sense of maximizing efficiency, effectiveness, and predictability.

For example, a principal might believe that less time could be spent in faculty meetings. The principal could count the hours spent in faculty meetings last year and then call in an OD consultant. After learning the new ways of conducting the meetings, the principal would then count the hours spent during the rest of the year. The principal could compare the person-hours per year spent in faculty meetings before and after the training. The principal could also multiply the salaries per hour by the hours saved and compare that with the fee paid the consultant. That would be means-end evaluation.

The *situational* direction takes the evaluator to the people engaged in OD or those who have a stake in it. Quite aside from the "goals of the project," the evaluator taking the situational direction examines the quality of the beliefs and feelings that participants and other people—the various audiences—have about their experiences with OD. The typical question is, "What satisfactions or lack of them do people find during OD?" Another would be, "What meanings for their working lives do people take from their experience with OD?" Situational evaluation looks for the new views of their working situation that participants develop. To situational evaluators, all groups (participants, stakeholders, audiences) have justifiable claims on their attention.

In a school district that has declining enrollment, for example, OD consultants might be asked to help with procedures for recruiting faculty and transferring teachers among schools. A means-end evaluator might measure the outcome by counting the number of formal complaints and suits brought against the district and comparing the count with those in similar districts with declining enrollment. The situational evaluator, however, would want to know whether transferred teachers had a voice in where they were assigned, whether they went into their new schools believing they could make a good working situation for themselves there, whether the schools receiving transferred teachers took steps to build morale among the faculty, and the like. The situational evaluator might also want to know whether the released teachers felt that their dismissal was a mark against their competence and whether they sought new jobs with confidence or fear.

The *critical* direction, Aoki says, reveals the "underlying human and social conditions that distort human existence" and alienate people from one another. Going beyond the present situation at work, the evaluator with the critical orientation asks what assumptions about people and community the project planners have in mind and what assumptions the participants have as they engage with one another in OD. What kinds of people are the participants now becoming, or failing to become? A typical question is, "What are the assumptions about human nature, or the nature of teachers and students, or about knowledge itself, that participation in OD implies?" For example, when you act within the requirements of an OD project, are you acting as if people will not work unless strictly supervised? Another question is, "Who are the chief beneficiaries of OD?" For example, does OD further the interests of the funders, the administrators, the taxpayers, the teachers, or the students? Does one group benefit at the expense of another?

Of Aoki's three orientations toward evaluation, the critical orientation looks farthest into the future. Critical evaluators ask us on what path to the future we have put our feet. They ask us not only whether original goals are achieved at reasonable cost, and not only whether participants find OD a comfortable way of working together, but also whether the future we are building is worthy of human aspirations.

For example, a school district might establish a cadre of organizational specialists. A critical evaluator would look beyond the money saved in fees for outside consultants and beyond the satisfactions the participants feel in working with colleagues. The critical evaluator would want to know how many people feel a new confidence that they and their colleagues are capable of solving their own problems, whether they are discovering new resources within themselves, whether they find one another more trustworthy, and whether they have a greater confidence that they can build their own future both at school and in the community. In sum, the critical evaluator asks whether participants have new beliefs about their own qualities and capabilities and those of their colleagues, their students, and their community.

To sum up, the ends-means orientation focuses on the particular project and its products, the situational orientation on the uniqueness of participants and their working situation, and the critical orientation on the deeper meaning of OD for self and community. The ends-means orientation asks whether an OD project produces a preconceived outcome, the situational whether participants and other stakeholders are brought into fulfilling ways of working together, and the critical whether school and community are being shaped to expand human potentiality. In practice, of course, most evaluations partake of all three orientations, but some lean most heavily on one or another.

Many evaluators are finding the ends-means kind of evaluation less satisfying than they once did. David Clark (1980), for example, writing about planning (which is the obverse of evaluation), says that the "traditional" view (the ends-means view) is that an educational organization is a "goal-driven, rational system in which operations can and should be programmed, sequenced, monitored, and evaluated in short-range and long-range planning cycles" (pp. 1–2). That view, Clark says, mistakenly assumes that (1) goals are prerequisite to action, (2) organizational life is rational and sequential, (3) fidelity in communication and the coupling among planned steps are adequate, (4) adequate information can be gathered, (5) events are reasonably predictable, and (6) the organization's goals sufficiently stabilize individuals' goals.

Many researchers on organizational life are now questioning those assumptions as follows:

1. A consensual goal is not a prerequisite to moving ahead with OD. Indeed, as we mentioned in Chapter 1, schools typically have multiple and unclear goals.
2. As we also pointed out in Chapter 1, schools are naturally beset by conflict and are highly permeable to their environments—conditions inimical to sequential, rational process.
3. In Chapter 3, we asserted that accuracy of communication is low in most schools, and in Chapter 1 we pointed out that the relation of schools to their publics almost demands some loose coupling internally.
4. The information necessary to reasoned decisions is often weak or missing. The variables inside and outside schools that affect what can be done in them are so many and of such variety that getting the relevant information often exceeds the time school people can spare, even when the information does exist somewhere.
5. Everyone knows how unpredictable events can be. No one, indeed, knows that better than the OD consultant. A project is started with teachers in a particular school, but then the school is selected as one to be closed because of declining enrollment, and the teachers are scattered among other schools in the district, and so on.
6. If evaluation of the attainment of prechosen goals is to be useful, people must care about the same goals at the end that they cared about at the beginning. But participants and stakeholders often discover new goals as they move along with OD.

Ends-means planning tries to *predict* in sequential detail what an organization (or an OD project) can be made to do. Not only Clark, but other theorists of organizational behavior argue that the aspirations of the ends-means planners are mostly hopeless. March and Olsen (1976) tell us that problems, solutions, and choice opportunities occur not sequentially, but in a jumble, as one might toss them all, along with the participants, into a large garbage can and stir them around. Weick (1979, pp. 18, 195, and 239) writes that goals usually come *after* action, not before. Planners who take the garbage-can, or goal-enactment, view try to *allow* for what can happen instead of assuming that they can *make* it happen. The new views of evaluation can be found in Scriven (1973), Stake (1975), Patton (1978), House (1980), Guba and Lincoln (1981), and Cronbach (1982).

GOALS FOR OD

Even though the goals of individuals and groups can differ and change, it is obvious that people can agree on certain directions well enough to accomplish worthwhile work. Common goals, however, are easier to establish and maintain when they can be reached in the near future and when they enlist small numbers of people. In contrast to goal-based planners, OD consultants choose goals that above all are attainable in the near future. Next, they accept the goals of individuals and groups as worthy, or at least as real and not to be ignored. Third, consultants' goals concern the *process* by which members of a school pursue their tasks. Finally, OD consultants usually care about the kinds of outcomes that situational and critical evaluators care about. They want participants to find greater satisfactions of achievement, affiliation, and power in their work; to find new possibilities in their relations with colleagues; and to explore new assumptions about human nature. They also want participants to find a new confidence in solving their own problems and to look for new potentialities in themselves and their students.

Evaluating curricula has its own technicalities. So does evaluation of other kinds of work in schools and districts with which OD consultants sometimes deal—public relations, personnel management, requisitions and supplies, voter turnouts, and so on. Those matters are beyond the scope of this book. We concentrate here on evaluating OD. The four metaskills—diagnosis, searching for information and resources, mobilizing synergistic action, and monitoring the first three skills—provide a frame within which to evaluate OD.

EVALUATING THE FOUR METASKILLS

Not all OD projects are large and long. Some have a duration of weeks or days. A team-building consultation, for example, might run for a dozen meetings, even fewer. For small projects, we think the skills discussed in Chapters 3 through 7 will serve well as the consultant's goals. We turn here to ways of evaluating larger OD projects in which it may seem reasonable to evaluate the school's capacity for problem solving. Ir Chapter 1, we set forth the four metaskills as the foundations for problem solving in the school. They are consonant with situational and critical evaluation; they are ways of enhancing capability.

In this section, we will put forward a series of questions as guides to data collection. They will read somewhat like questions to be used in an interview, but we do not necessarily mean them to be used just as they stand. We intend them as starting points from which you might write your own questionnaire or interview questions, or as suggestions for kinds of behavior you might observe, or as ideas for kinds of information you might look for in the school's files. We do not mean, either, that every questionnaire or interview should include questions of all the thirty-five sorts we show below. The kinds of information you will choose to gather will depend on the particular project. Use the questions below as a file of ideas.

Diagnosis

When we ask whether a school shows skill in diagnosis, we ask whether it systematically inspects its own current functioning. We do not mean that you merely ask whether the school seems to be getting along with or without troubles. We mean that you ask whether what the school is actually doing matches the way members talk about what they are doing, and then whether what they are doing is what they want to be doing. We want to know whether the school uses formal and informal diagnosis as often as is necessary to stave off radical, stressful reorganization in response to crisis. (Some actual diagnostic activities in schools are described in Runkel, Schmuck, Arends, and Francisco, 1979, pp. 74–79.) Here are some inquiries you might make about the school's skill in diagnosis:

GUIDES FOR EVALUATING THE SKILL OF DIAGNOSIS

1. Sometimes the descriptions a school staff gives of itself in handbooks for faculty and students or in public utterances do not match what actually goes on in the school. Are there discrepancies of that sort in your school?
2. Does your school have goals with which almost all staff members agree? (If yes:) Are the school's goals written down? (If yes:) Do you have a copy?
3. Have you received any information this year that has helped you judge how the school is moving toward its goals? Did you get the information informally, by chance, or through formal channels?

4. Most teachers test students at the end of a course. But usually less attention is given to assessing students' competencies at the start of a course or at the beginning of school. Does your school have a formal means of judging where students start?

5. Outside sources—federal government, state legislation, state department, municipal regulations, citizens' groups, and so on—make demands on schools. Some of their demands require extra effort from the staff; they become problems to solve. But a school must somehow choose the problems that should get the most attention. In your school, who chooses the problems that will receive the most effort? Is there a formal procedure for doing so?

6. Conflicts arise within schools over how to do things. Does your school leave it to the principal to uncover conflicts and do something about them, or is there a regularized means by which the staff finds conflicts and deals with them?

7. What recent projects have attracted students, staff, or parents? Was evidence on the effects of the project collected as part of the project or as part of the school's regular record keeping?

8. What recent projects failed, and what was the effect of the failure on students, staff, and parents? Was evidence collected as part of the project or as part of the school's regular record keeping?

9. Do you know of overloads or underloads among your colleagues? Are they known to others? Did you learn of them through formal or informal channels?

10. How would you gauge staff morale? What evidence do you have? Did the evidence come to you through formal or informal channels?

11. Most individuals have more skills and capabilities than are called for in their job descriptions. Does you school find out about those other abilities among staff, students, parents, or administrators?

12. Does your school assess its problem-solving effectiveness? Are there regularized ways for newcomers to learn the criteria for a well-solved problem—a plan of action with times and persons specified for reviewing results?

13. Do people in your school help one another handle a threatening situation by seeking additional resources for dealing with the threat, calling on others for analysis and suggestions, offering comfort and support to those who are fearful, or using systematic problem solving to reduce the difficulties?

14. Are there formal procedures in your school for discovering individuals being satisfied or frustrated in achievement, affection, or influence in their work? Are there occasions when

staff can examine the effects of the school's organization on motive satisfaction?

15. Are there formal procedures for keeping the various groups—departments, committees, and so on—informed about what the others are doing?

Searching for Information and Other Resources

By searching for information and other resources, we mean initiating searches within or outside the school whenever the information or other resources at hand seem inadequate for planning an effective solution to a problem. A skillful staff decides when a problem must be resolved, how to get the information to plan a resolution, and who will take the necessary steps. In addition to information, the skillful staff assesses the needs people have for status, affection, services, materials, and money. (Some actual resource-seeking activities in schools are described in Runkel, Schmuck, Arends, and Francisco, 1979, pp. 83–88.) Here are some inquiries you might make about the school's skill in searching for information and other resources:

GUIDES FOR EVALUATING THE SKILL OF SEARCHING FOR
INFORMATION AND OTHER RESOURCES

16. People often need more information than they have at hand to do a good job of solving a problem, but sometimes they go ahead without the information even though they could get it with reasonable effort. Do problem-solving groups here usually take time to get the information they need?

17. To anticipate new demands and possible overloads, do staff members know how to get information about new requirements of law? about changes in population? about community discontent with the school? about plans for desegregation? about staff morale?

18. Are there formal channels through which news can get to everyone about opportunities for skill training, staff development, organizational development, materials, services, or money? How many staff members make use of such resources?

19. Are some channels so overloaded that much information is ignored?

20. Do the ideas of mavericks, nonconformists, and radicals get a serious hearing?

21. Do problem-solving groups draw out the resources that their individual members can bring to the task, such as information influence in the district, friendly support, skill at parts of the

task, materials or access to materials, access to money, and so on?

22. Are there staff members with special skill in group processes? Does their skill get used in meetings? (See Chapter 4 for questionnaire items on using resources in meetings.)

23. Are consultants used appropriately?

Mobilizing Synergistic Action

Some schools are very good at planning and not good at all at taking action. By the skill of mobilizing synergistic action, we mean knowing when plans are adequate and then taking action even though the action may be risky and irreversible. An important aspect is the *group* skill of urging and supporting the individuals who must take the first steps. (Some actual examples of mobilizing synergistic action in schools are described in Runkel, Schmuck, Arends, and Francisco, 1979, pp. 90–94.) Here are some inquiries you might make about the school's skill in mobilizing synergistic action:

GUIDES FOR EVALUATING THE SKILL OF MOBILIZING
SYNERGISTIC ACTION

24. Do staff members with energy and optimism get isolated, or do they succeed in finding others with whom to work on solutions to problems?

25. Do staff members recognize overloads and collaborate in reducing them?

26. Do staff members collaborate to anticipate and cope with demands that come upon the school from outside? Or are those matters left to the principal or counselor?

27. When working together, do people express heightened satisfactions of achievement, affection, and power?

28. An effective group decides during problem solving either (1) that a feasible plan is unlikely to be achieved and therefore that it will postpone further work until a more auspicious time, or (2) that a feasible plan has been achieved and therefore that it will take action now. Do groups in your school show the ability to agree on when it is time to make the one decision or the other?

29. To help in taking action, do problem-solving groups draw out resources from their members and draw in relevant resources from outside?

30. When a group does take action, do members check on whether schedules and subgoals are met? Do they then feed back that

information to the group? Does the group alter plans and schedules appropriately?

31. Are people encouraged to use intuition and insight in problem solving as well as reason and logic?

32. When the staff suffers from excessive planning and a lack of action, does it call in a consultant to help?

Monitoring the First Three Metaskills

Monitoring the first three metaskills is the crowning skill a school needs to sustain a capacity for solving problems. This is the skill of being able to observe one's own group and ask, "Are we as skillful as we need to be in diagnosing, getting appropriate information and resources, and mobilizing our action synergistically? Are we able to move ourselves in the directions we want to go?" In addition to asking whether it is achieving its goals, the skillful staff also asks whether its goals are worth achieving.

When monitoring the first three metaskills, one asks whether the kinds of questions we listed above are indeed being asked.

GUIDES FOR EVALUATING THE MONITORING OF
THE FIRST THREE METASKILLS

33. Are there formal occasions when staff members ask one another the kinds of questions we listed above under "Diagnosis"?

34. Are there formal occasions when staff members ask one another the kinds of questions we listed above under "Searching for Information and Other Resources"?

35. Are there formal occasions when staff members ask one another the kinds of questions we listed above under "Mobilizing Synergistic Action"?

Formats

You can rewrite any of the thirty-five questions above to make them suitable for questionnaires, interviews, guides to culling the school's files, or counting instances of behavior you observe in meetings. If you ask a question in a way that allows the respondent to answer freely in his or her own words, you will get a lot of richness. Still, it is sometimes hard to judge whether the answer points one way or another. For example, it might be unclear whether the answer is in favor of a proposed course of action, against it, indifferent to it, or expresses no opinion.

You might rewrite Question 18, for example, like this: "What news have you heard lately about staff development?" That question could draw answers ranging from "Nothing" to a five-minute lecture on what has happened, what has not, and what ought to. To count the kinds of answers you get, you would have to "code" them. That is, you would have to find some categories that would separate the answers clearly into kinds and that would encompass all the answers. Classifying answers in this way is a lot of work, but it is sometimes worth the effort when you want to get the full flavor of the respondents' opinion.

Making counts is easier when you offer the respondents some ready-made answer choices. On a questionnaire, you might follow a question with these choices:

(   ) Almost all the time
(   ) Frequently
(   ) Sometimes
(   ) Rarely
(   ) Never or almost never

There are many more examples in the "Gathering Data" sections of other chapters. See also the remarks about keeping items short and simple under "K.I.S.S. and Pilot" in Chapter 9. In the example above, you could assign five points to the top answer, four to the next, and so on. Then you could quickly and easily see the range of answers in a group and calculate the average. If you have several questions that get at the same idea, you can add scores across questions. It is often useful, too, to include a choice for "I don't know" or "No opinion."

Numbers are often handy if you want to compare scores before OD with scores afterward, or scores in one school with scores in another. But if you want to know in the end *how good* an outcome is, you will be faced with using judgment whether you compile the information impressionistically or by numbers. How high is a "good" score? The answer will be up to you. You will have to make a judgment about the items you believe should be answered "yes" or "frequently" in your school and the minimum percentage of those answers you can accept without worry.

STUDY DESIGNS

Data on outcomes are usually more persuasive if you have compared outcomes in a school or group that had OD with outcomes in one or more that had not. For example, you might like to say, on the basis of your data, that OD improved the skill of participants in helping others to communicate clearly. You would like your data to rule out the possibility that the participants were already skillful at helping others to communicate clearly, and the OD work might have added nothing. You might like to rule out the possibility, too, that the participants would have done as well if they had merely spent the same amount of time talking together without any help from OD.

We will not, however, take space here to lay out the logic of using comparison ("control") groups. That topic is well treated in many books on research design—for example, Campbell and Stanley (1963), Ary, Jacobs, and Razavieh (1979, p. 247 ff.), Jung (1982, Ch. 3), Kidder (1981, Ch. 2 and 3), Nachimas and Nachimas (1981, Ch. 4 and 5), Runkel and McGrath (1972, Ch. 3), Simon (1978, Ch. 11 and 12), and Tuckman (1978, Ch. 6). But we will here consider some matters usually given short shrift by books on research or evaluation but especially pertinent to evaluating OD in schools.

Sequences

The sequence of causation from the beginning to the end of an OD project of large scope is too complicated for simple before-and-after assessments. Consultants should be able to present data justifying their claim that a given outcome took shape through a series of planned and deliberate steps, each of which was instrumental in making more advanced steps possible. To that end they should assess the condition and functioning of the client subsystem after every important step, noting the dates on which important interventions occurred; the dates on which pre-and postintervention assessments were made; the designations of the subsystems from which data were taken; and the abilities, qualities, or conditions assessed.

Careful documentation will reveal the causal chain leading from one step to the next. If a documentation can show that the steps exhibited immediate results that approximated, at each step and more or less in order, the interim outcomes that were planned, it is much easier for the consultant to claim that the OD or some part of it produced the final outcome, and that the outcome was not produced by some condition (such as the availability of extra money) that existed simultaneously with the OD. It will usually not be easy to argue that the outcome of any one particular step necessarily produced the right conditions for the next step to have its effect in turn. But if the interim outcomes can be shown to move fairly steadily toward the eventual outcome, it would be excessive for anyone to claim that the whole catenation fell together by chance or was produced by some background factor. The inference from such a chain is always stronger than an inference from any one of its links.

Consider, for example, a hypothetical consultation designed around the Imaging procedure (Chapter 7) to enable two opposing groups to agree on the mutual behaviors or subproblems that are obstructing the solutions of larger problems. Suppose that the consultant had been tracking and documenting the consultation over weeks and could point to the actual steps at which problems had been conceived in a new way, at which joint steps had been taken by groups that had never done so before, at which the two groups had joined in discussion and work that many had believed impossible at the start, at which they had appealed to information and skills presented during the consultation, and at which they had coordinated their actions by referring to their planning and comparing their actions with that planning. Because of the concatenation of these events and the clients' use of the "products" of the events for coordinating later events, a reasonable reader of your report would have to admit that the chain of events had had a strong causal effect on the outcome.

Time and Change

Assessing organizational problem solving does not necessarily require sophisticated techniques, but it often does require that one or several people linger long enough to count and chart typical rates of change. It takes considerable time to lift a school from its original level of capability to a level of high capability with regard to the four metaskills, and a school district can make an excellent investment in its future by setting aside resources for counting instances that evidence continued gradual growth in the metaskills. Unfortunately, however, someone must pay salaries, and it is difficult to persuade government agencies and the comptrollers, chairpersons, and boards of local school districts to provide money over a three-to ten-year period that would enable the effects of OD to be charted in respect to the metaskills.

In addition, schools show considerable variation in their year-to-year progress toward organizational problem solving. Studying the kinds of innovations reported by elementary school teachers in two school districts near Seattle over four years and four administrations of questionnaires, Runkel, Wyant, Bell, and Runkel (1980, Chapter 8) divided the innovations into five classes—structural, collaborative, curricular, cloistered, and none. Omitting answers of "none" and examining the class of innovation reported by the greatest percentage of teachers that gave data over at least two years in each of twenty-two elementary schools, those authors found that six schools reported the same type of innovation over three consecutive years, five schools reported the same type of innovation over two consecutive years, and eleven schools changed every year. Those statistics indicate that outcome evaluators should watch at least three elementary schools to find one sticking with one type of problem for as long as three years. Even then, we must recognize the fact that sticking with one type of problem does not necessarily mean solving it well.

Murray (1973) has presented data showing why we should not expect to make a reliable assessment of organizational change after only a year of effort.* Two elementary schools had made use of OD consultation to help them move from self-contained classroom structure to multiunit structure. Assessing several features of their organizational functioning before the consultation began (spring of 1970), after a year of continuing consultation (1971), and after a second year of discontinued consultation (1972), Murray's data revealed different sequences of effects in the two schools. Discussing these results, Schmuck, Murray, Smith, Schwartz, and M. Runkel (1975) write:

> Spartan and Palmer differed significantly in how the organizational change processes proceeded over a two-year period. The Palmer staff members began quickly to implement team teaching and other sorts of collaborative educational arrangements during the first year of the project. Later they ran into difficulties in maintaining these change attempts, and the following year saw the innovation beginning to fade. In contrast, the Spartan staff members first spent effort in developing communication skills, group norms, and problem-solving procedures, moving much more gradually than Palmer into the multiunit structure. After one year of consultation in OD, the Spartan staff was ready to benefit from technical consultation and multiunit structure. The Spartan staff then moved quickly in that direction and stayed there during the second year (p. 358).

> Successful establishment of a multiunit structure requires two school years. Consultation in organization development should be designed to last at least for the first year, with instructional innovations emphasized the second year . . . Gradual, incremental changes within the school may support more sustainable changes in structure than rapid alterations in staff arrangements (p. 191).

In brief, when assessing progress toward organizational problem solving, consultants or evaluators must always strive to ascertain a trend and refuse to be satisfied with an evaluation that takes data only once before OD and once afterward. Had Murray assessed the functioning of Spartan and Palmer schools only before and after, in 1970 and 1971, he

---

*Murray's results are abridged in Chapter 6 of Schmuck, Murray, Smith, Schwartz, and Runkel (1975).

would mistakenly have concluded that Spartan had improved slightly but that Palmer had leapt far ahead, whereas the 1972 assessment showed that Palmer had bitten off more than it could chew while Spartan had increased and made firm its gains. Ascertaining a trend in OD requires at least three years, and often more.

Directly Observable Evidence

Although conducting interviews and questionnaires at the end of a project will bring interesting information, the most direct route is to observe whether clients are actually doing what you hoped they would be doing: discussing problems in terms of situation, target, and plan; using the systematic problem-solving methods in choosing and trying out solutions; probing resources and playfully exercising abilities that are not usually demanded by their jobs; trying out courses of action instead of explaining away problems defensively; regularly assessing the progress of their action plans and testing whether they are going where they wished to go; and periodically reassessing their goals.

In addition to observing whether these things are being done, consultants must judge whether they are being done more often, more judiciously, and more successfully that they were being done before or in greater degree than they are done by those who have not received consultation. You will want to judge, too, whether the changes or the differences from other schools were worth the cost of mounting the project. Although your judgment will sometimes differ from that of your clients or of other audiences, the necessity for judging cannot be removed.

Judging whether clients are better off than they were or better off than others who have not availed themselves of OD consultation should be guided whenever possible by comparing rates or frequency of certain actions at the end of a project with those exhibited at the beginning of the project. Such comparisons are seldom numerical and are often intuitive, based on what "everybody knows" to be the typical rate in most schools or districts. Although some evaluators belittle nontallyable evidence, it often gets more directly to the point than data extracted from questionnaires, is frequently more convincing to some audiences than more scientific data would be, and can be used to validate data that are countable. The examples of directly observable evidence that follow make explicit or implicit comparisons with base rates.

Searching for Resources. Our first example of the use of resources seldom called forth in schools is from Schmuck and Runkel (1970):

As the Principal's Advisory Committee became more of a problem-solving group, they felt that meetings should last long enough to permit in-depth examination of problems. They got this block of time by meeting at 6:30 A.M. once a month at a local restaurant. These meetings ran for two and one-half hours. This schedule continued throughout 1968–1969. Members very rarely missed these meetings; when an area chairman could not attend, he asked a member of his subject area to take his place and he paid for the breakfast of his substitute. On several occasions, general faculty members were invited to attend these meetings; typically, two or three would appear and participate (p. 99).

Our next example is from Runkel, Wyant, Bell, and Runkel (1980). This extract describes an unusual use a superintendent made of the skills of a cadre of organizational specialists.

As the budget crisis broke over the district, the superintendent and his staff (the cabinet) agreed that communication at their meetings was poor. Participants were unsure of their roles, and norms did not permit healthy debate and disagreement. Few decisions were made publicly, and the cabinet was the object of confusion and mistrust throughout the district. The superintendent decided to open the meetings to broader participation, and several job groups were invited to send representatives to them: the superintendent instructed principals that any teachers who wished to attend a meeting should be released to do so. The Cadre was asked to send two observers to each meeting. The observers gave the cabinet feedback over the course of several meetings, and as a result, some important changes in group processes were made. The superintendent periodically stepped out of the role of presenter and convener to participate more freely in the discussion, while other cabinet members assumed leadership roles when appropriate. Agreements to help the meetings run more smoothly were made consensually. Time was allowed at the end of each meeting to debrief group processes and hear the specialists report their observations. As a result, there was much less criticism of the meetings by cabinet members, and the mistrust of the cabinet noticeably lessened throughout the district (p. 27).

Mobilizing Synergistic Action. The following example comes from Schmuck and Runkel (1970).

An incident in the latter part of February illustrated Highland Park's problem-solving abilities. The central office asked Highland Park if it could provide room for approximately 100 educators who would be participating in a conference sponsored by the Northwest Regional Educational Laboratory. Other schools in the district, citing insufficient space, turned down the central office.

The principal called together the area chariman for physical education, the cafeteria manager, the assistant principal for curriculum, the vice principal, and the chief custodian. A solution was found within an hour. A class in physical education, usually taught separately for boys and girls, could be taught with both groups together in the gymnasium except for the lunch periods, when the gymnasium had to be used as a dining hall. During these periods, however, the band room was available. The cafeteria manager decided she could provide lunch for the visitors with the addition of one temporary person to her staff. The plan was described to the central office, who sent a representative to meet with the Highland Park group and work out a detailed schedule for the occasion.

During the actual conduct of the visiting conference, the principal was out of town. The assistant principal for curriculum acted as host. Though there was some inconvenience to the music department, members of the conference expressed gratification with the hospitality they received. The central office sent the Highland Park staff a letter of appreciation, stating that it would not have been able to host the conference without the problem-solving ability of the Highland Park staff (pp. 99–100).

That example shows how a natural occurrence can fit nicely into the logic of the base rate. Other schools with no less space per student than Highland Park had been asked to host the conference, and all had the same eager support from the central office, had the same financial compensation (none), occurred at the same time of year, and so on. The other schools provided the base rate against which Highland Park stood out as unusual. Of course, one problem well solved does not bespeak organizational problem solving; but when a school solves several problems with unusual resourcefulness, one should take special notice.

Monitoring the First Three Metaskills. In the summer of 1969, the Center for Educational Policy and Management (then CASEA) established in a school district in the state of Washington a cadre of organizational specialists who became highly skillful at examining their goals, assessing their position in relation to their goals, planning and taking corrective action. Those skills became vital when the district suffered a severe financial setback the year after the cadre was formed. Quoting from the report by Runkel, Wyant, and Bell (1975), we briefly describe a few meetings from a longer series in which the cadre assessed its movement toward its goals. The point is not to show what assessments were made but to show the kinds of activities and occasions through which the cadre undertook to make assessments.

> 12–13 December 1969. Meeting of cadre for renewing group solidarity and refurbishing coordination. The crisis in the district (they said) pervades our conference. Furthermore, physical distance makes it difficult for us to communicate rapidly. When composing subteams

for interventions we must consider the personal acceptability of members. Will staff resent being asked to give extra time when their hours are already being overclaimed by budgetary stresses? Should we revise priorities?

27 May 1971. Meeting of entire cadre "to discuss status of the group at this time and where it is going." Ideas for future activities were generated. Consensus seemed to be that "the group feels it has a tremendous service potential, but it needs a boost from funding support, etc." No facilitator from outside was employed.

5 February 1972. Meeting of entire cadre for a self-renewal session to formulate goals, clarify expectations, choose maintenance tasks and projects, and plan budget. Maury Pettit of Central Washington State College was facilitator.

8–9 September 1972. Meeting of entire cadre for a self-renewal session on interpersonal blocks and goals for the future. Runkel and Murray . . . were facilitators. They reported: "In our opinion, the workshop was exciting and stimulating. They were very receptive to giving one another feedback and ready to proceed with work toward new goals. They showed great maturity and adaptability as an organization."

30 October 1972. Meeting of entire cadre to clarify the balance between goals and resources. Maury Pettit was facilitator.

7–8 September 1973. Meeting of the entire cadre for "team building." Twenty cadre members attended. John Goff and Bob McGlone were facilitators. Included exercises, lecture, and planning.

Testimonials

OD consultants are often tempted to accept complimentary remarks from their clients as a fair evaluation of their work. They are right in accepting compliments as part of the picture, but they are wrong if they leap to the conclusion that clients who did not speak felt the same as those who did. In one situation, those who are angry may be the more vocal; in another, the happier people may speak up. Testimonials can bring diagnostic information only if you give every sort of reaction an equal chance of reaching you. If you collect only the opinions of clients who initiate approaches to you, you are almost certainly allowing bias in one direction or another to affect the opinons you get.

The solution is to go after the data yourself, making sure to ask for opinions from every client or from a representative sample of them. At the end of a training day, for example, consultants can ask participants to form buzz groups and tell one another how things are better or worse than they were yesterday or before the training. Recording all the remarks will usually bring information of reasonable validity, but the important point is how the remarks are selected. If the consultant or evaluator selects them in a way that allows each remark an equal chance to be heard, the evaluation will be a fair one.

VALIDITY

How do you know, when you have collected information about your clients, whether your judgments about their condition, abilities, resourcefulness, and actions correspond to fact? How can you know, when you act on your newly formed judgments, whether the clients will behave as your judgments lead you to expect? The only way you can know for sure is to design an action based on your new judgments, carry out the action, and note the clients' reactions. That seems the merest common sense; yet it is easy to forget that the judgments we make from data are only inferences subject to the errors of human logic, desire, impatience, and fatigue that are common to us all. It is important always to treat inferences from data as hypotheses and to check every hypothesis against relevant data for the purpose of confirming, revising, or testing your conclusions further.

If, for example, you deduce from questionnaires that teachers in a school show a low level of readiness for collaboration, the next day at the school you could say to the first teacher you see, "I've sometimes worked on projects where the teachers took a year or two to build teaching teams and made them work pretty well. How would you react if one of your colleagues suggested an idea like that to you?" To the next teacher you might say, "Not long ago I visited a place where a half-dozen of the teachers figured out a way of scheduling classes so that they could include a two-week minicourse on about a week's notice and do it almost any time of the year. Do you know whether anyone here has tried anything like that or wanted to? If some teacher told you tomorrow that three or four teachers were going to try to figure out how to do something like that, would you feel like joining in?" You might ask the next teacher: "Has anything been getting under way here to bring parents more into the life of the school? Have any teachers gotten together as a group to work out a place for parents? How would you react if another teacher asked you whether you wanted to join a group working on an idea like that?"

Questionnaire results suggesting a low readiness for collaboration in the school would lead you to expect little enthusiasm in response to such questions. Your conclusion would be validated if you received answers like, "People never stick together on anything around here," or "I'd tell them that if they want to do it, they should go ahead on their own," or "That's not the way to get anything done. If the principal can do it, he should do it. If the principal can't do it, the teachers certainly can't." In this hypothetical example, you predicted a pessimistic answer and got it. Your conclusion from the questionnaires was given a further independent test and your confidence in your conclusion would have increased. If, on the other hand, you had got answers more optimistic than you had expected, you would have to revise your conclusion and give the new conclusion still another test.

Anticipating the kind of reaction you are going to get to a certain kind of action, taking that action, and watching to see whether you get the anticipated response is called *hypothesis testing*. When you get the second round of data by a different method, you are using the *multi-method strategy*.

Multiple Methods

When information gathered from one source or by one method agrees with information from another source or method, you are almost always justified in feeling more confidence in the validity of the information. Any method of data collecting is likely to have weaknesses, however, and information should never be discarded, no matter how unreliable its source, until you have clear evidence that it is faulty. Weak information does not weaken strong information. If it agrees with it, it may strengthen the strong information a bit; if it disagrees, it offers only a small challenge. Unless it has a noticeably spoiled odor, information of every sort should be added to your collection.

At the early stages of entry, for example, no alternative method of getting information is likely to have greater validity than that which the consultant carefully infers from face-to-face conversations. Multiple-choice questionnaires may bring greater objectivity to the scorer than do records of conversations; but objectivity is no guarantee of validity, and questionnaires have shortcomings as well. Without adequate rapport between interveners and clients, questionnaires offer an easy occasion for carelessness and dissembling. Many teachers and administrators, especially those working near universities, have been badgered with questionnaires until they have become cynical about them. Many teachers, facing still another questionnaire, will be reminded of other occasions that were followed by no return of information, no action taken on the basis of information they gave, no demand that they stand responsible for their answers, and no evidence that their answers were kept confidential, whatever the investigator's promises.

In these circumstances it is not surprising if disenchanted respondents write answers that are quick, noncommittal, or safe, or relieve their boredom by composing responses that they regard as humorous. Questions about interpersonal matters, especially, are likely to be resented and skipped. Even those who have had little previous contact with researchers, evaluators, or consultants may be suspicious about the use to be made of the data, so that they, too, may give answers that will be safe even if they reach the superintendent. During the early days of acquaintance between client and consultant or evaluator, most of these weaknesses apply to interviews and direct observation as well.

This is not to say that any one method is generally better than another. Even in the early stages of a project, one can strengthen information by getting the same sort of information from two or more sources or methods. In discussing problems informally with teachers in a high school, for example, we noted that teachers in one department never hinted at any conflict with teachers in another department, even though we knew that both departments depended on the same school budget and must sometimes have been in competition for scarce resources. But we also knew that the schedule of classes and other duties prevented the department heads from having time for conferences and that the principal wrote each year's budget single-handedly.

We concluded that the department heads communicated very little, even outside school hours; that they knew very little about how the principal balanced demands on the budget; and that if they displayed very little overt conflict, it was because the schedule allowed them no occasion on which a first exchange of information could occur. Another reason was that they had too little information about budgeting to express a sharp conflict, even if they had the occasion. To check our hypothesis, we arranged a meeting of five department heads, some pairs of whom could have had potentialities for conflict. The earlier conversations with teachers constituted one method and the meeting with department heads a second; the second method validated the first.

At the first meeting we said merely, "We asked the principal to make time in your schedules for this meeting specifically so that you could have time to discuss the question of whether there *is* anything that might be mutually profitable for you to discuss." After several questions about our own motivation (such as, "Are you getting a dissertation out of this?"), the department heads began to ask one another whether they had, in fact, any mutual concerns worth discussing. Before long, they decided that they wanted a regular time to meet together and wanted to know more about the school's budget. This lent further validity to our interpretation and also opened a point of entry for further work.

Another example of checking through different sources is the series of steps used by Wyant (1974) to ascertain whether schools had what he called "collaborative structure," by which he meant (1) a strong leadership team or an "Improvement-of-Instruction committee," (2) a sharply differentiated position for leaders of teaching units, and (3) stable, well-defined teaching teams to which all instructional personnel were assigned. To determine whether a school met or failed to meet these criteria, Wyant first asked central office personnel, such as the director of elementary education, to name the schools in the district that satisfied these criteria, and then asked the principals of the schools named whether their schools met the criteria. If the principal said yes, Wyant went to the leaders of the teaching units (if they existed) and asked once again about the criteria. Only those schools that passed the inquiry at all three steps were designated as having collaborative structure.

The Effects of Rapport Between Consultants and Clients

The relationship between consultants and clients constitutes a difference between OD projects and many purely research or innovative projects. In many research projects, from pretests through posttests, the attitude of school people toward the data collector is one of distant acquaintanceship and irritable tolerance. In even a very brief OD project, however, the client-consultant relationship becomes increasingly intimate, trusting, and committed as time passes, especially when clients feel that they are receiving a clear benefit. Consultants who are also the collectors of evaluative data will get different answers to the same questions at different times, not only because external factors may have changed in the interim, but also because clients who have grown more trusting will confide at a later date what they had been unwilling to confide earlier. Indeed, clients will often transfer this growing intimacy and trust to outside evaluators. When consultants first collect data on job satisfaction, and before they have carried out any consultation, respondents will season their answers with a large measure of protectiveness: "Sure, I like it here okay; I have no complaints." Given multiple choices, they will usually check a favorable item. They do that because, at first acquaintance, school people do not know whether their answers will be passed on to their superiors; parents (especially those in poverty) do not know whether their answers will be passed on to school authorities, social service agencies, or the police, and students have no way of knowing whether their answers will be passed on to all the above. Clients tend initially to withhold information about unhappy feelings, but as trust grows they begin to open up about their unhappiness with their school, their jobs, their working conditions, and the people with whom they work. Therefore, clients will frequently answer questions about satisfaction more unfavorably several months after consultation begins than before it begins, even though they may be feeling more hopeful than they felt before.

Another feature of OD work may exacerbate this effect. When social science researchers ask their "subjects" for information, for example, they have usually been authorized to do so because their entry into the organization has been legitimized by someone of authority within the organization: "Dr. Scaramouche is here from the university to conduct a very important study, and we can be a key source of information. I want you to give him your full cooperation." No matter how gently researchers may talk, this mode of entry inevitably gives them a measure of power or authority over the subjects—a relationship almost impossible to avoid as long as the researcher makes unilateral decisions about what to investigate, who will be studied, what the instructions will be, what will be done with the data, and so on.

In contrast, the consultant-client relationship gradually comes to approximate a partnership. At the beginning of an OD project, many if not most clients expect to be treated as they have been by researchers; at the end, they find themselves being treated as peers and allies, so it is not surprising that their later answers to questioning differ from their earlier ones. The point is that if, in striving for objectivity and uniformity in their relationships with subjects, researchers have reaped one kind of data contamination, OD consultants reap another kind as they grow into partnerships with their clients. For researchers and consultants alike, the important thing is to be alert for distortions of data.

ASSESSING SATISFACTION

Most of us believe that a strong, resilient organization that meets internal and external challenges with competence and vigor will be composed of people who come to work in the morning feeling confident and eager, who go home feeling good about their day, and who are in general well satisfied with their lives as part of the organization. Indeed, because work preoccupies so much of our lives, many people believe that being happy on the job is a worthwhile end in itself. For those reasons, many social scientists and industrial psychologists regard the satisfaction of organization members as a touchstone for organizational health and adaptability. For their part, OD consultants design interventions for change projects to include activities that bring immediate satisfactions so that participants will be encouraged to continue working toward a more satisfying organization.

Though the idea of assessing satisfaction has an immediate appeal, satisfaction is surprisingly difficult to measure in a way that yields useful information. One common method of assessing satisfaction is to ask respondents about their satisfaction with various features of school life. But any given feature of life at school has more importance to some people than to others. For example, people with inheritances or with working spouses may be less concerned about salary or job security than others. People who have no satisfying companionship elsewhere may be especially sensitive to friendliness at school. Some people may be unhappy because they do not have enough to say about the management of the school, and others because they are too often asked for their opinion about matters of management. And so on. Thus, the tally for satisfactions from one person might mean something quite different from that of another.

Then, too, satisfaction is always relative. In a school attended mostly by students of low academic aptitude, a teacher might feel gratified to have one class of "bright" students. But in a school attended mostly by students of high academic aptitude, the teacher with only one class of "bright" students might feel deprived. So one teacher's reason for satisfaction can be another's reason for dissatisfaction.

We propose here some ways of reducing the sources of ambiguity in data about satisfaction. We start with ways of phrasing questions.

Information Yielded by Various Types of Questions

Both in everyday conversation and in scientific studies, it is common to assess satisfaction by asking a direct question, such as

How satisfied would you say you are with your present job?
_____ Very satisfied
_____ Somewhat satisfied
_____ Neither satisfied nor dissatisfied
_____ Somewhat dissatisfied
_____ Very dissatisfied

The answer will usually give you a fairly good impression of how each individual feels about the overall satisfaction the job brings compared with what the respondent imagines it *could* bring. While useful surveys have been conducted using this kind of item, it works best when all or most of the dissatisfied respondents are dissatisfied for the same reasons and when all or most have roughly the same picture of the greatest degree of satisfaction that a job could bring. For it is in exactly those two ways that the item may yield misleading information.

"How satisfied" questions cannot tell you what to offer to make the dissatisfied respondent more satisfied. For example, should it be a shorter workday, or four ten-hour days a week? Does the respondent want more or less responsibility? and so on. "How satisfied" questions also cannot tell you what the respondent's aspirations are. If I find my job boring but think that it could never be otherwise, if I think that any job I might get would be equally boring, and if I am resigned to holding this kind of job for the rest of my life, then "very satisfied" might mean "about all I can expect." If, in contrast, my job is boring but I am taking a correspondence course with the hope of making it big in computers, I am going to answer something less favorable than "very satisfied."

Not surprisingly, people who express satisfaction with routine jobs in answering this question are usually those who have stayed in their jobs longer. Writing about jobs in industry, Argyris (1973, p. 162) says, "The greatest dissatisfaction on a routine job occurs during the first years. After three to five years, the individual becomes adapted and satisfied. . . . " That datum matches the fact that the greatest number of people who leave teaching do so after only a year or two of experience. In brief, "Very satisfied" may only tell us that the respondent has become resigned to the low satisfaction at work, not that he or she gets up in the morning eager to go to work.

We can use a different kind of question to find out more about the direction of change that would make a respondent more satisfied. Consider two items such as the following to ascertain the direction of the gap between the respondent's present condition and ideal condition:

How much opportunity to use your own judgment would your ideal job offer?

_____ A great deal of opportunity
_____ Some opportunity
_____ A little opportunity
_____ No opportunity

How much opportunity to use your own judgment does your present job offer?

_____ A great deal of opportunity
_____ Some opportunity
_____ A little opportunity
_____ No opportunity

If the answer is that the ideal job would offer "some opportunity" to exercise personal judgment and that the present job offers "no opportunity," we know what direction of change would bring greater satisfaction. That is useful information.

The defect in those paired questions is that they do not tell us about intensity. Respondents to those items can tell us whether there is a gap and its direction, but they cannot tell us whether they feel the gap to be trifling or terrible. The first kind of question (How satisfied . . . ?) tells us the degree of feeling but not what to do about it. The second kind (the paired items above) tells us the kind of change that would make the respondent more satisfied but not how much the respondent cares— that is, not whether the change is *worth* making.

Note that though the first kind of question does not require the respondent to specify a feature of the job, the second kind does. In our example, we specified the "opportunity to use your own judgment." If we had written the item about the ideal job without specifying some characteristic of the job, we would have had a silly question: "How satisfactory would your ideal job be?—very satisfactory?"

It is possible, of course, to ask and reap benefits from both kinds of questions. To do so, of course, we must specify some features of the job in the question. To begin constructing the combined kind of question, we write the idea of a gap and its direction into the answer choices offered. For now, we'll let X stand for the feature of the job we are asking about. Those things done, our item looks like this:

How much X do you get at work?

_____   I get about the amount I prefer.
_____   I'd like to get more.
_____   I'd like to get less.

That item tells us the direction in which the respondent would like X to be changed, if at all, to become more satisfied. Now, to get an indication of intensity, we add choices about that:

How much X do you get in your work?

_____   I get about the amount I prefer.
_____   I'd like to get more:
   _____   Only a little more
   _____   Some more
   _____   A lot more
_____   I'd like to get less:
   _____   Only a little less
   _____   Some less
   _____   A lot less

Now the item tells us both in what direction greater satisfaction lies and the amount of change the respondent wants. Other wordings of the answer's choices about intensity could also be used—for example: "But it is not very important to me," "And it is important to me," and "And it is very important to me."

If we must include in our questions some features of life at work, what features should they be? We turn to this matter next.

The Satisfaction of Needs

The features of school life about which one could ask are innumerable. But the interviewer or the questionnaire writer must not burden the respondent with long lists. We must find some way of asking respondents about features of their working lives (1) that they care about and (2) that suggest something we can do about the dissatisfactions we discover. Instead of listening to all the things people mention when they are talking about their gratifications or disgruntlements at school, we think we can do better by turning to theory.

In Chapter 1, we mentioned the three social motives that we believe bring everyone satisfaction—achievement, affection, and power. We will use those in our examples below. We think the satisfaction or frustration of those social motives underlies most of the reactions people have to particular conditions and events at school, whether the reactions are happy or unhappy.

To social motives, we will add two new sources of deprivation that exist in some schools—safety and salaries. Worries about physical safety can cause people to restrict the frequency of their interaction with others or to restrict their purpose in interacting simply to finding safety. Both kinds of restriction reduce people's opportunities for finding achievement, affection, and power in concert with others. Also, worries about money, of course, overwhelm other needs. In addition, money is often a symbol of status or achievement. We may "need" more money not because we are hungry, but because it signals our professional worth.

Some theorists include activity—the need to be up and doing—in their lists of basic needs. Just for good measure, we'll include that too.

Finally, because teachers spend almost all day in interaction with students, we will include relations between teachers and students. To a great extent, teachers find their satisfactions of achievement, affection, and power in the classroom—and students do, too.

In the lists below, we offer some illustrative items. They are phrased as if written for a questionnaire, but you can rephrase them for interviewing or use them as guides for collecting data by other methods. Furthermore, you can write similar items of your own.

We begin with safety, a fundamental concern.

Safety. Here we refer to sheer physical safety. This is a worry in some schools. If it is not so in the school you are evaluating, you will be able to find out quickly in a few informal conversations, and you can omit questions on the topic from your evaluation. Below are two examples of questions eliciting data on safety issues. In these items, we omit the choice of "I'd like less safety," because we assume that no one would pick that answer.

Do you worry about your physical safety in this school?

_____ No, I don't worry about it.
_____ Yes, I do worry:
    _____ But only a little.
    _____ I worry somewhat.
    _____ I worry a great deal.

Do you think faculty feel safe in this school?

_____ Yes, I think they do.
_____ No:
    _____ I think almost everyone feels *un*safe.
    _____ I think many feel unsafe.
    _____ I think a few feel unsafe.

The first item is a "harder" item, in the sense that it asks respondents to talk directly about themselves. Some respondents will be reluctant to admit that they are worried about their safety, even on an anonymous questionnaire. To the extent that is true, the item measures a lower limit of worry. The second item enables respondents to tell you their feelings about safety in the school without talking about themselves personally.

Salary. With regard to salary, it is not very useful to get actual dollar figures, for the reasons we gave earlier. We want an indication of the respondent's satisfaction with his or her financial position, whatever the actual dollar income and whatever the reasons. Here are two examples of items that might be used:

Does your salary here, along with other sources of income you may have, enable you to leave money worries at home?

_____ Yes, it's okay.
_____ No, I wish my salary were larger:
    _____ I feel pinched once in a while.

_____ I worry frequently.
_____ I worry every day, even at work.

Would you say your salary is a good match to your ability, your professional standing, your service to the community, and the like?

_____ Yes, it matches pretty well.
_____ No, my salary does not give me enough recognition:
      _____ My salary should show a little more recognition of me.
      _____ It should show substantially more recognition of me.
      _____ It should show a great deal more.
_____ No, my salary shows more recognition of me than I really expect:
      _____ My salary recognizes my ability and standing a little more than I feel comfortable with.
      _____ It recognizes me substantially more.
      _____ It recognizes me a great deal more.

The first item focuses on the adequacy of income to sheer subsistence and the distraction that worries about it might make. We omitted the answer choice of "No, I wish my salary were smaller," because we didn't think anyone would mark that answer. The second item focuses on salary as a symbol of recognition—status in the eyes of others. Maybe no one would mark the last choice there, either, but we put it in to catch the few who might.

Power. In general *power* means having control over one's important choices and reasonable control over one's own fate. On the job, it means being able to do the things one cares about without having to ask permission or having a judgment contradicted or overturned by someone else. In particular, it means having reasonable control over one's own actions within the agreed limits of the job.

How much independence (control over your own work) do you have in the way you go about your own teaching?

_____ I have about the amount that I prefer.
_____ I'd like more independence:
      _____ A little more
      _____ Somewhat more
      _____ A lot more
_____ I'd rather have less independence:
      _____ A little less
      _____ Somewhat less
      _____ A lot less

How do you feel about who makes the decisions about what you should do?

_____ I like the degree to which I myself make decisions about my work.
_____ Other people make too many decisions for me; I'd like to be making more on my own:
    _____ A little more on my own
    _____ Somewhat more
    _____ A lot more
_____ I am expected to make too many decisions; I'd like to leave more of them to others:
    _____ To leave a little more to others
    _____ Somewhat more to others
    _____ A lot more to others

Achievement. The next two examples can be useful in assessing the satisfaction of the need for achievement.

How much of your own ability, skill, or creativity can you put to use in your teaching (job)?

_____ I can put my abilities, skill, and creativity to use to about the degree that I want.
_____ I wish I could put more of my abilities to use than my job now allows:
    _____ A little more
    _____ Somewhat more
    _____ A lot more
_____ I wish my job did not demand as much of my abilities as it does:
    _____ I wish it demanded a little less
    _____ Somewhat less
    _____ A lot less

How much opportunity do you have in your work to feel proud of what you have done?

_____ I get ample opportunity to feel proud of things I do.
_____ I wish I had more occasion to do things of which I could feel personally proud:
    _____ I wish the occasions would come just a little more often.
    _____ I wish the occasions would come more often.
    _____ I wish they would come a lot more often.
_____ I wish there were fewer occasions when people expect me to take pride in what I do:
    _____ I wish the occasions would come just a little less often.
    _____ I wish the occasions would come less often.
    _____ I wish they would come a lot less often.

Affiliation. The need for affiliation is the most difficult to assess. Although we know that cooperative effort in achieving a shared goal typically evokes strong feelings of mutual trust and affection, there seems to be a norm in this country supporting the view that doing good work on the job is irrelevant to feeling warm and friendly toward co-workers. To assess the need for affiliation, consultants might begin with a few warm-up questions:

Some people think they work with a really great bunch of people; others don't feel that way at all. How do you think your bunch might compare with those in other schools?

When something really good happens at work, people sometimes give one another a big hug. Has that happened where you work?

Sometimes people think they have to work past or around other people, or be on the lookout, because certain other people might do them harm. On the other hand, people sometimes feel that there is a spirit of one for all and all for one. What's it like where you work?

After a few such warm-up questions, you might proceed to the following.

How do you feel about the friendliness of the people with whom you work?

_____ I like the amount of friendliness we have at work; it's not too much and not too little.
_____ I wish we had more of a feeling of friendliness and togetherness at work:
    _____ I wish we had a little more.
    _____ I wish we had somewhat more.
    _____ I wish we had a lot more.
_____ There is too much buddy-buddy (straining to be friendly) where I work:
    _____ There is a little too much.
    _____ There is rather too much.
    _____ There is a great deal too much.

Do you feel relaxed and warm with your colleagues at work?

_____ The bunch at work is a nice, comfortable group of people about whom I feel very good.
_____ The bunch at work are not very comfortable to be with. I wish they

could relax more, be less businesslike sometimes and more human-to-human:

_____ I wish they were a little more human.

_____ I wish they were somewhat more human.

_____ I wish they were a lot more human.

_____ The bunch at work is more chummy than I like. I sometimes wish they'd accept the school as a place where people work and let it go at that. We don't all have to be pals:

_____ I wish it were a little more worklike here.

_____ I wish it were somewhat more worklike.

_____ I wish it were a lot more worklike.

Activity. You might want to check on the available energy for initiative and exploration among your clients. By "activity," we mean the need to initiate, explore, and pursue curiosities or visions with vigor. Initiation, exploration, and vigorous pursuit can be either intellectual or physical, as the following items illustrate:

How do you feel about the amount of variety and new experience you get in your work?

_____ I get the amount of variety and new experiences I like.

_____ I wish my job had more variety and new experience in it:

_____ I wish it had a little more.

_____ I wish it had somewhat more.

_____ I wish it had a lot more.

_____ I wish my job had less variety and new experiences in it:

_____ A little less

_____ Somewhat less

_____ A lot less

How do you feel about the energy and vigor that your job calls for?

_____ I like the amount of energy and vigor that my job calls for.

_____ There isn't enough opportunity in my job to expend energy or to have a feeling of vigor:

_____ I wish it had a little more of that feeling.

_____ I wish it had somewhat more.

_____ I wish it had a lot more.

_____ My job calls for too much energy; I'd like to take it easier:

_____ I'd like to take it a little easier.

_____ Somewhat easier.

_____ A lot easier.

Relations with Students. Here we can recapitulate the items above, simply rephrasing them to ask about settings in which teachers (or administrators or counselors) work with students. To illustrate, here is an item about power:

In your classroom, to what extent are you able to choose on your own the sequence of topics, the activites for learning, and the like?

_____ I am able to choose the topics and activities to the extent I prefer.
_____ I wish I had more freedom to choose:
    _____ A little more freedom
    _____ Somewhat more
    _____ A lot more
_____ I wish I were not expected to make so many of my own choices:
    _____ I'd like to make my own choices a little less often.
    _____ Somewhat less often.
    _____ A lot less often.

Such a question could also be asked about extracurricular activities, counseling sessions, meetings of the student government, and so on. Here is an item about affiliation:

Does your classroom feel warm, comfortable, and friendly to you and your students?

_____ The amount of friendliness in my classroom is about the amount I prefer.
_____ I wish the feeling among my students or between them and me were more friendly:
    _____ A little more
    _____ Somewhat more
    _____ A lot more
_____ The students want more friendliness than I think is suitable for classroom work:
    _____ A little more
    _____ Somewhat more
    _____ A lot more

Those are examples of the kind of item we recommend for assessing satisfaction. You can, of course, use selected items from the list. You can also add some items to get at detail peculiar to the school you are evaluating. The items give you information on the direction of change that would bring respondents more satisfaction and the degree to which they yearn for change. The methods explained in other chapters can help you move in the directions the data indicate.

You will note that the items above can be as useful for diagnosis as for the evaluation of outcomes. That is a virtue, since information from these items is more useful if you ask the questions more than once and then track the changes. The chief disadvantage of the items is that despite their usefulness to consultants helping a school to make changes, their content will not usually be revealing to lay audiences—school boards, newspaper reporters, and even teachers—not directly involved in the change project. It takes some knowledge of theory to see the connections between such questions and the ordinary work of the school. And to that we turn next.

EFFECTS ON STUDENTS

The most direct effects on students occur in the classroom— in the immediate working situation in which they listen, talk, and write out their exercises; in which they work face to face in teams; and so on. Evidence is growing that "time on task"—the amount of time a student actually spends listening, reciting, or practicing—has direct and large effects on academic performance. Growing evidence also suggests that greater student achievement shows up when students are tested on what they are taught—that is, if the tests contain items matched to the actual content of the lessons. Neither of those findings is surprising. They illustrate what we mean, however, when we say that the direct effects are to be found in the classroom.

Evidence is growing, too, to show that the interpersonal relations in student work teams also have strong effects. A great deal of research has been done on the effects of competitive, cooperative, and individual-istic work by students. In some applications in actual workaday class-rooms, teams of students compete, but team members cooperate to solve arithmetic problems, design science experiments, label sentence struc-tures, and other topics. Researchers have found that cooperative tasks improve retention of information, mastery of concepts and principles, problem-solving ability, creative thinking, and other cognitive out-comes. Also improved are students' cooperative skill, awareness of their own capabilities, and ability to see things from others' viewpoints. Their democratic values, appreciation of cultural and ethnic differences, atti-tudes toward school, enjoyment of learning, and self-esteem are im-proved as well. Those outcomes, too, occur in the classroom. (For a book on cooperation, competition, and individualistic work, see Johnson and Johnson, 1975.)

Effects from Organization

The organization of the school can help or hinder classroom work. If students are to devote a maximum amount of time to their academic tasks, then administrators, counselors, and others must not interfere with class time. If a teacher takes too much time in class struggling with discipline, others must give help—but first they must be informed of the teacher's need. If test items are to test actual content taught, time must be arranged for teachers to make the tests or to learn to use tests developed elsewhere (for example, those of the Instructional Accomplishments Information Systems available from SWRL Educational Research and Development, 4665 Lampson Avenue, Los Alamitos, CA 90720). If teachers are to learn the appropriate uses of cooperative, competitive, and individualistic learning tasks, and if they are to learn how to manage work in groups, they must have time and help. Giving time and all those kinds of support calls for responsiveness from the organization: skill in diagnosing the present situation, in communicating effectively in and out of meetings, in setting goals, and in solving problems and dealing with conflicts that arise; trust in the professional behavior of others; skill in drawing out the staff's resources and in finding outside resources, in making decisions and taking synergistic action, and in monitoring the effectiveness of all those other skills.

That is only a quick sketch of the path from organizational effectiveness to the behavior of students (though drawn in reverse), but it will suffice to show that there are multiple paths, not a single one, and that the steps along the way are many. Furthermore, improving the organizational problem solving of a school takes time. Some years may go by—the number depending on the school's readiness at the outset—before the school can help teachers change what they do in the small settings. And making those changes, too, takes time.

We know of no study in schools that has itemized and numbered the links from organizational characteristics to individual performance. But we do know of such a study in industry. Brass (1981) studied the matter in a newspaper publishing company. One of his measures of organizational structure was "transaction alternatives"—the number of other people from whom each person could receive inputs or to whom he or she could distribute outputs. Brass also took measures of job characteristics—measures from the settings that would be analogous to classrooms in schools. One of his measures of job characteristics was "task support"—the degree to which other persons provide active support, help, and cooperation. Brass found that transaction alternatives correlated .24 with task support, and task support correlated .41 with performance, but transaction alternatives correlated only .11 with performance. Those figures illustrate the kind of relation we have described above. The strongest effect on performance (.41) was from a characteristic of the setting that was analogous to the classroom.

The weakest effect of the three (.11) was the link all the way from an organizational characteristic to performance. Brass found a similar effect on satisfaction. Satisfaction correlated .60 with task support but only .27 with transaction alternatives. The implication for consultants seems clear: arrange organizational structure so that it supports the small settings such as committees and classrooms that directly support performance. The implication for educators is the same.

Because of the lag from the first steps to the last, the effects of organizational renewal on outcomes among students may take longer to reveal themselves than many people are willing to wait. And by the time those outcomes improve, it may be difficult to marshall convincing data to show how the organizational changes were related to student outcomes. Making the case might require a long-term evaluation of considerable scope, with frequent data collection tracking changes in many norms and skills. Such an evaluation is expensive to mount and requires the commitment of people in many parts of school and district while personnel come and go.

For all those reasons, we do not recommend that consultants blithely tell their clients that organizational development will have effects on students—at least not without warning them that it will take a long time and that demonstrating the outcomes will require an evaluation of large scope.

The effects on students can be accelerated, of course, if students are included in the change project. That is not easy. So far, few OD consultants have worked with students. To our knowledge, no consultant has yet carried out a long and comprehensive project with students, though Alderfer and Brown (1975) came close. But it remains our theory and our faith that simultaneous work with students and faculty can considerably speed change. Accordingly, we turn next to assessing organizational conditions among students.

Assessing Outcomes Among Students

It is not always easy to elicit information from students, especially from those who believe that the staff cares little about them and is likely to misuse any information about them that they acquire. For this reason, it is vital to maintain anonymity in the data and a reputation for integrity in handling them.

If consultants include students in an OD project, they can monitor progress by using the suggestions for data gathering in Chapters 3 through 7, altered to suit the student's age and language comprehension. In pluralistic countries like the United States, the language of students contains many more dialects than the language of teachers. Thus, an interview written for tenth-graders will not work well with third-graders; an interview for inner-city black high school students will work less effectively for suburban white high school students; an interview written for students in Plaquemines Parish, Louisiana, will not work as well for those in Westchester County, New York. Evaluators who use the questions in this section, even though they are presented in the form of questionnaires, should convert them to interview schedules, guides to direct observation, topics to guide a search among documents, or to whatever form is best suited to their purpose and clientele.

If evaluation is needed concerning the relations between students and the rest of the school, evaluators will want to ascertain communicative relations between students' and staff's subsystems. They will want to know about the mutual responsiveness of students and staff and about how each makes use of the other's resources. They will want to know how students, staff, and parents join in mutual problem solving and assess progress toward their goals and how they decide when to do so.

Schmuck and Schmuck (1983) have described several straightforward ways of obtaining information about students and from students in classrooms, and Simon and Boyer (1967) have produced fifteen volumes describing systematic methods for observing students in classrooms. Evaluators can use techniques and instruments directly from those and other books or borrow ideas from them for constructing their own methods. In the same spirit, we offer two lists of questions below.

Organizational Functioning. In 1976 Warren Bell and Ann Burr developed a questionnaire to ascertain the functioning of the school organization from the point of view of students. Their questionnaire did not include the subheadings used below; those headings are included here for the convenience of consultants who may not wish to use the entire questionnaire.

Questionnaire for Students on Organizational Functioning _____

This is not a test. We want to find out about how it feels to be in your school. If the words seem to be true about your school, circle "Yes"; if they don't, circle "No." If you don't know what the sentence is about, circle "I DK" (I don't know).

Problem Solving   Circle your answer

People notice when something goes wrong;
they try to make it right.   YES   NO   I DK

There is no one here who will help me
when I have a problem.   YES   NO   I DK

Teachers plan a lot together when a
change needs to be made.   YES   NO   I DK

People here are interested in ideas from everyone.   YES   NO   I DK

Teachers don't solve problems; they just
talk about them.   YES   NO   I DK

Goals

People talk about the way they want the school to be.   YES   NO   I DK

I have certain things I want to do in school this year
and I have told someone else about them.   YES   NO   I DK

Parents were not asked to help set school goals.   YES   NO   I DK

What we do here is because of "goals."   YES   NO   I DK

This school does not try to get better.   YES   NO   I DK

Conflict and Variety

People listen to each other even if they are not friends.   YES   NO   I DK

No one else will help me if a teacher is unfair to me.   YES   NO   I DK

Most people here believe there is more than one way
to take care of problems.   YES   NO   I DK

The principal will not listen to our "side" of an argument. YES   NO   I DK

When we disagree here, we learn from each other.   YES   NO   I DK

Open Communication Up and Down

Teachers find it easy to talk to the principal.   YES   NO   I DK

I do not find it easy to talk to the teachers.   YES   NO   I DK

The principal talks with us frankly and openly.   YES   NO   I DK

I can easily get help from teachers if I want it.   YES   NO   I DK

People do not talk to each other here if they
are from different parts of the school.   YES   NO   I DK

Teachers say mean things about each other.   YES   NO   I DK

Decision Making

Teachers help decide which adults will work at this school. YES   NO   I DK

Parents do not help decide about new school programs.   YES   NO   I DK

People from this school give advice to the superintendent
and his staff before things are decided about the school.   YES   NO   I DK

I do not get to help decide what to do here in school.   YES   NO   I DK

None of the students gets to help decide what to do.   YES   NO   I DK

Responsiveness

In this school, it is OK to have a problem.   YES   NO   I DK

Teachers don't try "new" things here.   YES   NO   I DK

Students with special problems get help.   YES   NO   I DK

Students with new ideas are ignored.   YES   NO   I DK

The new things we do at this school are just what we need.   YES   NO   I DK

Attractiveness of the School

I would rather go to school here than in
most other schools in the city.   YES   NO   I DK

Students here have a good feeling about each other.   YES   NO   I DK

New students and new teachers are ignored or "put down."   YES   NO   I DK

Teachers and students feel good about each other.   YES   NO   I DK

People here do not care about one another.   YES   NO   I DK

Learning Environments. Anderson (1973) has made available for students a list of 105 questions in booklet form. In this booklet the student marks one of four answers: strongly disagree, disagree, agree, or strongly agree. Since at this writing the booklets are easily available from Anderson at small cost, we reproduce only a few examples here.

Questionnaire for Students About the Learning Environment

- The class has students with many different interests.
- Certain students work only with their close friends.
- The students enjoy their classwork.
- There is constant bickering among class members.
- The better students' questions are more sympathetically answered than those of the average students.
- Every member of the class has the same privileges.
- Most students want their work to be better than their friends' work.

- Students cooperate equally with all class members.
- The better students are granted special privileges.
- Only the good students are given special projects.
- Class decisions tend to be made by all the students.
- The students would be proud to show the classroom to a visitor.
- Some groups of students work together regardless of what the rest of the class is doing.
- A few of the class members always try to do better than the others.
- There are tensions among certain groups of students that tend to interfere with class activities.
- Students are asked to follow strict rules.
- The class is controlled by the actions of a few members who are favored.

FINAL ADVICE

Evaluate because you want to learn from unbiased, systematic data whether you knew what you were doing. But evaluate also because the information about the school made available to other audiences—such as administrators, school boards, and taxpayers' associations—can affect the school's welfare and fate.

Have in mind not only the goals of the OD project conceived by the designers at the start, but also the possible effects of the OD on the quality of work life and on the future of the participants and their community. Evaluate the four metaskills—diagnosis, gathering information and other resources, mobilizing synergistic action, and monitoring the first three metaskills. Always include directly observable evidence. And use multiple evaluative methods.

Beware of the pitfalls in measuring satisfaction. Beware of promising early effects on students. Both matters have subtleties. But don't let that stop you.

11

Institutionalizing OD in School Districts

On Thursday evening, the budget committee of the school board met. The total funds requested by various parts of the district had exceeded the expected revenue. A few budget items had to be cut. The committee came to a line in the budget that read, "Organizational support services." That didn't sound important. Besides, what did it mean? The committee crossed it out.

That line was in the budget to support the district's cadre of organizational specialists—an arrangement for providing OD consultation to the district.

The budget committee met again on Saturday morning to make final recommendations. The room was crowded with visitors who wanted to be heard. Many were members, clients, and friends of the district's cadre of organizational specialists. Principals told the committee how the cadre had helped save time in meetings, speed curricular changes, reduce conflicts, and improve relations with parental groups. Teachers told how the cadre helped them to work more effectively in teams. Several students who were members of the student government in a high school explained that they had learned from the cadre how to work with staff in ways that improved friendliness, trust, and accuracy of communication between students and teachers. They also reported that their attitudes toward the school as a whole had changed for the better. A researcher from the nearby university described how the cadre functioned and presented data on its effectiveness. In the end, the committee put back into the budget sufficient money to support the cadre.

That episode, an actual one, illustrates how easily support for OD in a school district can be lost. It also shows how support for OD can be marshalled. The clients of OD often give it its firmest support.

This cadre of organizational specialists had been active in the district for five years, but the budget committee had not heard about its work and could not estimate its value—or even interpret a reference to it in the budget. The voices of approval for the cadre's work did not reach them until the last moment. But the voices did reach them. Some members of the cadre had been present Thursday evening. They spent the rest of that night and most of Friday telephoning other members, clients, and friends. As a result, the breadth and intensity of the testimonials at Saturday's meeting impressed the members of the committee. The testimonials altered the committee's thinking about the cadre's usefulness to education in the district.

Those present on Saturday morning were people the budget committee cared about. They were people whose approval or disapproval was capable of making the committee members feel good or bad about their actions. From principals to students, the speakers were those the budget makers saw themselves as serving. The committee members would feel rewarded if they took an action that would bring praise and joy from those people.

To put it differently, some *norms* were at work. The committee and the audience agreed about many kinds of work in schools that they thought *ought* to be done—work they approved and saw as important. Also, the visitors showed strong and common approval of some further kinds of actions in the district designed to help the actions the committee already knew about and approved. In particular, the visitors showed strong support for OD and wanted the committee to show similar support.

When an action brings clear and agreed-on approval or disapproval from many people, and when the person acting cares about that approval or disapproval, then a norm is operating. When people show approval and disapproval to a person acting in an organizational capacity, they are sending messages about what they consider to be proper behavior on the part of that person. They are sending specifications, so to speak, for the person's behavior in his or her organizational role. To put it in a phrase, they are *role senders*. The visitors at the meeting on Saturday morning were role senders to the budget committee.

Organizational behavior is held in place by norms, and the norms are transmitted by role senders. OD is institutionalized in a district when role senders make it an approved and expected part of the district's activities. Several methods have been used in school districts to make consultation approved, expected, and customary. We will describe those ways and then return to the use of role senders in maintaining OD as an expected activity in the district.

METHODS OF MAINTAINING CONSULTATION

A lot of help giving goes on in schools. In fact, some jobs consist mostly of help giving: those of librarians, curriculum specialists, assistant principals, and custodians. And of course teachers and counselors are always helping students.

Consultation is one kind of help giving. The term *consultation* means giving information, giving advice, showing how, and guiding practice. Districts maintain the availability of consultation of one kind or another by various means. We will distinguish three kinds of consultation: content, process, and OD. Within each of those, we will distinguish inside from outside consultation.

Content Consultation

Most consultation in school districts is *content* consultation. An example is the in-service course or workshop in which an expert trains educators in such subject matters as reading, mathematics, social studies, or the arts. Other examples include psychologists who teach educators about child development, mathematicians who help teachers with new instructional strategies, mental health consultants who help teachers with students who have problems, and specialists in "precision teaching" who help teachers use various reinforcement techniques.

Inside Consultation. Districts maintain some consultants full time—curriculum specialists, for example. Frequently, districts maintain central-office departments of curriculum. For other kinds of consultation, schools call upon people who spend most of their time performing duties other than consultation but who are experts in needed topics. A teacher who is expert in "precision teaching," for example, may be called upon occasionally. Both those methods have also been used to maintain process consultation—both OD and the less systematic sort. (For the distinction, see Chapter 1, "Goals of OD.")

The advantages of inside consultation, both content and process, are that (1) the inside consultant is more easily available than the outsider; (2) the insider knows useful information about the setting, can get to the task faster than an outsider, and can avoid political mistakes an outsider might make; and (3) the insider shares a "common fate" with the clients and can inspire their immediate trust. Clients know that the insider will continue to be within easy reach and will have a continuing personal stake in achieving a favorable outcome and in avoiding discomfort to individuals.

The disadvantages of inside consultation are that (1) inside people usually have work loads calibrated to average demand and are therefore unable to undertake exceptionally large projects without putting aside other regular duties; (2) simply because they are locals, they may not be seen by the clients as experts; (3) their knowledge of the district may be biased; and (4) the very fact of their "common fate" with the clients may dissuade them from taking risks that a change project requires.

Outside Consultation.   The advantages of outside consultants are that (1) they can more easily take on large projects beyond the ready capacity of the district; (2) they have expert power; (3) they can collect information for an unbiased diagnosis uninfluenced by having been members of the district; (4) to the extent that they are trusted—and some people usually trust an outside expert immediately—some staff members will confide in them things they would be fearful of telling an insider; and (5) they are freer to take the risks of change.

The disadvantages are that (1) it takes time and effort to find the right consultant; (2) outside consultants require more time for getting to know a school or district regardless of how open some participants may be; (3) although some participants will trust them immediately, others may take longer to trust outsiders, worrying that outside consultants will be more likely than insiders to embark upon risky journeys; and (4) they require a cash outlay. We might also mention the risk of picking the wrong consultant, but that applies equally to insiders and outsiders.

Content consultation in education is important, of course. For making organizational changes in support of the content, however, the expertise does not lie in the content. The expertise rarely lies with the curriculum committee, the payroll department, or the bus schedule. It lies in the norms and skills of organizational development—in particular, in the four metaskills.

Process Consultation

Process consultation within a district aims to improve the interpersonal *procedures* used by school personnel to reach their educational objects. It focuses on the *how* of interpersonal interactions rather than the *what* of their content. Process consultants deal with such matters as the patterns of communication, leadership attempts, underlying group tensions, problem solving, and decision making. Examples of inside consultation include counselors meeting with a team of teachers to offer constructive feedback on the team's group procedures, an administrator acting as a third-party mediator between an angry parent and an uneasy teacher, and a curriculum specialist giving feedback to the class and teacher about their interaction patterns. The emphasis is on procedures; process consultants do not deal directly with the subject matter of interactions.

Inside Consultation. Like content consultation, process consultation can be provided from inside either by full-time or part-time people. Some districts have positions for "human relations." Counselors, school psychologists, mental health specialists, administrators, and others sometimes give process help.

Content consultants almost always deal with individuals (even when they work with groups), and unless they move into process consultation, they can have little effect on the norms that hold organizational procedures and structures in place. Since they deal frequently with interpersonal processes, process consultants can begin to affect organizational norms.

The advantages and disadvantages of process consultation from inside are much like those of content consultation. Since process consultants more often run afoul of organizational norms, however, they are likely to be weakened more by being embedded in the organization.

Much process consultation focuses on interpersonal norms. To the extent that it does so, it can be carried on with a subsystem in temporary isolation from the rest of the organization. An inside process consultant can train a committee in meeting skills, for example, while doing little about those skills in other groups in the school. But the procedures in the committee cannot be kept secret. Indeed, to the extent that the committee members find the new skills useful, they will want to use them elsewhere. They will probably talk about them in other groups. And to the extent that the new skills differ from the old, people who have not shared the committee's gradual transformation and the rewards its members found in the new skills will be leery, even frightened, of what they hear. These others may come to think of the committee members as people they want to avoid, and they may come to think of the consultant as an irritant, or even a danger, rather than a helper. In brief, it is easy for inside consultants, especially when they are dramatically successful with one part of the school, to find people in other parts fending them off.

To the extent that a process consultation deals with many parts of a district, the consultant will become known personally and gradually to people in those parts. Participants will come to know the consultant through direct experience rather than rumors. The consultant can move forward with each group at its own pace but at the same time maintain communication among groups, so that no group is suddenly surprised by what is happening in other groups. But it is difficult for an inside consultant to break the time loose to work with an entire school of any size, not to mention an entire district. And at the other extreme, if the consultant is a member of a very small school, the other disadvantages of being embedded in the organization are exacerbated.

Outside Consultation.   The advantages and disadvantages of process consultation from the outside, too, are much like those of content consultation. Again, however, because process consultation deals with interpersonal and organizational norms, there are some differences. The hat of the expert on process will be less persuasive to some participants than that of the content expert, because they will be unable to visualize what will come from under the process hat. They will know, or think they know, what a content consultant will do, but they will have little idea about what a process consultant will do. And the difficulties of gaining trust are magnified for the outside process consultant when the participants discover that the consultant seems bent on unhinging the existing norms.

OD Consultation

OD consultation is a kind of process consultation. To institutionalize it, we want to magnify the advantages of both inside and outside consultation, with due regard to the special delicacies of process consultation with intact systems. We want to put OD consultation into the hands of those who are close to influential members of the district. We want to reach administrators, of course, but we also want to reach teachers and others who are influential in informal ways. Those with informal influence are almost always important role senders to the administrators.

Inside Consultation.   Most districts have no member skilled in OD. Some have one or two but lack a formal structure to support OD. Somewhere between seventy-five and a hundred districts worldwide have a district capacity for OD, and some of those have a central-office department.

A central-office department for OD has advantages:

1. It is close to the heart of administrative power. Its members can communicate easily in one direction with the superintendent,

assistant superintendents, and directors, and in the other to the principals. If the OD department carries out consultation that pleases the central-office administrators, its direct links to them give OD the strength of their support.

2. The connection of the central-office department with authority brings its members immediate attention when they approach a school.
3. When the staff of the OD department is full-time, it has the advantage of being able to put large blocks of undistracted time into a project.
4. Because of their position near the top of the hierarchy, the OD staff gains an additional aura of expertness.
5. Clients can find the department easily.
6. Like all insiders, the OD staff accumulates first-hand knowledge of the district.

A central-office department also has disadvantages:

1. Its close connection with authority causes some people to treat OD with caution and initial distrust.
2. Because the superintendent and assistant superintendents see OD as part of the central administration, they are likely to believe that it should carry out their purposes. The fact that the OD office is in their suite reminds them that OD might be useful to them. They sometimes might press the OD staff to carry out projects in schools against the will of the people there. The price of refusal can be loss of support.
3. When the OD department does carry out a successful consultation, other people in the district may attribute the success only to the pressure of authority, not to the validity of OD.
4. As with the other insiders, the knowledge of the OD staff about the district may be biased and spotty. The information the OD staff gets from schools will usually be thinned by the careful editing organizational members give their communications to the top.
5. Frequently a superintendent and the assistant superintendents will not themselves use OD skills or adhere to its norms. Like other members of the district who have not had direct experience of OD, they may be fearful of norm changes and may press the OD staff to limit itself to innocuous and picayune projects.

All those constraints infect every OD department in one degree or another, because they stem from the characteristics of hierarchy. No amount of competence or skill on the part of the members of the OD department will erase them.

Outside Consultation. To the advantages and disadvantages of outside consultation mentioned earlier, we have two disadvantages to add in the case of OD. First, it is costly to hire a consultant for every OD project and a team of consultants for large projects. Second, OD consultants with experience in schools are hard to find. OD consultants with experience in other kinds of organizations can often be helpful, but it always takes them a while to learn about the special qualities of schools.

Fullan, Miles, and Taylor (1978) located 308 consultants who had been doing extensive OD with schools in the United States and Canada during the previous five years. That is a heartening number, but it is not enough to touch many of the 16,000 school districts in the United States, not to speak of Canada.

When OD consultants with school experience are not located nearby, they cannot respond quickly to sudden needs. Responding quickly can sometimes be crucial to the progress of a project. And if the distant consultant is to be on site frequently, travel costs mount.

ROLE SENDING AND INSTITUTIONALIZATION

Conducting OD in a district requires that some people take on the role of consultant and others that of client. To institutionalize OD, these roles must become expected and stabilized. A role is stabilized by norms about the proper behavior of the person acting in it. When people say, "That's the way we do things around here," or "That's *not* the way we do things around here"—that is, when they express approval or disapproval of an action—you know that norms are at work. OD becomes institutionalized when the norms support it—when the practice of OD itself causes no eyebrows to rise, when special skill in it draws compliments, and when deviations from its norms draw frowns.

The people who express approval or disapproval, who convey standards of behavior, are the role senders to the person in the role. Here, we will use the term *role sending* to abbreviate long phrases such as "expressing approval or disapproval of selected behavior on the part of a person acting in a particular organizational role." The best arrangement for maintaining OD in a school district is one that puts knowledgeable and supportive role senders in communication both with the central office and with potential clients in the schools.

But superintendents come and go, citizens' groups suddenly get riled, and the state department issues new regulations. What then? What can protect the norms of OD within a school from onslaughts by role senders who hold to contrary norms of organizational behavior? What we need, obviously, are role senders who can strongly support OD when others send disapproval. Furthermore, the role senders should be placed where they can be most effective.

A method of institutionalizing OD should make use of supportive role senders in schools who can voice approval for actions and opinions that go in the direction of OD and disapproval of contrary actions and opinions. Outside consultants cannot be those voices, since they are usually not in the schools between consultations. Nor can OD departments usually provide them, since department members rarely spend time in the teachers' lounge, the hallways, or at faculty meetings where they can affect role behavior. And even when they do, they may not be the people whose approval and disapproval the teachers care most about. The most effective role senders in support of OD in a school are school members who have had experience with OD either as clients or as consultants and who are present to speak when the topic comes up.

Further, a method of institutionalizing OD should put supportive role senders not only in the schools that are making use of OD, but also in schools that have not yet done so. Obviously, outside consultants do not spend time in schools where they are not consulting. Members of OD departments, too, spend most of their time in the schools that ask them for help.

A method of institutionalizing OD should include supportive role senders to central-office administrators. An OD department can usually do that very well. Outside consultants are weak in this respect owing to the sporadic nature of their visits.

Finally, a method of institutionalizing OD should entail role senders who can support OD in the schools when they interact with the community. Such role senders are most effective when they can actually help, for instance, conduct meetings, coordinate among groups, and solve problems with PTAs, youth groups, social service agencies, and so on. People who are active in community affairs are often those who attend and speak at school board meetings and who communicate directly with—that is, who are themselves role senders to—teachers, principals, and superintendents.

We turn next to a method of institutionalizing OD that puts knowledgeable role senders into closer contact with clients in schools, administrators, and community than either an OD department or outside consultants can do.

PEER CADRES

In J.D. Salinger's novel, *The Catcher in the Rye*, Holden Caulfield tells of his recurring dream of patrolling the edge of a high field of rye to keep the children playing there from falling over the cliff. Through that poetic image, Holden poignantly portrays for his little sister, Phoebe, the sort of job he would like to have as an adult. He would be the catcher in the rye, he says.

Metaphorically, school consultants catch administrators, teachers, students, and parents before they fall off organizational cliffs. They are catchers in the school. And like Holden Caulfield, OD consultants don't want to tell school people what games to play, where to stand, and where to run. They don't want to be breathing down their necks all the time. Rather, consultants want their clients to look around for help every now and then. If school people look for help, it will be easier for the catcher to catch them when they get too close to the edge.

Even if a catcher were available for every school district, however, the strategy of stationing one at the cliff's edge would contain an irreparable flaw. We and others have learned from experience that participants in OD can become too dependent on their consultants. The consultant's charisma and expertise, though advantageous in the short run, can become drawbacks in the long run. After all, the OD consultant has designed the diagnoses; designed the retreats and workshops; brought all staff members through the stages of problem solving; initiated the evaluation and feedback; and led the follow-up support to put new structures and procedures into place. It was the consultant who knew about the exercises and procedures, and it was the consultant who took leadership when events turned confusing or highly emotional. Under those circumstances, it is not surprising that participants come to depend on the consultant.

We have been concerned in our designing, therefore, with creating ways of gracefully disengaging from our consulting roles with the participants. We have sought to remove ourselves from dependency relationships, for example, by asking participants to take leadership in convening sessions for their own faculty. But even after successful year-long projects from which we gradually extricated ourselves from our powerful roles, we were sometimes not fully satisfied that the school had achieved a capacity for self-renewal.

In early 1969, we were well into a research project with an entire district we will call Keele. It became obvious that we would be unable to provide continuing consultation to the district, or even to one school, after we completed our research. Other suitable consultants in the region were scarce. And even had there been more consultants available, they would have suffered the disadvantages of outside consultants. It was then that Richard Schmuck conceived the idea of a peer cadre to provide continuing consultative help to a district (for his conception, see Schmuck, 1982; for other writings on peer cadres, see Schmuck, 1977, and in press).

In our project with the Keele district, we (and eleven assistants) carried out OD during 1968–1969 in two elementary schools, one junior high school, and two high schools. Then, in the spring of 1969, we informed Keele personnel that training would be offered in June for those wishing to become "communication consultants" for the district. A printed circular stated that the trainees would become knowledgeable and skilled in communication, simulations, diagnosis, feedback giving, problem solving, and OD designing. We solicited applications from all levels of the district; the twenty-three people eventually selected represented a wide cross-section of the district, including teachers, counselors, elementary and secondary principals, curriculum and student personnel specialists, and assistant superintendents who were members of the superintendent's cabinet.

We gave the Keele peer cadre its initial training during two weeks in June 1969. Then, from September 1969 to March 1970, we coconsulted with them, working side by side with them and helping them with their planning and consultations. We gave them constructive feedback during and after each of their interventions.

Ten rules for an OD cadre grew out of our work at Keele:

1. Draw members from all ranks and from throughout the school district. Since the initial peer-cadre project at Keele, cadres have been drawn from the following, in order from larger to smaller numbers: teachers, counselors, principals and assistant principals, central-office specialists, assistant superintendents, secretaries, and parents.
2. Assign members part time to the cadre—perhaps for 10 or 15 percent of their time.
3. Do not impose cadre services; let the cadre respond to requests. The cadre should, however, advertise its services and give demonstrations.
4. Do not assign cadre members to consult with units (schools, central-office departments, etc.) in which they are regularly employed.
5. Appoint a cadre coordinator to work at least half time.
6. See that the cadre has at least ten active members. A couple of dozen is better.
7. Train the cadre to provide services through temporary *teams* drawn from its memberships. A cadre member should consult alone only in exceptional circumstances.
8. Plan three weeks (fifteen full days) of initial training for cadre members and at-the-elbow help to teams of cadre members during their first consultations.
9. Give the cadre its own budget.

10. Provide time for the cadre's own self-renewal: recruiting and training new members, distributing information about the district among members, acquiring new skills, renewing the cadre's cohesiveness, planning for the future.

Rules 1 through 7 serve to maximize the advantages of both inside and outside consultants and to minimize their weaknesses. Because cadre members are employees of the district (Rule 1), they are perceived as insiders. They have a common fate with their clients. They cannot pull out and vanish; they must live with the outcomes of their consultations. That brings them trust more quickly than outsiders can give it. Because they continue to work most of the time in their regular jobs (Rule 2), they have a great deal of intimate information about what is going on in the district and about its history. That saves them from many mistakes, especially political mistakes, that outsiders might make, no matter how thorough their diagnosis might be. Because they work in all ranks in the district, their information is not screened as information is to a central-office department. They get the information that goes to teachers and secretaries as well as that going to central-office department heads. Their knowledge still has some of the bias to which insiders are prone, but the wide spread of its sources minimizes the bias. Rules 7 and 10 (working in teams and setting aside time for self-renewal) help the cadre to distribute information among its members.

Because the cadre has members throughout the district who can give accurate information, because it advertises its services and gives demonstrations of its work (Rule 3), and because it engages colleagues in all parts of the district in OD, it is less likely than a smaller group of consultants or a central-office department to suffer from the growth of antagonistic rumors—that is, to get walled off.

Because cadre members do not consult in their own units, but are always assigned to consult elsewhere in the district (Rule 4), they are outsiders to their clients. They collect systematic diagnostic data to learn what they need to know. They get the trust that some participants give to outsiders. They are willing to take some risks they would not take if they were members of the clients' unit. And they can come in with at least a little of the aura of the outside expert.

Because the cadre contains a fair number of members (Rule 6), it has flexibility in meeting demands. If the available time of some members is committed, others can be assigned. Because cadre members work only part time in that role (Rule 2), some can negotiate more released time when a project of large scope looms. The coordinator (Rule 5) facilitates those allocations. The flexibility of any cadre has its limits, of course. The available time of cadre members and the willingness of administrators to release more of their time can become overstretched.

On the whole, however, because cadre members are continuing members of the district (Rule 1), because the coordinator is in the district's phone book, and because of the other reasons we gave, the cadre can respond to most requests with alacrity.

The cadre's direct link to the central office through its coordinator has advantages and disadvantages. It makes the cadre easy to find, and it gives cadre members a formal place in the organization. And as long as the cadre does work of value to the central-office administrators, the coordinator can draw support for the cadre that is important to its morale and stability. On the other hand, the cadre can find itself pressed by administrators to go out and solve problems that are administrators' problems, not schools' problems, and it can further find itself pressed to limit itself to work that does not rock the boat. The coordinator can act as a buffer against that pressure, and the cadre can counterpose its clients' demands against those of the administrators. The latter defense is usually the better, especially if some administrators have participated in OD themselves. Nevertheless, pressures for conformity to administrators' demands will crop up intermittently, and the cadre must withstand them.

Finally, the cost of a cadre is moderate. Figures from some of the cadres we will describe below are representative. Start-up costs in Keele and Eugene were about $37,000 in 1982 dollars. The Boulder Valley cadre invested perhaps $9,000 during the first year, and the Cupertino cadre perhaps $6,000. One reason for the lower costs of the latter two is that those cadres spread initial training over a longer period than did Keele and Eugene.

Maintaining a cadre costs less than starting one up. Fullan, Miles, and Taylor (1978, vol. V, p. 12) say that the cost of a typical OD program is "perhaps one-half of one percent of total budget, and is comparable to amounts usually spent on in-service education." Some districts do use part of their staff-development funds for supporting their cadres. Annual maintenance costs in Eugene have varied between $25,000 and $40,000. Writing about the cadre in Buffalo, Milstein and Lafornara (1980) say,

> The actual cost of the direct maintenance of [the cadre] has been about $25,000 annually. Buffalo's 1979–80 budget was approximately $126,000,000. [The cadre's] cost, therefore, represents less than [two hundredths of one percent] of that budget. Another way of looking at the situation is to note that it would cost substantially more to support even one full-time change agent in a school district than it does to support a skilled internal change team of twenty teachers and administrators.

All those advantages of the cadre's structure help it to do good work. When it does good work, it gets approval from its clients, and it can influence persons who have power to keep it going or destroy it. In brief, the cadre can institutionalize itself. In their nationwide study of OD, Fullan, Miles, and Taylor (1978, vol. V, p. 7), report that " 'classical' OD, plus two other system-oriented, comprehensive approaches . . . were most likely to show clear impact, positive attitudes and institutionalization." The term "classical OD" characterizes cadres.

The way a cadre is organized puts role senders in important places. Members in all parts of the district (Rules 1 and 2) can voice their support of OD both in schools and in central-office departments. Because they have experience *outside* their own units (Rule 4), they are often seen to have a wider knowledge of the facts than their colleagues within the unit. Because they respond to requests from all over the district (Rule 3), they are not known as the captive agent of any one school, department, or faction. Since many of the cadre's members are connected to the bottom of the organization through their own jobs and to the top through their coordinator, they have an open channel for conveying role expectations from bottom to top and back again. Since they have various jobs in the district, they can convey the expectations of various groups.

Because the coordinator reports to someone in the central office (Rule 5), he or she can act as role sender from the cadre's members and clients to the central office. The coordinator can keep the central office informed of the demands for its services and of the satisfaction of its clients. It almost always happens, too, that the cadre is called upon by groups in the community. When that happens, the cadre stimulates role sending from community to school.

The many links and opportunities for communication and role sending by a district cadre promote its stability. In the example we gave at the opening of this chapter, the cadre almost lost its funding because it had not set out to influence the budget committee. But the cadre members were not out of touch. They knew the budget committee was meeting, they knew the meetings were critical, they knew when the proceedings would allow them to be heard, and they attended. When the need arose, they were able to round up clients—principals, teachers, students—overnight. Their presence at the meetings, their quick communications, and the support of their clients saved the day.

One test of stability is longevity. Our first cadre in Keele started operation in the fall of 1969. That November, an auditor discovered a shortage of $1.85 million in Keele's operating budget of $12 million. Programs were cut, jobs were eliminated, and administrators were moved back to classrooms. But the cadre survived. The superintendent wrote to us later to say that the OD delivered by us and the cadre there had been a major asset in helping the district to weather the crisis. Then, in the fall of 1971, a new superintendent arrived. When he encountered a conservative and vocal segment of the community who believed the cadre was doing "sensitivity training," he became first ambivalent about the cadre and then unsympathetic. The cadre's budget was cut and then abolished. Nevertheless, the cadre continued to receive requests from schools for OD, and it continued work (the varieties of its work are described in Runkel, Wyant, Bell, and Runkel, 1980). In the end, however, the difficulties of getting released time for cadre work without central-office support, the pressures of overtime work, and other matters became too much; the Keele cadre disbanded at the end of 1975. The fact that the Keele cadre was perceived as a help rather than a luxury during the terrible budget crisis, and the fact that it went on working for several years after it lost its budget, testify to its durability.

The cadre in Eugene began its work in the fall of 1971. It has survived four changes of superintendent, seven changes of coordinators, and budget cuts in recent years. It continues strong. The literature is full of accounts of educational innovations, particularly curricular changes, that fade away a year or two after the departure of the outside consultants. In view of that record, the staying power of the Eugene cadre is remarkable. We will tell about other cadres in the next section.

Rules 7 through 10 help the cadre to maintain its own internal strength. Rule 7 specifies consultation by teams, not individuals. Especially when cadre members are new at their work, they find it comforting to have a colleague alongside. Doing OD is stressful enough without having to be alone on the firing line. Even when cadre members are highly experienced, it is still useful to exchange informal diagnoses with partners, to discuss possible alterations in the plan for the next hour, and to give and get feedback about performance. Partners can divide the work, too. While one is leading a session, for example, another can be observing and noting participants' reactions to parts of the session. Finally, when making informal judgments about outcomes, the presence of two or more judges increases reliability.

Rule 8 specifies that cadre members be adequately trained before they are released to work on their own—still in teams, but without the trainer at the elbow. The training is necessary to build in the members an adequate repertoire of skills, but it is also necessary to develop confidence among cadre members in one another's skill and trust in their support. When they go to work in teams, each must feel that the other members will be a help, not a hindrance. The initial training includes many exercises requiring interdependence for success.

Rule 9 specifies a budget for the cadre. According to the information we have from several cadres, the biggest expense is usually for released time for clients and cadre members. In some cases, money for released time is part of the cadre's budget and is used to release both clients and cadre members. In other cases, clients request released time directly from the district. Some cadres get along on very little released time. Beyond released time, cadres need money for the coordinator's salary, secretarial time, supplies and materials, rental of space when the cadre mounts a session away from school property, and the occasional outside consultant when the cadre engages one to help it with its own self-renewal. Sometimes there are transportation costs as well. A cadre can hardly plan well without its own budget; we know of no cadre that has none. Besides the practical considerations, a cadre's budget serves as a symbol that the unit is a legitimate and honored part of the district.

Rule 10 provides time for the cadre to recruit and train new members, bring in outside consultants to teach old and new members new skills, exchange information about what is going on in the district, and plan for the future. This rule is also vital for renewing trust and solidarity among members—by resolving conflicts and coping with feelings of affront and injury. The work of a cadre never becomes routine, for the unit must continually make adaptations to changing circumstances. Every change in the district administration calls for a conference among cadre members. Every consultation by the cadre changes the climate of acceptance in the district—a little or a lot—and the impact of the change must also be assessed. Adaptability requires communication among cadre members that is frequent, accurate, quick, and honest, and it requires cadre members to trust that help and support, when they are needed, will be strong and quick. Time for self-renewal is vital in maintaining such communication and support.

Two other rules not only help the cadre to do good work and to become institutionalized, but also help it to maintain its internal strength and cohesiveness. Rule 1, drawing members from all ranks, enables the cadre to get support from all ranks. If a cadre discovers that it cannot recruit new members from some sectors, it should worry that it is losing support from those sectors. Drawing members from all ranks also brings the cadre direct information about its own status in the district.

Rule 5, having a coordinator, provides for a central person through whom arrangements can be made. Clients call the coordinator. The coordinator finds members to make up a consultation team—members who have the skills needed for the particular consultation, who will work well together, and who are personally acceptable to the client. Having a paid coordinator also adds legitimacy to the cadre.

EXAMPLES OF PEER CADRES

In this section we describe the organizational features and consultative activities of a number of cadres in school districts in the United States and elsewhere. Our information about the first five comes from published and unpublished documents and from our own experience. Information about the remainder comes from Kelsh (1983).

Keele

In the fall of 1967, the Keele district had just hired several new assistant superintendents to cope with the problems of a ballooning student population and an increased number of schools. The superintendent wanted us to clarify roles and improve the communication among departments, committees, and schools. We struck a bargain: we would do that if we could conduct research on OD as we went along. The full story of the Keele project, including displays of data on outcomes, is told by Runkel, Wyant, Bell, and Runkel (1980).

Entry and preparation of questionnaires for summative evaluation took place from August 1967 to January 1968. In January we collected data from Keele and from two neighboring districts for comparison; we did so again in May 1969, April 1970, and April 1972. We also collected diagnostic and formative data by means of interviews, observations, documents such as newspapers and district memos, and occasional brief questionnaires.

Our macrodesign included consultation with the superintendent's cabinet, three central-office departments, two high schools, one junior high, and two elementary schools during 1968–1969. In the spring of 1969, we recruited volunteers for the cadre of organizational specialists—the name they chose for themselves was "Communication Consultants." We sought people who, after training, would spend 10 percent of their time acting as OD consultants within the district. From the volunteers, we selected twenty-three for training.

The initial workshop for the cadre lasted two weeks in June of 1969. The first week was devoted to exercises to develop the cadre's skills in group work and to help it become cohesive. The neophyte specialists were also given experiences as cotrainers in exercises on particular consultative skills and then conducted them for their colleagues. During the second week, new temporary consulting teams formed, and members of each team shared resources and experiences. Then the cadre as a whole generated a list of potential clients for their consultations. Each team selected an actual client, made entry, gathered diagnostic data, and returned to the cadre's training site to review its data and design its consultations.

In the fall of 1969, cadre members found two schools in the district willing to become the cadre's first school-clients. Members of our own outside consulting team collaborated in the consultations. During the spring of 1970, we gradually withdrew our presence; we ceased active collaboration at the end of that school year. In the meantime, seven elementary schools had requested the cadre's services, and the cadre delivered OD to all of them in August 1970. Later, the cadre provided OD consultation to other elementary and secondary schools and to administrative groups. Cadre members taught several in-service courses in communication skills, which later turned out to be one of the best sources of future members for the cadre. In one way or another, the cadre also aided two schools in other districts, teachers' and principals' groups, PTAs, a League of Women Voters local, and social agencies.

The first coordinator of the Keele cadre was a curriculum coordinator. He and all later coordinators were drawn from the cadre membership. The cadre also organized a "decision-making group" of four or five members to aid the coordinator. That group decided things that came up between meetings of the whole cadre. Members of the decision-making group were highly trusted, but were also held to account at the meetings of the whole.

Eugene

In the spring of 1971, we were completing OD consultation with six elementary schools in Eugene and Springfield, Oregon (the project is reported in Schmuck, Murray, Smith, Schwartz, and M. Runkel, 1975). The Eugene cadre grew out of the interest in OD that arose in the Eugene district during that project.

Throughout that same spring, Richard Arends, Donald Essig, and the two of us recruited members for the Eugene cadre. We put a printed notice in the district's annual catalogue of summer workshops. We attended several meetings of the central-office staff, of principals, and of the teachers' association to inform people about the project. A great deal of information, we discovered, was spread informally at parties, in faculty rooms, in supermarkets, and so on. In all, seventy-two people responded. We invited the respondents to a two-hour meeting to hear about OD and how it works. After that meeting, we asked interested persons to fill out an application; fifty-one people handed one in. The four of us, along with the assistant superintendent of personnel, acted as a panel of judges. We selected twenty-seven respondents for initial membership: three assistant superintendents, six central-office coordinators, three secondary administrators, two elementary administrators, one secondary counselor, two elementary counselors, four secondary teachers, and six elementary teachers. We selected the twenty-seven on the basis of their educational experience in group dynamics, the nature of their interest in the cadre, and the diversity of role, sex, and race. The twenty-seven candidates represented fourteen of Eugene's forty-four schools and several different sections of the central office.

The formal training of the twenty-seven consisted of two two-hour introductions to OD in May of 1971, ten workshop days in June, five workshop days in August, and coconsultations with us throughout the 1971–1972 academic year.

Our intention in the June workshop was not to produce sophisticated consultants quickly, but to give the trainees a thorough introduction to communication skills, setting goals, working with conflicts, improving meetings, solving problems and making decisions in groups. We included lecturettes and some practice in entry and start-up, organizational diagnosis, designing, and evaluation. We made use of mimeographed sections from the manuscript of the first *Handbook* (Schmuck, Runkel, Saturen, Martell, and Derr, 1972).

Day 1. After introduction, cadre members formed triads to discuss "What I hope the cadre can do for me." We gave a lecture on paraphrasing and asked cadre members to overuse paraphrasing during the workshop. They then formed new triads to discuss "What I hope the cadre can do for the district." Next came a lecturette on the clients, issues, and strategies with which OD is concerned. Then, after we spoke briefly on the skill of behavior description, participants formed cross-role groups to list goals for the cadre in behavioral terms. We then lectured on describing one's own feelings, after which we formed new small groups to build Tinkertoy models of "What this district is like." Participants discussed what the models revealed about the district and the group processes they noted while constructing their models. We then held a discussion on checking one's impressions of another's inner state. Finally, we asked cadre members to fill out the questionnaire entitled Team-Expectations Survey (Chapter 3).

Day 2. We gave a lecture on the technique of survey-data-feedback, displayed data from the Team-Expectations Survey, and asked new small groups to design and administer brief questionnaires to the whole group. Together with the cadre members, we criticized the newly created questionnaires. Next, we asked the cadre members to list their personal goals and resources and then to exchange that information with one another. As homework, we assigned the *Handbook* chapters on clarifying communication and establishing goals.

Day 3. After lecturing on constructive openness and the interpersonal gap, we asked cadre members to form new triads to review their personal goals. Next, after· discussing the use of conflict to uncover problems, participants grouped with persons in jobs similar to theirs to practice the Imaging exercise. By the end of the day, they had completed Stage 1 (generating images of the other groups) and Stages 2 and 3 (clarifying the images with the other groups). We assigned for reading the chapter of the *Handbook* on improving meetings.

Day 4. After going on with the Imaging exercises through Stage 4 (listing own behavior from which others might have formed their images) and Stage 5 (clarifying the listed behavior), cadre members completed the exercise by forming cross-job groups to discuss problems in the district that were brought out by the exercise. The entire group discussed the strengths and limitations of the exercises. We then conducted the Planners and Operators exercise. We assigned for reading the *Handbook* chapter on making decisions.

Day 5. After we lectured on task and social-emotional processes in groups, cadre members discussed ways in which those processes are related to decision making. They formed small groups to list skills they would need as cadre members and then formed pairs of groups to exchange lists. Next, we lectured on techniques of process observation and feedback, after which each pair of groups formed a Fishbowl. The inner groups discussed restraints the cadre would encounter in using its skills in the district, while the outer groups acted as process observers. Then the roles and physical positions of the inner and outer groups were reversed to give everyone a chance to play both the content and the process functions. We asked participants to read the *Handbook* chapter on theory and technology.

Days 6 to 10. The second week contained a similar mix of lectures, procedures, exercises, simulations, and anticipations of future work. We gave lectures on entry and start-up, diagnosis, designing, types of consultations, and problem solving. For exercises and simulations, we used the Five-Square puzzle, Lost on the Moon, One-Way, Two-Way Communication, and again Planners and Operators. We used a lot of time in demonstrating *S-T-P* problem solving with the cadre's own anticipated problems. At the end of the week, the superintendent attended and expressed his support for the cadre.

Days 11 to 15. During the five days in August, we helped cadre members get ready to coconsult with us during the 1971–1972 school year. We wanted to move from the rehearsal of specific exercises and procedures toward the wider application of skills associated with making entry, building contracts, diagnosing clients' needs, macrodesigning and microdesigning, and evaluating members' consultative efforts.

We encouraged cadre members to discuss the norms that were being established within their group. We encouraged them to ask, Are we being open with one another? What does it mean to learn from others? How can we put resources within the group to best use? What commitments to one another have we made or are willing to make? In addition, we encouraged cadre members to become more self-analytic about the emerging structural arrangements for their cadre. We encouraged them to discuss these questions: What will the coordinator's role be? What sort of governance structure will direct the cadre's actions? How can the cadre work to be accepted by others in the district while at the same time maintaining its autonomy and neutrality?

On the first day, we divided the participants into six teams for the 1971–1972 consulting. Each team was made up of four or five members, and each team member typically held a job in the district different from those of his or her teammates. We asked the teams to discuss how their group composition would limit or enhance their ability to work effectively, and then to brainstorm ways of overcoming the group's potential limitations. In two teams, group memberships were changed. Then we devoted ten minutes to each of the following topics: problem solving, communication, consultation stages, organizational issues, OD procedures, OD exercises, and survey-data-feedback. We asked participants to spend the last two hours of the day making agreements in their teams about their preferred norms for working together, using the Group Agreement Exercise.

As the week continued, the cadre made agreements about the role of the coordinator, the role and composition of the steering committee, the decision-making procedures, matters of ethics, and the manner of functioning of the separate teams. Members also made plans for advertising the cadre's services. They selected one person from each team to serve on the steering committee. On the last day, the steering committee selected some future self-renewal events, and the cadre as a whole discussed and revised them. Schmuck (1982) gives more detail on these fifteen days.

After Day 15. From August to May 1972, we joined cadre members in carrying out some initial consultations with an assortment of client groups. Three teams provided follow-up consultation to schools with which we ourselves had already worked, and one team helped a secondary staff develop the skills and structure for participatory decision making. Another team consulted with the superintendent's cabinet to help it improve vertical and lateral communication in the district. A sixth team designed and started an in-service course on communication and problem solving for anyone in the district who might like to attend. Though this last group was not "doing OD," its work was deemed important both to inform a wider audience in the district about cadre skills and to motivate key teachers, counselors, and principals to request OD consultation in their schools. One of us or one of our advanced graduate students aided each of the consulting teams. After May 1972, our active involvement and leadership with the cadre ended.

As others have done, the Eugene cadre has focused its consultations on intact work groups such as school staffs, teaching teams, and administrative cabinets, helping them overcome interpersonal and organizational constraints to productive collaboration. The following are some examples of the kinds of tasks they have undertaken:

- Diagnosing communication skills
- Diagnosing general organizational functioning
- Convening (facilitating) meetings at schools and central office
- Training in communication skills
- Training in meeting skills
- Facilitating communication by direct observation and immediate oral feedback (i.e., "process consultation")
- Training in methods of group decision making
- Training in methods of systematic group problem solving
- Training in team building and team leadership skills
- Building cohesiveness and coordination in the faculty of a new school
- Facilitating conflict negotiations
- Helping choose near-term goals
- Intervening in units facing crisis and applying diagnosis, conflict management, and negotiation (crises have included interpersonal hostilities, financial shortages, communication lags between superintendent and staff, and the like)
- Providing instruction and guided practice in management and leadership styles
- Conferring with administrators or others to design a strategy for change
- Consulting on classroom management and implementation of programs
- Consulting in time management and scheduling
- Evaluating effectiveness of projects
- Teaching self-development classes in interpersonal communication, group processes, and meeting skills

The overall sequence of most OD projects by cadre members includes an initial period of start-up and contract-building followed by diagnosis and design. Then a series of sequential consultative sessions follows, interspersed with data collections for formative evaluation. A typical consultation will last from a few months to an academic year. Evaluative data serve as the springboard for redesign and more consultative sessions, until cadre and clients agree that the necessary structures and procedures for self-renewal have been built. Finally, data are often collected for purposes of summative evaluation and are offered to policy makers.

After the Eugene cadre had acquired some experience, and after new clients requested their services, the teams originally formed in the summer of 1971 no longer served. Since then, members have repeatedly sorted themselves into teams to suit new tasks as they have arisen. Members now typically choose the team to which they want to belong, using criteria such as willingness to work with others on the team, making a balance among the regular jobs of the members, and showing significant interest in the task to be done. It is fairly typical for individual specialists to focus their energies on such functions as designing interviews, training large groups, service as process facilitators, or coaching individual clients such as principals. All team members provide one another with helpful feedback and carry out continual evaluation as the interventions move along.

In 1983, the Eugene cadre contained one supervisor-consultant for training, one specialist in assessment and planning, three central-office coordinators, one computer specialist, one principal, three assistant principals, two counselors, fifteen teachers, four secretaries, and one receptionist.

Cash outlay for the Eugene cadre in 1981–1982 was about $4,000, not counting salaries, ordinary materials, telephone, rental space, and the like. The $4,000 paid for the cadre's continuing training, expenses of courses they taught in communication skills, and released time for conducting consultations during the school day. There had been an exceptionally low need for released time in 1981–1982; the cadre estimated that a cash outlay of about $7,300 would be needed in 1982–1983. In addition to those funds, the district designated half the coordinator's salary for cadre activities and the other half to his duties as director of staff development.

Cadre members volunteered time outside their regular work day during 1981–1982 to conduct thirty-three consultations and to attend cadre meetings and training sessions. At regular pay rates, the donated time was worth $37,000.

Buffalo

Some years ago, the Buffalo (New York) Public School District was presented with a court order to desegregate its schools. Having already encountered difficulties in desegregating its schools, and being aware of the difficulties encountered in Louisville, Boston, and other cities, the leaders of the Buffalo district knew that a "supportive institutional environment" would be necessary. They determined to provide to individual schools skill, encouragement, and social support for dealing with the myriad problems that they knew were inevitable. Michael Milstein, of the State University of New York at Buffalo, was asked to assist.

As a result, in 1977 the Buffalo district established the School Improvement Resource Team (SIRT). It was modeled on the kind of cadre of organizational specialists described above, but it took on a shape of its own suitable to its locality and its mission. In particular, under the pressure of the desegregation order, SIRT could not observe the rule of waiting for invitations from schools. Milstein and Lafornara (1980) explain:

> in urban school environments, . . . invitations are not readily forthcoming . . . Schools needing help are usually identified by central office administrators. . . . Efforts are [then] made to (1) explain how SIRT functions, (2) clarify . . . the issues at the school, and (3) obtain faculty-wide commitment. . . . SIRT's experience is that the involvement of entire school facilities is not practical, since interventions usually take place after school or at week-end sessions. SIRT's response . . . has been to rely on volunteers who are vitally interested in the issues involved. As a result, SIRT sessions typically draw from a minimum of four or five teachers up to a maximum of about 25 percent of a faculty.

In the spring of 1977, sixteen of sixty-five applicants for membership in SIRT were accepted. The group received three weeks of initial training that summer. The stressful conditions are indicated by the facts that five of the original members dropped out during the first week of training and that the central office pressed the team to take on tasks even before it was fully prepared. In August, nevertheless, SIRT conducted one-day workshops in three high schools and did a week of consultation with "liaison teams," which would in turn conduct in-service activities in eight other schools.

Beginning in the fall of 1977, SIRT met monthly for further training, to renew its internal dynamics, and to deal with business affairs. In the spring of 1978, ten of forty-five new applicants were added to SIRT, and the entire group received another two weeks of training in the summer of 1979. SIRT conducted numerous consultations in the spring of 1978 and throughout the 1978–1979 school year.

The operation of SIRT, its embedding in the district structure, the stresses it experienced in bringing itself to active and competent performance, and other matters have been reported by Milstein (1978), Milstein (1979), and Milstein and Lafornara (1980). The following descriptions of some of SIRT's 1980 projects are condensed from Milstein and Lafornara (1980).

The Student Relations Committee (SRC). SRC contained about fifty students from three academic high schools undergoing the greatest extent of desegregation. The students, their teacher-advisers, and a SIRT subteam met monthly for all-day sessions to develop skill and to deal with such issues as discipline, student morale, teacher-student relations, school spirit, and class cutting. SRC began in 1978; it replenished its ranks several times. In each of the three SRC schools, members maintained events calendars to keep students informed about school activities. Each SRC group met regularly with school administrators to discuss strategies for school improvement. Action committees dealt with issues and concerns unique to each school. For example, one SRC group formed an action committee to curb "hall walking" and false fire alarms.

High Schools. After the first workshops with high schools in 1977, SIRT discovered it would have to rely on volunteers at a time when the teachers' union was urging its members not to volunteer for any projects. Nevertheless, as many as 25 percent of a school's teachers volunteered to attend after-school meetings. At one school confronted with severe disciplinary problems, teachers at first focused their efforts on "hall sweeps," in which groups of staff members walked the halls to get students back into class and to remove those who were from other schools or who were dropouts "just visiting." The result was an immediate improvement in discipline and a more favorable perception of SIRT activities by other staff members. The school's administrators became actively involved, volunteers doubled in number, and the group expanded its work to nondisciplinary matters.

A second high school also initially focused on discipline, but developed another strategy. Volunteers at this school developed a schedule card to be carried by all students. This "Omega Card" served as a long-term solution to problems of student identification, hall walking, and class cutting. Other high school principals were contemplating similar methods.

This second high school was the city's newest. Under court order, it was slated to be closed as a secondary school and reopened as an elementary school. Before the court order was handed down, SIRT had been helping the school's faculty develop activities to strengthen school traditions and clarify special resource needs for grants-in-aid proposals. After the court order, SIRT turned its efforts to helping the school faculty to buoy up its sagging morale and minimize the impact of the pending closing on the educational programs. As a result of those efforts and the subsequent intercession of a board member, the school underwent a gradual phase-out instead of the abrupt one-year closing originally prescribed.

Elementary Schools. SIRT's work with elementary schools began in response to requests from schools that had one or more faculty members in SIRT. In one school, the staff asked for process help in refining their individualized mathematics program. The staff, meeting weekly for a semester, developed a schoolwide resource file for math materials, an individualized diagnostic test, and a procedure for assessing student progress in mathematics. A second school was faced with absorbing a junior high school staff. Teachers and ancillary staff met for a semester to develop new policies, disciplinary procedures, and report card procedures. The group was also successful in obtaining a small grant to develop a basic skills task force in the school.

During the spring of 1980, SIRT was called upon to help three elementary schools slated for closing. SIRT trained school-based liaison teams to help the schools close in orderly fashion.

Nonschool Interventions. SIRT helped a citywide citizens' advisory council establish goals and assess needs related to desegregation. Two projects were conducted with groups established by the board of education to monitor and recommend policy for schools in their areas. SIRT conducted several sessions with them to identify and resolve problems.

SIRT had not one coordinator, but two. Together, they oversaw SIRT's budget and kept tabs on the consultations. Other leadership activities were distributed among the members. At monthly meetings, the roles of convener, group-process helpers, and observers were rotated. Every consultation had its own leader. SIRT-wide functions such as overall evaluation and public relations were delegated to members.

At first, SIRT was assigned for administrative purposes to a central-office administrator in charge of school integration. He did not find much time for SIRT, and several important items of information failed to reach the right place in the hierarchy. Later, another central-office administrator was assigned who had been a participant in one of SIRT's early interventions; he had attended SIRT's meetings, observed interventions, and participated in budgetary decisions. That person served as an effective role sender to the central office.

After desegregation had been satisfactorily achieved, federal funds were withdrawn, and the district ceased to provide funds for released time or for training new members. The cadre no longer met as a formal organization. Milstein told us, however, that the associate superintendent for instruction still called on ex-members of the cadre for help with organizational problems. Milstein's own consultation with the district changed to giving aid with stress reduction, and ex-members of SIRT have often helped him with that consultation.

New South Wales

In 1976, the Director of Services in the New South Wales (Australia) Department of Education circulated a paper to his staff. It proposed that the Division of Services establish consultant teams for school improvement. William Cameron, an officer of the division, proposed to train a team of school heads to act as consultants and change agents to a number of schools. In early 1977, Cameron met with the director of the Macquarie North Region (a fictitious name), and they agreed to mount a project with the following characteristics (this list is abridged from Cameron, 1982):

1. Cameron would train a team of consultants. The team would assist faculties of schools to attain goals they would choose.
2. The consultants would be school heads.
3. The consultants would be released from their regular jobs for one-half day per week to carry out consultation in *other* schools.
4. The consultants would work in *pairs*, each pair to be assigned to one client school during the project.
5. The decision to participate in the project would be made by the school faculties.
6. The schools in the project would not receive any additional resources.
7. The project would run for about two years.

Cameron also obtained the support of the New South Wales Teachers' Federation for the project.

Cameron and the Director of Macquarie North selected three "experimental" schools in which pairs from the consulting team would intervene: Raworth Primary, with thirty faculty members; Blue Gum Primary, with thirty-two; and Redleaf High with seventy-five. They selected four comparison schools: Mountview Primary, with thirty faculty members; Highfield Primary, with twenty-five; Ridgeway Primary, with seventeen; and the Parklands High with seventy. Cameron visited the schools and explained the project to the faculties. He promised every school a survey-data-feedback diagnosis. He promised the experimental schools a weekend retreat and consultant support afterward for about two hours per week for two years. All school faculties voted by large margins to join the project.

The entry phase of the project ran from May to December 1977. It included survey-data-feedback, the selection of consultants, and the weekend retreats.

The Director of Macquarie North submitted to Cameron the names of twenty-five school heads who had been nominated by inspectors of schools. Cameron visited the nominees. From the eleven who were interested, he selected seven who had moderate needs for control, achievement, and affiliation, and who could act in a "reflective and supportive" role with the faculties in the schools. The seven-member consulting team received two days of training in July 1977 and three days near the first of November. Between the two sessions, members of the team carried out the survey-data-feedback on current school operations.

The faculty of each experimental school participated in a weekend retreat for training in problem solving: Raworth on 4–6 November 1977, Blue Gum on 18–20 November, and Redleaf on 2–4 December.

The active problem-solving phase of the project ran from November 1977 to August 1979. Temporary problem-solving groups were formed in each of the experimental schools. They were intended to place emphasis on task (rather than process), to use peer pressure to keep themselves on task, to represent interest groups in the school, and to be a link with the rest of the school. During the active problem-solving phase, the consultants demonstrated their competence as helpers and showed that they could be trusted by the faculties.

Each school formed three problem-solving groups, each group to undertake a particular task, as shown in Table 11-1. The problem-solving groups at the schools carried out a variety of activities that involved all staff members, but particularly the problem-solving group members, in gathering information, making decisions, and taking action. Activities included surveys, inventories, displays, resource purchasing, curriculum developing, role playing, mounting in-service courses, developing teaching aids, role negotiating, and outcome evaluating. Overall, a great deal of energy was expended by school staffs in planning and development in addition to their normal teaching duties.

Table 11-1. Problem-solving Tasks Undertaken by Three Schools in New South Wales

School	Team Number	Number of Members	Task
Raworth	1	9	Resource organization
	2	Unknown	Curriculum development in cultural activities
	3	7	Teaching methods
Blue Gum	1	7	Relationships within and among major work groups
	2	7	Pupil evaluations, including reports to parents
	3	7	Resource organization
Redleaf	1	8	Expectations for faculty
	2	9	Pupil behavior
	3	10	Pupil evaluation

As the time for withdrawal of the consultants approached, Cameron intended for the consultants and their schools to find teachers or others who would serve as internal consultants, gradually taking over the helping role from outside consultants. Little of that happened. In 1980, Cameron visited Redleaf and discovered that "nothing more had happened at the school with regard to collaborative problem solving." Principals at Raworth and Blue Gum, however, did continue to call the Division of Services for materials to aid staff development. Both reported that collaborative activities were continuing; Raworth's principal held another weekend retreat, and Blue Gum's principal asked Cameron for an after-school refresher course in problem solving. As late as March 1981, the two principals reported serving each other as consultants.

Boulder Valley

The cadre in Boulder Valley, Colorado, grew out of the district's Participative Option Development Project. Discussions began in 1970, and funding was obtained in 1974. In 1976, the project staff recruited twenty teachers, counselors, administrators, and parents to become a cadre of part-time OD specialists. The project staff began training the cadre in March 1976, and the cadre began its field work in the spring of 1977. Roark and Davis (1981) report that the cadre carried out thirty-five consultations during its first twelve months of field work.

When a school requested help from the cadre, a team from the cadre and a committee from the school merged to become a planning team to conduct a diagnosis and design the OD. Some examples of the cadre's work were (1) improving working relations among members of a department in a secondary school, (2) surveying community attitudes toward a secondary school, (3) helping a faculty state its goals and helping the principal find ways to aid the faculty in reaching them, (4) training parents as discussion leaders, and (5) facilitating a workshop on competency-based testing for the board of education, the accountability committee, and central-office personnel. Generally, the cadre gave aid in diagnosis, skill training, leadership consultation, planning, and team building. Teams from the cadre ranged in size from one to nine members.

In February 1978, the cadre began training new members. Forty-nine trainees were selected from seventy applicants. The new members came from seven elementary schools, three secondary schools, and the central office. The new members completed their training in January 1979. The district then suffered drastic budget cuts. The cadre did very little work in 1981–1982, and in 1983 it disbanded.

Jefferson County

In 1980, the Boulder Valley cadre helped establish a new cadre in the Jefferson County District—a suburban district west of Denver and the largest district in Colorado.

The Jefferson County District is divided into four areas, and the cadre is divided into four corresponding teams. Area teams meet about every four to six weeks, and the cadre meets as a whole about every two months. The cadre has about eighty members on its roster, of whom approximately forty are active.

The cadre's consulting is paid through individual schools. The district allocates annually $10 per faculty member to each school (a minimum of $300 to small schools) for staff development. The school can use that money to pay the cadre's expenses, including released time.

In 1983, about ten cadre members were working with schools to improve their school climate, seeking especially to change norms that were creating stress. Another project was dealing with drug abuse by establishing faculty teams to plan action in the individual school. Fifty faculty members in twelve schools were engaged in that project; ten of the fifty were cadre members. Many other projects were also in progress.

Polk County

The cadre in Polk County, Florida, came into being about 1977. It contained fourteen people, including the present superintendent. The cadre was expanded and reorganized in 1980–1981. The twenty-four members of the new cadre received training in the summer of 1980. The training used the program called "Preparing Educational Training Consultants" published by the Northwest Regional Educational Laboratory. Another training cycle began in February of 1983; it offered twenty-seven hours of training over a nine-week period. In addition to the twenty-four persons already in the cadre, eight potential recruits were also invited to attend.

The cadre follows the rules of consulting in teams and of refraining from consulting in members' own units. Cadre members volunteer to join consulting teams when the coordinator notifies members of requests. The cadre as a whole meets irregularly, chiefly to receive further training.

The cadre assists schools in assessment, goal setting, and other phases of school improvement. It also offers in-service workshops. In 1983, the district was suffering financial restrictions, and money for released time was not available. Nevertheless, the district office was supporting the cadre in other ways, and the coordinator reported "every possibility for success."

North San Mateo County

In 1977, Rich Gemmet was on the staff of the San Mateo County Office of Education, an office serving twenty-three districts south of San Francisco, California. Gemmet proposed a cadre to two small districts: Millbrae and Burlingame. He attended meetings of principals, teachers, and classified staff in those two districts and recruited twenty-two potential members.

Training for the cadre began in the fall of 1977, running for thirty hours in six evening sessions and using the *Second Handbook of Organization Development in Schools*. In addition, each person completed at least ten hours of internship. At the end, sixteen people chose to continue with the cadre. When, however, Gemmet left in March of 1979 to work in private industry, the cadre languished.

In March 1981, Gemmet returned to the San Mateo County Office as a private consultant. He discovered that fourteen of the original sixteen members wanted to revive the cadre. They brought in other potential members. The new cadre received training in October and November 1981, emphasizing contracting, diagnosis, and macrodesign. By December, with members from the Burlingame, Millbrae, and San Mateo school districts, the new cadre was formally established. In January 1983, the cadre had eighteen members and, Gemmet said, was "strong and healthy."

Redwood City

By January of 1982, news of North San Mateo County's cadre had reached Redwood City, California, in the southern part of the county. Rich Gemmet talked to the superintendent there and then met with the heads of the unions and associations of the teachers, principals, and classified staff. He asked them to invite suitable people to attend the initial cadre training and also held one-hour meetings with the three groups. Twenty-two people attended the six evening training sessions during January and February. Sixteen became cadre members.

The cadre's first projects were with parents' groups. Then, in January 1983, the cadre offered a workshop on problem solving. In addition to the sixteen cadre members, twenty-four other people attended, including some members of the school board. Subsequently, the cadre was asked to facilitate meetings of various kinds. Cadre members rotate among projects.

Gemmet found that the emphases he used in training the cadre for North San Mateo County were not suitable for Redwood City. Participants there were not ready to consider long-term organizational changes. Gemmet replanned the training to emphasize basic facilitation skills.

At this writing, the cadre continues to meet every other month.

Cupertino

In 1978, at the instigation of Associate Superintendent of Instruction William Zachmeier, the Cupertino Union School District established the position of Coordinator of Staff Development and hired Shareen Young for the job. Young built the Cupertino cadre.

Young got nominations for potential cadre members from principals. These recruits received two five-day blocks of training in the summer of 1978; the *Second Handbook of Organization Development in Schools* was used. Of the twenty-five persons attending the training, fourteen became the members of the cadre. Administrators, teachers, classified staff, and parents composed the group. Some further training was given during the cadre's monthly meetings. The cadre began field work in early 1979.

Rosemary Moore was coordinator during 1979–1980. The cadre advertised for new members in October and November 1979 and took in ten. Cadre members received little new training during 1979–1980, though monthly meetings continued.

Joy Weiss was coordinator during 1980–1981. Cadre members received little new training during this year, either. Monthly meetings continued, and in May 1981 the cadre held a retreat for business and group maintenance. During that same month, the cadre took in another ten new members. Of those, four were from the central office, and one was a principal. By August 1981, the cadre had thirty members, of whom twenty-five were active.

Marilyn Miller became coordinator in the fall of 1981. The cadre used 1981–1982 as a time for reorganization and consolidation; it added no new members. During November and December 1982, the cadre took in eight new members and established a training program for itself, with members who were among the original fourteen acting as the core trainers. A membership committee was established to regularize the recruiting procedure. Monthly meetings continued. In January 1983, the cadre had twenty-eight active and six inactive members. The cadre adopted the rule that inactive membership would be limited to one year, after which members would have to become active or resign.

The Cupertino cadre had work waiting for it at the start. School enrollments had been declining, and schools were facing closure or merger. During 1979–1980, the original fourteen members worked with staff, parents, and students to ease the stresses of closures and mergers. They also helped an organization of parents with its meetings. In addition, they taught courses in group dynamics, recommending that intact school groups attend. And they recommended that schools send groups composed of the principal and at least two teachers to the course on effective meetings.

During 1980–1981, the cadre continued its aid to school mergers. Members also facilitated conflict resolution in teaching teams, conflict resolution between staff and administrators, and meetings of the district's management team.

During 1981–1982, the cadre received fewer requests for aid than in earlier years, but its members nevertheless facilitated four school mergers. The superintendent required the principals of the schools to be merged to use the cadre's services at least once. Two of the four used the cadre's services extensively. In addition, in one school, members carried out a six-month project in role clarification.

At various times during its existence, the cadre also helped change teaching techniques in the junior high schools, aided conflict resolution among teaching teams, and gave further help to the parents' organization.

The Cupertino cadre has observed the rules of working in teams and refraining from consultation in members' own units. In addition, the custom has developed of asking that requests from school staff members be routed through the principal so that he or she is sure to be aware of why the cadre members are visiting the school.

The cadre has had the continuing support of the associate superintendent of instruction, who by 1983 had become acting superintendent. Also, the school board has continued to give strong support to staff development. The district has paid for all released time needed. In 1981–1982, as an example, the amount needed came to about $4,000.

Boise

The School Climate Cadre in Boise, Idaho, began as a joint project of the Teacher Resource Center, the Boise Education Association, and the school district. The purpose of the cadre was "to maintain and enhance the working atmosphere of our schools . . . primarily through the initiation of support groups within schools."

In August 1980, the nine-member cadre received its first training, partly from two members of the cadre in Eugene, Oregon. Training covered personal effectiveness, stress management, decision making, and problem solving. During 1980–1981, cadre members gave workshops on those topics to seven hundred members of the district.

In August 1981, the cadre, then numbering twelve, received more training. By October 1981, the cadre contained fourteen members: one assistant superintendent, two facilitators for the gifted and talented, two psychologists, one principal, two assistant principals, three counselors, two teachers, and a half-time coordinator.

In fall, 1982–1983, and again in the spring of that year, the Boise cadre offered, among other courses, one entitled "Management Techniques for a Positive Climate." Several local consultants participated in the instruction. The text used was the *Second Handbook of Organization Development in Schools*. In the fall session, one principal attended with six of his school's teachers.

In a flyer distributed in 1983, the cadre offered workshops in communication skills, effective meetings, team building, reaching consensus, problem solving, conflict resolution, increasing job satisfaction, nutrition, exercise, relaxation, stress and time management, dealing with difficult people, and developing assertive skills.

Though the Boise cadre started by offering workshops, it also began early to prepare itself to conduct OD consultations. In 1981–1982, the staff of an elementary school wanted to learn how to run its own meetings, and the principal approved. The cadre provided consultation to the staff. By the spring, the principal was telling the benefits to other principals.

The cadre's budget, not counting salaries, was $2,000 in 1980–1981, $4,000 in 1981–1982, and $8,000 in 1982–1983. One cadre member said that although the cadre was no doubt in its honeymoon period, everything seemed to be going well so far.

Like most others, the Boise cadre holds meetings monthly.

In the examples above, you can see variations on the prototype we described in the first part of this chapter. Also apparent are differing origins or precipitating conditions and similarities in the cadres' work style.

We have also heard of cadres or cardrelike groups in Santa Cruz and Palo Alto, California, in the provincial department of education in Manitoba, Canada, and in Trondheim, Norway, but we have only vague information about them.

THE DISTRICT'S READINESS FOR A PEER CADRE

Before launching a cadre, whoever is thinking of doing so should examine the clients' readiness in four areas: (1) the district's administrators, (2) the cadre's potential trainers, (3) the cadre's potential membership, and (4) the potential coordinator.

Administrative Readiness

First, as with other programs or projects, establishing a cadre requires the institutional legitimacy that only top-level decision makers can provide. Although a cadre need not be initiated by top administrators (in Eugene, for example, much of the early work to establish the cadre was done by the coordinators of another districtwide project), the superintendent and other key personnel in influential positions should acknowledge the project's usefulness and clearly state their commitment to support it.

Second, top administrators must be clear about where the cadre fits into the overall organizational structure. They must know to whom the cadre will go when it needs to explain its work or to request cooperation, and they must recognize, if the cadre is not to be viewed as simply an extension of top administration, that the cadre services should be equally available to all the district's subsystems.

Third, the superintendent and other central-office administrators should be very clear with the nascent cadre about the amount of money they will commit and then be determined to carry out the commitment. See the figures on budgets given earlier in the chapter.

Fourth, though it is not necessary for district personnel to have had extensive experience with OD, they should be aware of both its costs and benefits. A new cadre will get off to a good start if schools or other district subsystems are ready to ask for consultation as it is formed.

Fifth, administrators should feel a need for change and have confidence that crises can be averted through long-range efforts. Administrators of districts undergoing profound or pervasive crisis may believe they cannot afford the long view. If they believe they cannot, they should delay starting a cadre until emergencies seem less pressing.

Finally, the district must evidence the skills and norms necessary to build and maintain a new subsystem. Are people present who can plan where the new subsystem will fit in relation to other departments, projects, and programs? Are they willing to allocate resources to the project? Are they receptive to the idea of part-time work by cadre members, responsive to the interdependent needs of the new subsystems, and confident that their own resources are necessary?

The Readiness of Trainers

The skills needed in a cadre are best learned in real consultations under the tutelage of one or more experienced consultants who are also good teachers. Trainers should be ready to make a commitment of several months' duration.

Private consultants can serve during the first year of establishing a cadre. They are sometimes hard to find, especially in some locations, but with persistence it is possible to do so. You may not find a consultant nearby who has had experience in schools, but the experience of those who have worked in other human service organizations is often transferable to schools.

As you search for outside consultants, you might call the school districts of the cadres we have described in this chapter to ask them for aid from their own members or for referrals to other consultants. Or you might call the psychology department, sociology department, or college of education at the nearby university. People with the necessary skills can also be found at the Northwest Regional Educational Laboratory in Portland, Oregon.

The three professional organizations named below maintain lists of consultants, some of whom have the necessary skills. You can use these lists to find consultants in your region. Even if you reach people who have had no experience in schools or who show no interest in your project, they might be a good source of referrals.

Director of Program Management
NTL Institute
1501 Wilson Boulevard
P.O. Box 9155, Rosslyn Station
Arlington, VA 22209

Certified Consultants International
P.O. Box 573
Brentwood, TN 37017

The Organization Development Institute
6501 Wilson Mills Road, Suite K
Cleveland, OH 44143

Beginning in 1978, we have sponsored an Annual Conference for Facilitators of OD. This event has been attended by consultants in public and private schools, higher education, social service agencies, government, and industry. The names of those people and others are available from us at

Division of Educational Policy and Management
College of Education
University of Oregon
Eugene, OR 97403

Potential trainers of cadres need information to determine whether the project has clear objectives and goals, the support of key personnel, and other resources required to initiate and sustain a training effort. In exchange, the district's leaders will want to assess the motivation, competencies, and resources of outside consultants before contracting for training. At best, the contract should be a written document detailing the goals of the collaboration between consultant and district, the obligations of each, and a clear statement of the resources (money, prestige, logistical support) being exchanged.

The Readiness of Potential Cadre Members

Two categories of people should exist in a district before a cadre can be launched: individuals who want training and a few groups ready to use the services of a cadre once it is formed. When volunteers for the project are being recruited, it is important to inform the greatest number of people possible, giving potential members a chance to ask questions and to ascertain their commitment. Two-way communication is essential at this point, because many district educators will be unclear about organization development, and especially about the purposes of cadres and their manner of working. Those who view the training as an opportunity for personal growth may lack the commitment to serve as cadre members after training. Others may view the project as only another administrative push toward improving a specific curriculum or implementing another technical innovation.

As potential cadre members are selected for training, at least five considerations are important. First, because they will take on cadre duties in addition to their regular full-time jobs in the district, applicants should demonstrate special motivation and understand the extent of the commitment required of them. Second, potential cadre members should either have some consultation competencies already or have the ability to learn them. While many of the skills can be taught in workshops, the scope of the training task and the amount of time required to prepare the cadre will depend on the trainees' prior level of skill and understanding. Third, applicants should feel optimistic about their ability to influence others and change situations around them. Fourth, people who have previously exhibited leadership ability, who have participated in other innovative projects, who have high visibility in the district, and who have good rapport and a favorable reputation with persons in the administrative and teaching ranks should find it easier to help others.

Finally, the individual criteria for selection should be sufficiently relaxed to enable the creation of a fifteen- to twenty-five-member group representing all important role groups in the district. Role balance is important if cadre members are to help one another understand the district's organizational forces and problems, provide ready-made links to various groups within the district, and reduce the likelihood that they will be perceived as pursuing the interests of any particular group over others. For the same reasons, districts might also pay attention to factors of sex, race, age, years of experience in the district, membership in professional organizations, and building assignment. Some cadres include noncertified staff—secretaries, for example—among their membership. At least one has a parent or two. Expanding cadre membership to include parents and students would add to the task of coordination, but we believe the benefits to be gained would make the experiment worth the effort.

The Coordinator

Once the decision has been made to develop a cadre and firm agreements have been reached between the district and the outside consultants, the district must find someone to build support for the cadre and to recruit potential specialists and clients. This same person should later coordinate the cadre and link the specialists with the outside consultants, with others in the district, and with one another.

In Keele and Eugene, we found that this person had to understand organization development, have experience as a consultant, be familiar with the working arrangements of school districts and cadres, and have the skills necessary to coordinate the efforts of diverse individuals and groups. In addition, we sought a coordinator who had leadership and administrative talents, had earned a high degree of trust and respect from colleagues, and had demonstrated ability in working successfully with others at difficult tasks. Skill as a trainer or consultant is important but not paramount. The critical factor is the person's ability to link the cadre with other district groups and to coordinate its efforts.

People with these qualities are probably rare in school districts, although many of the skills are similar to those needed in convening adult task groups. Districts may look to their own personnel for someone who either has these qualifications or who could be trained to fill the position. A qualified coordinator from outside will need help in becoming settled and familiar with the district.

TRAINING THE CADRE

In training the Keele and Eugene cadres, we had the following four objectives—shared, we believe, by the trainers of the other cadres described above:

1. The cadre was to develop into a cohesive subsystem with clear goals, roles, norms, and procedures both for internal functioning and for delivering consultation within the district.
2. The specialist trainees were to feel enthusiastic about their tasks and their own potential influence as consultants.
3. They were to learn about OD theory, intervention designs, and techniques.
4. They were to develop skills in data collection, communication, problem solving, convening meetings, and managing conflicts, and to convert those skills into strategies and designs for helping others.

During the initial training, cadre members learned about OD by experiencing process analyses during their own team building. They received lecturettes and reading assignments designed to increase cognitive understanding, and the practice and experiential learning were used to teach skills. Most workshop activities were designed to be self-analytic, self-reflexive, and self-directed. Structured activities such as games, simulations, and role playing were used in the early days of training, but were gradually replaced by realistic procedures and skills that would often be more useful for accomplishing actual tasks. Cadre members worked in several different groupings during the initial training, enabling them to become well enough acquainted with one another to build functional interdependence and cohesiveness.

Doing OD in schools has its stressful episodes, which are not usually felt as poignantly by outside consultants. As an example, a principal of an elementary school once called one of our cadres to say that he had arrived that morning to find resignations on his desk from twelve of his teachers. In response, a cadre team interviewed the entire faculty. In a faculty meeting with the principal present, the team members reported the concerns they had discovered. They then helped to resolve the conflicts, and several days later all but two of the twelve teachers withdrew their resignations.

Another example of very high stress occurred in a district when the teachers went on strike. A few teachers and most administrators crossed picket lines to go to work. Some of the members of the cadre in that district found themselves having to look other cadre members in the eye as they crossed the lines. The strike put severe stress on the fabric of the cadre, but their cohesiveness was strong enough to enable them to understand that their conflicts during the strike were due to the system they were all caught in and to the role conflicts it forced upon them. The cadre had to use several of its meetings for members to air their emotions, but it survived the episode as strong as ever.

In addition to difficult consulting tasks and events in a district beyond a cadre's control, the way the cadre is embedded in the district will also bring episodes of stress. For example, supervisors will sometimes show reluctance or will refuse to permit a cadre member released time to carry out a consultation. Cadre members will sometimes find their work as consultants in conflict with that of their regular jobs. And sometimes one member will suddenly get sick and someone else will have to step into a consultation in which he or she does not feel competent.

Because of those inevitable and recurring stresses, it is important that the initial training enable cadre members to come to know one another much more deeply than colleagues at work usually do. They must feel fully confident that they know each other's hope and fears, strengths and weaknesses. They must know on whom they can count and for what. They must know that all the cadre's active members feel devoted to the welfare of the group and to that of its members as friends and admired colleagues. And they must know that when a sudden need arises, any active member will stretch an extra muscle and give up an hour of sleep to get the job done.

Cadre members cannot have those requisite attitudes and that confidence unless it actually becomes true that members will respond to one another's needs with solidarity. The initial training and the cadre's regular self-renewal sessions must enable solidarity to develop and continue. We have, therefore, always taken time in the initial training for participants to debrief thoroughly after the exercises—that is, to tell the feelings they had about one another during the exercise and the feelings they anticipate having about one another in an actual consultation. When a lack of trust or a lack of competence has surfaced, we have arranged further sessions to build new trust or competence. In doing so, we have been explicit about our reasons for making the rearrangements, thus modeling the honesty and openness necessary for maintaining a high level of competence among all members.

In brief, the strong emotions of solidarity become the armor against the strong emotions of threat and conflict the cadre will meet in its work.

MAINTENANCE AND RENEWAL

When a cadre is well trained at the outset, half the battle is won. But the other half—maintaining the strength and resilience of the cadre while replenishing its membership from year to year—goes on forever. We review here the most important matters requiring continued attention.

Structure

The organizational structure of a cadre radiates from the coordinator, who (1) participates as a team member in some of the cadre's consultations; (2) arranges demonstrations for potential clients; (3) assists in the entry and contract-building stages of consultations; (4) coordinates the various consultation teams; (5) explains the goals, methods, and work of the cadre to people in the district or community; (6) arranges for outside consultants when they are required; (7) links the cadre with the central office; and (8) links the cadre to groups outside the district, such as other cadres, universities, the state department of education, and research and development centers.

Every cadre forms committees to help with some of the coordinator's duties and with such tasks as organizing self-renewal sessions and recruiting new members. A cadre of much size, however—say more than ten members—also needs a decision-making body. In Eugene, membership in this body rotates among people currently active in consultation teams. In contrast, the Keele cadre used a four-person group elected at large. This central body, whatever it is called, copes with matters that must be decided between plenary meetings of the cadre. Also, it typically helps in preparing budgets, allocating resources, planning self-renewal events, deciding on responses to requests from clients, and recruiting new members.

When enough money is available, the question usually arises whether it might be advantageous to pay some members to work in their cadre roles half or full time. It might also be advantageous in a cadre of some size to rotate a few half-time assignments. That goes contrary to the egalitarian norm that is often strong in cadres, but it can work if cadre members watch for signs of resentment and cope with them promptly. It is desirable in any case to pay overtime for work outside regular school hours.

Every cadre finds that its members differ a great deal in the amount of time they can give to cadre work. Some find some kinds of work not to their liking. Others find that they had originally overestimated the amount of time people in their regular work units would suffer them to be gone. The Eugene cadre established three formal categories of membership: (1) "active members," those currently consulting in teams and attending most meetings of the cadre; (2) "supporting members," those who attend meetings only occasionally but speak and act in support of the cadre in their own units and elsewhere; and (3) "inactive members," those who have suspended all their activities with the cadre for a limited time. Persons who stop all activity without any estimate of a return date are dropped from the rolls.

Using teams, not individuals, to provide consultation is an important part of the cadre's structure. Working in teams enables cadre members to pool their skills, give one another emotional support, and demonstrate to clients by their own behavior that collaboration among people in different jobs is not only possible but actually enjoyable.

The consulting teams are not permanent. A new one is formed for each consultation. Each member of the cadre works with a variety of colleagues as the months go by. That rotation is one more structural feature that maintains the cohesiveness of the cadre. Using temporary teams also allows new members to join teams as apprentices to get practical experience gradually with helpful colleagues at their elbows.

Support from the Top

Lively support in the central office is vital to the cadre. Such support can help cadre members get released time from their regular jobs. Central-office support can also make a continuing budget more likely and give potential clients more confidence in asking for the cadre's help.

The coordinator is in large part responsible for the vital link between the central office and the cadre. But the coordinator cannot do it alone, and therefore the cadre maintains membership from all ranks in the district. In their regular jobs, cadre members are the grass roots to which most administrators are responsive; they are role senders. Beyond that, the central-office administrators who are also members of the cadre can influence other central-office people directly.

It often happens that central-office people who join a cadre find later that they cannot devote as much time to it as they originally hoped. In both Keele and Eugene, we noted some decrease, after the cadres were first established, in the percentage of central-office administrators active in the cadre's work. Most of the administrators, however, continued to attend meetings often enough to remain well informed about the cadre's doings, and they provided very important support for the cadre among their administrative colleagues. A cadre should cherish and nurture those connections.

Relationships with Clients

Doing good work is essential, of course, though a cadre can overcome the disappointments of some failures, especially if clients enter the consultation with a high awareness of the risks. Beyond good work, however, some other considerations are important.

Awareness. Although the cadre should not press its services on clients, it should advertise itself and give demonstrations of its kind of work. A cadre can use handouts, circulars, announcements in district newsletters, posters, and even slide-tape presentations.

A very effective way for the cadre to build informed awareness is to offer in-service courses in communication and group-process skills. The Eugene cadre has offered three courses of increasing complexity, each made up of ten three-hour sessions. Participants get actual experience with some of the kinds of work the cadre does. They can tell others about that work and about the competence with which the cadre members do it. If the unit in which they work considers asking for the services of a cadre team, participants are likely to show optimism about the cadre's helpfulness. The courses have those outcomes among almost all enrollees, because they acquire practical skills they can put to use quickly.

The Eugene cadre did a good job of building awareness. In a study of that cadre, Burr and Bell (1976) say,

> During the five years of the cadre's tenure, the 35 or 40 people who have been members (approximately two percent of district employees) have exerted a surprising amount of influence on this district of 2,000 staff. The results of the study show that a sizable amount of knowledge exists about the cadre, and 67 percent of their knowledge is accurate. Attitudes toward the cadre are substantially more favorable than unfavorable, particularly in schools where cadre interventions have taken place.

Collaboration. Intervening only when invited to do so lays the necessary foundation for good collaboration between the cadre and its clients. Never acting as a consultant to one's own unit also models collaboration, since the clients see that members of their own group who are also members of the cadre do not therefore set themselves apart, but collaborate with the cadre team just as the client group does.

A cadre maintains collaboration with clients throughout a consultation. Cadre members demonstrate that they value democratic and humanistic relationships by showing in their own behavior with clients the kinds of behavior they hope their clients will emulate: interdependence, collaboration, openness, and the use of rational inquiry for organizing and getting work accomplished. During each step of a consultation, they strive to remain open to feedback concerning their own performance and their helpfulness or unhelpfulness.

Long-term Work. Because organizational problems are a continuing part of school life, they are seldom resolved in a brief workshop; they almost always require extended consultation. Short-term efforts may lead to undesirable consequences. We have learned, for example, that fewer than about twenty-four hours of training with a school staff in communication skills can do more harm than good. Even when a short-term consultation seems highly successful, short-term gains usually fade quickly. Through demonstration and discussion, specialists reveal to potential clients the futility of quick interventions, and they refuse clients who desire one-shot events except as a means of demonstrating longer term consultation.

Telling clients that a short intervention will not get them what they want is discouraging to some clients, but it also impresses them with the cadre's sense of responsibility and integrity. Usually, a request for a short consultation with unrealistic goals can be converted into a short demonstration of the kind of work the cadre does, purposely giving the client direct experience upon which to base the choice of whether to undertake a longer consultation. If the client is still tentative, the consultation can be made tentative also, with the understanding that a new "contract" will be made after each part of a longer play is carried out. But if the client insists on an unrealistic contract, the cadre is better off to refuse it.

When the cadre takes the long-term view, clients know that the cadre cares about their own long-term welfare—that it is not just dipping in for some gain of its own. This stance also conveys to central-office administrators that the cadre cares about the long-term welfare of the district—that it is not just playing around.

Self-renewal

To remain effective, cadres must renew and upgrade their skills. They must be on the lookout for new ideas and methods, and they must solve problems that arise about their own internal coordination and that between themselves and parts of the district. Because they work in teams, each tightly interdependent but rotating in membership, they must do those things as a group. Cadres use monthly meetings on evenings or weekends, occasional seminars, summer workshops, and annual retreats for this sort of renewal.

Cadres periodically hire outside consultants. The outside consultants explain theory and methods of diagnosis or evaluation, show new OD techniques, and serve as facilitators at the cadre's longer convocations. As noted earlier, OD consultants who have worked with schools are hard to find, but it is much easier to find consultants nearby whose skills or experience can be *adapted* to use by the cadre. Cadres have shown themselves very capable of doing that.

The renewal meetings of a cadre differ, of course, from most staff-development activities. The distinguishing features are these:

1. A cadre initiates its own self-improvement. It determines its own needs, recruits its own outside consultants and usually helps design its own training. That fact heightens commitment, readiness to learn, and the readiness of cadre members to apply their learning.
2. The new learning is directed to group functioning, not to individual functioning. Training sessions for a cadre are usually devoted to skills to be exercised in teams, not by individuals.
3. Training sessions are not lectures, but practice. Lecturing and reading are used to illustrate practice, but it is practical skill that is emphasized. Any consultant from outside always has to answer the demand, "All right, that sounds good. Now can you show us how to *do* it?"
4. A cadre deals constantly with interpersonal relations among members. The strong emphasis on collaborative teamwork demands high levels of trust and confidence. If someone fails to do his or her part, others cannot take refuge in the claim that they have done their duty, leaving the weaker member to be cast out by some superior. The solution of the problem always requires airing feelings about how both the stronger and weaker team members act.

Maintaining a skilled, lively, and cohesive cadre takes time. We have some figures from a report made to the district in January 1983 by the coordinator of the Eugene cadre. Between July 1982 and January 1983, the Eugene cadre distributed its person-hours as follows:

Conducting interventions	71	
Planning for interventions	54	
Giving other kinds of consultation	47	
Total for consultations		172
Upgrading members' own skills	123	
Attending to cadre business	229	
Total for maintenance		352

During those months, the Eugene cadre spent about twice as many person-hours on maintenance as on consulting.

Recruiting

Cadres periodically send circulars around the district advertising openings in their ranks. They try to recruit more members than immediate prospects of consultation will require, because (1) having more members than are immediately necessary reduces the shock of sudden overloads, (2) some new members inevitably drop out for various reasons, (3) some become relatively inactive—that is, they become what the Eugene cadre calls supporting members—and (4) it is always useful to have members throughout the district as role senders.

Circulars always include a brief description of the cadre and of OD's goals and techniques. Many people in the district will not be knowledgeable about the cadre's methods, and many will not even have heard of the cadre. The circulars include the coodinator's telephone number, of course, for those who want more information. They may also include an application blank, though that stage can be left for later.

The circular does not ask people to commit themselves to joining the cadre. Rather, it invites them to attend a meeting where they can learn more about the cadre's work and ask questions. Many persons will lose interest after that first meeting. The remainder can be invited to a second meeting to go into more detail, or they can be interviewed individually. After that, a few more will drop away. Some of those who still want to join the cadre will be selected, and others will be advised to prepare themselves by enrolling in the in-service courses conducted by the cadre or by some other means.

Several cadres offer in-service courses both to spread skill in communication and group dynamics (or knowledge about them, at least) around the district and to generate a pool of likely recruits. Most "graduates" of these courses become useful role senders on behalf of the cadre.

OUTSIDE THREATS

Compared with many organizational innovations, cadres seem exceptionally sturdy. Nevertheless, not all cadres have survived the slings and arrows of outrageous fortune. Is it possible to design a cadre or some other arrangement that would be impervious to any possible outside threat? We think not.

Nor do we consider it a good idea to try. No human system is an island. Any human system is shaped not only by itself but also by the other human systems around it. If a school district changes, the cadre must change. If social problems change, districts and cadres must change. As budgets change, a cadre's mode of operation must change. And so on. Our hope in our design of the cadre is not that our ten rules will suffice forever. Rather, we hope that sufficient adaptability grows out of those rules to enable most cadres to bend and evolve, without shattering, as they meet challenges to their capabilities. We do not hope that every cadre will look as it does now twenty years from now—that it will be following the same ten rules. Instead, we hope that school districts will have institutionalized a way to help members deal cooperatively with their own organizational problems. If that kind of mutual help continues and grows, we may still see something recognizable as cadres in school districts twenty years from now, but we may not.

Our society exhibits two strong and opposite trends. One is the growing trend toward local self-sufficiency and participative democracy. That is the trend of which cadres partake. The other is the trend toward centralization and far-flung hierarchy. That is the trend of "big government," litigation, and accountability enforced from the top. When governmental regulations make life more difficult in a school district, they make the work of a cadre more difficult also. When a group of citizens demands that its own idea of education be enforced upon all families, the participative democracy (the nourishing pluralism) of the school district is threatened, and the cadre finds it harder to foster mutual self-help. When the courts issue rulings about what all schools must do, that much local self-sufficiency is nibbled away. We are not here taking sides about any one law, regulation, or court decision. We are pointing out that these two trends oppose each other and that the cadre, along with the school district, is pulled both ways. We think that this two-way tugging is the source of most of the severe conflicts to which districts and cadres must nowadays adapt.

We are often asked how a cadre or any other organizational arrangement can be made invulnerable to the turbulent organizational environment of today. Beyond urging districts (and other organizations) to build in as much adaptability as possible, we do not know the answer to that question. Indeed, we think there is a point of diminishing returns beyond which the effort to make an organization impervious to threat is effort wasted. It is better to turn the effort to sensing environmental trends and searching for ways of coping with new conditions. That may mean letting the old ways "fail" and vanish. The continuity comes in using the lessons learned to build anew. Individuals die, but the species continues. Old ideas become quaint, but the culture remains strong. Adaptability, we think, is not a suit of armor, but a phoenix.

THE ULTIMATE TARGET

Near the beginning of this chapter, we talked about the catcher in the rye. A disturbing aspect of that metaphor is that the catcher stands apart. The catcher is not a member of the group, but assumes the special role of savior, who saves the others from their own inadequacies. The role is paternalistic and even arrogant. When a consultant takes that stance and when the clients accept it, the latter become dependent upon the consultant, and the likelihood dwindles that the clients will ever learn to manage their own affairs. We would like to see school people managing their own affairs, even their own organizational self-renewal. We think the cadre is a large step in that direction.

Nevertheless, the danger remains that cadre members will fall into the same savior role as an outside consultant might. We think cadres can democratize the management of schools best if they encourage their clients in the district to become consultants to themselves in the same way that cadre members become consultants to themselves within the cadre—through open communication, using personal resources as the tasks demand, helping one another apply strengths and strengthen weaknesses, giving the supports of energy and loyalty when stresses mount, and rotating the process roles in helping. Conditions being right, the cadre can teach clients how to do without the cadre. We don't mean to be categorical about this, of course. Cadres do call upon outsiders occasionally to help them in their work, and people in schools should call upon the cadre occasionally even when they are themselves skillful in their own OD. But we want to encourage people all the way down the hierarchy—even students—who would otherwise depend on a catcher, to practice self-help.

At its best, OD offers concepts and procedures to carry democracy into the work place, where people seek achievement and productivity, control over their own work domain, and friendship and affection. To do that in schools, OD should come to include not only administrators and teachers, but also students, parents, classified personnel, and perhaps other citizens with a stake in the community's schools.

What steps might a cadre encourage?

First, the cadre might help principals learn how to initiate and support the norms, structures, and procedures needed for organizational problem solving. Although principals cannot easily remove themselves from the flow of school life, they can start the conditions necessary for communicating, goal setting, problem solving, and decision making.

It is not impossible, in fact, for a principal to step out of the authority position, at least temporarily, to act as a consultant to the staff. In one case we know of, the principal of a high school did just that: for an entire academic year while on sabbatical leave and studying for a doctorate, he served as an organizational consultant to his own staff and student body (for an account, see Flynn, 1976). Data from questionnaires answered by all the staff members indicated that the principal was able to step out of his role and be effective as a consultant with the majority of his staff. Thirty-four of fifty-eight staff members perceived him to be in the role of OD consultant throughout the experimental year; fourteen saw him in a halfway position; and only ten still saw him in the role of principal throughout the consultation. The thirty-four who saw him in the consulting role thought he was more competent, more facilitating, more open, and more willing to let the faculty members find things out for themselves than the last ten did. The latter had difficulty in viewing him as helpful. The evaluation also showed that the staff members' communication improved, their participation in group meetings and their initiation of influence attempts became more widespread, and by the end of the school year they were clarifying and developing a new, more participative decision-making structure.

Second, teachers, counselors, and resource persons might act as OD consultants within their own schools, at least in matters in which they do not have too strong a personal stake. They might act as observers and coaches in Fishbowl arrangements or as conveners or recorders in meetings, and they might regularly model communication skills and helping roles in groups. They might also form helping pairs to facilitate one another's professional growth, both as classroom teachers and as staff members, observing each other, giving each other feedback, and generally supporting one another through personal change.

In relation to OD for the entire school, teachers and others might serve as members of a schoolwide renewal committee to collect data on the systematic effectiveness of the school and to arrange to feed data back to the staff to stimulate collaborative problem solving. A few of the members of the renewal committee might also act as trainers in *S-T-P* problem solving. Goodlad (1984, p. 278) has recommended a similar body.

Third, it is not unreasonable to consider giving parents consultative functions in the school. As an arm of a schoolwide renewal committee, for example, they could collect questionnaire and interview data from other parents and citizens in the community, analyze those data and put them into tables and figures, and present the data to the staff with the collaboration of the principal and teachers. Moreover, parents could participate in staff and team problem solving, adding their thoughts to the general reservoir of ideas obtained during brainstorming. And there could be instances in which parents would be helpful consultants to helping pairs—for example, when a pair is wrestling with ways of increasing the involvement of particular parents in their children's education.

Finally, students remain an untapped resource as consultants to their own schools. At first, that concept sounds crazy, but it seems crazy only when students are viewed as the clients or as the "products" of the school. Consider students as organizational participants in some aspects of schoolwide diagnosis and planning, educational problem solving, and staff decision making. Indeed, a failure to consider students as organizational participants could partly explain low student motivation and high student alienation. Teachers and administrators can become so preoccupied with their own management efforts that they lose touch with the students. For their part, students can feel "put down," even oppressed, by imposed rules and become alienated when their ideas and energies have not been used.

Perhaps the most straightforward procedure for helping students participate in school organization is to use the social studies curriculum. A course has been developed by Arends et al. (1981) to help students understand the dynamics of the school as a formal social organization, to delineate their roles as potential organizational participants, and to teach the students the skills required to design and participate in a schoolwide improvement program. Through experiential activities, reading, and group discussions, students learn how the motives of affiliation, power, and achievement can be satisfied or frustrated through organizational participation. They practice communication skills to facilitate their discussions about interpersonal relations in the school. They explore the roles of individuals, groups, and the organization as a whole in carrying out the school's mission and in satisfying the needs of both students and adults. In one activity, students prepare "maps" of the informal structure of the school, designating the groups in which they spend their time out of school. They compare the maps with rosters of students in classrooms and discuss the congruence of friendship groups with work groups. In another activity, students collect questionnaires about the climate of the school from teachers, administrators, and other students. They analyze the data and present a summary in a colloquium for members of their class and interested adults in the school. That kind of activity offers an entry point for students to act not only as organizational participants, but also as consultants to their own school.

We believe that school participants, including students, can successfully act as OD consultants to themselves and that they can bring into being a self-renewing school without the need for large amounts of outside consultative help. Perhaps the concept of participants as consultants serving themselves is no more radical or outrageous than that of consciously watching the impact of one's own behavior or of being aware collectively of how a system is operating. After all, what the consultant offers is an organizational *mirror*. And once the participants can look at themselves in the mirror, they can manage changes in their own system. Self-renewal, one might say, is simply self-reflection accompanied by concerted, collaborative action to right the wrongs that are discovered. Can participants as consultants to themselves learn to hold up the organizational mirror together? We think they can.

References

Alberti, Robert E., and Michael L. Emmons. *Stand up, speak out, talk back!* New York: Pocket Books, 1975.

Alderfer, Clayton P. An empirical test of a new theory of human needs. *Organizational Behavior and Human Performance*, 1969, *4*, 142–175.

Alderfer, Clayton P. *Existence, relatedness, and growth.* New York: Free Press, 1972.

Alderfer, Clayton P., and L. Dave Brown. *Learning from changing: Organizational diagnosis and development.* Beverly Hills: Sage, 1975.

Allport, Gordon W., and Leo F. Postman. The basic psychology of rumor. *Transactions of the New York Academy of Sciences* (Series 2), 1945, *8*, 61–81.

Alutto, J., and J. Belasco. A typology for participation in organizational decision making. *Administrative Science Quarterly*, 1972, *17*, 117–125.

Amarel, Marianne, E. House, D. Langmeyer, D. Lortie, R. Meyer, L. McLean, and L. Sealey. Reform, response, and renegotiation: Transitions in a school change project. New York: Ford Foundation, 1979. Also available from Ontario Institute for Studies in Education, 252 Bloor Street West, Toronto, Ontario, Canada, M5S 1V6.

Anderson, Gary J. The assessment of learning environments: A manual for the "Learning Environment Inventory" and the "My Class Inventory." Halifax, Nova Scotia: Atlantic Institute of Education, 1973.

Aoki, Ted. Interests, knowledge, and evaluation: Alternative curriculum evaluation orientations. In T. T. Aoki (Ed.), *Curriculum evaluation in a new key.*

Edmonton, Alberta, Canada: Department of Secondary Education, Faculty of Education, University of Alberta, 1984.

Arends, Jane H. Organization development for the staff, parents, and students of an urban junior high school: A case study. Doctoral dissertation, University of Oregon, 1975.

Arends, Richard I., Jane H. Phelps, Martha Harris, and Richard A. Schmuck. *Organization development: Building human systems in schools.* Audio-slide presentation. Eugene, Oregon: Center for Educational Policy and Management, 1973.

Arends, Richard I., Jane H. Phelps, and Richard A. Schmuck. *Organization development: Building human systems in schools.* Eugene, Oregon: Center for Educational Policy and Management, 1973.

Arends, Richard I., R. A. Schmuck, M. Milleman, J. Arends, and J. Wiseman. *School life and organizational psychology.* New York: Teachers College Press, 1981.

Argyris, Chris. *Intervention theory and method: A behavioral science view.* Reading, Mass.: Addison-Wesley, 1970.

Argyris, Chris. Personality and organization theory revisited. *Administrative Science Quarterly,* 1973, *18,* 141–167.

Argyris, Chris. Reflecting on laboratory education from a theory of action perspective. *Journal of Applied Behavioral Science,* 1979, *15*(3), 296–310.

Argyris, Chris, and Donald A. Schön. *Organizational learning.* Reading, Mass.: Addison-Wesley, 1978.

Ary, Donald, Lucy Cheser Jacobs, and Asghar Razavieh. *Introduction to research in education* (2nd ed.). New York: Holt, Rinehart, & Winston, 1979.

Bachman, J., C. Smith, and J. Slesinger. Control performance and satisfaction: An analysis of structural and individual effects. *Journal of Personality and Social Psychology.* 1966, *42,* 127–136.

Bales, Robert F. *Interaction process analysis: A method for the study of small groups.* Reading, Mass.: Addison-Wesley, 1950.

Barker, Roger G., and Paul V. Gump. *Big school, small school: High school size and student behavior.* Stanford, Calif.: Stanford University Press, 1964.

Bass, Bernard. *A program of exercises for management and organizational psychology.* Pittsburgh: Management Development Associates, 1966.

Bassin, Marc, and Thomas Gross. Organization development: A viable method of change for urban secondary schools. Paper read at meeting of the American Educational Research Association, Toronto, 1978.

Bassin, Marc, Thomas Gross, and Patricia Jordan. Developing renewal processes in urban high schools. *Theory into Practice,* 1979, *18*(2), 73–81. Published by the Ohio State University.

Bavelas, Alex. Communication patterns in task-oriented groups. *Journal of the Acoustical Society of America,* 1950, *22,* 725–730.

Beckhard, Richard. *Organization development: Strategies and models.* Reading, Mass.: Addison-Wesley, 1969.

Belasco, J., and J. Alutto. Decisional participation and teacher satisfaction. *Educational Administrative Quarterly,* 1972, *8,* 44–58.

Bell, Warren E. Impact of organization development interventions conducted by an internal cadre of specialists on the organizational processes in elementary schools. Doctoral dissertation, University of Oregon, 1977. University Microfilms No. 780 2504.

Bell, Warren E. Obstacles to urban school renewal. *Theory into Practice*, 1979, *18*(2), 64–72. Published by the Ohio State University.

Bell, Warren E., and Ann M. Burr. The Eugene cadre: An internal group of OD specialists—Their impact on a school district. Eugene, Oregon: Center for Educational Policy and Management, 1976. (Mimeo).

Bell, Warren E., and Spencer H. Wyant. *Diagnosing a school's readiness for change: What to look for when starting an improvement effort* (2nd ed.). Santa Cruz, Calif.: Consulting Exchange, 1981.

Benedict, B. A., P. H. Calder, D. M. Callahan, H. A. Hornstein, and Matthew B. Miles. The clinical experimental method of assessing organizational change efforts. *Journal of Applied Behavioral Science*, 1967, *3*, 347–380.

Berlew, David E. Leadership and organizational excitement. In D. A. Kolb, I. M. Rubin, and J. M. McIntyre (Eds.), *Organizational psychology: A book of readings* (2nd ed.). Englewood Cliffs, N.J.: Prentice-Hall, 1974, pp. 265–277. Also in *California Management Review*, 1974.

Berman, Paul, and Milbrey McLaughlin. *Federal programs supporting educational change. The findings in review* (Vol. 6). Santa Monica, Calif.: Rand, 1975.

Bigelow, Ronald C. Changing classroom interaction through organization development. In R. A. Schmuck and M. B. Miles (Eds.), *Organization development in schools*. Palo Alto, Calif.: National Press Books (now Mayfield), 1971, pp. 71–85.

Boulding, Kenneth. *Ecodynamics*. Beverly Hills, Calif.: Sage, 1978.

Bowers, David G. OD techniques and theory in 23 organizations: The Michigan ICL study. *Journal of Applied Behavioral Science*, 1973, *19*(1), 21–43.

Brass, Daniel J. Structural relationships, job characteristics, and worker satisfaction and performance. *Administrative Science Quarterly*, 1981, *26*(3), 331–348.

Brown, L. Dave. Organizational change from the bottom up. *Education and Urban Society*, 1976, *8*(2), 159–171.

Buckley, Walter. *Sociology and modern systems theory*. Englewood Cliffs, N.J.: Prentice-Hall, 1967.

Buergenthal, D. A., and Michael M. Milstein. Modifications in attitudes, skills, and behaviors of administrators and teachers who are trained as organization development specialists. Paper read at a meeting of the American Educational Research Association, New York, 1977.

Burr, Ann M. The process of a principal's retirement and its effect on a school community. Doctoral dissertation, University of Oregon, 1977.

Burr, Ann M., and Warren E. Bell. The Eugene cadre: An internal group of OD specialists—their impact on a school district. Eugene, Oregon: Center for Educational Policy and Management, 1976. (Mimeo)

Callan, Mary F., and William P. Kentta. A backward glance over traveled roads: An evaluation of the Eugene cadre. Eugene, Oregon: Eugene School District 4J, 1979.

Cameron, William G. The in-service school development project: A case study in consultancy for planned change. Doctoral dissertation, University of New England (Australia), 1982.

Campbell, Donald T., and Julian C. Stanley. Experimental and quasi-experimental designs for research on teaching. In N. L. Gage (Ed.), *Handbook of research on teaching*. Chicago: Rand McNally, 1963, pp. 171–246.

Chapman, David W., and Sigrid M. Hutcheson. Attrition from teaching careers: A discriminant analysis. *American Educational Research Journal*, 1982, *19*(1), 93–105. Copyright 1982, American Educational Research Association, Washington, D.C.

Clark, David L. In consideration of goal-free planning: The failure of traditional planning systems in education. In D. L. Clark, S. McKibbin, and M. Malkas (Eds.), *New perspectives on planning in educational organizations*. San Francisco: Far West Laboratory for Educational Research and Development, 1980, pp. 1–15.

Coad, R. A., C. Miskel, and E. Van Meter. The effects of an organization development program on satisfaction, group process, climate, leadership and student achievement. Paper read at a meeting of the American Educational Research Association, San Francisco, 1976.

Coch, L., and John R. P. French. Overcoming resistance to change. *Human Relations*, 1948, *1*, 512–532.

Cohen, A., and H. Gadon. Changing the management culture in a public school system. *Journal of Applied Behavioral Science*, 1978, *14*(1), 61–78.

Cohen, Michael D., James G. March, and Johan P. Olsen. A garbage can model of organizational choice. *Administrative Science Quarterly*, 1972, *17*, 1–25.

Coleman, James S. Conflicting theories of social change. *American Behavioral Scientist*, 1971, *14*(5), 633–650.

Cooke, Robert A., and Robert J. Coughlan. Developing collective decision-making and problem-solving structures in schools. *Group and Organization Studies*, 1979, *4*(1), 71–92.

Cooperative Project for Educational Development (COPED, 3 vols.; final report of Project No. 8-0069 to the U.S. Office of Education under Grant No. OEG-3-8-080069-0043 [010]). Washington, D.C.: U.S. Office of Education, 1970.

Corprew, James C., and Herbert J. Davis. An organizational development (OD) effort to improve instruction at a university, with suggestions for successful implementation. *Educational Technology*, 1975, *15*(9), 41–44.

Croft, John C. Organizational development for Thornlea: A communication package and some results. *Journal of Applied Behavioral Science*, 1970, *6*, 93–106.

Croft, John C. Organization development and the planning interface. Toronto, Ontario, Canada: Ontario Institute for Studies in Education, 1971. (Mimeo.)

Cronbach, Lee J. (with the assistance of Karen Shapiro). *Designing evaluations of educational and social programs*. San Francisco: Jossey-Bass, 1982.

Davis, Louis E., and Albert B. Cherns (Eds.). *The quality of working life. Volume 1: Problems, prospects, and the state of the art*. New York: Free Press, 1975.

Davison, Ronald G., and Paul D. Longhofer. Organizational development training: A case study. *Educational Considerations*, 1977, *5*(1), 8–13.

DeCharms, Richard. *Personal causation*. New York: Academic Press, 1968(a).

DeCharms, Richard. Personal causation training in the schools. *Journal of Applied Social Psychology*, 1968(b), *2*(2), 95–113.

DeCharms, Richard. *Enhancing motivation: Change in the classroom.* New York: Irvington (distributed by Halstead Press), 1976.

Derr, C. Brooklyn. Organizational development in one large urban school system. *Education and Urban Society,* 1970, *2,* 403–419.

Derr, C. Brooklyn. Organization development and PPB for education. Paper read at the convention of the American Educational Research Association, 1971(a).

Derr, C. Brooklyn. An organizational analysis of the Boston School Department. Doctoral dissertation, School of Education, Harvard University, 1971(b).

Derr, C. Brooklyn. Conflict resolution in organizations: Views from the field of educational administration. *Public Administration Review,* 1972(a), *32*(5), 495–501.

Derr, C. Brooklyn. Surfacing and managing organizational power. *OD Practitioner,* 1972(b), *4*(2), 1–4.

Derr, C. Brooklyn. Successful entry as a key to successful organization development in big city school systems. In W. W. Burke and H. A. Hornstein (Eds.), *Social technology of organization development.* Fairfax, Va.: NTL Learning Resource Corp., 1972(c), pp. 41–52.

Dillon-Peterson, Patty (Ed.). *Staff development and organization development.* Alexandria, Va.: Association for Supervision and Curriculum Development, 1981.

Doll, Russell C., Barbara J. Love, and Daniel U. Levine. Systems renewal in a big-city school district: The lessons of Louisville. *Phi Delta Kappan,* 1973, *54*(8), 524–534.

Dowling, William F. Conversation: An interview with Fletcher Byrom. *Organizational Dynamics,* 1978, *7*(1), 37–60.

Duffin, Richard, Arnold Falusi, and Philip Lawrence. Organization development. Part 1: What's it all about? *School Progress* (Toronto), 1972, *41*(9), 34–36. Part 2: Problems can only be solved from the inside, 1972, *41*(10), 52–64.

Duncan, Robert B., Susan A. Mohrman, Allan M. Mohrman, Robert A. Cooke, and Gerald Zaltman. *An assessment of a structural task approach to organizational development in a school system* (final report to the National Institute of Education under Grant No. 6-003-0172). Evanston, Ill.: Northwestern University, 1977.

Ely, Vivian King. Collaboration for planned organizational change in a state vocational education agency. Doctoral dissertation, North Carolina State University at Raleigh, 1975.

Feitler, Fred C., and Lawrence L. Lippitt. A multi-district organizational effort. *Educational Technology,* 1972, *12*(10), 34–38.

Flanders, Ned A. Some relationships among teacher influences, pupil attitudes, and achievement. In B. J. Biddle and W. J. Ellena (Eds.), *Contemporary research on teacher effectiveness.* New York: Holt, Rinehart, & Winston, 1964, pp. 196–231.

Flanders, Ned A. *Analyzing classroom interaction.* Reading, Mass.: Addison-Wesley, 1969.

Flynn, C. Wayne. The principal as an organizational consultant to his own school. Doctoral dissertation, University of Oregon, 1971.

Flynn, C. Wayne. Management effectiveness by organizational development.

Bulletin of the National Association of Secondary-School Principals, 1974, *58*(382), 136–141.

Flynn, C. Wayne. Collaborative decision making in a secondary school: An experiment. *Education and Urban Society,* 1976, *8*(2), 172–182.

Foa, Uriel G. Convergences in the analysis of the structure of interpersonal behavior. *Psychological Review,* 1961, *68*, 341–353.

Foa, Uriel G., and Edna B. Foa. *Societal structures of the mind.* Springfield, Ill.: Charles C. Thomas, 1974.

Fosmire, Fred R. Some TDL-VOCOM tasks and their use in education and research. Psychology Department, University of Oregon, 1970.

Fosmire, Fred, and Carolin Keutzer. Task-directed learning: A systems approach to marital therapy. Paper presented at the meeting of the Oregon Psychological Association and the Western States Psychological Association, May 1968.

Fosmire, Fred, Carolin Keutzer, and Richard Diller. Starting up a new senior high school. In R. A. Schmuck and M. B. Miles (Eds.), *Organization development in schools.* Palo Alto, Calif.: National Press Books (now Mayfield), 1971, pp. 87–112.

Fox, Robert, R. A. Schmuck, E. Van Egmond, M. Ritvo, and C. Jung. *Diagnosing professional climate of schools.* Fairfax, Va.: NTL Learning Resource Corp., 1973.

Francisco, Richard P. The Documentation and Technical Assistance Project in urban schools. *Theory into Practice,* 1979, *18*(4), 89–96. Published by the Ohio State University.

French, John R. P., and Bertram H. Raven. The bases of social power. In D. Cartwright (Ed.), *Studies in social power.* Ann Arbor: University of Michigan Press, 1959, pp. 150–167.

Fullan, Michael, Matthew B. Miles, and Gib Taylor. *OD in schools: The state of the art* (5 vols.; final report to the National Institute of Education under contract Nos. 400-77-0051 and 400-77-0052). Toronto: Ontario Institute for Studies in Education, 1978. Three extractions from the original report appear elsewhere: (1) M. Fullan and M. B. Miles. OD in schools: The state of the art. In W. W. Burke (Ed.), *The cutting edge: Current theory and practice in organization development.* San Diego, Calif.: University Associates, 1978, pp. 149–174. (2) M. Fullan, M. B. Miles, and G. Taylor. Organization development in schools: The state of the art. *Review of Educational Research,* 1980, *50*(1), 121–183. (3) M. B. Miles and M. Fullan. The nature and impact of organization development in schools. In M. M. Milstein (Ed.), *Schools, conflict, and change.* New York: Teachers College Press, 1980, pp. 72–95.

Gardner, John. *Self-renewal: The individual and the innovative society.* New York: Harper & Row, 1963.

Gentry, Joe E., and J. Foster Watkins. Organizational training for improving race relations. In C. B. Derr (Ed.), *Organizational development in urban school systems.* Beverly Hills, Calif.: Sage, 1974, pp. 138–152.

Gibb, Jack R. Defensive communication. *Journal of Communication,* 1961, *11*, 141–148.

Goodlad, John. *A place called school.* New York: McGraw-Hill, 1984.

Goodson, Max R., and Warren O. Hagstrom. Using teams of change agents. In R. A. Schmuck and M. B. Miles (Eds.), *Organization development in schools.* Palo Alto, Calif: National Press Books (now Mayfield), 1971, pp. 155–184.

Gross, Thomas Frank. Illusions, crisis, awareness, and realignment: A case study of an organizational change project and a model of the consultant-client relationship. Doctoral dissertation, Harvard University, 1980.

Guba, Egon G., and Yvonna S. Lincoln. *Effective evaluation: Improving the usefulness of evaluation results through responsive and naturalistic approaches.* San Francisco: Jossey-Bass, 1981.

Hackman, J. Richard, and Greg R. Oldham. *Work redesign.* Reading, Mass.: Addison-Wesley, 1980.

Hale, James R., and R. Allen Spanjer. *Systematic and objective analysis of instruction training manual.* Portland, Oregon: Northwest Regional Educational Laboratory, 1972.

Hall, Jay. *Systems maintenance: Gatekeeping and the involvement process.* Monroe, Texas: Teleometrics International, 1969.

Hall, Jay. Decisions, decisions, decisions. *Psychology Today,* 1971, *5,* 51–54, 86, 88.

Harrison, Roger. Choosing the depth of organizational intervention. *Journal of Applied Behavioral Science,* 1970, *6,* 181–202.

Harrison, Roger. Role negotiation: A tough-minded approach to team development. In W. W. Burke and H. A. Hornstein (Eds.), *The social technology of organization development.* Fairfax, Va.: NTL Learning Resources Corporation, 1972, pp. 84–96. Another version appears in R. T. Golembiewski and W. B. Eddy (Eds.), *Organization development in public administration, Part 2.* New York: Marcel Dekker, 1978.

Harrison, Roger. *Materials for a training program in Personal Power and Influence.* Plymouth, Mass.: Situation Management Systems, 1977.

Harrison, Roger. How to design and conduct self-directed learning experiences. *Group and Organization Studies,* 1978, *3*(2), 149–167.

Harrison, Roger. A practical model of motivation and character development. In J. W. Pfeiffer and J. E. Jones (Eds.), *1979 Handbook for group facilitators.* San Diego, Calif.: University Associates, 1979, p. 207–220.

Harrison, Roger, and Jim Kouzes. The power potential of organization development. *Training and Development Journal,* 1980 (April), 44–47.

Hatley, Richard V., and Michael J. Tull. Effects of organization development of teacher effectiveness and teacher–student relationships. *Southern Journal of Educational Research,* 1978, *12*(3), 125–150.

Hedberg, Bo L. T., Paul C. Nystrom, and William H. Starbuck. Camping on seesaws: Prescriptions for a self-designing organization. *Administrative Science Quarterly,* 1976, *21,* 41–64.

Hirschman, Albert O. *Exit, voice, and loyalty.* Cambridge, Mass.: Harvard University Press, 1970.

Hornstein, H., D. Callahan, E. Fisch, and B. Benedict. Influence and satisfaction in organizations: A replication. *Sociology of Education,* 1968, *412,* 380–389.

House, Ernest R. *Evaluating with validity.* Beverly Hills, Calif.: Sage, 1980.

Jackson, Philip W. *Life in classrooms.* New York: Holt, Rinehart, & Winston, 1968.

Jamieson, David W. Organizational change and development in schools: An assessment of a structural-process strategy for redesigning and developing the management system. Doctoral dissertation, University of California at Los Angeles, 1976.

Janis, Irving L. *Victims of groupthink.* Boston: Houghton Mifflin, 1972.

Johnson, David W., and Frank P. Johnson. *Joining together: Group theory and group skills* (1st and 2nd eds.). Englewood Cliffs, N.J.: Prentice-Hall, 1975 and 1982.

Johnson, David W., and Roger T. Johnson. *Learning together and alone: Cooperation, competition, and individualization.* Englewood Cliffs, N.J.: Prentice-Hall, 1975.

Jung, John. *The experimenter's challenge: Methods and issues in psychological research.* New York: Macmillan, 1982.

Katz, Daniel, and Robert L. Kahn. *The social psychology of organizations* (1st ed.). New York: Wiley, 1966.

Katz, Elihu. The two-step flow of communication: An up-to-date report on an hypothesis. *Public Opinion Quarterly,* 1957, *21,* 68–78.

Kelsh, Bruce. Effects of a teachers' strike on an organization development cadre. Doctoral dissertation, University of Oregon, 1983.

Keutzer, Carolin S., Fred R. Fosmire, Richard Diller, and Mary Dell Smith. Laboratory training in a new social system: Evaluation of consulting relationship with a high school faculty. *Journal of Applied Behavioral Science,* 1971, *7*(4), 493–501.

Keys, Chris B. Renewal processes in urban parochial schools. *Theory Into Practice,* 1979, *18*(2), 97–105. Published by the Ohio State University.

Keys, Chris B., and Jean M. Bartunek. Organization development in schools: Goal agreement, process skills, and diffusion of change. *Journal of Applied Behavioral Science,* 1979, *15*(1), 61–78.

Keys, Chris B., and R. L. Kreisman. Organization development, classroom climate, and grade level. *Group and Organization Studies,* 1978, *8*(2), 224–238.

Kidder, Louise H. *Selltiz, Wrightsman and Cook's research methods in social relations.* New York: Holt, Rinehart, & Winston, 1981.

Knutson, Andie L. Quiet and vocal groups. *Sociometry,* 1960, *23,* 36–49.

Koberg, Don, and Jim Bagnall. *The universal traveler.* Los Altos, Calif.: William Kaufmann, 1974.

Kouzes, James M., and Paul R. Mico. Domain theory: An introduction to organizational behavior in human service organizations. *Journal of Applied Behavioral Science,* 1979, *15*(4), 449–469.

Krell, Terence C. The marketing of organization development: Past, present, and future. *Journal of Applied Behavioral Science,* 1981, *17*(3), 309–329.

Lake, Dale G., and Daniel M. Callahan. Entering and intervening in schools. In R. A. Schmuck and M. B. Miles (Eds.), *Organization development in schools.* Palo Alto, Calif.: National Press Books (now Mayfield), 1971, pp. 139–153.

Langmeyer, Daniel. An exploratory study of group effectiveness using two tasks and three populations differing in organizational history. Doctoral dissertation, University of Oregon, 1968.

Langmeyer, Daniel, Leonard Lansky, and W. Brendan Reddy. Organizational training in subsystems of a Midwest school district. In William Claiborn and Robert Cohen (Eds.), *School intervention* (Vol. I). New York: Behavioral Publications, 1973, pp. 191–205.

Lawrence, P. R., and J. W. Lorsch. *Organizations and environment: Managing differentiation and integration.* Boston: Harvard Business School, Division of Research, 1967.

Leary, Timothy. *Interpersonal diagnosis of personality.* New York: Ronald, 1957.

Leavitt, Harold J. Some effects of certain communication patterns on group performance. *Journal of Abnormal and Social Psychology*, 1951, *46*, 38–50.

Leavitt, Harold J., and Ronald Mueller. Some effects of feedback on communication. *Human Relations*, 1951, *4*, 401–410.

Lehman, Linda. Organizational change and the teacher. *Educational Technology*, 1972, *12*(10), 52–54.

Lewin, K. *Field theory in the social sciences.* New York: Harper & Row, 1951.

Lewin, Kurt, Ronald Lippitt, and Ralph K. White. Patterns of aggressive behavior in experimentally created "social climates." *Journal of Social Psychology*, 1939, *10*, 271–299.

Likert, Rensis. *New patterns of management.* New York: McGraw-Hill, 1961.

Likert, Rensis. *The human organization: Its management and value.* New York: McGraw-Hill, 1967.

Likert, Rensis, and Jane Gibson Likert. A method for coping with conflict in problem-solving groups. *Group and Organization Studies*, 1978, *3*(4), 427–434.

Longabaugh, Richard. A category system for coding interpersonal behavior as social exchange. *Sociometry*, 1963, *26*, 319–344.

Longabaugh, Richard. The structure of interpersonal behavior. *Sociometry*, 1966, *29*(4), 441–460.

Lortie, Dan C. *School-teacher: A sociological study.* Chicago: University of Chicago Press, 1975.

Luft, Joseph. *Group processes: An introduction to group dynamics* (3rd ed). Palo Alto, Calif.: Mayfield, 1984.

Luke, Robert A., Jr., and Dorothy Mial. An emergent interuniversity consortium for educational change. *Journal of Applied Behavioral Science*, 1971, *7*, 194–214.

Macbeth, Paul R. Preparing organizational specialists for a school district: Some effects of laboratory training within an organizational development project. Doctoral dissertation, University of Oregon, 1971.

McClelland, David C. Methods of measuring human motivation. In J. W. Atkinson (Ed.), *Motives in fantasy, action, and society.* New York: Van Nostrand, 1958, pp. 7–42.

McClelland, David C., J. W. Atkinson, R. A. Clark, and E. L. Lowell. *The achievement motive.* New York: Appleton-Century-Crofts, 1953.

McElvaney, Charles T., and Matthew B. Miles. Using survey feedback and consultation. In R. A. Schmuck and M. B. Miles (Eds.), *Organization development in schools.* Palo Alto, Calif.: National Press Books (now Mayfield), 1971, pp. 113–138.

McGregor, Douglas. *The professional manager.* New York: McGraw-Hill, 1967.

McMillan, Charles B. Organizational change in schools: Bedford-Stuyvesant. *Journal of Applied Behavioral Science*, 1975, *11*(4), 437–453.

Maier, Norman R. F. *Problem solving and creativity*. Belmont, Calif.: Brooks/Cole, 1970.

Manno, A. O. Group interaction as a means of inducing innovative teaching in elementary schools. Doctoral dissertation, Teachers College, Columbia University, 1969.

March, James G., and J. P. Olsen. *Ambiguity and choice in organizations*. Bergen, Norway: Universitetsforlaget, 1976.

March, James, and H. Simon. *Organizations*. New York: Wiley, 1958.

Maslow, A. J. *Motivation and personality*. New York: Harper & Row, 1954.

Meyer, John W., and Brian Rowan. Institutionalized organizations: Formal structure as myth and ceremony. *American Journal of Sociology*, 1977, *83*(2), 440–463.

Meyer, John W., and Brian Rowan. The structure of educational organizations. In M. W. Meyer and Associates, *Environments and organizations*. San Francisco: Jossey-Bass, 1978, pp. 78–109.

Miles, Matthew B. Organizational development in schools: The effects of alternate strategies of change. New York: Horace Mann-Lincoln Institute of School Experimentation, Teachers College, Columbia University, 1963. (Mimeographed research proposal.)

Miles, Matthew B. Planned change and organizational health: Figure and ground. In R. O. Carlson, A. Gallagher, Jr., M. B. Miles, R. J. Pellegrin, and E. M. Rogers (Eds.), *Change processes in the public schools*. Eugene, Oregon: CASEA (now Center for Educational Policy and Management), 1965, pp. 11–34.

Miles, Matthew B. Critique: Diffusing OD in schools. *Education and Urban Society*, 1976, *8*(2), 242–254.

Miles, Matthew B., P. H. Calder, H. A. Hornstein, D. M. Callahan, and R. S. Schiavo. Data feedback and organizational change in a school system. Paper read at meeting of the American Sociological Association, 1966.

Miles, Matthew B., Michael Fullan, and Gib Taylor. *OD in schools: The state of the art. OD consultants and OD programs in school districts* (Vol. III). Toronto, Ontario, Canada: Ontario Institute for Studies in Education, 1973.

Miles, Matthew B., Michael Fullan, and Gib Taylor. *OD in schools: The state of the art. Implications for policy, research and practice* (Vol. V). Toronto, Ontario, Canada: Ontario Institute for Studies in Education, 1978.

Miles, Mathew B., H. A. Hornstein, D. M. Callahan, P. H. Calder, and R. S. Schiavo. The consequences of survey feedback: Theory and evaluation. In W. G. Bennis, K. D. Benne, and R. Chin (Eds.), *The planning of change* (2nd ed.). New York: Holt, Rinehart, & Winston, 1969, pp. 457–468.

Miles, Matthew B., and Richard A. Schmuck. Improving schools through organization development: An overview. In R. A. Schmuck and M. B. Miles (Eds.), *Organization development in schools*. Palo Alto, Calif.: National Press Books (now Mayfield), 1971, pp. 1–27.

Miller, James G. *Living systems*. New York: McGraw-Hill, 1978.

Milstein, Michael M. Evolution of an internal change team: Expectations, design, and reality. Paper read at meeting of the American Educational Research Association, Toronto, Ontario, Canada, 1978.

Milstein, Michael M. Developing a renewal team in an urban school district. *Theory into Practice*, 1979, *18*(4), 106–113. Published by the Ohio State University.

Milstein, Michael M., and Paul A. Lafornara. The institutionalization of an internal change agent team: The Buffalo experience. Paper presented to the annual meeting of the American Educational Research Association, 1980.

Mohrman, Allan M., Jr., Robert A. Cooke, and Susan Albers Mohrman. Participation in decision making: A multidimensional perspective. *Educational Administration Quarterly*, 1978, *14*(1), 13–29.

Mohrman, Susan A., Allan M. Mohrman, Robert A. Cooke, and Robert B. Duncan. A survey-feedback and problem solving intervention in a school district. In P. Mirvis and D. Berg (Eds.), *Failures in organization development and change*. Toronto: Wiley-Interscience, 1977.

Murray, Donald G. Organizational development training for adopting multi-unit structure: A comparative case study of two elementary schools. Doctoral dissertation, University of Oregon, 1973.

Nachimas, David, and Chava Nachimas. *Research methods in the social sciences.* New York: St. Martin's Press, 1981.

Nelson, Jack E. Collegial supervision in multiunit schools: A study of an inservice program for primary teachers in newly formed units in schools which have received two forms of organizational development training. Doctoral dissertation, University of Oregon, 1971.

Nord, Walter R. Job satisfaction reconsidered. *American Psychologist*, 1977, *32*(12), 1026–1035.

Osgood, Charles E., and George J. Suci. Factor analysis of meaning. *Journal of Experimental Psychology*, 1955, *50*, 325–338. Reprinted in James G. Snider and Charles E. Osgood (Eds.), *Semantic differential technique: A sourcebook.* Chicago: Aldine, 1969, pp. 42–55.

O'Toole, James (Ed.). *Work and the quality of life.* Cambridge, Mass.: MIT Press, 1974.

O'Toole, James, and others. *Work in America.* Cambridge, Mass.: MIT Press, 1973.

Papagiannis, George J., Steven J. Klees, and Robert N. Bickel. Toward a political economy of educational innovation. *Review of Educational Research*, 1982, *52*(2), 245–290.

Patton, Michael Quinn. *Utilization-focused evaluation.* Beverly Hills, Calif.: Sage, 1978.

Pfeiffer, J. William, and John E. Jones (Eds.). *Handbook of structured experiences for human relations training* (Vols. I through IX). San Diego, Calif.: University Associates, 1969–present.

Pfeiffer, J. William, and John E. Jones (Eds.). *Annual handbook for group facilitators.* San Diego, Calif.: University Associates, 1972–present.

Phelps, Jane H., and Richard I. Arends. Helping parents and educators to solve school problems together: An application of organization development. (Technical report.) Eugene, Oregon: Center for Educational Policy and Management, 1973. Reprinted as "Bringing a school staff and parents into effective interaction" by Arends and Arends, in Schmuck, Runkel, Arends, and Arends, 1977, pp. 448–456.

Pilon, Daniel H., and William H. Bergquist. *Consultation in higher education: A handbook for practitioners and clients.* Washington, D.C.: Council for the Advancement of Small Colleges, 1979.

Poole, Edward Archie. A study of the effects of an organizational problem-solving intervention strategy on the development of self-renewing characteristics of a school faculty. Doctoral dissertation, Indiana University, 1971.

Porterfield, Robert W., and Illah J. Porterfield. School-based renewal coordinators. *Theory into Practice,* 1979, *18*(4), 82–88. Published by the Ohio State University.

Roark, Albert E., and Wallace E. Davis, Jr. Staff development and organizational development. In P. Dillon-Peterson (Ed.), *Staff development and organization development.* Alexandria, Va.: Association for Supervision and Curriculum Development, 1981, pp. 37–57.

Rogers, C. R. *Freedom to learn.* Columbus, Ohio: Charles E. Merrill, 1969.

Ross, F. D., and Terrence E. Deal. The effects of an externally directed organizational change intervention on the structure of a small elementary school district. Paper read at meeting of the American Educational Research Association, San Francisco, 1976.

Runkel, Philip J. Conditions for success and failure of organizational development in schools. *CEDR Quarterly,* 1975, *18*(4), 6–10.

Runkel, Philip J., and Warren E. Bell. Some conditions affecting a school's readiness to profit from OD training. *Education and Urban Society,* 1976, *8*(2), 127–144.

Runkel, Philip J., and Pamela Harris. *Bibliography of organizational change in schools: Selected, annotated, and indexed.* Eugene, Oregon: Center for Educational Policy and Management, 1983.

Runkel, Philip J., and Joseph E. McGrath. *Research on human behavior: A systematic guide to method.* New York: Holt, Rinehart, & Winston, 1972.

Runkel, Philip J., and Richard A. Schmuck. Review of research findings. In R. A. Schmuck, P. J. Runkel, J. H. Arends, and R. I. Arends, *Second handbook of organization development in schools.* Palo Alto, Calif.: Mayfield, 1977, pp. 33–38.

Runkel, Philip J., and Richard A. Schmuck. Group processes. In H. E. Mitzel (Ed.), *Encyclopedia of educational research* (5th ed.). New York: Macmillan, 1982.

Runkel, Philip J., Richard A. Schmuck, Jane H. Arends, and Richard P. Francisco. *Transforming the school's capacity for problem solving.* Eugene, Oregon: Center for Educational Policy and Management, 1979.

Runkel, Philip J., Spencer H. Wyant, and Warren E. Bell. *Organizational specialists in a school district: Four years of innovation.* Eugene, Oregon: Center for Educational Policy and Management, 1975. (ERIC order No. 111 107.)

Runkel, Philip J., Spencer H. Wyant, Warren E. Bell, and Margaret Runkel. *Organizational renewal in a school district: Self-help through a cadre of organizational specialists.* Eugene, Oregon: Center for Educational Policy and Management, 1980.

Salinger, J. D. *The catcher in the rye.* Boston: Little, Brown, 1951.

Saturen, Steven L. On the way to adaptability: Some conditions for organizational self-renewal in elementary schools. Doctoral dissertation, University of Oregon, 1972.

Saturen, Steven L. OD in Adams County School District No. 50. *Education and Urban Society*, 1976, *8*(2), 196–212.

Schein, Edgar H. *Organizational psychology.* Englewood Cliffs, N.J.: Prentice-Hall, 1965.

Schein, Edgar H. *Process consultation: Its role in organization development.* Reading, Mass.: Addison-Wesley, 1969.

Scheinfeld, Daniel. A design for renewing urban elementary schools. *Theory Into Practice*, 1979, *18*(2), 114–125. Published by the Ohio State University.

Schindler-Rainman, Eva, Ronald Lippitt, and J. Cole. *Taking your meetings out of the doldrums.* Columbus, Ohio: Association of Professional Directors, 1975.

Schmidt, W., and Robert Tannenbaum. How to choose a leadership pattern. *Harvard Business Review*, 1958, *36*, 95–101.

Schmuck, Richard A. Bringing parents and students into school management. In C. B. Derr (Ed.), *Organizational development in urban school systems.* Beverly Hills, Calif.: Sage, 1974.

Schmuck, Richard A. Peer consultation for school improvement. In C. L. Cooper and C. P. Alderfer (Eds.), *Advances in experiential social processes.* Sussex, England: Wiley, 1977, pp. 137–159.

Schmuck, Richard A. District cadres of OD consultants. In J. Alpert (Ed.), *Psychological consultation to schools: Case studies.* San Francisco: Jossey-Bass, 1982, pp. 247–274.

Schmuck, Richard A. Characteristics of the autonomous school. In D. Hopkins and M. Wideen (Eds.), *Alternative perspectives on school improvement.* Lewes, East Sussex, England: Falmer Press, 1984, pp. 21–32.

Schmuck, Richard A. Participants as consultants to themselves. In G. S. Harman and R. H. Millikan (Eds.), *Perspectives on educational consultation.* In press.

Schmuck, Richard A., and Matthew B. Miles (Eds.). *Organization development in schools.* Palo Alto, Calif.: National Press Books (now Mayfield), 1971. Reprinted in 1975 by University Associates with an annotated bibliography that includes reports of research published since 1971.

Schmuck, Richard A., Donald Murray, Mary Ann Smith, Mitchell Schwartz, and Margaret Runkel. *Consultation for innovative schools: OD for multiunit structure.* Eugene, Oregon: Center for Educational Policy and Management, 1975.

Schmuck, Richard A., and Philip J. Runkel. *Organizational training for a school faculty.* Eugene, Oregon: Center for Educational Policy and Management, 1970.

Schmuck, Richard A., Philip J. Runkel, Jane H. Arends, and Richard I. Arends. *Second handbook of organization development in schools.* Palo Alto, Calif.: Mayfield, 1977.

Schmuck, Richard A., Philip J. Runkel, and Daniel Langmeyer. Improving organizational problem solving in a school faculty. *Journal of Applied Behavioral Science*, 1969, *5*(4), 455–482.

Schmuck, Richard A., Philip J. Runkel, Steven L. Saturen, Ronald T. Martell, and C. Brooklyn Derr. *Handbook of organization development in schools.* Palo Alto, Calif.: National Press Books (now Mayfield), 1972.

Schmuck, Richard A., and Patricia A. Schmuck. *A humanistic psychology of education: Making the school everybody's house.* Palo Alto, Calif.: Mayfield, 1974.

Schmuck, Richard A., and Patricia A. Schmuck. *Group processes in the classroom* (4th ed.). Dubuque, Iowa: Wm. C. Brown, 1983.

Scriven, Michael. Goal-free evaluation. In E. R. House (Ed.), *School evaluation: The politics and process.* Berkeley, Calif.: McCutcheon, 1973.

Shalaway, Linda. Schools can create delinquency. *Educational R & D Report,* 1982–1983, *5*(4), 2–6.

Simon, Anita, and E. G. Boyer (Eds.). *Mirrors for behavior.* Philadelphia: Research for Better Schools, 1967.

Simon, Julian L. *Basic research methods in social science* (2nd ed.). New York: Random House, 1978.

Simon, S. B., L. W. Howe, and H. Kirschenbaum. *Values clarification: A handbook of practical strategies for teachers and students.* New York: Hart, 1972.

Simons, David L. Durability of organizational training for a school faculty. Doctoral dissertation, University of Oregon, 1974.

Smith, Mary Ann. A comparison of two elementary schools involved in a major organizational change, or You win a few; you lose a few. Doctoral dissertation, University of Oregon, 1972.

Smith, Gerald R., Thomas B. Gregory, and Richard C. Pugh. Meeting student needs: Evidence for the superiority of alternative schools. *Phi Delta Kappan,* 1981, *62*(8), 561–564.

South, Oron. Diffusing a system. *Education and Urban Society,* 1976, *8*(2), 183–195.

Stake, Robert E. (Ed.). *Evaluating the arts in education: A responsive approach.* Columbus, Ohio: Merrill, 1975.

Starling, William. An unsuccessful attempt to implement an educational innovation: A case study. Doctoral dissertation, University of Oregon, 1973.

Steefel, Nina, Mary Cook, and Brooks Brophy. Eugene cadre, substudy II: A cadre looks at itself. Eugene, Oregon: Center for Educational Policy and Management, 1976. (Mimeo.)

Tannenbaum, Arnold S. *Control in organizations.* New York: McGraw-Hill, 1968.

Thomas, Terrance A. The effects of laboratory training on the interpersonal relations of elementary school principals with their teaching staff. Doctoral dissertation, University of Oregon, 1969.

Torbert, William R. *Creating a community of inquiry: Conflict, collaboration, transformation.* New York: Wiley, 1976.

Tuckman, Bruce W. *Conducting educational research.* New York: Harcourt Brace Jovanovich, 1978.

Wallen, John L. Emotions as problems. In Charles Jung, Rosalie Howard, Ruth Emory, and Rene Pino (Eds.), *Trainer's manual: Interpersonal communications.* Portland, Oregon: Northwest Regional Educational Laboratory, 1972.

Walton, Richard E. *Interpersonal peacemaking: Confrontation and third-party consultation.* Reading, Mass.: Addison-Wesley, 1969.

Watson, Goodwin (Ed.). *Change in school systems.* Washington, D.C.: Cooperative Project for Educational Development, National Training Laboratories and National Education Association, 1967(a).

Watson, Goodwin (Ed.). *Concepts for social change.* Washington, D.C.: Cooperative Project for Educational Development, National Training Laboratories and National Education Association, 1967(b).

Weick, Karl E. Educational organizations as loosely coupled systems. *Administrative Science Quarterly*, 1976, *21*(1), 1–19.

Weick, Karl E. *The social psychology of organizing* (2nd ed.). Reading, Mass.: Addison-Wesley, 1979.

Williamson, John N. The inquiring school: Toward a model of organizational self-renewal. *Educational Forum*, 1974, *38*, 355–371, 393–410.

Wood, M. T. Power relationships and group decision making in organizations. *Psychological Bulletin*, 1973, *79*, 280–293.

Wyant, Spencer H. The effects of organization development training on intra-staff communication in elementary schools. Doctoral dissertation, University of Oregon, 1974.

Name Index

Subject Index